ARTHURIAN WRITERS

A Biographical Encyclopedia

EDITED BY LAURA COONER LAMBDIN AND
ROBERT THOMAS LAMBDIN

GREENWOOD PRESS
Westport, Connecticut • London

Library of Congress Cataloging-in-Publication Data

Arthurian writers : a biographical encyclopedia / edited by Laura Cooner
Lambdin and Robert Thomas Lambdin.
   p. cm.
  Includes bibliographical references.
  ISBN 978-0-313-34682-8 (alk. paper)
  1. Arthurian romances—Encyclopedias. 2. English literature—Bio-
bibliography—Encyclopedias. 3. English literature—English-speaking
countries—History and criticism. 4. English literature—History and
criticism. 5. Arthur, King—In literature. 6. Archetype (Psychology) in
literature. I. Lambdin, Laura C. II. Lambdin, Robert T.
  PR149.A79A78 2008
  809′.93351—dc22   2007026093

British Library Cataloguing in Publication Data is available.

Library of Congress Catalog Card Number: 2007026093
ISBN-13: 978-0-313-34682-8

First published in 2008

Greenwood Press, 88 Post Road West, Westport, CT 06881
An imprint of Greenwood Publishing Group, Inc.
www.greenwood.com

Printed in the United States of America

The paper used in this book complies with the
Permanent Paper Standard issued by the National
Information Standards Organization (Z39.48–1984).

10   9   8   7   6   5   4   3   2   1

To our precious warrior princesses,
Elizabeth Ann and Mary Nell,
and in memory of our beloved knight,
Charles S. Lambdin

Contents

Preface   ix

Introduction   xi

Gildas (c. 490–570)   1

Bede (c. 673–May 25, 735)   7

Nennius (c. early ninth century)   16

Wace (Robert?) (c. 1100–1183)   23

Geoffrey of Monmouth
(c. 1100–c. 1155)   30

Chrétien de Troyes (c. 1125–1191)   37

Layamon (fl. c. 1185–1225)   45

Hartmann von Aue
(c. 1160/1165–c. 1210/1220)   58

Wolfram von Eschenbach
(fl. c. 1200–d. c. 1216)   70

Jehan Froissart (c. 1337–c. 1410)   81

The *Gawain*-Poet (fl. c. 1350–1400)   90

Giovanni Boccaccio (c. June 1313–
December 21, 1375)   110

Geoffrey Chaucer (c. 1340–1400)   120

Sir Thomas Malory (c. 1400–March
14, 1471)   128

Edmund Spenser
(c. 1552–January 13, 1599)   138

Thomas Heywood
(c. 1573–August 16, 1641)   146

John Dryden
(August 9, 1631–May 1, 1700)   154

Matthew Arnold (December 24,
1822–April 15, 1888)   165

William Morris (March 24,
1834–October 3, 1896)   175

Algernon Charles Swinburne
(April 5, 1837–April 10, 1909)   185

Alfred, Lord Tennyson (August 6,
1809–October 6, 1892)   200

Mark Twain (November 30,
1835–April 21, 1910)   218

Edwin Arlington Robinson
(December 22, 1869–April 6,
1935)   230

T(homas) S(tearns) Eliot (September
26, 1888–January 4, 1965)   241

C(live) S(taples) Lewis (November
29, 1898–November 22, 1963)   249

John Steinbeck (February 27,
1902–December 20, 1968)   265

T(erence) H(anbury) White
(May 29, 1906–January 17, 1964)   276

Walker Percy (May 28, 1916–May
10, 1990)   288

Mary Stewart (September 17, 1916–)   301

Rosemary Sutcliff (December 14,
1920–July 22, 1992)   311

Thomas Berger (July 20, 1924–)   323

Marion Zimmer Bradley
(June 3, 1930–September 25, 1999)   334

Persia Woolley (November 8, 1935–) 351

Margaret Eleanor Atwood
(November 18, 1939–)   357

Arthurian Art   364

Selected Readings   379

Index   393

About the Editors and Contributors   399

PREFACE

*A*rthurian Writers: A Biographical Encyclopedia describes the lives and works of authors who have employed Arthurian legend in some significant way from the old English/medieval period to the present. This text is intended as a reference tool to serve university and advanced high school students. However, it is also perfect as a concise, yet thorough desk reference book for academics.

Volume entries are arranged chronologically from Gildas to Margaret Atwood. Each entry begins with a summary of the author's contribution to Arthurian literature. Next follows the author's biographical background, which can be scant, as in the case of Wace, about whom little information is known. The following section mentions an author's other writings as well, but focuses upon the distinguishing treatment of Arthurian legend, especially changes to the tradition, by objectively summarizing the significance of that rendition of the myth.

As expected in an encyclopedia, there is some overlap of analyses of prevalent themes and of other Arthurian works. Entry lengths vary based upon the writer's significance to Arthuriana, making the Marion Zimmer Bradley entry, for example, longer than the John Steinbeck entry. Character's names within each entry are spelled as that particular author presented them, demonstrating a distinct lack of continuity. Each entry also includes a list of works by that author as well as a list of well regarded texts concerning that author's works. There is also a longer, more inclusive list of "Selected Readings" at the end of the volume.

Included at the back of this text is an "About the Editors and Contributors" section providing a short summary of professional backgrounds. Scholars were chosen based upon their publication records and asked to participate based upon their academic expertise.

Although the emphasis is upon literature, a chapter about Arthurian Art has been included for interest. Other related topics, such as important political and religious leaders, wars, and movements, have been included within entries as needed.

INTRODUCTION

Arthurian legends are a complex reworking of previously existing narratives and ideologies that are ever both anachronistic and contemporary. The costumes, characters, and settings reflect some portion of the early medieval period, but the themes of fate, guilty passion, and loyalty are universal, not in the sense of timeless meaning, but because new writers and readers in each period care enough to mutate or reinvent the lesson to be gleaned about Camelot's tragedy; thus aesthetic judgments about the point of Arthuriana change based upon the historical present. Arthurian themes have ever lent themselves well as a veneer for social criticism; each new author pleads and persuades through language, making a particular point by shifting the narrative's focus to change the significance assigned by readers. While it is as impossible to assess an author's intentions as it is to predict a reader's response, we can note each author's particular alterations as a dialogue between past and present.

The basic Arthurian plot is as follows: Merlin influences the creation of Arthur, son of the mighty, warlike Uther Pendragon and Igraine, the beautiful wife of another powerful lord. The baby is hidden for years and finally, by pulling Excalibur from the stone on New Year's Day, Arthur is declared the rightful monarch. Fighting bravely but fairly, Arthur and his troops beat back the Saxons and unite Wales, Ireland, and Scotland. During a shining time of peace, a fellowship of knights sit equally at a Round Table and create the laws of civilized society until many of them leave on quests for the Holy Grail. Arthur marries the young Guinevere, who betrays him by committing adultery with Lancelot, the knight of greatest prowess. After Arthur is tricked into spending a night of incestuous passion with his half-sister, Mordred is born. Although Arthur orders all male babies in the kingdom killed, Mordred lives and eventually mortally wounds his father in battle. Arthur is carried away by three queens in a boat to the Isle of Avalon from where he will return when his people most need him. This powerfully tragic tale has been convincingly rewritten from every possible angle and versions of it are found from all parts of the world.

The legends reflect a complex weaving of Christian and pagan elements. Arthur, the best of kings who rides into battle under the banner of Christ, is destroyed by the worst of human characteristics: betrayal, adultery, incest, and patricide. There are also many religious figures such as monks, nuns, and religious hermits, but they are overshadowed by characters who rely more upon magic than God. Overall, the legends lack the reverent attitude typical of sacred texts, and an earthly and barbaric realism prevails despite the many magical and pagan elements. Dwarfs, giants, wizards, and witches such as Morgan Le Fay, The Lady of the Lake, and Merlin move the text forward in many places by forcing an action. Even the great sword Excalibur has a personality dependent upon the supernatural. The mystical, pagan elements are often cited as evidence of the legends' earliest sources, probably Celtic mythology—when the grail was a bubbling cauldron of plenty.

When an author reworks an existing narrative, the changes generally prove an intention to moralize on some ongoing theme, person, or place in his period. The narrative is a rhetorical performance, an attempt at the most authoritative persuasion through historical representation rather than a neutral discourse. Examination of epistemic/ontological choices reflect distinct ideological or political thought perhaps intended to encourage social change or comment upon a political leader. We can only guess what those changes might entail because interpretation is always anachronistic. Myths give comfort, lull the reader into accepting, through familiarity, choices that might seem repugnant if delineated in plain language. Critical choices between texts—new interpretation of old material—is particularly fascinating in the Arthurian legends and proves that no myth has a universal or timeless meaning. From remotest times, fiction about Arthur is found in the literature of England, France, Italy, Spain, Ireland, and Scotland. Parts of the legend also can be found far from Europe in parts of Asia and Africa.

Examining relationships between Arthurian texts—the traditional aspects as well as the creative twists—stimulates an appreciation for the historical moment that produced a particular work by an artist with a specific personal past and writing agenda. Whether Arthur existed as a real human being or not is insignificant inasmuch as his primary job is to provide, as a huge mythological figure, a unifying form for an enormous variety of stories about the early medieval period. The historicity, even if it does not accurately reflect historical reality, is one particularly fascinating aspect of Arthurian legends. The sociopolitical and economic orders defining that phase of human history are particularly vivid. Further, the legends reflect the realism of the various classes and their struggles by involving and reflecting the entire spectrum of social relations.

Scholars such as E. K. Chambers, David Dumville, and John Morris have tried to pinpoint an historical Arthur and answer the question was he real or simply a myth? Recent works aiming to prove that Arthur actually lived have named Riothamus as a likely model. Sent to Briton by Pope Leo I in 467 to counteract ongoing Saxon invasions, Riothamus's name may have been Anglicized to "Rigatamos," which translates roughly into "supreme king." The derivation of his name into Arthur may have been the result of his being given the name "Artorius" after his baptism. The main argument against Riothamus was that he was known to have campaigned in Gaul before he disappeared around 470 CE; thus, it does not seem feasible that he could have been the Arthur whom the Welsh document as dying in 539 CE at Camlann at the hands of Medraunt. Perhaps his deeds became overstated after he liberated the Britons. Tales about his triumphs would have become legendary among his grateful people, and his fame widespread. Thus, exploits attributed to Artorius could have occurred long after he died. Also, as Geoffrey

Ashe notes, Roman military units during this time were often named for individuals. If this is the case, then Artorius's unit could have kept the name well after his death until their demise at Camlann.

Critics continue to disagree about whether King Arthur was a man or a derivative of a mythological god. No deities names are similar, but the Roman name Artorius was known early in Britain and suggests that Arthur may have been a local engaged in a form of guerrilla warfare successful enough to unite other men. These people desperately needed a hero so they may have elevated this fighter to deity status by the oral transmission of tales that grew in each retelling. Since tales of Arthur deeds were spread largely through oral renditions, his deeds could have become exaggerated.

Catholic Church dogma dominated the medieval period and evidence of this influence is smattered throughout the tales. As the first Christian king, Arthur is concerned with religious values such as brotherhood, equality and fairness, as evidenced by the Round Table that gave no man precedence at meat. The quest for the grail, the legendary vessel used to collect Christ's blood as he hung on the cross, the cup brought to the British Isles by Joseph of Arimethea, is another significantly religious portion of the legends. The grail was underscored by medieval romances, and most writers of Arthuriana tend to view the grail as historical rather than literary invention. That the grail is found and returned to Heaven by the virgin Galahad, known in Arthuriana as a descendent of Jesus, is a fitting conclusion to that portion of the legend.

In the *Historia Britonum* (c. 800), written in South Wales by Nennius, we see Arthur mentioned as a battle leader in the period after the death of Hengist (c. 488). In Nennius's account, Arthur is a sort of general who fights for "Jesus Christ and Holy Mary his mother." *Historia Britonum* reflects a revival of Welsh nationalism wherein Arthur alone, a mythical warrior figure, slays 960 enemy fighters. The victory of Mount Baden is mentioned here as well as in other sources that establish the battle—without mentioning Arthur—as having definitely taken place at the end of the fifth century. That Arthur is still hailed as a hero one thousand years later by Thomas Malory is understandable as that battle changed the course of his people's history by allowing them peace and security for about 375 years. Recalling this perfect time may be the root of the messianic theme throughout Arthurian legends: Arthur lives on in Avalon and will return when his people most need him to unify and protect them once again.

The next extent mention of Arthur can be found in the *Annals of Wales* (c. 950), a short, anonymous work that underscores Arthur's large role in the Battle of Badon. This text further emphasizes Arthur's religious role, a trait that ultimately leads to later writers referring to him as the first Christian king. In the *Annals of Wales*, Arthur bears the cross of Christ on his shoulders while fighting. This chronicle notes that Arthur's death occurred at the Battle of Camlann (c. 539) and that Medraut died there also. Later in the legends Arthur and nephew/son Mordred inflict fatal stab wounds upon each other. Other early histories of this type read like headlines or outlines. The real fleshing out of Arthur's tale does not properly develop until the twelfth century chronicles that weave together the elements of both Irish and Welsh folklore that had previously been largely part of an ancient oral tradition. This seems a good time to pause and remind our reader that when dealing with materials as old as the roots of Arthuriana, scholars have precious little to work with as so many fragile documents have been lost or destroyed. It is impossible to know how much was written about any subject when extant manuscripts are so scarce. Of course, even more problematic is dating the beginning of a mythology passed along orally.

The legends were apparently solidified for the first time around 1136 with Geoffrey of Monmouth's *Historia Regum Britanniæ*. This text was accepted as historically accurate through the late medieval period and into the Renaissance. Geoffrey claimed to have translated his material from an ancient book given to him by Walter, archdeacon of Oxford; however, scholars doubt that this source existed as citing an ancient text was a common strategy or ploy among writers of medieval fiction to make their words seem more weighty. Further, because most of Geoffrey's details, such as names of characters and weapons, can be traced to early oral folkloric traditions, it seems unlikely that there was another chronicle. There are two extent Welsh poems containing the sort of material typical of what one might imagine to have been Geoffrey's starting point. In one, Arthur is asked by a gatekeeper to name his companions, and in the other Arthur and his men plunder an island where pagan gods live. Geoffrey traces England from the fall of Troy in a patriotic history seemingly devoted to making Arthur seem noble as a hero and legitimate as a ruler, perhaps imagining him as a latter day Charlemagne. The text is of particular value as the first time we see derisive, contemporary political aims furthered through the legend. This is different from the early fanciful mythological mixtures of pagan deities with a hero warrior.

Robert de Boron, who composed in the late twelfth or early thirteenth century, gave us much of the earliest information concerning the grail mystery in his three poems, *Joseph d'Arimathie*, *Merlin*, and *Perceval*, wherein the grail is used at the Last Supper by Jesus and later retrieved by Joseph of Arimethea after Christ's crucifixion. In this account, Joseph used the grail to collect Jesus's blood as he prepared the body for burial. De Boron's poems are significant because they transform the grail into the holiest of relics, making it an historical fact rather than an unsolved mystery. In de Boron's account, Joseph gives the grail to his brother-in-law, Bron, who takes the vessel west to the vale of Avalon. In *Merlin*, de Boron wrote that the great wizard knew of the grail's roots and purposefully continued its history. Indeed later renditions of the tales had the Round Table with thirteen chairs, including the famous *Siege Perilous*, Galahad's chair. Remember, it was Galahad who eventually found the grail. Thus, the grail is shifted into the Arthurian tradition, where it will play such a huge role. De Boron left the final part of the trilogy, *Perceval*, to be completed by someone else. In this poem, Perceval seeks the grail and his pursuits are filled with the usual adventures. The portion not completed by de Boron mentions Arthur's wars and Mordred's patricide/regicide, much in the manner of Geoffrey of Monmouth and Wace, but fails to include the relationship between Guinevere and Lancelot.

De Boron also had an idea for but did not compose a series of works about Arthurian tradition. This medieval literary masterpiece called the *Vulgate Cycle* (c. 1215–1235), an eight-volume set anonymously transcribed, is the first instance of the collation of the entire Arthurian story. Significantly, the *Vulgate Cycle* is composed entirely in prose and introduces the adulterous love affair between Lancelot and Guinevere as a key element in the downfall of Arthur and his kingdom. The first two sections of the *Vulgate* mirror de Boron's work. The third sections details the more common Arthurian themes, but establishes Guinevere and Lancelot's connection when she holds onto the handle of Lancelot's sword when he is knighted by Arthur. The *Vulgate* then pretty much echoes Chrétien de Troyes's depiction of Guinevere's being held hostage and her rescue by Lancelot. Following the revelation that Lancelot, because of his impurity, is no longer the greatest knight, Galahad steps in, passes the test of the Siege Perilous, thus proving that he is destined to fulfill the grail quest. The *Vulgate* is important in this area as it shows that the flawed knights—Lancelot, Perceval, Lionel, Hector, Gawain, Bohort, and others—are incapable of living up to the piety of the grail. Their worldliness disqualifies them from this quest. Thus, the most spiritual of the knights, such as Galahad, are able to grasp the conceptual complexity of the grail. In the end, only those whose spirituality has led them on their quests survive.

The *Vulgate* ends with the section detailing the death of Arthur and serves to unite the previous sections. The knights of the Round Table demonstrate they have come together to eliminate evil; theirs is a noble quest for goodness. Thus, as the demise of Arthur occurs because of his inability to overcome his worldly nature, as evidenced in the existence of his son/nephew Mordred, the knights are seeking the holiest of relics, the grail. Arthur is slain by Mordred, the result of his incestuous tryst with his half-sister and buried at the Noire Chapel. In the *Vulgate* Lancelot seeks repentance, but it is too late and he dies a broken man.

While the *Vulgate* works center around the deeds of Lancelot, Arthur is the character who unites the work. Here we see for the first time the knights and the Round Table as symbols of good; their quest for spiritual perfection plays off the sins of Arthur and the others. Thus, Galahad and Perceval become models of goodness. This plays especially well in the works as the characters are presented not only as nobles but also as humans. They have thoughts and emotions that they cannot comprehend.

Between 1150 and 1420 around fifty other chronicles were written; all seem to have been copied from Geoffrey of Monmouth's work. Also apparently using a copy or the original of Geoffrey's work, Wace, a Norman clerk, wrote the *Roman de Brut* (1154), a poem presented to the wife of Henry II of England, Eleanor of Acquitaine. To comprehend the writings of Wace and later Arthurian authors like Chrétien's works, one must have an understanding of the philosophical concept of courtly love that flourished in France and England during the thirteenth century. Scholars disagree as to its roots, but it is believed to be somewhat of a conglomeration of the works of Ovid, some Middle Eastern philosophy, and the songs of the troubadours. In this tradition a man, usually of high estate, would fall madly in love with a married woman. Things only get worse for the smitten who must first suffer for months pining for his unattainable beloved in silence before making the object of his adoration aware of his feelings. Once he has made his affections known, the knight must then prove his devotion by attempting daring deeds in her name and engaging in devoted service to her. Following this quest for her affection, the couple swear their allegiance to each other and vow to keep the affair a secret. While this may simply have been a way for bored, wealthy couples in court settings to justify adulterous affairs, it did provide rich fodder for authors of the age—especially Chrétien in his *Lancelot*—and for later parodies like Chaucer's "Miller's Tale."

Wace's poetic rendering in French couplets is especially valuable for containing the first extant mention of the round table as a device introduced to keep Arthur's fellowship from fighting about order of precedence as they sat to eat together. Wace's aristocratic audience would surely wonder about the protocol of seating arrangements and apparently the poet devised a brilliant scheme to get around an explanation of each warrior's station or value. The poet notes that there are twelve chieftains or barons at the table with Arthur, and it is interesting to recall that at this period in history it was assumed that Christ and his disciples sat at a round table for the Last Supper. Wace's Arthur is also the first to call out for help from God in battle. Many courtly elements are added, especially detailed descriptions of costumes and etiquette that had previously been unmentioned. Gone are the more gory, bloody battle scenes as well. Here, we see a sanitized Arthurian legend for the upper class. This early French author's concern with manners foreshadows Chrétien de Troyes's later texts that show the French interest in etiquette.

Layamon's *Brut* is the first extent English poem of Arthurian legend. Written around 1200 by a Worcestershire priest, the poem is composed in alliterative meter and is more dramatic and intense than Wace's version. Arthur is seen here as a member of the Saxon race that defeated the British years ago, but are now oppressed by Norman attackers. Emotions run high in direct discourse here; to avoid possible bloodshed or any mayhem caused by undemocratic seating, Arthur has a round table built that seats sixteen hundred. Amazingly, this giant table is also easily portable. Another fascinating element is the addition of Avalon as the place to which Arthur, after his mortal wound is inflicted by Mordred, is taken by the most beautiful of the fays or elves, Argante. This mighty fay intends to protect and heal Arthur so that he will be ready to return to the Britons later. Despite the intervention of a pagan fay in this ending, the *Brut* again underscores the messianic flavor of Arthur as a Christ-like figure and has many mentions of God and Mary—as one would expect to find in a poem composed by a priest of the Catholic Church.

The idea of Arthur as eternal hero who intends to return from Avalon is mentioned in several Breton lais, charming short fairy tales. These tales often use Arthur's court as a backdrop and mention him as the "Breton Hope," the one who never died and will be back. The most famous is *The Lay of Sir Launfal* (1175) by Marie de France. We see here a mixture of magic and chivalry at court, but Arthur's world involves moments of ugly backbiting making it contrast directly and poorly with the Fairies' beautiful kingdom.

It is in the elegant verse romance of the twelfth-century French poet Chrétien de Troyes that moved the Arthurian legends rapidly forward in numerous ways. Chrétien was closely connected to Countess Marie, daughter of Eleanor of Acquitaine, of the court of Champagne and therefore concerned with the interworkings of life among the aristocracy. Fairy tales and bloody battles take a back seat here to chivalry and courtly life. Settings change from fields to castles where characters illustrate correct court behavior, clothing, and polite conversation. We have four of Chrétien's Arthurian works—*Erec* (c. 1170), *Lancelot* (c. 1179), *Yvain* (c. 1179), and *Perceval* (c. 1180–1190)—but suspect more were composed. Much of these texts seems intended to teach the proper manners of a courtly lover and his lady.

The Fisher King, who was in charge of the grail, first appears in the works of Chrétien as the wounded keeper in the grail castle which has been identified by some as being in Glastonbury. The Fisher King's condition, usually observed to be a wounded leg or thigh, mirrors the decrepit condition of the castle and its surrounding area, which is usually regarded to be a wasteland. To restore the land to its pristine condition, all one needed to do was to ask the keeper about the grail procession. When Percival neglects to do so in his interaction with the wounded king, his failure results in the ongoing grail quest.

There are many differences between the initial literary works as they present the Fisher King. In Chrétien, he is nameless, while Wolfram calls him "Anfortas." Even his ancestry is not clear. Some critics find his roots in Celtic Mythology while others trace him back to Joseph of Arimethea's brother-in-law. Those who favor the Celtic origin point to the Fisher King as being Bran, the son of Lyr, the Irish sea god. Bran owned a magic cauldron that could bring the dead back to life. In a quarrel, Bran is wounded in the foot by a poisoned spear, and the cauldron is destroyed. The wound so bothers Bran that he orders his legion to cut off his head. After this deed is done, the head is returned to

Briton and remains in a state of suspended animation for seven years. Then, the head was moved to Grassholm where Bran's seven followers live as carefree partiers for eighty years—aware neither of time or aging—until one member breaks the castle's enchantment. The seven take the head for burial in London, where it is buried facing the channel to France.

In this rendition Bran, the leader, is given an unspeakable wound and loses possession of the life-giving cauldron. As a result of his misfortune, the others live a life of revelry, oblivious to the desolation that has affected the kingdom. All of these parallel the Fisher King legend. However, Jessie Weston places the origin of the Fisher King back to the Mystery Cults, most notably the story of the Salmon of Wisdom, where the boy, Finn is exposed to the Fish of Life by Finn Eger, who has been waiting seven years to capture the fish. Thus, we have the establishment of a mortal who is reborn as an immortal, again, much the same legend as the Fisher King.

Of note is the relationship of the fish symbol and Christ, who strews his nets and harvests his disciples whom he calls "fishers of men." Thus, the fish metaphor is equated with an uncountable wealth, that of everlasting life and prosperity. This spiritual notion also plays well with the idea posited in the Percival tale, especially in the Arthurian tales of the twelfth and thirteenth centuries where the sins of the nobles (and, therefore, the unknowing) lead to their demise while those seeking spiritual truth thrive. In another version, Joseph never leaves mainland Europe, and the grail is brought to Briton by Bron, Joseph's brother-in-law, who re-creates Jesus's miracle of the fish and feeds his entire entourage with one fish. Bron thus becomes known as the Rich Fisher, and his people settle in Avaron to await Alain, the grail's keeper. The temporary keeper becomes king and the grail knights are formed. Again, the story then varies as some tell of the keeper being wounded by a spear in the thigh because of the group's loss of faith; others believe the keeper is wounded because of the love of a woman, betraying the keeper's vow of chastity. The land becomes a wasteland, echoing the spiritual emptiness of the knights and mirrored in the wound; literally the land has become wounded. In the Hallows castle are found the three elements of the grail quest: a sword, a platter, and the lance, which became associated with Longinus, the Roman who speared Christ on the cross.

In any case, the tale of the Fisher King adds another stake in the resounding tragedy that is found in Arthurian tradition. The knights strive to achieve this spirituality, even when it is clear that they are unable to handle such a task, making the reader even more sympathetic to their flaws. In these knights are the human characteristics that keep most from achieving spiritual perfection. Thus, when Percival fails to ask the correct question about the grail procession, the knights of the Round Table are as doomed as the Fisher King and his wasteland. And, even more tragic, is the realization that their leader and beloved king is among the least spiritual who will betrayed by his incestuous son and by his best knight's coupling with his queen.

Clearly these influences would have played a huge role in the composition of the Arthurian works. While Arthur, Lancelot, and Percival were the focus of many of the early works, the story of Sir Tristan also is important. Especially in the Middle Ages, the story of Tristan and Iseult was hugely popular. The modern reader may be surprised to find that this tale has been retold so many times that only the works concerning Lancelot and Guinevere surpass it. The Tristan story encompasses a large part of Malory's *Morte*, but its roots run far earlier, back to the Celtic tradition. Some find Tristan to have originated in Cornwall or north Britain, but there is no tangible evidence of this. What is clear is that the Tristan stories that so delighted the medieval audiences arose from a compendium of sources, including classical and oriental. It is because of this infusion of worldly sources that the work became popular throughout Europe. There are many Norman, French, and German versions of the Tristan story, composed in both prose and verse. Among the first medieval versions were several that came from Brittany and France. Perhaps the first identified works were those of the Anglo-Norman writer Thomas d'Angleterre, whose twelfth century account of the legend became the basis for the German author Gottfried von Strassburg's early thirteenth century version, as well as the late thirteenth century "Sir Tristram," composed in metrical verse. Thomas's work also influenced Scandinavian versions, such as Brother Robert's 1226 work. These poetic compositions are considered to be the "courtly versions" of the works.

The earliest versions of the Tristan legend, which originated in Ireland, were independent of the Arthurian tradition and were eventually drawn into it. While many different examples of the story exist with subtle differences, for the most, the basic plot is the same. Tristan is sent to England to pick up and deliver Iseult the Fair to his uncle, King Mark, to whom she is betrothed. The unwitting couple swallow a potion that dooms them to an eternal undying love. In most works, the couple tries to deny their love; Tristan marries Iseult of the White Hands while the other Iseult marries King Mark. The love between Tristan and Iseult the Fair never wanes. Even on his death bed Tristan, who has been mortally wounded in battle, calls for his beloved, but he is deceived into thinking that she is not coming. This thought breaks his heart and he dies of despair. When Iseult the Fair arrives and finds her love dead, she, too, dies of a broken heart.

By the mid-thirteenth century, prose versions of the Tristan legend were developed. Here Tristan becomes a part of Arthur's court and a knight of the Round table. His tales are full of events typical in the medieval romances. The French *Tristan* was such a popular work that it was translated into Italian and Spanish, with many versions extant. It seems then that these romantic prose versions superceded the poetic texts in popularity. It was this work that Malory shortened for inclusion in his *Morte* in 1485. By the sixteenth century, really only the prose versions remained popular. It was not until Wagner reinvigorated the poetic tradition with his opera *Tristan und Isolde* in the nineteenth century that the works again became popular. When the stories of the Arthurian legend again became chic during the Victorian period, English authors such as Alfred, Lord Tennyson, Matthew Arnold, and Algernon Charles Swinburne composed versions of the Tristan tale.

Perhaps this is because of Tristan's appeal not only as a lover, but as a knight. In medieval art there are numerous images of him demonstrating his dazzling fighting skills, often while under the watchful eyes of the ladies of the court. While this may have appealed to the female audience, it is recorded that Tristan also had great prowess as a hunter, which would have endeared him to the male populace as well. Indeed many pieces of art from this time show Tristan hunting with his faithful dog, Husdent, an animal so delightful that Beroul included a good passage in his twelfth century *Tristan* describing the hound.

Finally, the Tristan myth is of great import in that in many ways it parallels the Arthurian story, as it is about a love triangle involving seduction of a queen and betrayal of a king. Here, we have characters of high rank who let passion to dictate their lives. This allows for two distinct interpretations. The protagonists, Tristan and Lancelot, can be seen as great models who are tragically fated to fail because of love or as pompous self-servers who act with little regard for the consequences of their deeds. Their tales of tragic adulterous love of a noble woman epitomize the fallacy of the courtly tradition.

French influences also seem to have reached the anonymous English author of *Sir Gawain and the Green Knight* (c. 1350). Beautiful alliterative poetry and many references to etiquette dominate this poem where Arthur's handsome, gallant nephew Gawain is the hero. French writers by this time had also become interested in a whole host of other Arthurian characters and sometimes dropped Arthur midway through the text or even entirely. Often they digressed into long moral treatises pondering unanswerable questions and unsolvable issues. Religious doctrine sometimes became the focus, so even the aristocratic audience was uninterested. In these tedious texts the storylines were in danger of being forgotten.

Sir Thomas Malory's *Morte d'Arthur* (1485) probably saved the legends from obscurity by packaging them neatly into an interwoven abridged version accounting for most of the original characters and adventures while dropping concerns with religion and etiquette. The simplified form and common man viewpoint, along with the use of Caxton's newly invented printing press, made this an Arthurian tale for the masses. Malory cites "the French book" as his source, but critics do not believe any one such text ever existed and credit Malory with deciphering and sorting several French works for his English audience. Malory also simplified the legends and made them more English by dropping most of the magic, religious mysteries, and emotional analysis. Action is presented directly with little comment from the narrator. The focus is upon the socio-political ramifications of civil strife in the kingdom, perhaps reflecting Malory's own involvement as a knight in the Wars of the Roses (1455–1485). Many critics agree that Malory's Arthur may have been intended as a tribute to Henry V's triumphant campaign in France. As a political tool, Arthur the first Christian and British king was wielded by nearly every monarchy until the Tudors eventually chose Alfred the Great as their hero because his existence was indisputable, while Arthur's lineage was questionable.

Reversing Chrétien's focus entirely in the *Morte*, Malory's Lancelot is not a courtly lover to Guinevere. Such elements are almost totally removed to reflect him as a Christian knight who has betrayed his king and brotherhood because of a momentary attraction. The concept of fraternal loyalty is pondered on many levels. Arthur knows he can have other queens, but that the brotherhood of his knights will not be as easy to mend once shattered by Lancelot and Guinevere's treasonous liaison. The *Morte*'s most brilliant portion is its conclusion, the battle between Arthur and Mordred caused by the disloyalty of many characters. Malory gives the tale eternal grandeur and unrelenting tragedy by exploring the forces that destroy the kingdom. The *Morte* still remains true to each character's traditional motivations but makes them more interlocking in humanism wherein sin radiates outward like the circles from a stone thrown into a pond: Arthur loves Lancelot and Guinevere, but must punish their treason because as king he is the chief lawmaker; Guinevere feels tenderness and respect towards Arthur, but is blinded by overwhelming passion for Lancelot; Lancelot is the strongest knight and his king's right arm, but fights against Arthur when the king condemns Guinevere to burn for adultery; Morgause feels rejected by her brother and conceives Mordred in an angry act of incest; Mordred remains unacknowledged by Arthur as his son, so his frustration makes him try to take over the kingdom, and ultimately, it makes him commit patricide. All the essential conflicts that one has come to expect from contemporary Arthurian texts were first pieced together, however primitively, by Malory.

It is impossible to know why the story of Camelot was essentially ignored following Malory's work until the latter half of the eighteenth century, but during that time, Arthuriana was scarcely noted. Classical learning and the Reformation were by nature alien to the Arthurian legends. Perhaps new writers felt that the *Morte* had covered all the matter beautifully or perhaps the lack of new Arthurian tales may be more adequately explained by hostilities from advocates of the rigorous of classical education and the Protestant attention upon simplified Christianity; neither would have welcomed the mystical, magical, or pagan portions of the legends. Also, historians of Tudor England were the first to question the accuracy of Geoffrey of Monmouth's chronicle and so deleted Arthur's name for the first time from the official list of kings because his monarchy was unverifiable. Further weakening interest beyond damage done by the close scrutiny of historians, was the popular interest in battles involving modern cannons rather than quaint swords and spears. Further, magic and romance did not meet the standards for literature mandated by the rationality of Neoclassicism. The Protestants of the Reformation found the grail quest offensive and lacking from a biblical standpoint; they also despised references to Catholic priests, relics, and religious masses referred to in the legends.

Edmund Spenser's *The Faerie Queen* (1590–1596) includes Arthur as prince but the material is invented about his birth and ascension to the throne. Arthur is a symbol of chivalry in Samuel Dryden's libretto for the composer Porcell's *King Arthur*. There was little written about Arthurian legend until the Gothic Revival and the romantics. Indeed one must look hard to find any mention; perhaps the idea that Sir Walter Scott, who was so intrigued by the Middle Ages, saw fit to compose only one minor poem with an Arthurian link, *The Bridal of Triermain* (1813) reflects the disdain most clearly. William Wordsworth's "The Egyptian Mind" (1836) and several other brief references kept the Arthurian legends alive in the public imagination; however, the story was not reborn until the poetry of Alfred, Lord Tennyson, who published his first Arthurian poem in 1832.

The Victorian poets, Tennyson, Arnold, Morris, and Swinburne, like most of their predecessors, employed Arthurian legends as a veneer for social criticism. Their works express particular moral stances and reactions to medieval England, Victorian England, and the human conditions that are dissimilar to the point of incompatibility. As poet laureate, Tennyson wrote to underscore the Victorian's emphasis upon Orthodox Christianity and to discourage unethical behavior. In the *Idylls* characters are Victorians in medieval costumes and the entire tragedy is blamed on Guinevere's passion for Lancelot, a love that leaves her groveling upon the cold floor of the nunnery at her unmerciful husband's feet. Tennyson's characters show the ill effects of other self-indulgent acts, but the emphasis is upon the corrosive nature of human sexuality.

Matthew Arnold's "Tristan and Iseult" (1852) seems less interested in overall Christianity because the emphasis is unwaveringly upon the value of family. The lovers indulge in their passion despite the wife and children Tristan leaves at home. Unlike earlier writers, Arnold does not excuse Tristan and Iseult's liaisons as the result of wine drugged with a love potion. Arnold's unwavering attention is upon the effects of adultery upon the abandoned wife Iseult of Brittany and her two small children. Immoral love in the domestic sphere is extremely unattractive and Arnold added the children to the picture to increase the vision of sin's pain.

Morris's Arthurian works, such as "The Defense of Guinevere" (1858), centered upon immoral sexual love, but the poet's response seems much more liberal and less judgmental. Morris's Guinevere narrates her own defense of how her feelings vacillated between sensual self-indulgence and spiritual Puritanism. The poet renders a realistic portrait of a woman lured by erotic passion to commit acts she still cannot believe are sinful. In her monologue Guinevere arrives at a point where she feels guilty and wants to burn for her crime—except that she fears God's wrath in the afterlife. Examining the difference between earthly and heavenly love seems to be Morris's focus; there is little judgment in terms of adherence to traditional Christian values.

As an iconoclastic atheist Swinburne wrote Arthurian poems such as *Tristrem of Lyonesse* (1862) and *The Tale of Balen* (1896) that reflect God as a product of fearful human imagination. The heroic characters are those who never deviate from a predetermined path and who glorify human passion by serving the true gods Love and Fate. In this world, characters are encouraged by eternal forces of nature who stress mutability moving towards peaceful death. For humans to gain permanence they had to become part of the organic unity of an afterlife in harmony with nature. They accept their destiny—even if it seems immoral to others—and have a position in the collective destiny of mankind. These four Victorian writers of Arthuriana show how well the legends lend themselves to serving opposite positions.

Nathaniel Hawthorne's poem of 1843, "The Antique Ring," began the American tradition of using Arthurian legend to comment upon current happenings or people. The trend of attacking through medieval characters continued in the work of Mark Twain, Raymond Chandler, and Donald Bartholome. This habit of critiquing historical, political, social, and cultural events and/or people through Arthuriana entered popular culture in World War II as "both right wing extremists who sympathized with the rise of totalitarianism and leftists who fought to defeat the Axis powers used elements of Arthuriana to advance their causes" (Mathis, 2). For example, in Foster's *Prince Valiant* comic strip, medieval knights battled Nazis disguised as Huns. Camelot endured in America as a prototype of leadership both monumentally effective and ultimately ineffective, a kind of government intended to be pure and stable, but destroyed in the end. From his Celtic background, military achievements, regal persona, and administration style to his brutal death, Camelot was the perfect symbol of John F. Kennedy and his presidency.

The modern outpouring of thousands of Arthurian novels, television programs, movies, and scholarly and popular articles proves that the habit of recreating the Camelot narrative to discuss social problems cannot be kicked. Feminist and/or pagan Arthurian worlds abound in modern literature and fantasy fiction. Perhaps in response to the many late twentieth century antifeministic terms used to describe Arthur's court, there are now many retellings with a feminist slant: women-oriented spiritualism, goddess worship, wicca groups, matriarchal communities led by three queens and tales of powerful, dominant women abound currently.

Elizabeth Sklar and Donald Hoffman note that "Like the Grail, holy or unholy, the Matter of Arthur may be seen as an empty receptacle, waiting to be filled with whatever substance may speak to the individual or cultural moment" (6). The commodification of Arthur was seen first in the uses of scenes from *Idylls of the King* on Victorian fireplaces, teapots, furniture, and trivets. The domestication of the legend continues in America, as Zia Isola notes, "Because Arthur is such a durable and malleable culture icon, Arthuriana has provided the American imagination with an infinite source of tropes and images, readily adaptable to a variety of uses from military campaigns to political ideology to digitized video games" (27). Books, merchandise, music, films, and even George Lucas' *Star Wars* have all contributed to keeping the actual storyline alive, but its the many uses of verbal and visual icons as part of our popular culture that keep Arthuriana in the foreground.

Sklar notes that "marketplace Arthuriana may be divided loosely into two broad categories: Promotional Arthuriana and Arthurian products" (10). "Promotional Arthuriana" means that words or images are used as attention-grabbing hooks to sell nonmedieval products, establishments, or services like trailer parks, restaurants, liquor stores, or hairstyling. The words most commonly used for these purposes are Camelot, Excalibur, Avalon, Merlin, Round Table, and King Arthur. While we admire the moral qualities implied by some aspects of the legends, Americans tend to use more Arthurian names as purely purposeful hooks than any other nationality, perhaps lamenting a lack of our own royalty. Despite the fact that there are more Americans of Germanic ethnic descent than any other, we are still greatly attached to England's national mythology (Mathis, 3). We ignored the mythology of our indigenous peoples and did little to promote stories like Johnny Appleseed and Paul Bunyan. Particularly our blue collar audience is enticed by noble sounding names that perhaps add an air of class and validity: also this may express a "suppressed desire to transcend commodities altogether" (Goodrich, 220). Chef Boy Ar Dee's Sir Changes-A-Lot canned pasta, Excalibur pies, Grail Ale, Toyota Avalon, and King Arthur Flour have names that suggest quality above similar products.

Arthurian verbal icons add a certain desired level of class to trailer parks, liquor stores, and apartments that they normally would not be afforded. Arthurian products like comic books, graphic novels, board games, and computer games all appeal to adolescent males which reminds one of the early Arthurian youth groups in England and America that influenced the development of the Boy Scouts. We have Avalon books and games, Camelot Casinos, and Round Table social organizations. There is a Hawaiian version of Round Table Pizza. However, one wonders about the necessity of such a hook with X-rated comics like Arthur Sex and Camelot uncensored or the Excalibur porn site. The Internet has expanded exponentially and with the Arthurian material, like most other areas, academic research areas have not covered this explosion. Now that there are more dot-com web sites than dot-gov or dot-edu, it is the commercial use of Arthurian words and images that is mind boggling. Donald Hoffman had a student whose Grandma from Ghana talked about Malory's Polomides as a Saracen knight. The ways the Internet incorporates Arthuriana has not changed much since Elizabeth Sklar noted in her 1993 article the commodification of Arthur. It really is impossible to count the sites as the Internet is not static like a book, so pages are constantly being added, deleted, and amended.

Each new user or writer may view the destruction of the Utopian empire as caused by a clash between repressed women and warriors; centuries of paganism and the new Christianity; the passion of Lancelot and Guinevere that caused disloyalty to the king; the incestuous coupling of Arthur and Morgause; Mordred's need for validation and power; or the expenses in manpower and equipment to continue the grail hunt. The resulting ideological stance always finds a new audience. Naturally each generation of writers and readers places a particular value upon each version. However, part of the interest of scholars in the bulk of Arthurian legend is in recreating what a particular reworking of the tale meant to a writer within his culture. At best, our understanding is a fusion of past and present because as readers we contribute our own history to give the words an extra layer of meaning. We can become caught in an infinite loop here wondering if the connection between art and ideology is conscious or unconscious. Style and form also suggest subtle but particular meanings to a specific society and period. Language, implicitly and explicitly, sends a message, and understanding that the original message mutates with time only adds more interest to a literary critic.

King Arthur is more than a character; he is an organizational, unifying device linking a series of anecdotal and mythological materials as old as time with significance as endless as life in Avalon. It is fine to enjoy the surface narrative, so long as we see into and through it as well. Assigning meaning from our defined viewpoint is complex enough. Interpreting a text based upon possible historical dialectic between literature and the critical readers that shaped the aesthetic object is the ultimate examination of coercion. Realizing that historical literature need not be mimetic, not an imitation of events in the world, but narrative designed as discourse about the world removes questions of King Arthur's actual existence as a man and allows us to focus upon his life as a symbol. Apparently even the modern commercial employment of King Arthur as product endorser has been unable to render him an empty signifier; the once and future king continues to reign.

Secondary Sources

Chambers, E.K. *Arthur of Britain* (London: Sidgewick, 1927); Dumville, David. "Sub-Roman Britain: History and Legend," *History* 62 (1977): 173–92; Goodrich, Peter H. "Merlin in the Public Domain," in *King Arthur in Popular Culture*, eds. Elizabeth S. Sklar and Donald L. Hoffman (Jefferson, NC: McFarland, 2002), 219–32; Hoffman, Donald L. "Arthur, Popular Culture, and World War II," in *King Arthur in Popular Culture*, eds. Elizabeth S. Sklar and Donald L. Hoffman (Jefferson, NC: McFarland, 2002), 45–58; Isola, Zia. "Defending the Domestic: Arthurian Tropes and the American Dream," in *King Arthur in Popular Culture*, eds. Elizabeth S. Sklar and Donald L. Hoffman (Jefferson, NC: McFarland, 2002), 24–35; Lupack, Alan, and Barbara Tepa Lupack. *King Arthur in America* (Cambridge: Brewer, 1999); Mathis, Andrew E. *The King Arthur Myth in Modern American Literature* (Jefferson, NC: McFarland, 2002); Morris, John. *The Age of Arthur* (New York: Scribner, 1973); Sklar, Elizabeth A. "Marketing Arthur: The Commodification of Arthurian Legend," in *King Arthur in Popular Culture*, eds. Elizabeth S. Sklar and Donald L. Hoffman (Jefferson, NC: McFarland, 2002), 9–23.

GILDAS

(c. 490–570)

As with King Arthur, what we know about the Celtic monk, Gildas, in legend is much more than what we can verify in historical fact. Not only is his place of origin unclear, but there is question over what his real name and status in life were. His writings of himself are so enigmatic that one cannot discern if he was a monk or a member of the secular clergy. It is also possible he used a pseudonym. He writes that he was sometimes called Badonicus because of the year he was born, the year the Britons defeated the Saxons in the Battle at Mount Badon (the date for which ranges from c. 490 to c. 520). He might have lived in the early part of the sixth century, possibly at the end of the fifth century as well. However, two documents verify when he died: *Annales Cambriae* and the *Annals of Tigernach* record his death in the year 570. There are two medieval hagiographies, each written several hundred years after Gildas's death: one was written in the eleventh century by an anonymous monk of the Abbey of Rhuys and the other was written in the twelfth century by Caradoc of Llancarfan, a Welsh monk. These documents differ in many details, including the point of Gildas's origins; however, the two hagiographies do agree in some areas. Additionally a few other documents that mention Gildas exist, as well as his own writings and numerous legends, which may hold some level of truth about him. Gildas is important to Arthurian studies because it was possible that he knew Arthur (if he existed); however, Gildas does not mention Arthur in his writings. Who was Arthur? Who was Gildas? The answer to the second question holds a possible answer to the first.

According to the *Vita Gildae auctore monacho Ruiensi* (c. eleventh century), by the anonymous monk of the Abbey of Rhuys in Brittany, Gildas was born the son of Caw in Arecluta (Strathclyde). He had five brothers and one sister—all hermits or ecclesiastics. He was educated in a monastery in Wales, under the tutelage of St. Iltut and in the

---

(St. Gildas the Wise, Sapiens; possibly also Badonicus, St. Gueltas of Ruys)

companionship of such other future saints as Samson and Peter of Léon. He traveled to Ireland after completing his studies. He moved on to North Britain where he preached. There is also a legend that he made a bell of pure tone while in Ireland. He then supposedly returned to North Britain before traveling on to Rome to give the bell to the pope. When the well-made bell mysteriously did not ring for the pope, it was decreed that it needed to be returned to Wales, which Gildas did. Gildas apparently retired to the small island of Houat (off the coast of Brittany), where he lived the life of a Celtic hermit until he was discovered by some fishermen, who persuaded him to help build a monastery in Rhuys. He was supposed to have done much missionary work, and possibly built several monasteries and churches. According to the anonymous monk of the Abby in Rhuys, Gildas died on January 29.

According to Caradog of Llancarfan's *Vita Gildae auctore Caradoco Lancarbanensi* (c. 1130–1150), Gildas knew Arthur. Gildas was born in Strathclyde, one of twenty-four warrior sons of King Nau of Scotland. He studied in Gaul, and returned home to preach in Dyfed. Caradog of Llancarfan writes that while Gildas was in Rome, a long-running dispute between Gildas's family and King Arthur climaxed with Arthur killing one of Gildas's brothers, Cuil (or Hueil). (If this is true—and there is no evidence—it may be why Gildas does not mention Arthur in his history, even though Arthur apparently did penance.) He visited Rome, and then spent some time on Flatholm Island (in the Bristol Channel). He served some time as a mediator between King Arthur and King Melwas, who had captured Arthur's wife, Guennuvar, before moving to Glastonbury. There, according to Caradog of Llancarfan, Gildas wrote *De Excidio et Conquestu Britanniae* (*The Ruin and Conquest of Britain*), which will be discussed below. At some point, Gildas took on the life of a hermit. Finally, Gildas was supposed to have been buried at Glastonbury Abbey.

Several interesting similarities exist between the two hagiographies, such as the visits to Ireland and Rome and the recognition in each of Gildas as a historian. While it is probable that St. Gueltas of Ruys is not the same person as St. Gildas of Britain, Gildas was believed to have traveled a great deal—even all the way to Rome—so many scholars believe the two are one and the same person. Furthermore, other sources also support parts of each of the above. For example, a similar story about Gildas making a bell is also mentioned in *The Life of St. Illtud.* That Gildas was a hermit seems likely. Columbanus, who was the first to mention Gildas in a letter to Pope Gregory the Great, referred to him as a consultant on how a monk might best become a hermit. It is said that he wore a hair-shirt under a cloak, increasingly limited his diet, and slept on the floor. Thus, he lived a Celtic sort of martyrdom of self-denial and isolation. According to St. Finian, Gildas became known as an esteemed scholar, and many people from many places sought his opinion.

Gildas's writing and reputation were powerful enough to have had a strong influence well into the Middle Ages, partly because his writings represented the most comprehensive history available. The Germanic tribal invaders were illiterate in the first two centuries of their conquest of Britain, so any historical records of the transition had to come from fragments recorded from their oral traditions, from works written by the literate and angry Celtic natives or else from foreigners getting information (along with misinformation) from afar. (Recently, archaeology has served to supplement these age-old records.) Bede labeled him as the "Historian of the British," sorting much of the history of early medieval Britain from Gildas's writing. Yet, today his work is more useful and interesting for its rhetoric than for its facts. It is possible that Gildas left us two other works: *Fragmentae* and *Poenitentiae*. The *Fragmentae* is a compilation of bits of letters attributed to Gildas. Some of the subjects that were covered in these letters parallel or repeat concepts relayed through *De Excidio et Conquestu Britanniae*: the role of the clergy, excommunication, and hermitage. The *Poenitentiae* (Monastic Rule) deals with similar issues, but also contains a collection of rules for members of the clergy to follow, reflecting Gildas's ideal monastic life. Regardless of who he was or what he wrote, it is clear that one person, named Gildas, wrote the passionate and feisty history of Britain, which we will now look at more closely.

Gildas is thought to have written *De Excidio et Conquestu Britanniae ac flebi castigatione in reges, principes, et sacradotes* (*The Ruin and Conquest of Britain or a Mournful Rebuke for Kings, Princes, and Priests*) forty-four years after the Battle at Mount Badon. (Mount Badon might be what is now known as Bath.) Although it is the only significant source written from the time of the Anglo-Saxon conquest, it does not qualify as an objective chronicle. *De Excidio et Conquestu Britanniae* is less a history and more a political and vengeful diatribe against the rulers of Britain, as its subtitle suggests. The work has a clear agenda: to chastise the five kings and the clergy for their supposedly numerous character flaws. He writes at the very beginning, "it is my present purpose to relate the deeds of an indolent and slothful race, rather than the exploits of those who have been valiant in the field." His writing does not conform to modern dating practices, so it is difficult to determine the chronological accuracy of his records. Some contemporary historians complain that Gildas mixed facts with misinformation. However, the tone of his writing seems to be more directed toward his contemporary readers than to posterity. It appears that his work might have been written somewhat in the spirit of the literary attacks of later British writers, such as Jonathan Swift and Alexander Pope, upon the nobility, although with much more directness and sobriety. Gildas's writing is metaphorical: he translates events into biblical examples and changes the names of those he slanders into puns. So, it was not only difficult to prosecute him for political or treasonous crimes back then, but it is today difficult to understand the "facts" he was recording into his diatribe. *De Excidio et Conquestu Britanniae* went beyond the close circles of Gildas's monastic community to influence how both friend and foe perceived the Britons for generations to come. However, it was not intended for the edification of posterity as much as it was for the edification of his fellow man.

Gildas's history of Celtic Britain is less a history and more a rant, full of sermonizing fire and brimstone on the surface, but clearly reflecting a deeper prosecutorial doctrine that follows the traditions of Roman law. To understand the voice and tone of *De Excidio et Conquestu Britanniae* it might be helpful to understand the author's time and audience. Gildas lived in an age of transition: Maximus had pulled the last of the Roman legions out, and the Anglo-Saxons had taken over the island. Gildas's history is one written after the island has been conquered and the Britons have been either marginalized, murdered, or otherwise oppressed. Apparently, the Britons were unable or even unwilling to fight against their oppressors, many of the more piously Christian Britons saw this invasion and consequential suffering as a well-deserved wrath of God. St. David of Pembrokeshire, one of Gildas's contemporary colleagues, founded a monastery in Menevia where a harsh and limiting life was enforced upon both him and the other members of his brotherhood. He inflicted hard labor (such as harnessing monks with ploughs), provided minimal food and water, and imposed other mortifying circumstances upon every one for the sake of redemption. Soon, his practices spread to other monasteries in Wales and even Ireland considered adopting this masochistic lifestyle.

Gildas seems to have also at least partially embraced this religious ideology. *De Excidio et Conquestu Britanniae* is both a patriotic and moralistic treatise, a woven story of political and amoral corruption with biblical lessons. For example, he begins Chapter 23: "Then all the councilors, together with that proud tyrant Gurthriger [Vortigern], the British king, were so blinded, that, as a protection to their country, they sealed its doom by inviting in among them (like wolves into the sheep-fold), the fierce and impious Saxons, a race hateful both to God and men, to repel the invasions of the northern nations." In other words, one should not place blame upon the Romans for removing their protection from the island. Nor should the blame be placed anywhere else except upon the "kings, princes and priests" of Britain.

Gildas also argues that the Britons deserved the ravaging of the Teutonic heathen invaders, that their suffering is a punishment from God, a punishment he argues that they deserve:

> Ever since it was first inhabited, Britain has been ungratefully rebelling, stiff-necked and haughty, now against God, now against its own countrymen, sometimes even against kings from abroad and their subjects. What daring of man can, now or in the future, be more foul and wicked than to deny fear to God, charity to good fellow-countrymen, honor to those placed in higher authority (for that is their due, provided, of course, that there is no harm to the faith). (translation from *Medieval Source Book,* chap. 3)

The Saxons flooding over the lands, pushing the Britons farther and farther to the west is, according to Gildas's so-called history, punishment for their sins. And Gildas chastises his contemporaries, stating that they must embrace this punishment for the sake of redemption. This is hardly an enthusiastically positive portrayal of the people of his Celtic homeland, but it is passionate and supportive in its harsh criticisms. Such writing is in the spirit of the Celtic monk who promotes martyrdom for the good of the faith, but clearly Gildas takes his preaching so far as to be almost hateful of any who have fallen from either the grace of country or the grace of God. In other words, the sermonizing qualities of his doctrine seem to be a cloak for an intensely political and legally binding set of accusations. Gildas's writing is also passionately patriotic, and victories in battle and other heroic acts are praised as reflective of what kind of people the Britons have been and might be again.

It is this writing that is tied to the Arthurian legends. In terms of Arthurian studies, Gildas does not even mention King Arthur by name. Gildas's contribution (and inspiration to the legends) is the descriptions of Vortigern's invitation to the eventually invading Saxons, the mentioning of Ambrosius Aurelianus, and of the Battle at Badon Hill. Because of the similarities between Gildas's description and Arthur's later descriptions, some believe that Ambrosius Aurelianus was actually Arthur. He writes that Ambrosius was one of the few Romans left alive in Britain, and argues that his "modest nature" is what allows him opportunities to defeat the invading Saxons.

> Their leader was Ambrosius Aurelianus, a gentleman who, perhaps alone of the Romans, had survived the shock of this notable storm. . . . Under him our people regained their strength, and challenged the victors to battle. The Lord assented, and the battle went their way. From then on victory when now to our countrymen, now to their enemies. . . . This lasted right up till the year of the siege of

Badon Hill, pretty well the last defeat of the villains, and certainly not the least. That was the year of my birth; as I know, one month of forty-fourth year since then has already passed. (translation from *King Arthur in Legend and History*, 3–4)

Later stories mention Badon Hill as the battle fought by Arthur, either under Ambrosius, or else Ambrosius's name is not mentioned at all. It is also possible that Ambrosius Aurelianus was a pseudonym for King Arthur, just as Badonicus was a pseudonym for Gildas. If Caradog of Llancarfan's story of Gildas is true, that Gildas and Arthur were both friends and foes, it is possible that Gildas might have had good reasons not to mention Arthur by name. Then again, Gildas seems to mention only kings and other leaders by name whom he wishes to attack as bad examples of leadership. So it is also possible that Arthur was not bad enough to be attacked and yet not worthy enough to be mentioned as an example of good leadership.

Regardless, it seems that for Gildas, the historical facts were better recorded under the sermonizing qualities of lessons to be learned from the events of a story. This type of rhetoric is elusive. While it is possible that Arthur is one of the many real leaders whose name Gildas changed in his metaphorical diatribe, it is also possible that Gildas was too angry to even mention Arthur at all. Or perhaps Gildas was not angry at Arthur? It is also possible that Arthur simply did not exist. Did Gildas know Arthur? Little more than speculation can be made. But Gildas's doctrine does verify certain surrounding facts of Arthur's time, and while that is not proof of Arthur's existence, it is proof of Arthur's time. Gildas's contribution is both historical and fictional, a little sermonizing, intensely political, which is part of the mystery.

PRIMARY WORKS

De Excidio et Conquestu Britanniae ac flebi castigatione in reges, principes, et sacradotes (The Ruin and Conquest of Britain or a Mournful Rebuke for Kings, Princes, and Priests, c. 540s). **Manuscripts:** There are five extant manuscripts, the earliest dating from the eleventh century; there are four other manuscripts that contain parts of this work. **First publication:** *De Excidio et Conquestu Britanniae ac flebi castigatione in reges, principes, et sacradotes*. England: printed by Polidore Virgil, 1525. **Standard edition:** In *Monumenta Germaniae Historica, Auctores Antiquissimi*, ed. Theodor Mommsen, 1894–1898. Reprint, Berlin, 1961; *The Ruin of Britain and Other Works*. In *History from the Sources*, vol. 7, trans. M. Winterbottom. Old Woking, 1978; *De Excidio Brittonum*. In *Six Old English Chronicles, of Which Two Are Now First Translated from the Monkish Latin Originals*, trans. John Allan Giles. London: George Bell and Sons, 1891. Also available at http://www.fordham.edu/halsall/basis/gildas-full.html; *The de excidio Britonum*, trans. Keith Matthews (based on Mommsen's version). Available at http://www.kmatthews.org.uk/history/gildas/frames.html.

SECONDARY SOURCES

Ashe, Geoffrey, ed. *The Quest for Arthur's Britain*. Chicago: Academy Chicago Publishers, 1987; Bachrach, Bernard S. "Gildas, Vortigern, and Constitutionality in Sub-Roman Britain." *Nottingham Mediaeval Studies* 32 (1988): 126–40; Bartrum, P. C. *Early Welsh Genealogical Tracts*. Cardiff, 1966; ———. *A Welsh Classical Dictionary*. Cardiff, 1993; Caradoc of Llangarfan. "The Life of Gildas." In *Two Lives of Gildas by a Monk of Ruys and Caradoc of Llancarfan*, Cymmrodorion Record Series, ed. and trans. Hugh Williams, 1899. Reprint, Felinfach, UK: Llanerch Publishers, 1990. Also available at http://members.aol.com/michellezi/translations/

LifeofGildas.html; Dark, Kenneth R. *Civitas to Kingdom: British Political Continuity, 300–800.* Studies in the Early History of Britain. Leicester, 1994; Dumville, David N. "The Chronology of *De Excidio Britanniae*, Book 1." In *Gildas: New Approaches*, ed. Michael Lapidge and David N. Dumville, 61–84. Woodbridge, UK: Boydell Press, 1984; ———. "Gildas and Maelgwn: Problems of Dating." In *Gildas: New Approaches*, ed. Michael Lapidge and David N. Dumville, 51–60. Woodbridge, UK: Boydell Press, 1984; ———. "Gildas and Uinniau." In *Gildas: New Approaches*, ed. Michael Lapidge and David N. Dumville, 207–14. Woodbridge, UK: Boydell Press, 1984; Higham, N. J. *King Arthur: Myth-Making and History.* London: Routledge, 2002; Ibeji, Mike. "King Arthur—British Resistance Legend." Available at http://www.bbc.co.uk/history/ancient/arthur_01.shtml; Jones, Michael E. *The End of Roman Britain.* Ithaca, NY: Cornell University Press, 1996; Morris, John. *The Age of Arthur: A History of the British Isles from 350 to 650.* 1973. Reprint, Rochester, NY: Boydell & Brewer, 1989; O'Sullivan, Thomas D. *The De Excidio of Gildas: Its Authenticity and Date.* Columbia Studies in the Classical Tradition, vol. 7. Leiden, 1978; Sims-Williams, P. "Gildas and the Anglo-Saxons." *Cambridge Medieval Celtic Studies* 6 (1983): 1–30; ———. "Gildas and Vernacular Poetry." In *Gildas: New Approaches*, ed. Michael Lapidge and David N. Dumville, 169–90. Woodbridge, UK: Boydell Press, 1984; Snyder, Christopher A. *An Age of Tyrants: Britain and Britons, AD 400–600.* University Park: Pennsylvania State University Press, 1998; Thompson, E. A. "Gildas and the History of Britain." *Britannia* 10 (1979): 203–26; White, Richard, ed. *King Arthur in Legend and History.* London: Routledge, 1997; Wood, Ian N. "The End of Roman Britain: Continental Evidence and Parallels." In *Gildas: New Approaches*, ed. Michael Lapidge and David N. Dumville, 1–26. Woodbridge, UK: Boydell Press, 1984.

CAROL L. ROBINSON

BEDE

(c. 673–May 25, 735)

Bede was an Anglo-Saxon monk and scholar of Northumbria (northern England). He was a notable historian, careful to cite sources and to put a wide variety of data together to form a cohesive narrative of events, and his work was groundbreaking in the now standardized methods of historiography. Perhaps indicative of his care as an historian, however, Bede does not provide a comprehensive narrative in his histories, recording only events for which he felt he had solid evidence. For example, nothing that directly supports the real existence of Arthur appears in his works. Bede was more than an historian, though, and this affected his recording of history. However, Bede's history provides a context for not only Arthurian history and legends, but also for Christian Anglo-Saxon perspectives of Celtic history. Both his recordings of history and his gaps of history perhaps are telling about Bede the scholar, his scholarship, and the fact or fiction of the Arthurian world.

Very little of Bede's origins and personal life is known. He was born in either 672 or 673 CE in what soon after became known as Northumbria. He was seven years old, and very likely an orphan, when he was placed by his relatives at the newly developed monastery of St. Peter at Wearmouth, under the care of Abbot Benedict. When he was approximately ten years old, the St. Paul monastery was established in Jarrow, and Bede was apparently transferred there and became the custody of Abbot Ceolfrid. That Bede excelled at his scholastic and religious studies is demonstrated by the fact that he was ordained a deacon at the age of nineteen (692)—six years under the minimum age decreed for such ordination by the ecclesiastical canons. Eleven years later in 703, Bede's scholarship and piety were again recognized, and at the age of thirty he was ordained a priest. He never became an abbot (perhaps due to a possible lack of noble birth). His life was consumed by his devotions to religion and scholarship at the monastery. He spent

(Bede the Venerable, Venerabilis Bæda, St. Bede the Venerable)

the majority of his life in Northumbria at the monastery in Jarrow, though he did leave it for infrequent visits to other monasteries, and it is probable that he visited the king of Northumbria, Ceolwulf. Despite a statement made by William of Malmesbury, there is little evidence that he ever visited the pope in Rome. He died in his early sixties in the spring 735. According to Cuthbert, who was one of Bede's protégés and an eyewitness to his death, Bede worked to the very end. He acquired the title Bede the Venerable (*Venerabilis Bæda*) sometime after his death. In a short autobiography at the end of his life titled *A History of the English Church and People*, Bede wrote, "And while I have observed the regular discipline and always sung the choir offices daily in church, my chief delight has always been in study, teaching, and writing."

The significance of Bede's care as a scholar is great, especially within the context of the Middle Ages and certainly in light of the question of Arthur's reality. He was prudent enough to cite sources, including passages borrowed from elsewhere, pleading to copyists to continue his documentation. Bede's historical and theological work demonstrates a formidable ability to cipher through much data, weeding out doubtful or weakly supported items, to form a cohesive and mostly factual narrative. At time his source is but a single work, and he is careful to note this, too. He is most known as a theologian, historian, and teacher, but he was also a hagiographer, a poet, a geographer, a scientist, a chronologist, and one of the few mathematicians of this period. Modern mathematics historians recognize Bede for his solitary writings on the computations for calendars and the method of counting and figuring with fingers. Following the system devised by the Greek monk, Dionysius Exiguous, Bede popularized the Anno Domini system of reckoning that is still used today. Bede established himself as a master chronologist, devoted to the pursuit of accurate computation, a skill that is also significant to the work of an historian. Citing him as a source would add credence to any later written history.

Bede is mentioned as a source for the history of King Arthur by Geoffrey of Monmouth, roughly four hundred years after Bede's death (and about 650 years after the probable time of Arthur's existence):

> Whenever I have chanced to think about the history of the kings of Britain, on those occasions when I have been turning over a great many such matters in my mind, it has seemed a remarkable thing to me that, apart from such mention of them as Gildas and Bede had each made in a brilliant book on the subject, I have not been able to discover anything at all on the kings who lived here before the Incarnation of Christ, or indeed about Arthur and all the others who followed on after the Incarnation.

Bede's *A History of the English Church and People*, also known as *Ecclesiastical History* (*Historia Ecclesiastica*, 731 CE), is almost certainly the book to which Geoffrey of Monmouth is referring, yet there is no mention of King Arthur in this book (much less in any other work by Bede).

Bede does not provide proof that Arthur did exist, nor does he provide proof that Arthur did not exist. Despite his skills and brilliance, Bede's scholarship was limited by numerous factors. While he is today most celebrated as a historian, Bede was best known during his lifetime for his ecclesiastical works. Furthermore, although Bede put much energy into the research and writing of a wide variety of fields, his true vocation was as a teacher. By the time he was ordained into the priesthood, his reputation as a devoted and excellent teacher had been already firmly established. In Bede's time, the only available formal education was monastic, and that Bede virtually grew up in a monastery further emphasizes his detachment from Anglo-Saxon, Celtic, Roman, and other secular works (written or oral). In terms of Arthurian scholarship specifically, Bede's access is also limited in terms of time and space. Bede was researching and recording events two to three centuries after the most likely time of Arthur's existence, and he was doing so in Northumbria, a predominately Anglo-Saxon land where the sermonizing writings of Gildas seem to have been his primary source.

But Bede's *A History of the English Church and People* does provide some significant surrounding data and confirmation for the period of Arthur's supposed existence. For example, the book provides some neglected details of the Anglo-Pictish alliance, made at about the same time as the battle against the Jutes at Aylesford in 455. *A History of the English Church and People* also confirms the Battle of Mount Badon, and adds to it some vital information (such as the names of Vortigern, Hengist, and Horsa).

According to Bede, once it became clear that the Roman Legion would no longer return to help the Britons fight back the invading Scots from the northwest (Ireland) and the Picts from the north (Scotland) "were quick to return themselves" and "bolder than ever." Bede wrote, "They were driven from their homesteads and farms, and sought to save themselves from starvation by robbery and violence against one another, their own internal anarchy adding to the miseries caused by others, until there was no food left in the whole land except whatever could be obtained by hunting."

This slaughter went on for years, but those Britons who did not surrender or die fought back. "Making frequent sallies from the mountains, caves, and forests, they began at length to inflict severe losses on the enemy who had plundered their country for so many years." For some time, then, there was a kind of peace from these invading raiders, and thus famine was reduced for awhile.

But then, not long after a terrible bout of the plague had struck, the Britons "consulted how they might obtain help to avoid or repel the frequent fierce attacks of their northern neighbors, and all agreed with the advice of their king, Vortigern, to call on the assistance of the Saxon peoples across the sea." According to Bede, in 449, either the Angles or the Saxons came over and "were granted lands in the eastern part of the island on condition that they protected the country." This bargain was upheld for a time, but then there was a change of heart, and the Germanic peoples decided to invite their native countries to invade and take over the Briton's lands for themselves. Clearly, Bede's bias comes through as he describes the Britons as "cowardly" and the Jutes, Angles, and Saxons as "the three most formidable races of Germany"—arguing that the Britons got what they deserved. Bede writes that the Jutes settled in Kent, the Isle of Wight, and in "the province of the West Saxons opposite the Isle of Wight." The Saxons settled in the rest of what is now Southern England, and the Angles settled the middle and northern parts of the island (East and Middle Anglia, Mercia, and Northumbria). "Their first chieftains are said to have been the brothers Hengist and Horsa." Soon after, Bede wrote that "the Angles made an alliance with the Picts, whom by this time they had driven some distance away, and began to turn their arms against their allies."

Then, several years later (roughly 493), the Britons had a new leader, Ambrosius Aurelianus, "a man of good character and the sole survivor of Roman race from the catastrophe." Under Ambrosius Aurelianus, the Britons won a battle, and from then on "victory swung first to one side and then to the other, until the battle of Badon Hill, when the Britons made a considerable slaughter of the invaders."

Although Bede was a careful historian, he was not the most objective. For example, he summarized the Anglo-Saxon invasion by commenting, "In short, the fires kindled by the pagans proved to be God's just punishment on the sins of the nation, just as the fires once kindled by the Chaldeans destroyed the walls and buildings of Jerusalem." *A History of the English Church and People* served as a historical compilation of lessons on human nature and how to live and not live one's life. Indeed, there are several hagiographies interlaced between recorded events. The book also served as a text of national unity. While the central focus was upon native Northumbria, Bede consistently made the point that the English people are a diverse people, all united in their devotion to Christ and their ties to the Roman Church. As even Bede's descriptions of where each race lived suggests, such unity—be it just among the Anglo-Saxons or among all the inhabitants of the island—was far from real, but his writing of this ideal helped to influence later generations. He described the country this way: "At the present time there are in Britain, in harmony with the five books of the divine law, five languages and four nations—English, British, Scots, and Picts. Each of these have their own language; but all are united in their study of god's truth by the fifth—Latin—which has become a common medium through the study of the scriptures." The book was clearly not mere nationalistic propaganda, and contemporary historians continue to affirm the accuracy of his presentation of English history. His last major work, it demonstrates his maturity as a scholar, priest, and teacher and represents the culmination of a lifetime of work.

But what of Arthur? This lack of recorded data has been the cause of much concern over the reality of Arthur's existence. For one thing, the missing data has often given credence to the interpretation that King Arthur never existed, except in the imaginations of storytellers and political propagandists. It is possible that the efforts to once again reunite the Britons against the Teutonic invaders was real, and that King Arthur was more a symbolic figure, like the United States's Uncle Sam. This missing data could also simply mean that, particularly since Bede lived the kind of monastic life that could shelter him from the political and cultural histories of the outside secular world, he could not find sufficient support to mention this idealistic and possibly non-Christian king, leaving it to others to find such proof. The conclusion of this argument is that, since no one other contemporary of Bede (much less from earlier times) provides sufficient proof, Arthur did not exist. But it is this silence that eludes contemporary historians who are unable to fill the void, either way.

Primary Works

De temporibus liber includens chronica minora (On Times Including a Short Chronicle, 703). **First publication:** In *Bedae presbyteri Anglosaxonis viri eruditissimi de natura rerum et temporum ratione*, ed. John Sichardus. Basel: printed by Henri Petrus, 1529. **Standard edition:** In *Corpus Christianorum Series Latina*, vol. 123C, ed. C. W. Jones, 579–611. Turnhout, Belgium: Brepols, 1980; *De natura rerum liber* (On the Nature of Things, c. 703). **First publication:** In *Bedae presbyteri Anglosaxonis viri eruditissimi de natura rerum et temporum ratione*, ed. John Sichardus. Basel: printed by Henri Petrus, 1529. **Standard edition:** In *Corpus Christianorum Series Latina*, vol. 123A, ed. C. W. Jones, 173–234. Turnhout, Belgium: Brepols, 1980; *Explanatio Apocalypsis* (On the Apocalypse, c. 703–709). **First publication:** In *Secundus operum Venerabilis Bedae ... tomus, in quo continentur eiusdem commentarii*. Paris: printed by Jodocus Badius Ascensius, 1521. **Standard edition:** In *Patrologia Latina*, vol. 93, ed. J.-P. Migne, 1850. Reprint, Turnhout, Belgium: Brepols, 1980, cols. 129–206. **Partial English edition:** *The Explanation of the Apocalyse by Venerable Beda*, trans. E. Marshall. Oxford: J. Parker, 1878; *De locis sanctis* (On the Holy Places, c. 703–709). **First publication:** In *Venerabilis Bedae opera omnia*. Basel: printed by John Herwagen, 1563. **Standard edition:** In *Corpus Christianorum*

Series Latina, vol. 175, ed. J. Fraipont, 245–80. Turnhout, Belgium: Brepols, 1965. **English edition:** *Bede: A Biblical Miscellany.* Translated Texts for Historians Series, vol. 28, ed. W. Trent Foley and Arthur G. Holder. Liverpool: Liverpool University Press, 1999; *Libri quatuor in principium Genesis* (On Genesis, Book 1a, c. 703–709; Books 1b, 2–4, c. 725–731). **First publication:** Book 1a in *Venerabilis Bedae opera omnia.* Basel: printed by John Herwagen, 1563. Entire work in *Bedae venerabilis opera quaedam theologica, nunc primum edita, necnon historica, antea semel edita*, ed. Henry Wharton. London: printed by S. Roycroft, 1693. **Standard edition:** In *Corpus Christianorum Series Latina*, vol. 118A, ed. C. W. Jones. Turnhout, Belgium: Brepols, 1967; *Liber hymnorum, rhythmi, variae preces* (Hymns, c. 703–731). **First publication:** In *Hymni Ecclesiastici.* Cologne: printed by Georgius Cassander, 1556 (includes eleven poems attributed to Bede). **Standard edition:** In *Corpus Christianorum Series Latina*, vol. 122, ed. J. Fraipont, 405–70. Turnhout, Belgium: Brepols, 1965; *Vita sancti Cuthberti metrica* (Life of Saint Cuthbert, in prose, c. 706–707). **First publication:** In *Antiquae lectionis*, vol. 2, ed. Heinrich Canisius. Ingolstadt: printed by A. Angermarius, 1604. **Standard edition:** *Bedas metrische vita sancti Cuthberti*, ed. Werner Jaager, in *Palaestra*, 198. Leipzig: Mayer & Müller, 1935; *Epistola ad Plegvinam* (Letter to Plegwine, 708). **First publication:** In *Venerabilis Bedae epistolae duae, necnon vitae abbatum Wiremuthensium & Girwiensium*, ed. Sir James Ware. Dublin: printed by John Crook, 1664. **Standard edition:** In *Corpus Christianorum Series Latina*, vol. 123C, ed. C. W. Jones, 613–26. Turnhout, Belgium: Brepols, 1980; *In Epistolas VII Catholicas* (On the Seven Catholic Epistles, c. 709). **First publication:** In *Secundus operum Venerabilis Bedae . . . tomus, in quo continentur eiusdem commentarii.* Paris: printed by Jodocus Badius Ascensius, 1521. **Standard edition:** In *Corpus Christianorum Series Latina*, vol. 121, ed. D. Hurst, 179–342. Turnhout, Belgium: Brepols, 1983. **English edition:** *Commentary on the Seven Catholic Epistles*, trans. David Hurst. Kalamazoo, MI: Cistercian Publications, 1985; *Expositio Actuum Apostolorum* (On the Acts of the Apostles, c. 709). **First publication:** In *Secundus operum Venerabilis Bedae . . . tomus, in quo continentur eiusdem commentarii.* Paris: printed by Jodocus Badius Ascensius, 1521. **Standard edition:** In *Corpus Christianorum Series Latina*, vol. 121, ed. M. L. W. Laistner, 1–99. Turnhout, Belgium: Brepols, 1983. **English edition:** *Commentary on the Acts of the Apostles*, trans. Lawrence T. Martin. Kalamazoo, MI: Cistercian Publications, 1989; *In Lucae evangelium expositio* (On the Gospel of Luke, c. 709–716). **First publication:** In *Secundus operum Venerabilis Bedae . . . tomus, in quo continentur eiusdem commentarii.* Paris: printed by Jodocus Badius Ascensius, 1521. **Standard edition:** In *Corpus Christianorum Series Latina*, vol. 120, ed. D. Hurst, 1–425. Turnhout, Belgium: Brepols, 1960; *De orthographia* (On Orthography, c. 710–731). **First publication:** In *Venerabilis Bedae opera omnia.* Basel: printed by John Herwagen, 1563. **Standard edition:** In *Corpus Christianorum Series Latina*, vol. 123A, ed. C. W. Jones, 1–57. Turnhout, Belgium: Brepols, 1975; *De arte metrica et de schematibus tropis* (On the Art of Metrics and On Figures and Tropes, c. 710–731). **First publication:** *Liber Bedae de schemate & tropo and Eiusdem vero ars de metris incipit feliciter.* Milan: printed by Antonius Zarotus, 1473. **Standard edition:** In *Corpus Christianorum Series Latina*, vol. 123A, ed. C. B. Kendall, 59–171. Turnhout, Belgium: Brepols, 1975. **English edition:** *Libri II De arte metrica et de schematibus et tropis: The Art of Poetry and Rhetoric*, from Saint Gall, Stiftsbibliothek 876, ed. and trans. Calvin B. Kendall. Saarbrucken, Germany: AQ-Verlag, 1991; *In primam partem Samuhelis* (On the First Book of Samuel, 716). **First publication:** In *Venerabilis Bedae opera omnia.* Basel: printed by John Herwagen, 1563. **Standard edition:** In *Corpus Christianorum Series Latina*, vol. 119, ed. D. Hurst, 1–287. Turnhout, Belgium: Brepols, 1962; *In Marci evangelium expositio* (On the Gospel of Mark, c. 720–725). **First publication:** In *Secundus operum Venerabilis Bedae . . . tomus, in quo continentur eiusdem commentarii.* Paris: printed by Jodocus Badius Ascensius, 1521. **Standard edition:** In *Corpus Christianorum Series Latina*, vol. 120, ed. D. Hurst, 427–648. Turnhout, Belgium: Brepols, 1960; *In Tobiam* (On Tobias, c. 720–731). **First publication:** In *Venerabilis Bedae opera omnia.* Basel: printed by John Herwagen, 1563. **Standard edition:** In *Corpus Christianorum Series Latina*, vol. 119B, ed. D. Hurst, 1–19. Turnhout, Belgium: Brepols, 1983. **English**

edition: *Bede: A Biblical Miscellany.* Translated Texts for Historians Series, vol. 28, ed. W. Trent Foley and Arthur G. Holder. Liverpool: Liverpool University Press, 1999; *In Proverbia* (On Proverbs, c. 720–731). **First publication:** In *Venerabilis Bedae opera omnia.* Basel: printed by John Herwagen, 1563. **Standard edition:** In *Corpus Christianorum Series Latina*, vol. 119B, ed. D. Hurst, 21–163. Turnhout, Belgium: Brepols, 1983; *In Habacuc* (On Habakkuk, c. 720–731). **First publication:** In *Bedae venerabilis opera quaedam theologica, nunc primum edita, necnon historica, antea semel edita*, ed. Henry Wharton. London: printed by S. Roycroft, 1693. **Standard edition:** In *Corpus Christianorum Series Latina*, vol. 119B, ed. J. E. Hudson, 370–409. Turnhout, Belgium: Brepols, 1983; *In Cantica Canticorum* (On the Song of Songs, c. 720–731). **First publication:** In *Venerabilis Bedae opera omnia.* Basel: printed by John Herwagen, 1563. **Standard edition:** In *Corpus Christianorum Series Latina*, vol. 119B, ed. D. Hurst, 175–375. Turnhout, Belgium: Brepols, 1983; *Homeliarum evangelii libri II* (Homilies on the Gospels, c. 720–731). **First publication:** In *Homiliae Bedae presbyteri Anglosaxonis ... aestivales (hyemales) de tempore & de sanctis*, 2 parts. Cologne: printed by Joannes Gymnicus, 1534. **Standard edition:** In *Corpus Christianorum Series Latina*, vol. 122, ed. D. Hurst, 1–378. Turnhout, Belgium: Brepols, 1965. **English edition:** *Homilies on the Gospels*, 2 vols., trans. Lawrence T. Martin and David Hurst. Kalamazoo, MI: Cistercian Publications, 1991; *Vita sancti Cuthberti prosaica* (Life of Saint Cuthbert, in prose, c. 721). **First publication:** In *Venerabilis Bedae opera omnia.* Basel: printed by John Herwagen, 1563. **Standard edition:** In *Two Lives of St. Cuthbert*, ed. and trans. Bertram Colgrave, 141–307. Cambridge: Cambridge University Press, 1940. **English edition:** In *The Age of Bede*, ed. D. H. Farmer, trans. J. F. Webb, 39–102. Harmondsworth, UK: Penguin, 1983; *De tabernaculo et vasis eius ac vestibus sacerdotum* (On the Tabernacle, c. 721–725). **First publication:** In *Venerabilis Bedae opera omnia.* Basel: printed by John Herwagen, 1563. **Standard edition:** In *Corpus Christianorum Series Latina*, vol. 119A, ed. D. Hurst, 1–139. Turnhout, Belgium: Brepols, 1969. **English edition:** *On the Tabernacle*, trans. Arthur G. Holder. Liverpool: Liverpool University Press, 1994; *De temporum ratione liber includens chronica maiora* (On the Reckoning of Times, Including a Long Chronicle, 725). **First publication:** In *Bedae presbyteri Anglosaxonis viri eruditissimi de natura rerum et temporum ratione*, ed. John Sichardus. Basel: printed by Henri Petrus, 1529. **Standard edition:** In *Corpus Christianorum Series Latina*, vol. 123B, ed. C. W. Jones, 239–544. Turnhout, Belgium: Brepols, 1977. **English edition:** *Bede: The Reckoning of Time.* Translated Texts for Historians Series, vol. 29, trans. and ed. Faith Wallis. Philadelphia: University of Pennsylvania Press, 2000; *In Regum librum XXX quaestiones* (Thirty Questions on Kings, c. 725). **First publication:** In *Venerabilis Bedae opera omnia.* Basel: printed by John Herwagen, 1563. **Standard edition:** In *Corpus Christianorum Series Latina*, vol. 119, ed. D. Hurst, 289–322. Turnhout, Belgium: Brepols, 1972. **English edition:** *Bede: A Biblical Miscellany.* Translated Texts for Historians Series, vol. 28, ed. W. Trent Foley and Arthur G. Holder. Liverpool: Liverpool University Press, 1999; *Retractatio in Actus Apostolorum* (Retraction on Acts, c. 725–731). **First publication:** In *Venerabilis Bedae opera omnia.* Basel: printed by John Herwagen, 1563. **Standard edition:** In *Corpus Christianorum Series Latina*, vol. 121, ed. M. L. W. Laistner, 101–63. Turnhout, Belgium: Brepols, 1983; *In Ezram et Neemiam* (On Ezra and Nehemiah, c. 725–731). **First publication:** In *Venerabilis Bedae opera omnia.* Basel: printed by John Herwagen, 1563. **Standard edition:** In *Corpus Christianorum Series Latina*, vol. 119A, ed. D. Hurst, 235–392. Turnhout, Belgium: Brepols, 1969; *Historia abbatum* (History of the Abbots, c. 725–731). **Standard edition:** In *Venerabilis Baedae opera historica*, vol. 1, ed. Charles Plummer, 1896. Reprint, Oxford: Oxford University Press, 1956. **English edition:** In *The Age of Bede*, ed. D. H. Farmer, trans. J. F. Webb, 183–208. Harmondsworth, UK: Penguin, 1983; *Martyrologium* (c. 725–731). **First publication:** In *Acta sanctorum quotquot toto orbe coluntur, vel a catholicas scriptoribus celebrantur quae ex latinis et graecis, aliarumque gentium antiquis monumentis*, vol. 2, ed. Godefroid Henskens and Daniel van Papenbroeck, viii–xl. Antwerp: printed by John van Meurs, 1688. **Standard edition:** In *Édition practique des martyrologes de Bède, de l'anonyme lyonnais et de Florus*, ed. Jacques DuBois and Geneviève Renaud. Paris: Éditions du Centre

National de la Recherche Scientifique, 1976; *De templo* (On the Temple, c. 729–731). **First publication:** In *Venerabilis Bedae opera omnia*. Basel: printed by John Herwagen, 1563. **Standard edition:** In *Corpus Christianorum Series Latina*, vol. 119A, ed. D. Hurst, 141–234. Turnhout, Belgium: Brepols, 1969; *Historia ecclesiastica gentis Anglorum* (Ecclesiastical History of the English People, 731). **Manuscripts:** More than 150 extant manuscripts include the complete text; many others include excerpts. The standard edition by Colgrave and Mynors (1969, 1991) is based on two classes of early manuscripts. The C group is represented by Landesbibliothek, Kassel, theologicus Q. 2 (Northumbrian, late eighth century); British Library, MS. Cotton Tiberius C. II (southern England, late eighth century); and an early-eleventh-century manuscript in the Bodleian Library, Oxford, MS. Hatton 43 (4106). The M group includes two Northumbrian manuscripts written soon after the time of Bede: Cambridge University Library Kk. 5. 16 (c. 737) and Public Library, Leningrad, Q. v. I. 18 (c. 747). **Facsimiles:** *The Moore Bede: Cambridge University Library MS. Kk. 5. 16*, Early English Manuscripts in Facsimile, vol. 9, ed. Peter Hunter Blair and Roger A. B. Mynors. Copenhagen: Rosenkilde & Bagger, 1959. *The Leningrad Bede*, Early English Manuscripts in Facsimile, vol. 2, ed. O. Arngart. Copenhagen: Rosenkilde & Bagger, 1952. Six extant manuscripts transcribe the Old English version in whole or in part; Miller's edition (1890–1898) is based largely on Tanner 10 (tenth century) in the Bodleian Library at Oxford. **Facsimile:** *The Tanner Bede: The Old English Version of Bede's "Historia ecclesiastica," Oxford Bodleian Library Tanner 10*, Early English Manuscripts in Facsimile, vol. 24, ed. Janet Bately. Copenhagen: Rosenkilde & Bagger, 1992. **First publications:** Latin version, *Historia ecclesiastica gentis Anglorum*. Strasbourg, c. 1475–1480. Old English version, in *Historiae ecclesiasticae gentis Anglorum libri V, a venerabilis Beda presbytero scripti*, ed. Abraham Whelock. Cambridge: printed by Roger Daniel, 1643. Modern English version, *The History of the Church of Englande Compiled by Venerable Bede, Englishman*, trans. Thomas Stapleton. Antwerp: printed by John Laet, 1565. **Standard editions:** *Bede's Ecclesiastical History of the English People*, 2nd ed., ed. and trans. Bertram Colgrave and R. A. B. Mynors. Oxford: Clarendon Press, 1991. *The Old English Version of Bede's Ecclesiastical History of the English People*, ed. and trans. Thomas Miller, EETS, o.s. 95–96, 110–111, 1890–1898. Reprint, 1959. **English edition:** *Ecclesiastical History of the English People, with Bede's Letter to Egbert and Cuthbert's Letter on the Death of Bede*, trans. Leo Sherley-Price, rev. R. E. Latham, with translations of the minor works by D. H. Farmer. London: Penguin, 1990. *The Ecclesiastical History of the English People, The Greater Chronicle, and Bede's Letter to Egbert*, ed. and trans. Judith McClure and Roger Collins. Oxford: Oxford University Press, 2000; *Aliquot quaestionum liber* (On Eight Questions, c. 731–735). **First publication:** In *Venerabilis Bedae opera omnia*. Basel: printed by John Herwagen, 1563. **Standard edition:** In *Patrologia Latina*, vol. 93, ed. J.-P. Migne, 1850. Reprint, Turnhout, Belgium: Brepols, 1980, cols. 455–462. **English edition:** *Bede: A Biblical Miscellany*. Translated Texts for Historians Series, vol. 28, ed. W. Trent Foley and Arthur G. Holder. Liverpool: Liverpool University Press, 1999; *Epistola ad Ecgbertum Episcopum* (Letter to Egbert, November 5, 734). **First publication:** In *Venerabilis Bedae epistolae duae, necnon vitae abbatum Wiremuthensium & Girwiensium*, ed. Sir James Ware. Dublin: printed by John Crook, 1664. **Standard edition:** In *Venerabilis Baedae opera historica*, vol. 1, ed. Charles Plummer, 1896. Reprint, Oxford: Oxford University Press, 1956. **English edition:** *Ecclesiastical History of the English People, with Bede's Letter to Egbert and Cuthbert's Letter on the Death of Bede*, trans. Leo Sherley-Price, rev. R. E. Latham, with translations of the minor works by D. H. Farmer. London: Penguin, 1990.

Collected Editions

Venerabilis Bedae opera omnia. In *Patrologia Latina*, vols. 90–95, ed. J.-P. Migne, 1850–1851. Reprint, Turnhout, Belgium: Brepols, 1980; *Bedae venerabilis opera*. In *Corpus Christianorum Series Latina*, vols. 118–23, 175–176 (to date), various editors. Turnhout, Belgium: Brepols, 1955–.

SECONDARY SOURCES

Ashe, Geoffrey, ed. *The Quest for Arthur's Britain*. Chicago: Academy Chicago Publishers, 1987; Blair, Peter Hunter. *Northumbria in the Days of Bede*. New York: St. Martin's Press, 1976; ———. *The World of Bede*. Cambridge: Cambridge University Press, 1990; Bolton, W. F. "Bede." In *A History of Anglo-Latin Literature, 597–1066*, vol. 1, 101–85. Princeton, NJ: Princeton University Press, 1967; ———. "A Bede Bibliography, 1935–1960." *Traditio* 18 (1962): 436–45; Bonner, Gerald. "Bede and Medieval Civilization." *Anglo-Saxon England* 2 (1973): 71–90; ———, ed. *Famulus Christi: Essays in Commemoration of the Thirteenth Centenary of the Birth of the Venerable Bede*. London: SPCK, 1976; Bonner, Gerald, David Rollason, and Clare Stancliffe, eds. *St. Cuthbert: His Cult and His Community to AD 1200*. Woodbridge, UK: Boydell, 1989; Boyer, Carl B. *A History of Mathematics*. Princeton, NJ: Princeton University Press, 1985; Brown, George Hardin. *Bede the Venerable*. Boston: Twayne, 1987; ———. "Royal and Ecclesiastical Rivalries in Bede's History." *Renascence: Essays on Values in Literature* 52, no. 1 (Fall 1999): 19–33; Campbell, James. "Bede." In *Latin Historians*, ed. T. A. Dorey, 159–90. London: Routledge & Kegan Paul, 1966; Carroll, M. Thomas Aquinas. *The Venerable Bede: His Spiritual Teachings*. Washington, DC: Catholic University of America Press, 1946; Chambers, R. W. "Bede." In *Proceedings of the British Academy*, vol. 22, 129–56. London: Oxford University Press, 1936; Cowdrey, H. E. J. "Bede and the 'English People.' " *Journal of Religious History* 11 (December 1981): 501–23; Davidse, Jan. "The Sense of History in the Works of the Venerable Bede." *Studi Medievali*, third series, 23 (December 1982): 647–95; Dionisotti, Anna Carlotta. "On Bede, Grammars, and Greek." *Revue Bénédictine*, 92, nos. 1–2 (1982): 111–41; Duckett, Eleanor Shipley. "Bede of Jarrow." In *Anglo-Saxon Saints and Scholars*, 217–336. New York: Macmillan, 1948; Eckenrode, Thomas. "The Venerable Bede: A Bibliographical Essay, 1970–1981." *American Benedictine Review* 36 (June 1985): 172–94; Farrell, Robert T., ed. *Bede and Anglo-Saxon England: Papers in Honour of the 1300th Anniversary of the Birth of Bede, Given at Cornell University in 1973 and 1974*. British Archaeological Reports, vol. 46. Oxford: British Archaeological Reports, 1978; Goffart, Walter. *The Narrators of Barbarian History, AD 550–800: Jordanes, Gregory of Tours, Bede, and Paul the Deacon*. Princeton, NJ: Princeton University Press, 1988; Harris, Stephen J. "The Alfredian World History and Anglo-Saxon Identity." *Journal of English and Germanic Philology* 100, no. 4 (October 2001): 482–510; ———. "Bede and Gregory's Allusive Angles." *Criticism: A Quarterly for Literature and the Arts* 44, no. 3 (Summer 2002): 271–89; ———. "Bede, Social Practice, and the Problem with Foreigners." *Essays in Medieval Studies* 13 (1996): 97–109; Higham, N. J. *King Arthur: Myth-Making and History*. London: Routledge, 2002; Holder, Arthur G. "Allegory and History in Bede's Interpretation of Sacred Architecture." *American Benedictine Review* 40 (June 1989): 115–31; Irvine, Martin. "Bede the Grammarian and the Scope of Grammatical Studies in Eighth-Century Northumbria." *Anglo-Saxon England* 15 (1986): 15–44; Jones, Charles W. "Some Introductory Remarks on Bede's Commentary on Genesis." *Sacris Eruditi* 19 (1969–1970): 115–98; Kendall, Calvin B. "Bede's *Historia ecclesiastica*: The Rhetoric of Faith." In *Medieval Eloquence: Studies in the Theory and Practice of Medieval Rhetoric*, ed. James J. Murphy, 145–72. Berkeley: University of California Press, 1978; King, Margot H., and Wesley M. Stevens, eds. *Saints, Scholars, and Heroes: Studies in Medieval Culture in Honour of Charles W. Jones*. Vol. 1, *The Anglo-Saxon Heritage*. Collegeville, MN: St. John's Abbey and University, 1979; Kleinschmidt, Harald. "Bede and the Jutes: A Critique of Historiography." *NOWELE: North-Western European Language Evolution* 24 (August 1994): 21–46; Laistner, M. L. W. "Bede as a Classical and a Patristic Scholar." *Transactions of the Royal Historical Society*, fourth series, 16 (1933): 69–94. Reprinted in *The Intellectual Heritage of the Early Middle Ages*, ed. Chester G. Starr, 93–116. Ithaca, NY: Cornell University Press, 1957; Laistner, M. L. W., and H. H. King. *A Hand-List of Bede Manuscripts*. Ithaca, NY: Cornell University Press, 1943; Ledoyen, Henri. "St. Bède le Vénérable." *Bulletin d'histoire Bénédictine* 10 (1979–1984): 712–18; Loyn, H. R. "Bede's Kings: A Comment on the Attitude of Bede to the Nature of Secular Kingship."

Trivium 26 (1991): 54–64; Martin, Lawrence. "Bede as a Linguistic Scholar." *American Benedictine Review* 35 (June 1984): 204–17; McClure, Judith. "Bede and the *Life of Ceolfrid.*" *Peritia* 3 (1984): 71–84; Palmer, Robert B. "Bede as Textbook Writer: A Study of His *De Arte Metrica.*" *Speculum* 34 (October 1959): 573–84; Ray, Roger. "Bede and Cicero." *Anglo-Saxon England* 16 (1987): 1–15; ———. "What Do We Know about Bede's Commentaries?" *Recherches de Théologie Ancienne et Médiévale* 49 (1982): 5–20; Rosenthal, Joel T. "Bede's Use of Miracles in *The Ecclesiastical History.*" *Traditio* 31 (1975): 328–35; Speed, Diane. "Bede's Creation of a Nation in His Ecclesiastical History." *Parergon: Bulletin of the Australian and New Zealand Association for Medieval and Renaissance Studies* 10, no. 2 (December 1992): 139–54; Stephens, J. N. "Bede's Ecclesiastical History" *History* 62 (February 1977): 1–14; Thompson, A. Hamilton, ed. *Bede: His Life, Times, and Writings—Essays in Commemoration of the Twelfth Centenary of His Death.* Oxford: Clarendon Press, 1935; Wallace-Hadrill, J. M. *Bede's "Ecclesiastical History of the English People": A Historical Commentary.* Oxford: Clarendon Press, 1988; Ward, Benedicta. *The Venerable Bede.* Wilton, CT: Morehouse, 1990; Whitelock, Dorothy. *From Bede to Alfred.* London: Variorum, 1980; Wormald, Patrick, Donald Bullough, and Roger Collins, eds. *Ideal and Reality in Frankish and Anglo-Saxon Society: Studies Presented to J. M. Wallace-Hadrill.* Oxford: Blackwell, 1983; Wright, Neil. "Bede and Vergil." *Romanobarbarica* 6 (1981–1982): 361–79.

CAROL L. ROBINSON

NENNIUS

(c. early ninth century)

Nennius was a ninth-century monk, a follower of Elford the Bishop of Bangor in Northern Wales. The name "Nennius" is a latinized version of the native Welsh appellation "Nynniaw." He is known to the contemporary world for his authorship of the *Historia Brittonum (History of the Britons)*, a primary text written in Latin and documenting events of the fifth and sixth centuries. Although the authorship of the text is still disputed, historians are generally content to attribute the work to Nennius since there is a dearth of other plausible authors. For example, the sixth-century writer Gildas has also been credited with the work, yet he was dead before many of the events described in the text took place. That aspect of the chronicle that has drawn the most interest is the inclusion of events suggesting the historical reality of King Arthur.

Many early manuscripts of the *Historia Brittonum* are extant, suggesting that Nennius's work was well known and widely read. The text, for instance, was appropriated by Geoffrey of Monmouth in the composition of his *Historia Regum Britanniae*, the most well known of the early Welsh chronicles. The existing manuscripts also include a variety of innovations, revealing that the work was revised periodically. Indeed, one theory is that Nennius merely revised a preexisting work, possibly written by the above-mentioned Gildas. The main manuscript is held in the British Library, cataloged as Harley 3859, also known as the *British Historical Miscellany*, which contains several other manuscripts. The collection may have been compiled in the mid-tenth century at St. David's scriptorium.

Historia Brittonum is not a reliable text by modern standards of scholarship. It includes material that is clearly spurious and does not demonstrate a rigorous historical method. Indeed, those portions that are of most interest to contemporary readers (the Arthurian allusions) are also the most likely to be fanciful. Two narrative techniques considered unreliable by contemporary historians are employed in the document: synthesizing and synchronizing history. Synthetic history involves the mixing of the legitimate and the legendary, of fiction and nonfiction, a technique that renders the historical accounts suspect. Most scholars of the period regard the inclusion of events associated with the historical Arthur as an intrusion of the legendary into the actual. Synchronizing history is also untrustworthy, involving an effort to create a deceptively fluid and comprehensive account of events by presenting the available materials in fashion that suggests coherence and continuity. Nennius does this by suggesting specious cause/effect relations between events that in all probability were entirely isolated. Synchronizing history also involves an effort to create a consecutive and comparative account of the histories of varying groups. Nennius acknowledges his composite: "I have gathered together all that I could find not only in the Roman annals, but also in the chronicles of the holy fathers ... and in the annals of the Irish and English, and in our native traditions." The authors efforts to synchronize materials is not altogether successful; the text is discontinuous. He admits, "I have made a heap of all that I have found."

A brief account of the historical context in which Nennius wrote will be useful in understanding the *Historia Brittonum*. In contemporary vernacular, the term "Briton" would seem to allude to all the people of the British Isles; however, in the British Isles of the first millennium AD, the appellation "Briton" referred to the native Celtic people who inhabited the island before the Romans and Anglo-Saxons. Nennius's work is a history of the Britons living in the area that is modern day Wales. The military conflicts documented in the work are waged against the English, the pagan tribes of Angles and Saxons migrating from Northern Europe in the fifth and sixth centuries. *Historia Brittonum* offers an account of the gradual encroachment of the English into formerly Celtic territory. The account of Arthur's twelve battles that constitutes the fifty-sixth chapter of Nennius's work is a quasi-historical rendering of conflicts in which the Britons temporarily triumphed over the Saxons.

The *Historia Brittonum* can be subdivided into seven sections. The first involves a speculation regarding the age of the world, beginning with Adam and concluding with "Edmund King of the Angles"; it also includes an enumeration of the ages of the world. The second section records the history of Britons concluding with an account of the life of King Vortigern. The third portion offers a narrative of St. Patrick's life and works, and the fourth an account of Arthur's twelve battles. The final three sections include the ancestry of Saxon kings, a record of towns inhabited by the Britons, and a tract referred to as the *Mirabilia*, which includes a catalogue of extraordinary places and events. Of course, the primary focus of this discussion will be on the events of the fifty-sixth chapter, the twelve battles of Arthur, as well as other allusions to the Arthurian legend.

The references to the so-called historical Arthur in the fifty-sixth chapter begin with the statement that he "fought against them in those days." The ambiguity of this statement has been a catalyst for much speculation about whom he fought. The context seems to suggest that he battled the Saxons, since the mention of Arthur is immediately preceded by a statement that the Saxons had multiplied greatly in Britain. Thus, Arthur would be a Welshman who fought against the conquest of Celtic territory by invading Germanic tribes. The context may also suggest that he fought only against the kings of Kent, or the dynasty of Octa, the progenitor of subsequent kings in that region.

The initial allusion to Arthur also raises a question about his title. The text states that he was "dux bellorum," a phrase that means "duke of battles." It is a matter of speculation whether "dux bellorum" was an official title or merely a description of the significant role he played in defeating the Saxons. The additional statement that he fought "with the kings of the Britons" could imply that he was not a king himself. The context suggests that while the other notable combatants were kings, he was simply a successful commander in the wars or an individual who had distinguished himself for valor.

The catalogue of the twelve battles and victories of Arthur is considered by historians to be of dubious historical merit. One theory is that Nennius listed the battles of the Britons and Saxons with which he was familiar and then arbitrarily credited Arthur with them. A more plausible theory is that he paraphrased the entire account of Arthur's battles from a pre-existing Welsh poem celebrating the legendary Celtic hero. Nennius was clearly familiar with early Welsh poets, his work considered one of the first accounts of the emerging Welsh literature. He names five poets in the *Historia Brittonum*: Talhaearn Tad Awen, Aneirin, Taliesin, Blwchfardd, and Cian. The battle-catalogue poem was a tradition within Welsh poetry, and the aforementioned Taliesin is credited with such poems, but no evidence exists to suggest that he is the source for Nennius's battle list.

Most scholarly commentary on Arthur's battles has attempted to identify the specific locations of his labors in order to determine the veracity of the events: if the battles are historical, then Arthur may be as well. Unfortunately, historians have concluded that none of the locations can be identified with any certainty; each could be associated with several alternative sites. Moreover, in none of the accounts does Nennius reveal the specific opponent that Arthur faces. Indeed, Nennius devotes only a single sentence to each of the first eleven battles, and in most, he identifies only the number of the battle and the place name.

The first five of Arthur's battles are conflicts associated with rivers. The first is identified as taking place "at the mouth of the river Glein." The name is drawn from the Celtic term that signifies clarity and purity, and there is general agreement that the battle might have occurred at one of two locations: the river Glem of Lincolnshire or the Glen in Northumberland. The next four battles are identified with a second river, "the Dubglas in the region Linnuis." The effort to identify this particular river is even more vexing than that of the "Glein," and the use of the qualifier "Linnuis" does little to narrow the possibilities. "Dubglas" means "blue-black," a term that could be merely descriptive. There is justification for associating "Dubglas" with a legion of potential river names, including "black stream," "Devil's Brook," or "Blackwater." "Linnuis" may be a variation on two derivative words meaning "people of Lindum" ("Lindenses") or "land of Lindum" ("Lindensia"). Linnuis is in all likelihood the area known as "Lindsey," which contains the old Roman town of "Lindum," recognized today as "Lincoln." The name "Lindsey" is derived from "Lindensia." This location would be certain if there were any rivers in the area that can be associated with a derivation of the name "Dubglas." Moreover, there is a second town known as Lindum, this one in Scotland, near Loch Lomond and the Douglas glen.

The association of four battles with a single site suggests that the spot was of great consequence to each of the warring groups. It was perhaps the line upon which the Britons sought to repel further incursion of the Saxons into their territory; however, this additional assumption does not offer many plausible alternatives. If the location is Lindsey, then the Britons would be opposing the Saxons where the latter's power was concentrated. Moreover, such a battleground would not be defensive site since the Saxons had occupied the region for a considerable period of time. Of course, this could suggest a heroic incursion into the very heart of Saxon civilization, an effort to win back Celtic territory rather than simply deter further aggression. These might even be the types of conflicts sufficient to win a figure such as Arthur legendary status. However, even if he was victorious in these battles, it cannot be argued that he was successful in expanding the area of Celtic influence for a sustained period. The location near Loch Lomond may have been a plausible spot for waging a campaign against the Scots. A third possibility is the North Dorset Downs where there are two rivers named Dubglas and where it is conceivable that the Saxons were driving west to occupy new territory.

Nennius tells us that the sixth battle was fought on the river Bassas, but there is no river with a related name. There is, however, a rock in North Berwick known as "The Bass," and some believe that the engagement took place here. Another possibility is the Lusas river in Hampshire. Nennius's account of the tenth battle offers equally meager detail. He indicates that the battle took place on the "banks of the river Trat Treuroit." The possible locations include the Ribroit in Somersetshire or the Ribble in Lancashire. It is worth noting that none of the suggested locations for the sixth and tenth battles retain much scholarly credibility.

The alternative locations for the eighth battle are equally unlikely. He locates the battle near castle Gurnion, but there is no such structure on record. The most probable location may be Garionenum, an old Roman outpost in Norfolk. Other options are associated with Cornwall and Durham. What makes the eighth battle more interesting than some of the others is the inclusion of additional provocative information:

The eighth was near Gurnion castle, where Arthur bore the image of the Holy Virgin, mother of God, upon his shoulders, and through the power of our lord Jesus Christ, and the Holy Mary, put the Saxons to flight, and pursued them the whole day with great slaughter.

Arthur's carrying of the Virgin Mary's image is indicative of his Christian piety and humility since he acknowledges the necessity of a favorable providence in his victory. There is, however, general agreement that the placement of the image on Arthur's shoulder is improbable. The scribe might have mistook the Welsh word "scuit" (shield) for "scuid" (shoulder). This clarification lends some historical credibility to the event since it was common for soldiers to adorn their shields and since carrying an image on his shoulders might hinder his performance in battle. Nennius is clear that the battle was of great importance, but the conflict has not been successfully identified with any account in the verifiable historical record.

The location of battle seven is the one for which there is the most scholarly agreement, but even here the consensus extends only to the general area of Scotland. Nennius says that the struggle took place "in the wood of Celidon, which the Britons call Cat Coyt Celidon." Historians concur that Celidon (or the forest of Caledonia) is in Scotland, but the accord dissolves with efforts to be more specific. Some maintain that the battle must have occurred in the northern Highlands, the homeland of the tribe of Caledonii. In contrast, the Welsh located Coit Celidon near Carlisle in the southern Uplands. Speculation over the particular antagonist for Arthur's advances does not resolve the disagreement. His antagonists could have included Picts, Scots, or Angles.

The various extant manuscripts of *Historia Brittonum* offer conflicting details regarding the ninth and eleventh of Arthur's military engagements. The ninth took place in the "city of the legion, which is called Cair Lion." The later qualification of "Cair Lion," which is not included in all of the manuscripts, strongly suggests that the ninth battle took place at Caerleon in Monmouthshire where the Romans had maintained a fortress. Yet the expression "Cair Lion" can also be associated with Chester. The eleventh battle was fought "on the mountain Breguoin, which we call Cat Bregion." Some of the manuscripts locate the battle at "Agned," and some use both names. "Agned" is believed to be Edinburgh, but historians and geographers have not been successful locating the battle any more precisely. The effort to identify "Breguoin" has been just as difficult. The place name may be a derivation of the Roman fortress Bremenium, which would locate the battle at Rochester. On the other hand, a simple translation error, the replacing of an "o" for an "e," could have obscured the name "Breguein," which is associated with the Latin "Bravonium," a clear allusion to Herefordshire, specifically the town of Leintwardine. Rochester is a reasonable location for hostilities since it could be the site where Arthur would repel an invasion from Bernicia; however, Herefordshire is an improbable setting for a conflict.

The twelfth battle is the one for which Nennius provides the most detail. As in the eighth, he affirms Arthur's Christian piety, suggesting that he was armed with providential strength to scourge the heathens. Nennius tells us that Arthur slew nine hundred and forty Saxons with only God's assistance and that "Arthur penetrated to the hill of Badon," a phrasing that suggests the acquisition of substantial Saxon territory. Immediately following the catalog of battles, the chronicler reveals that Arthur's victories, particularly the last, caused alarm among the Saxons, compelling them to bring reinforcements from Germany in number so large that they eventually overran the Britons. Despite the obvious exaggeration of Arthur's prowess in battle (nine hundred and forty killed by his hand), the twelfth battle is the single one for which there is a high level of historical credibility. In other words, the first eleven battles may be mythical rather than historical, but the twelfth is likely to be actual. Historians' confidence in the reality of the clash at the "hill of Badon" is bolstered by documentation of the event from an independent source, namely Gildas, a Welsh monk writing in the middle of the sixth century. While Gildas mentions the battle of Mount Badon in his *De Excidio et Conquestu Britanniae*, he does not acknowledge Arthur's involvement, a fact that may undermine the credibility of the catalog. However, Gildas does insist that the hostilities were waged between the Britons and the Anglo-Saxons, a detail that can contribute to the effort to identify the scene of the conflict. Some scholars associate the name "Badon" with Badbury, derived from the Anglo-Saxon "Baddanbyrig," or "Badda's fort." One of the problems that arises from this association is that there were five hill forts known as "Badda" or "Badbury" in southern part of the island, where a battle between Britons and invading Saxons is likely to have taken place in the centuries that Nennius documents. Another probable location is the city known today as Bath. The "d" in Badon was probably pronounced as a "th," a consistent linguistic difference that still exists between English and German to this day (witness the linguistic cognates "think" and "denken"). With this consideration, the evolution of Badon into Bath seems simple, yet the city of Bath is located in a valley, so the site of the struggle would have to be the surrounding hills.

Nennius's *Historia Brittonum* is also a source for the early development of the mythology surrounding Merlin. Nennius related the tale of Vortigern and Ambrosius Aurelianus, both of whom were historical personages following the Roman occupation. Vortigern was a ruler of the Britons who was instructed by his wise men to build a fortress to defend his land against the invading Saxons. Having discovered a defensible summit in Northern Wales, he set about gathering the materials to construct his citadel. However, each night the building materials disappear and have to be gathered again. Vortigern consults his wise men who insist that he must find a boy who was born without a father and sacrifice him, dripping his blood in the foundation of the citadel. Only after he has completed this task will he be able to complete his city. At length, the boy, Ambrosius, is discovered in the region of Glevesing, contemporary Monmouthshire, and his mother confesses that she is a virgin.

The messengers convey the boy to Vortigern who explains his motivations. When Ambrosius confronts the wise men himself, he advises them to dig in the foundation where they will find a pool at the bottom of which are two vases. Within the vases are two folded tents, and within the tents are two dragons, a red one and a white one. When the dragons are discovered, they begin to fight each other. The white dragon repeatedly drives the red dragon to the center of the tent and occasionally to the very edge. Eventually, however, the red one rallies and drives the white dragon out of the tent and through the pool. Ambrosius then explains the nationalistic symbolism of his discovery. The white dragon is the Saxons; the red is the Britons; the tent is the island of Britain, and the pool is the world. Thus, the allegory of the dragons predicts the vanquishing of the Saxons from the land of the Britons. Ambrosius then prophesies that Vortigern must abandon his project on the hill, leaving the visionary boy at the site. The Welsh leader must then find another location for his citadel. Vortigern obeys, following the boy's instructions and founds a city named Cair Guorthegirn in the region of Gueneri. Some believe this location is Palmecaster in Carlisle, while others insist it is Chepstow in Monmouthshire.

Those familiar with Arthurian legend will note the resemblance between the story of Ambrosius and those later associated with the activities of Merlin. Geoffrey of Monmouth includes the tale in his *Historia Regum Britanniae*; however, he changes the name of the boy to Merlinus. Formerly, legends surrounding Merlin and Ambrosius were two separate traditions, but they were united by Geoffrey's work. Nennius offers little evidence for the veracity of Ambrosius's prophecy. Immediately following the account of Vortigern, he tells of the victory of Vortigern's son, Vortimer, over the Saxons, driving them to the edge of the island, but he then explains that the Saxons summon reinforcements from Germany with tragic consequences for the Britons. There is then no affirmation of the prophecy that the Britons will chase the Saxons out of the "pool."

The final allusions to Arthurian legend can be found at the conclusion of Nennius's *Historia* in that section known as the *Mirabilia* (*Marvels*). Here the historian recounts two local Welsh legends that reveal that the mythology surrounding Arthur was already beginning to take shape in the ninth century. One of the *Marvels* lies in the Buelt region of Wales; here a mound of stones bears a dog's print that is said to belong to Arthur's hound Cabal, who left this mark while hunting the boar, Troit. Arthur later assembled the stones that retain his dog's print and named the spot Carn Cabal. The *Mirabilia* also includes an allusion to the burial place of Arthur's son, Amir. Legends surrounding the tomb suggest that it miraculously changes size.

Despite the contested veracity of Nennius's *Historia Brittonum*, it remains a compelling lens through which the contemporary reader can view the growth of early Arthurian folklore. While there is little reason to believe that Nennius's work demonstrates the historical reality of Arthurian mythology, it may confirm that there was indeed a historical leader of the Britons named Arthur who was important enough to inspire the growth of legend. Whether or not Arthur fought twelve battles is not the pertinent criteria to apply to the *Historia* since clearly Nennius was comfortable including fanciful tales among his authentic historical events. The work is interesting because it perpetuates a lore that eventually becomes the most enduring and beloved mythology of the British Isles, a collection of tales that has been a source of nationalistic pride for centuries.

PRIMARY WORKS

Historia Brittonum. From the early twelfth century. **Manuscript:** British Library MS. Harley 3859. Included in this manuscript are the *Annales Cambriae* and a collection of Welsh genealogies.

SECONDARY SOURCES

Alcock, Leslie. *Arthur's Britain*. New York: St. Martin's, 1971, 55–73; Ashe, Geoffrey. *The Discovery of King Arthur*. New York: Garland Press, 1986, 501–2; ———. *King Arthur's Avalon: The Story of Glastonbury*. New York: Dutton, 1958; *Bibliography of Critical Arthurian Literature*. New York: Modern Language Association, 1931; Brengle, Richard L., ed. *Arthur, King of Britain: History, Chronicle, Romance, and Criticism, with Texts in Modern English, from Gildas to Malory*. Englewood Cliffs, NJ: Prentice-Hall, 1964; Bromwich, Rachel, A. O. H. Jarman, and Brynley F. Roberts, eds. *The Arthur of the Welsh: The Arthurian Legend in Medieval Welsh Literature*. Cardiff: University of Wales Press, 1992; Bruce, J. Douglas. *The Evolution of Arthurian Romance from the Beginnings Down to the Year 1300*. Gloucester, MA: P. Smith, 1958; Dumville, David E. "The Historical Value of the *Historia Brittonum*." *Arthurian Literature* 6 (1986): 1–26; ———. "Sub-Roman Britain: History and Legend." *History* 62 (1977): 173–92; Edwards, Thomas Charles. "The Arthur of History." In *The Arthur of the Welsh*, ed. Rachel Bromwich, A. O. H. Jarman, Brynley F. Roberts, 15–32. Cardiff: University of Wales Press, 1992; Hopkins, Annete Brown. *The Influence of Wace on the Arthurian Romances of Crestian de Troies*. Menasha, WI: Banta, 1913; Jackson, Kenneth Hurlstone. "The Arthur of History." In *Arthurian Literature in the Middle Ages*, ed. Roger Sherman Loomis, 1–11. Oxford: Clarendon, 1959; ———. "Once Again Arthur's Battles." *Modern Philology* 43 (1945–1946): 44–57; Jarmon, A. O. H. *The Legend of Merlin*. Cardiff: University of Wales Press, 1960; Jenkins, Elizabeth. *The Mystery of King Arthur*. New York: Coward, McCann & Geoghegan, 1975; Knight, Stephen T. *Arthurian Literature and Society*. New York: St. Martin's Press, 1983; Korrel, Peter. *An Arthurian Triangle: A Study of the Origin, Development, and Characterization of Arthur, Guinevere, and Modred*. Leiden: Brill, 1984; Lacy, Norris J., ed. *The Arthurian Encyclopedia*. New York: Garland, 1986; ———. *The New Arthurian Encyclopedia*. New York: Garland, 1991; Lacy, Norris J., and Geoffrey Ashe, eds. *Arthurian Handbook*. New York: Garland, 1988; Loomis, Roger. *Celtic Myth and Arthurian Romance*. New York: Columbia University Press, 1927; Phillips, Graham. *King Arthur: The True Story*. London: Century, 1992; Starr, Nathan Comfort. *King Arthur Today: The Arthurian Legend in English and American Literature, 1901–1953*. Gainesville: University of Florida Press, 1954; Whitaker, Muriel A. *The Legends of King Arthur in Art*. Rochester, NY: D. S. Brewer, 1990; Wilhelm, James J. *The Romance of Arthur*. New York: Garland, 1984; ———. *The Romance of Arthur II*. New York: Garland, 1986; ———. *The Romance of Arthur III: Works from Russia to Spain, Norway to Italy*. New York: Garland, 1988.

JAMES KELLER

WACE (ROBERT?)
(c. 1100–1183)

O ne may only speculate what would have become of the Arthurian legend were it not for the contribution of Wace, the twelfth-century author of the *Roman de Brut*. Wace's references to Arthur as a great king significantly increased the audience's assumptions about the character's historical significance. Wace provided material that is probably imaginary enough to seem real and, thus, kept the legends alive. While Wace is a key contributor to Arthurian legend, much of his own biography is shrouded in speculation because little tangible evidence exists concerning his life. What is known comes mainly from a brief passage in his *Roman de Rou*, where Wace notes simply that he was born on the isle of Jersey and educated in Caen, France.

Given this sparse information, critics have generally pieced together three different theories about the life of Wace. There appears to be no doubt that he was born in Jersey sometime between the late eleventh and early twelfth centuries. References in his works have lead scholars to believe his birth to be sometime around 1100. Since there is no birth record of Wace from Jersey during this period, most of the rest of his biography is based solely on speculation.

Many believe that Wace was the grandson of Duke Robert I of Normandy's (Robert the Magnificent) chamberlain, Toustein. If this is true, then Wace would most likely have been a man of means, and he would have been educated with a good background in history. This would help explain the historical references in his texts. Also, as a child of wealth, he would have had more opportunity to be schooled abroad, as there was no real formal education available in Jersey. While educated in Caen, Wace would have become fluent in Latin, the language of many of his works, before taking his holy orders. This would also add to the likelihood that he lived the bulk of his life in Caen.

Conversely, others feel that Wace may have come from a family of little means. It has been proposed that Wace's father may have been a carpenter. The isle of Jersey was noted for its shipbuilding industry and seaport community and little else. If Wace's father was in the carpentry business, Wace would have had firsthand knowledge of shipbuilding and the travails of the seamen. Since the seaport was populated mainly by working class farmers and fishermen, there would have been little opportunity for the poor to escape their lot. Perhaps the only way out of this life would have been entering the priesthood. To someone who had grown up seeing the harsh reality and the brutality of life on the sea or farming the rugged, rocky soil, the impoverished life of a cleric could have been an attractive alternative. His father's vocation as a carpenter is also significant for scholars who hypothesize that his father participated either directly or indirectly in the Norman Conquest; the knowledge of the Conquest evident in his works suggests that Wace must have had access to someone who had been involved in this great action. The only part of Wace's childhood that is not argued is that he must have grown up near a seaport, specifically Jersey; his work shows a great understanding of the sea and the vessels that sailed upon it.

Some of the earliest documentation of Wace's life shows that he was an appointed cleric lisant in Caen in 1130. Since his position as the assistant to a maistre lisant apparently had no specific duties, the situation would have been ideal for Wace as a writer. A trained cleric would have been at least somewhat literate and able to compose; most clerics had some form of correspondence as a part of their daily regimen. Furthermore, Wace would have been trained as an educator, as those who were literate were expected to teach. As a clerc lisant, Wace would have been a step below the master teachers of Caen, and thus in a good position to learn from the masters. Wace later attained the rank of maistre lisant, a title often mentioned in his works. Of the fifteen references to himself in his text, he is simply "wace" in five of them. In the other ten references, he calls himself "Maistre Wace," an indication of his elevation in status. Additionally, there is evidence that his works were popular among his peers because they were copied and preserved. The early works of Wace tended to be translations from Latin into *romanz*, or Old French. Of such extant texts, only three can be certainly attributed to him: *La Vie de St. Marguerite*, a fragment of some 420 lines, the 1,500 line *La Vie de St. Nicholas*, and *La Conception Nostre Dame*. All three of these works were signed either "G[u]ace" or "Maistre G[u]ace" (Kibler, 501).

In addition to his clerical duties, it is also clear that Wace was given the patronage of Henry II, and also served as a canon at Bayeux. During this time Henry would have been the ruler of both Normandy and England. Evidently Henry was made aware of Wace's first work composed in verse in 1155, *Le Roman de Brut*, the piece wherein Wace included some startling new details concerning Arthurian legend. The *Brut* may have been dedicated to Henry's queen, Eleanor of Acquitaine, for Layaman states this in his *Brut*; however, no definitive proof exists. Wace's work is written in octosyllabic verse and presents a somewhat romanticized account of Geoffrey of Monmouth's *Historia Regum Britannia* (c. 1138). Like its predecessor, the *Brut* attempts to recount the history of Britain in some detail. As with Geoffrey's work, the *Brut* traces the history of Britain from the Trojan War, specifically Brutus. While he was true to a great deal of Geoffrey's text, Wace's work is important because of the changes it made in Arthurian legend. Wace's *Le Roman de Brut* is a somewhat looser version of Geoffrey of Monmouth's *Historia Regum Britanniae*, covering the history of Britain from its perceived founding by Brutus to the death of Cadwallader. In the twentieth century the poem was exhaustively studied by such renowned critics as Robert Huntington Fletcher, E. K. Chambers, J. S. P. Tatlock, and Jean Blacker-Knight. Their results highlight the comparative nature of both Geoffrey's and Wace's works and serve to distinguish many of the unique aspects of Wace's rendition of the myth.

Geoffrey's *Historia* contains the germ of Arthurian legend, but Wace's *Brut* varies in that it is somewhat more sympathetic to the Normans and has a much freer style. The *Brut* is perhaps the first work that presents Arthur as a real rather than mythological character. Wace's work was among the earliest to introduce Celtic matter into the French language. The principal source for *Brut* may have been the *Britannici sermonis liber vestustissmus*, a work most probably written by Walter of Oxford (Kibler, 501). Wace made three major changes. First and foremost, Wace's is the first extant work that provides a development of the previously unelaborated upon concept of Arthur's Round Table intermingled with the ancient Celtic traditions of rank and import in connection with the individual's place in relation to the leader. He also provided the name "excalibur" for Arthur's sword, and finally, he was responsible for creating the unified concept of Christian Knights democratically ruling from a Round Table.

Some critics have posited that Wace may not have been able to acquire a copy of Geoffrey's work and so had to rely primarily on the *Britannici sermonis liber vetustissimus*, a work probably composed by Walter of Oxford. This does not mean that he would have been unaware of the contents of Geoffrey's work Whatever the true source, several critics believe Wace may have been interested in helping the Celts establish a heroic lineage. By combining Wace's work with other Welsh chronicles, as well as those of Nennius, the Celts could trace their roots to the great Trojan Aeneas. According to these works, Brutus, Aeneas's great-grandson, led the Trojans from their Greek captors to Britain. Thus, the Celts could rejoice in the idea that they were descendants of great antiquity. This would have helped them cope with the cultural insults about their lack of heritage in relation to the Normans, whose civilization was steeped in tradition. Whether because it promoted Celtic pride or for other reasons, Wace's *Brut* must have been popular for today there are eighteen extant manuscripts.

In lines 9,747–58 of the *Roman de Brut*, Wace notes the origin of Arthur's Round Table as a preventative device. Arthur used the edgeless table as a means of forestalling spats concerning the precedence of his earls based upon their rank; thus all felt more of a sense of equality. However this novel idea did not totally solve the problem because Arthur the king did have to sit somewhere, and naturally those seated closer to him would be perceived to be somewhat nobler that the others. Nevertheless, the roundness of the table was crucial because as Wace notes in the *Brut*, each of the earls thought themselves to be the best. Since there were no corners to differentiate rank, all would consider themselves to be equals while seated at the table. Thus in theory they all were equals and peers; petty disputes over status were virtually eliminated because none of the nobles were able to boast about their position relative to the king.

In his adaptation of Wace's work, Layamon, in his thirteenth century *Brut*, would expand the source with his inclusion of an argument about seating precedence during a holiday feast that occurred because of the limited space around the table. The aftermath of this bloody confrontation left many dead or sorely wounded. Upon hearing of this tragedy a Cornish carpenter decided to create a massive yet portable round table capable of seating 1,600 people. Both Wace and Layaman attribute Breton storytellers as the sources of their explications concerning the Round Table. While it seems dubious and hyperbolic to believe that a table could be carved large enough to seat 1,600 people and, yet, remain portable in that unsophisticated day, there may be no reason to doubt the existence of a round table having to do with Arthur and his warriors. There is a plethora of material demonstrating that the ancient Celts customarily had warriors sit in circles around the king. Many other Celtic influences are obvious in Wace's writing, so while such a huge and lightweight table may be an overstatement, there was probably some smaller round table. Interestingly, early versions of Jesus' Last Supper place Christ and his twelve disciples at a round table.

However, it is also clear that at least the notion of the Round Table was already present in many early Celtic sources of which Wace may have been aware. But Wace's inclusion adds significant twists to the Arthurian saga. The table itself becomes a metaphor demonstrative of the Arthurian knights and their interrelationships. Later authors would run with this conceit; Malory's additions relate the table to an image of the splintering that was occurring in Camelot during its decline. This fracturing caused by the relation of each knight's place at the table and his proximity to the king shows the frustrations that ran rampant during the Wars of the Roses. Malory's focus is upon fraternal loyalty and the aftereffects of disloyalty continuing on like concentric circles in a pond after a rock is thrown into it.

Loyalty, and so nationalism, in terms of feudalism, is a theme in Wace's work. The distinct relationship between a lord and his vassals is of interest. The knights, men in positions of honor, had the special job of serving and protecting the general populace of Britain. The hierarchy is defined but also turned upside down. Here the knights are in elevated positions yet they serve for the good of the general populace. This is a vision of a society through the eyes of a poet seeing the knights of the Round Table including men hailing from all over the known world. The author's incorporation of foreign knights with their British counterparts is both novel and noble. This union of Normans and Britons in Wace's work may have been symbolic of the possibilities available to the Britons since the Norman invasion of 1066. The national identity provided here remained a rallying point for the British for centuries to come.

One of the *Brut's* most enduring changes from the text of Geoffrey of Monmouth is Wace's implementation of the name Excalibur for Arthur's sword. Geoffrey referred to the sword as "Caliburnis," a derivative of the Latin word "*chalybs*" or "steel." Chrétien de Troyes seized upon this expansion of the tale in his *Perceval* and prose *Lancelot*. Thus, through much of the medieval French tradition, Excalibur is the name of Arthur's sword, a name that has stuck through contemporary Arthurian writings. Chrétien would go on to add that the sword previously belonged to Gawain, but most works had it belonging exclusively to Arthur. Previously several authors had placed it in the stone; the young Arthur pulls it out to be crowned the king of England. Interestingly, this strays from the traditional origin of Excalibur, such as conveyed in Malory's *Morte*, wherein Arthur receives the sword from and returns it to the Lady of the Lake. Oddly, when Merlin takes Arthur to receive the sword from the Lady of the Lake, he informs Arthur that the jewel-encrusted scabbard is far more valuable than the sword itself.

Without Wace's inclusion of the sword Excalibur, perhaps one of the great scenes in literary history would not exist. This occurs in Sir Thomas Malory's *Morte d'Arthur* when the fatally wounded Arthur orders his bereaved knight Bedivere to toss Excalibur back to the Lady of the Lake. The first time Bedivere does not throw the sword into the lake and is rebuked by the king. The second time he throws Excalibur's scabbard into the lake; again the mortally wounded Arthur is angered by this disregard of his final orders. Finally, Bedivere tosses Excalibur into the lake where it is caught by the white hand of the Lady of the Lake and Arthur is able to begin his trip to Avalon with the weeping queens surrounding him.

While Wace's *Brut* remains true to much of Geoffrey's source material, it omits certain elements such as several minor characters. Even if Wace lacked a copy of Geoffrey's work, he would have been keenly aware of its content due to the popularity of the *Historia.* Wace abbreviates much of the religious history found in *Historia Regum Brittanniae.* And, some of the more graphically disturbing passages, such as Arthur brutalizing the Picts and the Scots, are dropped. Additionally several passages concerning courtly love are added, perhaps reflecting the patronage of Eleanor of Acquitaine. One reaction typical of the courtly lover is seen when Uther Pendragon immediately becomes smitten when he espies Ygerne. At the same time Wace strives to deliver a message about the harsh consequences of both love and passion, exemplified by the adulterous relationships of Locrin and Modred. Also, many of the mysticism and dark craft images found in Geoffrey's text are eliminated. Merlin rarely prophesizes and many of the supernatural elements have been either ignored or purged from the text.

Critics have noted the effectiveness of Wace's reductive technique, especially concerning Geoffrey's work. To overcome his narrowing of the work, it seems that Wace included some storytelling elements into his version. Instead of the straightforward accounts of previous authors, Wace delivers dramatic conventions and additional intrigue. These variations were expanded by later writers of Arthurian legend. When Uther Pendragon meets Gorlois and Igerne, the lady becomes the focus of Uther's attention rather than Gorlois, the Earl of Cornwall. This connection continues after the feast when Uther follows Igerne and Gorlois with the intent of gaining his desire—Igerne. Wace's version of this episode is novel in that he blurs the line between reality and fiction, adding hazy detail to the eventual cuckolding of Gorlois.

It seems that in his *Brut*, Wace added details which may have been based on his own travels and travails in southwest Britain. But remarkable in the *Brut* is Wace's additional comments upon Arthur as being the "Breton Hope," developing in grand style Arthur's potentially incredible exegetic return from Avalon to save his people. This addition of a messianic hero was a turning point in the development of Arthurian legend. Wace's skills in description, as well as his seemingly honest treatment of the material in a lively style, makes the legend very vivid.

The popularity of Wace's treatment is clear from the number of editions and expansions of Arthurian legend that were composed after his *Brut* became available. The writings of Chrétien de Troyes and Marie de France clearly have their seeds in Wace's work. Further, a massive collection of anonymous Arthurian works followed both in England and on the Continent. Soon after, around 1200, Layaman adopted Wace's *Brut to* Middle English, expanding his predecessor's volume to more than 32,000 lines. Henry II became aware of Wace's *Brut* and was immediately taken by its presentation and style. If, as hypothesized, the text was presented by Layaman to Eleanor of Acquitaine, Layamon would most certainly have intended it to appeal to the king. Regardless of the verity of this notion, Henry offered to be a patron for Wace and hired him to compose a work about the deeds of the dukes of Normandy. Wace would have been ingratiated to the king for this measure of largesse. Clerics would have been in dire need of funding, and the king's endorsement probably would have been a welcome additional income for Wace.

During the next fourteen years Wace worked on the *Roman de Rou*, a work that was based on real events and real people. Named after the founder of the Normans, the *Rou* is composed in octosyllabic couplets and monorhyme stanzas of alexandrines; it is a history of the Norman dukes from Rollo (c. 911) to Robert II Curthose (1106). In 1162 Wace accompanied Henry to Fecamp while the remains of Richard I and Richard II were removed, showing that for a while at least he remained in favor with the king. However, after fourteen years the king removed his commission and gave the work to one of Wace's rivals, Benoit de Ste. Marie, who was instructed to finish the job.

Although it is incomplete, the *Rou* is detailed, covering most major happenings up to and including the Norman Conquest of 1066. This time and event is extremely important to Wace, as this is considered the first important event in the history of the island. However, as with many other works from this era, it must be recalled that by the time Wace composed the *Rou*, six other dukes of Normandy had ruled over the Channel Islands. Thus, Wace was far removed from this major event, as well as the other times recalled in his verse. This makes it seem unlikely that the work is accurate historically. His creative and lively account of the Norman Conquest makes for good reading, but it is doubtful that it is a reliable version of the actual events. This point is strengthened when it is recalled that he was trying to please his benefactor with his writing, likely skewing any sense of proportionality in his account.

Sometime between 1160 and 1170 Wace was promoted to canon of Bayeux. This date can be verified because he clearly states in his work that when he began the *Rou* he was a cleric; in the second part of the work, probably composed after 1170, he notes that he was elevated in position and granted by Henry II a prebend in the church of Bayeux.

When he stopped work on the *Rou* around 1174, most traces and references ceased. It is thought that he died after 1174, although some date his death to 1183. Little information about the later years of Wace's life exists. While his literary collection of extant works is small, his role in the development of Arthurian legend cannot be downplayed. Wace's conscious determination to make Arthur a real character established a clear foundation for the great amounts of Arthurian material that would follow shortly. The artistry of the *Brut* would provide not only substantial stylistic devices to later writers, especially the verse romances that were so popular in the later centuries, but it also inspired a bevy of imitators, most notably Layamon. What Wace did was to pave the way for authors, such as Chrétien de Troyes, Thomas Malory, and many anonymous authors to take the character of Arthur and treat him as a man rather than a mythical hero. Because he took some liberties with his model and added such important details as Excalibur and the significance of seating at the Round Table, Arthur the king and the man became much more interesting than when he was a mystical character.

Wace must have been a well-known writer during this time. It is important to remember that medieval writers placed great emphasis upon the notion of imitation that was so popular during this time. A good story could not be told often enough. Indeed, the most popular ones were not only copied repeatedly, but later transcribers would add their slants to the story. It is impressive, given that there are eighteen extant volumes of Wace's *Brut*, because of the diligence that was needed to reproduce manuscripts during this time. The fact that so many imitated his works shows that Wace's *Brut* is a key text in the growth of Arthurian legend. Without Wace's transcription of the Latin work into the French, along with his additions, it is possible that the Arthurian legend as it is known today would not exist.

PRIMARY WORKS

La Vie de Sainte Marguerite (The Life of Saint Marguerite, c. 1135). **Manuscripts:** Three extant manuscripts containing the saint's life—two from the thirteenth and one from the fourteenth century. **First publication:** *La Vie de Sainte Marguerite.* Calirvaux, France: Jean Bouhier, 1781. **Standard edition:** *La Vie de Sainte Marguerite,* ed. Hans-Erich Keller. Tubingen, Germany:

Niemeyer, 1990; *La Conception Nostre Dame* (1130–1140). **Manuscripts:** Eighteen contain sections of the text; they are composed in numerous dialects. **First publication:** *La Conception Nostre Dame.* Caen, France: Mancel & Trébutien, 1842. **Standard edition:** *The Conception of Nostre Dame of Wace,* ed. William Ray Ashford. Chicago: University of Chicago Libraries, 1933; *La Vie de Saint Nicolas* (c. 1150). **Manuscripts:** Five extant in England and France. **First publication:** *La Vie de Saint Nicholas.* Bonn: Delius, 1850. **Standard edition:** *The Life of Saint Nicholas,* ed. Mary Sinclair. Philadelphia: University of Pennsylvania Press, 1923; *Le Roman de Brut* or *Brut d'Angleterre* (c. 1155). **Manuscripts:** Twenty-two extant from the thirteenth through the fifteenth centuries. Usually in collections with other chronicles, such as the British Library Sous le n.13.A.XI from the thirteenth century. Perhaps the best reproduction of this is the *Le Roman de Brut: A Reproduction of MS. 2603, folios 1–100b in the National Library Vienna.* New York: Modern Language Association of America, 1927. **First publication:** *Le Roman de Brut,* ed. Le Roux de Lincy, 2 vols. Paris: Frére, 1836–1838. **Standard edition:** *Le Roman de Brut,* ed. Ivor Arnold, 2 vols. Paris: Société des Anciens Textes Francais, 1938–1940. **English edition:** In *Arthurian Chronicles,* trans. Eugene Mason. London: Dent & Sons, 1962; *La Roman de Rou* (c. 1174). **Manuscripts:** Four extant—two from the thirteenth century, one from the fourteenth century, and one from the fifteenth century. **First publication:** *Le Roman de Rou et des Ducs de Normandie,* ed. Frederick Pluquet. Rouen, France: Frére, 1827–1829.

SECONDARY SOURCES

Ashe, Geoffrey. *The Discovery of King Arthur.* Garden City, NY: Anchor Press, 1985; ———. *King Arthur's Avalon: The Story of Glastonbury.* New York: Dutton, 1958; *Bibliography of Critical Arthurian Literature.* New York: Modern Language Association, 1931; Brengle, Richard L., ed. *Arthur, King of Britain: History, Chronicle, Romance, and Criticism, with Texts in Modern English, from Gildas to Malory.* Englewood Cliffs, NJ: Prentice-Hall, 1964; Bromwich, Rachel, A. O. H. Jarman, and Brynley F. Roberts, eds. *The Arthur of the Welsh: The Arthurian Legend in Medieval Welsh Literature.* Cardiff: University of Wales Press, 1992; Bruce, Douglas J. *The Evolution of Arthurian Romance from the Beginnings Down to the Year 1300.* Gloucester, MA: P. Smith, 1958; Cummins, Walter Arthur. *King Arthur's Place in Prehistory: The Great Age of Stonehenge.* Wolfeboro Falls, NH: A. Sutton, 1992; Dean, Christopher. *Arthur of England: English Attitudes to King Arthur and the Knights of the Round Table in the Middle Ages and the Renaissance.* Toronto: University of Toronto Press, 1987; Hopkins, Annete Brown. *The Influence of Wace on the Arthurian Romances of Crestian de Troies.* Menasha, WI: Banta, 1913; Jenkins, Elizabeth. *The Mystery of King Arthur.* New York: Coward, McCann & Geoghegan, 1975; Kibler, William W. "Wace." In the *Arthurian Encyclopedia,* ed. Norris J. Lacy. New York: Garland, 1986; Knight, Stephen T. *Arthurian Literature and Society.* New York: St. Martin's Press, 1983; Korrel, Peter. *An Arthurian Triangle: A Study of the Origin, Development, and Characterization of Arthur, Guinevere, and Modred.* Leiden: Brill, 1984; Lacy, Norris J., ed. *The Arthurian Encyclopedia.* New York: Garland, 1986; ———. *The New Arthurian Encyclopedia.* New York: Garland,1991; Lacy, Norris J., and Geoffrey Ashe, eds. *Arthurian Handbook.* New York: Garland, 1988; Loomis, Roger. *Celtic Myth and Arthurian Romance.* New York: Columbia University Press, 1927; Phillips, Graham. *King Arthur: The True Story.* London: Century, 1992; Starr, Nathan Comfort. *King Arthur Today: The Arthurian Legend in English and American Literature, 1901–1953.* Gainesville: University of Florida Press, 1954; Whitaker, Muriel A. *The Legends of King Arthur in Art.* Rochester, NY: D. S. Brewer, 1990; Wilhelm, James J. *The Romance of Arthur.* New York: Garland, 1984; ———. *The Romance of Arthur II.* New York: Garland, 1986; ———. *The Romance of Arthur III: Works from Russia to Spain, Norway to Italy.* New York: Garland, 1988.

ROBERT THOMAS LAMBDIN AND LAURA COONER LAMBDIN

GEOFFREY OF MONMOUTH
(c. 1100–c. 1155)

Geoffrey of Monmouth was born c. 1100; his full name may have been Geoffrey Arthur, but that is unsubstantiated. Alhough there is no record of his birth, he is considered to be "of Monmouth" for several reasons, not the least of which he refers to himself as Geoffrey of Monmouth in several of his works, including the *Viti Merlini*. It is thought that he was either born in the town or educated in its priory. Little is known of his family, again due to sparse records. However, Geoffrey is one of the most valuable authors in the development of the Arthurian legends because he wrote *Historia Regum Brittanniae* (*The History of the Kings of England*). Completed in 1138, the *Historia* exists as one of the earliest known accounts of the first British rulers. In the *Historia* Geoffrey claims to be recounting the lives of rulers from Britain's beginning with Brutus, around 1100 BC, to Cadwallader's fall around 689 AD. Moreover, the *Historia* was the first to put Arthur in the line of British kings; many events concerning Arthur related by Geoffrey have become common to readers ever since. In his *Prophetiae Merlini* (*The Prophecies of Merlin*), which was composed before the *Historia* in about 1135, Geoffrey introduced the character of Merlin the Wizard. Geoffrey later used much of the *Prophetiae Merlini* text as Book VII of the *Historia*. The *Prophetiae Merlini* contains prophesies from a wizard, Myrddin, who is in many ways a compilation of both pagan and Christian ideals. While his prophecies were treated seriously at the time, Wace later rejected them, although Wace would use three early French translations in his own works. Geoffrey's work was later translated into Welsh and Icelandic.

Geoffrey's *Historia* was novel in that he elevated the Britons in status, placing them as equals with the Romans and the Greeks. This approach found a receptive audience, as the *Historia* quickly became accepted by a people hungering for a sense of nationalistic pride. This work served as the truest account of British history (a position it held for some six centuries until its verity crumbled under close scrutiny). During this period Arthur was considered a real king rather than a successful warlord. Perhaps the most important element of the *Historia* was its effect on the perceptions of the French and continental Europeans about Arthurian legend. Previously Arthur and his followers had been seen as merely barbarous, inconsequential hooligans—and unworthy of a cultured person's attention. Geoffrey's work became the germ for the rapid growth of Arthurian legend both in England and on the Continent.

Geoffrey was probably Welsh, but little is known of his life. In five charters he is referred to as "Galfridus Arturus"; this in itself is curious because "Arturus"(from which "Arthur" may be derived) was an uncommon name. This leads some to posit that this was his father's name. Historians note that Geoffrey became prior of the abbey of Monmouth around 1125 before he moved to Oxford, where he was made a secular canon of the college of Augustinian Canons of St. George. Over the next twenty years his signature is found on six charters related to religious houses located near Oxford. The same "Walter" whom Geoffrey notes provided him with the "ancient book" that he used as his source for the *Historia* co-signed five of the documents. It is unlikely that the book truly existed, inasmuch as this form of citing sources was a common medieval ploy when one author wished to give his text greater authenticity by pretending that his information was from the text of an earlier writer.

Geoffrey's loyalties must have been pulled in two directions in his efforts to relate British history. He was comfortable in the Norman ways, having been given a Norman education, but his heritage was still Welsh. Geoffrey knew that the Welsh had been routed, invaded, and overrun by invading hordes for centuries, and, therefore, they had little or no heritage of their own. Perhaps this is why he wished to create a venue wherein the past of the original Britons (at least from his perspective) was extolled.

Robert de Chesney, to whom Geoffrey dedicates the *Vita Merlini*, became the bishop of Lincoln in 1148. It was sometime during his period at Oxford that Geoffrey composed all three of his works; only after their completion did he gain the preferment he sought so diligently. While the dates of his compositions are conjectured, there are some details of his life that have been confirmed. In 1151 Geoffrey was elected bishop of St. Asaph in North Wales. He was never able to reside in his diocese, however, because the warring Welsh occupied it. Only three years later, in 1155, Geoffrey died.

While he does not seem to have been a prolific author, his *Historia* is significant, whether it is based in fact or fiction. Regardless of its verity—the work was almost immediately known to be historically untrustworthy—it was a very popular work. References to its inaccuracies appeared as early as the twelfth century, but the *Historia* was quickly translated into other languages, including French. The works of Bede and Gildas were sources for the *Historia*, and the works of Nennius might also have influenced Geoffrey. Further, the *Annales Cambriae* and works of the historian William of Malmesbury seem to have been partial sources for the *Historia*. Others find that the greatest source for the Arthurian sections of the *Historia* were Geoffrey's vivid imagination.

While the *Historia* may fail as a work of reliable history, it is still regarded as a great story. The tale begins around 1100 BC when Brutus, the great-grandson of Aeneas, leads his people to the British Isles and is crowned its first king. Geoffrey's use of this device serves an important purpose, for all of the great European countries of this time claimed Brutus as their founder. The Celts, the French, and the Romans all traced their lineage to this Trojan exile. Geoffrey's chronicle contains a roster of kings who are unknown today. One of the key elements of the *Historia* may be the sections on Arthur, Books 9–11. Geoffrey devotes nearly one-fifth of the *Historia* to Arthur. According to Geoffrey, the warlords of Britain splintered the country after the Romans left Britain in the fifth century; thus, pockets of powerful men mercilessly gained at the expense of the poor. Prior to the books that center on Arthur, Geoffrey goes through great lengths to detail the events that lead to Arthur's birth. Especially of import here is that the great leader, Vortigern, exiled Uther and Ambrosius to Brittany; Vortigern then signed a treaty with the Saxons for the protection of Britain.

The Saxons violated the treaty and began expanding their claims while eliminating or chasing away many of the Briton king's allies. Vortigern escaped to Wales where he encountered a young Merlin, who foretold of Arthur as the savior of all Britain. Through a series of twists and murders, Uther Pendragon returns to England from exile in Breton and becomes ruler. Unlike his predecessors, though, Uther listens to and heeds the words of Merlin. However, Uther's downfall begins when he meets Ygerna, the wife of Gorlois, the Duke of Cornwall, at a feast and covets her. Gorlois recognizes Uther's attraction to his wife and decides to avoid an ugly confrontation by returning to his castle at Tintagel in Cornwall. This action, while noble, serves only to enrage Uther, who, brimming with desire for the beautiful Ygerna, considers Gorlois's actions an insult. In a passionate rage, Uther calls up his army to invade Tintagel.

Some forward men bring Gorlois word of Uther's pursuit, and the Duke of Cornwall responds by first hiding Ygerna and then countering Uther's offensive with his own troops. Geoffrey here gives the first real glimpse of Merlin's abilities, which will be a force throughout Arthurian literature. While he would later use his powers to serve as the main seer and adviser to the youthful Arthur, here he uses them to deceive Ygerna directly and Gorlois indirectly. Ironically, the cruel deception Merlin creates is the means through which the true-born king of all Britain, Arthur, is conceived.

At Tintagel, Merlin magically transforms Uther into the image of Gorlois so that Uther may enter the castle unquestioned. Simultaneously, the real Gorlois is battling Uther's army in a bloodfest. In the chaos, Uther walks past the guards, enters the castle, and finds Ygerna. Merlin's work on Uther has been so precise that Ygerna has no reason to question his presence. Thinking him to be the true Gorlois, she believes her brave husband has conquered the attacking horde, and Tintagel is safe. Thus, in her relief and her pleasure, the two have a ravenous tryst.

This is the rather dubious manner whereby Arthur was conceived. While this life was being created, Gorlois found himself becoming overrun by Uther's army. Gorlois is killed without knowing that his wife had unwittingly cuckolded him or that in his absence, a child had been conceived. Ygerna is initially confused when she hears the news of the time of her husband's death, but nine months later she gives birth to Arthur.

Geoffrey continues that Arthur, at the age of fifteen, ascends to the throne of Britain. The young king learns his craft well, pushing back the Saxons and conquering much of known Britain, as well as Iceland. After this successful campaign, he marries Ganhumara (Guinevere). For twelve years Arthur's is rule is somewhat peaceful, for he has established a sort of representative government for the good of the people, a far cry from the previous lawlessness. He and his army then conquer other parts of Scandinavia, including Denmark and Norway. Thinking his world to be in control, the king again returns to his court. Arthur is shocked when the Roman emperor demands tribute of the Britons. This action enrages the king who refuses to send tribute to anyone. Arthur immediately marches his army into France to take on the Romans. Arthur's troops are on the verge of victory when he hears to him that Modred, his nephew, has taken Ganhumara as his queen and has usurped the throne.

This treasonous act cuts Arthur's continental campaign short. He is forced to return to Britain and confront the evil Modred. Their final bloody battle takes place in Cornwall by the Camel River. In the climatic final, Modred is killed by Arthur, but not before he mortally wounds the monarch. The dying king is taken to the Isle of Avalon with the proviso that he will return to take control of Britain again. The crown is given to Constantine, Arthur's cousin, but none can rule as well as Arthur, and eventually Arthur's line is defeated and the crown is lost. This forms a sort of anticlimax to the great tale of Arthur. Following victories by Malgo, Cadwanus, and later Cadwallo, who actually defeated the Saxons and ruled in London for many years, Cadwaller is eventually forced to retreat to Brittany. He eventually retires to Rome, becoming a monk. Thus, the defeated ruler can leave the governing only of Wales to his son, Ivor. It is here that the book chronicling the reign of the kings of the Britons ends.

Geoffrey had a wealth of sources from which he could have drawn. However, he opted to include information gleaned from the oral accounts of both the Britons and the Welsh to create his Arthur. This would be only natural given Geoffrey's apparent heritage. Yet Geoffrey is novel in that he opted to integrate tales from throughout the area in to his *Historia*. "The Matter of Britain," as literary texts related to early British history are called, are firmly rooted in the *Historia*. The sources Geoffrey could have used, including Gildas's *De Excidio Brittaniae (On the Ruin of Britain)* and Nennius's *Historia Brittonum (History of the Britons)*, all vary a bit in their retellings.

Additionally, Geoffrey introduced several key elements to Arthurian legend. He is among the first to directly provide a name for Arthur's shield, "Pridwen." His sword, "Caliburnus," would become better known as "Excalibur." Even his lance, "Ron," was given a name. While Geoffrey may be legitimately chastised for what he depicted as historical "fact," he must also be recognized for touches such as these that individualized his work. Thus one must be careful when judging the literary quality of a manuscript so obviously steeped in exaggeration, hyperbole, and outright embellishment. The important thing is that Geoffrey gave credence to Arthur. He brought a figure from the shadows and gave him life; the two dimensional Arthur of Nennius and Gildas became the three dimensional figure of Geoffrey. Arthur had noble blood and a place of birth. Arthur was a successful general and gave to the later populace something that they had previously lacked: a symbol of what they had been and what they could be again. No longer would they have to wish for a distinguished history. Geoffrey's *Historia* chronicled the adventures of a king on a par with the great French rulers. The empire of Arthur spanned from the British Isles to Scandinavia and the continent. At one time, Arthur's empire even challenged Rome for greatness. Thus, Geoffrey's *Historia* provided its audience with an invaluable sense of legitimacy. Geoffrey manipulated his sources to create a figure who not only achieved power, but maintained it. Each passing generation added attributes to Arthur's character that would appeal to contemporary audiences. All are clearly indebted to Geoffrey of Monmouth.

While the heritage of the *Historia* remains questionable, there is no doubt that Geoffrey had great knowledge of the workings of the Bretons. Some critics posit that the *Historia Brittanica* may have been the "very old book" that Walter had given to him as a source. Others mention a late tenth-century work titled *Livre des faits d'Arrthur* as the source. Recently others have speculated that the *Vita Goeznouei* from 1019 served as the basis for Geoffrey's work.

Geoffrey's final work, *Vita Merlin*, was dedicated to his friend Robert de Chesney, who had become the bishop at Lincoln. (The previous bishop had been unreceptive to Geoffrey's calls for patronage, so Geoffrey must have been thrilled at his friend's promotion.) In the *Vita*, a middle-aged Merlin goes into seclusion following the deaths of his companions in battle. Hearing an odd chorus of music, the magician is lured from the woods. In his travails away from the woods, the wizard is successful in a multitude of tasks. At one point, he reveals a queen to be an adulteress. Later, Merlin gives his wife Guendoloena permission to leave him and to remarry, thus allowing him to return to the woods to live again. As a wedding gift he kills a deer to give to the newlyweds, but then, strangely and suddenly, Merlin murders his Guendoloena's new husband with the antlers of a deer. He does not deny his guilt in this crime and is taken into custody. While incarcerated, Merlin prophesizes concerning Rhydderch, the king; when the prophecies are verified, he is freed, and again retires to the woods. His sister, Ganieda, builds him a large home and invites astronomers to share it with him. While there he again prophesizes about the fate of Britain. At this point he meets Taliesin, a bard, who tells him of Arthur's voyage to Morgan le Fay's island, Avalon, in hopes of recovering from Modred's fatal wound. Merlin, who has gone mad, is cured when he washes in a spring of water. The newly appreciative Merlin talks with Taliesin about the joys of nature, only to be interrupted by another madman, Maeldin. This lunatic is also cured by the spring, and the three determine to spend the duration of their lives happily exploring the spiritual powers of the forest and of nature.

The root of *Vita Merlini* was sown when Geoffrey was writing his *Historia*. Important for the later Arthurian legends, he learned about a northern bard, Myrddin, whose name he latinized into the "Merlin" who went to Vortigern's court and astounded the king's magicians. Welsh works tell us that Myrrdin went mad in 575, roaming through the northern forests while prophesizing. As is customary with Geoffrey, he strays from the official dates to make his work more functional. His introduction of Taliesin is important in that he sends the bard with Arthur's body to Avalon, where the cunning Morgan, who would evolve into Morganna le Fay in later works, reigned over a family of nine sisters. However, unlike the later Morganna, this Morgan is compassionate; her only concern is the welfare of the king.

Yet it is the *Historia* for which Geoffrey is most remembered. It was perhaps the seminal work of its time, and few works from this period could match it in its instantaneous popularity. Proof of this widespread favor is evident in the more than two hundred extant manuscripts copied in several different languages. The *Historia* would be a great factor in the works of many later authors. Geoffrey's work influenced Wace, who translated the work in the late twelfth century. Wace's work was then translated by Layamon. Later, the work was chronicled by Robert of Gloucester. The works of Thomas Bek and Robert Mannynge in the fifteenth centuries are based upon other translations of Geoffrey. Geoffrey's works would also fuel the fire of Arthurian legend for centuries to come. Writers such as Thomas Malory, Edmund Spenser, Alfred, Lord Tennyson, and William Morris would continue the tradition. Often these authors would add to the legends to make points concerning their respective societies.

While much of Geoffrey's work may be spurious, there is no doubt that his works are important in the foundation of Arthurian legend. Prior to Geoffrey's work, Arthur existed as a hero in the oral tradition, but it seems as though there was little written about him in the literary sense. Geoffrey devoted little space to the bloody wars that became prevalent in the later Arthurian legends. Geoffrey's audience may have been the first provided with a hint that there was a tragic love between Arthur and his queen—a notion that would be so embellished by later writers that it became the focal point of many of the works. Thus, the *Historia* is seminal because it provides the seed of a great legend that would flourish for centuries and die out, only to be resurrected time and time again by different generations longing for a hero to whom they could relate.

PRIMARY WORKS

Prophetie Merlini (*The Prophecies of Merlin*, composed c. 1135). **Manuscripts:** While it was later printed as a part of Geoffrey's *Historia regum Britannie*, *Prophetie Merlini* is found independently in some eighty manuscripts. About ten others also have the *Merlini* as an insertion; *Historia regum Britannie* (*The History of the Kings of England*). Two versions: Vulgate (c. 1138) and Variant (c. 1155). **Manuscripts:** At least 215 Latin manuscripts are extant of both versions. Most are Vulgate editions, and the best known is Cambridge University Library MS. 1706, fols. 1r–128v (twelfth century); also Burgerbibliothek (Stadtbibliothek), Bern, MS, 568, fols. 18r–83r (twelfth century) and Trinity College, Cambridge, MS. 1125, fols. 5r–117v (late thirteenth century). Variant editions (eight extant) British Library MS. Harley 6358, fols. 2r–58v (late twelfth century). **First publication:** *Britannie utriusque regum et Principe orig. et Gesta insignia AB Galfrido Monemutensi*, ed. Ivo Cavellatus. Paris: Jodocus Badius Ascensius [Josse Bade], 1508; revised 1517. **Standard editions:** Vulgate: *The Historia Regum Britannie of Geoffrey of Monmouth*, ed. Neil Wright. Cambridge: Brewer, 1985. Variant: *The Historia Regum Britannie of Geoffrey of Monmouth, the First Variant Version: A Critical Edition*, ed. Neil Wright. Cambridge: Brewer, 1988. **English edition:** *The History of the Kings of Britain*, trans. Lewis Thorpe. London: Penguin Books, 1966; *Vita Merlini* (*Life of Merlin*, c. 1140). **Manuscript:** One complete version—British Library MS. Cotton Vespasian E. iv, fols. 112b–138b (late thirteenth century). **First publication:** *Gaufridi Arthurii Archdiaconi postea vero episcopi Asaphensis, de vita et vaticiniis Merlini Calidonii carmen heroicum*, ed. William Henry Black. London: printed by William Nicol for the Roxburgh Club, 1830. **Standard edition:** *Life of Merlin*, ed. Basil Clarke. Cardiff: University of Wales Press, 1973. **English edition:** *Life of Merlin*, trans. Basil Clarke. Cardiff: University of Wales Press, 1973.

SECONDARY SOURCES

Ashe, Geoffrey. "Camelot." *British Heritage* (March 1998): 30–37; ———. *The Discovery of King Arthur*. Garden City, NY: Anchor Press, 1985; Ashe, Geoffrey. *King Arthur's Avalon: The Dream of a Golden Age*. London: Thames & Hudson, 1990; ———. *The Landscape of King Arthur*. New York: Henry Holt, 1987; ———. *The Traveller's Guide to Arthurian Britain*. Glastonbury, UK: Gothic Image, 1997; Barber, Richard. *The Arthurian Legends: An Illustrated Anthology*. Woodbridge, UK: Boydell Press, 1996; Bromwich, Rachel, A. O. H. Jarman, and Brynley F. Roberts, eds. *The Arthur of the Welsh: The Arthurian Legend in Medieval Welsh Literature*. Cardiff: University of Wales Press, 1992; Castleden, Rodney. *King Arthur: The Truth Behind the Legend*. London: Routledge, 2000; Coghlan, Ronan. *The Illustrated Encyclopedia of Arthurian Legends*. Rockport, MA: Element, 1993; Curley, Michael J. *Geoffrey of Monmouth*. New York: Twayne, 1994; Huntley, Dana. "The Quest for the Historical Arthur." *British Heritage* (March 1998): 12–15; Lacy, Norris J., and Geoffrey Ashe, eds. *Arthurian Handbook*. New York: Garland, 1988; Leckie, R. William. *The Passage of Dominion: Geoffrey of Monmouth and the Periodization of Insular History in the Twelfth Century*. Toronto: University of Toronto Press, 1981; Otter, Monica. *Inventiones: Fiction and Referentiality in Twelfth-Century English Historical Writing*. Chapel Hill: University of North Carolina Press, 1996; Peck, M. Scott. *In Search of Stones*. New York: Hyperion, 1995; Pennar, Meirion, trans. *The Black Book of Carmarthen*. Felinfach, UK: Llanerch Enterprises, 1989; Phillips, Graham, and Martin Keatman. *King Arthur: The True Story*. London: Century, 1992; Quennell, C. H. B., and Marjorie Quennell. *Everyday Life in Roman and Anglo-Saxon Times*. New York: Dorset Press, 1987; Reno, Frank D. *The Historic King Arthur*. Jefferson, NC: McFarland and Co., 1996; Smith, Lucy Toulmin. *Leland's Itinerary in Wales*. London: George Bell and Sons, 1906; Snell, F. J. *King Arthur's Country*. New York: E. P. Dutton, 1926; Snyder, Christopher. *An Age of Tyrants*. University Park, PA: Pennsylvania State University Press, 1998; Stone, Brian, trans. *King Arthur's Death: Morte Arthure and Le Morte Arthur*. London: Penguin, 1988; Tatlock, John S. P. *The Legendary*

History of Britain: Geoffrey of Monmouth's Historia Regum Britanniae and Its Early Vernacular Versions. Berkeley: University of California Press, 1950; Thorpe, Lewis, trans. *Geoffrey of Monmouth: The History of the Kings of Britain*. London: Penguin, 1966; White, Paul. *King Arthur: Man or Myth?* Cornwall, UK: Tor Mark Press, 1998.

LAURA COONER LAMBDIN AND ROBERT THOMAS LAMBDIN

CHRÉTIEN DE TROYES
(c. 1125–1191)

T he romances of the medieval French poet Chrétien de Troyes are significant for exploring the ideals of courtly love and chivalry in Arthurian settings. He also was the first poet to create separate important adventures for Arthur's knights Gawain, Yvain, Erec, Lancelot, and Perceval in individual works. Our conception of the Arthurian legends was molded by Chrétien's pen; he transformed brutal warriors into elegant statesmen and lovers. The psychological insights are profound, but never overshadow the action and high adventure. It is unlikely that Camelot would have had such an enduring impact upon Western thought had Chrétien's works been less popular and pervasive.

Of Chrétien's biography we know little beyond his association with the court of Champagne and the Countess Marie, daughter of Eleanor of Acquitaine and Louis VII. Probably born at Troyes around 1135, Chrétien gained a classical education most likely in training to be a cleric. We know that he was from Troyes because his material is signed Chrétien "of Troyes" and because of certain distinct dialectal features. Troyes was the capital of the courts of Champagne, a cultural center that had many medieval fairs as well as a large talmudic center. The possibility that Chrétien was Jewish has been suggested, primarily to account for his odd name. Marie was his patroness sometime around 1160 to 1172, when he lived and wrote at court. The ideal of courtesy grew into the cult of courtly love probably because of Chrétien's octosyllabic rhyming couplets. The four romances he composed form the most complete rendering of French chivalry available. Extant works definitely by Chrétien are *Erec et Enide*, *Cligés*, *Yvain*, and *Lancelot*. Another poem, *Perceval*, was probably only partially composed by Chrétien. Two short lyrical poems, "Guillaume d'Angleterre" and "Philomena," may have been written by him, but the evidence is inconclusive.

It is generally understood that the Arthur who was a guerilla warfare chieftain around 500 AD had little in common with the glamorized King Arthur of Chrétien. So little material is extant from the period known as the "Dark Ages" that Chrétien's transformation of the character and his comrades seems almost magical; the Celtic prototypes and the heroes of the French romance bear little resemblance to each other. However, because from its inception to the modern time, Arthuriana has ever lent itself well as a veneer for contemporary criticism, it seems likely that Chrétien transformed Arthur and his knights to teach his readers to be as attentive and courteous as his characters; the poetry is intended to instruct the court about ideal behavior. Tracing Chrétien's sources has proven impossible, but while he may have had Latin or French literature no longer available, such material likely would have been very different in focus.

While others were surely written prior to it, *Erec et Enide* is the oldest surviving Arthurian romance in any language; it was probably written between 1160 and 1170. One must note, above and beyond the significance of plot and protagonists, that Arthur's court is shown as the center of civilization, where all knights meet. Erec is a knight of Arthur's court who adores his bride Enide so much that he neglects his knightly duties to remain with her. Erec's obsession leads him to suspect his innocent wife of infidelity. The patient Griselda theme of folklore runs rampant through the work as Enide's loyalty is tested. She is ever the good, wise, beautiful, and faithful wife. She repeatedly warns her husband that his knightly reputation will be lost if he remains by her side, but this only fuels his desire to stay home to enjoy his wife's charms and watch her, lest she stray.

Setting out on an adventure, Eric has Enide ride silently before him. She disobeys several times to warn him of peril ahead. Erec wants his wife to prove her loyalty by heeding his commands; Enide wants to show her devotion by helping to protect her husband. Ultimately, the couple learns to act in a manner more befitting a feudal lord and his lady who must serve those whom they rule. When their faithfulness is proven, the pair are made heirs to the kingdom.

Erec et Enide reflects a common question running throughout Chrétien's work about how a courtly couple is expected to respond to society. Clearly the answer is not to selfishly enjoy the pleasures of love to the exclusion of all else. Chrétien's characters always show some growth in understanding, a growing up or accepting of service to others despite the self sacrifice involved. Chivalry included questing for adventure and gaining a reputation as a great protector by helping those in peril. Erec's overwhelming devotion to his wife is underscored repeatedly as unbeneficial to others and to the couple. The lovers must wonder and endure many hardships before the lesson unfolds. Because Enide is more devoted to protecting her husband's life than to her own comfort, she is the perfect example of the courtly wife and teaches Erec about the service one is expected to render upon joining the knighthood. Erec realizes her great love for him and his own responsibilities to society from her selfless actions. While Chrétien's poems appear to be about courtly love, they actually stress moderation and duty to others.

Erec is introduced as a knight of the Round Table, a member of an esteemed fellowship of some fifty men whose names Chrétien lists. Sloth and uxorious dalliance is unexpected from a hero like Erec; equally odd given his perfect courtly lover status are his cruel and violent outbursts at his beautiful wife. Erec's ardent love causes him to lose objectivity both as a knight and as a courtly lover. Another explanation may be that Chrétien never adopted the Provençal worship of women as God's representatives on earth through the cult of the Virgin Mary. Erec's worship of his wife causes gossip and slander at court and sorrow to his wife and friends. When he understands he is deeply hurt, but must prove his manliness and courage by taking the dangerous adventure to vindicate himself and to test Enide's love. His strength is ultimately proven and soon after his father dies, Erec is crowned king in an elaborate ceremony.

The character of Enide represents a literary advancement for women because she is a fully developed female character. Enide solves the problem of the White Stag kiss competition by being the most beautiful woman at Arthur's court; much detailed are her physical attributes and clothing—both her early rags and the gown given to her by Queen Guenevere. However, the real triumph for her gender is the psychological insight ascribed to Enide. Also significant are her courage and devotion; she is not the weakened prisoner bound by love that her husband so hideously becomes. Instead, she is strengthened by love.

It is possible that this romance was not composed at Troyes because he signed it "Chrétien of Troyes," implying that he was elsewhere. Sometime after 1168, Chrétien apparently returned to Troyes and began his association with Countess Marie, wife of Count Henry of Champagne. This couple had set up an experimental salon type of court setting that was the seat of heightened civilization at the time.

We have no chronological list of Chrétien's writings; however, it seems likely that of the works we have extant, *Cligés,* was written next after *Erec et Enide.* Oddly, this romance about the hero Cligés begins with a history of his father and contrasts the two generations' responses to courtly love. Alexander, the father, indulges in tortured internal monologues about his beloved. His language is not courtly and his anguished tone lacks the smooth sophistication of his son's rhetoric.

Cligés's parents, Alexander, son of the king of Greece and Soredamor, the niece of King Arthur and sister of Gawain, are both beautiful. Alexander sails from Greece to Arthur's court, where he befriends the king and queen. He sails to Brittany and meets Soredamor on the ship. The queen believes they are seasick rather than feverishly in love because of their trembling, sighing, and paleness. Readers know better because of the long monologues about hope and fear for love. Finally, the queen guesses the couple's true state; they are married and produce a son named Cligés. Alexander's throne is taken by his brother Alis, who never promises to wed so Cligés will be heir to the throne. However, Alis became betrothed to the daughter of the emperor of Germany, Fénice, whom Cligés must rescue from twelve opponents.

Cligés and Fénice fall so in love and are so beautiful that their radiance fills the castle of the German emperor. Fénice refuses to share her body or heart with another, so Alis must be tricked. She drinks the magic herbal potion, is buried, and resurrected secretly by Cligés. First, she does actually marry Alis and he is served a potion by Fénice's maid that gives him dreams of such amorous satisfaction that he believes he has enjoyed full carnal love with his bride.

Cligés is a sort of anti-Tristram hero because, although his love affair with Fénice in some ways echoes the story of Tristram and Iseult, he seeks to avoid their tragic fates. Just as Isolde was married to Marc, who was Tristram's uncle, Fénice is married to Cligés's uncle Alis. Fénice, despite her love for Cligés, refuses to be like Isolde by being with one man while her heart belongs to another. Employing an ancient solution that was later used by William Shakespeare in *Romeo and Juliet,* Chrétien solves the couple's problem via a potion that makes Fénice appear to have died. Fénice is then free to live with Cligés and love him freely without having to endure the sort of death in life that had been Isode's fate at Marc's court. While this seems unethical at best to modern audiences and no real improvement over Isolde's predicament, the problem was apparently appropriately solved to Chrétien and his contemporary audience, as long as Fénice was true to her heart.

In *Yvain* the problems of courtly love and marriage are examined again. Yvain desperately wants to make a name for himself at court, so much so that he unnecessarily foolishly and repeatedly risks his life. Further, he needs to settle down and act more courteously to his lady after their marriage because he is no longer a bachelor with only his personal renown to consider. Chrétien reinforces the value of reputation by linking Yvain to King Arthur "who was of such renown that people speak of him near and far; and I agree thus far with the Bretons that his name will live forever." Yvain, like Arthur and Tristram, is one of the few characters of Arthurian romance whom scholars believe actually existed. His name was Owain, son of King Urien, and both warriors are recalled in Welsh memory as mighty warriors.

The hero puts his desire to avenge his cousin's honor before his duty to the brotherhood of knights and his reputation. Arriving at a fountain in the forest of Brocéliande, Yvain pours water on the stone causing Escaldos, lord of a nearby castle, to attack him. Yvain wounds Esclados and chases him into the castle he shares with his wife, Laudine. There the hero is hidden by a servant named Lunete. Yvain is able to kill Esclados and falls in love with Laudine, the grieving widow. Yvain becomes the new champion of the fountain and marries Laudine. Arthur and his knights arrive and invite Yvain to go questing with them. Despite their recent marriage, Yvain is ready to go and begs Laudine to allow him to leave. She grants permission, but he must be back within one year or he will lose her forever. Yvain returns late and is driven insane when he is told that his wife has renounced him.

Despite the madness that causes Yvain to live naked in the forest, he is kind to a hermit and a lady. The lady uses a magic balm to make Yvain sane again. A lion, whose tail is stuck in a serpent-dragon's mouth, is freed by Yvain and becomes his faithful champion. Yvain is now called the Lion Knight. Naturally the lion, whose rump was being scorched by dragon flames, is grateful. It shows the traditional nobility of lions by standing on its hind legs and bowing to Yvain after he cuts the dragon in half. The lion guards Yvain by night and provides food by day. When Yvain swoons at one point, the lion thinks he is dead and tries to commit suicide. The lion character provides comic relief while embodying the qualities of gratitude, loyalty, and courage.

Yvain is driven insane when his wife banishes him forever from her realm because she imagines him to be faithless. The good, courtly lover is attentive and would never neglect or fail to respond to his lady's rule. The male must worship, adore, and serve his lady, so Yvain must win back Laudine's love. Yvain wastes time by becoming suddenly slavishly devoted after he has lost Laudine; he is so absorbed by his passion that madness overtakes him for years, forcing him to live like an animal in the forest. The knight gains a reputation for kindness and valiant deeds, one of which is rescuing Lunite the servant who had once saved him. Lunite, in turn, agrees to help Yvain win back his wife's love. Eventually Laudine consents to his return to her kingdom and bed. Their reconciliation, restoring their natural status as husband and wife, is accomplished finally by her forgiveness upon seeing his valor and subjugation.

The romance is well structured and nearly the mirror image of *Erec et Enide* in some ways. Both are happily married couples, but Erec won't leave Enide while Yvain begs to leave to go questing for adventure as soon as he and Laudine are married. Just as Enide taught Erec how a loving spouse should act, the lion shows Yvain what perfect devotion and servitude should be so he becomes a better courtly lover-husband. *Yvain* and *Erec* are concerned with marriage, while Chrétien's next work *Lancelot* or *The Knight of the Cart* is about courtly love outside of marriage. Chrétien, perhaps because he was a cleric, seems uncomfortable condoning adultery and explains that Countess Marie asked for this text.

Like the Classical story of Helen of Troy, *Lancelot* is a tale of abduction and rescue. Meleagant arrives and wants to take the queen as tribute, minotaur style, but Kay tries to stop him through combat. Guinevere is abducted by Meleagant and locked up with other prisoners he has previously abducted. Several knights try to rescue her, but ultimately Lancelot crawls over a bridge of sharp knife blades to win the release of his arrogant queen. Lancelot is enslaved by her every whim and powerless in her presence. Lancelot is shamed and humiliated at every turn, mostly because of Guinevere's cruelty. She torments him for her pleasure and her cruelty quickens his heart. The story is mainly concerned with tests of his courage, endurance, and love. The agony and delight of his passionate worship of the queen is the point, and it would no doubt please Chrétien's patroness. Such ruthless behavior became en vogue among those women aspiring to be fashionable. Testing the true sincerity of adoration by the level of bravery and fear of fatal consequences—or at least discovery—is part of courtly love's system.

The story of Lancelot and Queen Guenevere is flagrantly immoral, but in Chrétien's hands well expresses the devotion and courtesy of courtly love. Moral decadence seems less offensive when it is put in the elegant terms of a master storyteller describing the most perfect lover. Initially Lancelot's troubles began because he momentarily was not Guinevere's idea of the courtly devoted knight. She has been kidnapped, and to rescue her quickly, Lancelot must ride in a cart designed for carrying criminals. Thinking of his reputation, Lancelot hesitates before stepping into the cart. Despite his many superhuman efforts on her behalf, Guinevere continues to punish Lancelot for considering his reputation before her safety. The poem's remainder is a series of tests of his fidelity. Lancelot repeatedly shows himself willing to be humiliated for his queen's sake. Guinevere is impetuous and haughty as she commands her lover to newly ridiculous tasks designed to embarrass him, such as having him purposefully lose a tournament. Lancelot's devotion may seem foolish to a modern reader and his attempted suicide downright insane given the situation, but the point was to express the knight's obsessive attachment as a courtly lover.

Guinevere returns to Arthur's court, leaving Lancelot imprisoned and does nothing to facilitate his release. Nor does Lancelot receive aid from any of the others he rescued like Gauvain. He is, however, helped by maidens, whom he later protects. For reasons unknown, Chrétien stopped writing towards the end of the romance and it was finished by Godefroy de Leigny. In medieval romantic literature, Guinevere is not condemned for her sin, and criticism of Lancelot is rare, although he betrays his king and best friend. Arthur's position as the cuckolded husband is unflattering in *Lancelot*, even though Chrétien had praised the king in *Cligés* and *Erec et Enide*. The tale's recreation seems intended to reinforce the free love encouraged at Marie's court. Chrétien explained that the subject and style were given to him by the countess, and no doubt his patroness had every reason to enjoy a story of Lancelot's utter subjugation to his mistress's every whim. This daringly explicit tale of adulterous love is immoral and would have been objectionable to Chrétien if he was a cleric. Perhaps this is why Chrétien left the work unfinished.

Chrétien also did not finish his last and longest romance, *Perceval* or *The Story of the Grail*, finishing only about a third, no later than 1191, because it is dedicated to Philip of Alsace, Count of Flanders, who died that year. Chrétien says that Count Philip gave him a book that was about the grail and asked him to tell the tale in verse. It is the story of the young and naive knight Perceval's visit to the grail castle. The most overtly religious of Chrétien's poems, *Perceval* teaches of knightly spirituality. Leaving his mother to die in the forest so that he could become a knight is the sin that Perceval must rectify by performing penitence before he can learn the secrets of the grail castle. Later in the romances, the character of Perceval was developed into a chaste virgin hero and the grail became the most sacred relic of Christ's suffering. However, Chrétien's Perceval begins as a crass buffoon who easily takes the maid Blauncheflor into his bed. Boyish ignorance excuses much of his behavior, but the grail scene—where not questioning the maimed keeper causes the continued desolation of the land—is the inevitable final straw. The grail riddle has bewildered scholars for years and because Chrétien died mid-sentence, *Perceval* does not solve the problem nor does he reconcile the inconsistencies.

The story begins with Perceval leaving his widowed mother in tears to follow his dream of becoming one of King Arthur's knights, even though the lad knows nothing of chivalry. Because Perceval is a simple country boy whose manners are atrocious, he even insults a maiden. A helpful mentor knight educates Perceval about how to use his weapons and keep his mouth shut. Perceval defends a castle and falls in love with Blancheflor. Next he watches an odd procession containing a bleeding lance and a jeweled grail; because he has been told that his speech reflects his lack of education, Perceval does not ask the questions he longs to ask: "Why does the lance bleed?" and "Whom are they serving with the grail?" If he had asked, the Fisher King's father and the country would have been healed. Back at Arthur's court, Perceval chooses to return to the grail castle and ask the correct questions. He wanders for five years, thinking no Christian thoughts until on Good Friday he meets his uncle, who is a hermit. The uncle explains that because Perceval left his grieving mother, he has committed the great sin of the unasked questions. The hermit also explains that the Fisher King's father is a man so holy that he has been fed nothing but mass wafers from the grail for years.

After some of Gawain's adventures are realted, presumably to contrast with Perceval's attitudes, the story is interrupted, and we learn that Chrétien is dead and cannot finish the tale. Probably the story would have returned to Perceval who had repented of his shabby treatment of his mother and taken communion, thus making him fit for the grail quest. Perceval, who was once indifferent to others, has been taught true Christianity. In legend, the grail is the dish of the Last Supper, which was used by Joseph of Arimethea to collect Christ's blood. In *Perceval*, it is used to feed the Fisher King's father, but because Perceval lacks the courtesy required to ask about the grail, he cannot heal the older man's wound. The ruler remains unhealed, so the land becomes more and more desolate; this reflects ancient fertility beliefs that the ruler's prowess would be reflected in the abundant yield of the land. The idea that a knight must be spiritually pure, and thus able to heal, was most likely a new twist in the ideal of chivalry as are the elements of penitence and charity; however, the idea of the leader's physical situation being reflected in his lands', animals', and people's fertility is as old as time. Traditionally, the king's wound is a sexual maiming. Chrétien's is the earliest known version of the grail story, and the source he claimed to use has been lost.

Other lost manuscripts include several works Chrétien claims to have written. In *Cligés* he gives us a list of his other writing: a translation of Ovid's *Remedia Amoris* from Latin into French, an adaptation of Ovid's *Metamorphoses*, and a version of the Tristan story (*Conte du rol Marc et d'Iseult la Blonde*). Extent is a pious adventure story by Chrétien called "Guillaume d'Angletene" and a lyric poem "Philomena." Forty-five copies of his manuscripts remain. The documents date from about one hundred years after Chrétien's death and were composed from about 1275 to around 1325. Further, ten of the manuscripts are illustrated with miniatures containing gold leaf and lapis lazuli, indicating their value as literary works.

While the plots of Chrétien's romances differ widely, they have many similar elements. One link is that the knights are all Arthur's men and, while the king is never a main character, he is the main judge of everyone's actions. The protagonists all need to be taught lessons involving relationships to a lover, the community, or God. Chrétien did not just compose interesting episodic narratives, because his intent was to instruct.

The inventive powers in Chrétien's works are remarkable in two ways: the narratives and the form. The stories are apparently new, as is the genre of poetic romance. His multifarious form may have sprung from unknown Irish, Welsh, Cornish, or Breton tales that commingled over the six hundred years since Arthur probably lived. Chrétien barely mentions Merlin, and it may be that the scant references to this character can be explained by the poet's natural bent toward realism rather than enchantment. His creative genius was shaped by Latin classical tales of noble heroes, military strategy, and enduring love. The only thing superhuman about most of Chrétien's protagonists is their courage.

Early medieval epics are violent and cruel. They contain no love stories or charming feminine details. Even the early French epics are uninspired though written in a more refined tone. With the establishment of a chivalric code of nobility, Christianity, courtesy, and respect, a poet of Chrétien's caliber had something significant to write about.

PRIMARY WORKS

Erec et Enide (c. 1165–1170). **Manuscripts:** There are seven extant manuscripts of *Erec et Enide*: Perhaps the best are in Paris: Bibliotéque Nationale de France, f. fr. 375; Bibliotéque Nationale de France, f. fr. 1376; Bibliotéque Nationale de France, f. fr. 1420; Bibliotéque Nationale de France f. fr. 1450; Bibliotéque Nationale de France, f. fr. 24403. Fragments are rather plentiful in both private and public collections. **Standard editions:** *Erec et Enide*, ed. Wendelin Foerster. Vol. 3 of *Chrétien de Troyes: Sämtliche Werke nach allen bekanntn Handschriften*. Halle: Niemeyer, 1890; reprint, Amsterdam: Rodopi, 1895. *Erec et Enide*, Classiques Français du Moyen Age, no. 80, ed. Mario Roques. Paris: Champion, 1952. **Standard modern French edition:** In *Œuvres Completes de Chrétien de Troyes,* Bibliothéque de la Pléiade, no. 408, ed. Daniel Poirion, 1–90. Paris: Gallimard, 1994. **English editions:** In *Arthurian Romances by Chrétien de Troyes*, trans. W. Wistar Comfort, 1–90. London: Dent, 1914. In *Chrétien de Troyes: Arthurian Romances*, trans. D. D. R. Owen, 1–92. London: Dent, 1987. *Erec et Enide*, trans. Carleton W. Carroll. New York: Garland, 1987. *Erec et Enide*, trans. Dorothy Gilbert. Berkeley: University of California Press, 1992; *Philomena* (c. 1170). **Manuscripts:** Chrétien's *Philomena* is found in nineteen manuscripts of the *Ovide Moralisé*, a fourteenth-century text. **Standard edition:** In *Philomena: conte raconté d'après Ovide*, ed. Cornelis de Boer. Paris: Geutherner, 1909. **Standard modern French edition:** In *Œuvres Completes de Chrétien de Troyes,* Bibliothéque de la Pléiade, no. 408, ed. Daniel Poirion, 915–52. Paris: Gallimard, 1994. **English edition:** In *Three Ovidian Tales of Love: Piramus et Tisbé, Narcisus et Danaé, and Philomela et Procné*, trans. Raymond Cornier, 183-265. New York, Garland, 1986; *Cligés*. **Manuscripts:** There are eight extant manuscripts. Perhaps the best are in Paris: Bibliotéque Nationale de France, f. fr. 375; Bibliotéque Nationale de France, f. fr. 1374; Bibliotéque Nationale de France, f. fr. 1420; and Bibliotéque Nationale de France, f. fr. 12560. Fragments are rather plentiful in both private and public collections, especially Oxford, Bodleian Library, Michael 569 (SC 24064). **Standard editions:** *Cligés*, ed. Wendelin Foerster. Vol. 1 of *Chrétien de Troyes: Sämtliche Werke nach allen bekanntn Handschriften.* Halle: Niemeyer, 1890; reprint, Amsterdam: Rodopi, 1895. *Cligés*, Classiques Français du Moyen Age, no. 84, ed. Alexandre Micha. Paris: Champion, 1954. *Cligés*, Arthurian Studies, no. 28, ed. Stewart Gregory and Claud Luttrell. Cambridge: Brewer, 1994. **Standard modern French edition:** *Cligés, Chrétien de Troyes édition critique du manuscrit B, N. fr. 12560*, ed. Marie-Claire Gérard-Zai, trans. Charles Méla and Olivier Collet. Paris: Livre de Poche, 1994. **English editions:** In *Arthurian Romances by Chrétien de Troyes*, trans. W. Wistar Comfort, 91–179. London: Dent, 1914. In *Chrétien de Troyes: Arthurian Romances*, trans, D. D. R. Owen, 93–184. London: Dent, 1987. *Cligés: Chrétien de Troyes*, trans. Burton

Raffel. New Haven, CT: Yale University Press, 1997; *Le Chevalier de la Charette, ou Lancelot* (c. 1180). **Manuscripts:** There are eight extant manuscripts of *Le Chevalier de la Charette, ou Lancelot*. Perhaps the best are in Paris: Bibliotéque Nationale de France, f. fr. 794; Bibliotéque Nationale de France f. fr. 1450; Bibliotéque Nationale de France, f. fr. 12560. The best fragment of *Le Chevalier de la Charette, ou Lancelot* is Paris: Bibliotéque de l'Institut de France, 6138. **First publications:** *Roman van Lancelot (XIIIe eeuw)*, 2 vols., ed. W. J. A. Jonckbloet. The Hague: Stickun, 1846. *Le roman du chevalier du la charette*, ed. Prosper Tarbé. Reims, 1849. **Modern French edition:** *Guillaume d'Angleterre*, trans. Jean Trotin. Paris: Champion, 1974; *La Conter du Graal, ou Perceval* (c. 1181–1190). **Manuscripts:** There are fifteen extant manuscripts of *La Conter du Graal, ou Perceval*. Perhaps the best are in Paris: Bibliotéque Nationale de France, f. fr. 794; Bibliotéque Nationale de France, f. fr. 1429; Bibliotéque Nationale de France, f. fr. 1450; Bibliotéque Nationale de France f. fr. 1453; Bibliotéque Nationale de France, f. fr. 12576 and Bibliotéque Nationale de France f. fr. 12577. Complete manuscripts are also found in Edinburgh, Scotland; London, England; and Florence, Italy. **First publication:** *Perceval le Gallois ou le conte du Graal*. 6 vols., Société Bibliophiles Belges, no. 21, ed. Charles Potvin. Mons: Dequesne-Maquillier, 1866–1871. **Standard editions:** *Le Roman de Perceval ou le Conte du Graal*. ed. William Roach. Geneva: Droz, 1956. *La Conter du Graal (Perceval)*, Classiques Français du Moyen Age, nos. 100 and 103, ed. Félix Lecoy. Paris: Champion, 1973-1975. **Modern French edition:** In *Œuvres Completes de Chrétien de Troyes*, Bibliothéque de la Pléiade, no. 408, ed. Daniel Poirion. Paris: Gallimard, 1994. **English editions:** *The Story of the Grail (Perceval)*, trans. Robert Whie Linker. Chapel Hill: University of North Carolina Press, 1952. In *Chrétien de Troyes: Arthurian Romances*, trans. D. D. R. Owens, 374–495. London: Dent, 1987. *The Story of the Grail (Lli Contes del Grail), or Perceval*, ed. Roger T. Pickens, trans. William W. Kibler. New York: Garland, 1990; *Chansons*. **Manuscripts:** The standard edition of the *Chansons* is based on fourteen manuscripts. Perhaps the best are in Paris: Bibliotéque Nationale de France, f. fr. 765; Bibliotéque Nationale de France, f. fr. 844; Bibliotéque Nationale de France, f. fr. 845; Bibliotéque Nationale de France f. fr. 847; Bibliotéque Nationale de France, f. fr. 1591; Bibliotéque Nationale de France f. fr. 12615; Bibliotéque Nationale de France, f. fr. 20050; and Bibliotéque Nationale de France f. fr. 24406. Copies are also found at the Oxford Bodleian Library and at the Vatican. **Standard edition:** *Les Chansons de Chrétien de Troyes*, ed. Marie-Claire Zai. Bern: Lang, 1974. **Modern French edition:** In *Œuvres Completes de Chrétien de Troyes*, Bibliothéque de la Pléiade, no. 408, ed. Daniel Poirion, 1037–49. Paris: Gallimard, 1994.

SECONDARY SOURCES

Busby, Keith, et al., eds. *Les manuscrits de Chrétien de Troyes / The Manuscripts of Chrétien de Troyes*. 2 vols. Amsterdam: Rodopi, 1993; Duggan, Joseph J. *The Romances of Chrétien de Troyes*. New Haven, CT: Yale University Press, 2001; Frappier, Jean. *Chrétien de Troyes*. Paris: Hatier, 1957; Kelly, Douglas. *Chrétien de Troyes: An Analytic Bibliography*. London: Grant and Cutler, 1976; ———, ed. *The Romances of Chrétien de Troyes: A Symposium*. Lexington, KY: French Forum, 1985; Kelly, Douglas, et al. *Chrétien de Troyes: An Analytic Bibliography, Supplement I*. Woodbridge, UK: Boydell, 2002; Krueger, Roberta L., ed. *The Cambridge Companion to Medieval Romance*. Cambridge: Cambridge University Press, 2000; Lacy, Norris J. *The Craft of Chrétien de Troyes*. Leiden: Brill, 1980; Lacy, Norris J., Douglas Kelly, and Keith Busby, eds. *The Legacy of Chrétien de Troyes*. 2 vols. Amsterdam: Rodopi, 1987–1988; Maddox, Donald. *The Arthurian Romances of Chrétien de Troyes: Once and Future Fictions*. Cambridge: Cambridge University Press, 1991; Nykrog, Per. *Chrétien de Troyes: Romancier Discutable*. Geneva: Droz, 1996; Pickens, Rupert T., ed. *The Sower and His Seed: Essays on Chrétien de Troyes*. Lexington, KY: French Forum, 1983; Topsfield, Leslie. *Chrétien de Troyes: A Study of the Arthurian Romances*. Cambridge: Cambridge University Press, 1981.

LAURA COONER LAMBDIN AND ROBERT THOMAS LAMBDIN

LAYAMON
(fl. c. 1185–1225)

Layamon is the first author to write the story of Arthur in the English vernacular. His *Hystoria Brutonum* or *Brut* is an early Middle English version of the history of Britain. At its core lies a poetic paraphrase and elaboration of Wace's *Roman de Brut* (a French poetic retelling of Geoffrey of Monmouth's Latin *Historia Regum Britanniae*). Layamon's use of Anglo-Saxon poetic techniques and his energetic elaborations on Wace's original poem have ensured him an important place in the annals of Arthurian literature and chroniclers of the history of Britain. He colors his poem with an intense love of the early inhabitants of Britain and tells of the various battles and conquests that contributed to Britain becoming the country it was in the centuries just prior to the Norman conquest. Layamon offers frequent negative commentary on foreign conquests of his native Britons, but he presents a continuum in which all Englishmen should feel pride in their country and remember their noble ancestors.

Critical opinion of the *Brut* has varied between an acceptance of it as a major innovation in English chronicling to relegation of it to the status of mere paraphrase translation, although contemporary opinion favors the former. Layamon's elaborations concerning Merlin, Arthurian conquests, and the Round Table, as well as his innovative use of techniques from Anglo-Saxon poetry, support an estimation of him as one of the greatest writers of his day, possibly surpassing both Wace and Geoffrey in terms of literary technique.

All that we know about Layamon's life is presented to us by him at the opening of his poem.

An preost wes on leoden; Layamon wes ihoten.
he wes Leouenaðes sone; liðe him beo Drihten.
He wonede at Ernleze; at æðelen are chirechen.

(Laweman, Lawman)

vppen Seuarne staþe; sel þar him þuhte.
on-fest Radestone; þer he bock radde.
Hit com him on mode; & on his mern þonke.
þet he wolde of Engle; þa æðelæn tellen.
wat heo ihoten weoren; & wonene heo comen.
þa Englene londe; ærest ahten.
æfter þan flode; þe from Drihtene com.
þe al her a-quelde; quic þat he funde.
buten Noe & Sem; Iaphet & Cham.
& heore four wiues; þe mid heom weren on archen.
Layamon gon liðen; wide zond þas leode.
& bi-won þa æðela boc; þa he to bisne nom.
He nom þa Englisca boc; þa makede Seint Beda.
An-oþer he nom on Latin; þe makede Seinte Albin.
& þe feire Austin; þe fulluht broute hider in.
Boc he nom þe þridde; leide þer amidden.
þa makede a Frenchis clerc;
Wace wes ihoten; þe wel couþe writen.
& he hoe zef þare æðelen; Ælienor
þe wes Henries quene; þes hezes kinges.
Layamon leide þeos boc; & þa leaf wende.
he heom leofliche bi-heold. liþe him beo Drihten.
Feþeren he nom mid fingren; & fiede on boc-felle.
& þa soþere word; sette to-gadere.
& þa þre boc; þrumde to are.
Nu bidde[ð] Layamon alcne æðele mon;
for þene almiten Godd.
þet þeos boc rede; & leornia þeos runan.
þat he þeos soðfeste word; segge to-sumne.
for his fader saule; þa hine for[ð] brouhte.
& for his moder saule; þa hine to monne iber.
& for his awene saule; þat hire þe selre beo. Amen. (1–35)

A translation of the opening to the Caligula manuscript of Layamon's *Brut* might run thus: (There was a priest living in this land, who was called Layamon. / He was the son of Leovenath, Lord be merciful to him! / He had a living at Areley, at a noble church, / on the banks of the River Severn—he thought it pleasant— / close by Redstone, where he read books. / It came to his mind, a most splendid idea, / that he would tell of England's noble men: / What each was called and from what place they came, / those who first possessed the land of England, / after the flood that came from our Lord God, / which killed all living creatures that it found here, / except Noah and Shem, Japhet and Ham, / and their four wives who were on the ark with them. / Layamon went traveling widely through this land, / and obtained the splendid book which he took as a model: / He took the English book which Saint Bede had made; / another he took in Latin made by Saint Albin, / and the blessed Augustine who brought baptism here; / a book he took as his third source, and laid this among the others, / a French cleric made it, / Wace he was called, who well knew how to write; / and he gave it to the noble Eleanor, / who was the queen of Henry, that great king. / Layamon laid out these books and he leafed through them. / He beheld them gratefully—the Lord be gracious to him! / He took a quill pen in hand and wrote on parchment. / And truthful words he set together, / and combined the three books into one. / Now Layamon bids each and every good man / for almighty God's sake, / that those who may read this book and learn from its secrets, / that he should those truthful words say together / for the sake of the soul of the father that brought him forth, / and for his mother's soul that bore him male, / and for his own soul that he may be better for it. Amen.)

From this sole source of biographical information, we can ascertain for certain several things about Layamon's life and speculate as to others. Layamon was the son of Leovenað. He lived at Areley Kings, a village located about ten miles up the Severn from Worcester near where the Severn runs through red rock cliffs. His village would have been located near where Astley and Arely parishes met. Quite possibly he was a learned scholar, as the books he claims to use for his source are in Old English, French, and Latin, but if he could read all of these languages fluently, he was far better educated than the average rural priest of his day. His statement that "he read books" could mean an involvement with a scholarly life or could refer to his having a position in the church where he read aloud parts of the service for the congregation.

The three books to which Layamon directly refers are almost certainly an Anglo-Saxon translation of the Venerable Bede's *Historia Ecclesiastica* (the "English Book"), Bede's Latin original of *Historia Ecclesiastica* (which mentions Albin and Augustine prominently in its opening and first chapter) and Wace's *Roman de Brut* (itself a French translation of Geoffrey of Monmouth's Latin *Historia Regum Britanniae*). Scholarly debate continues around whether Layamon ever consulted either of the first two books while writing the *Brut,* but all agree that the primary influence on Layamon is Wace's *Roman de Brut,* which was written less than one hundred years prior to Layamon's writing his *Brut.* Noticeably absent from Layamon's list is Geoffrey's *Historia Regum Britanniae,* a widely popular book it its own and Layamon's day. It is not uncommon for Middle English authors to refer to authorities that they do not actually use, in an attempt to bolster acceptance of their text, so the first two books mentioned by Layamon may be merely for show. Because Layamon used Wace, who translated Geoffrey, it is difficult to show Geoffrey's direct influence on Layamon, but some critics have found that Layamon must have seen Geoffrey's text and possibly even corrected his own account against the *Historia Regum Britanniae.* Additionally, it is difficult to document the influence of other texts on the *Brut*, although there is a consensus that Welsh and or Celtic source stories influence some of Layamon's original passages.

Also questionable from Layamon's short account of the making of his book is his traveling widely throughout the land. He almost certainly never toured England, although his knowledge of south and southwest England and Wales could come from personal experience. His descriptions of the English countryside invariably come across more authentic than Wace's descriptions, which frequently transpose elements of the French countryside onto English locales.

It is difficult to date Layamon's *Brut* with any real precision. Obviously it must have been written some time after Wace completed his *Roman de Brut* (c. 1150), and we know the *Brut* itself was used to write another chronicle, *The Chronicle of Robert Cloucester* in 1320. Probably the latest it could have been composed is 1260. However, merely limiting the dates of the *Brut* to a 110-year period seems fully dissatisfying, and most scholars can agree to a much smaller range of dates.

Based on Layamon's use of the past tense after naming Wace (line 21), numerous critics assume that the manuscript must have been written after Wace's death, and we know

Wace was still alive in 1170. Layamon also mentions either Eleanor or Henry II or both Eleanor and Henry II in the past tense (lines 22–23). This might indicate the poem was written after Henry II's death in 1189 or after Eleanor's death in 1204, and it may imply he wrote before the ascension of Henry III to the throne in 1216, owing to Layamon's lack of distinction about which Henry he is discussing. A competent and reliable dating of the manuscript would range from 1185 to 1225, with a high probability that it was written during the first few decades of the thirteenth century.

The *Brut* exists in two separate manuscripts, both of which were copied from a single earlier manuscript. The Cotton Caligula A ix manuscript (located in the British Museum) is the earliest and longest of the two manuscripts and was probably copied about fifty years after Layamon wrote. Other than eighty original lines found in the Otho manuscript (which the Caligula scribe probably mistakenly skipped), the Caligula manuscript contains the most accurate rendition of what Layamon wrote. At 16,096 lines the Caligula *Brut* is the longest poem in English prior to Spenser's *Faerie Queene*. It consists of 192 leaves of double column writing by two different scribal hands. The columns generally contain thirty-four lines each and character names appear in red lettering. The syntax, vocabulary, and spelling are often archaic and probably retain Layamon's original intention to recapture some of the antique beauty of Anglo-Saxon poetry. The Cotton Otho C xiii manuscript (also located in the British Museum) is accepted to be an attempt at both modernizing and condensing the manuscript from which both it and the Caligula were copied. The Otho was some three thousand lines shorter in its original form and suffered fire damage in 1731 (in the same fire that damaged the *Beowulf* manuscript). The Otho manuscript is the work of one scribe who generally restricts himself to more factual and fewer imaginative details from the *Brut*. Although the Caligula manuscript is the text upon which most versions of the Brut are based, there are a few slight differences in the Otho manuscript (especially in the opening lines) that bear mentioning. The poet's name in the Otho is spelled Laweman, and this probably stems from a translation of the name Layamon into an approximation of its meaning in Middle English, that is, "Lawman." Some critics use this difference in spelling to postulate that "Layamon" was more a designation of someone involved with the law than a name in the strictest sense, but arguments of this sort are notoriously difficult to prove. Additionally, Laweman is identified as a priest who lives "wid þan gode cniþte (with a good knight)," which could indicate that Layamon was not just a simple country priest, but a chaplain to a nobleman in Areley where he might have had the freedom to study and read texts in Old English, French, and Latin.

Even though the Caligula text is accepted as the most reliable, the Otho scribe's mention of Layamon's working for a knight answers one of the most important questions about the *Brut:* For whom was Layamon writing? Would a simple country priest have had the leisure to pursue his interest in British history to the extent of a 16,096-line poetic text? If Layamon were a chaplain to a noble, he might have been writing for this knight, or some other noble, as his patron. A patron could have made possible the leisure time needed to travel, collect books, and write such a massive undertaking. Whether he wrote for a patron or not, or lived with a knight or not, we can surmise some things about The *Brut*'s audience. Layamon must have expected his audience to have pride in their Briton ancestry because he depicts the natives of England as the most heroic of peoples. Layamon is certainly not appealing to the ruling class Normans of the England of his day. One common feature of the *Brut* is its disdain for whoever is the most current invader of England. As earlier invaders are assimilated into the culture some of the disdain is assuaged, but Layamon consistently presents the most recent invaders of England as ruthless opportunists.

The language of the *Brut* is an early Middle English, but its poetic form, vocabulary, and style are reminiscent of the classical Anglo-Saxon period. English was pretty far along in its transition from Old English to Middle English in Layamon's day, but the *Brut* is intentionally archaic, possibly in order to harken back to a time when Britain was free from the Normans. One rather interesting fact about the *Brut's* vocabulary is that it uses very few French loan words—far fewer than other texts written during the same time period. Also, it uses a number of Anglo-Saxon terms that had probably been out of use for more than a century, and it often appears similar to an Anglo-Saxon heroic poem, but only superficially. Bernard Ten Brink succinctly makes this point, "of all English Poets after the conquest none approach the Old English epos as close as [Layamon]" (quoted in Gillespy, 366). Working from a French, rhyming, octosyllabic model, Layamon attempts to re-create, years after the language has moved on, the look and feel of the model for great English poetry: Anglo-Saxon heroic verse. Although beautiful and innovative, Layamon's poem does not successfully re-create the grandeur of the poetry of his past, but he does create an amazing alliterative and rhyming hybrid verse that is uniquely suited to his heroic chronicle celebrating the glory of England's past. And, although Layamon's language is entirely Middle English, it is probably more akin to Anglo-Saxon than to the English used by Shakespeare.

Numerous studies of Layamon's style have been conducted and some of the more basic structural facts merit repeating. Of the *Brut's* more than sixteen thousand long alliterative lines (each line approximately twice as long as Wace's shorter rhyming lines), almost half follow the Anglo-Saxon pattern of two alliterative half-lines per line, with two stresses per half-line. About one third of the poem's lines have some variety of rhyming either within lines or between different lines. Although Layamon does a good job of giving his poem an Anglo-Saxon appearance, there is no direct antecedent for many of his recurrent poetic phrases (or formulas) and compound words. Layamon simply knew that Old English used these devices and seems to have created his own. He seems to have had significant exposure to epic and heroic poetry, although some of his techniques seem more similar to the Latin *Aeneid* than to the Anglo-Saxon *Beowulf*. For one thing, he uses few or no kennings (Anglo-Saxon tag phrases composed of compound words) and he uses numerous extended similes (which are common in Latin epics, but not in Anglo-Saxon poetry). Nevertheless, Layamon's pseudo-Anglo-Saxon style has compelled different theorists to consider if he might have read *Beowulf* and been consciously imitating its now-archaic language.

The influence of Anglo-Saxon heroic poetry on Layamon is especially interesting owing to the often oral formulation of Anglo-Saxon poems. We know for a fact that Layamon composed the *Brut* as a written literary response to an earlier written work, and so the oral poetic elements of the *Brut* are as interesting as they are unnecessary. The result is that, although it is entirely a literary creation, the *Brut* partakes of the Anglo-Saxon musicality and rhythm of orally performed poems. Scholars have often mentioned the probability that Layamon expected the poem would be read aloud to his countrymen as a form of entertainment, and the poem's incidents are broken down in to stories of varying length, which could be read and aurally appreciated within different settings.

Although a number of critics have been tempted to show the poem's affinities to *Beowulf*, one more likely Anglo-Saxon model for the poem is theorized by S. K. Brehe, who finds that Aelfric's Old English *Lives of the Saints,* with its loosely alliterative and sometimes rhyming prose, might have been a more accessible text for Layamon. In fact, owing to its being written late in the Anglo-Saxon period, Aelfric's text is closer to Layamon's in terms of literary style and vocabulary. With this in mind, Brehe can assert that the structure of the *Brut* is more like Middle English free verse.

The possible stylistic and source influences on the *Brut* differ depending on how well-read and well-traveled we suppose Layamon to be. We know he used Wace's *Roman de Brut,* and a few scholars have found that Layamon corrects changes Wace makes to Geoffrey of Monmouth's original *Historia Regum Britanniae,* so he probably knew this immensely popular work. Quite possibly he also knew Geoffrey's *Vita Merlini,* which could have served as a source for some of the material about Merlin and his prophecies about Arthur. Harder to pin down is how Celtic, Welsh, and Germanic source stories are able to resonate in some of Layamon's more detailed elaborations on Wace. In his discussion of Arthur's armor alone, Layamon introduces Germanic and Celtic smith deities while using some distinctly Welsh terms. Layamon's living in close proximity to Wales probably resulted in his knowing a number of Celtic stories, which he was able to integrate into his presentation of the magical attributes of Arthur. Possibly Layamon had a textual source for these stories, but they also were circulated in oral form by minstrels.

Some of the changes that Layamon makes to people and place names in Wace reflect Layamon's greater familiarity with Welsh terminology, although he probably did not speak Welsh. His bias toward native Britons also reflects a Welsh influence as the Britons were consistently driven west by invaders. It is Layamon's underlying sense of native pride (which some have called patriotism) that probably drew him to retelling the story of his people in their own language. And it may be that the recurring emphasis on evil invaders was meant as a commentary on England's most recent invaders: the Normans. Regardless of his national pride, Layamon's text makes available to the masses in their own language stories of their ancestors' greatness.

In addition to his Arthurian content, which constitutes either a third or half the poem depending on whether the story of Uther Pendragon (Arthur's father) is considered Arthurian material, the *Brut* contains numerous stories that are taken up by later writers and reflect Layamon's deep sense of pride in British sovereignty. The chronicle begins (as both Geoffrey and Wace begin) with the founding of Britain by Brutus the great-grandson of Aeneas (of Trojan War fame). Even though Brutus travels to Greece and avenges the wrongs done to Trojans, he chooses to leave the Mediterranean in search of a land where he and his people can establish their own country in relative safety from their traditional enemies. Throughout his account of the founding of Britain, Layamon offers etymological reasons for the naming of cities and regions based on heroes and battles from wars long ago.

Layamon is the first writer to tell the story of King Leir and Cordoille (Shakespeare's Lear and Cordelia) in English (lines 1451–1885). Much of Shakespeare's main plot is contained in Layamon, except in Layamon's version Leir and Cordoille successfully regain power over England and rule in peace for three years. The original lacks the grand tragic structure given it by Shakespeare, although Layamon's story ultimately ends with a tortured Cordoille's suicide. Layamon also makes available in English the story of Dunwallo Molinus, the first crowned king of England, who united the country from Scotland to Cornwall through valiant behavior and generous diplomacy. Dunwallo developed the first codified set of laws for the country and his reign was characterized by prosperity for all, from nobles to peasants. Almost nine hundred lines of poetry (2140–3036) are devoted to the reign of Dunwallo's two sons, Belin and Brennes. Layamon chronicles their feud, Brennes's exile, their reunification, and their eventual conquering of all of Europe and the Roman empire. These early British rulers' claim to Rome is made to predate any Roman entitlement to tribute from England. Later rulers, including Arthur, can assert that it is not England that owes tribute to Rome, but Rome that owes tribute to England, owing to Belin's and Brennes's conquests. But Layamon does not only tell of British triumphs and victories, he records the adversities which befell England. Sometimes good kings had evil kin or offspring, but more often foreign invaders weakened and overpowered British resolve.

Julius Caesar was the first Roman to attempt to conquer Britain. Caesar attacks the British king Cassibellanus and is repelled twice. However, after a disagreement between Cassibellanus and one of his nephews, Androgeus, Caesar is aided by Androgeus to subdue Britain and make Cassibellanus pay yearly tribute to Rome. At times the relationship between Rome and England was mutually beneficial; Androgeus's nephew, Cymbeline, was educated and made a knight in Rome. It was during Cymbeline's rule of Britain that Jesus Christ is born and the Briton wizard/advisor Taliesin prophesizes the importance of Christ's birth. Although Cymbeline was a powerful ruler, he sent tribute to Rome all the years of his life, but his son Wither sternly refused to be a subject of Rome. Angered by Wither's arrogance, Claudius Caesar invades Britain. He is unsuccessful for a time, but ultimately succeeds and forms an alliance with Arviragus (Wither's brother) after Wither's death. Claudius and Arviragus reunited all of England under Arviragus's rule. Arviragus marries Claudius's daughter, Genius, and Claudius takes a Briton bride before returning to Rome.

The ties between Rome (the most successful ruling power of all time from the medieval point of view) and England are continually reasserted throughout Layamon's narrative. When Arviragus refuses to pay tribute to Claudius's successor, Vespian, Genius reminds him that Britain and Rome are tied together through their marriage. When Rodric and his Pictish warriors invade, it is Arviragus's Roman-educated son Maurus who defeats them and returns England to order. It is Maurus's grandson, Luces, who is king when Pope Eleutherius sends bishops from Rome to convert the Britons to Christianity in the early second century.

Eventually Basian, son of Caesar Severius and a Briton woman, becomes king. He is betrayed by a fellow Briton, Carrais, who tries to turn Rome against Basian and enlist the help of the evil Picts in defeating Basian. It is the Cornish Duke Asclepidiot who next repels Roman forces and creates a reign of peace among the Britons. Rule shifts between noble and corrupt Briton- and Roman-born rulers for many years. Eventually King Octaves of Wales and Adolf Earl of Kent kill all the Romans and humble the great. When the ailing Octaves asks his nobles for their opinions as to whom should marry his only daughter, they are divided between Conan Earl of Kent or Maximien of Rome. When Maximien is chosen, Conan declares war, enlists the help of the Scots, and eventually flees to Brittany and becomes king there. It is here we have another of Layamon's significant departures from his source in Wace. Conan sends to the Athionard, regent of Britain, and asks for Athionard's daughter, Ursula, to be his queen. Twenty-seven ships of women accompany Ursula on the journey. A storm destroys all but fifteen of the ships, and Ursula and her female followers are captured by the pirate warlords Melga of Hungary and Wanis of Scythia, who rape and kill the women and turn Ursula into a ship's whore.

The accumulated loss of so many native Britons to war, exile in Brittany, and emigration to Rome leaves Britain depleted of defensive resources and ripe for invasion by Melga and Wanis. Again, Rome intervenes sending Gracien—who subdues the country, but establishes a depraved reign. Eventually Melga and Wanis conquer England, and Rome renounces any claim to Britain to conserve its resources on the continent. The

Archbishop of London, Guenceline, appeals to Conan's heirs in Brittany, and Constantine arrives with two thousand knights of Brittany to battle Melga and Wanis. In the aftermath of the defeat of Melga and Wanis, the British women rip to pieces any remaining followers of the evil pair. The victorious Constantine calls an assembly of all the British lords and is made king of all England. After his treacherous murder, England is left without a king and the nobles must chose between his two oldest sons (Constance and Aurelius). His third and youngest son, Uther, was still an infant. Lord Vortigern, who controlled half the Welsh lands, corrupts and supports Constantine's eldest (Constance) and subdues much of England; eventually, Constance is murdered and Vortigern becomes king. Uther and Aurelius are raised in Brittany for their own safety, while Vortigern rules England. It is Vortigern who first welcomes the Saxons (lead by Hengest and Horsa) into England and uses them to defend his kingdom from the Scots and Picts. Vortigern slowly imports more and more Saxons and their pagan ways; he eventually relinquishes his own Christianity. The British reject the idea of a pagan king and select Vortimer (Vortigern's son by his Christian wife) as their king. Eventually Vortimer and his British forces defeat Vortigern and the Saxons. However, while Vortimer's stepmother implores his mercy, she secretly poisons him, allowing Vortigern to regain control of Britain. When Vortigern recalls Hengest and some of his Saxon allies, Hengest brings many more than the one hundred knights Vortigern suggested. The Briton's fear Hengest's forces, but he promises he will send them home and remain with just a small force to live with Vortigern. At a truce where both sides were to meet unarmed, Hengest secretly arms his men, slaughters the Britons, and captures Vortigern. Hengest forces the captive Vortigern to give him the lands now known as Essex, Wessex, and Middlesex. Vortigern, once free, flees across the Severn into Wales. He has little power, but still much gold. After encountering difficulty building a castle in Wales, he is encouraged by counselors to sacrifice a fatherless boy upon the site. This is how we are first introduced to Merlin, a character that Layamon treats in greater detail and with greater sympathy than Wace. Layamon uses some information from Geoffrey of Monmouth's texts to broaden his presentation of Merlin, but also presents details wholly original to his story.

In the absence of a clear ruler, Aurelius and Uther are welcomed back by their native Britons, and they quickly subdue the country and burn Vortigern in one of his castles. Aurelius and Uther then turn toward Scotland, where Hengest has fled. After a number of battles, Hengest is beheaded, and Aurelius is made king. He makes Merlin his advisor and, at Merlin's prompting, determines that the massacre of Britons by Hengest at Amesbury should be memorialized by a stone ring. Uther and Merlin—with many troops—travel to Ireland to steal a giant stone ring. The Irish are easily defeated by the better equipped English; the savage Irish wear no armor, nor even breeches. Using incantations, Merlin lightens the stones so they may be transported back to England, where Stonehenge is then erected. While Uther is off quelling an uprising caused by Gillomaur, king of Ireland and Vortigern's son Passent, a traitor hired by Passent poisons Aurelius. With Merlin's counsel, Uther defeats Passent and becomes king. Uther then subdues all dissenting factions and is aided greatly by Gorlois of Cornwall. However, Uther lusts after Gorlois's wife, Igerne, and causes Gorlois to rebel. Because Igerne is so virtuous and cannot be corrupted, Merlin is enlisted to win her for Uther. Using magic, Merlin changes Uther's appearance to that of Gorlois. While Gorlois is away, Igerne is impregnated by the disguised Uther and conceives Arthur. After Gorlois's death, Uther takes Igerne as his queen.

Whereas Wace translated and elaborated on Geoffrey but retained the basic proportions of his tale, Layamon takes the information on Arthur in his sources and expands what was one-fifth of the tale in Wace and Geoffrey into one third of his 16,096-line *Brut*. It is with the Arthurian material that Layamon makes some of his longest and most poetic elaborations. Many times Layamon is adding a few details to more clearly depict the time or place of an event. He often offers exact numbers for lines wherein Wace merely indicates "many" or "few." Moreover, sometimes for hundreds of lines Layamon is not referring at all to his French model, but instead is extending the story, characters, and dialogue using his understanding of Anglo-Saxon heroic poetry and the Welsh oral tradition.

By elaborating on events and bringing characters to life through vivid speeches, Layamon makes available to a popular audience the stories of his more esoteric sources for Arthur and his knights. He recounts for the first time in English the story of Arthur's conception and birth; his unification of England, Scotland, and Wales; the conquest of all the British Isles, Scandinavia, Germany, and France; his single combat with Frollo, king of France; and his defeat of the lustful giant of St. Michel. Layamon creates the first English-language catalog of English knights, and he attributes characteristics to individual knights that serve to inspire many future writers. Gawain is shown to be the most Christian of all knights and very loyal to his king. And, it is from Layamon that the first British audiences can hear of their great king's near defeat of Rome and betrayal by his nephew and queen. Arthur is depicted with detail afforded to no other character in the *Brut*, and Layamon's treatment far exceeds his mention in any previous sources. Layamon's Arthur is clearly superior to any other British chronicle character and predestined to be England's greatest ruler.

Immediately upon introducing Arthur, Layamon begins adding details that emphasize the king's majesty and destiny as England's savior. The following original lines continue the magical influence initiated by Merlin at the boy's conception, but presage the remarkable achievements of the best leader Britain has ever had.

> Sone swa he com an eorðe; aluen hine iuengen.
> heo bigolen þat child; mid galdere swiðe stronge.
> heo zeuen him mihte; to beon bezst alre cnihten.
> heo zeuen him an-oðer þing; þat he scolde beon riche king.
> heo ziuen him þat þridde; þat he scolde longe libben.
> heo zifen him þat kine-bern; custen swiðe gode.
> þat he wes mete-custi; of alle quike monnen.
> þis þe alue him zef; and al swa þat child iþæh. (9808–15)

(As soon as he [Arthur] came to earth, fairies attended upon him. / They enchanted that child with exceedingly strong magic. / They gave him might, to be the best of all knights; / they gave him another thing, that he should be a great king; / they gave him a third gift, that he should live long; / they gave him, that royal child, such exceedingly good qualities / that he was the most courteous of all living men; / these things the fairies gave him, and so that child prospered.)

The idea that Arthur has a destiny appointed by supernatural creatures adds to the greatness of the king and also partakes of the elements of folklore and fairy tale that Layamon would have known from exposure to Welsh and Celtic sources. These same sources undoubtedly influence Layamon's discussion of Arthur's Armor:

> þa dude he on his burne; ibroide of stele.
> þe makede on aluisc smið; mid aðelen his crafte.

he wes ihaten Wygar; þe Witeze wurhte.
His sconken he helede; mid hosen of stele.
Calibeorne his sweor[d]; he sweinde bi his side.
hit wes iworht in Aualun; mi[d] wizele-fulle craften.
Halm he set on hafde; hæh of stele.
þer-on wes moni zim-ston; al mid golde bi-gon.
he wes V[ð]eres; þas aðelen kinges.
he wes ihaten Goswhit; ælchen oðere vnilic.
He heng an his sweore; ænne sceld deore.
his nome wes on Bruttisc; Pridwen ihaten.
þer wes innen igrauen; mid rede golde stauen.
an on-licnes deore; of Drihtenes moder.
His spere he nom an honde; þa Ron wes ihaten. (10543–57)

(Then he put on his corset of woven steel / made by an Elvish smith with all his noble skill. / He was called Wygar, that wise wright. / His legs he girded with hose of steel. / Caliburn his sword he hung by his side; / it was made in Avalon by magic craft. / A steel helm he placed high on his head, / on which there were many jewels all set in gold; / it had been Uther's—that noble king. / It was called Goswhit; there was no other like it. / On his neck he hung a costly shield / that was called Pridwen in the British tongue. / On the inner side there was engraved in red gold / a splendid likeness of God's Mother. / His spear that he took in hand was called Ron.) This donning of magical armor (common to epic heroes) reinforces Arthur's grandeur. And although elements that make the "historical" Arthur awe-inspiring exist in Layamon's sources, it is in the added details about Arthur that sets Layamon apart from earlier chroniclers as one thoroughly committed to commemorating the greatness of Britain's past for future generations.

The Round Table is a perfect example of Layamon's handling of detail. Whereas Geoffrey does not even mention the Round Table, and Wace includes just a few lines concerning it (the table was part of folk tradition about Arthur), Layamon devotes more than one hundred lines to his discussion of why the table was made and how it was made. It is one of Layamon's longest elaborations on an idea briefly mentioned by Wace. Layamon posits that the table had to be created because Arthur had so many important knights at his feasts that it was impossible to know who should be seated at the tables of highest honor. After one disastrous banquet during which a food fight actually transpires, owing to certain nobles feeling slighted about the order in which they were served, a skilled craftsman from Cornwall makes a remarkable round table which can seat more than sixteen hundred knights and can be disassembled for travel. Layamon makes clear that having this table makes Arthur the envy of other kingdoms and helps assure Arthur's fame for posterity.

Another of Arthur's amazing kingly attributes is his gift for prophetic dreaming. Most Arthurian stories include at least a few mildly veiled prophetic dreams, but Layamon as one of the earliest writers on Arthur has a flair for recounting vivid dreams full of portent regarding Arthur's destiny. A good example of this would be Arthur's dream prior to what he hopes will be his final, definitive assault on Rome. He tells his trusted counselors:

Me imette þat mon me hof; uppen are halle.
þa halle ich gon bi-striden; swulc ich wolde riden.
alle þa lond þa ich ah; alle ich þer ouer sah.
and Walwain sat biuoren me; mi sweord he bar an honde.

þa com Moddred faren þere; mid unimete uolke.
he bar an his honde; ane wiax stronge.
he bigon to hewene hardliche swiðe.
and þa postes for-heou alle; þa heolden up þa halle.
Þer ich iseh Wenheuer eke; wimmonnen leofuest me.
al þere muche halle rof; mid hire honden heo to-droh.
Þa halle gon to hælden; and ich hæld to grunden.
þat mi riht ærm to-brac; þa seide Modred Haue þat.
Adun ueol þa halle; & Walwain gon to ualle.
and feol a þere eorðe his ærmes brekeen beine.
& ich igrap mi sweord leofe; mid mire leoft honde.
and smæt of Modred is hafd þat hit wond a þene ueld.
And þa quene ich al to-snaðde; mid deore mine sweorede.
and seo[ð]ðen ich heo adu[n] sette. in ane swarte putte. (13984–14001)

(I dreamed that I was seated upon a high hall, / bestriding the hall as if I would ride it; / all the land that I possess, I looked out over it all. / And Gawain was before me, my sword he bore in hand. / Then Mordred marched there with numerous folk; / he bore in his hand a strong battleaxe. / He began to hew very strongly, / and cut through all the posts that held up the hall. / There I also saw Guinevere, my dearest woman, / pulling down the hall's roof with her hands. / The hall began to sway, and I fell to the ground / so that my right arm broke. Then Mordred said "Take that!" / and the hall collapsed, and Gawain fell down / upon the earth, breaking both his arms. / And I grasping my beloved sword with my left hand, / smote off Mordred's head so that it rolled on the ground. / And the queen I cut to pieces with my dear sword, / and then I thrust her down in a dark pit.)

Arthur goes on to describe the reaction of his subjects and some symbolic beasts he encounters in the woods after this event (all original in Layamon), but the crux of this portentous dream is clear. Mordred (who Arthur appointed regent before leaving on his quest to subdue most of Europe) will betray the king, and Guinevere will support Mordred's treachery. Layamon uses this relatively simple dream to highlight not only Arthur's rather dark destiny, but also one of the few failing of this severe, Saxon-style ruler. When Arthur asks his loyal knights to interpret his dream, they tell him:

Lauerd þu hauest un-riht.
ne sculde me nauere sweuen; mid sor zen are[c]chen.
u ært þe riccheste mon; þa rixleoð on londen.
and þe alre wiseste; þe wuneð under weolcne.
zif hit weore ilu[m]pe; swa nulle hit ure Drihte;
þat Modred þire suster sune; hafde þine quene inume.
and al þi kine-liche lond; isæt an his azere hond.
þe þu him bitahtest; þa þu to Rome þohtest.
and he hafde al þus ido; mid his swike-dome.
þe zet þu mihtest þe awreken; (14022–31)

(Lord, you are mistaken; / nor should one ever ominously interpret dreams. / You are the most powerful man, the ruler of this land / and the wisest of all that dwell under heaven. / If it were to happen–and Lord forbid it!,— / that Mordred, your sister's son has taken your queen / and all your possessions and land into his own hand— / that you left to him when you planned to go to Rome, / and he had done all this through his treachery— / you might still avenge yourself.)

In this case Layamon shows the negative repercussions of Arthur's near omnipotence; his men dread giving him bad news. The king who subdues all he attempts may have just foretold his own downfall, but his men will only discuss this in the most guarded of manners. The long "If" clause makes clear that they want to inform him, but its presence also betrays their underlying fear of Arthur's disapproval.

After Arthur's removal to Avalon, Layamon reminds his audience of Merlin's prophecy concerning Arthur. Layamon presents as a certainty what Geoffrey and Wace present somewhat skeptically, that Arthur will never die and will return at some future date to rule all of England. In the aftermath of Arthur's death, we have a number of power struggles for king; there were numerous bad kings. Even King Malgus, who unites the whole country, has what Layamon sees as a severe flaw—he is homosexual. Eventually England falls to the African king, Gurmond, who destroys Christianity. Later, Pope Gregory sends to the English king, Ethelbert, Augustine who re-institutes Christianity to the sometimes reluctant English. Layamon moves through a succession of British kings until he ends with Caldwalader, whom he calls the last British king, implying that all subsequent rulers are not native English.

Although the genre of the *Brut* is undoubtedly chronicle, Layamon's history is significantly more like fiction than what twenty-first century readers think of as history. His flair for dramatic speeches and his penchant for creating details in support of a past he believed existed often push Layamon's writings toward the realm of historical fiction or epic or heroic poetry. The *Brut* though possibly redundant or lacking in consistency by modern standards. Probably achieved its purpose to dramatize and make real the lives of the great humans (men mostly) who established England as a country. Numerous writers are suspected to have been influenced by Layamon's work. Some scholars assert that Chaucer knew of Layamon; Chaucer's mention of an "English Geoffrey" might not be an allusion to Geoffrey of Monmouth, but to the writer who brought Geoffrey of Monmouth's story into the English tongue, Layamon. The *Brut* definitely served as a starting point for some later chronicles (such as the 1320 *Chronicle of Robert Cloucester*). It is a source for some of the *Alliterative Morte D'Arthur,* and its influence can be seen in Thomas Malory's *Le Morte Darthur* and *Gawain and the Green Knight.* In addition we know that Alfred, Lord Tennyson alludes to Layamon in his poem about Guinevere and the Scottish historical novelist Sir Walter Scot had a copy of the *Brut* in his library.

Layamon's contribution to Arthurian literature cannot be overstated. Although the basis for his stories existed before the *Brut* was written, the recognition of Arthur's importance to native Britons is for the first time made apparent when Layamon, for whatever reason, chooses to devote more than sixteen thousand lines of carefully crafted poetry to recounting the life of an English hero in English. Moreover, Layamon's contribution is more than just translation and elaboration in that he invents incidents (such as those concerning Arthur's knights and round table) that have been taken up by numerous subsequent writers. Layamon's passion to present a vital and interesting super-hero king has undoubtedly contributed to continued richness of Arthurian stories.

PRIMARY WORKS

Manuscripts: British Museum Ms. Cotton Caligula A. ix. ff. 3–194v.; British Museum Ms. Cotton Otho C. xiii. ff. 1–145. **Standard editions:** *Layamon's Brut, or Chronicle of Britain,* 3 vols., ed. Frederic Madden. London: Society of Antiquaries of London, 1847. *Layamon's Brut:*

Selections, ed. Joseph Hall. Oxford: Oxford University Press, 1924. *Layamon's Brut: Edited from British Museum MS. Cotton Caligula A. ix and British Museum MS. Cotton Otho C. xiii*, 2 vols., ed. G. L. Brook and R. F. Leslie, 1963. Reprint, London: Oxford University Press, 1978. *Selections from Layamon's Brut*, ed. Joseph Hall, 1963. Reprint, Oxford: Clarendon, 1983. *Layamon's Arthur: The Arthurian Section of Layamon's Brut*, ed. and trans. W. R. J. Barron and S. C. Weinberg. Austin: University of Texas Press, 1989. *Layamon: Brut or Hystoria Brutonum,* ed. and trans. W. R. J. Barron and S. C. Weinberg. New York: Longman, 1995. *Brut* (MS Cotton Caligula), University of Virginia Library Electronic Text Center, November 1, 1995. Available at http://etext.libvirginia.edu/mideng.browse.html/LayBruC. *Brut* (MS Cotton Otho), University of Virginia Library Electronic Text Center, January 1, 1994. Available at http://etext.libvirginia.edu/mideng.browse.html/LayBruO. **Recordings:** Burton, T. L., reader. *Extracts from Layamon's Brut.* Provo, UT: Chaucer Studio, 1990. **English editions:** *Brut*, trans. Donald G. Bzdyl. Binghamton, NY: Center for Medieval and Early Renaissance Studies, 1989. *Lawman Brut*, trans. Rosamund Allen. London: J. M. Dent, 1992. *Arthurian Chronicles: Wace and Layamon*, trans. Eugene Mason. Toronto: University of Toronto Press, 1996. *The Life of Arthur*, trans. Judith Weiss and Rosamund Allen. London: Everyman, 1997.

SECONDARY SOURCES

Allen, Rosamund. Introduction to *Lawman Brut.* London: J. M. Dent, 1992; Barron, W. R. J., and S. C. Weinberg. Introduction to *Layamon's Arthur: The Arthurian Section of Layamon's Brut.* Austin: University of Texas Press, 1991; Bennet, J. A. W. *Middle English Literature.* Oxford: Clarendon, 1986; Brook, G. L., and R. F. Leslie. *Layamon Brut.* London: Oxford University Press, 1963; Donahue, Dennis P. *Lawman's Brut, an Early Arthurian Poem: A Study of Middle English Formulaic Composition.* Lewiston, NY: Edwin Mellon Press, 1991; Gillespy, Frances Little. "*Layamon Brut:* A Comparative Study in Narrative Art." *University of California Publications in Modern Philology* 3, no. 4 (1916): 361–510; Glowka, Arthur Wayne. "The Poetics of Layamon's *Brut*." In *The Text and Tradition of Layamon's Brut*, ed. Francoise H. H. LeSaux, 57–64. Cambridge: D. S. Brewer, 1994; LeSaux, Francoise H. H. *Layamon's Brut: The Poem and Its Sources.* Cambridge: D. S. Brewer, 1989; ———, ed. *The Text and Tradition of Layamon's Brut.* Cambridge: D. S. Brewer, 1994; McNelis, James I. "Layamon as Auctor." In *The Text and Tradition of Layamon's Brut*, ed. Francoise H. H. LeSaux, 253–72. Cambridge: D. S. Brewer, 1994; Paton, Lucy Allen. *Arthurian Chronicles: Represented by Wace and Layamon.* London: J. M. Dent, 1928; Roberts, Jane. "A Preliminary Note on British Library Cotton MS Caligula A ix." In *The Text and Tradition of Layamon's Brut*, ed. Francoise H. H. LeSaux, 1–14. Cambridge: D. S. Brewer, 1994; Stanley, E. G. "Layamon's Un-Anglo-Saxon Syntax." In *The Text and Tradition of Layamon's Brut*, ed. Francoise H. H. LeSaux, 45–56. Cambridge: D. S. Brewer, 1994.

RICHARD B. McDONALD

HARTMANN VON AUE
(c. 1160/1165–c. 1210/1220)

Although not much is known about the Middle High German author Hartmann von Aue, as no historical document reports anything about him, he offers considerable information about himself in the prologues to the various narratives and in his courtly love poems. Hartmann introduced the Arthurian material to German speaking audiences by translating and adapting two of the major Arthurian romances by Chrétien de Troyes, *Erec* (c. 1180) and *Iwein* (c. 1203) into Middle High German. Whereas *Erec* proves to be a fairly independent version and reveals remarkable differences to the Old French source, *Iwein* follows Chrétien's text much more carefully. Hartmann must have had a good command of French, unless he relied on a translator, but there is no indication of such a procedure, and it would have been highly unusual for a Middle High German poet of Hartmann's caliber. In fact, Hartmann worked so carefully with the French sources, changing them subtly and at times quite radically, that one can assume his thorough familiarity with that language. In all likelihood he had gotten hold of copies of the French texts from some of his patrons and worked from them directly.

Hartmann hailed from Swabia in the southwest of Germany, as specific aspects of his own language and references to Hartmann as a "Swabian" by later authors confirm. There is no way, however, to identify the precise location, as the term "von Aue" means "of the meadow," a phrase often used in that region as a suffix in the name of various places and towns ("au"). In his verse novella *Der arme Heinrich* (*Lord Henry*, c. 1190) the narrator introduces himself as "Hartmann ze Ouwe" (vv. 4–5) and emphasizes that he was so learned that he could read books (vv. 1–2). He studied many texts to find a tale worthy for the spiritual and religious illumination of his audience, and begs his readers/listeners to pray for him after his death. The protagonist of his tale, Lord Henry, ("Heinrich von Ouwe," vv. 48–49) originates from Swabia as well, meaning that Hartmann either intended to create a literary document glorifying his own family or composed his tale in honor of his lord in whose service he stood as a "ministerialis." Basically the same information is included in the prologue to Hartmann's *Iwein* (vv. 21–30), whereas nothing can be gleaned from Hartmann's *Erec* as its prologue and introduction are missing.

Gottfried von Strassburg, author of *Tristan* (c. 1210), praises Hartmann as one of the best German poets still alive. On the other hand, Heinrich von dem Türlin, author of *Diu Crône* (c. 1220/1230), lists Hartmann as one of the great poets from the past. Considering what is known about Chrétien de Troyes's life, about references to Hartmann's work in the poems and narratives of later poets, and also taking into account the political, economic, and cultural circumstances (the time of the Hohenstaufen family in Germany), Hartmann's life dates have been approximately set at c. 1160/1165–c. 1210/1220. In the famous *Manesse* songbook, also known as *Große Heidelberger Liederhandschrift* (Large Heidelberg Songbook), and in the *Weingartner Liederhandschrift* (Weingarten Songbook; both early fourteenth century), Hartmann is depicted in large-page illustrations as a fully decked knight on a horse carrying a banner on his lance. It would be almost impossible, however, to draw any conclusions from this fantasy portrait, especially as the coat of arms on the banner showing three white eagles's heads on a blue or black background cannot be identified with any contemporary coat of arms. The Swiss family Wespersbühler in Thurgau displayed the same coat of arms since 1238, but there is no family member connected with the name of Hartmann von Aue.

According to his "Crusading Song," "Ich var mit iuweren hulden, herren unde mâge" (MF 218, 5), Hartmann seems to have joined the Third Crusade against the Egyptian Sultan Saladin, led by Emperor Fredrick Barbarossa (1189–1192), which was aborted after the accidental death of Frederick. But perhaps it was the Fourth Crusade from 1197–1198, at first led by Emperor Henry VI until his early death, and then resumed in 1202 until 1204. Whereas in all his previous works Hartmann had idealized courtly life and secular culture, in this poem he expresses a profound change of mind, as he turns away from the material world toward the spiritual.

In his *Lord Henry*, Hartmann identifies himself as "dienstman" (v. 5) or *ministerialis*, but the possible range of social ranks among this class was extensive. He could have been the administrator of a castle or a simple employee; he could have been an imperial diplomat or the manager of a farm or an estate. In his courtly love song "Sît ich den sumer truoc riuwe unde klagen" (MF 205, 1; "Since I felt sorrow about and lamented the passing of summer") the poet deplores the death of his lord (MF 205, 14), but he does not provide any concrete biographical information. The same applies to "Dem kriuze zimet wol reiner muot" (MF 209, 25; "He who wants to bear the cross must have a pure mind"), where the death of his lord has caused him deeply felt heart pains (MF 210, 23-24). Although he never identifies any of his patrons, the Swabian Dukes of Zähringen (Berthold IV and Berthold V) are likely contenders for this role in Hartmann's life, especially since they had close contacts with those French aristocratic families that sponsored Chrétien de Troyes. Insofar as some *Iwein* manuscripts survive within the domain of the Welf family (Upper Swabia), these also might have supported the poet. It is not known where Hartmann received his education, but it is certain that he acquired a considerable degree of education, including both French and Latin with the corresponding literature and philosophy.

No other Middle High German poet has produced such a wide variety of texts belonging to different genres as Hartmann. In each genre he proved his mastery, which his contemporaries quickly recognized and acknowledged in their own texts. In *Tristan* (c. 1210), Gottfried sings the most impressive song of praise of Hartmann:

Hartmann der Ouwaere,
âhî, wie der diu maere
beide ûzen unde innen
mit worten und mit sinnen

durchverwet und durchzieret!
wie er mit rede figieret
der âventiure meine!
wie lûter und wie reine
sîniu cristallînen wortelîn
beidiu sint und iemer müezen sîn!
si koment den man mit siten an,
si tuont sich nâhen zuo dem man
und liebent rehtem muote.
swer guote rede ze guote
und ouch ze rehte kan verstân,
der muoz dem Ouwaere lân
sîn schapel und sîn lôrzwî. (4621–37)

(Ah, how Hartmann of Aue dyes and adorns his tales through and through with words and sense, both outside and within! How eloquently he establishes his story's meaning! How clear and transparent his crystal words both are and ever must remain. Gently they approach and fawn on a man, and captivate right minds. Those who esteem fine language with due sympathy and judgement will allow the man of Aue his garland and his laurels [Hatto, 105].) This opinion was echoed by many other poets throughout the next centuries. Not surprisingly, Hartmann has always been considered one of the major contributors to Middle High German literature, particularly as he impresses his readers/listeners with his lucid, elegant, and poetic language, his remarkable narrative skill, and his choice of topics through which fundamental aspects of twelfth-century society pertaining both to material and spiritual problems are addressed.

In his *Diu Klage* (The Lament) or *Das Büchlein* (The Little Book), probably the first work composed by Hartmann sometime around 1180 and only preserved in one early sixteenth-century manuscript, the *Ambraser Heldenbuch* (c. 1504–c. 1516), the poet has his heart and his body discuss with each other exploring the significance of courtly love. No German precedents or sources are available, but similar debate poems can be found in French literature, known as *complaintes d'amour* and *saluts*. The body complains to the heart for being forced to seek love, which has caused him to experience innumerable types of pains, but the heart points out that the eyes have allowed the image of the lady to enter the body, triggering the love pains. To solve the problem for the body, the heart suggests the *krûtzouber von Kärlingen* (root magic from France), which would allow the body to gain love from God and his society. This magic implies the development of the fundamental courtly values, such as generosity, disciplined behavior, modesty, loyalty, constancy, purity, and dependable manhood.

The most important literary works from Hartmann's pen are his two Arthurian tales, *Erec* and *Iwein*, both derived from Chrétien de Troyes (*Erec et Enide* [c. 1170–1185] and *Le Chevalier au lion* [c. 1175–1180]), representing the most significant Middle High German Arthurian epics introducing the *matière de Bretagne* to German audiences. *Erec* was composed only a short time after 1180, whereas the *Iwein* was written around 1200, more or less parallel to the Old Norse *Ivens-Saga* and the Maginobi *Owen*, further adaptations of the *Iwein* material. Although Hartmann follows Chrétien's model much more closely in his *Iwein*, both the theme and the poetic style exerted the greatest influence on Hartmann's contemporaries and successive generations. Whereas the text of *Erec* has been preserved only once in almost complete form in the aforementioned *Ambraser Heldenbuch* (today Vienna, cod. ser. nov. 2663) and in three thirteenth and fourteenth-century fragments (Wolfenbüttel, Koblenz, Vienna), *Iwein* has come down to us in thirteen complete manuscripts and seventeen fragments from the thirteenth to the sixteenth centuries. In addition, individual scenes were copied into tapestries and frescoes at Castle Rodenegg, South Tyrol; the "Hessenhof" (an urban residence) in Schmalkalden, Thuringia; in the Malterer tapestry, Augustinusmuseum, Freiburg; and at Castle Runkelstein, South Tyrol. Moreover, there are significant illustrations and images in the Princeton University Library manuscript Garrett 125; in Paris, Bibliothèque Nationale fr. 1433; and also in late-medieval English misericords. The latter, however, were probably influenced by Chrétien's romance or oral traditions and not the German text.

With these two romances Hartmann created the classical model of Arthurian epics for the history of German medieval literature. Both show the same structural concept of the hero winning all desired glories in a first round of adventures (*cursus*), but who then falls from his high station into utter disgrace. Next he embarks on a new and much more extended journey (second *cursus*) during which he eventually recovers his fame and gains a much more profound understanding of his role as knight within the context of courtly society. In both romances the protagonist marries, and his wife soon emerges as the catalyst for his own personal development. Nevertheless, serious tensions between individual ideals and social requirements quickly threaten to destroy their marriage. In fact, the gender conflict proves to be a decisive element that forces the hero to question all his personal values and those of Arthurian society. In both *Erec* and *Iwein*, only once Erec and Iwein have learned to accept their wives as equal partners, and have also begun to fight for women and other people in dire need, do they grasp what chivalry truly means. Intriguingly, Hartmann has his two heroes go through the almost opposite development during the first circle of adventures (*cursus*). Erec returns home after having won the tournament at King Arthur's court and having married Enite. He assumes his father's throne, but he is so passionate about his wife that he spends almost all his time in bed with her, neglecting all his duties as ruler and knight. Quickly the entire court culture disappears because the hero has turned into a shadow of his previous self, lost to sensuality and egocentricity, a process called "verligen" (v. 2971). Later this process will be satirically portrayed by Gawein when he warns Iwein about the potential dangers for a freshly married knight to forget the ideals of chivalry because of his uxoriousness (*Iwein*, vv. 2806–50). One day, however, when Enite laments her husband's failures, not being aware that he is not fully asleep while lying in her lap, the hero realizes the danger for himself and his kingdom (although at first he seems to blame everything on his wife in a traditionally misogynist fashion). At this point begins the second round of adventures in which both Erec and Enite have to go through much suffering, but eventually both find each other, reestablish their love, and Erec recovers his fame—actually he achieves a much higher esteem because he has turned away from himself and toward the external world where many challenges had been waiting for him. Eventually Erec reestablishes the famous "Joie de la curt" (v. 9601; "joy of the court") by defeating the ultimate opponent, the knight Mabonagrin, then he returns to King Arthur, and subsequently to his home country.

In *Iwein* there is a similar process, but after Iwein has married Laudine, Gawein warns the protagonist not to follow Erec's negative example who "durch vrouwen Êniten verlac" (v. 2794; "lying idle because of Lady Enite"). Consequently, Iwein requests from his wife to let him go on a round of tournaments for a whole year before settling into married life, to which she complies, but she also warns him that if he were not to return in time she would never forgive him (v. 2928). Almost inevitably, however, this is just what happens as Iwein completely forgets about his wife and so suffers from the process called "verrittern" (turning into a knight with a total disregard for any other aspect in life). When Laudine's chambermaid Lunete finally arrives at King Arthur's court more than a year later and finds Iwein amidst the Arthurian knights, she severely reprimands him for his failure and announces that Laudine will never see him again (vv. 3190–92). This shocks Iwein to such an extent that he immediately leaves the court, loses his mind, sheds his clothing, and begins a life as a wild man in the forest. Eventually, however, he is rescued by a nun who applies a magical salve to his body while he is asleep, helping him to recover his mind. Iwein embarks on his second round of adventures and learns similar lessons as Erec. After having helped many people in their misery and need (and also a lion who then becomes his loyal companion), Iwein is reintegrated into the world of King Arthur and wins back his wife, Laudine. She resists for a long time to accept him again, but when he pretends that her country is attacked, she finally submits to his pleadings and that of her her chambermaid Lunete. Whereas Iwein has to learn especially the meaning of *triuwe*, or loyalty, to gain the full respect a knight deserves, Laudine (who is forced by a trick to accept her husband as her companion, insofar as she does not know who the so-called Knight with a Lion [Iwein] truly is) needs to understand to show more compassion and understanding of human weakness. He asks to be forgiven by her, as he has repented and would never again commit the sin of ignoring and forgetting her. Ultimately, the couple is reconciled and finds happiness with each other because they have gained fully developed personalities and matured into loving adults.

Although both *Erec* and *Iwein* focus on individual heroes, they are intimately connected with the world of King Arthur and prove to be complimentary to each other. The protagonists's actions, failures, and triumphs shed important light on the court of King Arthur as they serve as his representatives in the outside world. Both Erec and Iwein hail from kingdoms outside of Arthur's realm, and after short but significant stays at his court at various times throughout the romances, they return home and assume their royal rulership.

In *Erec* one sees the hero at first in the company of Queen Guinevere when they encounter an unknown knight and his aggressive dwarf, who shames both Guinevere's damsel and Erec by whipping them for asking about his lord's name. As they have no weapons with them, they cannot defend themselves against this violent treatment. Erec is immediately determined to avenge himself and departs from the queen, who is deeply concerned about his well being because he is not armed and of such young age. But he triumphs at Duke Imain's tournament with the help of the armor and weaponry provided to him by his future father-in-law, Koralus, and with the help of Enite, Koralus's daughter, and can thus restore his honor when he defeats the unknown knight, later identified as Iders. In the meantime King Arthur has hunted and captured the symbolic white stag himself and is about to choose the woman whom he will be entitled to kiss when Guinevere begs for a delay as she has not heard news from Erec. Soon the latter's opponent, Sir Iders, arrives and reports how he has been defeated by Erec. His request for atonement and forgiveness is accepted in return for his pledge to join the queen's retinue. Erec, on the other hand, is splendidly welcomed by the royal couple and the knights of the Round Table when he arrives the next day. Queen Guinevere takes particular care of Enite, giving her a bath and dressing her splendidly. Next, the narrator introduces all the knights of the Round Table and all the other knights at court by name. He finishes the account with King Arthur kissing the young bride as the most beautiful woman at court, according to the custom established by Arthur's father, Uterpandragon. The wedding itself takes place there as well, as Arthur wants all his lords and princes to be present at this festive event. The narrative abounds with splendid descriptions of the wealth, prowess, culture, and power displayed at the Arthurian court, including minstrels performing and a tournament organized for the knights where they demonstrate their bravery, skill, and strength. But the narrative focus remains on Erec, whereas Arthur stays in the background as the host.

After Erec has embarked on his second quest to regain his lost honor, he also comes across King Arthur's court again. His first encounter with the court seneschall Keii ends in a fiasco for the latter, but Keii at least reports about this meeting to the court. Arthur sends out Gawein to lead the stranger to him, but Erec refuses, so Gawein secretly asks the court to relocate to a spot where Erec would be forced to run into them. Once again the knight errant and his wife are heartily welcomed and treated with greatest sustenance and comfort, but Erec stays only the shortest time possible and continues his journey the next day. Only at the conclusion of *Erec* does one hear of King Arthur again. This time Erec returns there voluntarily because he has accomplished his chivalric goals; has established peace with his wife Enite; has defeated Mabonagrin, thereby recovering the "Joie de la curt"; and has liberated the wives of the slain knights. Arthur exceedingly praises him for his enormous deeds:

> wan dû hâst wol gemret
> unsers hoves wünne.
> swer dir niht guotes engünne,
> der enwerde nimmer mre vrô. (9947–50)

("you have indeed enhanced the splendor of our court. May any man who begrudges you his favor be evermore a stranger to happiness!"). But once again Erec does not stay long and finally returns to his kingdom, which brings the romance to its conclusion.

In *Iwein* one is confronted with more or less the same portrait of King Arthur's court as in *Erec*, although the narrative setting differs remarkably. In the prologue to *Iwein*, King Arthur is praised as the perfect example of a person filled with knightly spirit who wears a crown of honor. But the narrator immediately emphasizes that the days of King Arthur have long passed, though his fame and renown live on until the present. Next, the reader learns of another festival at Karidol of utmost splendor and lavishness, but the details are passed up; instead the audience is told that the royal couple has gone to their sleeping chambers to rest together. Six knights sit down outside of their walls and listen to Kalogrenant's unfortunate adventure at a magical fountain. At this point the queen silently joins the group and becomes the cause of a fight between Kalogrenant and Keii, who mocks the former for his attempt to demonstrate particular courtly manners in jumping up and bowing before the queen. Guinevere, however, reprimands Keii for his rude behavior, his envy, and his bitterness toward all good knights. Kalogrenant also joins the queen in her criticism, but Keii mostly ignores him and insists that he should continue with his tale. After they have learned all details, another squabble breaks out with Keii, but then King Arthur appears. Once he has gained knowledge of Kalogrenant's adventure, he swears that the entire court would travel to the magical fountain and learn about its secret powers. At this point, Iwein decides to proceed alone and win the prize of honor, and so the Arthurian court resurfaces again only much later when Iwein (as the new ruler of the fountain) and Arthur and his retinue meet. After Iwein has successfully defended himself, he invites the court to stay at his place and celebrate, but it happens at these festivities that Gawein warns his friend Iwein about the danger which Erec had suffered from, and not to forget the primary function of chivalry. The protagonist's subsequent life takes him far away from his wife, whom he completely falls out of sight. Once Lunete has reminded him of his failure, he is driven into lunacy, and only later does he manage to return to the path of knighthood. King Arthur and his court do not assume any particular function for the hero's personal development, but it is here where Iwein forgets about his promise to his wife and becomes guilty of an inordinate passion for chivalry for chivalry's sake. By contrast, it is here as well where Iwein finally fights on behalf of a maiden and now proves once and for all that he has matured and become a fully responsible adult and member of the courtly world. The last thing we hear of King Arthur is that he and his wife took care of Iwein and Gawein until their wounds are healed. But Iwein's ultimate achievement proves to be, of course, his reunification with his wife, Laudine, but that takes place outside of the Arthurian court.

Although both romances strongly emphasize the gender conflict and outline fundamental ways of how man and woman can find each other in order to form a harmonious and joyful union, Hartmann also expresses a strong religious devotion and frames his Arthurian romances with clear references to God, who guides and determines the knights's destiny. This becomes much more apparent in two other works, the one a religious tale, the other a secular love story.

In his *Gregorius* from the late twelfth century, Hartmann introduces a fantastic tale of a young man who enters this world as the product of incest committed by a brother and sister, the Duke of Aquitaine's children, after their parents's death. To do penance, the brother goes on a pilgrimage to the Holy Land, but dies on the way, having pined away for his sister. In the meantime, she sends the child away in a basket, which has been entrusted to the water. Gregorius, as the child is called, is found by fishermen, who hand him over to an abbot who raises him in the hope of finding a successor in him. The young man, however, desires for chivalry and leaves the monastery, but only—in close parallel to the ancient Oedipus story—to come to the rescue of a queen who is besieged by a nobleman who wants to force her to marry him. Gregorius defeats the opponent and is married to the queen without knowing anything about his blood relationship with her, as she is his own mother. As he regularly studies the tablet that his mother had originally put into the basket and on which she had written an outline of her son's origin, his true identity is soon found out. Totally in despair, Gregorius abandons the throne, leaves the kingdom, and disappears in the wilderness. A fisherman who thoroughly mistrusts this alleged penitent takes him to a lonely rock in a lake, and upon his request, locks him to the rock, and throws the key into the water. Gregorius survives, however, with the help of God for seventeen years when two noblemen from Rome receive a dream that Gregorius has been chosen as a successor. They search for him and eventually find him on his rock. The night before, the fisherman serves them a fish in whose stomach he discovers the key with which he had chained the penitent to the rock. When the emissaries reach the rock the next day, Gregorius at first refuses to come along as he still considers himself a sinner, but the rediscovered key demonstrates to him that God indeed has forgiven and chosen him as the new pope. When they also find the tablet again, which Gregorius had forgotten in the fisherman's house on the way to the rock, they know that Gregorius has turned into a holy man indeed worthy of being the next pope. He produces many signs and wonders on his way to Rome, and after a while his mother also arrives and receives God's forgiveness through her long-term penitence and through her son's help.

It is not known which source Hartmann used for his religious tale, but there are six versions of the Old French *Vie du Pape Gregoire* (Life of Pope Gregory) extant. Yet, the Middle High German author did not make use of any of them, as one can tell on the basis of extensive differences in the plot, but he might have relied on some oral sources or on a now lost manuscript. The connection to the ancient *Oedipus* tragedy by Sophocles is obvious, and yet the variations are significant enough to question any theory claiming direct influence. Gregorius does not, for instance, kill his father; he is portrayed as a deeply religious penitent. Moreover, there are many tales of incest in the history of medieval literature, and Hartmann could have easily modelled his tale after a variety of them.

Remarkably for a vernacular text from the High Middle Ages, *Gregorius* was soon translated into Latin by Abbot Arnold of the St. John Convent in Lübeck (sometime before 1212), followed by two more fourteenth-century Latin translations by unknown authors, and a German prose version contained in a fourteenth-century collection of religious narratives, *Der Heiligen Leben* (Life of Saints, first printed in 1471). Nineteenth- and twentieth-century scholars and writers were also deeply impressed by Hartmann's tale, best documented in *Der Erwählte* (The Selected, 1951) by Thomas Mann, the winner of the Nobel Prize for Literature in 1929.

One of the most fascinating and intriguing medieval verse narratives is Hartmann's *Der arme Heinrich* (Lord Henry) from c. 1190, preserved in its complete form in three manuscripts (Straßburg, Heidelberg, Geneva-Cologny) and as a fragment in three other manuscripts (Berlin, Munich [two manuscripts]). Verses 199–204 were also copied in a Freiburg manuscript. Here as well the religious theme dominates, but the novella also offers many elements of eroticism, gender conflicts, and illuminates medieval medical practices.

Young Lord Henry is at the peak of his life when leprosy strikes him. The local doctors cannot help him, and even a visit to Montpellier does not yield any results. When he travels to Salerno (southern Italy) to consult with the ultimate medical experts, he is told that there might indeed be a cure for him, but it would have to be the blood from the heart of a nubile woman who voluntarily would give up her life to rescue the sick man. Considering this to be an impossibility, Henry abandons all hope, disseminates his worldly treasures, and retires to a loyal farmer to await his death there. One of the farmer's daughters strikes a close relationship with him, and when she learns of the condition for Henry's recovery, she quickly decides to become the victim and to give her life for him. The novella includes powerful dialogues between the girl, her parents, Henry, and even the doctor in Salerno, but nobody can argue against her and all begin to believe that the Holy Spirit must be speaking through her. The curious aspect, however, is that during the three years prior to these events, Henry and the girl had developed more than pure friendship, as his erotic gifts for her and her almost intimate relationship with him, indicate.

The girl argues that Henry's life would be more important than her own, and if he were to die, her parents would be in danger of getting a much worse lord, who could cause them much hardship or take away their farm. Moreover, she desires to give her young life for her lord as she wants to enter heaven and hopes to avoid any sins in her adult life. In fact, she indicates fear of life itself, as for her it only represent dangers and temptations for the soul's salvation. Every positive thing in life would lead to suffering, all happiness would turn to pain. Surprisingly, the girl also expresses fear of getting married to a farmer, to deliver babies, and suffer from the problems affecting a peasant's existence. By contrast, she longs for the union with the Godhead, whom she calls a free farmer who desires her (v. 775); to be with him would mean freedom of personal suffering, death, and pain, and also freedom of unbearable heat, cold and hunger, of fear that the farm animals might die, and of crying children.

Finally, both the parents and Henry agree, and the girl is equipped for the journey as if she were going to her wedding. The dramatic climax takes place in Salerno, where the surprised doctor soon prepares the operation to cut out the girl's heart. While he is sharpening the knife, Henry is waiting outside of the room and develops a strong desire to see what is happening inside. When he finds a little hole in the wall he gazes onto her beautiful naked body, and, inflamed by love, he stops the doctor and rejects the girl's sacrifice. Although she angrily fights against him and feels cheated out of the promise to achieve sanctity already as a young woman, Henry realizes that he is not entitled to her life for his own sake. Perhaps he also has suddenly understood that he loves her, but most important proves to be his learning process as he suddenly understands that each person has to accept one's own existence, and so one's own suffering and pain. The sick man now also knows that he cannot justify the death of such a beautiful creature for the recovery of his own miserable life. When Henry and the girl return home, God helps the young prince to regain his health because He has seen the fundamental change of heart in Henry. After the latter has been reinstated as Duke of Swabia and the question comes up whom he should choose as his future wife, he convinces his councillors that the farmer's girl saved his life and deserves to be raised in social rank, making her available for him as a wife. As she has stayed at his court since their return—another noteworthy factor normally not observed by scholarship—he hugs her and declares her his bride.

Both the religious and the erotic element in this novella are obvious and can be easily identified. Similarly, the parallels to the biblical Job, but also the symbolic significance of Henry's sickness, the young woman's awe-inspiring willingness to sacrifice herself as an example of an extremely altruistic attitude, and Hartmann's criticism of secularized life at the courts lacking spirituality have been pointed out. On an anagogical level, the interpretation of both characters as representatives of body and soul, would also be a possibility, especially as Henry suffered physically because he showed spiritual failing, and regained his health after he had looked from outside of the wall into the operation room where he saw the most beautiful creature in this world, the unnamed and naked girl. Once he has rescued her from certain death, God also recognizes the internal healing process and allows his body to return to its previously healthy condition. In other words, Hartmann's novella proves to be a masterpiece in medieval narrative as it offers powerful insights in many different aspects of man's worldly and spiritual existence, and yet is not exclusively dominated by religious ideals, as Henry and his wife's marriage is greeted by all of his people and also receives God's blessings.

Finally, Hartmann's significant courtly love poems also deserve to be mentioned. There are sixty strophes in *Die Manessische Liederhandschrift*, or *Große Heidelberger Liederhandschrift* (see above), ten strophes in *Die kleine Heidelberger Liederhandschrift*, and twenty-eight strophes in the *Weingartner Liederhandschrift*. The individual songs differ in their arrangement from manuscript to manuscript, but Hartmann seems to have composed eighteen songs in total, some of which are Crusade Songs such as "Dem kriuze zimet wol reiner muot" (MF 209, 25; "The cross is fitting for a pure mind") and "Ich var mit iuweren hulden" (MF 218, 5; "I travel with your grace"), whereas the majority follows the traditional model of *Minnesang* or courtly love poetry. The singer often complains about his lady's inaccessibility ("Ich sprach, ich wolte ir iemer leben," MF 207, 11; "I said I always wanted to live for her"); describes his love service ("Mîn dienst der ist alze lanc," MF 209, 5; "My service takes much too long"); laments about the love pain that affects him ("Ez ist mir ein ringiu klage," MF 213, 29; "It is only a little complaint"); but also praises the experience of love, which provides profound happiness ("Ich muoz von rehte den tac iemer minnen," MF 215, 14; "It is proper that I always love the day"); and argues that love service for ladies of lower social rank might be more fruitful than for arrogant, high ranking ladies who despise the courtly love poet ("Maniger grüezet mich alsô," MF 316, 29; "Many greet me in such a way").

Gottfried von Strassburg was not the only one to praise Hartmann von Aue as one of the best Middle High German poets. Others, such as Wirnt von Grafenberg (c. 1210), Heinrich von dem Türlin (c. 1225), Rudolf von Ems (c. 1235), Der von Gliers (middle of thirteenth century), Der Pleier (second half of the thirteenth century), Konrad von Stoffeln (late thirteenth century), and Albrecht (von Scharfenberg? c. 1270) also expressed their great admiration for Hartmann's literary accomplishments. Modern scholarship has also recognized Hartmann's many accomplishments, both as a poet and as a social critic who challenged the traditional concept of knighthood with its inherent violence, and who argued for improved communication and a better relationship between the genders.

PRIMARY WORKS

Die Klage or *Das Büchlein* (c. 1180). **Manuscript:** *Die Klage* is found in one manuscript: Ambraser Heldenbuch (Österreichische Nationalbibliothek, Vienna; cod. Vind. ser. nov. 2663). **First publication:** *Der arme Heinrich*, ed. Johann Jakob Büsching. Zürich: Drell, Flüssli, 1810. In *Die lieder und Büchlein, und Der arme Heinrich, eine altdeutsche Erzählung*, ed. Moriz Haupt. Leipzig: Weidmann, 1842. **Modern editions:** *Die Klage Das (zweite) Büchlein aus dem Ambraser Heldenbuch*, ed. Herta Zutt. Berlin: De Gruyter, 1968. *Das Klagebüchlein Hartmanns von Aue und das zweite Büchlein*, ed. Ludwig Wolff. Munich: Fink, 1972. *Hartmann von Aue: Das Büchlein; nach den Vorabeiten, von Arno Schirokauer zu Ende geführt und herausgegeben*, ed. Petrus W. Tax. Berlin: Schmidt, 1977. **English edition:** In *Arthurian Romances, Tales, and Lyric Poetry: The Complete Works of Hartmann von Aue*, trans. Frank Tobin, Kim Vivian, and Richard H. Lawson, 1–27. University Park: Pennsylvania State University Press, 2001; *Eighteen Songs*. **Manuscripts:** Three major manuscripts contain strophes of Hartmann's songs. Sixty are in *Die Manessische Liederhandschrift* (Universitätsbibliothek, Heidelberg; cpg 848); ten are in *Die kleine Heidelberger Liederhandschrift* (Universitätsbibliothek, Heidelberg; cpg 357); and twenty-eight strophes are in *Die Weingartner Liederhandschrift* (Württembergische Landesbibliothek, Stuttgart; cod. HB XIII 1). **First publication:** In *Sammlung von Minnesingern aus dem schwaebischen Zeitpuncte, CXL, Dichter enthältend: durch Ruedger Manessen, wieland ds Rathes der wralten Zyrich, aus der Handschrift der königlich-französoschen Bibliothek herausgegeben*, 2 vols., ed. Johann Jakob Bodmer and Johann Jakob Breitinger. Zurich: C. Orell, 1758–1759. **Standard edition:** *Des Minnesangs Frühling*, ed. Karl Lachmann and Moriz Haupt. Leipzig: Hirzel, 1857. Revised by Hugo Moser and Helmut Tervooren, 2 vols., 38th rev. ed. Stuttgart: Hirzel, 1988. **Modern German edition:** *Lieder: Mittelhochdeutsch/Neuhochdeutsch*, ed. Ernst von Reusner. Stuttgart: Reclam, 1985. **English editions:** In *Old German Love Songs*, trans. Frank C. Nicholson. London: Unwin, 1907. In *The Minnesingers*, vol. 1, trans. Jethro Bithell. New York: Longmans, 1909. In *Medieval German Lyrics*, trans. M. F. Richey. Edinburgh: Oliver & Boyd, 1958. In *The Songs of the Minnesingers*, trans. Barbara G. Jackson and J. W. Thomas. Urbana: University of Illinois Press, 1966. In *Arthurian Romances, Tales, and Lyric Poetry: The Complete Works of Hartmann von Aue*, trans. Frank Tobin, Kim Vivian, and Richard H. Lawson, 29–50. University Park: Pennsylvania State University Press, 2001; *Erec* (c. 1180). **Manuscript:** The only complete edition, save several lines, is in Ambraser Heldenbuch (Österreichische Nationalbibliothek, Vienna, Cod. Vind. Ser. nov. 2663, fol. 30rb-50vb). **First publication:** *Erec: Eine*

Erzählung von Hartmann von Aue, ed. Moritz Haupt. Leipzig: Weidmann, 1839. **Standard edition:** *Hartmann von Aue: Erec*, ed. Albert Leitzmann. Halle: Niemeyer, 1939. Revised by Christopher Cormeau and Kurt Gärtner. Tübingen: Niemeyer, 1985. **Modern German edition:** *Erec, Mittelhochdeutscher Text und Übertragung*, 19th ed., ed. Thomas Cramer. Frankfurt: Fischer, 1997. **English editions:** *Erec*, trans. J. Wesley Thomas. Lincoln: University of Nebraska Press, 1982. In *The Narrative Works of Hartmann von Aue*, ed. R. W. Fisher. Stuttgart: Kümmerle, 1983. *Erec*, trans. Michael Resler. Philadelphia: University of Pennsylvania Press, 1987. In *Arthurian Romances, Tales, and Lyric Poetry: The Complete Works of Hartmann von Aue*, trans. Frank Tobin, Kim Vivian, and Richard H. Lawson, 51–163. University Park: Pennsylvania State University Press, 2001; *Gregorius* (c. 1187). **Manuscripts:** Six full manuscripts and five fragments exist, from the thirteenth to the fifteenth centuries. The standard manuscript is *J* (Staatsbibliothek Stiftung PreuBischer Kulturbesitz, Berlin; Ms. germ. qu. 979). **First publication:** *Gregorius: Eine Erzählung von Hartmann von Aue*, ed. Karl Lachmann. Berlin: Reimer, 1838. **Modern German edition:** *Gregorius der gute Sünder*, ed. Burkhard Kippenberg. Stuttgart: Reclam, 1976. **English editions:** *Gregorius: A Medieval Oedipus Legend*, trans. Edwin H. Zeydel and Bayard Q. Morgan. Chapel Hill: University of North Carolina Press, 1955. *Gregorius: The Good Sinner*, trans. Sheema Z. Buehne. New York: Ungar, 1966. In *Arthurian Romances, Tales, and Lyric Poetry: The Complete Works of Hartmann von Aue*, trans. Frank Tobin, Kim Vivian, and Richard H. Lawson, 165–214. University Park: Pennsylvania State University Press, 2001; *Der arme Heinrich* (c. 1190). **Manuscripts:** The work is preserved in three manuscripts and four fragments from the thirteenth century. **First publication:** In *Samlung deutscher Gedichte aus dem XII., XIII. und XIV. Jahrhundert*, vol. 1, ed. Christoph Heinrich Myller. Berlin, 1784. **Standard edition:** *Der arme Heinrich von Hartmann von Aue*, ed. Herman Paul, 16th rev. ed., ed. Kurt Gärtner. Tübingen: Niemeyer, 1996. **Modern German edition:** *Der Arme Heinrich: Mittelhochdeutscher Text und Übertragung*, ed. Helmut de Boor. Frankfurt: Fischer, 1967. **English editions:** Dante Gabriel Rossetti paraphrased the work as *Henry the Leper*, 2 vols. Boston: printed for members of the Bibliophile Society, 1905. *Peasant Life in Old German Epics: Meier Helmbrecht and Der arme Heinrich*, trans. C. H. Bell. New York: Columbia University Press, 1931. "Poor Heinrich," in *The Best Novellas of Medieval Germany*, trans. J. Wesley Thomas. Columbia, SC: Camden House, 1984. In *Arthurian Romances, Tales, and Lyric Poetry: The Complete Works of Hartmann von Aue*, trans. Frank Tobin, Kim Vivian, and Richard H. Lawson, 215–34. University Park: Pennsylvania State University Press, 2001; *Iwein* (c. 1200). **Manuscripts:** Fifteen complete manuscripts and seventeen fragments exist, dating from the thirteenth to the sixteenth centuries. **First publication:** In *Samlung deutscher Gedichte aus dem XII., XIII. und XIV. Jahrhundert*, vol. 1, ed. Christoph Heinrich Myller. Berlin, 1784. **Standard edition:** *Iwein der riter mit dem lewen getihtet von dem hern Hartmann dienstman ze Ouwe*, ed. Georg F. Benecke and Karl Lachmann. Berlin: Reimer, 1827. Revised by Ludwig Wolff, 7th ed. Berlin: De Gruyter, 1968. **Modern German edition:** *Iwein: aus dem Mittelhochdeutschen übertragen*, trans. Max Wehrli. Zurich: Manesse, 1988. **English editions:** *Iwein*, trans. J. Wesley Thomas. Lincoln: University of Nebraska Press, 1982. *Iwein*, trans. Patrick McConeghy. New York: Garland, 1984. In *Arthurian Romances, Tales, and Lyric Poetry: The Complete Works of Hartmann von Aue*, trans. Frank Tobin, Kim Vivian, and Richard H. Lawson, 235–321. University Park: Pennsylvania State University Press, 2001.

SECONDARY SOURCES

Clark, Susan. *Hartmann von Aue: Landscapes of Mind*. Houston: Rice University Press, 1989; Classen, Albrecht. "Schweigen und Reden in Hartmanns 'Erec.'" In *Erec, ou l'ouverture du monde arthurien: Actes du Colloque du Centre d'Etudes Médiévales de l'Université de Picardie—Jules Verne*, ed. Danielle Buschinger and Wolfgang Spiewok, 25–42. Greifswald: Reineke-Verlag, 1993; ———. *Verzweiflung und Hoffnung: Die Suche nach der kommunikativen Gemeinschaft in der deutschen Literatur des Mittelalters*. Beihefte zur Mediaevistik, no. 1. Frankfurt:

Peter Lang, 2002; Cormeau, Christoph, and Wilhelm Störmer. *Hartmann von Aue: Epoche-Werk-Wirkung*. Munich: Beck, 1985; Fischer, Humbertus. *Ehre, Hof und Abenteuer in Hartmanns Iwein: Vorarbeiten zu einer historischen Poetik des höfischen Epos*. Forschungen zur Geschichte der älteren deutschen Literatur, no. 3. Munich: Fink, 1983; Hasty, Will. *Adventure as Social Performance: A Study of the German Court Epic*. Untersuchungen zur deutschen Literaturgeschichte, no. 52. Tübingen: Niemeyer, 1990; ———. *Adventures in Interpretation: The Works of Hartmann von Aue and Their Critical Reception*. Literary Criticism in Perspective. Columbia, SC: Camden House, 1996; Heinen, Hubert. "The Concepts *hof, hövesch*, and the Like in Hartmann's *Iwein*." In *The Medieval Court in Europe*, Houston German Studies, no. 6, ed. Edward R. Haymes, 41–57. Munich: Fink, 1986; Kaiser, Gert. *Textauslegung und gesellschaftliche Selbstdeutung: Aspekte einer sozialgeschichtlichen Interpretation von Hartmanns Artusepen*. Frankfurt: Athenäum, 1973; McConeghey, Patrick. "Women's Speech and Silence in Hartmann von Aue's *Erec*." *PMLA* 102 (1987): 771–83; McFarland, Timothy, and Silvia Ranawake, eds. *Hartmann von Aue: Changing Perspectives*. London Hartmann Symposium, 1985. Göppinger Arbeiten zur Germanistik, no. 486. Göppingen: Kümmerle, 1988; Mertens, Volker. *Laudine: Soziale Problematik im "Iwein" Hartmanns von Aue*. Beihefte zur Zeitschrift für deutsche Philologie, no. 3. Berlin: Schmidt, 1978; Ruh, Kurt. *Höfische Epik des deutschen Mittelalters*, vol. 1. Grundlagen der Germanistik, no. 7. Berlin: Schmidt, 1967; See, Geoffrey. "An Examination of the Hero in Hartmann's *Erec*." *Seminar* 27 (1991): 39–54; Spaarney, Hendricus. *Hartmann von Aue: Studien zu einer Biographie*. 2 vols. Halle: Niemeyer, 1933–1938; Wapnewski, Peter. *Hartmann von Aue*. 5th ed. Stuttgart: Metzler, 1972.

ALBRECHT CLASSEN

WOLFRAM VON ESCHENBACH

(fl. c. 1200–d. c. 1216)

Among the greatest medieval vernacular authors, such as Chrétien de Troyes, Hartmann von Aue, Gottfried von Strasbourg, Dante Alighieri, Boccaccio, Petrarch, Geoffrey Chaucer, and Juan Ruiz, we also find the Middle High German poet Wolfram von Eschenbach. Wolfram was born in or around Eschenbach, a little town in Franconia east of Ansbach and south of Nuremberg, renamed Wolframseschenbach in 1917 in honor of the poet. He refers to his birthplace many times in his texts, such as in *Parzival* 114, 12; 185, 7; 827, 13, and in *Willehalm* 4, 19. Other towns and locations nearby are also mentioned often, supporting the claim that Wolfram was thoroughly familiar with that region. In *Parzival* the narrator once comments on the foolishness of the Bavarians, using the first person plural, "us Bavarians" (121, 7), but this might well have been a comment with tongue-in-cheek, as in the Middle Ages Franconia was an independent territory and not forcefully merged with Bavaria until 1806. Although not much is known about Wolfram in concrete terms—there are no historical documents referring to him—he has provided us with several clues in his texts that shed some light about his life and allow us to sketch a rough biography. Wolfram mentions the Count of Wertheim (*Parzival*, 184, 4), lord of the Wildenburg in the Odenwald, a large and mountainous forest area south of the Main and east of the Rhine valley. The reference in the text implies that his lord, obviously his first patron, commands over many riches, and that his wealthy court proves to be the very opposite to the famine-plagued kingdom of Brôbarz, where the literary figure Parzival meets his future wife, Condwîr âmûrs. Above all, in his courtly epic *Parzival* Wolfram mentions vineyards that had been destroyed during a siege of Erfurt (379, 18–20). This siege took place during a war between King Philipp of Swabia (1198–1208) and Landgrave Hermann of Thuringia (1190–1217), his second, and most important patron, in the summer of 1203 or 1204; this implies that Wolfram composed his courtly epic shortly thereafter. In the last book of his *Willehalm,* Wolfram has his narrator say that Hermann, who had commissioned him to compose a German version of this text, had died (417, 22). The actual date of Hermann's death was April 25, 1217, and consequently Wolfram must have worked on his *Willehalm* during and after that date. Wolfram's contemporary Gottfried von Strasbourg, who composed his famous *Tristan* around 1210, makes a derogatory remark about another poet's obscure writing style (vv. 4665–90). In all likelihood, Gottfried specifically criticized his competitor Wolfram, which would specify the year when he finished *Parzival*, close to 1205.

Wolfram also wrote a fragmentary verse narrative, *Titurel* (after 1217), and seven dawn songs. Although he belonged to the class of lower nobility (*Parzival*, 115, 11ff), he often complained about his poverty (*Parzival*, 184, 29–185, 9). Nevertheless, judging by his slightly arrogant tone of voice with which he addressed other poets, such as the goliard Walther von der Vogelweide (*Willehalm*, 136, 7ff; 286, 19ff), and considering the tone of familiarity that he used among highly ranking ladies (*Parzival*, 403, 26–404, 9), we may assume that he considered himself of higher nobility. After all, in *Parzival* the narrator stresses his status as a knight: "schildes ambet ist mîn art" (115, 11; "to hold the office of a knight [with a shield] is my privilege"). Moreover, he underscores that, according to his social role, he has to win a lady's favor by means of chivalric deeds (115, 15–20).

Immediately following, Wolfram emphasizes that he is illiterate (*Parzival*, 115, 27; see also *Willehalm*, 2, 19–22), but this does not have to mean that he could not read and write. As scholarship has confirmed, this ironic statement implies a deliberate distancing from the classical learned tradition so powerfully represented by Gottfried von Strasbourg, whereas he seems to have been an autodidact and was obviously somewhat familiar with Arabic, Hebrew, and occult sciences. It remains a highly intriguing, yet not fully demonstrable thesis that Wolfram had spent time in Toledo, Spain, where he might have been in contact with Arabic and Hebrew scholars. Nevertheless, Wolfram insists that he composed his *Parzival* without the guidance of any book (115, 30), which again has to be read ironically, as the poet definitely relied on Chrétien de Troyes's *Perceval*, among other sources. It seems unlikely that he would have learned about it only through oral channels, but when he claims not to know books, he probably refers to scholastic books written in Latin.

Apparently Wolfram had acquired a considerable degree of learning, especially of occult sciences, as he has the Gral (Grail) messenger Cundrie in *Parzival* display astonishing knowledge about astrology, lapidary science, biology, theology, law, and geography. We also know that some of the medical practices applied by heroes, such as Gawan in *Parzival*, represent the state of art in medical science as developed particularly at the Universities of Salerno (southern Italy) and Toledo (Spain). Here, the Christian doctors had begun to adopt Arabic medicine after relevant treatises, which originally had been translated from ancient Greek into Arabic, were made available in Latin. By contrast, Gottfried of Strasbourg does not indicate in his *Tristan* that he was particularly interested in medicine as he followed the more traditional school of thinking when such matters emerged in his book.

In the famous early fourteenth-century Manesse manuscript, the *Große Heidelberger Liederhandschrift*, which contains a large selection of Middle High German lyrical poems from the late-twelfth and thirteenth centuries copied on behalf of the Zurich Manesse family, Wolfram, armed with a sword as a symbol of his knightly rank, is depicted standing next to a horse clad in chivalric armor, holding a banner in the right hand and a shield in the left. A squire controls his horse, which is covered with a blanket that displays the same symbols as the banner, shield, and even the knight's helmet. Nothing reveals the poet's individuality, as his face is covered by a helmet whose visor is closed. As in all other cases in this famous manuscript, the illuminator created a fantasy image of the highly admired poet and created a coat of arms that has no relationship with any existing noble family. As far as the poet's personal situation is concerned, he only refers to his family in general terms. He would not like to take his wife to King Arthur's court (*Parzival*, 216, 26–217, 6); he also mentions his own daughter (*Willehalm*, 33, 24–26), but remains silent about his parents and other relatives, and hardly divulges anything about his personal situation.

Wolfram was well known in his time and enjoyed a high esteem, as we can tell from the surprisingly large number of the manuscripts that have survived. His *Parzival* has survived in as many as eighty-three manuscripts, of which seventeen contain the complete text, whereas the other sixty-six preserve the verse epic only in fragmentary form. Wolfram's *Willehalm* has been transmitted in seventy-six manuscripts, of which twelve offer the complete text and sixty-four contain only a fragment. By contrast, his dawn songs have survived in only three manuscripts, exactly the same number as in the case of his *Titurel*, but both these songs and the latter have exerted considerable influence in other ways. Moreover, many of Wolfram's contemporary poets and his successors such as Herman der Damen, Regenbogen, Ulrich von Türheim, Ulrich von dem Türlin, The Pleier, Konrad von Stoffeln, Ulrich von Etzenbach, and Johann von Würzburg voiced their strong admiration of Wolfram's art. In the fifteenth and sixteenth centuries the urban Meistersingers identified him as one of the twelve ancient masters of their art, creating a legendary fiction of Wolfram whose true accomplishments were little known and even less understood already at that time. Nevertheless, Wolfram's *Parzival* was copied by hand as late as the sixteenth century when the manuscript tradition finally broke off. It was rediscovered in the late eighteenth-century (first modern edition in narrative form by Johann Jacob Bodmer in 1753) and has enjoyed an ever-growing popularity and respect by lay audiences and scholars since then. Bodmer was also the first to bring Wolfram's *Willehalm* to light by editing the text in a narrative paraphrase in 1774 and by translating a section from the prologue in 1781. The first full edition was prepared by Willhelm Johann Christian Gustav Casparson in 1784. Johann Gustav Büsching was the first to retell Wolfram's *Titurel* in 1814. Richard Wagner's opera *Parsifal,* published in 1877, fully established this text, at least in Wagner's version, as a national cultural icon.

In all his literary works Wolfram made remarkable contributions to the specific genre within which he was writing. With the exception of the *Titurel,* all other texts are somewhat based on literary sources, but Wolfram succeeded in rewriting and reconceptualizing them in such a way as to create entirely new texts. Chrétien de Troyes was the first to compose the *Perceval* narrative, *li Comtes del Graal,* with which in turn Count Philipp of Flanders had familiarized him through a *livre.* We do not know for sure the origin of this source, but as in other cases Chrétien seems to have been charged to translate and reconstruct an ancient Celtic account.

Wolfram's *Parzival* consists of sixteen books or chapters, of which Book III to the middle of Book XIII are closely modeled after Chrétien's *Perceval.* Wolfram added the significant accounts of Parzival's father, Gahmuret and his step-brother, Feirefiz; he also changed many of the names or gave names to his characters—there are 222 named characters in the German text versus just a few in the French text—and developed the Gralmotif quite differently. Whereas Chrétien's romance begins the narrative *in medias res* focusing on the young hero Perceval, Wolfram offers a highly intriguing, but also opaque introduction in which he discusses human nature, the difficulty of distinguishing between good and evil, and people's ability (or inability) to understand their world. Subsequently, he outlines in great detail the life of Parzival's parents, Gahmuret and Herzeloyde. The huge family tree varies considerably from the one in Chrétien's text, and Wolfram refers to a new, perhaps fictional, but perhaps also verifiable source, Kyot.

The Provençal Kyot, while studying in the library of Toledo, had found an account of the Gral written in Arabic. The Heathen astronomer Flegetanis, a descendent from Solomon, had been able to read about the Gral in the constellation of stars and had recorded his findings. Kyot later followed this trail and learned everything about the Gral family in an Anjou chronicle (453–55). Wolfram might have created this fictional source to establish some authority for his text, as the majority of Wolfram-scholarship assumes, but we cannot entirely exclude the possibility that he might indeed have been to Toledo and encountered a scholar there who could have told him something about the Gral myth and the Gral family. At any rate, Wolfram projected an intricate relationship between Arthurian chivalry and a divinely inspired Gral community where religion and knighthood uniquely join hands.

Parzival's father, Gahmuret, is the second son and does not inherit property or wealth from his own father. Although his brother Galoes offers him money and a place in his household, he declines it all and seeks his good fortune as a knight. After having gained much fame in heathen lands, he liberates the black Queen Belacane from a siege set up by Vridebrant of Scotland, a kinsman of Isenhart who had died in his attempts to win Belacane's love. Gahmuret also falls in love with the queen despite her black skin color and creates a baby with her who will be called Feirefiz. But his unquenchable love for knighthood drives him away, although Belacane would have converted to Christianity if he only had asked her. After Gahmuret's departure she delivers her son who is checkered black and white and who later gains highest triumphs as a knight and king. Gahmuret, on the other hand, travels to Spain where he encounters Herzeloyde and marries her. When she is pregnant with Parzival, her husband abandons her as well for new chivalric adventures somewhere in the Orient. This time, however, he dies because an opponent had used goat's blood to soften his otherwise impenetrable diamond helmet. Herzeloyde grieves so much about his death that she withdraws into the woods of Soltane to protect her son from the dangers of knighthood and human society. When Parzival has grown up, he happens to run into some knights and soon leaves his mother—who, unknown to him, immediately dies of a broken heart—to find King Arthur. For a long time Parzival displays a disconcerting degree of ignorance and foolishness, badly hurting Lady Jeschute and killing Ither for his armor, not recognizing him as his uncle. An old knight, Gurnemanz, provides him with the basic teachings of knighthood, which helps him to liberate Condwîr âmurs from a hostile suitor and to win her love and hand. But the lesson also prevents him soon after from asking the crucial question while he observes the Gral miracle and does not understand the expressions of suffering on castle Munsalvaesche. Nevertheless, subsequently he proves his outstanding qualities as a knight and achieves a great reputation that makes him a celebrated hero at King Arthur's court.

The romance here takes a dramatic turn to the tragic. The Gral messenger Cundrie arrives and criticizes Parzival for his failure on Munsalvaesche to ask the expected question, which would have demonstrated his sympathy with King Anfortas's suffering. Parzival expresses his disappointment with God rejecting him outright, and departs from King Arthur's court. At this point the narrative shifts the focus to Gawan, whose honor and chivalry are also challenged. Books VII and VIII, and X through XIV deal exclusively with his many knightly adventures and his wooing of Lady Orgeluse, whereas in Book IX and XV to XVI the narrator returns to Parzival's destiny.

After many trials and tribulations, the protagonist meets his uncle Trevrizent who provides him with the fundamental Christian teachings and also assumes, almost like a Christ figure, his guilt of not having asked the question and of having unknowingly committed crimes against his nearest relatives. Parzival also meets his half-brother, Feirefiz, who in the meantime has become the mightiest king in the East. Both begin a deadly fight and almost would have killed each other, but at the end Parzival's sword breaks and Feirefiz graciously yields to the stranger, whom he respects for his chivalric virtue. The half-brothers recognize each other, and both return to King Arthur's court. Once again Cundrie joins the company and declares that Parzival has been given a second chance to free his uncle Anfortas from his pain. Once he has asked the decisive question, joy and happiness return both to the Gral community and to the rest of the world, as Parzival replaces Anfortas as the new Gral king. Feirefiz accepts baptism and marries Repanse de Schoye, a member of the Gral family. At the end Parzival's wife, Condwîr âmurs, arrives with their two children, Loherangrin and Kardeiz, whereas Feirefiz departs with Repanse heading for his kingdoms in the East where he introduces the Christian religion. His son is later to become the famous Prester John, whereas Loherangrin briefly marries the Duchess of Brabant who, however, loses him when she asks him about his origin, breaking the vow never to do that. In a way Wolfram does not fully conclude his narrative, but instead fleetingly opens the perspective toward future accounts about the next generations of the Gral family.

Although deeply Christian in its fundamental concept, Wolfram's *Parzival* also reveals significant interest in and understanding of other cultures, peoples, and religions. Gahmuret marries a black queen, their son Feirefiz grows up as a heathen, but when he is baptized, his conversion to Christianity seems to be more a matter of convenience that allows him to marry Repanse. Nevertheless, Feirefiz carries Christianity to the Indian subcontinent, and his son John establishes the mythical kingdom traditionally associated with this "Prester John." Parzival at first grows up without any knowledge of God, if we disregard his mother's one helpless and inappropriate effort, and later, once Cundrie has publicly condemned him for his failure, he entirely abrogates his religion and service under God. Nevertheless, Parzival regains his belief with the help of Trevrizent and recovers the frail Gral community, leaving the world of King Arthur behind where religion does not play any significant role.

The shining model knight Gawan has to go through life-threatening experiences in his wooing of Orgeluse, but he eventually succeeds and restores happiness in the Arthurian universe. Most disturbingly, almost all women experience profound pain and suffering, many die because of wrong actions by their men, and only few see the light at the end of the tunnel. Wolfram projects a highly troubled world thrown into an existential crisis as both chivalry and courtly love, not to speak of King Arthur and his court, fail to live up to the public expectations. Violence, the abandonment of women, ill-treatment of those in need of protection, despair, rape and betrayal seem to dominate, but Parzival's (but also Gawan's) unfailing virtues and abilities as knight, his various teachers, the love of his wife, and, above all, God's calling, prove to be the catalysts in rescuing an endangered world.

Willehalm is an epic poem in the tradition of the *chansons de geste,* specifically *Aliscans* which deals, like many other texts, with the struggles of Count Guillaume d'Orange against Arabic enemies. The historical basis can be traced to Count Guillaume de Toulouse, who fought under Charlemagne against the Basques and Saracens in Northeastern Spain and conquered Barcelona in 801. He founded the monastery Gellone near

Montpellier, joined it in 806, and died there around 812 or 814. There are close to twenty different epic poems from the twelfth and thirteenth centuries that treat this legendary figure, but we do not have available the one text that had been Wolfram's source and which Landgrave Hermann of Thuringia had secured for Wolfram as a basis for a translation. Nevertheless, Wolfram's adaptation of the *Stoff* transformed it so thoroughly that his *Willehalm* has to be considered a highly unique and remarkably innovative contribution to this genre. Whereas in all the *chansons de geste* versions Guillaume assumes center position, Wolfram focused the attention on Willehalm and his wife, Giburg, who is eventually made into a saint.

The epic begins with a prayer to St. Willehalm, and at the end, the last book (IX) sets in with a prayer to St. Giburc. *Willehalm* is no longer a heroic poem in the traditional sense, instead it combines heroic elements with those typical of courtly love poetry and the religious legend.

The Provençal Margrave Willehalm has to fight against vast armies of heathen enemies defending his own territory, religion, and his wife. After having been captured by the Saracen King Terramer, he met his daughter Arabel; both had fallen in love with each other and then had escaped to his home country (although she had originally been married to Tibalt, another Saracen ruler). After her voluntary conversion to Christianity, she is renamed Giburg and marries Willehalm. Her enraged father and former husband try with all their enormous might to recapture her, leading to catastrophic battles at Alischanz between the Christians and the Saracens. Willehalm is the only one to survive and fights his way through the opponents using the armor of King Arofel, whom he had slain in a gruesome and totally unmerciful manner, and by means of his knowledge of Arabic. His wife at first does not recognize him and forces him to identify himself before she allows him to enter the castle. Giburg advises Willehalm to seek help from his brother-in-law, the French King Loys, and with the help of Arofel's armor, he finds his way through the siege. But the French court in Laôn at first proves to be very hostile, especially his sister who wants to deny him any help. In his rage, Willehalm almost would have decapitated her, but when his niece Alyze begs him to calm down and to forgive her parents, and when the queen has learned of the uncountable scores of casualties, the conflict is settled. The king summons an army in support of Willehalm, who now emerges as the defender not only of his territory, but of all of France and of Christianity. The next day Willehalm observes a huge kitchen boy, Rennewart, who later turns out to be Giburg's long lost brother who had been kidnapped by merchants and sold to the king. Because Rennewart had refused baptism, he was forced to work in the kitchen despite his noble origin. He considers his treatment as highly humiliating, but he also harbors strong hatred against his family, believing that they neglected to search for him and free him from captivity. Willehalm communicates with him in Arabic and asks for his release, taking him into his own service. Rennewart proves to be invaluable as he has the strength of a giant and is entirely dedicated to Willehalm's cause. At one point he prevents the desertion of the French army, forcing them to march forward.

Before the second battle at Alischanz, the council meets to deliberate their strategies. It is here where Giburg gives a famous speech in which she develops early ideas of tolerance. She points out her personal dilemma as she has friends, family, and loved-ones on both sides of the conflict, and she reminds her listeners that God had created all people, irrespective of their beliefs. She points out that all people become God's children through baptism, but not all heathens are automatically condemned to Hell, especially as God might feel mercy and spare them from their destiny. Whatever evil the heathens might have done to the Christians, as Giburg emphasizes, the latter should remember that even Christ forgave those who killed him. Consequently, she appeals to them to exert mercy even in the midst of battle. On a very personal note, she also underscores that she had left her children and her husband behind who all were completely free of any guilt, and at the same time she laments the death of so many brave warriors on the Christians' side. She explains the theological issue that people can hope for God's forgiveness, whereas the evil angel (Lucifer) cannot, as people were misled by the devil, but the angels followed their own wrong decision.

Giburg does not call for an end of fighting, and she does not develop the notion of tolerance as we know it today, especially as she fully embraces Christianity, but her speech clearly lays the foundation for a broader, more inclusive view of people with different religions.

The second half of Wolfram's *Willehalm* is dominated by extensive descriptions of the battle, which ultimately is won by the Christians under Willehalm's leadership. Rennewart plays a leading role, killing nine kings all by himself, not even sparing his own heathen brother Kanliun, whose identity remains unknown to him, but the fragmentary ending leaves the question open what happened with this young hero. Once the enemies' banner has come down, the Christians' victory is secured. Terramer is seriously wounded in a last battle with Willehalm, but his men rescue him in time and take him to his ship. The final and truly remarkable feature of Wolfram's epic poem, however, consists of the treatment of the defeated heathens at the hand of the Christian warriors. Although the battle itself is characterized by utmost brutality, portrayed in gruesome detail, the protagonist laments all dead men irrespective of their religion and ethnic and national origin. He even raises the crucial question: "Is it a sin to slaughter like cattle those who have never received baptism? I say it is a great sin, for they are all the creatures of Gold's Hand, and He maintains them, with their seventy-two languages" (218). Willehalm deeply grieves the devastation resulting from this war, and he treats King Matribleiz, Giburg's relative and one of the few surviving kings, with great respect and even honor. He praises the opponents for their bravery, loyalty, and steadfastness, and he requests from Matribleiz that he and his surviving men gather the corpses of the killed heathen kings so they may receive an honorable burial according to their own religion and customs. He goes so far as to offer balsam, strong mules, and anything else needed for their proper burial, as he knows that someone loved the deceased, and that they are, even in their death, human beings. In other words, the protagonist realizes that despite the difference in religion, all warriors share in their humanity, and so he acknowledges Giburg's heathen family and allows the defeated army to return home.

Willehalm's victory, however, remains a Pyrrhic victory, as too many beloved ones have died on both sides. Wolfram has him express his wish that the heathens had simply stayed where they had come from, as then the world would not have experienced such an Armageddon. Despite the profound grief and pain that permeate this epic, Wolfram also indicates that although the world is divided into Christianity and heathendom, both sides are related to each other in concrete and general terms, and deserve to live their own lives, as long as they do not threaten each other with violence—a clear condemnation of the prevalent crusade mentality of the time.

If these two monumental epics were not enough to establish Wolfram's world fame, he also composed a highly enigmatic, yet profound and meaningful fragmentary text, *Titurel*, sometime between 1217 and 1220. Here the author returns to some lose narrative threads in *Parzival* and develops them further. There are two fragmentary pieces, the first consisting of 131 and the second of thirty-nine stanzas. Sometime during the thirteenth century an otherwise unknown author Albrecht (von Scharfenberg?), obviously intrigued by the ideas developed in Wolfram's text, created a monumental epic out of the fragments, *Der Jüngere Titurel* (*The Younger Titurel*). In Wolfram's verse narrative, the destiny of Parzival's aunt Sigune and her lover Schionatulander is explored in greater detail. Here we learn the background of the Gral family, how God had sent the Gral to Titurel, who handed it down to his son, and so forth, and how finally tragedy struck leading to a quick decline of the entire Gral community. In the first fragment the two young people Sigune and Schionatulander fall in love with each other, and after a certain testing period—Schionatulander accompanies Gahmuret on his second military campaign to the East where the latter will be killed—they are given permission to be lovers. The second fragment, much shorter than the first, offers a truly innovative theme, which was never developed before and after by any other medieval poet. The two young people enjoy time together in a courtly arranged camp in the middle of the woods, when they hear a dog barking in the distance. Schionatulander, though barefoot because he had tried to catch fish in a creek, runs after the dog and catches him. Sigune discovers to her great delight and excitement that the enormous dog leash is covered with gems which, read together, form letters and these in turn words. She immediately begins to read the text and learns that the dog is called "Gardeviaz," or "Stay on the Trail." Moreover, the leash reports of tragic lovers whose destiny evokes great sympathy in Sigune. Anxiously, she undoes a knot in the collar with which the dog was tied to a tent pole as she wants to keep reading. Gardeviaz immediately frees himself following his animal instincts and runs away, soon only heard barking in the distance. Schionatulander again tries to capture the dog, but this time he fails and returns empty handed but with bloody feet. Significantly, Sigune's palms are bloody as well because the gems cut into her skin when she tried to hold on to the leash. She forces Schionatulander to pursue the dog with all his might, as she would grant him her love only once he returned with Gardeviaz. Tragically, however, the reader is aware of Schionatulander's destiny of doom, knowing from *Parzival* that he will encounter the knight Orilus and die in a joust with him to regain the dog. In *Parzival* Sigune is shown throughout the text as holding Schionatulander's corpse and lamenting both his and her destiny. The first time Parzival meets his aunt, Schionatulander just has suffered his death; later Sigune will move into the territory of the Gral community and transform into an anchorite, who laments the by then embalmed body of her lover. The appearance of this *pietà* figure has a great significance for Parzival's slow development and learning process, whereas in *Titurel* we are informed about the cause of Schionatulander's death and Sigune's life-long suffering.

Most important, though, proves to be the highly unique motif of a text on a dog leash. It contains not only profound ethical and moral warnings ("Gardeviaz"), but also an account of two tragic couples who experience death because of too high demands of the lovers. Wolfram seems to be the first, and maybe only, medieval poet who explicitly experimented with the concept of the fragment, as the text on Gardeviaz's leash disappears, just as Wolfram's own text comes to an abrupt ending. In other words, the internal fragment is paralleled by the external fragment, and the readers/listeners are challenged to continue with the tale and to think for themselves about the meaning of Gardeviaz's running away and Sigune's obsession with the text. If she loves Schionatulander, why does she impose such a life-threatening task upon him? To what extent is knightly love service justified and appropriate? And finally, whereas Sigune was able to read the enigmatic words on the leash, why does she fail to read the bloody letters inscribed on her own skin by the gems, and on Schionatulander's legs written by the thorns and brambles that prevented him from catching the dog? In a way, Sigune understands the significance of the account on the leash, but she miscalculates its importance for her own life: "If I don't get to read that to the end, my whole land of Katelangen will be meaningless to me" (165, 2). Despite is brevity and fragmentary nature, *Titurel* easily proves to be one of the most fascinating literary experiments ever realized in the Middle Ages and illustrates once more why Wolfram must be counted among the most famous medieval poets.

Wolfram also composed seven remarkable dawn songs, which belong to the best of their kind in the entire Middle Ages. In *Parzival* he mentions that he knows how to compose poetry (114, 12–13), but he also utters a disclaimer that has to be read as tongue-in-cheek (115, 11–14). Dawn songs can be found in almost all medieval European languages, but also all over the world throughout time, as they deal with the erotic situation of two lovers who have spent a night together and are forced to separate at dawn. Nevertheless, Wolfram once again proved to be one of the best lyric poets in this genre as his dawn songs bristle with innovative images and powerful, emotional expressions. We are made into direct witnesses of the sad moment when the lovers realize that the end of their happiness has come. We hear them cursing the arrival of the new day, lamenting the passing of the night, and bewailing their destiny. The poet includes surprisingly intimate images of the lovemaking and portrays intense scenes of love. Particularly song III, "Sîne klâwen," impresses with its astonishing poetic language: "Its talons / are thrust through the clouds. / It rises up with great force." Wolfram was also the first to inject a completely new thematic orientation in his song "Der helnden minne ir klage" (no. IV) as he suggests within the dawn-song context that lasting happiness in love could be achieved if the lovers were married, which would make it unnecessary for the man to leave the woman early in the morning to avoid being caught by the court: "a man's sweet wife, acknowledged openly, / is able to provide such love" (IV, 2, 9–10). It was to take several hundred years until later poets followed Wolfram's lead.

Whereas Wolfram's *Willehalm, Titurel,* and his dawn songs do not contain any references to King Arthur, *Parzival* is intimately connected with the Arthurian world. As unbelievable as it might seem, Wolfram developed a faint but indisputable family connection between the Gral world and the Arthurian world. Arthur's father, Utepandragun, was the son of Brickus, who in turn was Mazadan's son. Brickus's brother Lazaliez's son and grandson are called Addanz and Gandin, respectively. The latter's daughter, Rischoyde, is married to Frimutel, who in turn is Titurel's son and at the same time Parzival's grandfather. Gahmuret, however, has nothing to do with King Arthur, whereas Parzival's career as a knight begins at Arthur's court where a serious conflict has erupted with the knight Ither. At that moment the young and naive Parzival arrives at the scene and requests Ither's armor from King Arthur who at first rejects him, but then, spurred on by his court steward Keye, gives him permission to take it. Ither does not expect that the young man might represent a danger and kicks him off his horse with the blunt end of his lance. Filled with wrath, Parzival uses his javelin and kills Ither by shooting it through his eye into his brain.

Undoubtedly, chivalry has come to an end and is crudely dishonored through the still very boorish hero and others such as his uncle Ither. Moreover, the court as well is diminished through internecine strife and conflicts. Lady Cunnewâre, for instance, breaks out in laughter at the sight of young Parzival, though she had sworn never to laugh again until she would see the one knight who would be destined to achieve the highest triumphs—a prophetic realization, though in total ignorance of the future events through which Parzival will indeed transform into the savior of the world. Keye, however, beats Cunnewâre because he believes that she has shamed the court by identifying the ridiculous stranger as the prophesied "messiah." Moreover, the deaf Antanor, whose muteness is directly linked with Cunnewâre's promise never to laugh until the arrival of the true hero, suddenly speaks up and says to Keye that Parzival would one day revenge this ill treatment. Antanor is also savagely beaten, but the narrative outcome will prove both absolutely right, as Keye will soon receive reports of Parzival's outstanding chivalric accomplishments and will also be badly defeated by him in a joust.

The second time Parzival and King Arthur meet takes place later after Parzival has left his wife to visit his mother, not knowing that she had died from a broken heart when he had departed from Soltane. Once during May, Arthur and his court have heard so many news of Parzival's knightly deeds that they embark on a journey to find him. One evening a falconer goes hunting, but loses his bird. In the early morning Parzival, not knowing that Arthur is camped just ahead of him, comes across an unexpected patch of snow with three drops of blood from a goose that the falcon had tried to kill in vain. These drops remind Parzival of his wife, Condwîr amûrs, whom he misses deeply, making him to fall into a trance. When Arthur's knights wake up and see the strange apparition of Parzival, first Segramors, then Keye, try in vain to defeat the unknown warrior. Especially Keye fails miserably, because Parzival, who by now perfectly displays all knightly skills, makes the steward fall off his horse and break his right arm and left leg—an appropriate punishment for Keye's bad behavior at Parzival's first visit at Arthur's court. Only Gawan understands that the hero is lost in a trance because of love, covers the drops of blood and leads his friend to the camp.

Parzival meets King Arthur and his court a third time after his decisive battle with his half-brother Feirefiz. Once they have made peace, the two ride to King Arthur and are welcomed as the best heroes in the world. Soon, Cundrie arrives and announces that Parzival has been chosen by God to assume the throne of the Gral kingdom. This gives him the chance to ask Anfortas the long-expected question, and thus free him from his suffering.

Wolfram heavily relies on King Arthur to structure his romance, but the Arthurian court proves to be only an intermittent stage on Parzival's path from childhood to adulthood, and from boorish young man to the perfected knight. Ultimately, however, the world of King Arthur fades away, as it remains within the dimension of human affairs, whereas Parzival succeeds as King Anfortas, the ruler of the Gral world.

PRIMARY WORKS

Seven Songs (c. 1200?). *Seven Songs* are extant in three major manuscripts from the twelfth and thirteenth centuries. The Kliene Heidelberger Liederhandschrift (Heidelberg, Universitätsbibliothek, cpg 357) contains four strophes in A; the Weingartner Handschrift (Stuttgart, Württembergische Landesbibliothek, HB XIII, 1) has three songs in B; the Manessische Heidelberger Liederhandschrift (Heidelberg, Universitätsbibliothek, cpg 848) and the Munich manuscript of *Parzival* (Munich: Bayerische Staatsbibliothek, cgm 19) contain two songs in G. **First publication:** Two songs in *Auswahl aus Den Hochdeutschen Dichtern des Dreizehnten Fahrhunderts: Für Volesungen und zum Schulgebrauch*, ed. Karl Lachmann. Berlin, 1820. **Modern German edition:** In *Titurel: Lieder: Mittelhochdeutscher Text and Übersetzung*, ed. and trans. Wolfgang Mohr. Göppingen: Kümmerle, 1978. **English editions:** In *Eos: An Inquiry into the Theme of Lover's Meetings and Partings at Dawn in Poetry*, trans. Arthur T. Hatto, 448–55. London: Mouton, 1965. In *The Medieval German Lyric, 1150–1300*, trans. Olive Sayce, 211–16. Oxford: Clarendon, 1982. In *Wolfram von Eschenbach: Titurel and the Songs*, trans. Marion Gibbs and Sidney M. Johnson, 70–111. New York: Garland, 1988; *Parzival* (c. 1210). **Manuscripts:** There are some eighty extant manuscripts; sixteen are complete. The two best are D

(St. Gall, Stiftsbibliothek, 857) and G (Munich, Bayerische Staatsbibliothek, cgm 19). **First publication:** *Parzival.* Strasbourg: printed by Johann Mentelin, 1477. **Modern German editions:** *Parzival,* trans. Wolfgang Mohr. Göppingen: Kümmerle, 1977. *Parzival,* 2 vols., trans. Wolfgang Spiewok. Stuttgart: Reclam, 1981. **English editions:** *Parzival,* trans. Helen M. Mustard and Charles E. Passage. New York: Vintage, 1961. *Parzival,* trans. Arthur T. Hatto. Harmondsworth, UK: Penguin, 1980; *Wilhelm* (c. 1220). **Manuscripts:** This unfinished work appears in more than seventy manuscripts, twelve of which contain all that Wolfram completed. The earliest compete manuscript is the St. Gall (St. Gall, Stiftsbibliothek, 857) from the thirteenth century. The oldest fragments, from the early thirteenth century, are found in the Munich Bayerische Staatsbibliothek, cgm 193 III. **First publication:** *Wilhelm der Heilige von oranse: Zweyter Theil von Wolfram von Eschenbach, einem Dichter des schwäbischen Zeitpuncts,* ed. Wilhelm Johann Christian Gustav Casparson. Cassel, 1784. **Modern German edition:** *Wilhelm aus dem Mittelhochdeutschen übertragen,* trans. Reinhard Fink and Friedrich Knorr. Jena: Diedereichs, 1941. **English editions:** *The Middle High German Poem of Wolfram von Eschenbach,* trans. Charles E. Passage. New York: Unger, 1977. *Willehalm,* trans. Marion Gibbs and Sidney M. Johnson. Hammondsworth, UK: Penguin, 1984; *Titurel* (c. 1217). Three extant manuscripts have *Titurel.* Both fragments are found in the *Parzival* manuscript G (Munich, Bayerische Staatsbibliothek, cgm 19); the first sixty-eight strophes are in the H, the Ambraser Heldenbuch (Vienna, Östereichische Nationalbibliothek, 2663); and forty-eight strophes are located in M (Munich: Univeritätsbibliothek, Ms 154). **First publication:** *Titurel.* Strasbourg: printed by Johann Mentelin, 1477. **Modern German edition:** In *Titurel; Lieder: Mittelhochdeutscher Text und Übersetzung,* trans. and ed. Wolfgang Mohr. Göppingen: Kümmerle, 1978. **English editions:** *Titurel, by Wolfram von Eschenbach: Translation and Studies,* trans. Charles E. Passage. New York: Ungar, 1984. In *Wolfram von Eschenbach: Titurel and the Songs,* trans. Marion Gibbs and Sidney M. Johnson. New York: Garland, 1988.

SECONDARY SOURCES

Blamires, David. *Characterization and Individuality in Wolfram's "Parzival."* Cambridge: Cambridge University Press, 1966; Bumke, Joachim. *Die Blutstropfen im Schnee: Über Wahrnehmung und Erkenntnis im "Parzival" Wolframs von Eschenbach.* Tübingen: Niemeyer, 2001; ———. *Wolfram von Eschenbach.* 7th ed. Stuttgart-Weimar: Metzler, 1997; Classen, Albrecht. *Utopie und Logos: Vier Studien zu Wolframs von Eschenbach Titurel.* Heidelberg: Carl Winter, 1990; Green, Dennis Howard, and Leslie Peter Johnson. *Approaches to Wolfram von Eschenbach: Five Essays.* Bern: Peter Lang, 1978; Hall, Clifton D. *A Complete Concordance to Wolfram von Eschenbach's Parzival.* New York: Garland, 1990; Hasty, Will. *Adventure as Social Performance: A Study of the German Court Epic.* Tübingen: Niemeyer, 1990; Haug, Walter. *Strukturen als Schlüssel zur Welt: Kleine Schriften zur Erzählliteratur des Mittelalters.* Tübingen: Niemeyer, 1989; Heinzle, Joachim. *Stellenkommentar zu Wolframs Titurel.* Tübingen: Niemeyer, 1972; Jones, Martyn H., and Timothy McFarland. *Wolfram's Willehalm: Fifteen Essays.* Columbia, SC: Camden House, 2001; Mertens, Volker. *Der deutsche Artusroman.* Stuttgart: Reclam, 1998; Parshall, Linda B. *The Art of Narration in Wolfram's Parzival and Albrecht's Jüngerer Titurel.* Cambridge: Cambridge University Press, 1981; Przybilski, Martin. *Sippe und geslehte: Verwandschaft als Deutungsmuster im "Willehalm" Wolframs von Eschenbach.* Wiesbaden: Reichert, 2000; Schröder, Werner. *Wolfram von Eschenbach: Spuren und Werke.* Kleinere Schriften, 1956–1987, vol. 1. Stuttgart: Hirzel, 1989; Stevens, Sylvia. *Family in Wolfram von Eschenbach's Willehalm: mîner mâge triwe ist mir wol kuont.* New York: Peter Lang, 1997; Wapnewski, Peter. *Die Lyrik Wolframs von Eschenbach: Edition, Kommentar, Interpretation.* Munich: Beck, 1972; Wynn, Marianne. *Wolfram's Parzival: On the Genesis of Its Poetry.* Frankfurt: Peter Lang, 1984; Young, Christopher. *Narrativische Perspektiven in Wolframs "Willehalm."* Tübingen: Niemeyer, 2000.

ALBRECHT CLASSEN

JEHAN FROISSART
(c. 1337–c. 1410)

Jehan, or Jean, Froissart was a French historian and poet; he is perhaps the most famous of medieval chroniclers, famous for his account of the Hundred Years' War between France and England, covering the events of 1340–1400. Froissart's legacy to medieval history is without question, as he one of the most detailed observers of his times (if not always completely accurate by modern standards of fact). Froissart is also one of the most ardent champions of chivalry and the courtly life, which is amply displayed in all of his writings, especially his *Chronicle* and his long Arthurian romance, *Meliador*. Widely traveled and fascinated by the political and social turmoil of the wars of Europe, Froissart created in his prose *Chronicle* a text that is a sumptuously detailed political and military history, with a bit of memoir thrown in. His *Meliador* builds on the same background. Most importantly, Froissart's entire body of work reflects his conviction that chivalry was the noblest society civilization offered. Whether recorded actual historical events (*Chronicles*) or creating legendary exploits of perfect knights (*Meliador*), Froissart never wavered in his adulation of chivalry.

Froissart's work as a poet is less widely known, or for that matter, valued, but is worthy of more extensive study and certainly deserving of more appreciation than it has received. Among his underrecognized works is the long verse romance *Meliador*, which is both typical and atypical of the Arthurian cycles it mirrors. Of all his poetical works (which include lyrics and verse histories), *Meliador* has too often been treated with particular contempt. Renowned historian Johan Huizinga derisively views this critical endeavor of Froissart's as a mere "super-romance," while Raymond Kilgour refers to it in even more explicitly dismissive terms as an "interminable romance." Neither of these are uncommon opinions about *Meliador*. Even one of Froissart's admirers, a translator of his *Chronicles*, repeats this typical reaction to Froissart's poetry: Geoffrey Brereton states that Froissart wrote poetry "prolifically but not very memorably." Such opinions overlook the complexity of *Meliador*, its creativity (most of its characters are peculiar to this poem), and the way in which this poem is reiterating what Froissart does in his more respected *Chronicles*, promoting chivalry. Furthermore, *Meliador* is particularly important amongst the late medieval Arthurian texts in that most of the characters (and certainly all of the central characters) and actions do not appear in other Arthurian works; *Meliador* is part of the Arthurian tradition without repeating tales created by other poets. It is also the last in the long tradition of medieval French Arthurian romances.

Little is known about Froissart's family background or youth. Even his birth date is speculative; it may be as early as 1333. He was born at Valenciennes, which was then part of Hainault, now northeastern France, but which was then considered to be part of the Netherlands (although Froissart's native tongue was French). This reflects the complicated, and fluid, national identities that one finds in the fourteenth century. Froissart seems to have little interest in national prejudices; he judged people by more class than national affiliation, in that he always privileges the noble, whatever country that noble came from. Froissart probably died at Chimay; the poet was also a priest, and Chimay was his last parish benefice. In the years between those two events, Froissart traveled throughout France, Flanders and the Netherlands, to England, Scotland, Wales, and Italy. Of his own class, Froissart is suspiciously silent. He certainly views the nobility as the most exemplary class, but does not seem to have been of noble birth himself. Given his birthplace, it is likely his family were in the business of banking. In fact, privileging of the aristocracy, as Froissart does repeatedly in the *Chronicles* and his poems, especially his Arthurian romance, most likely indicates his envy of them. By 1361, when he was approximately twenty-four years old, Froissart had taken the tonsure (he would later take full ecclesiastical vows and become a priest), preparing himself for noble service. If he was not born noble, he would at least devote his life to working for the nobility, recording and applauding their values, and living exclusively in their world. He is plainly contemptuous of lower classes; the chronicler who fawned over every act of the knight on the battlefield has little positive to say about the archer or the foot soldier. The villein, or peasant/laborer, could never be a hero for Froissart. Even his own role as priest was defined as an servant of the nobility, not in terms of his ministry. His choice of the Arthurian themes as the focus of his lengthy poem reflects his preference for the stories of knights over that of commoners.

Fortunately for future biographers, Froissart was an extremely self-referential writer (in comparison with many writers of the late Middle Ages); more is known about his personal life and interests after he began writing professionally. He is not the cipher he could be because he includes his own story into that of his characters. He frequently refers to himself and his own life in the *Chronicles*, and one of his earliest verse works was the essentially autobiographic *"l'Epinette Amoureuse"* ("Prisoner of Love"). There is also some, albeit slight, corroborating evidence as to Froissart's status as a professional historian and poet in the form of financial records of stipends paid benefices that were granted to Froissart by his patrons or by other nobles to whom they introduced the priest/poet. Froissart's career as a writer was fairly typical for his times; he survived on the largess of aristocratic patrons and the benefices they found him once he took holy vows, by 1373.

One of his first appointments was at the court of Queen Philippa of Hainault, wife of Edward III (1327–1377) of England; there it is presumed his clerical training and education proved most useful. Philippa and Edward were just two of many royal and noble figures with whom Froissart would become acquainted, and whose lives he would record for posterity in his astonishingly comprehensive *Chronicles*; his first patron may have been John of Hainault, uncle to the Count of Hainault. It was probably John who recommended that Froissart go to England and meet with Philippa.

Froissart's personal and professional fortunes were closely tied to the war, as he records in his *Chronicles*. He gained the attention of his first patron, Philippa of Hainault, because of a verse narrative recounting the battle of Poitiers, in 1356, in which Philippa's son, Edward the Black Prince (1330–1376), proved himself so heroically. Sadly, this verse chronicle has been lost. As recorded by Froissart in the later prose *Chronicle*, which can be assumed to reflect the earlier version, the battle of Poitiers became a shining moment of chivalrous endeavor, and the prince a singular example of glorious knighthood: a "raging lion" who could not be touched by the opposing French, so strong in battle was he. Even the defeated French knights are the "finest flower" for Froissart. The poet brought his verses directly to Philippa, who hires him to be her secretary and who encouraged him to accompany various diplomatic missions around Britain. Froissart's life as an adventurer poet had begun, as well as his career as a professional scribe, sent by his patrons to discover and record events throughout western Europe.

For the next six years, until 1367, Froissart explored England and Scotland, meeting with such exalted personages as the King of Scotland, David Bruce. In that year he returned to the continent, first to Bordeaux with the Black Prince, and then on to Milan with Lionel, the Duke of Clarence (second son to Edward III), interrupting these trips with a brief return journey to London. In Milan Froissart attended Clarence's marriage to a wealthy Italian heiress, daughter of the Viscount of Milan. This event was also attended by two of Froissart's greatest artistic contemporaries, Chaucer and Petrarch, although Froissart tells his readers nothing about those two great poets. What are immediately obviously from Froissart's descriptions of the more personal royal and noble events he witnessed is how comfortable he feels in the noble world, and how much he idealized it. Critics have argued that Froissart does not see the flaws in the code of chivalry and the nobility's obsession with military glory at all costs, even while his *Chronicles*, in recording realistic details, presents the nasty reality of medieval warfare. This will again be reflected in his understanding of the Arthurian mythology; the importance of the noble knights of Camelot and their code of chivalry, not in the questionable utility of their need to joust and tournament all over Europe to prove their honor and manhood.

By 1369 Froissart had returned to Valenciennes, only to receive disturbing news: Philippa had died. Not only was she an early patron of Froissart, she was also a fellow expatriate of Hainault (in fact, she had been born in the same town as Froissart). Fittingly, he recorded this event and his feelings in the *Chronicles* (which he had just begun) and in a lay, or short narrative poem entitled "*Lay de la mort la royne diangleterre*" ("Lay on the Death of the Queen of England"). Froissart's feelings for his patrons were always notably personal; he idealized them individually as much as he did their lifestyles. Although grieving, Froissart needed to ensure his professional future, and to find a patron to allow him to continue the *Chronicles*. In 1369 Froissart acquired a new patron, Wenceslaus of Bohemia, Duke of Luxembourg and Brabant (b. 1337), with whom the poet would remain until the duke's death in 1381. The relationship between Froissart and Wenceslaus again reflects the centrality of the Hundred Years' War to the poet's career; Wenceslaus had gained his titles upon the death of his father, the Blind King of Bohemia, who died at Crécy in 1346. The king stands as one of many figures in the wars' battles that Froissart will applaud his chivalrous bravery (such as insisting on fighting although already blinded). It is with Wenceslaus that Froissart began *Meliador*. It was Wenceslaus who commissioned *Meliador* from Froissart; according to the poet's own words in the *Dit dou Florin*, the duke paid him to write a romance of chivalry, inspired no doubt by the romantic view Froissart takes of chivalry in the *Chronicles*. The duke's interest in

Meliador was highly personal; he was himself a poet and gave Froissart lyrics that were incorporated into the final poem. The duke died shortly before *Meliador* was finished.

At the death of Wenceslaus, Froissart briefly visited the court of Gaston Phoebus, Count of Foix; by 1389 he was in the company of the Duke of Berry. In 1392 Froissart returned again to London; there he offered some verses to Richard II; in 1367 Froissart had been at the court of the Black Prince in Bordeaux when Richard was born, and near the end of his *Chronicles* he would record the events that led to Richard's deposition by Henry IV. Between 1392 and his death sometime around 1410, Froissart tells his readers little more about his life, concentrating on the fourth and final part of the *Chronicles* and on rewriting *Meliador*.

In its final form (and it must be noted that Froissart repeatedly revised sections of the text even as he added new parts), the *Chroniques de France, d'Angleterre, d'Ecosse, de Bretagne, de Gascogne, de Flandre et lieux circonvoisins* (*Chronicles of France, England, Spain, Brittany, Gascony, and Flanders and Neighboring Countries*) was divided into four books, and seems to have been revised by its author at least three times. The material covering the years from 1340–1361 was based on a verse chronicle by Jean Le Bel, whom Froissart calls "wise and venerable . . . generous, honorable, and chivalrous." Le Bel is particularly important as a source for Froissart. Most simply, le Bel's *Chronicle* (which exists for the modern reader in a single manuscript with no indication of its author) covered a period of time before Froissart was born, the history of Edward I and Edward II of England. Equally crucial, however, was le Bel's own "chivalrous" character; unlike the scholarly, priestly Froissart, le Bel more than just a poet, as he was also a soldier and a knight. He thus encapsulated the highest Froissart ideals: scholarship, poetry, and chivalry. Le Bel is yet another figure that Froissart idealizes in the *Chronicles*. The opening passages of Froissart's text copy verbatim much of le Bel's *Chronicle* (and thus preserving it for the future generations), and Froissart openly acknowledges that he indebted to le Bel. Froissart also had his own verse chronicle of the Battle of Poitiers, given to Philippa, as a source for the earliest years of the war; which is fortunate, because it was not a battle that le Bel describes in any great detail. Beyond that, Froissart relies on the nobles he works with and for, gathering firsthand accounts. Using actual witnesses as sources seems to have been important to Froissart. Even in *Meliador*, which is not meant to be history, Froissart states in places that "as I have heard," implying that the poet used realistic surroundings for his fictional characters.

The first version of the first book of the *Chronicles* was completed by 1379; the second version of that book was completed before 1400, during which time he also composed the first drafts of books two, three, and four; a third version of the first book was finished after 1400. The *Chronicles* was immediately popular with Froissart's contemporaries, and throughout the fifteenth and sixteenth centuries was recopied many times, from elaborately illuminated manuscripts to a complete English translation under the Tudors. Although it never lost favor, interest in it—and in Froissart personally—was revived in the nineteenth century, when studying the Middle Ages became popular.

In each stage of writing or rewriting Froissart had a different patron, and his biases toward the combatants of the war were determined by which side his patrons were from, and which side he had the most firsthand information on. The first redaction of book one was written from a pro-English point of view, reflecting his close relationship with the English royal house. However, although he seems to have begun the *Chronicles* under his second patron, Robert of Namur, who was not English but was a nephew of Philippa of Hainault and thus connected to the Count of Flanders, an English ally. Notably,

Robert was also a former crusader, who would provide a model for the knights errant in *Meliador*. The second redaction was composed under the patronage of Guy de Chatillon, Count of Blois (who brought Froissart to Blois and to Flanders, expanding the chronicler's firsthand experience of those places so central to the war between England and France). This second version is markedly pro-French in tone, perhaps reflecting Guy's relationship to the French royal line, yet it stops short of disparaging the English (for whom it must be presumed Froissart still had fond memories). At this time, Blois also provided Froissart with his first parish as a newly ordained priest. As the tide of war turned, Froissart's third version reflects an increasingly antagonistic assessment of the English. Yet he will still acknowledge any outstanding example of knighthood, disregarding nationalism in favor of promoting chivalry whenever possible.

Throughout the creation of the *Chronicles*, Froissart worked in three other poetic genres, the lyric, the *dit* (longer than a lyric, a dit is a allegorical narrative), and the romance. While all three reflect the *Chronicles'* reverence for the nobility, it is with the last, in the romance of *Meliador,* that Froissart is at his most obviously eulogistic. While the *Chronicles*, which reads at times as ovation to knights, still retains a realistic understanding of the brutality and futility of war, the romance does not. *Meliador,* given its romance structure and mythological characters (most of which are atypical of the Arthurian saga; the usual suspects—such as Arthur himself—are relegated to the sidelines or do not appear at all) is the most pro-chivalry of Froissart's entire body of work.

Meliador has an even more interesting history than the *Chronicles*; some critics view its history as more interesting than the poem itself. Although scholars knew for centuries that Froissart wrote a romance, because he himself mentioned it in several of his other works (including the *Chronicles*, where he significantly refers to *Meliador* by name), the poem itself was lost until 1891. In that year, Auguste Longnon was examining seventeenth-century copies of law registers, and noticed that the bindings contained fragments of an older poem. It was not uncommon in the seventeenth century to use manuscript from earlier periods as binding and cover material. Longnon gathered together the fragments, indexed the names of the characters, noting that one was called *Meliador*. Familiar with Froissart's *Chronicles*, he recognized the name and knew that he had discovered remnants of the poet's lost romance. Other names that he listed as appearing in the fragments included Camel and Hermondine, who were the antagonist and central heroine, respectively, in *Meliador*. Longnon quickly published the fragments. Two years later, Longnon found a more complete version of the poem in the Bibliothéteque Nationale, the greatest archive of medieval manuscripts in France. Longnon discovered that the Bibliothétique Nationale has indexed a manuscript as *Roman de Camel et d'Hermondine* (Romance of Camel and Hermondine); until Longnon noticed it in 1893, no one had studied it. Because he recognized the names Camel and Hermondine from his 1891 fragment, Longnon knew that he had discovered Froissart's *Meliador*. Longnon published the poem in a three volume edition sponsored by the Society of Ancient French Texts, between 1895 and 1899. As it exists in this manuscript and published edition, the poem is 30,771 lines long, yet it is incomplete.

The dating of the rediscovery of *Meliador* is thus quite clear. In contrast, the dating of the poem's composition is less certain; it is best determined by sources outside the poem. Composing the poem was apparently a lifelong effort for Froissart, which either speaks to its length or to the importance with which he viewed the subject matter. Froissart seems to have worked on it before his began his more famous *Chronicles*, and completed other (and significantly shorter) poems before completing the romance. Froissart must have begun the romance sometime between 1369 and 1381, when he had Wenceslaus of Brabant as his patron and collaborator on the poem. Another clue to the start of *Meliador* is found in the *Dit dou Florin*, where Froissart records that Wenceslaus had commissioned *Meliador*, which means the poem has to have been written after 1369, when the duke became Froissart's patron. In the *Chronicles* Froissart states that he met Gaston Phoebus, in 1388, to whom he read *Meliador*. By 1389, while at the court of Foix Froissart composed the *Dit dou Florin* (Poem of the Florins) in which he describes reading *Meliador* to the count; that for three months he (Froissart) read seven pages of *Meliador* to his host until he reached the end of the narrative. In the *Dit dou Florin* Froissart describes *Meliador* as complete, it is clear that the poem was finished before 1389. A more precise completion date can be fixed at 1383, when Wenceslaus died. In the *Dit*, Froissart implies that poem was finished shortly before or immediately after the death of Wenceslaus. Froissart was apparently hoping Gaston would replace the late Wenceslaus as his patron, but the Gaston does not offer to buy the poem he has just enjoyed listening to, although he does pay Froissart eight florins for the reading.

The plot of *Meliador* is even more complicated than its textual history. Some critics, including Longnon, the discoverer and first editor of the published *Meliador,* view the poem as overly discursive and as particularly lacking in organization. It is possible that the missing portion, which Longnon believed contained more than 2,700 verses, contained not only a summation of the major plot lines (which are several), but also served to resolve the apparent digressions by drawing them into a central theme. However, this possible summation remains speculation as long as the text remains incomplete. Given the rather surprising discovery of the *Meliador* manuscript at the Bibliothétique Nationale, it is not inconceivable that the missing conclusion will itself someday be discovered. Until then, readers of *Meliador* must make do with what is known. It is certainly not an easy poem to navigate or even to summarize.

At the center of *Meliador* is the practice of chivalry. Meliador is the title character and may be called the protagonist, but the poem often leaves him to focus on other figures. Personal valor, love, and the quest, are the primary themes of the poem. It begins with the dilemma of Hermondine, daughter of the King of Scotland, who is her father's only heir, and thus brings with her hand in marriage the entire kingdom. Froissart is less interested in the political problem of a king without a male heir, and more interested in the opportunity afforded him: the chance for the finest flower of Arthurian knighthood to prove themselves worthy of the hand of Hermondine and the crown of Scotland. Thus, Froissart creates a series of situations that allow chivalrous young men to test and display their mettle, much as he witnessed in reality during the Hundred Years' War. Meliador, son of the Duke of Cornwall, will eventually win the hand and the love of Hermondine, as well as the crown; in order to do so he proves himself to be the most chivalrous of knights. Froissart creates a foil for Meliador in Camel, who is the initial suitor of Hermondine and whose interest in the young princess forces her father to send out a call for all ambitious knights to compete. Camel is ardent in his desire for Hermondine, and expresses himself with typical Froissardian lyricism, but he is meant to represent an antichivalrous knight, unable to control either his emotions or even his own body (he suffers from sleepwalking, a sign of moral weakness in the fourteenth century).

If left there, with the Meliador-Hermondine-Camel plot, the poem would be fairly straightforward. A tournament is called, in which Meliador defeats Camel. But Froissart has more in mind. As he alludes to in the poem, the real goal is not Hermondine or even Scotland; it is reputation, and chivalrous glory. A much larger stage is necessary than just one tournament. The poem is arranged around a series of five tournaments, over the course of five years (one tournament per year), with the initial tournament in Scotland. The series is arranged by the king of Scotland and King Arthur. The tournaments, which are held in Scotland, Cornwall, and Camelot (the final tournament which was presumably described in the fifth, missing, book) were designed to identify the greatest knight in Europe. Meliador will win the title, although he does not participate in all the tournaments (such as the one in Cornwall). The two kings, Hermont of Scotland and Arthur of Brittany, represent the guardians and advocates of chivalry by sponsoring these tournaments and relying on their results for such an important decision as the future ruler of Scotland.

In addition to Meliador and Hermondine, other knights and ladies are paired up during the course of the tournaments. Love is presented as fairly simple in this poem, and without much tension or conflict. The focus of the poem is not a romance in the modern sense; it is more concerned with the military world of men (the jousting, the feats of arms, traveling) than the domestic world of marriage or even of women. Women do not seem to have much role to play in Froissart's writings in general; as befits their role in the courtly society, they are inspiration and ideals, not actors. Women may not be entirely passive figures in Froissart's poem (it is, in fact, a woman, Floree, the cousin of Hermondine, who arranges the tournament series), but they are certainly not the main players.

Further complicating the plot are the discursive journeys, including one fairly long, rambling, adventure between the second and third tournaments, in which Sagremor, the son of the King of Ireland, explores the realm of Arthur. The kingdom of Arthur is presented through the eyes of Sagremor, whose own land is wild, uncourtly, lacking the literate and scholarly character of Brittany, or even Cornwall or Scotland. The contrast is reinforced by Meliador's own adventures in Ireland. Sagremor and his adventures, in addition to affording Froissart yet another chance to promote chivalry as the most just system, are also used to describe the career opportunities available to the chivalrously inclined youth: the role of "chevaliers errans" (l. 3023), or knight errant. It is a reinforcement of the poem's youthful milieu; *Meliador* is not the story of Arthur but of the young knights who represent the future of his Round Table values, which Froissart had already praised in his *Chronicles*.

Meliador is also broken up by the inclusion of the *rondel*, a rhymed poem of approximately seven lines, which have been given to Froissart by his patron Wenceslaus. There are seventy-nine of Wenceslaus's *rondeaux* included in the extant *Meliador*. There are also several ballads and other lyrics by the duke in the poem. None of the Wenceslaus interpolations add significantly to the plot of *Meliador,* but they do function as a reminder of the courtly nature of this poetry, for all that the plot is concerned with adventures and chivalrous competitions. One might view the contribution of the *rondeaux* as creating ambiance for the poem as a whole. They can also be viewed as an homage to Wenceslaus, who played such a pivotal role in the existence of *Meliador*.

Finally, one needs to consider the geography of *Meliador*. Not surprisingly, it reflects the geography that Froissart was himself familiar with; most of the central action in the tournaments, takes place in locales that Froissart has had personal experience with. For instance, much of the poem takes place in Scotland, where Froissart had spent several months in 1365. He adds to this territory that others have described to him, or that do not need to be particularly realistic (such as the description of Ireland) because they represent nonchivalrous and thus "less real" lands. However, the geographic choices that Froissart makes are not simply a matter of convenience for the poet. By placing *Meliador* in the same physical space as his *Chronicles,* Froissart is alluding to the correlation between the mythological and the historical; for Froissart the figures of his own world are just as much part of the Arthurian cycle as the heroes of the Round Table. Both worlds are united by the code of chivalry.

All of Froissart's writings, especially the *Chronicles* and *Meliador,* reflect his confidence in the code of chivalry and the values of the noble court. His was a courtly world; he moved amongst the most refined and cultured nobles of his day, many of whom were poets and scholars themselves. Several became his employers and patrons; one at least (Wenceslaus, Duke of Brabant) would also be a contributor of verses to *Meliador,* Froissart's elegy to the nobility of the Arthurian mythology. This courtly milieu was obviously one in which Froissart was comfortable. The significance of chivalry to Froissart is reflected in his writings; by the way he describes the heroes of the Hundred Years' War, the heroes of the Arthurian tournament, and of his society in general. The heroes of *Meliador* are archetypes for the heroes Froissart will describe in his *Chronicles.*

PRIMARY WORKS

Ballades et rondeaux, ed. Rae S. Baudouin. Geneva: Droz, 1978; *Chronicles,* trans. Geoffrey Brereton. London: Penguin, 1978; *The Chronicles of Jean Froissart,* ed. and trans. Gillian Anderson and William Anderson. London, 1963; *Chroniques de France, d'Angleterre, d'Ecosse, de Bretagne, de Gascogne, de Flandre et lieux Circonvoisins.* There are a considerable number of printed editions of this work, although none are complete. The most significant French editions are: *Chroniques,* 4 vols. Paris: Antoine Verard, c. 1498. *Les Chroniques de sire Jean Froissart,* ed. J. A. C. Buchon, 3 vols. Paris: Pantheon Littéraire, 1824–1826. *Chroniques,* Livre I, 4 vols., ed. George Diller. Geneva: Textes Littéraires Francais, 1991–1993. **English editions:** *The First Volume of Syr Johan Froissart,* 2 vols., ed. and trans. John Bourchier Berners. London: Wyllyam Myddylton, 1545. *Chronicles,* 2 vols., ed. and trans. Thomas Johnes. London: 1801–1802; *"Dits" et "Débats,"* ed. A. Fourrier. Geneva: Droz, 1979; *L'Espinette Amoureuse,* ed. Anthime Fourrier. Paris: Klincksieck, 1974; *Froissart: Ballads and Other Poems,* ed. and trans. Philip Pendleton Cooke. Philadelphia: Carey & Hart, 1847; *Meliador,* 3 vols., ed. Auguste Honore Longnon. Paris: Firmin Didot, 1895–1899. Reprint, New York: Johnson Reprint, 1965; *Poesies,* ed. J. A. Buchon. Paris, 1829; *La Prison Amoureuse,* ed. and trans. Laurence de Looze. New York: Garland, 1994.

SECONDARY SOURCES

Ainsworth, P. F. *Jean Froissart and the Fabric of History: Truth, Myth, and Fiction in the Chroniques.* Oxford: Clarendon, 1990; Allmand, C. T. "Historians Reconsidered." *History Today* 16 (1966): 841–48; Bastin, Julia. *Froissart: Chroniquer, Romancier, et Poete.* Brussels: 1948; Cerquiglini-Toulet, Jacqueline. "Fullness and Emptiness: Shortages and Storehouses of Lyric Treasure in the Fourteenth and Fifteenth Centuries," trans. Christine Cano and John Jay Thompson. *Yale French Studies* 10 (1991): 224–39; Coulton, G. G. *The Chronicler of European Chivalry.* London: Studio, 1930; Darmesteter, Mary. *Froissart.* Paris: Hanchette, 1894; Dembowski, Peter. *Jean Froissart and His Meliador: Context, Craft, and Sense.* Lexington, KY: French Forum, 1983; ———. "*Meliador* de Jean Froissart, Son Importance Littéraire: Le Vrai dans la Fiction." *Etudes Francaises* 32 (1996): 7–19; Diller, George. "Froissart: Patrons and Text." In *Froissart: Historian,* ed. J. Palmer, 145–60. Woodbridge, UK: Boydell, 1981; ———. "Froissart's Chroniques, Knightly Adventures, and Warrior Forays: 'Que Chacun se Retire en sa Chascuniére.'" *Fifteenth-Century Studies* 12 (1987): 17–26; Diverres, A. H. "The Geography of Britain in Froissart's '*Meliador.*'" In *Medieval Miscellany,* ed. F. Whitehead, A. H. Diverres, and F. E. Sutcliffe, 97–112. Manchester, UK: Manchester University Press, 1965; ———. "The Two Versions of Froissart's *Meliador*." In *Studies in Medieval French Language and Literature*, ed. Sally Burch North, 37–48. Geneva: Droz, 1988; Huizinga, Johan. *The Waning of the Middle Ages*. New York: St. Martin's Press, 1924; Kelly, D., ed. *Medieval Imagination: Rhetoric and the Poetry of Courtly Love*. Madison: University of Wisconsin Press, 1978; Kilgour, Raymond Lincoln. *The Decline of Chivalry as Shown in the French Literature of the Late Middle Ages*. Cambridge, MA: Harvard University Press, 1937; Macaulay, G. *Chronicle and Romance: Froissart, Malory, and Holinshed*. New York: P. F. Collier, 1910; Saint-Leger, F. *Froissart and His Times*. London, 1832; Shears, F. S. *Froissart, Chronicler and Poet*. London: Routledge, 1930; Zink, M. *Froissart et le Temps*. Paris: Presses Universitaires de France, 1998; ———. "Littératures de la France Médiéval." *Annuaire du Collège de France* 96 (1996): 915–37.

Candace Gregory-Abbott

THE *GAWAIN*-POET
(fl. c. 1350–1400)

Scholars customarily refer to the anonymous writer of the four poems of the British Library Cotton Nero A.x. Article 3 manuscript as the "*Gawain*-Poet" or "*Pearl*-Poet." *Pearl*, *Patience*, *Cleanness* (or *Purity*), and *Sir Gawain and the Green Knight* rank among the finest literary achievements of late fourteenth-century England. However, unlike his great contemporaries Geoffrey Chaucer, William Langland, and John Gower, the *Gawain*-Poet exercised practically no influence on English literary tradition until the unique manuscript containing his work was rediscovered in the nineteenth century. These three contemporaries, who also wrote during the reign of King Richard II, the so-called Ricardian Age, appear to find Arthurian tradition remote and mostly irrelevant, even though French Arthurian romance was the most popular literary entertainment for the English aristocracy at this time. *Sir Gawain,* by contrast, ranks among the greatest monuments of Arthurian literary tradition, but despite many attempts no scholar has convincingly identified the *Gawain*-Poet, although scholars seem to agree that he was a man. Nor has it been possible to prove that the same person wrote all four poems in Cotton Nero A.x., though again most scholars strongly support the notion. This combination of circumstances sets the *Gawain*-Poet apart from all other major contributors to Arthurian legend. *Sir Gawain* is the only ostensibly Arthurian work among the four poems in the same manuscript, but many scholars regard these four poems as a single work. Cotton Nero A.x. Article 3, a quarto volume of vellum with writing by one hand in the dialect of the Northwest Midlands, is the only extant manuscript collection consisting entirely of Middle English poems and the earliest illuminated manuscript in Middle English; the twelve somewhat crude illustrations were added to the manuscript some time after the text was completed.

The features all four poems share support the theory of common authorship, contribute to an understanding of the anonymous author's life, and point to what makes *Sir Gawain* both similar to and distinct from other Arthurian texts. The arrangement of the poems in the manuscript—in the order *Pearl, Cleanness, Patience,* and *Sir Gawain*—follows a structural master plan. Each poem mirrors, as a kind of microcosm, the *mise en abyme* pattern of the entire manuscript, a pattern common in orally transmitted texts. *Mise en abyme* is the literary equivalent of the series of mirror images that appear over a range of scales when a viewer looks at the image of a mirror reflected in another mirror. The core of each individual poem in this manuscript, like the core of the manuscript considered as a whole (the central poems *Cleanness* and *Patience*), reflects an earlier literary tradition that the rest of the poem and manuscript frames in terms of more recent literary and cultural traditions. The two central poems, based primarily on the Old Testament, are framed by two poems based primarily on the New Testament. In each individual poem, earlier prosodic (verse), Arthurian, or theological traditions evoked by paraphrases or echoes of earlier texts are presented in terms of late fourteenth-century literature and culture. Each individual poem is triadic like the entire manuscript, which has two New Testament wings around an Old Testament core.

The circular form of each poem in the manuscript mirrors the circular arrangement of the four poems within the manuscript. In *From "Pearl" to "Gawain"* (1995), Robert J. Blanch and Julian N. Wasserman note that the events depicted in the poems, as arranged in the manuscript, together form a chronological circle. Likewise, the end of each individual poem in the manuscript echoes its beginning by way of repeating words and phrases. And similar links between the beginning and end of subsections of individual poems mirror the circular form of the manuscript and of the entire poems. This *mise en abyme* structure, also termed onion-skin, envelope, or fractal structure, as well as ring (annular) composition, helps performers memorize texts and helps audiences follow oral recitation of texts. Formal similarities, like similarities in theme, diction, imagery, and point of view, provide strong circumstantial evidence that the same person wrote all four poems.

An early theory holds that the same author also wrote an alliterative poem known as *Saint Erkenwald*, also written in the Northwest Midlands dialect, which survives uniquely in another manuscript, British Library manuscript Harley 2250. This theory is generally held to have been disproved by Larry D. Benson in "The Authorship of *St. Erkenwald*" (1965), though the attribution of the Cotton Nero A.x. poems to a John de Mascy or Hugh Mascy, based in part on perception of an anagram of the supposed author's name in *Saint Erkenwald*, temporarily revived it, and recent books by Jim Rhodes and John M. Bowers give attention to the poem.

Although many attempts have been made to identify the *Gawain*-Poet, none has convinced more than a handful of scholars; William Vantuono provides a concise overview of the ten or so identifications proposed thus far in his revised edition of *Sir Gawain* (1999). The most recent and most convincing theory attributes the four poems to a John de Mascy or Hugh Mascy, on the basis of a pun on the word *mascelle* and an acrostic signature in *Pearl*, an anagram in *St. Erkenwald*, perception of the signature "j. Macyh" in the marginal decoration of two folios, the superscript "Hugo de" in the upper margin of the recto of the first leaf of *Sir Gawain*, and other evidence. Vantuono notes that as a priest and civil servant, John de Mascy of Sale in Northern Cheshire, may have had the knowledge of theology and law evidenced in the four poems.

Michael J. Bennett's *Community, Class and Careerism: Cheshire and Lancashire Society in the Age of "Sir Gawain and the Green Knight"* (1983) discusses the dialect region, historical background, and probable life circumstances of the *Gawain*-Poet; like Bowers and Rhodes, Bennett focuses on how the poet sets older traditions within the late fourteenth-century. For Bowers, *Pearl* reflects the politics of the Ricardian court. For Rhodes, the works of this poet reflect late fourteenth-century theology, particularly the form it took in England.

Although no scholarly consensus links the manuscript to any one place within the Northwest Midlands counties of Lancashire, Derbyshire, Cheshire, and Staffordshire, recent studies most often mention Cheshire. The extant manuscript is not an autograph (original manuscript by the author), but the dialect of the author differs only slightly from that of the most recent copyist, suggesting that the author lived somewhat to the south of the scribe; the spelling of alliterating and rhyming words preserves features of the author's dialect that contrast with aspects of the scribe's dialect. The manuscript has been dated to about 1400. Because standard English today has its roots in the language of the south of England employed by Chaucer, the language of the *Gawain*-Poet now seems unfamiliar to most English speakers. The Northwest Midlands represented a border territory whose Middle English dialects reflect a variety of influences, including that of Norse diction, a survival from the Danish Viking conquests.

The poet was probably a cleric in minor orders, many of whom served as chaplains, scribes, and administrators to the nobility. At this time, some sort of clerical status was required to gain access to the institutions that provided education, but men could enter minor orders without being ordained as priests. At the conclusion of *Pearl*, the narrator refers to a priest in a way that suggests that he is not one. The *Pearl* dreamer appears to have had a daughter; members of minor orders could marry and have children. In the prologue of *Patience*, the narrator presents himself as a member of a congregation hearing a reading from the gospel rather than as a preacher, and he refers to the possibility of being sent to Rome by his liege lord, a frequent requirement of clerics in minor orders serving nobles. The narrator of the *Patience* prologue appears to address himself rather than address his audience from a position of authority. Readers have detected signs of male identity in the narrative voice of all four poems. His mastery of the Latin Vulgate translation of the Bible and of commentaries and contemporary sermons, especially as evidenced in *Cleanness*, suggests a clerical background; in *Cleanness* the narrator's reference to having read the work of "high clerks" (193) suggests that he is a cleric but not in major orders. (All translations from *Cleanness*, *Pearl*, and *Sir Gawain* are based on the most recent translation of each by Vantuono, and all *Patience* translations are by Borroff, 2001.) Without at least minor clerical status, the author would probably not have been exposed to the range of French and Italian secular literature whose influences have been detected in his work. His knowledge of secular culture makes it unlikely that the poet lived much or any of his life in a monastery.

Nowhere in his writings does the poet identify himself, his profession, or his environment, nor has any documentation of his life survived outside of Cotton Nero A.x. Based on the familiarity with court life evidenced in his poems, many early scholars presumed that the poet resided at a major aristocratic court in his own dialect region. In the *"Gawain"-Poet* (1956) Henry L. Savage speculates that the poet served under Enguerrand de Coucy, the French Earl of Bedford, who was brother-in-law of John of Gaunt, Duke of Lancaster. Elizabeth Salter suggests in *Fourteenth-Century English Poetry* (1983) that the poet was attached to the household of John of Gaunt at Clitheroe Castle.

In his book Bennett observes that few aristocrats resided for any length of time in the Northwest Midlands, and that the *Gawain*-Poet may have spent more time composing his works in a metropolitan setting than in a provincial setting. Many Cheshire and Lancashire retainers served at the court of Richard II in London, and the region provided many soldiers for the Hundred Years' War and many of the clerks who performed scribal and administrative duties in London at this time. The poet appears to have been exposed to continental texts, whose influence in England is not thought to have reached beyond London. Some early scholars presumed that *Sir Gawain* was a translation of a lost French original. But the *Gawain*-Poet reflects a convergence of Anglo-Saxon, Celtic, and continental traditions, as well as the increasingly urbane culture that characterized Ricardian English literature. And his poetry distinguishes itself from that of his contemporaries by borrowing extensively from a variety of dialects—including French, Anglo-Norman, northern English, and Old Norse—to create an artificial poetic language unlike any spoken dialect.

Perhaps the poet had so little influence on subsequent literary tradition because the high status Cheshire retainers enjoyed under Richard II vanished suddenly after Henry IV usurped the throne in 1399. Some readers detect echoes of *Sir Gawain* in the work of Cheshire poet Humphrey Newton, and a fifteenth-century reworking of the basic plot of *Sir Gawain* entitled *The Grene Knight* has survived. The first known owner of the Cotton Nero A.x. manuscript is Henry Savile of Banke; later it passed into the library of Sir Robert Cotton, which was acquired by the British Museum in 1753. In 1824 the poet's work is first brought to public attention in a footnote by editor Richard Price in Thomas Warton's *History of English Poetry*.

The meter of all four poems by the *Gawain*-Poet is mostly a Middle English survival of Old English (Anglo-Saxon) alliterative meter. Like Old English verse, Middle English alliterative verse is accentual, not syllabic: a line of verse is determined by the number of stressed (tonic) syllables, not the total number of stressed and unstressed syllables. Unlike the syllabic verse that Chaucer established as the norm for English poetry, lines of alliterative verse do not each contain a fixed number of metrical "feet" with the same combination of stressed and unstressed syllables. Each line of Old and Middle English alliterative verse usually contains four stressed syllables and a variable number of unstressed syllables. Each line of Old English verse is divided by a caesura, or pause, such that each half-line contains two stressed syllables. In Old English verse, usually the two stressed syllables of the first half-line and the first stressed syllable of the second half-line alliterate; that is, all three begin with the same consonant or with a vowel. The so-called "alliterative long lines" of most Middle English alliterative verse are longer and more flexible than lines of Old English poetry; the caesura is often less pronounced and alliteration is less regular but often more frequent. The alliterative long lines of *Cleanness* and *Patience* adhere most closely to Anglo-Saxon verse forms, but their arrangement in four-line syntactic units recalls continental quatrains. The alliterative scheme is subordinated to a continental, syllabic rhyme scheme in *Pearl*'s twelve-line stanzas. The verse form of *Sir Gawain* falls somewhere in between: its alliterative long lines form stanzas of varying length, each of which concludes with five shorter alliterative lines known as a "bob and wheel," which rhyme in the scheme *ababa*. All four poems in Cotton Nero A.x. show strong influence from numerological patterns then popular in continental verse.

The poet employs technical jargon from a variety of fields, including nautical language in *Patience*, legal and mercantile language in *Sir Gawain*, and theological language in *Pearl*. In *The "Gawain" Country* (1984), R. W. V. Elliott documents the poet's mastery of local vocabulary, often influenced by Old Norse, for geographical features of the Northwest Midlands, the setting of *Sir Gawain*. Another important feature of the poet's diction is his tendency to use many of the same leitwords (e.g., *cortaysye*, *trawþe*, and *clannesse*), recurring key words whose semantic range underscores the poems' main themes and the poems' relationship to each other.

The genres of the four poems represent another way in which the author transforms old forms into new forms. Each of the four poems appears to represent an original poetic genre composed of a hybrid of traditional genres.

It has not been possible to determine conclusively the order of composition of the four Cotton Nero A.x. poems. This essay considers the poems in this order: *Patience*, *Cleanness*, *Pearl*, and *Sir Gawain*. This arrangement presumes that *Patience* and *Cleanness* are both inferior and therefore earlier poems (although there is no consensus on which of the two was written first) and that *Sir Gawain*, as the poet's masterpiece, is most likely to have been written last.

Patience has the same structure as the other three Cotton Nero A.x. poems. The first line of *Patience* is repeated with slight variation in the last line, and parallels among three main settings mirror the circular form of the entire poem and manuscript.

Scholars have long applied to *Patience* the genre labels verse homily (sermon in the form of poetry) and biblical paraphrase. *Patience* resembles medieval sermons featuring a prologue followed by an *exemplum*, a narrative illustrating the moral teaching of the prologue. The prologue of *Patience* stresses the importance of the virtue of patience, and most of the fifty-three-line poem paraphrases the Old Testament story of Jonah, which may serve as a so-called negative *exemplum*, highlighting Jonah's lack of patience.

The three main settings within the exemplum are the ship Jonah boards to sail to Tarshish after God commands him to go to Ninevah, the whale that swallows Jonah after the sailors throw him overboard, and the booth Jonah builds for himself outside of Ninevah after the Ninevites repent in response to his prophesying. All three main settings are enclosing spaces that serve as shelters, and within all three Jonah encounters a shelter-within-a-shelter. The narrator specifically compares the *hyrne* (nook) within the ship, where Jonah falls asleep, to the *hyrne*, where Jonah takes refuge within the belly of the whale (178, 289–93). After God commands a gourd to grow and provide shade over the booth, the booth also functions as a shelter-within-a-shelter. These three enclosures-within-an-enclosure mirror the enclosing (circular) structure of the entire poem and manuscript on a smaller scale.

The prologue conflates the versions of the Beatitudes in the gospels of Matthew and Luke, underscoring the special relationship Augustine perceives between the first and last Beatitudes in order to highlight the interdependence of patience and poverty. Beginnings and endings are "fashioned in one form, the first and the last" (38); the form of the poem thus mirrors New Testament texts as well.

Unlike its biblical sources, *Patience* features a first-person narrator, and unlike most medieval sermons, *Patience* focuses more on achieving contentment in this world than on salvation. The poet's choice of Jonah as a negative exemplar for a sermon about patience has no theological precedent; much more consistent with medieval theology would have been the choice of Job as a positive exemplar of patience. The poet thus offers a fresh perspective on a time-honored virtue, but his portrayal of Jonah as a type of Christ and Everyman reflects traditional interpretation of the biblical source.

Cleanness, encompassing 1,812 lines, was long considered a poetic failure, a loosely organized collection of biblical paraphrases, but recent scholars find much to admire in *Cleanness*. Like *Patience*, it is a verse homily and biblical paraphrase, a sermon that features narrative *exempla*. As in *Patience*, *Cleanness* centers on a virtue denoted by the key word editors have adopted as the title, the prologue paraphrases New Testament material to introduce that virtue, and paraphrased Old Testament narrative in the form of a negative *exemplum* features behavior that contrasts with that virtue. As in *Patience*, in

Cleanness the prologue paraphrases the New Testament Beatitudes, though here the central virtue derives from the sixth Beatitude in the gospel of Matthew: "Blessed are the clean at heart: for they shall see God." The prologue to *Cleanness* also paraphrases the parable of the wedding feast in the gospels of Matthew and Luke.

In "The Architectonics of *Cleanness*" (1993), Donna Crawford discerns mathematically precise relationships among manuscript divisions based on the golden section, a ratio that underlies the geometry of the pentangle in *Sir Gawain*. The triadic annular form shared by all four poems was first identified in *Cleanness*, where it is most obvious. The title of Israel Gollancz's early edition of *Cleanness* (1921) calls attention to the triadic form of the poem, as do the concluding lines of the poem. William Vantuono first identifies the "triple-three structure for *Cleanness*" in *Manuscripta* (1984). Instead of the single Old Testament negative *exemplum* in *Patience*, *Cleanness* features three groups of Old Testament negative *exempla*, each of which contains one major *exemplum* and two minor *exempla* related in some way to the major *exemplum*. The three major *exempla* are based, respectively, on the Genesis accounts of the Flood and of the destruction of Sodom and Gomorrah, and on the account of Belshazzar's feast in Daniel. The first two minor *exempla* are the stories of the fall of Lucifer and of the fall of Adam, which chronologically precede the major *exemplum* of the Flood. The second two minor *exempla* contain the story of God's visit to Abraham and Sarah and the story of Lot and his family, which precede the major *exemplum* of the destruction of the two cities. The minor *exempla* of the third group which recounts Nebuchadnezzer's seizure of the Temple vessels and of his subsequent conversion and death, frame the major *exemplum* of Belshazzar's feast and death. The triadic form of the poem extends to at least one of its *exempla*: as W. A. Davenport observes in *The Art of the "Gawain"-Poet* (1978), the story of Lot contains three distinct scenes.

The link between the opening and closing lines of *Cleanness* is less obvious than that in the other three poems in the manuscript. Jane K. Lecklider notes in *"Cleanness": Structure and Meaning* (1997) that the poem begins and ends with liturgical material used at Advent, and that the whole poem is patterned on the structure of the liturgical year. This annular form based on the liturgical year resembles that of *Sir Gawain*, whose beginning and ending are associated with the Feast of Circumcision, and of *Pearl*, which begins and ends on the same "hy_ seysoun" (39), probably the Feast of Lammas (August 1).

As in the poet's other works, in *Cleanness* diction underlies form. The semantic range of *clannesse* (and its opposite, *fylthe*) expands in the course of the poem. The *fayre formes* of *clannesse* are contrasted with their opposite, *kark and combraunce huge* ("great distress and disaster," 3–4), much as *trawpe* and *untrawpe* are contrasted in *Sir Gawain* (all quotations from Cotton Nero A.x. based on revised edition by Andrew and Waldron, 1987). In the prologue of *Cleanness*, the sixth Beatitude refers to being clean "in the heart," but the parable of the wedding feast that follows emphasizes the cleanliness of clothing and of the outside of the body: the laborer who arrives at the feast with soiled garments is cast into prison. The allegorical significance of the wedding feast as a story about the relationship between God and humankind bears on the transitional passages between the three groups of *exempla*; each transition returns to the image of God as king in a court, and to *clannesse* as a prerequisite to seeing God (545–600, 1049–1148). The stories of Adam's fall, the Flood, and Sodom extend the concept of cleanliness to include sexual purity. The story of Adam's fall also focuses on obedience as a form of *clannesse*, as do the stories of Lucifer's defeat and of Lot's wife. In the third group of *exempla*, the accounts of the seizure of the sacred temple vessels by Nebuchadnezzar and of their subsequent defilement by Belshazzar further extend the semantic range of this key word. *Trawþe* recurs in connection with *clannesse* throughout *Cleanness*: those who fail to maintain *trawþe* include the protagonists of the six minor exempla: Lucifer, Adam, Sarah, Lot's wife, Zedekiah, and Nebuchadnezzar. The fusion of narratives sharing similar themes in *Cleanness* anticipates the fusion of folk motifs (beheading game, temptation, exchange of winnings) in *Sir Gawain*; and the fusion of homily with biblical paraphrase and other genres in *Cleanness*, as in *Patience*, anticipates the fusion of literary genres in *Pearl* and *Sir Gawain*.

The poet expands a great deal on his biblical sources in his detailed description of humans and animals drowned in the Flood (372–434) and of the destruction of Sodom and Gomorrah (890–972, 1001–48). The added details seem designed to evoke reader sympathy for the suffering of sinners not favored by an authoritative God, and are consistent with late-fourteenth century conceptions of authority reflected in *Pearl* and *Sir Gawain*. The poet's handling of the wedding feast in the introduction similarly evokes readers' sympathy for the guest who is condemned for wearing inappropriate clothing.

Pearl begins with the male narrator grieving the loss of his "pearl" in the garden where he lost it. After falling asleep on a mound or hill within that garden, he dreams that he is moving through a landscape that features the trees, singing birds, and streams that often appear in medieval portrayals of earthly paradise. But this paradise is unnatural compared to standard medieval portrayals; the birds are colored in flaming hues, the trees are indigo blue with leaves like polished silver, and the gravel underfoot consists of pearls. This paradise may also be regarded as a stylized version of the earthly garden where the dreamer sleeps. When he reaches the stream, he sees a young maiden adorned with a crown and pearls on the other side. The two characters then engage in a long dialogue that addresses, among other issues, her identity (Is she the pearl he lost?) and her status in heaven. The dreamer is then granted a vision of the New Jerusalem on a hill on the other side of the stream, an even more stylized and unnatural version of the first two gardens, in which the maiden appears among 144,000 maidens worshiping the Lamb of God. When the dreamer attempts to cross the stream, he awakens back in the initial earthly garden setting.

As in the other poems, annular form in *Pearl* is triadic, featuring three main settings. Because the first dream landscape is contained, in effect, within the head of the dreamer sleeping in the initial earthly garden setting, Andrew concludes in *New Perspectives* (2000) that it is a setting-within-a-setting, and that the New Jerusalem serves as a setting-within-a-setting-within-a-setting because the dreamer views it from a position within the first dream landscape. The structure of the text itself is annular: The first line of *Pearl*, "Perle pleasaunte, to prynces paye," is echoed by the final line, "Ande precious perlez vnto His pay." The opening and concluding passages, set in the initial earthly garden, enclose passages that describe the two dream settings, which together bracket a long dialogue between dreamer and maiden, which in turn encloses a paraphrase of the vineyard parable from the gospel of Matthew. The annular form of *Pearl* mirrors the biblical source reworked at its core: the maiden paraphrases the principle that "the first shall be last" in the vineyard parable from Matthew's gospel to explain how a girl who like herself dies as an infant can have equal status with the Virgin Mary and others who died at a later age. The pearl maiden recalls Matilda and Beatrice in cantos 18–31 of *Purgatorio* and canto 1 of *Paradiso*; the form of *Pearl* and the other poems by this poet resembles the triadic annular design of Dante's *Divine Comedy*.

As with the other poems in its manuscript, generic classification of *Pearl* has presented problems. Early *Pearl* scholars argued vigorously about which of two generic labels best suits the poem: elegy, written by a father for a dead infant, or allegory. Today scholars most often classify *Pearl* as a dream vision. In *The Realism of Dream Visions* (1967), Constance B. Hieatt identifies triadic ring composition as the basic structure of dream vision, which portrays the stages of increasing abstraction humans experience as they undergo platonic reversion or Christian resurrection. The paraphrase of the dream vision of the Apocalypse on which the second dream landscape is based, like the paraphrase of the vineyard parable from Matthew, provides an ancient prototype for the form of *Pearl*.

Like the other poems *Pearl* offers a late fourteenth-century perspective on older traditions. Its alliterative scheme is incorporated within a metrical form much more continental than the alliterative long lines of the other three poems: ballade stanzas of twelve iambic tetrameter lines with the end-rhyme scheme *ababbcbccdcd*. Its elaborate numerical design also reflects continental poetic fashion. Stanzas are arranged into groups of five (except for one group containing six), with a total of 101 stanzas and 1,212 lines. Bowers traces parallels between the paraphrase of the vineyard parable in *Pearl* and wage issues that resulted from the labor shortage after the Black Plague. Within the dialogue of *Pearl*, Rhodes traces influence from challenges to theological orthodoxy mounted by the Lollards, followers of John Wycliff. Richard II showed great interest in fine craftsmanship and luxurious display, and appears to have been especially fond of pearls; the dreamer's craft in *Pearl* puts him in opposition to the Lollards, who urged that all luxury crafts should be abolished.

Although the influence of *Sir Gawain* on Arthurian legend has been minimal, its ability to assimilate many aspects of that legend with much that is peculiar to the late fourteenth century establishes *Sir Gawain* as a landmark in Arthurian tradition. An acquaintance with the other poems in its manuscript makes it easier to identify both what *Sir Gawain* has in common with the rest of Arthurian literary tradition and what makes this poet's take on Arthurian tradition distinctive.

In *Sir Gawain* the classic quest structure of Arthurian courtly romance is of a piece with the triadic annular form evident in the poet's other works, so the *Gawain*-Poet serves as an especially important guide to the relationship between Arthurian romance and other genres. Though *Sir Gawain* has long been admired for its formal intricacy, its master plan or deep structure resembles the structures from oral tradition incorporated into the poet's other works. Its preoccupation with annular form at a thematic level is reflected in the narrator's warning to Gawain that "Þe forme to þe fynisment foldez ful selden" ("The beginning and the end accord hardly ever," 499), and at a symbolic level in the circular images of the pentangle and green girdle. Like the three other poems, *Sir Gawain* has three main settings—Camelot, Bertilak's Castle, and the Green Chapel— each of which is identified with a separate quest. The narrator indicates early in the poem that it is intended for oral performance (30–32). Most editions of the text follow Frederick Madden, its first editor, in dividing the text into four "fitts," but Vantuono divides it into three parts. The fact that the *Sir Gawain* text features nine large manuscript initials is consistent with a triadic scheme.

The basic design of *Sir Gawain*, like that of other Arthurian romances, is the quest: a knight-errant (Gawain) moves from the court to the otherworld in order to fulfill an obligation, then returns to the court. In the course of a series of trials that test the martial abilities and virtue of its knightly representative, the reputation of the Arthurian court is tested as well. Many scholars believe that the basic form of the classic Arthurian romances by Chrétien, Hartmann von Aue, and others is a double quest: from court to otherworld to court to otherworld to court. In *Sir Gawain* the classic double quest is assimilated to the tripartite ring structure of the poet's other works.

In an elaborated version of the verbal parallels that link the very first and very last lines of *Patience* and *Pearl*, the last several lines of *Sir Gawain* feature a series of echoes of the first several lines in reverse order. Discussed by Dale B. J. Randall in *Modern Language Notes* (1957), it creates an entire sequence of concentric rings at the edges of the text; the opening and concluding references to the Trojan prehistory of the tale are a standard Arthurian feature. This device exemplifies the general tendency in *Sir Gawain* to elevate the form it shares with the other three poems to a greater level of complexity, one of the features that suggest *Sir Gawain* was composed last. Martin Camargo's description of the triadic annular form of *Sir Gawain* in *Comparative Research* (1987) is consistent with the tendency in *Sir Gawain* to offer more complex versions of the form of the other poems. Camargo identifies a different quest with each of the three main settings. He argues that medieval audiences would first perceive in the set of parallels between the first two settings the traditional structure of the double quest and then, as a third set of parallels associated with the third setting emerged, the audience would be surprised to discover that the poem contains three quests.

The action begins with a New Year's Feast at King Arthur's court at Camelot. In a gesture familiar from the First Continuation of *Perceval* and other Arthurian romances, a youthful Arthur insists that some marvel take place before he eats. Immediately after, the Green Knight enters the hall on horseback. He is large ("half-giant," 140), and he and his horse are elegantly attired: his body, his attire, his horse, and his horse's attire are green. He proposes a game, an exchange of blows: He will allow a member of Arthur's court to attempt to cut off his head with one blow with the axe, if that same knight will submit his neck to a similar blow by the Green Knight himself one year later. Arthur begins to accept the challenge, but Gawain then asks and is given leave to represent the court in this contest. Gawain beheads the challenger with one blow, the challenger retrieves his head, and the head speaks, instructing Gawain to meet him at the Green Chapel in a year to receive a return blow to the neck. Thus ends the first quest.

After the passing of the seasons is described (a traditional topos in French romance) comes the account of the sad day of Gawain's departure to fulfill his agreement. Passages describing the season (500–533), Gawain's commitment to action (534–49), and a criticism of that commitment (550–65, 672–86) parallel similar passages in the first quest (respectively, 60–84, 85–106, and again 85–106), suggesting the beginning of a second quest structurally similar to the first one. Here the extended description of the arming of Gawain (566–669) parallels the extended description of the Green Knight (136–220); both descriptions subdivide into passages featuring the hero's attire, horse, and one or more talismans. The arming of the hero and lamented departure is another topos from French romance. The Green Knight's talismans are a holly bob and an axe adorned with green lace; Gawain's talisman is his shield, featuring an image of the Virgin on the inside and a pentangle, whose significance receives minute attention, on the outside. (The elaborate description of the pentangle has no precedent in romances the poet is likely to have read.) Gawain departs, rides to the northwest through a harsh wintry landscape to Wales and then through the wilderness of Wirral, engaging a variety of natural and supernatural enemies in battles merely mentioned in passing, but no one he asks can tell him where the Green Knight and his chapel are located (701–24). On Christmas Eve, he prays to the Virgin for some refuge where he may hear Mass and matins the next morning, promising to recite the Paternoster, Ave Maria, and Creed, and crying. After he crosses himself three times, he sees an imposing castle (763–803); the description of this first glimpse is traditional in French romance. He approaches the castle and is received with great honor by its inhabitants (again a romance topos, which typically includes an elegant robe for the knight and provision for the horse)—notably, its lord Bertilak, Bertilak's beautiful lady, and an unidentified old crone of high status (807–1104); these passages parallel the arrival of the Green Knight at Camelot (134, 221–31) and the welcome he receives there (232–55). The ensuing feast has precedents in English romance. In response to Gawain's query, Bertilak tells Gawain that the Green Chapel is nearby, and invites Gawain to remain at his castle until New Year's Day.

To help pass the last three days before New Year's Day, Gawain agrees to take part in an "exchange of winnings" game proposed by Bertilak: each day Gawain will rest in the castle while Bertilak hunts outdoors, and at the end of each day the two will exchange whatever they may have acquired that day. Like Arthur, Bertilak entertains a guest and presides over a Christmas game. Gawain does not realize that the outcome of the beheading game of the first quest depends on the outcome of this game. Each of the three days of the test has three parts: the early morning hunt by Bertilak and his men, which resembles hunting scenes in many English romances, a visit to Gawain's bedroom by Bertilak's lady in which she attempts to seduce Gawain, and a return to the hunting scene in which the slaying and dismemberment of the prey is described. At the end of the first day, Gawain exchanges a kiss he received from the lady for the carcass of a deer, and on the second day he exchanges the two kisses he received for the carcass of a boar. On the third day Gawain fails to hand over the green girdle he received from the lady in exchange for the carcass of a fox, presumably because the lady told him it would protect his life. Like the first quest, this one ends with a recapitulation of the bargain (2345–68) and Gawain's departure (2471–78). Andrew (2000) explains that the bedroom and outdoor scenes each function as settings-within-a-setting (the main setting being the castle and its surrounding land), like the settings-within-settings in *Patience* and *Pearl*. Like *Pearl*, *Sir Gawain* features extensive dialogue between male and female characters in a setting-within-a-setting, the castle bedroom. Later, Gawain confesses to the chaplain at Hautdesert without mentioning his deception of Bertilak.

Camargo identifies Gawain's adventure at the Green Chapel on New Year's Day as the third quest, whose components create parallels with the first two quests. A description of the season (1998–2005) and of Gawain's commitment to action (2006-8) as well as a criticism of that commitment (2089–2155) parallel the first three components of the first two quests. Parallels with the second quest include: a three-part arming sequence featuring attire (2015–29), horse (2047–50), and talisman (green girdle, 2030–42); Gawain's departure from the apparent security of Bertilak's castle (2060–76); his journey over harsh terrain on the way to the Green Chapel (2077–88); and his prayer prior to arrival (2156–59). His arrival at the Green Chapel (2160–2216) and welcome by the Green Knight (2217–44) parallel the arrival and welcome in the prior quests. The triadic form of the test here recalls the triadic test of the second quest, the three days of temptation at Bercilak's castle: When Sir Gawain lowers his head to receive the blow he owes his challenger as part of the beheading contest, the Green Knight makes two feinted blows with the axe before making a slight nick on Gawain's neck with a third blow. The Green Knight then reveals that he is Bertilak in an enchanted form made possible by Morgan la Fay, whom he reveals to be the revered crone at his castle; she devised this test in an attempt to sully the reputation of Arthur's court. The Green Knight also reveals that the outcome of the beheading contest has depended on Gawain's conduct during the three days of the exchange of winnings at his castle. The two feints with the axe reward Gawain for upholding his end of the bargain on the first two days, and the nick on his neck represents a mild punishment for withholding the green girdle from Bertilak on the third day. The punishment is mild because Gawain violated their agreement in an attempt to save his own life. Gawain responds with a brief misogynistic tirade, citing ancient and biblical women famous for having attempted to bring a man down; similar tirades by Gawain occur in *Le chevalier à l'épée* and *La vengeance Raguidel*. Gawain also confesses to Bertilak his failure to uphold his end of their bargain, a parallel to the confession at Hautdesert. These lines (2331–2470) parallel the recapitulation element in the prior two quests, as does Gawain's subsequent departure (2471–78) for Camelot, which follows his polite refusal of Bertilak's invitation to rejoin him at Bertilak's castle. Gawain's return to Camelot at the same season with which the poem began at Camelot brings the poem full circle. Gawain announces that henceforth he will wear the green girdle as a reminder of his failure to uphold *trawþe* in the exchange of winnings game, but the other members of the court receive him with great joy and honor, and all resolve likewise to wear the girdle themselves.

As in the poet's other works, the tripartite annular form of *Sir Gawain* establishes relationships with a variety of older traditions. By the late fourteenth century, the beheading contest and the temptation had long pedigrees as plot devices, but *Sir Gawain* is the first work known to combine these two with the plot device of the exchange of winnings; the seamless integration of these three devices contributes to the triadic patterning in the text. The parallels between the elements of the first and third quests, which constitute the beheading game, in turn invoke parallels with the elements of the second quest, which constitutes the temptation and exchange of winnings.

The first known appearance of the beheading game is in the eighth-century Old Irish *Bricriu's Feast*. In the two versions of this game it contains, the hero Cuchulainn, his older brothers, and a courtier are challenged to an exchange of blows by a shapeshifter in the form of a *bachlach*, or boorish lout, an Irish word that reminds R. Loomis of the name Bertilak (or Bercilak) in *Celtic Myth* (1927). The challenger is decapitated, walks away with his head, and returns the next day with his head restored to its place. Cuchulainn is proclaimed champion after he, unlike the other characters, keeps his part of the "champion's bargain," receiving feinted blows from the challenger's axe. In the second episode, there are three feints of the axe as in *Sir Gawain*. Like Gawain, Cuchulainn is a king's sister's son identified symbolically with the sun. The beheading game is one of many Celtic influences transmitted to Arthurian romance by way of traveling Breton storytellers, who adapted Celtic myth to courtly taste in France, England, and elsewhere in Europe. The plot of *Bricriu's Feast* survives in various Arthurian romances. Probably the *Gawain*-Poet is most familiar with the version in the First Continuation of Chrétien's *Lancelot*. In it, Caradoc beheads a challenger in Arthur's court after Arthur announces that he is waiting for a marvel to happen, and Caradoc must by contract endure a blow from the same stranger one year later at the same location. The challenger is a tall knight, not a huge and ugly churl. The challenge is accepted by just Caradoc, rather than the three successive heroes of the Irish version; Caradoc, like Gawain, is Arthur's nephew and accepts the challenge after protesting his unworthiness. Like *Sir Gawain*, this French romance mentions the grief the court feels for the hero and requires the hero to wait a year rather than a day to fulfill the contract. The challenger, whom Caradoc discovers to be his enchanter father, strikes his blow with the flat side of his sword. Another French romance, *Perlesvaus*, also offers parallels to the beheading game in *Sir Gawain*, but the protagonist is Lancelot and the setting is Waste City. In *Perlesvaus*, as in *Sir Gawain*, the challenger sharpens his axe with a whetstone, and the hero is rebuked for shrinking from the blow. Gawain first appears under his own name in Caradoc's role in *La mule sanz frain*. In *Hunbaut* Gawain faces another churl in a beheading contest, but avoids having to receive his own blow by holding his challenger's body away from its severed head until it dies.

The temptation is also a familiar plot in Arthurian romance. In French romance, often a daughter or wife of the host attempts to seduce their knightly guest, and as in *Sir Gawain*, often an ulterior motive underlies the attempt. In Ulrich von Zatzikhoven's *Lanzelet*, translated into German from Anglo-Norman shortly after 1194, the daughter of a forester visits her father's guests as they lie in bed, and there are three successive temptations; like Bertilak's wife, she makes the offer of a ring, but in this story the temptress acts on her own free will and her advances are accepted. *Lanzelet* also contains a challenge that resembles the beheading contest. In the Old French Vulgate *Lancelot*, an enchantress attempts to seduce the hero three times without success, then sends a younger version of herself for another three attempts; these two female characters may parallel the two hostesses at Hautdesert. In *Hunbaut*, a host encourages Gawain to kiss the host's daughter after the daughter flirts with Gawain. In *Le chevalier à l'épée*, Gawain receives a light sword wound to the skin, like that Gawain receives from the Green Knight, after his host offers a night with his daughter in an enchanted bed along with a warning about the sword. The hero of the Anglo-Norman *Yder* agrees with a king that he must resist the advances of the queen in order to be knighted, and does so by kicking her in the stomach. The Old French *Perlesvaus* also contains a version of the temptation. Like the beheading game, the temptation has Celtic origins. The earliest surviving medieval version that parallels that in *Sir Gawain* occurs in the eleventh-century "Pwyll, Prince of Dyfed" in the Welsh *Mabinogi*; the story serves as the nearest Celtic parallel to the temptation in *Sir Gawain*, but could not have directly influenced *Sir Gawain*. In it, the otherworld king and hunter Arawn arranges for Pwyll to lie with Arawn in the shape of Arawn's wife every night for a year to test Pwyll's chastity and loyalty. Pwyll, like Gawain, meets a supernatural challenger at a water crossing after one year; Pwyll's chastity ensures his success at that meeting. Arawn, like the Green Knight, is the same color as his horse, in this case gray; R. Loomis (1927) argues that the green color of challenger and horse in *Sir Gawain* derives from the Irish word for the color gray. In the fifteenth-century Middle English *Sir Gawain and the Carl of Carlisle*, the host places Gawain in bed with the host's wife, demands that he kiss her three times but do nothing more, and rewards him for his obedience with the host's daughter. *Lanzelet*, *Hunbaut*, *Le chevalier à l'épée*, and *Sir Gawain and the Carl of Carlisle* bring motifs of beheading and sexual temptation together in some fashion without integrating them as seamlessly as *Sir Gawain*.

Scholars usually cite only one literary antecedent for the exchange of winnings game, in the twelfth-century Latin *Miles gloriosus*; the Latin poem appears to have more in common with French *fabliau* than with courtly romance, just as the three bedroom scenes in *Sir Gawain* contain *fabliau* elements. No such bargain is involved in the other versions of the temptation. Plot devices from aristocratic romance are thus seamlessly integrated with a plot from the bawdy genre of *fabliau*.

While the earliest scholarship on the relationship between *Sir Gawain* and French Arthurian literature focused primarily on French antecedents of the beheading game and the temptation, more recently (1995) in *"Sir Gawain"* Ad Putter has related the poem much more broadly to French antecedents. Putter focuses particularly on concerns with manners and interpersonal relations and on a common stock of motifs and conventions *Sir Gawain* shares with earlier French romances. As in those romances, the setting of *Sir*

Gawain contrasts wilderness and civilization, and its aristocratic characters practice a complex etiquette and possess a knowledge of romance tradition, evidenced in their conversations about the conventions of that tradition.

Another important body of scholarship relating *Sir Gawain* to broader Arthurian tradition focuses on the evolution of the character Gawain, the most popular hero in that tradition. He is a major hero in early Celtic texts; the story of Culhwch and Olwen in the *Mabinogi* says Gawain never returned home without having achieved the quest he sought, and he is associated with the Welsh Gwalchmei in the *Triads*. Gawain is also an important figure in the early chronicles. William of Malmesbury refers to Gawain's renown as a strong warrior, his decisive characteristic in early chronicle tradition, and the fact that he is Arthur's sister's son. According to Geoffrey of Monmouth, Gawain leads a delegation to the Roman emperor and commands the forces against Mordred, his brother. The Anglo-Norman *Brut* by Wace joins the other chronicles in praising Gawain's strength in battle, but Wace also introduces Gawain's reputation as a lover. Wace has Gawain speak of the superiority of love over war as knightly activities; Layamon omits this aspect of Gawain's character in adapting Wace to create an English *Brut*. Wace also treats Gawain's reputation for courtesy in terms of his service as a page to the Pope Sulpicius. At the beginning of Arthurian romance tradition in French and Anglo-Norman, Gawain represents an ideal with which other characters, including the title characters of Chrétien's romances, are compared. The two main characteristics for which he is most consistently praised in this early tradition are his prowess in battle and his ideal status as a lover.

In romance tradition, Gawain's status as ideal lover inspires some maidens to create images of him in their bedroom to worship. In *Hunbaut*, a *chatelaine* has installed in her bedroom a statue of Gawain so lifelike that when Kay sees it he swears it is Gawain. In the First Continuation of *Perceval*, the Pucele de Lis has a wall-hanging embroidered with scenes from Gawain's life running all around her bedroom; when Gawain arrives, she has him remove his armor and only surrenders herself because he resembles the embroidered images. In some instances, Gawain's physical presence is no match for women's idealized image of him. In *La vengeance Raguidel*, a lady Gawain previously disdained prepares a trap to kill him, but when he appears she spares him because she does not recognize him. In *Li chevalier às deus éspées*, when a girl's parents bring an unknown knight to her bed as a reward for his services, she protests that she has reserved her virginity for Gawain; when the knight, who is in love with her, reveals himself to be Gawain, she refuses to believe him and he spends the night in bed with her to no avail. At a later meeting with Gawain, the girl says she did not believe him to be Gawain that night because Gawain would never be so discourteous as to let a woman escape his advances. In the bedroom at Hautdesert in *Sir Gawain*, likewise, Bertilak's wife suggests that if Gawain were really who he says he is, he would not refuse her advances, but Gawain's association with the chastity of the Virgin Mary (painted on the inside of his shield in *Sir Gawain*) is at odds with most of Arthurian tradition. In early Arthurian romance, Gawain is also a paragon of courtesy; in *Sir Gawain*, he confronts the Green Knight only after asking permission to leave his place at the table (343–46) and after expressing his own unworthiness for the task (354–55). He also asks that he be pardoned if he has misspoken in any way (360–61). When he arrives at Hautdesert, its residents expect him to teach them refined manners and speech, especially "love-talking" (916–17).

In *Arthurian Literature* (Loomis, 1959) Robert W. Ackerman notes that English romances featuring Gawain as hero evidence more independence from early French romances than English romances featuring other heroes; he divides the English Gawain poems into three overlapping groups, with an obvious bearing on *Sir Gawain*. One group features the decapitation of a main character. In *The Carl of Carlisle*, Gawain breaks a spell that had turned a man into a hideous giant by courteously obeying the host giant's requests to throw a spear at him, kiss his wife three times but no more (the temptation described earlier), spend the night with his daughter, and cut off his head. In *The Turk and Gawain*, an enchanted knight in the form of a dwarf similarly challenges Gawain to behead him to break a spell.

A second group of English Gawain romances concerns itself with the performance of vows (e.g., *The Avowing of Arthur*, *The Carl of Carlisle*, and Chaucer's *Wife of Bath's Tale*). In these romances, the central importance of fidelity to one's word parallels the emphasis on *trawpe* in *Sir Gawain*. These romances reflect a moral code characteristic of this transitional period between the Middle Ages and Renaissance that advocated *trawpe* as the most important virtue of the knightly code.

A third group of English Gawain romances links Gawain to a loathly hag (Chaucer's *Wife of Bath's Tale*, *The Wedding of Sir Gawen and Dame Ragnell*, and *The Marriage of Sir Gawain*). In this group, a beautiful woman enchanted in the form of a hideous old woman must convince a handsome knight to marry her in order to break the spell. Usually the knight is given a year to find out what women most desire in order to save his own life; the correct answer, "to have the sovereignty," reflects the link between sovereignty and the hag in Celtic tradition.

English Gawain poems adapted from French Arthurian romances in order to appeal to the British admiration for Gawain include *Ywain and Gawain* from Chrétien's *Yvain*, and both *The Gest of Gawain* and *Golagrus and Gawain* from Chrétien's *Perceval*. As Thomas Hahn observes in *Sir Gawain* (1995), practically all English Gawain romances are set near Carlisle, in Cumbria, in the northwest of England near the border with Scotland. Inglewood Forest and the lake called Tarn Wathelene, near Carlisle, are frequently the principal romance setting. The status of Carlisle as a border territory, populated in turn by Celts, Romans, Anglo-Saxons, and Scandinavians, accounts for the multiple cultural influences on *Sir Gawain* and other English Gawain romances.

In the later Arthurian romances in French (and, to a lesser degree, German), Gawain serves more often as main character and loses some of the ideal status he previously enjoyed as a more peripheral character; this change is evident in *La vengeance Raguidel*, *L'atre perilleux*, *Li chevaliers as deus espées*, *Gliglois*, and *La mule sans frein*. Lancelot replaces Gawain as the paragon of knighthood. As part of this deterioration, Gawain is transformed from ideal warrior and lover to cowardly and discourteous womanizer. The prose *Lancelot*, the prose *Tristan*, and the *Suite de Merlin* depict Gawain as the worst knight in the world, cruel and treacherous. In the English tradition of Arthurian romance, Gawain's deterioration and replacement by Lancelot occurs more slowly. By the late fourteenth century, the English Gawain is still a paragon of knightly virtue. But by the time of Malory, who portrays Gawain as a fanatical murderer, the English Gawain becomes the treacherous character he had already become in French romance by the late fourteenth century. The evolving characterization of Gawain may reflect a decline of chivalry in the late Middle Ages, but the question of whether chivalry was declining may also be an aspect of the self-conscious nature of chivalric literature itself.

Scholars have long pointed to *Sir Gawain* as illustrative of the differences between the Gawains in English romance and the Gawains in French and German romances, but recent studies have suggested a more nuanced relationship to the broader tradition of Arthurian romance. In *Deutsche Vierteljahrschrift* (1981) Joerg O. Fichte takes *Sir*

Gawain to be an inversion of the classical Arthurian romances of Chrétien that questions the Arthurian ideal by describing a protagonist's journey to defeat rather than to victory. The hero's reintegration into his applauding society at the end, standard in continental Arthurian romances, serves in *Sir Gawain* to bring the worthiness of that society into question. The temptation in *Sir Gawain* inverts the quest to win a bride that is also the Arthurian norm. The moral crisis Gawain faces parallels that faced by Chrétien's Erec, Yvain, and Perceval, but it occurs later in the narrative, resulting in a less conclusive celebration at the end of the story. Unlike many Middle English Arthurian romances, *Sir Gawain* features a number of romance set pieces, including descriptions of the arming of the hero, hunts, and courtly feasts. These features make *Sir Gawain* more similar to continental models than most British romances, but its inversions of continental features are in keeping with the British tendency to modify the French Arthurian model. In general, the *Gawain*-Poet shows an awareness of inconsistencies in traditional portrayals of Gawain, and chooses which aspects of tradition to emphasize; aside from *Perlesvaus*, there was little precedent for a chaste Gawain, but ample precedent in chronicle and early romance respectively for portraying Gawain as a successful warrior and paragon of knighthood. *Sir Gawain* downplays traditional emphasis on Gawain's prowess as warrior and lover, preferring to focus on his honesty in social transactions.

Scholars have traced the character of the Green Knight to a range of older traditions. In *Celtic Myth and Arthurian Romance* (1927), R. Loomis associates him (and Gawain) with Irish solar deities, and other scholars link the Green Knight to old beliefs in vegetation demons or gods, and thereby also to the green man of British May festivals, pictured in medieval cathedral iconography. In *Art and Tradition* (1965), Benson finds in the Green Knight reminiscences not only of the green man, but also the so-called wild man, a common figure in medieval literature and iconography associated with mummer's plays. Evidence against vegetable associations include the fact that in no version of the beheading game antedating *Sir Gawain* is the challenger a green giant dressed in green. Some readers speculate that the Green Chapel is an ancient burial mound like the many other funeral barrows in the poet's dialect region, and that the Green Knight recalls the Norse literary tradition of mound dwellers who represent death. This notion supports an interpretation of Gawain's tripartite quest as a journey to the realm of death, like Dante's journey through a tripartite hell in *Inferno*. Gawain's quest, like the *Pearl* narrator's dream vision and Jonah's descent to and return from "hell's womb" within the whale in *Patience* (306), are all tripartite journeys in which the protagonist undergoes a figurative death and resurrection. The Green Chapel also resembles the fairy mounds, which provide access to the otherworld in Celtic literature. The protagonist's trip to the otherworld is a standard feature of the romance quest, as when Chrétien's heroes go to Logres in *Perceval* and *Lancelot*; the latter work features a magnificent otherworld king that resembles Bertilak. The Green Knight's intrusion at Arthur's feast parallels similar intrusions by Meleagant and the Red Knight in *Lancelot* and *Perceval*.

The structure of *Sir Gawain* guides readers to the oldest traditions it contains in another way as well. Alliterating words are less likely than other words in the poem to have changed form as any scribe or scribes speaking a somewhat different dialect transmitted the poem, and many place names, for example survive as alliterating words in *Sir Gawain*. The alliterative verse of *Sir Gawain*, like that of the poet's other works, shows his mastery of Anglo-Saxon poetic form and his ability to combine Anglo-Saxon and continental verse forms: stanzas with a variable number of unrhymed alliterative long lines (between twelve and thirty-seven) conclude with the five shorter rhyming lines of the "bob and wheel" in the scheme *ababa*. This hybrid stanza form has no precedent among French romances, most of which are written in octosyllabic couplets.

Even more than in the poet's other three works, in *Sir Gawain* this hybrid of old and new poetic structures is a vehicle for conveying a great deal of information about late fourteenth-century England. *Sir Gawain* may offer a minutely detailed portrayal of Ricardian court life. Reflections in *Pearl* of the monarch's obsession with fine, ornate craftsmanship, especially that involving pearls, and reflections of his obsession with hygiene in *Cleanness* offer a mere glimpse of contemporary aristocratic culture compared to *Sir Gawain*. The attire and ornament of the nobility receives close attention in *Sir Gawain*, particularly that of the Green Knight and his steed on their first entry into Arthur's court, and that of Sir Gawain and his horse Gringolet in the description of his arming that precedes his departure from Camelot. Both descriptions overlay traditional associations. Gawain's near-death experience at the winter solstice recalls his association with the sun in those French romances in which his strength increases until noon and wanes thereafter. Although the fashionable elegance of the Green Knight's attire may appear at odds with any association with vegetation deities or wild men, this overlay of newer onto older traditions is a hallmark of this poet. The poet's treatment of Gawain's attire overlays the traditional set piece of the arming of the hero. The detailed account of the feast following Gawain's arrival at Bertilak's castle, like that of Belshazzar's feast in *Cleanness,* may reflect familiarity with contemporary aristocratic practice. The fact that when Gawain first glimpses Bertilak's castle it appears to be "cut out of paper" (802) may suggest the contemporary custom of placing miniature paper castles over individual dishes at a banquet. The poet's familiarity with aristocratic culture is also reflected in the long description of the butchering of the deer (1324–64); knowledge of proper procedure in such matters was, again, a requisite of aristocratic breeding. The motto of the Order of the Garter founded by Edward III, "Hony soyt qui mal [y] pence" ("Evil be to him who thinks evil"), appears at the end of the manuscript, though it may be a late addition. As Thomas J. Farrell argues in *Arthurian Interpretations* (1988), the Green Knight's blow to Gawain's neck may figure as a ceremony inducting Gawain into a new order of knighthood represented by the green girdle, superior to the order represented by the pentangle. (The origin of the girdle, featured elsewhere in Arthurian literature, is Celtic; lances and arrows bounced off Cuchulainn's "battle-belt.") Gawain's confession of his *untrawþe* to the Green Knight after receiving the cut to his neck may likewise supersede the confession Gawain offers earlier to Bertilak's priest. In the Wasteland of *La queste del saint graal,* hermit-priests sometimes hear the confession of knights.

Evidence of the poet's deep familiarity with aristocratic culture, in light of his extraordinary learning and literacy, is consistent with the assumption that he was a cleric in minor orders, possibly a chaplain in an aristocratic household. While his knowledge of the Vulgate Bible is most obvious in the other three works, and his command of contemporary theology is most clearly reflected in *Pearl*, *Sir Gawain* ranks among the most theological of Arthurian romances; it compares in this respect to the thirteenth-century German *Parzival* by Wolfram von Eschenbach. The substitution of the green girdle for the pentangle as an emblem for Gawain and Arthurian society is consistent with the poet's tendency to create empathy with imperfect human characters elsewhere, such as in his descriptions of the Sodomites and the victims of the Flood in *Cleanness*, and the sympathy he builds for the dreamer's challenges to the maiden's stern orthodoxy in *Pearl*. The liturgical structure of *Sir Gawain* resembles that of *Cleanness* and *Pearl*; the poem begins and ends with a wound to the neck figuring as a circumcision on New Year's

Day, when the Feast of Circumcision was celebrated. The virtues represented by the pentangle (619–65) derive from penitential and moral literature.

Sir Gawain, like the poet's other works, combines several literary genres. The bedroom encounters between Gawain and Bertilak's lady bring to mind the typical adulterous situations in Old French *fabliaux*, although no adultery takes place here. Their dialogue recalls the sample dialogues of Andreas Capellanus's twelfth-century *Art of Courtly Love*, an ironic love manual. Their dialogue also reminds readers that chivalry was a code governing not only warfare, but also relationships between men and women, as evidenced in Christine de Pizan's *Le livre des faits d'armes et de chevaerie*, and courtesy books like it, and in Jean Froissart's chronicles. In *The Matter of Courtesy* (1985), Jonathan Nicholls traces influences from medieval courtesy books in all four poems. *Sir Gawain* refers to itself as a lay (30), a short romance associated with the Bretons featuring marvelous events and aristocratic characters, and compares the Green Knight's decapitation to an interlude (472), a brief dramatic piece performed between the courses of a feast.

Like the poet's other works, *Sir Gawain* has inspired valuable studies from the perspective of gender. The obvious starting place for such studies is the Green Knight's late revelation that lady Bertilak worked with him to test Gawain (2361–62), prompting a diatribe by Gawain against women's wiles (2411–28), after which the Green Knight reveals that he is Bertilak in an enchanted form devised by "the goddess" Morgan la Fay (2452) to test the renown of the Round Table and inflict pain on Guenevere. Sheila Fisher in *The Passing of Arthur* (1988) and Geraldine Heng in *PMLA* (1991) have attempted to correct the consensus among the earliest male scholars that this abrupt use of *dea ex machina* constitutes a flaw in an otherwise well-structured poem. What the earliest scholars found most jarring—the abrupt attribution of great importance to two female characters who say nothing in the poem (Morgan la Fay and Guenevere) and to a female character who is only named by way of her relationship to her husband (Bertilak's lady)—is reinterpreted by some recent readers in light of the handling of gender elsewhere in the manuscript. The female characters appear all the more important for having motivated the plot without speaking a single line (Guenevere, Morgan la Fay) or without being named (Bertilak's lady). Morgan la Fay, whose origins have been traced to Celtic mythology, is the standard archvillainess of Arthurian romance, and medieval readers of romance knew her story well. Bertilak's statement that Morgan had a love affair with Merlin during which she learned his magical arts refers to an episode in the prose *Lancelot* of the Vulgate cycle; there Morgan's affair with a cousin of Guenevere prompts Morgan's exile from Arthur's court and her plan to exact revenge. Morgan builds a chapel at her residence in the Val sans Retour that traps knights who have been faithless in love. That chapel, with its wilderness setting, anticipates the Green Chapel, and the tests of faithfulness she administers there (also by way of a younger version of herself), thus anticipating the test of Gawain's *trawþe* in *Sir Gawain*. As in *Sir Gawain*, in that source Morgan is called a goddess. The appearance of Bertilak's lady at the center of the poem, bracketed by references to Guenevere and Morgan at the beginning and end of the poem, is a feature of triadic annular form. In *Machaut's World* (1978), Richard R. Griffith argues that Bertilak's lady has a precedent in the "false Guenevere" of Robert de Boron's thirteenth-century Vulgate *Merlin* and its anonymous continuation here she administers a similar chastity test, and that Bertilak is anticipated by the character "Bertolais" in those sources. Some readers perceive Morgan la Fay and Guenevere as doublets, two sides of the same character, in a relationship that parallels that between Bertilak and the Green Knight. Such doublets, two-faced female figures (one beautiful, one ugly) derive from treatments of the figure of sovereignty in Celtic literature and of the goddess Fortuna, traditions that survive in the figure of the loathly hag transformed into a beautiful lady in medieval romance.

Sir Gawain is set in the early history of Arthur's court, but its characters know the later history recounted in romance tradition, thus the Gawain Bertilak's wife has heard of is the Gawain of a more mature Camelot. Morgan la Fay, Fisher argues, attempts to intervene at an early stage of the Arthurian story to prevent the later, tragic fall of Camelot. The brief portrait of Guenevere in *Sir Gawain* contains no hint of the adulterous behavior that at a later stage of the story will contribute to the decline of the court. The testing of Gawain by Bertilak's wife anticipates Lancelot's adultery with Guenevere and Mordred's attempt to marry Guenevere in the later history of Camelot. It also may bring to mind the birth of Mordred by way of the incestuous union of Arthur and his sister Morgause. As Moorman observes in *The "Pearl"-Poet* (1968), the poem thus comments on the entire Arthurian history rather than presenting an isolated adventure of Gawain. Guerin suggests the poem functions as a "prequel" to the Arthurian story, that Hautdesert resembles Arthur's court as it appears in texts that describe a later phase of its history. Hautdesert rivals Camelot in its magnificence: Bertilak is more mature than Arthur, and Bertilak's wife is "more beautiful than Guenevere" (945).

Sir Gawain particularly lends itself to semiotic analysis. The pentangle is a sign of *trawþe* (625–26), and Gawain adopts the green girdle as a sign of his transgression (2433), a *token of vntrawþe* (2509). In effect, Gawain replaces the pentangle, the emblem of a moral code that allows for no flaw, with the green girdle, which he embraces as an emblem of his own imperfection. But in adopting it for themselves, Arthur's court appears to interpret the green girdle as a more positive sign (2513–20). Al Shoaf associates the pentangle with the perfection of platonic form, noting that both the pentangle and the green girdle are knots; the green girdle, unlike pentangle, can be untied, and both are figures for poetry (1984). Another study of medieval sign theory in *Sir Gawain* has been offered by Ross G. Arthur in *Medieval Sign Theory and "Sir Gawain and the Green Knight"* (1987); he draws on the fourteenth-century tracts of the terminist logicians, on works of speculative geometry, and on doctrinal and homiletic material concerning the relation of sign to referent. Because the geometry of the pentangle and green girdle so clearly pertain to the same tradition as the pearl symbol, such semiotic approaches clarify the relationship between *Sir Gawain* and *Pearl*. The pentangle, green girdle, and pearl are all presented as images of enclosure, so they may also be interpreted in light of the controlling image of the vessel in *Cleanness*, as investigated by Charlotte C. Morse in *The Pattern of Judgment* (1978), and in terms of the three main enclosures in *Patience*, the ship, whale, and bower. Sometimes such analysis points to very specific parallels between enclosures in two poems, so that, for example, both the whale in *Patience* and the Green Chapel serve as diabolical chapels. The semiotics of enclosure in all four poems is of a piece with the annular form they share.

PRIMARY WORKS

Sir Gawain and the Green Knight; Pearl; Cleanness. or Purity; and Patience. **Manuscript:** A unique manuscript contains the four poems attributed to the *Gawain*-Poet: British Library MS. Cotton Nero A.x., Article 3, late fourteenth century. **Facsimile edition:** *Pearl, Cleanness, Patience, and Sir Gawain: Reproduced in Facsimile from the Unique MS. Cotton Nero A.x. in the British Museum*, EETS, o.s.162, with introduction by Sir Israel Gollancz, 1922. Reprint, London: Oxford

University Press, 1971. **First publication:** "Sir Gawain and the Green Knight," in *Syr Gawayne: A Collection of Ancient Romance-Poems by Scotish [sic] and English Authors, Relating to That Celebrated Knight of the Round Table,* Bannatyne Club Publications, vol. 61, ed. Sir Frederic Madden. London: printed by R. & J. E. Taylor, 1839. *"Pearl, Purity,* and *Patience,"* in *Early English Alliterative Poems in the West-Midland Dialect of the Fourteenth Century,* ed. Richard Morris. London: Trübner, 1864. 2nd ed., 1869. Reprint, Oxford: Oxford University Press, 1965. **Standard editions:** *Pearl,* ed. E. V. Gordon. Oxford: Oxford University Press, 1953. *"Cleanness": An Alliterative Tripartite Poem on the Deluge, the Destruction of Sodom, and the Death of Belshazzar by the Poet of "Pearl,"* ed. Israel Gollancz. London: Oxford University Press, 1921. Reprint, with English translation, Cambridge: D. S. Brewer, 1974. *Sir Gawain and the Green Knight,* EETS, o.s. 210, ed. Israel Gollancz. 1940 (i.e., 1938). *Sir Gawain and the Green Knight,* ed. J. R. R. Tolkien and E. V. Gordon, 2nd ed., rev. Norman Davis. Oxford: Oxford University Press, 1967. *The Poems of the Pearl Manuscript: "Pearl," "Cleanness," "Patience," "Sir Gawain and the Green Knight,"* ed. Malcolm Andrew and Ronald Waldron. London: Arnold, 1978. Rev. ed., Exeter Medieval English Texts and Studies. Exeter: University of Exeter Press, 1987. *"Sir Gawain and the Green Knight": A New Critical Edition,* ed. Theodore Silverstein. Chicago: University of Chicago Press, 1984. **Modern English editions:** *Sir Gawain and the Green Knight,* ed. and trans. W. R. J. Barron. Manchester, UK: Manchester University Press, 1974. Rev. ed., Lanham, MD: Barnes & Noble, 1998. *The "Pearl" Poems: An Omnibus Edition.* Vol. 1, *"Pearl" and "Cleanness."* Vol. 2, *"Patience" and "Sir Gawain and the Green Knight."* The Renaissance Imagination, vol. 5, ed. and trans. William Vantuono. New York: Garland, 1984. *The "Pearl" Poem in Middle and Modern English,* ed. and trans. William Vantuono. Lanham, MD: University Press of America, 1987. *"Sir Gawain and the Green Knight": A Dual Language Version,* ed. and trans. William Vantuono. New York: Garland, 1991. Rev. ed., Notre Dame, IN: University of Notre Dame Press, 1999. *The Complete Works of the "Pearl" Poet,* ed. Andrew Waldron and Clifford Peterson, trans. Casey Finch. Berkeley: University of California Press, 1993. *"Pearl": An Edition with Verse Translation,* ed. and trans. William Vantuono. Notre Dame, IN: Notre Dame University Press, 1995. *"Sir Gawain and the Green Knight," "Patience," and "Pearl": Verse Translations,* trans. Marie Borroff. New York: Norton, 2001.

SECONDARY SOURCES

Andrew, Malcolm. "The Diabolical Chapel: A Motif in Pat and SGGK." *Neophilologus* 66, no. 2 (1982): 313–19; ———. *The "Gawain"-Poet: An Annotated Bibliography.* Garland Reference Library of the Humanities, vol. 129. New York: Garland, 1979; ———. "Setting and Context in the Works of the *Gawain*-Poet." In *New Perspectives on Middle English Texts,* ed. Susan Powell and Jeremy J. Smith. Woodbridge, UK: D. S. Brewer, 2000; Arthur, Ross G. *Medieval Sign Theory and "Sir Gawain and the Green Knight."* Toronto: University of Toronto Press, 1987; Bennett, Michael J. *Community, Class, and Careerism: Cheshire and Lancashire Society in the Age of "Sir Gawain and the Green Knight."* Cambridge Studies in Medieval Life and Thought, 3rd series, vol. 18. Cambridge: Cambridge University Press, 1983; Benson, Larry D. *Art and Tradition in "Sir Gawain and the Green Knight."* New Brunswick, NJ: Rutgers University Press, 1965; ———. "The Authorship of *St. Erkenwald.*" *Journal of English and Germanic Philology* 64 (1965): 393–405; Blanch, Robert J. *"Sir Gawain and the Green Knight": A Reference Guide.* Troy, NY: Whitston, 1983; Blanch, Robert J., and Julian N. Wasserman. *From "Pearl" to "Gawain": "Forme" to "Fynisment."* Gainesville: University Press of Florida, 1995; Bowers, John M. *The Politics of "Pearl": Court Poetry in the Age of Richard II.* Cambridge: D. S. Brewer, 2001; Brewer, Derek, and Jonathan Gibson, eds. *A Companion to the "Gawain"-Poet.* Arthurian Studies, vol. 38. Cambridge: D. S. Brewer, 1997; Burrow, J. A. *The "Gawain"-Poet.* Writers and Their Work. Horndon, UK: Northcote, 2001; ———. *A Reading of "Sir Gawain and the Green Knight."* London: Routledge, 1965; Camargo, Martin. "Oral Traditional Structure in *Sir Gawain and the Green Knight.*" In *Comparative Research on Oral Traditions: A*

Memorial for Milman Parry, ed. John Miles Foley, 121–37. Columbus, OH: Slavica, 1987; Crawford, Donna. "The Architectonics of *Cleanness.*" *Studies in Philology* 90 (1993): 29–45; Davenport, W. A. *The Art of the "Gawain"-Poet.* London: Athlone Press, 1978; Elliott, R. W. V. *The "Gawain" Country.* Leeds Texts and Monographs, no. 8. Leeds, UK: University of Leeds Press, 1984; Farrell, Thomas J. "Life and Art, Chivalry and Geometry in *Sir Gawain and the Green Knight.*" *Arthurian Interpretations* 2 (1988): 17–33; Fichte, Joerg O. "The Middle English Arthurian Verse Romance: Suggestions for the Development of a Literary Typology." *Deutsche Vierteljahrsschrift für Literaturwissenschaft und Geistesgeschichte* 55 (1981): 567–90; Fisher, Sheila. "Leaving Morgan Aside: Women, History, and Revisionism in *Sir Gawain and the Green Knight.*" In *The Passing of Arthur: New Essays in Arthurian Tradition*, Garland Reference Library of the Humanities, vol. 781, ed. Christopher Baswell and William Sharpe, 129–51. New York: Garland, 1988; Griffith, Richard R. "Bertilak's Lady: The French Background of *Sir Gawain and the Green Knight.*" In *Machaut's World: Science and Art in the Fourteenth Century*, Annals of the New York Academy of Sciences, vol. 314, ed. Madeleine Pelner Cosman and Bruce Chandler, 249–66. New York: New York Academy of Sciences, 1978; Guerin, Victoria M. "*Sir Gawain and the Green Knight.*" In *The Fall of Kings and Princes: Structure and Destruction in Arthurian Tragedy*, 196–232. Stanford, CA: Stanford University Press, 1995; Hahn, Thomas. *Sir Gawain: Eleven Romances and Tales.* Middle English Texts. Kalamazoo, MI: Medieval Institute, 1995; Heng, Geraldine. "Feminine Knots and the Other: *Sir Gawain and the Green Knight,*" *PMLA* 106 (1991): 500–514; Hieatt, Constance B. *The Realism of Dream Visions.* The Hague: Mouton, 1967; Lecklider, Jane K. "*Cleanness*": *Structure and Meaning.* Cambridge: D. S. Brewer, 1997; Loomis, Roger Sherman, ed. *Arthurian Literature in the Middle Ages: A Collaborative History.* Oxford: Oxford University Press, 1959; ———. *Celtic Myth and Arthurian Romance.* New York: Columbia University Press, 1927; ———. *The Development of Arthurian Romance.* New York: Norton, 1963; Marti, Kevin. *Body, Heart, and Text in the "Pearl"-Poet.* Studies in Mediaeval Literature, vol. 12. Lewiston, NY: Mellen, 1991; ———. "Dream Vision." In *A Companion to Old and Middle English Literature*, ed. Laura Cooner Lambdin and Robert Thomas Lambdin, 178–209. Westport, CT: Greenwood, 2002; ———. "Traditional Characteristics of the Resurrected Body in *Pearl.*" *Viator* 24 (1993): 311–35; Moorman, Charles. *The "Pearl"-Poet.* Twayne's English Authors Series, vol. 64. New York: Twayne, 1968; Morse, Charlotte C. *The Pattern of Judgment in the "Queste" and "Cleanness."* Columbia: University of Missouri Press, 1978; Nicholls, J. W. *The Matter of Courtesy: A Study of Medieval Courtesy Books and the "Gawain"-Poet.* Woodbridge, UK: D. S. Brewer, 1985; Putter, Ad. *An Introduction to the "Gawain"-Poet.* Longman Medieval and Renaissance Library. London: Longman, 1996; ———. "*Sir Gawain and the Green Knight" and French Arthurian Romance.* Oxford: Clarendon, 1995; Randall, Dale B. J. "A Note on Structure in *Sir Gawain and the Green Knight.*" *Modern Language Notes* 72 (1957): 161–63; Rhodes, Jim. *Poetry Does Theology: Chaucer, Grosseteste, and the "Pearl"-Poet.* Notre Dame, IN: University of Notre Dame Press, 2001; Salter, Elizabeth. *Fourteenth-Century English Poetry: Contexts and Readings.* Oxford: Oxford University Press, 1983; Savage, Henry Lyttleton. *The "Gawain"-Poet: Studies in His Background and His Personality.* Chapel Hill: University of North Carolina Press, 1956; Shoaf, R. A. *The Poem as Green Girdle: "Commercium" in "Sir Gawain and the Green Knight."* University of Florida Monographs–Humanities, no. 55. Gainesville: University Press of Florida, 1984; Spearing, A. C. *The "Gawain"-Poet: A Critical Study.* Cambridge: Cambridge University Press, 1970; Stainsby, Meg. "*Sir Gawain and the Green Knight": An Annotated Bibliography, 1978–1989.* Garland Medieval Bibliographies, vol. 13; Garland Reference Library of the Humanities, vol. 1495. New York: Garland, 1992; Vantuono, William. "A Triple-Three Structure for *Cleanness.*" *Manuscripta* 28 (1984): 26–32; Warton, Thomas. *The History of English Poetry.* 4 vols. 1774–1790. Reprint, New York: Johnson, 1968.

KEVIN MARTI

GIOVANNI BOCCACCIO
(c. June 1313–December 21, 1375)

Giovanni Boccaccio is often described as the father of European narrative or the father of Italian prose, a writer whose masterpiece *The Decameron* justifies his ranking alongside Dante and Petrarch as one of the most important and influential writers of the Italian *trecento*. Although *The Decameron* was admired during his lifetime, it was his scholarly Latin works that initially brought Boccaccio his fame. Despite periods in which his shorter vernacular works were considered salacious and briefly fell out of favor, today he is widely acknowledged as having made significant contributions to the development of Western literature. From the fourteenth century onward, Boccaccio's work was considered a model for prose style and influenced writers as diverse as Machiavelli and Chaucer. Boccaccio's *Decameron* stories are retold in many later literary works, and his *ottava rima* poetic form is imitated in Spenser's *Faerie Queen*. As an early exponent of humanistic studies, Boccaccio also helped initiate the interest in classical studies that defined the European Renaissance.

None of Boccaccio's works focus exclusively on Arthurian material, but five—*L'amorosa visione* (1342), *Elegia di Madonna Fiammetta* (1343), *The Decameron* (1349–1351), *Corbaccio* (1354), and *De casibus virorum illustrium* (1356)—contain Arthurian allusions, narratives, or influences. Arthurian legend was familiar to Medieval Italian writers, as Antonio Viscardi and Edmund Gardner have demonstrated and as the famous passage in canto V of Dante's *Inferno* clearly demonstrates. The Matter of Britain became well known in *trecento* Italy through several literary traditions: the French works of Chrétien and Marie de France, the Vulgate and the prose *Tristan*; the Latin prose work on courtly love, *De Amore* by Andreas Capellanus; and the Italian *Tristano Riccardiano* and *La Tavola Ritonda*. The Italian *cantari* (medieval narrative poems performed in public) also related Arthurian stories. As a writer conversant in Latin, French, and Italian literary traditions, Boccaccio drew on Arthurian material in interesting and varied ways. In fact, Daniela Branca has recently asserted in *Boccaccio e le storie di re Artù* (*Boccaccio and the Tales of King Arthur*)—the only book-length study on the subject—that the influence of Arthurian material on Boccaccio was decisive in how he treated the concepts of pure love, romance as subversion of authoritative conventions, and the victory of true love over death. Later, in the context of the Humanism emerging during the mid century, Boccaccio mined the Arthurian legends for a rich vein of parody, example, explicit and implied reference, and stylistic and thematic influences.

Giovanni Bocaccio was born in June or July 1313, probably in Tuscany (Florence or Certaldo), as the illegitimate son of Boccaccio di Chellino, a Florentine merchant who adopted him. No record of Boccaccio's mother exists. As a young boy, Boccaccio showed a talent for reading and writing, reportedly composing poetry as early as the age of seven. His father supported Boccaccio's boyhood study with Giovanni di Domenico Mazzuoli da Strada in order to prepare his son for a career as a merchant. A six-year apprenticeship with a merchant allowed Boccaccio to travel in France and Italy, but he decided not to pursue his father's profession. He spent the following six years apprenticed to a professor of canon law, but ultimately he realized his interest in writing surpassed all other vocations.

In 1327 Boccaccio left Florence with his father for Naples, where he remained until 1340. During this period, Boccaccio moved within the court circles of King Robert of Anjou and began to write vernacular poetry drawing on the courtly love tradition. Scholars agree that the French literary tradition, which would have included the Arthurian elements cited earlier in this essay, had a profound effect on the young Boccaccio. In 1330 he began studies at the Studio Napoletano with Cino da Pistoia and began frequenting the magnificent royal library. His lifelong admiration for Dante and his use of the *dolce stil nuova* (sweet new style) also began during this period. These were idyllic years, as Boccaccio would later describe them, and initiated his literary career, starting with the letters (*Epistole*) and the 150 poems (*Rime*) that he would continue writing throughout his life. Boccaccio also composed four noteworthy works in the Italian vernacular: *La caccia di Diana* (1334), *Filostrato* (1335), *Filocolo* (1336), and *Teseida* (1339).

La caccia di Diana (*Diana's Hunt*) consists of eighteen cantos of terze rima. The narrative begins with a male speaker's description of one of Diana's hunts in which the huntresses are actual Neopolitan ladies. Boccaccio constructs a lengthy catalog praising the women and then describes how the ladies rebel against Diana at the conclusion of the hunt, refusing to pay homage to the chaste goddess. Instead, they ally themselves with Venus, who rewards them by transforming their captured animals into young men.

Boccaccio's next poem, *Filostrato*, is written in nine sections of ottava rima and tells the well-known story of Troilus and Criseida, in which Criseida eventually betrays her lover and he is killed by Achilles. The influence of the French courtly love tradition on this poem has been frequently noted. This work also introduces the character of Fiammetta (little flame), who appears in several of Boccaccio's subsequent works as an object of desire, a narrator, or a minor character. Nineteenth and early twentieth-century critics, who were reading Boccaccio's works as autobiographical, identified Fiammetta as Maria d'Aquino, the illegitimate daughter of King Robert. However, this interpretation was disproved in the 1930s and 1940s as Vittore Branca and others noted the lack of historical evidence to support an autobiographical reading, and began to argue, as Janet Smarr has recently, that Fiammetta functions as a literary trope, rather than an autobiographical figure.

Filocolo (*Labor of Love*) is Boccaccio's next work, a prose romance in five books that begins with the male narrator recounting his initial meeting with Fiammetta. The work develops as he attempts to please her by recounting the tale of Florio and Biancifiore, subjects of Italian and French folk traditions. The young protagonists fall in love, are separated, reunited, convert to Christianity, and are married. During his search to be reunited with his beloved, Florio assumes the nickname "Filocolo."

The last major work of this period, *Teseida* (*Book of Theseus*), is an ottava rima poem written in twelve books and clearly influenced by classical ideas of the epic. Boccaccio provides notes for his allusions, giving the work a scholarly tone, but the subject matter is still love. The poem relates the story of Arcita and Palemone's love for Emilia, the sister-in-law of Theseus. After a protracted rivalry, Arcita wins the right to marry Emilia through a tournament, but he is fatally wounded and ultimately has Emilia promise to marry his rival after his death. This work is a significant source for Chaucer's "Knight's Tale."

Boccaccio reluctantly left Naples and returned to Florence in 1340 to assist his father with his business. Scholars observe that following this move his writing appears to become more strongly influenced by the allegorical and didactic Tuscan tradition. His first major work after returning to Florence is the allegorical pastoral *Il ninfale d'Ameto*, written between 1341 and 1342. Also known as *Comedia delle ninfe fiorentine* (*Comedy of the Florentine Nymphs*), it is composed of both terza rima and prose. The narrative chronicles the hunter Ameto's initial meeting with the nymph Lia, his love for her, the experiences of the other nymphs as they recount them to Ameto, and his resulting transformation after his final encounter with Lia. The nymphs allegorically represent the seven Christian virtues, and their previous lovers represent human weaknesses.

L'amorosa visione (*The Amorous Vision*), an allegorical dream vision written in 1342, is Boccaccio's first work to allude to the Arthurian tradition. Boccaccio's Arthurian sources are more likely to be the popular Italian versions of the Matter of Britain than the French traditions, argue the translators of the English edition. The poem, constructed of fifty cantos of terza rime, is described as ahead of its time by Vittore Branca for its humanistic evocation of the classical world through the medieval tradition of the spiritual dream vision. The narrator begins his journey with a mysterious female guide, who some critics identify as Celestial Love and others as Reason. She leads him to a castle and ultimately two doors: a narrow door, which leads down the path of a righteous life and a wide door, which leads to earthly fame. Despite the guide's urging to follow her through the narrow door, the narrator chooses the wide door and embarks on a journey during which he sees famous historical and mythological figures presented in a series of four allegorical triumphs: Wisdom (cantos IV–V), Glory (cantos VI–XII), Wealth (cantos XIII–XIV), and Love (cantos XV–XXIX). The influence of Arthurian legend first appears in the Triumph of Glory (canto XI, 1–54). The narrator begins this section describing the joyous appearance of the knights "della Tavola ritonda" (of the Round Table). King Arthur leads the procession, followed by Percival and Galahad. Other figures from Arthurian legend are listed, including Gallehault, Astorre, Yvain, Amoroldo, and Mordred, but while these characters are briefly mentioned, it is the two pairs of famous lovers who receive detailed descriptions: Lancelot and Guenevere (10–27) and Tristan and Isolde (38–51). The language used to describe the lovers draws on both secular and spiritual traditions. Lancelot casts a "longing look" at the "lovely lady, / whom he greatly wished to touch," and Guenevere rides beside Lancelot "in an honorable fashion" as a light shines "from her face" resembling a star. She seems "more beautiful than anyone ever was," smiles with compassion, and speaks discreetly and quietly. Tristan and Isolde also ride side by side, and her hand is "joined fast with his." Her expression reveals that she is "wounded by the power of love," and her language is an ironic echo of the narrator's guide at the poem's opening:

> Turn in my direction, I pray you, your
> compassionate face, so that I may enjoy my lovely
> paradise; toward it, secure, I follow such a path.

The attention given to these lovers in a canto devoted to Glory (rather than to love) is surprising until one considers the larger context of the work as Vittore Branca describes it: the "great theme of the Tuscan tradition, namely Love as an ennobling and transfiguring force." The two pairs of lovers appear again in the Triumph of Love (canto XXIX, 37–42). While Lancelot and Tristan are named, Guenevere and Isolde are alluded to as "her in whom so long he gloried" and "the one of whom he was / enamoured more than of any other," respectively. It is clear that *L'amorosa*'s narrator greatly enjoys his visions of the lovers, but their significance for the meaning of the work is not a matter of critical consensus. Robert Hollander describes Lancelot and Tristan as "exempla of lustful passion," but Vittore Branca reads their role more positively. Janet Smarr and others find the conclusion of the dream vision ambiguous, in terms of whether or not the narrator will return to the narrow door with his guide or continue to lead her astray. Despite its grounding in the dream vision tradition, *L'amorosa visione* is a work that ultimately focuses more on secular than spiritual love.

Boccaccio's next work, *Elegia di Madonna Fiammetta* (*Elegy of Madonna Fiammetta*), written in 1343, alludes to the Arthurian tale of Tristan and Isolde. The *Elegia* is a nine-chapter prose narrative told from the perspective of Fiammetta, tracing the downward spiral of her despair after her lover Panfilo abandons her. Despite the advice of her elderly servant, Fiammetta is trapped in a kind of psychological hell. Chapter Eight is of special interest to Arthurian scholars for Fiammetta's comparison of her own situation with that of the Arthurian lovers. The paragraph-length commentary on Tristan and Isolde occurs within a long catalog of lovers who have suffered tragic fates. The source for this passage seems to be the work of Chrétien and the French troubadours. Fiammetta begins by expressing some distrust in French romances, noting that "if they can be trusted," they claim that the young lovers' feelings for each other surpassed the love of all others. Because Tristan and Isolde shared their love during their lives and believed that they would be together after death, Fiammetta asserts that their fate is not as tragic as her own. Tristan and Isolde "ended pleasures and pains at once" with their deaths, but Fiammetta experiences only unending torment caused by her lover's betrayal. Several critics describe the *Elegia di Madonna Fiammetta* as the first modern psychological novel, and in a recent translation, Mariangela Causa-Steindler argues that the work "successfully bridge[s] the gap between allegory and introspective narrative by giving shape to a character who encompasses realistic and archetypal qualities." The contrast between the idealization of courtly relationships and the realistic exploration of the narrator's suffering reflects the tension between medieval and humanistic depictions of love during Boccaccio's lifetime. The use of Arthurian courtly ideals to contrast with Fiammetta's obsessive, destructive, adulterous behavior creates an interesting dialogue in the work.

From 1344 to 1346 Boccaccio wrote *Il ninfale fiesolano* (*The Nymph of Fiesole*), a poem in ottava rima, which explainsthe origins of two rivers, the Africo and Mensola. The youth Africo falls in love with a nymph Mensola, pursues and wins her, but them loses her when she repudiates him fearing Diana's wrath. When Africo kills himself, his blood becomes a river with his name. Mensola gives birth to their son and is later also transformed into a river as she tries to flee from Diana. The son of Africo and Mensola later becomes the founder of Fiesole.

Boccaccio began his most famous work, *Decameron: O, Prencipe Galetto*, in 1349, following the plague of 1348 that ravaged Florence and decimated half its population, including Boccaccio's father and stepmother. Although *The Decameron* does not focus exclusively on the Matter of Britain, it does contain Arthurian allusions and, as Daniela

Branca has argued, it is substantially influenced by Arthurian themes. This collection of one hundred stories is framed by the narrative of ten young people fleeing the city to escape the plague. The title ("ten days") refers to the length of their exile from the devastation of the plague, which Boccaccio describes in vivid detail in his introduction. During the ten days, the young men and women tell stories to help pass the time.

The *Decameron*'s subtitle "Prencipe Galeotto" (Prince Galehaut) is the first indication of its thematic connection with Arthurian material. The subtitle may, as Viscardi suggests, refer to Galehaut's role in the thirteenth-century prose *Lancelot* as a friend to lovers, or it may, as Mazzotta argues, refer to Dante's use of the term in *Inferno* V to mean a literary work as an erotic go-between. The *Decameron* is dedicated to women and offers advice on love. Daniela Branca finds the connection to the Lancelot story significant, for she asserts that for Boccaccio, Lancelot and Tristan stand as examples of proper lovers, imbued in the sacred spirit of love. Accordingly, they serve as Boccaccio's models of beautiful lovers (just as the *Decameron* should serve as the "Galeotto" to more lovers), and the romantic ethos these models occupy is thematically central to the way the *Decameron* should be received by its readers. As Branca points out, the Fourth Day of the *Decameron* is the pivotal section, in terms of Arthurian themes. The story of Ghismonda and Guglielmo immediately shows parallels to Tristan and Isolde though the enemy of true love is a cruel father rather than a husband. Many of the other stories told during Day Four concern thwarted true lovers, dying for love, and the fate of true lovers to be united in the tomb or in heaven. The Classical tradition is modified in that death is not typically by suicide, but the proverbial wasting away from love. Because the Christian heaven offers lovers final and pure solace, suicide, of course, would bring them damnation and eternal separation. Many of the stories in Day Four also show characters confronting and identifying with the Lancelot and Tristan legends and an ideology of refined feelings of love. Branca suggests that the lovers even serve as models of comportment for *trecento* readers who are unhappy in love. This behavior is especially an influence of Marie de France's refined concept of courtly love. Besides Ghismonda and Guglielmo (IV, 1), examples of such lovers in Day Four include Gabriotto and Andrevuola (IV, 6), Pasquino and Simona (IV, 7), and Girolamo and Salvestro (IV, 8). The ninth story of the Fourth Day has a thematic parallel with Thomas's *Tristan*, as the cruel husband feeds the wife, who is grieving for her true love, the true lover's heart. Though she destroys herself, technically a suicide, the story suggests that the "sin" rests fully on the husband who greatly offends against the more sacred ties of the true lovers. The lovers are laid in the same sepulchre, and though their union in Heaven is left open to question, they are eternally joined in the tomb as the "disloyal" husband flees for his life.

In addition to the overall thematic connections with Arthurian material, the *Decameron* also makes some specific allusions to the Matter of Britain. In Day Ten, story six, twin daughters, Ginevra and Isotta, are given names that are the Italian equivalents of Guenevere and Isolde. Day Three, story seven has an interesting parallel to the legend of Tristan, as a young Florentine in exile for love returns to his home from Cyprus after hearing a song he himself had composed for his love, although with humorous and ironically amorous consequences that could only be marginally related to the spirit of the Matter of Britain. Another specific allusion occurs in the story of Guiscardo and Ghismonda (IV, 1), mentioned above, when a hollow piece of cane is used to communicate the offer of a lover's tryst, parallel to a Tristan legend of Marie of France. These specific allusions, joined with the larger thematic connections, demonstrate the importance of Arthurian legend as a source for the *Decameron*.

A significant shift takes place in Boccaccio's writing after 1350. With the exception of the *Corbaccio*, his works are scholarly rather than fictional and are predominantly written in Latin rather than the Italian vernacular. Scholars advance various theories for this change. Some argue that the economic and social upheaval that resulted from the plague's devastation, as well as the loss of family and friends, contributed to the increasingly moralistic and didactic tone in Boccaccio's works. Boccaccio's illness in 1355 may have also influenced his increasing focus on serious subjects. Others argue that his relationship with Petrarch, whom he met in 1350 and with whom he began a lifelong friendship, caused his shift away from vernacular writing toward Latin, humanistic works. Another factor may have been his increasingly important role in Florentine politics, which included diplomatic trips to Romagna, Ravenna, Tyrol, and Naples, as well as a diplomatic mission to the pope in 1354.

Boccaccio's first Latin work during this period is *Genealogie deorum gentilium* (1350–1375), a fifteen-book treatise on antiquity and classical mythology. This text uses genealogy to describe the ranks of the classical Gods and provides allegorical readings of some myths and their possible relationship with later Christianity. Books XIV and XV contain a defense of poetry that considers the relationship of poetry to morality. After a discussion of the nature and origin of poetic inspiration, Boccaccio argues that the purpose of poetry is ultimately edification through truth.

Trattatello in laude di Dante (*Treatise in Praise of Dante*), begun around 1351 and revised in later versions, tells the story of Dante's life through narration of events that serve as *exempla* for the reader. The biography is written in Italian as a tribute to Dante's own work. *Trattatello* describes Dante's troubled relationship with Florence, his love for Beatrice, his writing, and praises his contributions to Italian literature.

Boccaccio returned to Latin with *De montibus, silvis, fontibus lacubus, fluminubus, stagnis seu paludibus, et de nominbus maris* (1355–1374), a reference guide to major geographical features of real and fictional sites in Europe, Africa, and parts of Asia. Attention is given particularly to places mentioned in his own works, in biblical narrative, and in classical works. Judith Serafini-Sauli notes that the work's emphasis on classical literature and its validation of geographical locations through literary tradition make *De montibus* "a Humanistic treatise."

Around 1355, Boccaccio wrote the *Corbaccio*, a satirical prose dream vision in the tradition of anti-woman literature. The title combines the word for crow ("corvo") with a pejorative ending ("accio"), and the negative reference is to one of the narrative's central characters, a widow. The title may also refer to the ugly nature of the work itself, as Robert Hollander has suggested. The narrator, who has just been rejected by the widow, has a dream that begins like a traditional dream vision, in which a guide leads the narrator toward a spiritual enlightenment or a journey of self discovery. The guide, however, is the spirit of the widow's dead husband. In order to lead the narrator away from his obsession with the widow, the spirit regales him with examples of the woman's gross immorality, all couched in the terms of existing misogynist satire. Arthurian legend is introduced through brief allusion or specific example and is used in several sections either to provide contrasts for the widow's behavior or to highlight her immorality. The Arthurian tradition is introduced early in the narrator's journey when the desolate valley in which he initially finds himself is described as the "Valley of Sighs and Woe," a term editor Anthony Cassell associates with the "valley of false lovers" common in Arthurian romances. This allusion connects the widow with a tradition of lovers who betray others. Later in the text, the widow is contrasted with Arthurian heroes when the spirit of her former husband describes her braggadocios behavior by saying, "she thinks she excels Galehaut of the Distant Isles or Febus in bravery," the former of which is best known as the previously-mentioned go-between for Lancelot and Guenevere. On another occasion, the spirit invokes Lancelot's father, King Ban of Benwick, as an emblem of noble lineage that would be "sullied" by loving the widow. In two other sections, the spirit explains the widow's interest in Arthurian legend, noting that the knightly "prowess" in which she delights is not utilized in "public squares" such as sites of battle or tournaments, but is "used in the boudoir" where she would consider any man a Lancelot or Tristan if his "lance does not bend for six, eight, or ten jousts in one night." "Morold of Ireland," or Morholt, another Arthurian character is also mentioned in this passage. The spirit goes on to provide more detail about his former wife's lascivious interest in Arthurian legend noting that "her prayers and paternosters are French romances and Italian songs" about the famous lovers Lancelot and Guenevere, and Tristan and Isolde. The widow takes particular delight in the secret trysts of the lovers and "goes all to pieces because she thinks she can see what they are doing and would willingly do as she imagines they do." Daniela Branca asserts that the satire of the widow only works if the Arthurian ideology of love is assumed to be lofty so that the contrast between her behavior and that of Arthurian lovers is ironic enough to highlight the widow's grotesqueness. Scholarly opinion is varied about the meaning and intent of this unusual work. For some, it is a virulent attack on women; for others, it is an ironic attack on anti-feminism that mocks men who hold the views expressed by the husband. Janet Smarr argues that the work attacks a state of mind (lust without reason) rather than a gender. Whether the subject of satire in *Corbaccio* is a specific woman, the female sex, or a state of mind, Arthurian legend is used to demonstrate the depth of the widow's self-delusion and immorality by describing her focus on the salacious details of Arthurian romance rather than the heroic or idealistic features.

In 1356 Boccaccio returned to Latin scholarly texts with *De casibus virorum illustrium* (*The Fates of Famous Men*). Like *Amorosa visione*, *De casibus* draws on both fact and fiction and utilizes characters from Arthurian legend. The Arthurian material appears to be partly drawn from Geoffrey of Monmouth and the concluding romance of the Lancelot Grail cycle, according to Daniela Branca. The juxtaposition of Arthurian characters with historical figures in Latin scholarly texts was not unusual during this period. Antonio Viscardi notes that other medieval scholars writing in Latin place Lancelot and Tristan "beside the great figures of biblical and historical literature and the characters of Ovid, Vergil, Lucan, and Statius" so that they "represent a synthesis of the refined, loyal lover of troubadour lyrics with the mighty warrior of the *chansons de geste*." In his introduction, Boccaccio explains that the characters in *De casibus* are those whom God or Fortune has overthrown, and they are intended to serve as exempla for fourteenth-century political leaders to remind them of "the shiftiness of Fortune." The book is divided into chronological sections that relate the fates of famous figures from biblical, classical, and medieval history and myth. The didactic tone of the work is reinforced by passages inserted between stories to make a moralizing point. The Arthurian legend that comprises all of Book Eight differs from Boccaccio's earlier use of Arthurian material in its attention to its characters' political fate rather than their romantic adventures. In fact, Tristan, Isolde, Lancelot, and Guenevere are not mentioned in this section, for the focus is entirely on Arthur and his betrayal and death at the hands of his son Mordred. Boccaccio qualifies his description of Arthur's fame by noting that although "we" (presumably educated Europeans) do not give complete credence to English tales of Arthur's "greatness and his fate, ... the whole world seems to have given witness to him." This observation highlights the pervasiveness of Arthurian legend in European culture during this period. After an account of Arthur's genealogy and his ascendancy to power, Boccaccio describes the establishment of the Round Table and its twelve rules, which he admires as "praise-worthy" and "strictly observed." The text attributes Arthur's reversal of fortune to his pride, which motivated him to invade Gaul, leaving England under the care of Mordred. The remainder of this section describes Mordred's betrayal of his father, their fatal encounter in battle, and Arthur's final voyage to Avalon. Boccaccio notes the mysterious circumstances surrounding Arthur's death and the belief in Britain that Arthur may return. The section concludes both with praise for Arthur's Round Table and with condemnation of the rebellion that led to its destruction. The moral at the conclusion of Book Eight is that "From this example people can learn, if they wish, that in this world only the humble things endure."

The next decade of Boccaccio's life is marked by opportunities for travel, including the diplomatic trips to Ravenna in 1357, Avignon in 1365, and Rome in 1367, as well as visits with Petrarch in 1359 and 1368. Records indicate that in 1360 Boccaccio received a papal dispensation for his illegitimate birth, and in 1361, he left Florence for a semiretirement in Certaldo. Boccaccio continued to write poetry and letters and to enlarge and revise many of his works during these years.

In 1361 Boccaccio composed *De mulieribus claris*, a Latin work in praise of women. Starting with Eve, *De mulieribus* provides a biographical survey of one hundred and four fictional and historical women whose stories are followed by moral lessons. Boccaccio dedicates the work to Andrea Acciaiuoli and notes that he hopes its positive *exempla* will please her. The work draws on sources such as Ovid and Tacitus, and it utilizes allegory in a manner similar to the *Genealogie*.

In 1373 the city of Florence commissioned Boccaccio to write a scholarly treatise on Dante's works for a series of public lectures beginning on October 23. During the following year, Boccaccio wrote the lectures, titled *Esposizioni sopra la Commedia di Dante*. Judith Serafini-Sauli identifies several methods Boccaccio uses in these lectures to justify his readings of non-Christian subjects in Dante: allegory, *auctoritas* (Christian and Classical authorities), and etymology. The lectures were both praised and subjected to some criticism for their support of literature written in the vernacular. Illness interrupted Boccaccio's work on canto XVII of the *Inferno*, and he died in Certaldo, on December 21, 1375. In his epitaph, "sweet poetry" is described as his passion.

Giovanni Boccaccio's diverse and substantial body of work made important contributions to the development of Western literature and the founding of Humanist scholarship. In addition to the achievements for which he is most well known, his use of the Matter of Britain is significant for several reasons. First, the diversity of his usage demonstrates the extent to which Arthurian legends were known and accepted at all levels of fourteenth-century Italian society. The five works that utilize Arthurian material— *L'amorosa visione* (1342), *Elegia di Madonna Fiammetta* (1343), the *Decameron* (1349– 1351), *Corbaccio* (1355), and *De casibus virorum illustrium* (1356)—range from Italian romantic verse, through psychological prose narrative, to lively short fiction, scathing satire, and finally scholarly Latin treatise. Second, Boccaccio's Arthurian materials help illustrate the tension between medieval and Renaissance humanistic ideas about the function of literature either as a means of moral improvement or as a Galehaut, a go-between for lovers, possibly contributing to their downfall. Boccaccio's use of Arthurian legend as part of this debate is the subject of ongoing critical discussion. Some scholars, like Hollander, see Boccaccio as a moralist who ultimately rejected Arthurian illicit love as a belief system that would make a "religion of love." Daniela Branca, on the other side, asserts that

Boccaccio's equation of Arthurian myth and legend with classical Latin myth and legend and their interrelationship in the same works, shows he felt that the Matter of Britain was in no sense degraded, but instead worthy of the highest respect. Boccaccio's multi-faceted use of Arthurian material in his works, despite possible contradictions, is a measure of its ongoing importance to the lifelong work of this complex and versatile writer.

PRIMARY WORKS

Rime (c. 1330–1375). **First publication:** *Le rime,* first published integrally in 1802. **Standard edition:** *Le rime, Caccia di Diana,* ed. Vittore Branca. Padua: Liviani, 1958. Reprinted in *Opere di Giovanni Boccaccio,* ed. Cesare Segre. Milan: Mursia, 1966; *Epistole* (c. 1330–1375). **Standard edition:** *Opere in versi, Corbaccio, Trattatello in laude di Dante, prose latine, epistole,* ed. Pier Giorgio Ricci. Milan: R. Ricciardi, 1965; *La caccia di Diana* (c. 1334). **First publication:** *Caccia di Diana.* Florence, 1832. **Standard edition:** *Caccia di Diana* in *Tutte le opere,* vol. 1, ed. Vittore Branca. Verona: Mondadori, 1967. **Modern Italian edition:** *Le rime, Caccia di Diana,* ed. Vittore Branca. Milan: Mondadori, 1990. **English edition:** *Diana's Hunt: Boccaccio's First Fiction,* ed. and trans. Anthony K. Cassell and Victoria Kirkham. Philadelphia: University of Pennsylvania Press, 1991; *Il filostrato* (c. 1335). **First publication:** *Filostrato.* Venice, 1480–1483. **Standard edition:** *Filostrato* in *Tutte le opere,* vol. 2, ed. Vittore Branca. Verona: Mondadori, 1964. **Modern Italian edition:** *Filostrato e il Ninfale fiesolano,* ed. Vincenzo Pernicone. Bari: Gius, Laterze & figli, 1937. **English edition:** *Filostrato,* trans. Robert P. Roberts and Anna Bruni Seldis. New York: Garland, 1986; *Il filocolo* (c. 1336). **First publication:** *Filocolo.* Florence, 1472. **Standard edition:** *Filocolo* in *Tutte le opere,* vol. 1, ed. Antonio Enzo Quaglio. Verona: Mondadori, 1967. **Modern Italian edition:** *Filocolo,* ed. Salvatore Battaglia. Bari: Laterza, 1938. **English edition:** *Filocolo,* trans. Donald Cheney, with Thomas Bergin. New York: Garland, 1985; *Teseida o Le nozze di Emilia* (c. 1339–1341). **First publication:** *Teseida.* Ferrara, 1475. **Standard edition:** In *Tutte le opere,* vol. 2, ed. Alberto Limentani. Verona: Mondadori, 1964. **Modern Italian edition:** *Teseida,* ed. Salvatore Battaglia. Florence, 1938. **English edition:** *The Book of Theseus or The Marriage of Emilia,* trans. Bernadette Marie McCoy. New York: Medieval Text Association, 1974; *Il ninfale d'Ameto* (c. 1341–1342). Also known as *Comedia delle ninfe fiorentine.* **First publication:** *Comedia delle ninfe fiorentine: Ameto.* Rome, 1478. **Standard edition:** In *Tutte le opere,* vol. 2, ed. Antonio Enzo Quaglio. Verona: Mondadori, 1964. **Modern Italian edition:** *Comedia delle ninfe fiorentine,* ed. Antonio Enzo Quaglio. Florence, 1963; *L'amorosa visione* (c. 1342–1343). **First publication:** Milan, 1521. **Standard edition:** In *Tutte le opere,* vol. 3, ed. Vittore Branca. Verona: Mondadori, 1974. **Modern Italian edition:** *L'amorosa visione,* ed. Vittore Branca. Milan, Mondadori, 2000. **English edition:** *L'amorosa visione,* trans. Robert Hollander, Timothy Hampton, and Margherita Frankel. Hanover, NH: University Press of New England, 1986; *Elegia di Madonna Fiammetta* (c. 1343–1344). **First publication:** Padua, 1472 (first dated edition). **Standard edition:** In *Opere di Giovanni Boccaccio,* ed. Cesare Segre. Milan: Mursia, 1966. **Modern Italian edition:** In *Tutte le opere,* vol. 5, ed. Maria Pia Mussini Sacchi. Milan: Mursia, 1987. **English edition:** *The Elegy of Lady Fiammetta,* ed. and trans. Mariangela Causa-Steindler and Thomas Mauch. Chicago: University of Chicago Press, 1990; *Il ninfale fiesolano* (1344–1346). **First publication:** Venice, 1477 (first dated edition). **Standard edition:** In *Tutte le opere,* vol. 3, ed. Armando Balduino. Verona: Mondadori, 1974. **Modern Italian edition:** In *Opera,* ed. Cesare Segre. Milan: Mursia, 1980. **English editions:** *The Nymph of Fiesole,* trans. Daniel J. Donno. New York, 1960. *Nymphs of Fiesole,* trans. Joseph Tusiani. Rutherford, NJ, 1971; *Decameron: O, Prencipe Galetto* (1349–1351). **Manuscript:** The two most frequently consulted manuscripts are the Mannelli, Laurenziano 42, I. 1384, and the Berlin, Hamilton 90. c. 1370. Branca has proven that the latter is Boccaccio's autograph. **First publication:** *Decameron: O, Prencipe Galetto. Deo Gratias* edition, c. 1470. **Standard edition:** In *Tutte le opere,* vol. 4, ed. Vittore Branca. Verona:

Mondadori, 1976. **Modern Italian edition:** *Decameron*, ed. C. S. Singleton. Baltimore, 1974.
English edition: *Decameron*, trans. Guido Waldman. Oxford: Oxford University Press, 1993;
Genealogia deorum gentilium (c. 1350–1375). **First publication:** Venice, 1472 (first dated edition). **Standard edition:** *Genealogia deorum gentilium*, ed. V. Romano. Bari: Laterza, 1951.
Modern Italian edition: *Opere in versi, Corbaccio, Trattatello in laude di Dante, prose latine,*
epistole, ed. Pier Giorgio Ricci. Milan: R. Ricciardi, 1965. **English edition:** *Boccaccio on Poetry,*
Being the Preface and Fourteenth and Fifteenth Books of Boccaccio's Genealogia Deorum Gentilium,
trans. Charles G. Osgood. Princeton, NJ: Princeton University Press, 1930. Reprint, New York:
Liberal Arts Press, 1956; *Trattatello in laude di Dante* (1351, 1360, 1373). **Modern Italian edition:** *Opere in versi, Corbaccio, Trattatello in laude di Dante, prose latine, epistole,* ed. Pier Giorgio Ricci. Milan: R. Ricciardi, 1965. **English edition:** *The Life of Dante,* trans. Vincenzo Zin
Bollettino. New York: Garland, 1990; *De montibus, silvis, fontibus lacubus, fluminubus, stagnis*
seu paludibus, et de nominbus maris (c. 1355–1374). **First publication:** Venice, 1473 (first dated
edition); *Corbaccio* (c. 1354/1355). **First publication:** Florence, 1487. **Standard edition:** In
Opere, ed. Cesare Segre. Milan: Mursia, 1980. **Modern Italian edition:** *Opere in versi, Corbac-*
cio, Trattatello in laude di Dante, prose latine, epistole, ed. Pier Giorgio Ricci. Milan: R. Ricciardi, 1965. **English edition:** *The Corbaccio,* trans. and ed. Anthony K. Cassell. Urbana:
University of Illinois Press, 1975; *De casibus virorum illustrium* (1356–1374). **First publication:**
Strasbourg, 1475. **Standard edition:** In *Tutte le opere,* vol. 9, ed. Pier Giorgio Ricci and V.
Zaccaria. Verona: Mondadori, 1983. **Modern Italian edition:** *Opere in versi, Corbaccio, Tratta-*
tello in laude di Dante, prose latine, epistole, ed. Pier Giorgio Ricci. Milan: R. Ricciardi, 1965.
English edition: *The Fates of Illustrious Men,* trans. Louis Brewer Hall. New York: Frederick
Ungar, 1965; *De mulieribus claris* (c. 1361–1375). **Standard edition:** In *Tutte le opere,* vol. 10,
ed. V. Zaccaria. Verona: Mondadori, 1970. **English edition:** *Famous Women,* trans. Virginia
Brown. Cambridge, MA: Harvard University Press, 2001; *Esposizioni sopra la Commedia di*
Dante (1373–1374). **Standard edition:** In *Tutte le opere,* vol. 6, ed. Giorgio Padoan. Verona:
Mondadori, 1965.

SECONDARY SOURCES

Almansi, Guido. *The Writer as Liar: Narrative Technique in the Decameron.* London: Routledge &
Kegan Paul, 1975; Branca, Daniela Delcorno. *Boccaccio e le storie di re Artù.* Bologna: Il
Mulino, 1991; ———. "Tradizione arturiana in Boccaccio." *Lettere Italiane* 37 (1985): 425–
52; Branca, Vittore. *Boccaccio: The Man and His Works,* ed. Dennis McAuliffe and trans. Rich-
ard Monges. New York: New York University Press, 1976; ———. "Introduction."
In *L'amorosa visione,* trans. Robert Hollander, Timothy Hampton, and Margherita Frankel,
ix–xxviii. Hanover, NH: University Press of New England, 1986; Cassell, Anthony K. "Notes
to the Translation." In *The Corbaccio,* trans. and ed. Anthony K. Cassell, 79–151. Urbana:
University of Illinois Press, 1975; Causa-Steindler, Mariangela. "Introduction." In *The Elegy of*
Lady Fiammetta, ed. and trans. Mariangela Causa-Steindler and Thomas Mauch, xi–xxvi. Chicago: University of Chicago Press, 1990; Gardner, Edmund G. *The Arthurian Legend in Italian*
Literature. London: E. P. Dutton, 1930; Hollander, Robert. *Boccaccio's Last Fiction "Il Corbac-*
cio." Philadelphia: University of Pennsylvania Press, 1988; ———. *Boccaccio's Two Venuses.*
New York: Columbia University Press, 1977; Kirkham, Victoria. *The Sign of Reason in Boccac-*
cio's Fiction. Florence: Leo S. Olschki, 1993; Mazzotta, Giuseppe. "*The Decameron*: The Mar-
ginality of Literature." *University of Toronto Quarterly* 42 (Fall 1972): 64–81; Serafini-Sauli,
Judith Powers. *Giovanni Boccaccio.* Boston: Twayne, 1982; Smarr, Janet Levarie. *Boccaccio and*
Fiammetta: The Narrator as Lover. Urbana: University of Illinois Press, 1986; Viscardi, Antonio.
"Arthurian Influences on Italian Literature from 1200 to 1500." In *Arthurian Literature in the*
Middle Ages: A Collaborative History, ed. Roger Sherman Loomis, 419–29. London: Oxford
University Press, 1959.

SIGRID KING AND MICHAEL JAMES DENNISON

GEOFFREY CHAUCER
(c. 1340–1400)

Geoffrey Chaucer is frequently called one of the most important English poets. During his life, he was much more than just a poet. Chaucer was also a translator, squire, ambassador, tax collector, forester, clerk of public works, and pensioner. More important from the literary perspective is that all these civil service occupations allowed Chaucer to observer the spectrum of humanity. His work was astonishingly groundbreaking in its use of English as a literary language and its inclusion of middle-class characters.

Chaucer was born in London around 1340 into a family of successful vintners. Nothing is known about the earliest years of his life or of his formal education, but there were three schools near the Chaucer home. Since some of his works show a great familiarity with Latin classic texts, it can be postulated that he received some type of formal schooling. As a youth, Chaucer served as an attendant to the household of the Countess of Ulster, who had a strong connection to the royal family of England. This early service would lead into a lifelong occupation in civil service and important connections to English royalty. He left the countess's household to serve in the army with her husband Prince Lionel, second son of Edward III. In 1359 Edward's army, including his sons and Chaucer, invaded France. During the campaign, Chaucer was captured and in 1360, Edward had to pay sixteen pounds to secure Chaucer's release. There is then a gap in the records of Chaucer's life until 1366, when it is documented that he was traveling in Spain. By 1367 Chaucer was an esquire to the house of King Edward III. The following year Chaucer wrote his first major poem, *The Book of the Duchess*, an elegy on the death of Blanche, first wife of John of Gaunt. The poem was favorably received and earned Chaucer an annual pension of twenty marks.

During the years 1372–1373, Chaucer journeyed to Genoa and Florence on the king's business. In Italy he would have been exposed to the works of Petrarch, Boccaccio, and Dante and may have obtained copies of these authors' works. Indeed, Petrarch and

Boccaccio were in Italy while he visited, although there is no evidence that Chaucer met them personally. Also at this time, Chaucer's wife, Philippa, was one of the ladies-in-waiting to Gaunt's second wife. She, too, was awarded an annual pension. The Chaucers were then made financially independent at the bequest of both Edward III and John of Gaunt. On April 23, 1374, the king granted Chaucer a daily pitcher of wine; on May 10, he was furnished with a rent-free house. Later, on June 8, he was appointed controller of customs, where he was responsible for collecting taxes on shipping exports. Finally, on June 13 he and Philippa were given a life annuity of ten pounds. All of these grants combined made the Chaucers very prosperous.

In the 1380s, Chaucer relocated to Kent and served as a member of parliament. By the time Philippa died in 1387, Chaucer had gradually separated himself from the court in London and was in semi-retirement. This changed again in 1389, when he took on the responsibilities of clerk of the king's works. In this position he was responsible for overseeing the building and maintenance of royal properties, including Westminster Palace, the Tower of London, and the king's other palaces, estates, and properties. As a part of this job he would have been responsible for overseeing vast sums of money and a huge staff. Indeed, during this time Chaucer was robbed no less than three times in four days in 1390. He was beaten and injured during these robberies, which may account for his resignation form this position in 1391. At the same time, he also carried out the duties of a forester maintaining the king's hunting lodges and game preserves.

Several years later, Chaucer seems to have had financial problems. Even though Richard II gave Chaucer a new annuity of twenty pounds, records show that he was sued for debt. Also during this period it is known that Chaucer sold property and borrowed money. However, in 1399, Henry IV at his coronation effectively ended Chaucer's money woes when he doubled the poet's annuity to forty pounds. Additionally, Chaucer signed a fifty-three-year lease at an estate in Westminster. One of the final documents relating to Chaucer shows that he received his last bit of wine on September 29, 1400.

It is believed that Chaucer died on October 25, 1400; his burial plot in Westminster Abbey began the section that would later come to be known as "Poets' Corner." However, he left behind a lasting legacy that remains with us today. Chaucer was the first English poet to create art in his native language. His closest contemporaries were still using Latin, Italian, and French as the language for literary productions. Chaucer held a number of civil posts during his life and enjoyed close connections with Edward III, Richard II, and Henry IV. Even through politically tumultuous times, Chaucer managed to stay on the favorable side of royal attention. Oddly, it appears that Chaucer did most of his writing during the period that he had the most duties as an administrator. In his twelve years as controller, which also included many trips abroad, he wrote the *House of Fame*, the *Parliament of Fowls*, and *Troylus and Criseyde*. During his retirement, he began *The Legend of Good Women* and *The Canterbury Tales*. By the time of his death, his writing had almost ceased; indeed all of his final works seem to be short poems.

One of the greatest English poets made precious little use of the greatest English literary tradition, the Arthurian myths. Chaucer refers to Arthurian materials only four times in *The Canterbury Tales*. "The Squire's Tale," "The Tale of Sir Thopas," and "The Nun's Priest Tale" each contain minor references to specific Arthurian characters; "The Wife of Bath's Tale" is placed in an Arthurian setting and presents an obviously altered form of a traditional Arthurian episode. In each of these instances, the reference to Arthurian material is included satirically to criticize some element of the Arthurian romance genre. Because of its very limited presence in *The Canterbury Tales*, there has been very little critical attention paid to Chaucer's use of Arthurian materials, with the exception of "The Wife of Bath's Tale" that has been closely examined by critics as a commentary on the institution of marriage and the role of women in medieval society. However, as the purpose of this entry is to examine Chaucer's use of Arthurian materials, it is necessary to point out every use throughout the work.

Chaucer's character of the perfect knight would be the ideal candidate to contribute a retelling of some Arthurian legend. His credentials are impressive, worthy of Round Table fellowship himself, and he "loved chivalrie, / Trouthe and honour, freedom and curteisie" [I, 45–46]. But instead of the Arthurian legends, which should be able to provide fertile ground for these qualities, "The Knight's Tale" draws upon classical material, setting his tale in Athens rather than Camelot, and having the action unfold under the rule and wisdom of Theseus rather than King Arthur. If the knight had told an Arthurian tale, it would have suggested that Chaucer held this literary tradition in high esteem. As an evolutionary descendant of the model of chivalric behavior that received its ideal form of expression in King Arthur's court, the knight's telling of an Arthurian tale would have been an ideal comment on the timeless values that exist in the Arthurian romances. Also, since "The Knight's Tale" is told first, and it is the longest tale, the Arthurian tradition would have been given a place of prominence among all the tales and the variety of forms and genres that they are drawn from. It is therefore critical to note that by not having the knight tell an Arthurian tale, especially after the way the character of the knight is introduced in the "General Prologue," Chaucer is showing his lack of regard for these traditions. Paul Olson provides a detailed discussion of the reception of Arthurian model of knighthood in "Chaucer's Epic Statement and the Political Milieu of the Late Fourteenth Century." The best-known expression of the Arthurian model of knighthood could be found among the order of the Knights of the Garter. By the time that Chaucer was writing *The Canterbury Tales* this model of knighthood was falling out of favor due to skepticism about the conduct of the Round Table knights, disillusionment from the Hundred Years' War, and the emergence of new types of warfare that displaced the mounted knight. New models of knighthood were based on religious models. Chaucer's the knight's career is modeled after the great Christian hero Peter of Cyprus. Chaucer's audience would have been aware of the incongruity between what the character of the knight should tell, and what he actually does tell.

This incongruity is further heightened when the knight's son, who is described in the "General Prologue" as "a yong Squier, / A lovyere and a lusty bacheler" [I, 95–96] tells his tale. The squire intends his tale to be a stirring chivalric romance, but what he actually tells is a repetitious parody of that genre which is such a failure that the Host and some of the other pilgrims feel compelled to interrupt his tale. In addition to serving as an example of exactly how bad chivalric romance can be, "The Squire's Tale" makes two brief references to Arthurian characters that comment on the extreme distance of the world of King Arthur and his knights from present reality, and of the exaggerated luxurious sensuality of those romances.

"The Squire's Tale" begins in the court of the great Mongolian king Cambyuskan (Genghis Khan). Into this court comes the hero of the squire's narrative, a knight who was so impressive in his speech and in his appearance that he looks as if Sir Gawain "with his olde curteisye, / Though he were comen ayeyn out of Fairye." Chaucer points out the notable discrepancy between the typical courtly mannerisms of "real" knights to those that inhabit Arthur's court. The degree of difference does not serve as an ideal to be met, but instead illustrates the ridiculous impossibility of such behavior.

Later in "The Squire's Tale," the hero knight is observing a strange dance of lovers. Here the squire interrupts his narrative to apologize for his inability to describe the dance itself to his listeners. The dance is so sensual, so full of passionate expressions and dissimulations that "no man but Launcelot" [V, 297] could depict it in detail. Lancelot, of course, was Arthur's closest friend and most important knight and was directly responsible for bringing about the end of Camelot because of his inability to end his adulterous affair with Arthur's queen, Guenevere. Dropping Lancelot's name into the tale in this context recalls his destructive role as a sensual adulterer, and not a paragon of the chivalric ideal.

Chaucer's inclusion of himself as a character in *The Canterbury Tales* is one of the most brilliant literary strategies of the entire work, and it should be obvious that there is some importance to the specific tales that Chaucer assigns himself within the narrative framework of *The Canterbury Tales*. It is therefore remarkable that the first tale that the character of Chaucer tells is a chivalric romance in verse called "Sir Thopas." This tale attempts to follow in the tradition of chivalric romance, but what results is a strange mixture of forms and genres that Larry Bensen describes as "thumping doggerel" (3).

The tale of "Sir Thopas" tries to imitate all those elements of an Arthurian romance, but gets everything wrong. The description given of Thopas is not something that one would expect of a knight; instead, he is described in a way that is typically reserved for the depiction of fair damsels. Chaucer draws attention to Thopas's fine white complexion, rosy lips, and brightly colored clothing. He excelled at activities like archery and wrestling, which are definitely not typical knightly qualities. He is also described as being so chaste that he is able to resist the advances of all the women who pine for his affection. The tale presents a complete reversal on the traditional knightly qualities. While this absolutely had a humorous affect that encourages the audience to laugh at Chaucer, it also effectively satirizes Arthurian romance by telling of the adventures of a gentleman that desperately tries to live up to the knightly code of chivalric romance but just cannot quite make it.

The satire of the tale of "Sir Thopas" continues to get stronger and more outrageous. Thopas meets a giant who threatens to slay his horse, but Thopas has to put off the giant's challenge because he is not wearing his armor at the time. The giant will not honor Thopas request to withdraw, and Thopas is forced to flee as the giant throws rocks at him. The story continues in this vein until Sir Thopas is compared to Sir Percyvell (Perceval). At this point, Harry Bailey refuses to hear any more and cuts off the tale. In the Arthurian tradition, Sir Perceval was a popular hero who, in most versions of the tale, is witness to the grail procession, but does not ask the Fisher King the correct question. He is later replaced by Galadad as the purest knight. Perceval is an archetype for near-perfection. He is almost pure, nearly achieves the grail, but ultimately falls just short of the prize. Much like Chaucer's tale of "Sir Thopas" that is not quite good enough to keep the attention of the pilgrims.

"The Nun's Priest's Tale" contains the next reference to Arthurian material, which is very minor. At this point in *The Canterbury Tales,* Harry Bailey, the host and guide of the pilgrims, pleads with the Nun's Priest to tell a comedy to lighten the tension that is building between certain members of the group. The Nun's Priest goes on to tell a mock epic about Chauntecleer, the heroic rooster that has a dream vision about his own demise in the hungry jaws of a fox. This tale is based the common beast fable handed down from the works of Aesop and which were popular in the Middle Ages. The result is a well-constructed mock epic where the rooster hero is learned and courtly and, like any adventuring hero, is captured by the villainous fox, and then uses his wits to escape complete destruction. Like typical chivalric heroes, Chauntecleer will not listen to the advice of women. His wife, the hen Pertelote, listens to his distress about the dreams he has been having, and is convinced that he needs a purgative. Chauntecleer is angered by his wife's discounting his dreams and claims that his story is as true "as is the book of Launcelot de Lake, / That women holde in ful greet reverence" [VII, 3312–3313]. The best that Chauntecleer can do to convince his wife of the validity of his story is to compare it to a romance that is highly prized by courtly ladies, which is not very high praise at all.

The most important representation of Arthurian materials in Chaucer's work exists in "The Wife of Bath's Tale." Her tale is set "In th'olde dayes of the King Arthour" [III, 857] and is about a young knight that rapes a maiden he has come upon. There is a public outcry against this crime brought to King Arthur with a demand for justice. The case was to be decided by Arthur's queen and a court of ladies who decree that, as just punishment, the knight has one year and one day to answer the question: "What thing is it that women most desiren"? Failure to return with a satisfactory answer will mean death for the knight. He travels all over the kingdom asking all the women he encounters but does not get any consistent answers. Eventually he comes upon a loathly lady who promises him she can tell him the answer to the question he seeks if he promises to do anything she asks of him. The knight agrees to the hag's offer and returns to court with the lady and his answer. The knight reports to the assembled court that the thing that women most desire is to have sovereignty over men. The hag then immediately announces to the court that this knight has promised to obey her and demands that he marry her. The court is stunned, but the knight must keep his word and agrees to do so. The knight and the hag are wed and on the wedding knight she lectures the knight on virtue, and then explains that she had been cursed and the knight must now make an important choice. He can choose to have her remain old and foul but be a faithful and humble wife, or he can choose for her to be young and beautiful and risk being a cuckold. The knight's decision is to allow her to choose for herself. In giving her mastery of this issue, the curse is broken and the tale has a happy ending as he gets a wife that is beautiful and faithful.

There has been some question among critics as to the appropriateness of this tale for the character of the wife. As one example, in *The Wife of Bath's Prologue and Tale*, James Winney claims it "improbable" that Chaucer would have assigned such a tale to the Wife of Bath. Many believe that the Wife of Bath was supposed to tell something bawdy, like "The Shipman's Tale." General consensus seems to be that "The Shipman's Tale" was originally intended to be The Wife of Bath's tale, but that Chaucer replaced it intentionally. After this, there is not very much agreement among critics as to why Chaucer would have replaced the original tale with what finally became known as "The Wife of Bath's Tale."

Helen Cooper believes that even though Chaucer himself held the Arthurian legends in low esteem, he realized that his audience would have been familiar with the substance of them. In the *Oxford's Guide to the Canterbury Tales,* Cooper discusses the two fifteenth-century analogues to "The Wife of Bath's Tale" and argues that the popularity of this particular Arthurian legend, the "loathly lady" story, would have been popular as folklore outside of its formal literary tradition. The audience would have been aware of how the Wife of Bath departs from the popular models of this story and some statement about the wife can be inferred from those changes.

The nearest sources to the "Wife of Bath's Tale" are both fifteenth-century compositions. One is "The Weddynge of Sir Gawen and Dame Ragnell" and the other is a ballad "The Marriage of Sir Gawaine." Unlike the wife's version featuring an anonymous hero,

Sir Gawain is the central hero in both of these texts. In both versions, Gawain undertakes the quest because Arthur's life or honor is in jeopardy unless he can answer the riddle. In "The Wife of Bath's Tale," the knight is trying to save his own life. In the wife's version, the queen and a court of women adjudicate the situation. Finally, the most obvious departure from the analogues is that there is not a rape in any other version. According to Cooper, Chaucer's audience would have been very aware of these departures from the traditional version of these stories and she argues that Chaucer does this in order to undermine the wife's character by showing how she perverts the Arthurian material to suit her own needs.

Sarah Disbrow holds a view similar to that of Cooper. In "The Wife of Bath's Old Wives Tale" she argues that Chaucer's use of Arthurian material "is intended to play a symbolic role in the tale, subverting its message and undermining the wife's reputation as a 'noble prechour'" (69). By referring to a literary tradition that had fallen into disrepute, and then telling the story incorrectly, the wife shows her ineptitude as a preacher and textual commentator. An interesting alternative interpretation of this is advanced by Beryl Rowland in her article, "The Wife of Bath's 'Unlawful Philtrum.'" Rowland posits that the wife is a learned country dame who draws as much of her wisdom from folklore as from biblical and classical authorities.

Another interesting suggestion is that Chaucer used "The Wife of Bath's Tale" to explore the position of women in society, particularly the problematic legal concepts of *raptus*, or seizure and rape. Corinne Saunders argues that rape, or the threat of rape, is an inherent and necessary component of Arthurian romance. The decision to rape can serve as an ethical test of a knight's virtue, the threat of rape can serve as an indicator of the physical beauty of a woman, and it can also be used to define the strength of a kingdom by its ability to protect its women from seizure and rape. Chaucer uses the Arthurian material in "The Wife of Bath's Tale" to explore the problematic legal issue of rape and seizure, which is something that he had first had knowledge of. Cecily Chaumpaigne accused Chaucer of *raptus* in 1380. The charges were later dropped and modern scholars are not able to definitively conclude if the charge was of sexual rape or seizure, which would have been similar to the modern notion of kidnapping. The wife's tale is not set in a time when women were safe from rape and seizure, but in a time when *raptus* was romanticized. Chaucer uses the Arthurian setting in the wife's tale to show a time when rape was taken more seriously and women were better protected. Unlike the lax attitude in Chaucer's own time that typically viewed rape as a crime against property, the queen and her ladies have imposed a difficult punishment and threat of death against the rapist knight.

One of the immediate effects of using Arthurian materials in "The Wife of Bath's Tale" is the sense of distance that it gives the tale. By giving the story a "Once upon a time" quality, Chaucer is able to use the material nostalgically and emphasize the passing of that mythical golden age. Mary Carruthers suggests that the character of the wife herself is aware of that quality and uses the Arthurian materials to parody the youthful romantic notions she once held. The Wife of Bath is a woman of experience who had gone through a number of careers and a number of husbands. When we encounter her she is firmly entrenched in her attitude about work and marriage. Carruthers argues that the wife is pointing out the youthful naiveté that she once possessed, which was of the same kind that can be found in Arthurian romance. Alas, the wife is no longer that young and innocent girl that can find satisfaction in Arthur's world. She has moved beyond it. Chaucer's intimation may be that, like the Wife of Bath, his literary culture has also moved beyond Arthur's world and must leave it behind as well.

This sense of the passing away of the Arthurian romance is echoed in the critical work of Louise Fradenburg, who takes the position that "The Wife of Bath's Tale" is about the end of the romance genre in a post-feudal society. She draws attention to the strong sense of nostalgia that seems to be present in the wife's treatment of the Arthurian materials indicate that the time for this genre has passed away for good.

One issue that all these critical views seem to have in common is the acknowledgment that Chaucer and his audience were well aware of the division between their own world and that of the Arthur, and it was a time when that difference could no longer be ignored. As Olson and Disbrow point out in their respective works, there was a decline in the popularity of Arthurian material. Evidence drawn from such sources as library records and estate inventories confirm a decline of interest in Arthurian romance. The major English court writers—Chaucer, Gower, and Clanvowe—did not use Arthurian materials except to satirize them. Models for heroic characters and ideals were coming from epics and hagiographies instead of romances. Camelot had passed, and in the works of Chaucer, the Once and Future King passed away and out of literary prominence.

PRIMARY WORKS

Guillaume de Lorris, *The Romance of the Rose* (Fragment A and possibly Fragment C translated by Chaucer before 1372). **Manuscript:** *Romaunt of the Rose* exists in a unique manuscript: Hunterian Museum MS V.3.7. **First publication:** *The Workes of Geffray Chaucer Newly Printed, with Dyuers Workes Neuer in Print Before*, ed. W. Thynne, London: printed by T. Godfray, 1532; *The Book of the Duchess* (c. 1368–1372). **Manuscripts:** Bodleian Library, MS Fairfax 16, MS Tanner 346, and MS Bodely 638. **First publication:** *The Workes of Geffray Chaucer Newly Printed, with Dyuers Workes Neuer in Print Before*, ed. W. Thynne, London: printed by T. Godfray, 1532; *The Canterbury Tales* (c. 1375–1400). Although some of the minor works that would later be included in *The Canterbury Tales* (e.g., "The Second Nun's Tale," "The Monk's Tale," "The Knight's Tale") may have been written as early as 1375, most of the *Tales* date from 1388–1400. **Manuscripts:** There exist more than eighty transcriptions of the *Tales*, and most are drawn from two manuscripts: the Hengwrt MS in the National Library of Wales, and the Ellesmere MS at the Huntington Library, Long Beach, CA. The Hengwrt MS is older and dated closer to the time of Chaucer's death. The Ellesmere is more complete and is the standard for modern editions. **First publication:** *wHan that Apprill with his shouris sote* Westminster: printed by William Caxton, 1477; *The House of Fame* (c. 1378–1380). **Manuscripts:** Bodleian Library, MS Bodleian 638 and MS Fairfax 16; and Magdalene College, MS Pepys 2006. **First publication:** *The Book of Fame Made by G. Chaucer*, ed. William Caxton. Westminster: printed by William Caxton, 1483; *The Parliament of Fowls* (c. 1380–1382). **Manuscripts:** There are fourteen manuscripts containing *The Parliament of Fowls*. Most modern editions are based upon Cambridge University Library MS Gg 4.27, and Bodleian Library MS Fairfax 16. **First publication:** *The lyf so short the craft so loge to lerne*. Westminster: printed by WIlliam Caxton, c. 1477; Boethius, *Consolation of Philosophy (Boece*; translated by Chaucer in the 1380s). **Manuscripts:** There are ten manuscripts containing Chaucer's translation of *Consolation of Philosophy*. Cambridge University Library, MS Ii.i. 38 and MS Ii.iii.21 are the basis for most modern editions. **First publication:** *Boecius de consolacione*. Westminster: printed by William Caxton, c. 1478; *Troilus and Criseyde* (c. 1382–1386). **Manuscripts:** There are more than twenty manuscripts containing *Troilus and Criseyde*. Most modern editions are based on Corpus Christi College, Cambridge MS 61, and the MS Morgan 817 in the Pierpont Morgan Library, New York. **First publication:** *the [sic] double sorrow of Troylus to telle*. Westminster: printed by William Caxton, 1483; *The Legend of Good Women* (c. 1386). **Manuscripts:** Bodleian MS Fairfax 16, and Cambridge MS Gg 4.27. **First publication:** *The Workes of Geffray Chaucer Newly Printed, with Dyuers Workes Neuer in Print Before*, ed. W. Thynne, London: printed by T. Godfray, 1532.

Collected Editions

The Canterbury Tales. William Caxton, 1478; *Troylus*. William Caxton, 1483; *The Canterbury Tales*. Wynkyn de Worde, 1498; *The Canterbury Tales*, 5 vols., ed. Thomas Tyrwhitt. 1775–1778; *The Complete Works of Geoffrey Chaucer*, 7 vols., ed. Walter W. Skeat. Oxford: Clarendon, 1894; *Canterbury Tales by Geoffrey Chaucer*, ed. John M. Manley. New York: Holt, 1928; *The Text of The Canterbury Tales, Studied on the Basis of All Known Manuscripts*, 8 vols., ed. John M. Manley and Edith Rickert. Chicago: University of Chicago Press, 1940; *The Works of Geoffrey Chaucer*, ed. F. N. Robinson. Boston: Houghton, 1933; *Chaucer's Major Poetry*, ed. Albert C. Baugh. New York: Appleton, 1963; *The Tales of Canterbury*, ed. Robert Pratt. Boston: Houghton Mifflin, 1974; *Chaucer's Poetry: An Anthology for the Modern Reader*, 2nd ed., ed. E. Talbot Donaldson. New York: Ronald, 1975; *The Complete Poetry and Prose of Geoffrey Chaucer*, ed. John H. Fisher. New York: Holt, Rinehart & Winston, 1977; *The Riverside Chaucer*, ed. Larry D. Benson. Boston: Riverside Press, 1987.

SECONDARY SOURCES

Carruthers, Mary. "The Wife of Bath and the Painting of Lions." *PMLA* 94 (1979): 209; Cooper, Helen. *Oxford's Guide to the Canterbury Tales*. New York: Oxford University Press, 1989; Disbrow, Sarah. "The Wife of Bath's Old Wives' Tale." In *Studies in the Age of Chaucer*, vol. 8, ed. Thomas J. Heffernan, 59–71. Knoxville, TN: New Chaucer Society, 1986; Fradenburg, Louise O. "The Wife of Bath's Passing Fancy." In *Studies in the Age of Chaucer*, vol. 8, ed. Thomas J. Heffernan, 31–58. Knoxville, TN: New Chaucer Society, 1986; Olson, Paul. "Chaucer's Epic Statement and the Political Milieu of the Late Fourteenth Century." *Mediaevalia* 5 (1979): 61–87; Roland, Beryl. "The Wife of Bath's Unlawful Philtrum." *Neophil* 56 (1972): 206; Saunders, Corrine J. "Women Displaced: Rape and Romance in Chaucer's Wife of Bath's Tale." In *Arthurian Literature*, vol. 13, ed. James P. Carley and Felicity Riddy, 115–32. Cambridge: D. S. Brewer, 1995.

JOHN DENNIS GROSSKOPF

SIR THOMAS MALORY
(c. 1400–March 14, 1471)

Because of its scope and because it was one of the early English works reproduced by moveable type, Thomas Malory's *Le morte d'Arthur* (1485), with the
help of the great printer, William Caxton, became the most well-known English version of the story of King Arthur and his knights. It is the source—directly or indirectly—for the Arthurian legend in significant works of later poets, storytellers, and
filmmakers. Malory is the chief source for Alfred Tennyson's *Idylls of the King,* for T. H.
White's *The Once and Future King*, for Mark Twain's *A Connecticut Yankee in King
Arthur's Court,* for John Steinbeck's *Acts of King Arthur and His Noble Knights*, and for
the once celebrated but now almost forgotten Arthurian trilogy of Edwin Arlington Robinson. Countless other writers—among them Algernon Charles Swinburne and T. S.
Eliot—have drawn inspiration from Malory. King Arthur and his knights show up in
numerous stage and film productions. John Boorman's memorable *Excalibur* is based on
Malory, and the musical and film *Camelot*—regardless of its distinctly nonmedieval ambitions—draws from Malory by way of T. H. White.

For a highly creditable, albeit controversial, view of Malory's life, the serious scholar
should consult P. J. C. Field's *The Life and Times of Sir Thomas Malory* (1993). The following survey of Malory's biography relies heavily on Field's extensive research and provides only an overview, with short explanations of medieval literary and political history,
for beginners in medieval literary studies. It is also important to note that Thomas
Malory's birth date, life, and even his attributed authorships are still subjects of question
and debate among medieval scholars.

This said, it is almost certain that Sir Thomas Malory of Newbold Revel in Warwickshire is the notorious author of a series of Arthurian legends that were penned and
printed in the mid- to late fifteenth century. This is a curious time in English literary history, seemingly a valley (or at least something of a depression) between great heights of
literary accomplishment—notably Chaucer, whose works were written roughly a century
earlier, and Shakespeare, whose works appear a little over a century after *Morte d'Arthur*.

What fifteenth-century England lacked in literary accomplishment, it made up for in real and sustained political and martial conflict, thus making the period an inexhaustible topic of interest for historians. Two famous and highly complex historic events overlapped the life of Malory. The first was Henry V's (1413–1422) great campaign in France during the Hundred Years' War, particularly his victory at Agincourt, after which he won back (or commandeered, depending upon which side one views it from) French lands that had once been held by England. The second event was the War of the Roses (1455–1485), a civil war that resulted from an internal argument among members of the English royal family over regal lineage.

Henry V's successful French campaign no doubt added some gusto to the self-image of men of name in England. Perhaps this focus on heroism influenced Thomas Malory, but—as outlined below—it is doubtful that Malory actually participated. More important to the actual life of Malory were the intrigues resulting from the War of the Roses. For a tumultuous period, the English aristocracy was split into those who supported either the Lancasters and those who supported the Yorks, as both branches made claim and fought viciously for the right to the English throne. The convoluted details of the divide are not as pertinent to this discussion as is the simple fact that the struggle demanded allegiances down the line and, down the line, a host of ancillary intrigues brewed among nobles of lesser rank. In Malory's case, it seems that his inability to sustain an allegiance to either side (at the right time) weighed greatly on the course of his life.

Returning for a moment to possible relationship between Henry V and Malory, early biographers have held that Malory participated in Henry's campaign. In fact, traditional wisdom holds that Malory served with Richard Beauchamp at the siege of Calais during King Henry V's war with France. Field, however, debunks this assertion because his research places Malory's birth "between the end of 1414 and June 1418" (64). Thus, according to Field, Malory would have been too young to serve with Beauchamp.

The misconceived association with Beauchamp is due to mostly the old siren's song— the biographer's attraction to possible unities between a given author's life and his work—that has historically drawn Malory biographers from fact. In Malory's case, the thought that a heroic esquire attached to Beauchamp may be the very person to have later penned a distinctly English version of the Arthur story has been too alluring. One might see, too, how the association between Malory and Henry's French campaign would provide an attractive secondary literary connection: first, between Malory and the esteemed story of Henry V, popularized a century later by Holinshed in his *Chronicles* (1577) and, second, between Malory's possible military connection with the memorable dramatic episodes of Shakespeare's *Henry V*.

Field's counterargument, comprising as it does trenchant cross-referencing of fifteenth-century records, is compelling. The birth year of 1416 that Field proposes places Malory at a more suitable age to be carrying through on both the heroic and unheroic events in his life (64). Although Malory did not make a direct contribution to Henry's military successes in France, he was certainly influenced by chivalric precedents and traditions.

Malory's family can be traced from a succession of landowners and knights who held land the English Midlands for two hundred years prior to Thomas's birth. Field maintains that Thomas was the son of John and Philippa (62–63). Malory's parents, by record, were respectable members of the country gentry and as such would have retained household servants and would have had the means to provide—at least from a fifteenth-century perspective—comfortable upbringings for Thomas and his siblings.

Extant records only refer to Malory as an adult, so we can only speculate about his childhood. He most probably grew up at his family home in Newbold Revel, with his parents and his three known sisters (and perhaps more siblings) and the family servants. Malory's father, John, appears to have been are hard worker, involved as he was in managing estates in three counties and also apparently involved in "local and national affairs" (Field, 65). This would have been a busy household: according to Field, Malory's home would have been a place where the family would have "to hear Mass before daybreak if they were to hear it at all" (65). At least on a local level, Thomas's father would have had some power, and Thomas, no doubt, would have been influenced by the respect his father received from those under his direction.

Thomas had a number of close relatives, and, in Field's view, two of his uncles may have had an influence on his upbringing and on his later writings. Thomas's uncle, John Chetwynd—often confused with the heroic John Chetwynd who fought with Henry V at Agincourt—was actually a lawyer who lived a humble life. Though the latter John Chetwynd would have made a more fitting mentor to the young Arthurian author-to-be, the former John Chetwynd's influence may have accounted for the basic legal knowledge Malory demonstrates in his writing (68).

The second avuncular influence is Thomas's possible youthful association with Sir Robert Malory, which might account for the strong interest that Thomas developed in exemplary military and political conduct. After a distinguished military career, Sir Robert became prior of the hospital of St. John of Jerusalem from 1432 to 1439 or 1440.

According to Field, "more than any other man in England in the late Middle Ages," Sir Robert "stood for the political standards that were most respected, if not always acted upon, by his fellow-countrymen" (68). Because Malory's *Morte d'Arthur* follows the distinctly medieval habit of describing the exemplary actions of exemplary men, it is tempting to see Robert as a real-life role model for the young Malory.

We know far more about Malory's adult life than his childhood. The first public record in which his name appears is a settlement he witnessed for his cousin, Sir Philip Chetwynd on May 23, 1439 (Field, 83). Scholars of the fifteenth century, including Field, have used this document to speculate that Malory was well-affiliated with the Warwickshire gentry and perhaps also a youngish man with sparse means who was looking toward his future.

He was apparently married by this time to Elizabeth Walsh of Wanlip in Leicestershire, with whom he had at a son, Robert, born in 1547–1548 (Field, 94). Given that Malory would have retained little income from his family's estate (and that his wife would not have been left much from her father's estate), it would make sense that he might have to prove himself in the field. Field points out that Malory's above-mentioned cousin, Sir Philip, had provided notable service for the crown in Gascony and that it would have made sense for Sir Philip "to have recruited his junior officers among his family and friends" (86). Though only speculation, Malory was apparently in an good position to advance himself through martial service to Sir Philip. Too soon, though, Malory lost his probable connection with the nobleman when Sir Philip died on May 10, 1444 (87).

Sir Philip's death was not such a setback that it prohibited Malory's advancement in reputation and in politics. Sir Thomas was knighted in 1442, a sign at that period of significant martial accomplishment, and he was elected to Parliament in 1445. Field provides strong evidence that Malory may have aligned himself politically during the following years with the Duke of Buckingham (Field, 94–96). Given the complexities of local politics during these turbulent years of King Henry's reign and the scarcity of factual record, one can still speculate that Malory's alleged later misdeeds may have been motivated by a possible falling out with Buckingham. If so, then Malory joined the ranks of the many political dissidents on all levels of society at this time. It is fair to assume, however, that, until the 1450s, Malory had been serving his lineage well with probable heroic and certain civic accomplishments. Then his life seems to have taken an unsavory course.

In the 1450s, numerous records of Malory's misdeeds have understandably led biographers to ponder Malory's sudden turn to malicious criminal behavior, a turn taken with a great degree of apparent enthusiasm. As Jeffrey Helterman puts it, Malory was a "well-known ne'er-do-well" in fifteenth-century records, who was accused of conspiracy to murder, robbery, and even rape and, who, from 1451, spent successive stints in jail and escaped twice "by violent means" (258).

Malory was indeed charged with a number of offenses, including lowbrow and even violent crimes. These records reflect glaring inconsistency with Malory's apparent early aspirations as a soldier and public servant. The chief charge against Malory was that he ambushed and attempted to murder the Duke of Buckingham. He was also accused of "rape" (in the complex fifteenth-century sense of the term) and theft.

This crime spree seems out of kilter, placed as it is between being knighted and becoming an author who focused on the exemplary values of knighthood. Field brings to light how Malory's political allegiances, perhaps more on the local than the national level, may provide an alternative view of Malory's criminal career, one that seems more in keeping with the author of *Morte d'Arthur*.

After demonstrating how easy it is to confuse identity while surveying fifteenth-century records—there are many local Malory's of variant spellings and several Thomas Malory's on record—Field concedes that the fifteenth-century allegations against Sir Thomas Malory of Newbold Revel "were not wholly invented" (106). However, Field hints strongly that Malory's actions were not necessarily driven by criminal motives, but were possibly the outgrowth of local feudal protocols being carried out in a time and place that was intermittently govern more by tribal conspiracy than by jurisprudence.

Field concludes on the whole that the "comprehensiveness" of the allegations against Malory "makes it plain that someone looked for people with grievances against Malory and organised them into court, and presumably encouraged them to make the most of their grievances" (106). Most of Malory's life from 1451 was spent in prison, aside from possible escapes or furloughs. One report show that, with a distinct Arthurian flare, he went on a swashbuckling "horse stealing expedition," was caught, jailed, and then escaped using swords and daggers (Field, 116).

Until his death in 1471, Malory was caught in the mercurial fifteenth-century legal system. The War of the Roses was in high gear, and it is doubtless that the often-treacherous politics of allegiance thoroughly compromised the judiciary. Malory appears to have been in the wrong place at the wrong time and under the jurisdiction of the wrong people. His first imprisonment in 1452 occurred under the auspices of the Lancastrian loyalists during the reign of Henry VI (1422–1461). Malory was related to Richard Neville, the Earl of Warwick, and the Yorkist loyalist made famous by Shakespeare in Henry VI. There were efforts from that side to gain him pardon or reprieve that ultimately failed.

After the succession of Edward IV (1461–1471), Malory did receive a regal pardon. Field holds that he gained his freedom in 1462 long enough to become a "knight companion" of the king in battle. However, his ties to the Yorkist side went sour because of his possible associations with plotting Lancastrians and because of his certain association with the revolt of the Earl of Warwick against the new Yorkist King. Malory's affiliation with Warwick, weak though it may have been, then made Malory a "dangerous Lancastrian" (31). Malory, by name, was excluded from regal pardons in 1468 and, in 1470, he was listed among other Lancastrians who were ineligible for pardons (Field, 117).

It is almost certain that Malory's troubles with the law were a direct result of his precarious position in a political culture that had gone topsy-turvy. Although the exact details of Malory's transgressions are now impossible to establish, his seeming inconsistent allegiances as knight, when place beside his interest in knightly loyalty as an author, brings to light another inconsistency between the life of Malory and the subject matter of his writing.

In Malory's own text he refers to himself as a knight-prisoner, so one must assume that *Morte d'Arthur* was written on the inside. He died in 1471, presumably still in prison. Malory must have had access to a library or libraries that could have provided the copious source material that he referenced in his rendition of the Arthur story. Helterman holds that Malory, when he was at Newgate Prison from 1460–1462, had access to a "nearby monastic library" (258). Field suggests that Malory, later in his imprisonment, may have even had access to Anthony Wydeville's prominent collection. Wydeville, Lord Scales, was the king's brother-in-law—no less—and also William Caxton's influential patron (145–46). There is no doubt that Malory was, at least for periods, comfortable enough to write in prison and availed of the appropriate resources. He wrote abundantly: his Arthurian tales are made up of eight romances and run roughly nine hundred pages in the Oxford edition. He finished the last tale in "in the ninth year of Edward IV" (1469–1470), shortly before his death.

With the help of William Caxton (1422–1491), Sir Thomas Malory's version of the Arthurian legend was the first to see print and, one assumes, the first to enjoy wide distribution. Caxton introduced moveable type to England after studying the art on the continent. Also the publisher of Chaucer and Gower, Caxton's efforts had an enormous influence on the preservation of medieval texts on later generations. Field holds that Caxton may have come by Malory's manuscript by way of the above-mentioned William Wydeville, but it is certain that the right people already considered the manuscript a significant contribution to letters regardless of how Malory's work reached the printer. Using the name of the final tale, Caxton published Malory's work as *Le morte d'Arthur* on July 31, 1485, fourteen years after Malory's recorded death.

Caxton's printing suggested a more unified work than Malory may have intended. Until W. F. Oakeshott discovered the Winchester Manuscript of Malory's work in 1934, the printed version by Caxton had been the only authoritative source. The Winchester Manuscript—although the work of two separate scribes—is arguably closer to Malory's original work and authorial intentions. When compared with the manuscript version, Caxton's edition does show significant editorial intervention. In short, Caxton wished to present Malory's work as a "hoole book" (to use Malory's own term), rather than as a simple collection of legends from various and diverse sources.

Eugene Vinaver, in his 1947 edition based on the Winchester Manuscript, argues convincingly that Malory wished to portray the Arthur stories as separate entities. Others, notably R. M. Lumiansky, have argued that the *Morte* should be treated as a single work, Vinaver's assertions notwithstanding. Certainly Vinaver based his judgments on a work that had been probably been altered by the later scribes, and, as Carol Meale shows, Vinaver himself made editorial decisions that again frame the presentation of the text in the image of the editor's own beliefs. Meale asserts, sensibly, that, "given the lack of an authoritative copy of the work, it is necessary to conclude that the exemplar which lay behind the sole surviving manuscript may be as much the product of editorial intervention as Caxton's or Vinaver's versions" (17).

We may never know exactly if Malory intended his work to be received as a single book, as an anthology of sorts, or if he changed his mind about the overall scheme as he was completing the project. Admittedly, the whole book, when taken as a unified work has seeming flaws. At certain points, the narrative even takes on a post-modern flavor. Antedating the habit of modern soap operas (and the 1994 movie, *Pulp Fiction*), characters appear in later tales who had died earlier. The high-minded motives of the knights, in some cases, anticipate Monty Python in their ungainly outcomes. As Helterman points out in his clever reading of Malory, "Arthur's early knights embrace chivalry with unbridled passion and rush off on a series of quests that lead to unmitigated disaster" (259). Included among the noble quests are missions to avenge the deaths of Gawain's dogs and Pellinor's horse. These flaws might be attributed to the obvious stresses and distractions facing our "knight prisoner" as he grapples to manage dozens of multifarious legends stuffed with more dozens of characters and genealogies.

These textual and narrative problems have inadvertently given later storytellers more creative freedom to frame the legend as they see fit. Indeed, this freedom to recreate the Arthurian legend—to color the legend via the tastes of the author or to tell the story as a reflection of current cultural tastes—is the distinguishing mark of Arthurian storytelling.

Before Malory's compendious collection saw print, the Arthur story had been recorded in England and on the continent in a scattered variety of culturally and linguistically variegated manners. Each version is a retelling of the legend with special features designed— one assumes—to make the stories both pertinent and entertaining to then current audiences. With obvious cross-hybridization, they appear in a number of formats and presentations. As Elizabeth Archibald puts it, "Arthur appeared in Celtic folktales, in Latin and vernacular chronicles and 'historical' accounts of early English rulers, and also in Latin and vernacular narratives of adventure starring either the king himself or individual knights of his court" (133). The "Ur" text for the story is arguably the *Mabinogion,* a collection of Welsh prose tales composed sometime during the eleventh, twelfth, and thirteenth centuries, that chronicle a much older oral tradition of the Arthurian legend in folklore. How the legend spread throughout Europe is unclear. The stories became part of the troubadour tradition in France and at that point took on the highly stylized features of the then popular courtly love convention.

Following a literary pattern established by Chaucer and other fourteenth- and fifteenth-century English writers, Malory drew primarily from French Arthurian romances (the Vulgate Cycle) and somewhat from several English sources, notably the Alliterative *Morte Arthure* and Geoffrey of Monmouth's *History of the Kings of Britain.* Unlike Chaucer (or Chretien de Troyes, in the French tradition), Malory was more concerned with being comprehensive than with being poetically refined. Rather than fashioning a courtly love drama or bringing lyric cohesion to the escapades of a single knight or story, Malory compiled something of a grand encyclopedia, in prose, of extant Arthurian narratives.

Malory's focus was not on the polite (or even bawdy) conceits of earlier versions of the tales but in providing a rational delivery of copious legends in a straightforward manner. The following exchange between Arthur and Merlin wastes no words. Arthur learns from Merlin—who has appeared to Arthur as a fourteen-year-old boy—the disturbing truth about Arthur's true parentage:

Right so came by him Merlin like a child of fourteen year of age, and saluted the king, and asked him why he was so pensive. I may well be pensive, said the king, for I have seen the marvellest sight that ever I saw. That know I well, said Merlin, as well as thyself, and of all thy thoughts, but thou art but a fool to take thought, for it will not amend thee. Also I know what thou art, and who was thy father, and of whom thou wert begotten; King Uther Pendragon was thy father, and begat thee on Igraine.

That is false, said King Arthur, how shouldest thou know it, for thou art not so old of years to know my father? Yes, said Merlin, I know it better than ye or any man living. I will not believe thee, said Arthur, and was wroth with the child. So departed Merlin, and came again in the likeness of an old man of fourscore year of age, whereof the king was right glad, for he seemed to be right wise. (37)

Another writer might see an opportunity to add more dramatic force to this passage, to explore perhaps the inner psychology of a great king who learns that he was the product of an adulterous relationship. Malory's King Arthur, however distraught, responds to Merlin by saying, "I will that my mother be sent for that I may speak with her; and if she say so herself then will I believe it" (37).

Perhaps Arthur's character is developed through the emotions that are absent from this terse response. In the next chapter, we do see him weep when Igraine admits to him that she is his mother, and we do learn that Arthur is so taken by this knowledge that he called for a great feast that lasted eight days.

These two scenes, even in the context of our modern exposure to the rapid sequencing of movie making, would tempt the poet or creative artist to provide far more emotional reflection that the two sentences here uttered by the hero. Malory has other fish to fry, however. After the feast—which is described in one sentence—Arthur, in the next sentence, is off to another venue where he is sponsoring new knights in conflict.

Of course Malory's prose could not be sidetracked by stylistic conventions than were, in the medieval period, specific to poetry. In a work with the scope of *Morte d'Arthur*, the foremost purpose was to tell the whole extant story of Arthur in one go, and Malory's success in doing so is chief among his accomplishments. Without doubt Malory did give a sense of form to the many scattered legends he assembled. This fact alone probably is what caught Caxton's attention and in turn assured the prominent survival of Malory's version of the legend into modern times.

Much of the framework of *Morte d'Arthur* is already familiar to us from current popular culture. The work contains the basic story of Arthur and the Knights of the Round Table. It begins with the birth and upbringing of the king who did not know he was a king until he unwittingly pulls the sword, Excalibur, from the stone. As the story continues, other familiar features come into focus: the continued interventions of Merlin and Merlin's undoing, the establishment of Camelot and the Round Table, the introduction of Launcelot and the knight's quest for perfection, and stories of exemplary (and unexemplary) deeds of the knights of the realm.

Later the tale of the Holy Grail, with its extraordinary symbolism and fabulous imagery, unfolds and ends with Sir Galahad's attainment of the Grail and his conveyance to Christ by the angels. The Grail section is followed by the story of the fall of Camelot, the illicit love and demise of Guinivere and Launcelot, the "hurting to the death" of Arthur in his battle with his illegitimate son, Mordred, and the deaths of Guinivere and Launcelot.

Much of *Morte d'Arthur*, however, would seem obscure and perhaps even tiresome to the modern reader. There are difficult genealogies and an endless cast of characters presented through countless episodes. There are a number of kings (read warlords) and knights with attendant alliances to keep track of and abundant seeming digressions into multifarious scenes and settings.

The section of *Morte d'Arthur* that focuses on Tristram De Lyons is hardly tiresome although it is not as familiar in current popular culture. The Tristram tales contain the highly engaging and intriguing affair of Tristram and Isoud (or Isolde in other spellings) and comprise roughly one-third of the entire book. Tristram's illicit love affair with the wife of his king and his ensuing madness parallels Launcelot's story, but this love affair clearly plays second fiddle to the Camelot love triangle. The story is not as familiar to us probably because it seems an enormous digression from the Arthur cycle and has not survived in later retelling of the Arthurian legend in film and popular writing.

Although on the margins of the main Arthurian legend, the pitiable love affair of Tristram and Isoud has made a significant impact on nineteenth- and twentieth-century literature. Perhaps because of its special mythic features—including a love potion that is inadvertently taken by Tristram instead of King Mark—it has a special historic place among illicit love stories and has been picked up again and again by a number of prominent writers. Tennyson includes a morally indignant version in his *Idylls*. Both Matthew Arnold and Swinburne re-created versions of the story independently, and the story has been told or has influenced a number of noteworthy modern writers, including Thomas Hardy, John Masefield, Martha Kinross, Don Marquis, Sir Arthur Quiller-Couch, John Erskine, and John Updike. It is one of the chief sources of critical inspection in *Love in the Western World*, Denis De Rougemont's brilliant disclosure of the persistence of medieval mythic expectations in modern love and marriage.

Malory's contribution to literary history is far more profound, however, than the simple provision of useful source material for later writers and authors. The specific features of his version have had an enduring impact on the Arthurian tradition in literature and in the arts. Malory expands on the character of Merlin and on Merlin's magical interventions on history through the mentoring of the king. Thus, the intriguing and morally ambiguous character of Merlin has become a mainstay in the history of literary consciousness.

Malory also places, one might argue, a modern emphasis on the secular order of knighthood via distinct codes of knightly behavior. The emphasis on loyalty and betterment sets the legend as an exemplary instructional manual for the more modern soldiers in training. The narrative, in fact, begins with political and military conflicts, all set in the unheroic and chaotic atmosphere of suspicious lineage, broken allegiances, and hopelessly convoluted claims to lands and power. There is no strong chain of command or ethos of good soldierhood. With the ascendancy of Arthur and Camelot, the political and military structure become more organized and the narrative focus shifts to individual tales of knightly challenges, culminating, of course, with the grail quests, all placed before the backdrop of Round Table worthiness or unworthiness. Malory's King Arthur is, above all, only looking for "a few good men."

Moral judgment as it circumscribes the Arthurian tale is also unique in Malory in that bad behavior is reported with little emotion and with no apology for the characters when they act wrongfully. This seems odd, given a story line was culled primarily from romances that focus relentlessly on the passions of characters caught in the overwhelming grips of illicit and thus passionate love. Love overwhelms heroes and brings personal and often political disaster. The chief thematic feature of courtly love stories is that they implore us to suspend our moral judgment in lieu of the sublime and grand eloquent emotions of larger than life characters rendered helpless by emotions that are transcendent, even supernatural, in force. In the end, the lovers are pitied, regardless of their wrongdoing.

Morte d'Arthur, however, sets a distinctly unromantic tone that shows a clear thematic departure from the source material. In Malory, kings and knights are not stylized into the apologetics of courtly love. King Uther's desire for Igraine, wife of the Duke of Cornwall, is merely reported: "The king [Uther] liked and loved this lady [Igraine] well . . . and desired to have lain by her. But she was a passing good woman, and would not assent unto the king" (1). With Merlin's help, Uther appears to Igraine in the likeness of her husband and sleeps with her. The matter-of-fact manner in which these acts are reported in Malory sets a harsh, even dismal tone for this part of the tale. Similarly, Malory's description of Launcelot's wooing of Queen Guinivere is dismal in its succinctness: "And then they [Launcelot's and Guinivere] made either to other their complaints of many divers things, and then Sir Launcelot wished that he might have come into her" (417). Poets have given hundreds of line to the above-mentioned "complaints" when they occur. In fact, one of the desired results of courtly love poetry is to develop fully the earnest nature of the characters through such complaints. In Malory's brusque descriptions, however, passions come off as simply lust, delivered as they are through simple, unadorned language that makes *Morte d'Arthur* reminiscent of certain fatalistic Old Testament stories. The atmosphere of the narrative is, on the whole, unforgiving.

The emotional austerity of Malory's presentation may be in the end what distinguishes *Morte d'Arthur* from any other version of the legend, before or after. Malory recognizes that the legend, as hopeful and aspiring as it might be at times, has an essentially tragic disposition. Arthur is faced with the classic hero's desperate struggle against inevitable doom and destruction, perhaps not from fate but from the cycle of deception and betrayal that circumscribes the story. Arthur, who was conceived by a deceiving father, is deceived by his sister, the enchantress, into conceiving the child, Mordred, who eventually destroys Arthur. Arthur is betrayed, memorably, of course, by his wife and best friend. Arthur is exemplary but by no means perfect. When he learns from Merlin that he is to be destroyed by one born on May Day (Mordred was born on May Day), he orders—with Roman flare—that all the children of nobles born on May Day be placed on a ship and sent to sea for certain death.

In *Morte d'Arthur*, we are not in the cycle of Medieval French romance or in the fantasy world of Lerner and Loewe's *Camelot*. We are not in the world of Christian moral allegory either. Malory's version of the legend examines the hard facts, leaving style and the psychology of justification to other writers. *Morte d'Arthur* is not about the inner thoughts of its characters; it is a book of acts and deeds. Though placed in a Christian framework, the good, when it is achieved, is brought about by humans acting on a secular code of personal betterment—by knights seeking to be the good knights through extraordinary deeds. Galahad, the pure or virginal knight, attains the kingdom of Christ because he does good and avoids doing bad. Similarly, bad events result from bad actions and deeds—whether direct and malicious acts of vengeance from a jealous kinsperson or ruler or the "dirty deed" resulting from mistaken (or not so mistaken) identity in bed.

As mentioned above, Malory's factual approach to the Arthurian legend tempts the biographer to draw parallels between fictional narrative and real political life in England during Malory's time. It is certain that *Morte d'Arthur* probes into the essence of regal and civic order. The lack of such order during the fifteenth century in England—the lack of a strong king who could consolidate power and cultivate loyalty—certainly could have provoked a knight-prisoner into a rediscovery of the Arthurian legend. Although Malory's work is difficult to frame as a direct political allegory, legends that explore such themes as knightly friendships ending in personal and political betrayal—or misguided trusts leading to disastrous conflict over regal lineage—certainly reflect the political climate that seemingly caused Malory's undoing.

In any case Malory's effort preserves and carries forward themes that have had and that continue to have enduring artistic, and even political, resonance. In sum, because of its innovations in narrative and presentation and because of its impact on later artists, Malory's *Morte d'Arthur* is certainly the most important, once-and-future monument in the history of Arthurian storytelling in English.

PRIMARY WORKS

Manuscript: The Winchester Manuscript, British Library. Add. MS. 59678. **Facsimile editions:** *The Winchester Malory: A Facsimile,* EETS, Supplemental series 4, ed. N. R. Ker. New York: Oxford University Press, 1976. *Le morte Darthur: The Winchester Manuscript,* ed. Helen Cooper. New York: Oxford University Press, 1998. **First publication:** *Thus endeth thys noble and Ioyous book entitled le morte Darthur.* Westminster: printed by William Caxton, 1485. **Facsimile edition:** New York: Scolar, 1976; **Standard editions:** *Le morte d'Arthur,* ed. John Matthews. London: Cassell, 2000. *Caxton's Malory: A New Edition of Sir Thomas Malory's Le Morte Darthur, Based on the Pierpont Morgan Copy of William Caxton's Edition of 1485,* ed. James W. Spisak. Berkeley: University of California Press, 1983. *The Works of Sir Thomas Malory,* 3 vols., ed. Eugene Vinaver. Oxford: Clarendon Press, 1947. 3ed ed., rev. P. J. C. Field. Oxford: Clarendon Press, 1990. *Le Morte Darthur: Sir Thomas Malory's Book of King Arthur and of His Noble Knights of the Round Table,* 2 vols., ed. William Caxton, A. W. Pollard, and Sir Edward Strachey. New York: Macmillan, 1903; available at http://etext.lib.virginia.edu/modeng/modengJ.-browse.html. *Sir Thomas Malory: Le Morte D'Arthur,* ed. Janet Cowen. New York: Penguin, 1969. *Le morte d'Arthur: King Arthur and the Legends of the Round Table,* ed. Keith Baines. 1962. Reprint, New York: Signet, 2001.

SECONDARY SOURCES

Archibald, Elizabeth. "Beginnings: The Tale of King Arthur and the Emperor Lucius." In *A Companion to Malory,* ed. Elizabeth Archibald and S. G. Edwards, 133–51. Cambridge: D. S. Brewer, 1996; Field, P. J. C. *The Life and Times of Sir Thomas Malory.* Cambridge: Boydell and Brewer, 1993; ———. "The Malory Life-Records." In *A Companion to Malory,* ed. Elizabeth Archibald and S. G. Edwards, 133–51. Cambridge: D. S. Brewer, 1996; Helterman, Jeffrey. "Sir Thomas Malory." In *Dictionary of Literary Biography.* Vol. 146, *Old and Middle English Literature,* ed. Jeffrey Helterman and Jerome Mitchell, 257–68. Detroit: Gale Research, 1994; Meale, Carol M. "'The Hoole Book.'" In *A Companion to Malory,* ed. Elizabeth Archibald and S. G. Edwards, 3–17. Cambridge: D. S. Brewer, 1996.

THOMAS WINN DABBS

EDMUND SPENSER
(c. 1552–January 13, 1599)

Between the middle ages and the rise of romanticism, the classical spirit ruled and was by nature alien to medievalism. That England's greatest poet since Geoffrey Chaucer chose to include Arthur in a romantic epic had great significance. While the overall quest belongs to the infallible Arthur in *The Faerie Queen*, he is certainly not the most important nor the most interesting character of Edmund Spenser's incomplete allegorical poem. Further, this is invented material about the blank period in the character's life, from his birth to his ascension to the throne. The name is the same, but the character is not the traditional king of Camelot. In terms of Arthuriana, Spenser's contribution is scant on the surface, but of enduring significance under scrutiny: as a Matter of Britain writer in the sixteenth century, Spenser kept the name of Arthur alive during a period when classical influences frowned upon such fancy. It had been proven that Arthur was never actually king of England (or anywhere else) so attitudes of pre-Enlightenment historical correctness generally frowned upon him. Smatterings of mentions were in fact all that kept the legends alive until the nineteenth century when Alfred, Lord Tennyson wrote *Idylls of the King* and the Pre-Raphaelite Brotherhood forged an obsession with medievalism.

Edmund Spenser was born around 1532 to a middle-class family. Little is known about his family, but it is likely that the Spenser's roots were in Lancashire and that Spenser had an unknown number of siblings. As a pre-teen, Spenser attended the Merchant Taylors' school, where he would have been exposed to a classical education with an emphasis on rhetoric. Additionally, Spenser was trained in the scholarly languages of Latin, Greek, and Hebrew. It was while he attended Merchant Taylors' that Spenser was first encouraged to write in verse. During his tenure at the school he met Thomas Kyd, Lancelot Andrewes, and Thomas Lodge, who were his fellow classmates. A short time later, in May 1569, Spenser left Merchant Taylors' and went to Cambridge, where he entered Pembroke Hall. His studies at Cambridge were supplemented by a monthly stipend of ten shillings presented to him by Robert Newell, who had also supplemented Spenser's tuition at Merchant Taylors'. Because of Newell's generosity, Spencer needed only work for his meals and housing.

During his tenure at Pembroke, Spenser found that he had a great interest in verse. He began composing original works, sharing them among his peers. He must have been pleased with his verses as he seems to have composed a great amount of work while he was there. Perhaps as important as his newfound love for poetry were the many good connections Spenser made at Cambridge. The acquaintances he made there became some of the central figures in his life. Perhaps the most important figure Spenser met during this period was his good friend Gabriel Harvey, who served as the liaison between Spenser and a number of future patrons, including Robert Dudley, Earl of Leicester. After three years of study, in 1573, Spenser graduated from Pembroke with a bachelor of arts degree.

He did not immediately leave Cambridge after graduating, opting instead to work on his master's degree. In 1576 Spenser took his master of arts, and he then left for Kent. Again he took advantage of his connections to rejoin with one of his former classmates, John Young. Young was the Bishop of Rochester, and Spenser served as his secretary. It was at this time that Spenser probably composed *The Shepheardes Calender*. Many critics have posited this to be a work, including characters clearly based upon Spenser's circle of friends. Of more import is the idea that this served as the first work to demonstrate Spenser's penchant for the medieval motifs he so admired and which he felt were being usurped by a growing movement towards humanism.

In 1579 Spenser took employment with the Earl of Leicester. His work was noticed by the preeminent author of the time, Sir Philip Sidney. Queen Elizabeth and her court considered Sidney of great cultural and artistic value, so Spenser admired him also. Indeed, Sidney often sang praises of Spenser in letters to their mutual acquaintance, Gabriel Harvey. This growing notoriety seems to have encouraged Spenser, but he realized that he would have a difficult time making a living solely as a writer. With assistance from Leicester, Spenser was appointed secretary to Lord Grey of Wilton in 1580. While this was a promotion, it did require that Spenser become a part of Britain's foreign service, and he left for Dublin in August. Prior to his leaving, the *Shepheardes Calender* was entered onto the Stationer's Register in June 1579. Arriving in Dublin, Spenser received the first glimpse of what he perceived to be a necessary English domination of a country. While Ireland had been claimed by England, it was hostile to the British and the natives refused to be subjugated. Spenser perceived the Irish to be radical rebels, a perspective he would later discuss in his *View of the Present State of Ireland*, a work written in 1596, but not published until some time after Spenser's death.

Spenser served the Crown well and spent the next decade or so in Ireland; his disdain for the Irish never abated. In 1586 Spenser was awarded some three thousand acres near Doneraile, including the old castle at Kilcolman. In June 1588 he was appointed to the post of clerk of the Council of Munster, residing near Cork. His tenure in Ireland took him to many locales until sometime around 1589, when Spenser met and began a friendship with Sir Walter Raleigh, who was living in Munster while he served as the mayor of Yougal. It was during this time that Spenser completed what would become the first three books of his most celebrated work, *The Faerie Queen*.

At this time Raleigh had the full support of the queen and her court as a writer of intensity and depth. Raleigh read a draft of Spenser's *The Faerie Queen*, and became so intrigued by Spenser's promise as a poet that he suggested that they travel together to London in 1590. During this campaign, Raleigh was invited to Buckingham Palace, where he personally presented Spenser to Queen Elizabeth. Good fortune continued to smile on Spenser, who found a publisher for the first three books of *The Faerie Queen*. Indeed, Spenser thought that he was on his way to literary prominence, but this was not to be. His work became well received, which brought him a brush with fame, but for reasons unknown, he could not secure the patron he so desired who would enable him to devote his life to his writings. Sadly, he came very close in this endeavor, only to taste the failure that would endure throughout his life. Queen Elizabeth herself had offered Spenser a large pension—one big enough to sate his literary appetite. Unfortunately, this fell through when the queen was pressured by a Lord Burghley to withdraw her offer. In 1591 Spenser took some vengeance when he cast the lord in a bad light in his *Complaints*. The *Complaints* so offended the court and the lord that they were deemed scandalous, and the work was quickly recalled by its publisher. Spenser was forced to return to Ireland empty handed, and he returned to his estate at Kilcolman.

Perhaps because of this scandal, Spenser was continually denied in his attempts to secure the financial favor of any member of the court; he did, however, seem to sway the monarch somewhat because he was granted the much smaller, fifty-pound annual stipend from Queen Elizabeth. In February he completed *Colin Clouts Come Home Again*; in January 1592 he published *Daphnaïda*. Also, Cuthbert Barbie published Spenser's attempt at a Platonic dialogue, *Axiochus*, which had the translation of it ascribed to one "Edw. Spenser." Spenser returned to Kilcolman, and was followed by good fortune and seemingly bad news. The year 1593 saw the death of Arthur, Lord Grey de Wilton, one of Spenser's closest acquaintances. Spenser was distraught by Arthur's passing, but he quickly recovered and fell in love with and courted Elizabeth Boyle, daughter of James Boyle, a relative of the first earl of Cork. They were married on June 11, 1594. Spenser's *Amoretti and Epithalamion*, published in London in 1595, is a recount of the couple's love. Spenser also finished the next three books (Books IV–VI) of *The Faerie Queen*. While the works were done before his vows, this version of *The Faerie Queen* was not to be printed until 1596.

Spenser used the publication of the revised version of *The Faerie Queen* as a reason to return to London. He must have remained there for about a year. While there, Spenser was well treated as the guest of the Earl of Essex. He was not idle during his time, as he began to work on *A vewe of the present state of Irelande*, which would not be published until after his death. He also was able to publish some of his shorter works, including *Fowre Hymnes* and *Prothalamion* during this time. Perhaps this was the height of Spenser's literary influence.

However, in Ireland, rebel forces were growing in both strength and anger against the British. They resented the empire building of the British occupiers and longed for their independence. By 1595 Hugh O'Neill, the Earl of Tyrone had been condemned by the British as a traitor for his efforts to lead Irish uprisings. Meanwhile, in London, Spenser once again was rebuffed in his efforts to secure a patron. Since he had failed to acquire a commitment that would allow him to stay in England as a writer, Spenser returned to his estate at Kilcolman, in April 1598. In September, Spenser was appointed sheriff of Cork County by order of the Privy Council. However, he only held this position for a short term, as O'Neill had led the Irish to a great victory over the British army at the Yellow Ford of the Blackwater in August 1598. This led to great unrest in Ireland as the people gained some hope that they could overthrow their occupiers, and within a month, all of Munster was in rebellion.

Spenser and his family fled back to the city of Cork to escape the dangerous horde. The president of Munster, Sir Thomas Norris, then sent Spenser to London to tell the

Privy Council the problems of the area. While he was away, the Irish rebels burned Spenser's estate at Kilcolman to the ground. Ben Jonson wrote that Spenser even lost his third child in the carnage. The tragedy became complete when Spenser arrived in London in late 1598 carrying messages concerning the upheaval in Ireland. He took up residence on King's Street and, according to Jonson, died "for lake of bread," on a Saturday in January 1599. He died as a pauper, for his funeral expenses were covered by the Earl of Essex, and poets carried his coffin. His tomb is situated adjacent to that of Geoffrey Chaucer in the Poet's Corner at Westminster Abbey. It remains a great mystery as to how someone of Spenser's stature could have died a pauper. With his connections to both the worlds of politics and the arts, it is inconceivable that he could have starved to death in poverty.

In his life Spenser completed perhaps a little more than one-half of his romantic epic *The Faerie Queen*. King Arthur is the hero of this poem; Spenser wanted Arthur to be both the ideal nobleman and representative of what Spenser termed "magnificence," his conception of the Aristotelian virtue of magnanimity. In this way, virtue becomes the sum of all the rest of one's attributes. *The Faerie Queen* begins when Arthur's father, Uther Pendragon, is attacked by Octa, the son of Hengist, and Octa's relative Eosa. At this time, Arthur is still a prince; he sees Gloriana, the Faerie Queen, in a dream and falls in love with her. He then begins a quest to locate the Faerie Queen; during his travels he meets many adversaries who unsuccessfully attempt to expose his lack of virtue and prowess.

Because Spenser died before completing the poem, we do not really know how it would have ended. The poet explained in a letter to Raleigh that the poem was supposed to be composed of twelve books. Each of these was intended to treat one of Aristotle's moral virtues here represented in the figure of a knight. But Spenser must have decided to amend his plan as by the fourth book the idea of each knight representing a single virtue has been abandoned. However, the theme of each book does seem to stick to this plan. More importantly, Spenser begins including virtues that were not Aristotelian. Too Spenser never deviates from the idea that virtue is a means by which we may see the moderate path between being excessive or deficient.

Additionally, Spenser loads *The Faerie Queen* with allusions to classical texts—both Latin and Greek—as well as biblical ones. And the work seems to have a strong base in Ludovico Ariosto's *Orlando furioso*. Spenser stays somewhat true to the Italian's tone and ideation, but eliminates much of Ariosto's irony and skepticism, instead opting to make the work a place to discuss his high morals and those of his monarch. Thus, *The Faerie Queen* is transformed from a simple book espousing courtesy to one that distinguishes what creates the ideal Christian man. Spenser even invented the stanza form he used. Spenserian stanza is composed of nine lines; the first eight lines have ten syllables (iambic pentameter) and the rhyme scheme ABAB BCBC. The ninth line has twelve syllables (iambic hexameter) and echoes the C rhyme.

Book I is perhaps the most well known of all *The Faerie Queen*. It concerns the Red Cross Knight, also known as the Knight of Holiness. He is a true knight and follows most closely Spenser's plan in composing the epic. The Red Cross Knight is asked to expunge a ferocious dragon from the kingdom of Una. This is no easy task, but the Red Cross Knight slowly develops all of the attributes needed for him to be both chivalric and stalwart in virtue. While initially seemingly doomed to failure, the Red Cross Knight eventually gains the attributes mandated to slay the wily beast.

Similarly straightforward is Book II. In it Sir Guyon is the Knight of Temperance—moderation, abstinence, and restraint. He suffers a series of setbacks, but learns from the experiences, thus enhancing his awareness of his title. He notes that temperance is greatly affected by the sins of excess and the defects it causes, both physically and mentally. The hideous notion of self-indulgence makes Guyon more and more aware of his task, which is overcome only when he realizes the folly of inhuman brutality. He initially is overpowered by the allegorical foe he opposes, but in the end Guyon is able to reject the pleasures thrust at him in the Bower of Bliss.

Books III and IV have different themes, Chastity and Friendship, but both are filled with a sort of appropriation of the Renaissance conception of platonic love. This shows that the allegorical methods acknowledged by Spenser have begun to change from the personal love found in his *Amoretti and Epithalamion*. This may be because the virtues are a bit more complicated than the initial two. Chastity is a much more complicated idea than physical love because one must reconcile the idea that in being chaste, even though carnal relations are not an option, carnal feelings do indeed exist. This the question arises as to how one deals with this seeming paradox. In this section, Spenser shows that carnal needs differ entirely from the idea of being gallant; the notion of serving for one's spiritual pleasure. Here the earlier characters return in brief intervals, perhaps to reinforce their previous tenets. Instead of telling the audience the import of Chastity, Spenser uses an tortuous web of characters to posit his consideration. He accomplishes this by presenting grand examples that offer comparisons and contrasts to the idea that chastity is much more than sexual abstinence. Chastity is the realization that one is drawn closer to a divine revelation only after understanding the glory of the perception of beauty that must be coupled with experience bound in love. This is a concept termed "mutuality," and it is shown when Scudamour is unable to accomplish his quest until acknowledging that Britomart must contribute and play a key role in his development.

This is countered by the premise in Book IV that offers insight into the difficult essence of friendship. There are always intrusions that cause leaks in the buttresses of commonality, but as the book explains, even these can be overcome, especially in the noblest of all friendships, that between a man and a woman. The way Book IV plays off of Book III is interesting in that one would usually think that friendship would be a good precursor, or at least a healthier alternative to the call for chastity. There are great frustrations in dealing with friends; however, the annoyances are kept personal, especially when between the sexes. In spite of the human annoyances conveyed throughout Book IV, the work grandly portrays both the pitfalls and the grandiose elements of friendship.

Artegall is the hero of Book V. Here Spenser demonstrates his conception of politics and attempts to forward a bit of a philosophy concerning it. He notes that justice must be the end result of all conflicts. In its pursuit of truth, justice must be inflexible and unyielding. This should not be a difficult abstraction but a way of life that leads to wise governing. Of course, if this were true, many conflicts could have been avoided. Therefore, Spenser uses Book V to show both the glory of wise decisions and the trauma of the unwise. In the truest of Aristotelian terms this is among the most difficult concepts to illustrate given that one person's good is another's bad. The stern structure of Book V offers a stark contrast to the less stringent somewhat pastoral treatment of courtesy found in the previous books in chivalric terms, and Sir Calidore attempts to learn this grace.

While the work was not completed, it can be supposed that Arthur would have found and been united with Gloriana. This seems to be a metaphor for the re-emergence of the glory of the Tudors. The work seems to have been composed on three levels concerning the characters. On the first level, the work seems to be a courtly romance. On another level, the characters become metaphors for various ideals, such as Christianity or truth. On the third level, the characters have been found to represent real people from Spenser's inner circle. Because many of these levels are esoteric, modern readers have a difficult time with the text.

The Arthurian legend serves Spenser well as a framing device for his tale; however, the actual characters from Camelot serve secondary functions in the work. Spenser uses very little traditional Arthurian legend in *The Faerie Queen*; indeed Arthur and Merlin are the only figures from the legends who have roles of any substance. Oddly Spenser bases Arthur's quest for Gloriana on that odd tale from Geoffrey Chaucer, *The Tale of Sir Thopas*, which is actually probably best described as an anti-Arthurian work parody.

Sir Tristram is the only other Arthurian character with a role, and even this is tiny. In essence, Spenser depends upon what his audience would have known without having to retell the legendary stories of Arthur to shroud his metaphorical intent. Obviously the work is meant to compliment the Tudors in general, Elizabeth I in particular, as Gloriana, the reigning monarch, is depicted splendidly. Spenser alters the Order of the Garter to become the Order of Maidenhead—Gloriana's knights—and to take on the role of the Round Table. Spencer's Arthur is given quite a burden. He must be infallible and thus invincible; because of this there is nothing interesting about his character, and he is easily overlooked as one of *The Faerie Queen*'s essential pillars. Thus, it must be noted that this work is not a very good Arthurian poem. Critics disagree over its merits as a poem outside the realm of Arthurian legend. However, this piece is extremely important in the continuation of Arthurian legend from the sixteenth century onward.

Spenser earned the title "the prince of poets" as the English considered his creations to be on a par with Virgil's Latin works. What is remarkable about Spenser is his versatility as a writer. He is known to have composed great works in many different genres of poetry, including: pastoral, elegy, and epithalamion. His prose treatise on the reformation of Ireland was unpublished until 1633, but it foreshadowed the problems facing English government in Ireland, which exist even today. Too it demonstrated that he could write prose as well as poetry. Other authors, including no less than John Milton, were influenced by Spenser. Milton claimed Spenser was as valuable as Thomas Aquinas in terms of what he taught him. Yet it is his *Faerie Queen,* with its theme of good versus evil, that catches the attention of the modern reader. Although unfinished, the extant portion shows that it had the potential to be quite the epic poem, and he pulls the reader into the work by his allegorical treatment of the moral virtues. More importantly here is that Spenser keeps the tradition of the Arthurian legend alive because he opted to use the unfashionable figure at a time when the canon was rejecting medievalism. Even though the poem is incomplete, it is an invaluable work showing the ongoing quest for an understanding of love.

PRIMARY WORKS

The Shepherdes Calendar Conteyning Twelve Æglogues Proportionable to the Twelve Monethes; Entitled to the Noble and Vertuous Gentleman Most Worthy of All Titles Both of Learning and Cheualrie M. Philip Sidney. London: printed by Hugh Singleton, 1579; *Three Proper and Wittie Familiar Letters: Lately Passed between Two Vniversity Men: Touching the Earthquake in April Last, and Our English Refourmed Versifying and Two Other Very Commendable Letters of the Same Mens Writing: Both Touching the Foresaid Artificial Versifying, and Certain Other Particulars.* London: H. Bynneman, 1580; *The Faerie Queen. Disposed in Twelve Books, Fashioning XII Moral Virtues.* Contains Books I–III. London: printed for William Ponsonby, 1590; *Complaints Containing Sundrie Small Poems of the Worlds Vanite . . . By Ed. Sp.* London: Imprinted for William Ponsonby, 1591; *Daphnaïda. An Elegie upon the Death of the Noble and Vertuous Douglas Howard,*

Daughter and Heire of Henry Lord Howard, Viscount Byndon, and Wife of Arthure Gorges Esquier. Dedicated to the Right Honourable the Lady Helena, Marquesse of Northampton. By Ed. Sp. London: printed for William Ponsonby, 1595; *Colin Clovts Come Home Again. By Ed. Sp.* London: printed for William Ponsonby, 1595; *Amoretti and Epithalamion. Written Not Long Since by Edmunde Spenser.* London: printed for William Ponsonby, 1595; *The Faerie Queen. Disposed into Twelve Bookes, Fashioning XII. Morall Vertues.* Contains Books I–VI, with a revised ending for III. London: printed for William Ponsonby, 1596; *Foure Hymnes, Made by Edm. Spenser.* London: printed for William Ponsonby, 1596; *Prothalamion Or A Spousall Verse Made by Edm. Spenser. In Honour of the Double Marriage of the Two Honorable and Vertuous Ladies, the Ladie Elizabeth and the Ladie Katherine Somerset, Daughters to the Right Honourable the Earl of Worcester and Espoused to the Two Worthie Gentlemen M. Henry Gilford, and M. William Peter Esquyers.* London: printed for William Ponsonby, 1596; *The Faerie Queen. Disposed into Twelve Bookes, Fashioning XII. Morall Vertues,* 2 vols. London: printed for H[enry] L[ownes] for Matthew Lownes, 1609–1613; *A Vewe of the Present State of Ireland,* in *The History of Ireland, Collected by Three Learned Authors, viz. Meredith Hammer ... Edmund Campion ... and Edmund Spenser, Esq.*, ed. Sir James Ware. Dublin: printed by the Society of Stationers, 1633.

Collections and Editions

Spenser's "Faerie Queen," 2 vols., ed. J. C. Smith. Oxford: Clarendon Press, 1909; *Spenser's Minor Poems,* ed. Ernest de Selincourt. Oxford: Clarendon Press, 1910; *The Works of Edmund Spenser: A Variorum Edition,* 11 vols., ed. Edwin Greenlaw et al. Baltimore: Johns Hopkins University Press, 1932–1957; *Books I and II of "The Faerie Queen," The Mutability Cantos, and Selections from the Minor Poetry,* ed. Robert Kellogg and Oliver Steele. Indianapolis: Bobbs-Merrill, 1965; *The Mutablitie Cantos,* ed. S. P. Zitner. London: Nelson, 1968; *"The Faerie Queen," 1596,* 2 vols., ed. Graham Hough. Menston, UK: Scholar, 1976; *The Faerie Queen,* ed. A. C. Hamilton. London: Longman, 1977; *The Faerie Queen,* ed. Thomas P. Roche, Jr. London: Penguin, 1978; *Edmund Spenser: The Illustrated "Faerie Queen"—a Modern Prose Adaptation,* ed. Douglas Hill. New York: Newsweek, 1980; *The Yale Edition of the Shorter Poems of Edmund Spenser,* ed. William A. Oram et al. New Haven, CT: Yale University Press, 1989; *Edmund Spenser's Poetry,* Norton Critical Edition Series, 3rd ed., ed. Hugh Maclean and Anne Lake Prescott. New York: Norton, 1993.

SECONDARY SOURCES

Alpers, Paul J. *Elizabethan Poetry: Modern Essays in Criticism.* New York: Oxford University Press, 1967; ———. *The Poetry of the Faerie Queen.* Princeton, NJ: Princeton University Press, 1967; Aptekar, Jane. *Icons of Justice: Iconography and Thematic Imagery in Book V of The Faerie Queene.* New York: Columbia University Press, 1969; Bender, John B. *Spenser and Literary Pictorialism.* Princeton, NJ: Princeton University Press, 1972; Bennet, Josephine W. *The Evolution of "The Faerie Queene."* New York: B. Franklin, 1960; Berger, Harry. *The Allegorical Temper: Vision and Reality in Book II of Spenser's Faerie Queene.* Hamden, CT: Archon, 1967; ———. *Spenser: A Collection of Critical Essays.* Englewood Cliffs, NJ: Prentice Hall, 1968; Bernard, John D. *Ceremonies of Innocence: Pastoralism in the Poetry of Edmund Spenser.* New York: Cambridge University Press, 1989; Cavanagh, Sheila T. *Wanton Eyes and Chaste Desires: Female Sexuality in the Faerie Queene.* Bloomington: Indiana University Press, 1994; Cheney, Donald. *Spenser's Image of Nature: Wild Man and Shepherd in The Faerie Queene.* New Haven, CT: Yale University Press, 1966; Cory, Herbert E. *The Critics of Edmund Spenser.* New York: Haskell House, 1964; Crampton, Georgia Ronan. *The Condition of Creatures: Suffering and Action in Chaucer and Spenser.* New Haven, CT: Yale University Press, 1974; Cullen, Patrick. *Infernal Triad: The Flesh, the World, and the Devil in Spenser and Milton.* Princeton, NJ: Princeton University Press, 1975; ———. *Spenser, Marvell, and Renaissance Pastoral.* Cambridge, MA: Harvard University Press, 1970; Davies, Stevie. *The Feminine Reclaimed: The Idea of Woman in Spenser, Shakespeare, and Milton*. Lexington: University Press of Kentucky, 1986; DeNeef, A. Leigh. *Spenser and the Motives of Metaphor*. Durham, NC: Duke University Press, 1982; Dundas, Judith. *The Spider and the Bee: The Artistry of Spenser's Faerie Queene*. Urbana: University of Illinois Press, 1985; Dunseath, T. K. *Spenser's Allegory of Justice in Book V of the Faerie Queene*. Princeton, NJ: Princeton University Press, 1968; Eustace, Bernard C. *Edmund Spenser: A Critical Study*. New York: Russell and Russell, 1962; Evans, Maurice. *Spenser's Anatomy of Heroism: A Commentary on the Faerie Queene*. Cambridge: Cambridge University Press, 1970; Fletcher, Angus John Stewart. *The Prophetic Moment: An Essay on Spenser*. Chicago: Chicago University Press, 1971; Fowler, Earle Broadus. *Spenser and the System of Courtly Love*. New York: Phaeton Press, 1968; Freeman, Rosemary. *The Faerie Queene: A Companion for Readers*. Berkeley: University of California Press, 1970; Frushell, Richard C. *Contemporary Thought on Edmund Spenser: With a Bibliography of Criticism of The Faerie Queene, 1900–1970*. Carbondale: Southern Illinois University Press, 1975; Gleckner, Robert F. *Blake and Spenser*. Baltimore: Johns Hopkins University Press, 1985; Gray, Margaret Muriel. *The Influence of Spenser's Irish Experiences on the Faerie Queene*. Folcroft, PA: Folcroft Library Editions, 1977; Greenlaw, Edwin A. *Studies in Spenser's Historical Allegories*. New York: Octagon, 1967; Guillory, John. *Poetic Authority: Spenser, Milton, and Literary History*. New York: Columbia University Press, 1983; Hamilton, A. C. *Essential Articles for the Study of Edmund Spenser*. Hamden, CT: Archon, 1972; ———. *The Structure of Allegory in the Faerie Queene*. Oxford: Clarendon Press, 1961; Hankins, John Erskine. *Source and Meaning in Spenser's Allegory: A Study of the Faerie Queene*. Oxford: Clarendon Press, 1971; Harper, Carrie Anna. *The Sources of the British Chronicle History in Spenser's Faerie Queene*. New York: Haskell House, 1964; Horton, Ronald Arthur. *The Unity of The Faerie Queene*. Athens: University of Georgia Press, 1978; Hough, Graham Goulden. *A Preface to The Faerie Queene*. New York: Norton, 1963; Kane, Sean. *Spenser's Moral Allegory*. Toronto: University of Toronto Press, 1989; King, John M. *Spenser's Poetry and Reformation Tradition*. Princeton, NJ: Princeton University Press, 1990; Lockerd, Benjamin G. *The Sacred Marriage: Psychic Integration in the Faerie Queene*. Lewisburg, PA: Bucknell University Press, 1987; Lotspeich, Henry Gibbons. *Classical Mythology in the Poetry of Edmund Spenser*. New York: Gordian Press, 1965; MacCaffrey, Isabel Gamble. *Spenser's Allegory: The Anatomy of Imagination*. Princeton, NJ: Princeton University Press, 1976; McNeir, Waldo F. *Edmund Spenser: An Annotated Bibliography, 1937–1972*. Pittsburgh: Duquesne University Press, 1975; Mikics, David. *The Limits of Moralizing: Pathos and Subjectivity in Spenser and Milton*. Lewisburg, PA: Bucknell University Press, 1994; Millican, Charles Bowie. *Spenser and the Table Round: A Study in the Contemporaneous Background for Spenser's Use of the Arthurian Legend*. New York: Octagon, 1967; Nelson, William. *The Poetry of Edmund Spenser: A Study*. New York: Columbia University Press, 1963; Nohrnberg, James Carson. *The Analogy of the Faerie Queene*. Princeton, NJ: Princeton University Press, 1976; O'Connell, Michael. *Mirror and Veil: The Historical Dimension of Spenser's Faerie Queene*. Chapel Hill: University of North Carolina Press, 1977; Osgood, Charles Grosvenor. *A Concordance to the Poems of Edmund Spenser*. Gloucester, MA: P. Smith, 1963; Parker, Pauline. *The Allegory of the Faerie Queene*. Oxford: Clarendon Press, 1960; Rix, Herbert David. *Rhetoric in Spenser's Poetry*. Folcroft, PA: Folcroft Press, 1969; Rose, Mark. *Spenser's Art: A Companion to Book One of the Faerie Queene*. Cambridge, MA: Harvard University Press, 1975; Sale, Roger. *Reading Spenser: An Introduction to the Faerie Queene*. New York: Random House, 1968; Sipple, William L. *Edmund Spenser, 1900–1936: A Reference Guide*. Boston, G. K. Hall, 1984; Tonkin, Humphrey. *Spenser's Courteous Pastoral: Book Six of the Faerie Queene*. Oxford: Clarendon Press, 1972; Waller, Gary F. *Edmund Spenser: A Literary Life*. New York: St. Martin's Press, 1994; Warton, Thomas. *Observations on the Fairy Queen of Spenser*. New York: Greenwood, 1968; Williams, Arnold. *Flower on a Lowly Stalk: The Sixth Book of the Faerie Queene*. East Lansing: Michigan State University Press, 1967; Williams, Kathleen. *Spenser's World of Glass: A Reading of the Faerie Queene*. Berkeley: University of California Press, 1966.

ROBERT THOMAS LAMBDIN AND LAURA COONER LAMBDIN

THOMAS HEYWOOD
(c. 1573–August 16, 1641)

Thomas Heywood (also spelled "Haiwood" and "Haywood[e]") was a well-respected author, poet, and playwright, both prolific and versatile. In his selective study of the writer, Frederick S. Boas comments that "no leading Elizabethan dramatist except Shakespeare had so continuous a professional connection with the stage" (15), spending more than forty years acting on and writing for the stage. Boas goes on to explain that *A Woman Killed with Kindness*, first produced by the Earl of Worcester's Men in 1603, "set the seal on his reputation as a dramatist" (39). Based in part on his experience as an actor, Heywood wrote *An Apology for Actors* (1612) to defend the men who worked as actors; this treatise was so successful that three years later an author referred to as "J. G." wrote *A Refutation of the Apology for Actors* in response. In his reference guide to the author, Michael Wentworth comments on Heywood's two most popular works as follows: "*Fair Maid of the West* is often cited as the finest adventure-romance in the language," and "critics have almost unanimously praised *A Woman Killed with Kindness* as the greatest English domestic tragedy" (xi). Although various critics over the years have attempted to assign Heywood's name to numerous plays and other works, the ones listed here are accepted as being his without question.

Thomas Heywood apparently was born in Lincolnshire, England, somewhere between July 1573 and the end of 1575. Evidence gathered by Arthur Melville Clark for his 1931 critical biography of the playwright indicates Heywood was probably the oldest son of Elizabeth and the Reverend Robert Heywood, rector of Rothwell and Ashby-cum-Fenby from 1575–93. As Frederick Boas and Barbara Baines remind readers in their books on the author, in his tract titled *An Apology for Actors* (1612), Heywood writes about spending time living in Cambridge, where he has an opportunity to see a variety of plays on the stages there; in fact, Clark suggests Heywood may have been one of the actors. Records for Emmanuel College in Cambridge, according to Boas, indicate a Thomas Heywood entered there "as a pensioner about 1591" and left in 1593 (12), which would have been when records indicate the reverend died, adding credibility to this connection of the playwright with the college.

When Heywood left Cambridge, he headed for London, obtained a job as an actor and found himself involved in revising some of the dramas being presented, including Christopher Marlowe's *The Jew of Malta*. By 1598 he was under contract as an actor with the Admiral's men; Barbara Baine's chronology in her book on the author indicates that Henslowe's *Diary* records payment that year to Heywood for a play now lost, *War Without Blows and Love Without Strife*, followed a year later by Parts 1 and 2 of *Edward IV*. In 1601 as a popular actor, and apparently for a share of the profits, Heywood joined the Earl of Worcester's company (the Queen's Servants Company in some lists), which would become Queen Anne's company (referred to in lists as the Queen's Company II) in 1603 after the death of Queen Elizabeth. While there, he penned *How a Man May Choose a Good Wife from a Bad* (1602), *The Royal King and the Loyal Subject* (1602), *A Woman Killed with Kindness* (1603), Parts 1 and 2 of *If You Know Not Me, You Know Nobody* (1604–1605), and the five parts of *The Ages* (1609–1612) among others. After completing *The Ages*, Heywood retired from the stage and took a break from writing plays until 1624, when he began writing for Lady Elizabeth's men who performed *Captives, or the Lost Recovered* at the Cockpit Theater. The company reformed itself in 1625 as Queen Henrietta's theatrical company (Queen's Men III in the lists) and performed *The English Traveller*, among others. In 1631 Heywood began an association with the trade guilds that lasted to 1639, writing pageants commissioned by the various guilds like the Drapers and the Haberdashers in honor of a member of that guild's being elected as Lord Mayor. Most of the pageants, as Boas describes them, have Heywood's classical interests at their core, with scenes, stories, and characters from classical literature placed in a London context. His 1634 masque written at the invitation of Queen Henrietta for King Charles I's birthday benefited from collaboration with famed set designer Inigo Jones for the scenic effects.

Even though Heywood is known today primarily as a playwright (and though in 1596 *Oenone and Paris*, his poem imitating Ovid, was published), the first book he prepared specifically for publication was actually a translation of a work by Crispus C. Sallustius: *The Two most worthy and notable Histories which remain unmained to Posterity: (viz.) The Conspiracy of Catiline, undertaken against the government of the Senate of Rome, and The War which Jugurth for many years maintained against the same State* (1608; sometimes listed as the separate parts, *The Conspiracy of Catiline* and *The War of Jugurtha*). This translation was followed in 1609 by *Troia Britannica or Great Britain's Troy*, which Boas describes as Heywood's first important original nondramatic work (58). After completing *Gunaikeion, or Nine Books of Various History Concerning Women* in 1624, Heywood wrote a prose history of Queen Elizabeth's life ... *from the Cradle to the Crown* (1631) followed by a couplet version that covered the period ... *from the womb to the Tomb, from her Birth to her Burial* (1639) and *The Hierarchy of the Blessed Angels* (1635). Finally, in 1640 Heywood's attention turned to Merlin's prophecies, which he apparently believed were authentic.

The full title of the piece is *The Life of Merlin, Surnamed Ambrosius, his Prophecies, and Predictions interpreted: and their truth made good by our English Annalls*. Part One provides *"A Chronographical History of the Kings of Britaine, from the first plantation of this Island by* Brute, *and his Cousin* Corinæus, *to the Reigne of King* Vortiger: *In whose time* Ambrosius Merlinus *began to utter his Predictions."* As the subtitle indicates, the overview of significant events begins with the arrival of Brute, a descendant of Troy through

Æneas, who settles the island with a small band of followers 1,136 years before the birth of Christ. The summary continues over six chapters through the story of King Leir (Lear) and his three daughters to the arrival of Julius Cæsar, eventually reaching Constantine, who comes to power in 433 CE and whose third son Vterpendragon is too young to succeed his father. Constantine is followed by Vortigerus (or Vortigernus) during whose reign Ambrosius Merlinus was born.

Part Two turns to "A true Historie of the strange Birth of *Ambrosius Merlin*, and his wonderful Prophesies." After addressing the circumstances of Merlin's birth to the virgin daughter of King Demetius (Merlin's father was an incubus), the story presents a brief history of prophecies to create a context for Merlin's prophecies that follow. The first prophecy arises out of Merlin's meeting with Vortiger. The king's attempt to build a castle on a hill west of the Grana River has been hindered by a sinking foundation. When Merlin is brought in to solve the problem, he points out the architects were attempting to build over a subterranean lake; if they would dig further down and drain the lake, they would discover "two hollow Rocks of stone, and in them two horrible Dragons fast sleeping" (22). The architects do as directed, releasing the dragons—one red, one white—who fight violently until only the white one remains. When the king questions what he has just seen, Merlin responds with his first prophecy, revealing that the Saxons (the white dragon) would come as friends, but they would eventually overpower the Britains (the red dragon) and squelch the worship of Christianity. However, the prophecy concludes, "out of Cornwall shall proceed a Bore, / Who shall the Kerk to pristine state restore, / Bow shall all Britaine to his kingly beck, / And tread he shall on the white Dragons neck" (23–24), fortelling King Arthur's arrival and eventual salvation of the country. The next four prophecies continue presenting early British history, including the Saxon invasion through Cadwallo and the civil wars that result after his death. The subsequent twenty-two prophecies start with Hardy Canutus the Dane being crowned King of England in 1041, and continue through William the Conquerer, Kings Stephen, Henry II, Richard I, John, Henry III, Edward I–III, Richard II, Henry IV–VI, Edward IV–V, Richard III, Henry VII–VIII, and Edward VI to Queen Mary and Elizabeth, ending with James I.

Heywood's chronicle originally ends with King Charles I coming to power March 27, 1625, leaving that king's reign to future chroniclers. The 1651 revision of the book ends with the funeral of James I, removing all reference to Charles and Queen Henrietta. On August 16, 1641, Thomas Heywood, Poet, was buried in the church of St. James at Clerkenwell, bringing to an end a career filled with mixed success.

Very little has been written critically specifically about Heywood's *Life of Merlin* (1640). Writing for the May 1928 issue of *Modern Language Notes*, Louis B. Wright points out that Heywood's nondramatic publications provide the essence of the author's contribution to literature. In "Heywood and the Popularizing of History," Wright emphasizes Heywood's awareness "of the value of history for its patriotic teaching," desiring "to present it in a brief and accurate form for the benefit of the general public" (288). Heywood wrote *Life of Merlin* to popularize historical knowledge in what Wright describes as a "straightforward and unprejudiced" manner (288), reporting facts without personal bias, even through the passages dealing with religious controversy, making Heywood a very "modern" writer in Wright's eyes. The value of Heywood's nondramatic work is echoed by Sarah Evelyn Jackson; the abstract of her 1959 dissertation on four of Heywood's nondramatic works (including *Life of Merlin*), indicates Heywood, in her eyes, was careful to "blend instruction with delight" while penning works that would appeal to the middle class masses who were purchasing his works (1788).

Taking a slightly different approach while writing for *The Journal of Modern History*, Wright considers in his 1931 article "The Elizabethan Middle-class Taste for History" why writers like Heywood might have chosen to attack the topic of England's past. Pointing out that the middle classes were the predominate market of the time, and they were fascinated by history, Wright explains that for centuries, the study of history played a key role in proper training of a gentleman; therefore, studying history was also deemed central to instill comparable qualities in the sons of the middle-class shopkeepers. In addition, "histories were hailed as the perfect literature of the middle class" (179), in part because of the elastic boundaries of the word "history"—even fictional tales could be and frequently were included. In the preface to *Life of Merlin*, Heywood clearly indicates his indebtedness to several popular chronicles of the day: those by Robert Fabyan (printed in 1516), Raphael Holinshed (died in 1580), and the *Universal Chronicle* (or *Polychronicon*) by Ranulf Hidgon who died in 1364. Wright concludes his analysis of various chronicles by observing that Heywood made special effort to present "accurate historical and biographical material in readable form" (196), striving to present a better quality of work than hack writers of his day were putting forth.

In his biography of the author, Arthur Melville Clark indicates "Heywood's interest in Merlin's prophecies was partly temperamental, for he was as credulous as a child of the strange and wonderful" (184). In his *Life of Merlin*, Heywood states that his work is based upon "*Jeffery* of *Monmouth*" (8), whose "Prophecies of Merlin" were originally printed as a separate pamphlet before being incorporated into his *History of the Kings of Britain* as part V or section vii, depending upon the edition used. Geoffrey's work ends with Cadwallader's death in 689, so Heywood had to expand upon the material available to him in order to bring the history up to date. According to Clark, Heywood is actually indebted to Alanus de Insulis's 1603 edition of *Prophetia Anglicana Merlini Ambrosii Britanni (Prophecies of the Anglican Merlin Ambrosius of Britain)* for a significant portion of the work, which might explain the additional prophecies. The historical matter, however, belongs to Fabyan's *The Concordance of Histories*, which, according to Clark, Heywood "quotes for pages at a time" (185), supplemented with Chronicles written by Holinshed, Polychronicon (i.e., Higdon), and Speed, according to Heywood's preface to the reader.

Because his plays were not collected into a single volume, as Ben Jonson's were in 1616 and William Shakespeare's were in 1623, as Boas observes in his study of the author, "only a relatively small proportion of his prolific dramatic output has survived and can be identified" positively as belonging to Heywood (16). According to Boas, essayist Elia Lamb described Heywood as "a prose Shakespeare" (157), apparently, Boas opines, based solely upon Heywood's work as a dramatist. Boas, in contrast, places Heywood's significant contribution with his poems, *Troia Britannica* and *The Hierarchy of the Blessed Angels*, while Wright places it with his histories. Supporting Lamb's focus on the primacy of drama, Otelia Cromwell's 1928 study of the author's drama focuses on Heywood's preoccupation with depicting the burgeoning middle-class of sixteenth and seventeenth century England within his plays.

Ultimately, Boas sums up the general critical attitude toward Heywood by observing that "although much about the life of Thomas Heywood must remain conjectural, the prefatory letters, prologues, and epilogues to his plays and the self-reflecting digressions in the nondramatic works provide valuable information about his attitude toward his profession and about his sense of achievement" (5). Heywood maintains an important part in the study of Elizabethan and Jacobean drama because, according to Boas, "he contributed substantially to our understanding of his fellow playwrights" through his *An Apology for Actors* (6). When the full extent of his canon is considered—plays dealing with history, comedy, tragedy, tragicomedy as well as myths; plus poetry and prose reflecting a similar breadth of interest—readers find an author whose work represents, as Baines sums up, "the richness and variety of [the] Renaissance" (158).

PRIMARY WORKS

Play Productions

The Four Prentices of London: With the Conquest of Jerusalem, London, unknown theater, Admiral's Men, c. 1592–1600; *The Fair Maid of the West, or A Girl Worth Gold* Part I, London, unknown theater, c. 1597–1610; *War without Blows and Love Without Strife* (lost play), London, Rose Theater, Admiral's Men, December 6, 1598; *Joan as Good as my Lady* (lost play), London, Rose Theater, Admiral's Men, February 10, 1599; *King Edward the Fourth* Parts I and II, London, Curtain Theater?, Earl of Derby's Company, c. 1592–1599; *How a Man May Choose a Good Wife from a Bad*, London, Boar's Head Theater, Earl of Worcester's Men, c. 1601–1602; *Albere Galles* (possibly the same play as *Nobody and Somebody*), with Wentworth Smith, London, Rose Theater, Worcester's Men, September 4, 1602; *Lady Jane* (lost play?), with Smith, Henry Chettle, Thomas Dekker and John Webster; London, unknown theater, Worcester's Men, October 15, 1602; *How a Man May Choose a Good Wife from a Bad*, London, unknown theater, Worcester's Men, c. 1602; *The Royal King and the Loyal Subject*, with Smith (possibly the same play as *Marshal Osric*), London, Rose Theater, Worcester's Men, autumn 1602; *Christmas comes but once a year* (lost play), with Chettle, Dekker, and Webster, London, Boar's Head or Rose Theater, Worcester's Men, November 1602; *The Blind Eats Many a Fly* (lost play), London, Rose Theater, Worcester's Men, November 24, 1602; *The London Florentine* (lost play), with Chettle, London, unknown theater, Admiral's Men, December 18, 1602; *A Woman Killed with Kindness*, London, Rose Theater, Worcester's Men, February 12, 1603; *If You Know Not Me, You Know Nobody* Parts I and II, London, Boar's Head or Curtain Theater, Queen's Men II, 1603–1605; *The Wise Woman of Hogsdon* (identical to *How to learn of a Woman to Woo* at Court, December 30, 1604), London, Curtain Theater, the Queen's Men II, 1605; *The Rape of Lucrece, A True Roman Tragedie*, London, Red Bull Theater, the Queen's Men II, 1607; *Fortune by Land and Sea*, with William Rowley, London, Red Bull Theater, Queen's Men II, c. 1607–1609; *Appius and Virginia*, with Webster, London, Red Bull Theater, the Queen's Men II, 1608; *The Golden Age*, London, Red Bull Theater, Queen's Men II, c. 1609–1611; *The Silver Age*, London, Red Bull, Black Friars and Globe Theaters(?), Queen's Men II and Kings Men, c. 1610–1612; *The Brazen Age*, London, Red Bull Theater, Queen's Men II, c. 1610–1613; *The Iron Age* Part I and Part II, London, Red Bull Theater, Queen's Men II, c. 1612–1613; *Captives, or The Lost Recovered*, London, Cockpit Theater, Lady Elizabeth's Company, September 2, 1624; *Calisto, or The Escapes of Jupiter* (scenes from *The Golden Age* and *The Silver Age*) London: unknown theater, c. 1625; *The English Traveller*, London, Cockpit Theater, Queen's Men III Company, c. 1625–1627; *Dick of Devonshire*, London, Cockpit Theater, Queen's Men III, summer 1626; *The Fair Maid of the West* Part II, London, Cockpit Theater, Queen's Men III Company, c. 1630–1631; *London's Jus Honorarium*, streets of London, pageant for the Haberdashers' Company, October 29, 1631; *Londini Artium & Scientiarum Scaturigo: or London's Fountain of Arts and Sciences*, streets of London, pageant for the Haberdashers' Company, October 29, 1632; *Londini Emporia, or London's Mercatura*, streets of London, pageant for the Clothworkers' Company, October 29, 1633; *A Maidenhead Well Lost*, London, Cockpit Theater, Queen's Men III, c. 1633; *Sir Martin Skink* (lost play), with Richard Brome, London, unknown theater, King's Men?, c. 1633–1641; *The Late Lancashire Witches* with Brome, London, Globe Theater, King's Company, summer 1634; *Love's Mistress: Or, The Queen's Masque*, London, at Court and the Phoenix Theater, Queen's Men III, November 19, 1634; *A Challenge for Beauty*, London, Black

Friars and Globe Theaters, the King's Company, c. 1634–1636; *Londini Sinus Salutis, or London's Harbour of Health and Happiness*, streets of London, pageant for the Ironmongers' Company, October 29, 1635; *Londini Speculum: or London's Mirror*, streets of London, pageant for the Haberdashers' Company, October 30, 1637; *Porta Pietatis, or the Port or Harbour of Piety*, streets of London, pageant for the Drapers' Company, October 29, 1638; *Londini Status Pacatus, or London's Peaceable Estate*, streets of London, pageant for the Drapers' Company, October 29, 1639; *Love's Masterpiece* (lost play), London, unknown theater, May 22, 1640.

Books

None and Paris, S.R. May 17, 1594. London: printed by Richard Jones, 1594; *The Four Prentices of London: With the Conquest of Jerusalem*, S.R. June 19, 1594. London: printed by Nicholas Okes for John Wright, 1615; *The First and Second Parts of King Edward the Fourth*, S.R. August 28, 1599. London: printed by John Windet for John Oxenbridge, 1599; *How a Man May Choose a Good Wife from a Bad*. London: printed by Thomas Creede for Matthew Lawe, 1602; *A Woman Killed with Kindness*, S.R. February 12, 1603. London: printed by William Jaggard for John Hodgets, 1607; *Nobody and Somebody, With the true Chronicle History of Elydure, who was fortunately three several times crowned King of England*, S.R. March 12, 1605/1606. London: Sold by John Trundle, 1606; *If You Know Not Me, You Know Nobody* [Part I] *or The Troubles of Queen Elizabeth*, S.R. July 5, 1605. London: printed by Thomas Purfoot, Jr., for Nathaniel Butter, 1605; *If You Know not Me, You Know Nobody* [Part II], *with the Building of the Royal Exchange, and the Famous Victory of Queen Elizabeth in the year 1588*, S.R. September 14, 1605. London: printed by Thomas Purfoot, Jr., for Nathaniel Butter, 1606; *The Rape of Lucrece, A True Roman Tragedy*, S.R. June 3, 1608. London: printed by Edward Allde for John Busby, sold by Nathaniel Butter, 1608; *Troia Britannica or Great Britain's Troy*, S.R. December 5, 1608. London: printed by William Jaggard, 1609; *The Golden Age, or the lives of Jupiter and Saturn*, S.R. October 14, 1611. London: printed by Nicholas Okes for William Barrenger, 1611; *An Apology for Actors*. London: printed by Nicholas Okes, 1612; published as *The Actor's Vindication* by William Cartwright, 1658; reprinted for the Shakespeare Society, 1841, J[ohn] Payne Collier, editor; *A Marriage Triumph in Memory of the happy nuptials betwixt the high and mighty Prince Count Palatine and the Most Excellent Princess, the Lady Elizabeth*, S.R. February 15, 1613. London: printed by Nicholas Okes for Edward Marchant, 1613; *The Silver Age*. London: printed by Nicholas Okes for Benjamin Lightfoote, 1613; *The Brazen Age*. London: printed by Nicholas Okes for Samuel Rand, 1613; *A Funeral Elegy Upon the Death of Henry Prince of Wales*, S.R. December 23, 1613. London: printed by Nicholas Okes for William Welbie, 1613; *Gunaikeion or Nine Books of Various History Concerning Women*. London: printed by Adam Islip, 1624; republished as *The General History of Women, Containing the Lives of the Most Holy and Profane, the Most Famous and Infamous in All Ages*. London: printed by William Hunt? for William Hope, 1657; *A funeral elegie upon the much Lamented Death of the Trespuissant and unmatchable King, King James of Great Britain, France and Ireland, Defender of the Faith*, S.R. April 4, 1625. London: printed by Eliot's Court Press for Thomas Harper, 1625; *The Iron Age*, Part I and Part II, S.R. August 2, 1630. London: printed by Nicholas Okes, 1632; *England's Elizabeth: Her Life and Troubles During Her Minority, From the Cradle to the Crown*, S.R. April 26, 1631. London: printed by John Beale for Philip Waterhouse, 1631; *The Fair Maid of the West, or A Girl Worth Gold*, Parts I and II, S.R. June 16, 1631. London: printed by Miles Flesher for Richard Royston, 1631; *London's Jus Honorarium*, S.R. October 29, 1631. London: printed by Nicholas Okes, 1631; *Londini Artium & Scientiarum Scaturigo: or London's Fountain of Arts and Sciences*, S.R. October 29, 1632. London: printed by Nicholas Okes, 1632; *The English Traveller*, S.R. July 15, 1633. London: printed by Robert Raworth, 1633; *Londini Emporia, or London's Mercatura*, S.R. October 29, 1633. London: printed by Nicholas Okes, 1633; *A Pleasant Comedy Called a Maidenhead Well Lost*, S.R. June 25, 1634. London: printed by Nicholas Okes for John Jackson and Francis Church, 1634; *The Late*

Lancashire Witches with Brome, S.R. October 28, 1634. London: printed by Thomas Harper for Benjamin Fisher, 1634; *The Hierarchy of the Blessed Angels: Their Names, Orders, and Offices. The Fall of Lucifer with his Angels*, S.R. November 7, 1634. London: printed by Adam Islip, 1635; *Philocothonista, or the Drunkard, Opened, Dissected, and Anatomized*, S.R. May 26, 1635. London: printed by John Crouch for Robert Raworth, 1635; *Pleasant Dialogues and Dramas*, S.R. August 29, 1635. London: printed by Richard Oulton for Richard Hearne, sold by Thomas Slater, 1637; *Love's Mistress: or The Queen's Masque*, September 30, 1635. London: printed by Robert Raworth for John Crowch, sold by Jasper Emery, 1636; *Londini Sinus Salutis, or London's Harbour of Health and Happiness*, S.R. October 29, 1635. London: printed for Robert Raworth, 1635; *The Wonder of this Age: or The Picture of A Man Living who is One Hundred Fifty two years old, and upward*, S.R. November 12, 1635. London: printed by John Okes, 1635; *A new-years gift presented at Court from the Lady Parvula to the Lord Minimum. commonly called Little Jefferie her Majesties servant, with a letter written by Microphilus.* London, 1636; *The Life and death of Sir Richard Whittington*, S.R. January 25, 1636/1637. London: printed by John Okes, 1637; reprinted as *The famous and remarkable history of Sir Richard Whittington, three times Lord Mayor of London.* London: printed by William Wilson, sold by Francis Coles, 1656; *The Phoenix of these late times: or The life of Mr. Henry Welby, Esq.*, S.R. January 25, 1636/1637. Printed by John Okes, 1637; *The Three Wonders of this Age*, S.R. April 8, 1636. London: printed by John Okes for Michael Sparke, Jr., 1636; *A True Discourse of the Two infamous upstart Prophets, Richard Farnham, Weaver of Whitechapel, and John Bull, Weaver of St. Butolph's Aldgate, now Prisoners, the one in Newgate, and the other in Bridewell: with their Examinations and Opinions taken from their own mouths*, S.R. June 7, 1636. London: printed by Nicholas Okes for Thomas Lambert, 1636; *A Challenge for Beauty*, S.R. June 17, 1636. London: printed by Robert Raworth, sold by John Becket, 1636; *A Curtain Lecture: as it is read By a Country Farmer's wife to her Good Man*, S.R. July 6, 1636. London: printed by Robert Young for John Aston, 1637; *A True Relation, of the Lives and Deaths of the two most Famous English Pirates, Purser, and Clinton; who lived in the Reign of Queen Elizabeth*, S.R. February 15, 1637/1638. London: printed by John Okes, 1639; *The Royal King and the Loyal Subject*, S.R. March 25, 1637. London: printed by Nicholas and John Okes for John Becket, 1637; *A True Description of His Majesties Royal Ship, Built this year 1637 at Woolwich in Kent*, S.R. September 15, 1637. London: printed by John Okes for John Aston, 1637; *Londini Speculum: or London's Mirror*, S.R. October 30, 1637. London: printed by John Okes, 1637; *A New Book of Mistakes, Or, Bulls with Tales, and Bulls Without Tales, But No Lies by Any Means.* London: printed by Nicholas Okes, 1637; *The Wise Woman of Hogsdon*, S.R. March 12, 1638. London: printed by Marmaduke Parsons for Henry Shephard, 1638; *Porta Pietatis, or the Port or Harbour of Piety*, S.R. October 29, 1638. London: printed by John Okes, 1638; *The Life and Death of Queen Elizabeth, From the Womb to the Tomb, from her Birth to her Burial*, S.R. March 28, 1639. London: printed by John Okes, 1639; *The Exemplary Lives and Memorable Acts of Nine the Most Worthy Women of the World*, S.R. September 19, 1639. London: printed by Thomas Cotes for Richard Royston, 1640; *Londini Status Pacatus, or London's Peaceable Estate*, S.R. October 29, 1639. London: printed by John Okes, 1639; *Machiavel as He Lately Appeared to His Dear Sons, the Modern Projectors*, S.R. January 25, 1640/1641. London: printed by John Okes for Francis Constable, 1641; extract appears in *Hogs caracter of a Projector*, S.R. July 15, 1642. London: printed for George Tomlinson, 1642; *The Rat Trap: Or The Jesuits taken in their own Net*, S.R. February 9, 1640. London, 1641; *Love's Masterpiece*, S.R. May 22, 1640. London: printed by John Okes, 1640; *The Life of Merlin, Surnamed Ambrosius, his Prophecies, and Predictions interpreted: and their truth made good by our English Annalls. Being a Chronographicall History of all the Kings, and memorable passages of this Kingdome, from Brute to the Reign of our Royall Soveraigne King Charles*, S.R. July 13, 1640. London: printed by John Okes, sold by Jasper Emery, 1641; *The lives of king Henry the Eight, Cardinal Woolsey & Queen Mary*, S.R. March 29, 1641 (lost manuscript); *Sir Martin Skink*, with Brome, S.R. April 8, 1654 (lost manuscript); *Appius and Virginia* with Webster, S.R. May 13, 1654. London, 1654; *Fortune by Land and Sea* with

Rowley, S.R. June 20, 1655. London: printed for John Sweeting and Robert Pollard, 1655; *The Captives: or The Lost Recovered,* ed. Alexander Corbin Judson from a British Museum manuscript. New Haven, CT: Yale University Press, 1921.

Translations

Ovid's *De Arte Amandi or The Art of Love* and *De Remedio Amoris or Love's Remedy,* published as *Love's School.* Amsterdam: Nicholas Jansz Visscher, 1600? Sallust's *The Conspiracy of Catiline,* S.R. February 15, 1607. London: Constable, 1924; Sallust's *The War of Jugurtha,* S.R. February 15, 1607. London: Constable, 1924.

SECONDARY SOURCES

Baines, Barbara J. *Thomas Heywood.* Boston: Twayne, 1984; Boas, Frederick S. *Thomas Heywood.* London: Williams and Norgate, 1950; Clark, Arthur Melville. *Thomas Heywood: Playwright and Miscellanist.* 1931. Reprint, New York: Russell and Russell, 1967; Cromwell, Otelia. *Thomas Heywood: A Study in the Elizabethan Drama of Everyday Life.* 1928. Reprint, New York: Archon, 1969; Greg, Walter W. *A Bibliography of the English Printed Drama to the Restoration,* 4 vols. London: Bibliographical Society, 1939–1962; Jackson, Sarah Evelyn. "'Aut Prodesse Solent aut Delectare': A Study of Four Nondramatic Works by Thomas Heywood." Ph.D. dissertation, Emory University, 1959. Abstract in *Dissertation Abstracts International* 20 (1959): 1787–88; Pollard, A. W. and G. R. Redgrave, eds. *A Short-Title Catalogue of Books Printed in England, Scotland, and Ireland and of English Books Printed Abroad, 1475–1640,* 3 vols., 2nd ed., rev. W. A. Jackson, F. S. Ferguson, and Katharine Pantzer. London: Bibliographical Society, 1976–1991; Watson, George. ed., *The New Cambridge Bibliography of English Literature.* Vol. 1. *600–1600.* Cambridge: Cambridge University Press, 1974; Wentworth, Michael. "Introduction." In *Thomas Heywood: A Reference Guide,* xi–xxvii. Boston: G. K. Hall, 1986; Wing, Donald. ed. *A Short-Title Catalogue of Books Printed in English, Scotland, Ireland, Wales, and British America and of English Books Printed in Other Countries, 1641–1700,* 4 vols., 2nd ed., rev. Timothy J. Crist et al. New York: Modern Language Association, 1982–1998; Wright, Louis B. "The Elizabethan Middle-Class Taste for History." *Journal of Modern History* 3 (June 1931): 175–97; ———. "Heywood and the Popularizing of History," *MLN* 43 (May 1928): 287–93.

PEGGY J. HUEY

JOHN DRYDEN

(August 9, 1631–May 1, 1700)

John Dryden is one of the most versatile writers in English literary history, gifted as a dramatist, poet, literary critic, and translator. The dominant literary figure of the Restoration, Dryden became the first poet laureate in 1668 and was made historiographer royal in 1670. As a dramatist, Dryden wrote successfully in every major genre, including comedy, tragedy, and opera. His plays, including an Arthurian opera, contributed greatly to the development of English drama and to the popularity of the Restoration stage. As a poet, Dryden perfected the heroic couplet as a form of narrative expression and logical reasoning, and he is regarded as one of the masters of formal verse satire. As a literary critic, he composed the first major body of critical writings in England. Known as the father of English criticism, he created principles of taste in drama and poetry that influenced writers throughout the eighteenth century. As a translator, Dryden made the works of classical poets like Homer, Theocritus, Virgil, Ovid, as well as medieval writers like Chaucer and Boccaccio, available to contemporary English readers.

Dryden was born on August 9, 1631, in Aldwincle, Northamptonshire, the son of gentleman Erasmus Dryden and Mary Pickering. A prosperous family of Puritan faith and conservative political views, the Drydens sided with Parliament over the monarchy of Charles I. John Dryden received his early classical education as a king's scholar at the Westminster School, where he trained under the eminent Dr. Richard Busby. While at Westminster, Dryden published his first poem, an elegy in tribute to Henry Lord Hastings, in a poetic collection entitled "Lachrymae Musarum" (1649). Dryden entered Trinity College, Cambridge, as a Westminster scholar in July 1650 and graduated with a bachelor of arts degree in January 1654. After inheriting a small estate from his father, he continued to reside in Cambridge until 1657, and then moved to London to pursue his career as a professional writer. In London, Dryden worked as a translator and aide for the commonwealth. It is likely he became acquainted with the poets John Milton and Andrew Marvell at this time, for they were also employed in the same department.

Dryden's first important poem was written in 1658 upon the death of Lord Protector Oliver Cromwell, "Heroic Stanzas on the Late Lord Protector."

The year 1660 marked the end of the Protectorate (1649–1660), the commonwealth military government led first by Oliver Cromwell and then by his son Richard after the execution of King Charles I in 1649. The restoration of the English monarchy to the throne with Charles II in 1660 ended twenty years of civil strife and rebellion. To ensure the return of order, Charles II concealed his own Catholic sympathies, reestablished the Anglican Church, and barred Protestant dissenters and Catholics from public life. Although Dryden originally sided with Parliament over the king, he welcomed the return of peace and stability to his country, and he celebrated Charles II's restoration in two poems, "Astrea Redux" (1660) and "Panegyric on the Coronation" (1661). After these public pledges of support for the Stuart dynasty, Dryden was to remain a faithful royalist for the rest of his life.

In 1662 Dryden commenced writing plays for the newly reopened theaters (which had been closed during the Protectorate) to supplement his income, and soon he became the leading dramatist of the Restoration period. His earliest play, *The Wild Gallant* (1663), was a comedy based on Spanish sources that failed in both its Vere Street Theatre and court performances. In 1664, Dryden fared better with *The Rival Ladies*, a tragicomedy also based on a Spanish drama and including several scenes composed in rhyming verse. In his dedication in *The Rival Ladies*, Dryden defended the use of rhyme in dramatic tragedies to facilitate memorization, rhetorical emphasis, and imaginative restraint. He achieved success again with his first original drama, *The Indian Queen* (1664), cowritten with his wife's brother, Sir Robert Howard. Howard was aware of the king's penchant for verse plays in the French tradition, and *The Indian Queen* was the first heroic drama in Restoration England to consist entirely of rhymed couplets. Dryden followed this success with a popular sequel, *The Indian Emperour* (1665), another rhyming heroic tragedy based on accounts of the Spanish conquest of Mexico.

In June 1665 an outbreak of bubonic plague forced the closing of the London theaters for eighteen months. Dryden and his wife, Elizabeth Howard, retired to her family estate in Wiltshire until the epidemic passed and the theaters were reopened in December 1666. While in Wiltshire, Dryden composed three of his major works in poetry, drama, and criticism. *Annus Mirabilis* (1667) was a heroic poem written to memorialize crucial events of the year 1666, especially the English victory in the Dutch naval war and the Great Fire of London. The poem also defended the monarchy against its detractors and prophesied a grander era to come. Dryden's play *Secret Love* (1667) was a tragicomedy that became a favorite of both the public and of King Charles II. And in *An Essay of Dramatick Poesie*, published in 1668, Dryden wrote the first major work of English literary criticism.

An Essay of Dramatick Poesie was written in dialogue form and presented a debate on dramatic theory and production, ancient to modern. The four fictional participants are Crites, who argues in favor of ancient drama; Eugenius, who defends modern drama; Lisideius, who prefers French to English drama; and Neander, who values English over French drama and approved of rhyming verse in plays. Thinly disguised as Neander, Dryden expresses his own taste for English dramatic variety over classical and French regularity. For example, the classical unities of time, place, and action adhered to by modern French playwrights are disparaged by Neander as restricting and artificial impositions. In noting that William Shakespeare violated all the classical precepts by mixing genres, adding subplots, and extending the time and geographical settings covered in his plays, Neander also judge him to be the most pleasing of dramatic artists. Always proud of his national heritage, Dryden helped establish the English literary tradition in his dramatic criticism by evaluating and praising the achievements of leading playwrights, such as Shakespeare, Ben Jonson, Francis Beaumont, and John Fletcher. *An Essay of Dramatick Poesie* sparked many debates about drama among Dryden's contemporaries and resulted in some satirical attacks on his judgment by Robert Howard and Thomas Shadwell. Dryden's literary tastes, however, have generally stood to the present time.

Having pleased the king with his recent compositions, Dryden was named as poet laureate in 1668 and appointed to be royal historiographer in the following year. Many of his works were written to support royalist views. To supplement his royal stipend, he continued to write other prefaces, prologues, and plays. In 1669 he also became a shareholder in the King's Theatre Company, for which he agreed to write three plays a year. Dryden's first productions for the new theater, *Tyrannic Love* (1669) and *The Conquest of Granada* (1670), are classic examples of the Restoration heroic tragedy in rhyming couplets. Though successfully received by the public, these plays brought Dryden some notoriety for their bombastic speeches, melodramatic plots, and unlikely character types. In 1671 Dryden and his heroic dramas became the butt of ridicule in a satirical drama called *The Rehearsal*, written by the Duke of Buckingham. *The Rehearsal*, though popular, did little to tarnish Dryden's reputation. However, when the text of Dryden's play *The Conquest of Granada* was published in 1672, he included a preface, *Of Heroick Plays*, that defended his use of heroic verse in tragedy and the development of his heroic plots and characters.

Dryden was largely dedicated to writing plays in the 1670s and produced a large body of drama that varied in style and theme. In 1671 he wrote what is considered his finest achievement in comic drama, *Marriage A-la-Mode*. His next comedy, *The Assignation; or, Love in a Nunnery* (1672), proved an immediate failure. Dryden's prose tragedy *Amboyna* (1673) treated the subject of the Dutch war and was also rejected by playgoers. Next, he composed a stage adaptation of Milton's *Paradise Lost*, an epic poem in blank verse based on the story of the fall of Adam and Eve in Genesis. Entitled *The State of Innocence* (1674), Dryden's version was never performed on stage. He wrote his final, and many consider his best, heroic tragedy with *Aureng-Zebe* in 1675. Its prologue announced the author's declining preference for rhyming verse in heroic plays, as Dryden was beginning to rethink some of his earlier critical principles. Milton's work also inspired epic ambitions in Dryden, who began to contemplate the idea of writing an original new epic based on the legends of King Arthur.

In 1677 Dryden wrote *All for Love*, a tragedy adapted from Shakespeare's *Antony and Cleopatra*. Composed entirely in blank verse, it is considered the masterpiece of Dryden's dramatic works and is the only one he claimed to have personally pleased him. In adapting his source, Dryden gave unity to the play's setting and action, and developed complex personalities in his characters. In 1679 Dryden adapted the classical Greek play *Oedipus* with fellow writer Nathaniel Lee, and in the same year adapted Shakespeare's *Troilus and Cressida*. In December 1679 Dryden was critically injured when ambushed and beaten near his home by hired thugs. No one has ever been certain of Dryden's offense, although it has been speculated the attack was arranged by one of the many persons who felt insulted by Dryden's writings or perhaps by someone of Whig sympathies in retaliation for Dryden's Tory alliance. After Dryden recuperated in the following year, he was ready to put his abundant literary talents to use in defense of his political beliefs, as he would do in his Arthurian opera.

The year 1680 brought the so-called Popish Plot and Exclusion Crisis to the forefront of the political scene in England. When the Reverend Titus Oates described a Jesuit plot to murder King Charles and take control of the throne, the public grew hysterical.

Protestant supporters attempted to pass the Exclusion Bill in Parliament, a bill that denied the right of succession to Charles's Catholic heir and brother James, Duke of York. Prominent Whigs called on Charles to yield succession to his illegitimate son James Scott, Duke of Monmouth and a Protestant. Dryden responded with a bold new tragicomedy, *The Spanish Friar* (1680), which affirmed his conservative stance on the royalist succession. He followed the play in 1681 with the first of his major satirical poems, *Absalom and Achitophel*. Considered the greatest political satire in literature, Dryden brilliantly adapted the biblical story of David and Absalom in Second Samuel to the principal players in the contemporary crisis: King David represented Charles II; David's rebellious son Absalom represented Monmouth; and the wicked Achitophel represented the Whig politician Shaftesbury, a leader in the Exclusion Bill movement. After Shaftesbury's acquittal on charges of treason, Dryden attacked him again in another satirical poem entitled "The Medal" (1682).

In 1682 Dryden composed another major poem, *Religio Laici*. Meditating on religious faith and intolerance, the poem promoted the middle way of the Anglican Church as opposed to the extreme views of Protestant Dissenters, Catholics, and Deists. Also in 1682 Dryden wrote another of his great verse satires, *Mac Flecknoe; or, A Satire on the True Blue Protestant Poet, T. S.*, in which he retaliated for a personal attack against him by Whig politician and fellow poet Thomas Shadwell. In mock-heroic style, *Mac Flecknoe* depicts Shadwell as succeeding his fictional father Richard Flecknoe, the minor Irish poet, in rule over the mythical realms of nonsense. Years later, the great English poet Alexander Pope used *Mac Flecknoe* as the model for his own famous mock-heroic poem *Dunciad* (1728). In 1682, Dryden also contributed to a sequel of *Absalom and Achitophel*, written largely by Nahum Tate.

In 1685 Dryden collaborated with composer Louis Grabu on an operatic version of the King Arthur legends. Written initially as a prologue, *Albion and Albanius* assumed the proportions of a full-length production. Early in 1685 while rehearsing *Albion and Albanius* for the stage, Charles II died, and his Catholic brother James II ascended the throne. When the opera was finally performed in June 1685, it was interrupted again after just ten days when Monmouth attempted his rebellion. Nevertheless, the play had already been judged a flop due to its unfortunate music and ill-suited rhymes. With this failure, Dryden stopped writing plays for several years, although he carried with him the goal of composing another opera in tribute to King Arthur.

During the fifteenth and sixteenth centuries, the Tudor monarchy used the Arthurian legends to validate their claims to the English throne. For example, King Henry VII declared himself to have descended from Arthur and thereby maintained that Merlin's prophecy of Arthur's return was fulfilled in his own reign. Later, Queen Elizabeth successfully used the Arthurian predictions of a restored golden age to reassure the English people of the legitimacy of her title. Her successor, James I, a Stuart, also believed in the critical need to establish himself in the Arthurian tradition, and he therefore emphasized his British descent. King Arthur's reign had been a period of union, and James's union of England and Scotland was promoted as further evidence of the Arthurian prophecy fulfilled. The writer Ben Jonson was among those who praised James as Arthur's heir and as a king even greater than Arthur. Such an emphasis helped win widespread approval for James's accession in 1603.

In the course of the seventeenth century, Arthurian legend reflects contemporary politics and the struggles between the English monarchy and Parliament. As Parliament grew in power, interest in the historical laws and customs of the Saxons developed among those who wished to advance the rights of commoners. This led many to doubt the legitimacy of Brutus's settling of Britain, to attack King Arthur's reputation as the national hero, and to condemn the Arthurian stories as mythological. After 1603 when James was established on the throne, he asserted the privilege of the divine right of kings and regarded himself as above the law. Resentment to James's absolutism grew, raising debate on the question of ultimate authority: the king's supremacy or common law, to which the king himself was subject. The conflict intensified until 1620 when James dissolved Parliament. James's successor, Charles, renewed the antagonism of Parliament with his own claim to divine privilege. Charles's eventual execution and the English Civil Wars of the mid-century were justified by Milton, among others, who concluded from his study of ancient Saxon tradition that the people were legally entitled to judge their king. These issues were directly to influence Dryden when he later composed his original version of the Arthurian legend.

After the monarchy was restored in 1660, Dryden had been a faithful supporter to both Charles II and James II. However, when the Glorious Revolution of 1688 ended the reign of James II and brought William and Mary to the throne, Dryden refused an oath to the new government. Not surprisingly, he lost his position and pension as poet laureate and royal historiographer. To earn his living, he turned again to writing plays and also to translating the classics. In 1689 Dryden wrote the play *Don Sebastian*, his longest tragedy. Written in blank verse and prose, *Don Sebastian* is considered second only to *All for Love* in Dryden's theatrical corpus. In *Don Sebastian*, Dryden subtly dramatized in the character of Dorax the struggle between individual and political loyalties that divided the nation in the time of the Revolution. Dryden's next play, a comedy, was also among his great successes. *Amphitryon* (1690), based on a play by Molière, jests at the hypocrisy of nobles, lords, and political rulers. When staged, the play was accompanied with songs written for the production by Henry Purcell, sometimes considered England's greatest composer. The popularity of the musical drama renewed Dryden's interest in opera, and soon he began reworking the Arthurian opera he had set aside five years earlier in 1685, in hopes of bringing it to the stage once more.

Dryden's opera *King Arthur; or, The British Worthy*, written in blank verse with music by Henry Purcell, was first performed at Dorset Garden in London in June 1691. It was an immediate success. The opera, or rather semi-opera since many of its passages are not accompanied by music, was not based on the traditional legends and romances of the Arthurian cycles, but was a new tale by Dryden, inspired by his readings in Bede's *Ecclesiastical History of the English Nation* and in Geoffrey of Monmouth's *History of the Kings of Britain*. Dryden had also studied the rites and customs of the pagan Saxons in Samuel Bochart's *Geographia Sacra*. Dryden had originally composed his Arthurian opera in 1684–1685 as a tribute to Charles II, with parallels between the fictional hero and the contemporary king intended to flatter and venerate the current regime. In revising the work, Dryden claimed he deleted its political innuendoes, and in his preface to the printed version he writes that Queen Mary read and approved the play before its first performance. In fact, as some scholars have noted, its innuendoes seem to have been merely softened so that accusations of Jacobite sympathies against Dryden were difficult to substantiate.

The plot of Dryden's operatic *King Arthur* centers on Arthur's war with the Saxon leader Oswald for the control of Britain and the hand of the beautiful daughter of the Duke of Cornwall, Emmeline. Arthur performs admirably in a series of adventures, modeled on epic events in the works of Spenser and Tasso, in which he undertakes to free Emmeline from captivity in an enchanted forest. Merlin the magician is present in the story, intervening on Arthur's behalf and battling his own nemesis in the figure of the evil sorcerer Osmond. Osmond controls the forest with evil spirits, sets spells on Arthur, and places fleshly temptations in Arthur's way. Arthur is ultimately successful, however, gains victory over the Saxons, and wins Emmeline for his own. Merlin magically restores her vision, and the play concludes with Arthur uniting the British people in peaceful alliance: "Britons and Saxons shall be once one People; / One Common Tongue, one Common Faith shall bind / Our Jarring Bands, in a Perpetual Peace."

Scholars are divided over the issue of how well Dryden's revised *King Arthur* is believed to have supported the Stuart monarchy and the tradition of royal authority. The original version of Dryden's opera was unambiguous in its praise of Charles II; the revised play was clearly pleasing to the new government, as it received Queen Mary's endorsement. Some have suggested that Charles II's victory over Parliament at the time of the Exclusion Crisis likely inspired Dryden's choice in making Arthur's enemy the Saxon Oswald from the kingdom of Kent, due to the widespread belief in the seventeenth century of parliamentary rights as having originated with the Saxon civilization in Kent. On the other hand, in the revised and staged opera, King Arthur seeks the council of others, calls for a harmonious union of all Britains and Saxons, and entreats all people in England to support King William.

Staged as a lavish spectacle when first performed in 1691, Dryden's *King Arthur* featured Thomas Betterton in the title role and garnered enthusiastic reviews in such publications as *The Gentleman's Journal*. It was presented again on many occasions in the last years of the seventeenth century and throughout the eighteenth. There are known performances in 1695, 1698, 1701, and 1706; and the opera's music was often played in concert in the years 1704–16. Adaptations of *King Arthur* were staged in 1726, 1736, and 1741 in London. In 1770 David Garrick revised the opera for a new premiere, and it regularly appeared onstage in the 1770s and 1780s. To the present day, the opera has been revived and performed numerous times in Europe and the United States.

Dryden continued to write plays as a source of income, and his next work was *Cleomenes* (1692). Influenced by French classical tragedy, this drama was based on a tale in Plutarch of an exiled ruler and was a characterization that many felt betrayed Dryden's lingering sympathies to James II. For political reasons, *Cleomenes* was banned from performance. Dryden's final production for the stage, a tragicomedy entitled *Love Triumphant* (1694), was also a dismal failure. At this time, with Dryden's dramatic talents apparently waning, his work in translating classical texts began to occupy him increasingly. Translating ancient literature from the classic languages into English was a standard exercise in the education of young men from the upper classes, and Dryden's poetic talent helped him to excel in the art. The English public was enthusiastic for newly translated works, and in this Dryden found a more dependable source of livelihood than in drama.

Dryden produced some early translations of Ovid and other ancient poets in 1680, and in the first and second *Miscellanies* of 1684 and 1685. In 1693 appeared his translations of Juvenal and Persius, classical Roman authors of satire. Dryden included with the published translations his famed dedicatory essay called "Discourse concerning the Original and Progress of Satire," in which he surveys the genre of satire from its origins to the present, summarizing and evaluating the works of various writers. The purpose of satire, asserts Dryden, is to teach and delight, while exposing folly, correcting vice, and tempting to virtue. In the course of the essay, Dryden discusses his unfulfilled ambition of writing an original epic for the glory of England, in the tradition of national poets like Spenser and Milton. Dryden names King Arthur as his choice of subject for the English epic, just as Milton had once considered as a possible subject before selecting the biblical account of Adam's fall in Genesis for his story in *Paradise Lost* (1667). Dryden also expresses his great disappointment in not having composed this epic work.

The third and fourth *Miscellanies* of 1693 and 1694 included Dryden's translations of selections from Ovid's *Metamorphoses,* Homer's *Iliad,* and Virgil's third *Georgic.* In 1694 Dryden conceived the idea of translating Virgil's Latin epic *Aeneid* in its entirety, along with the complete *Pastorals* and *Georgics.* Dryden finished the work in three years. One of his most rewarding professional and financial successes, the translations of Virgil were sold by subscription, and Dryden gained fame and profited handsomely. Dryden would always lament his inability to produce an Arthurian epic to honor England, and therefore he tried to take consolation that in translating the great Virgilian epic he had yet honored his country. Currently in favor with citizens of all political and religious persuasions, Dryden was requested to write the ode for the November 1697 celebration of the St. Cecilia's Day festival, a privilege he had not enjoyed since 1687 when he wrote "A Song for St. Cecilia's Day" in his last year as poet laureate. Dryden responded to the request for the new song with *Alexander's Feast* (1697), an ode in the classical Pindaric fashion, considered as one of his finest original poems.

Dryden's last great literary achievement was a volume of several original new poems and seventeen newly translated classics, *Fables, Ancient and Modern* (1699). Along with works from Homer and Ovid, Dryden added poetry from the medieval Italian poet Giovanni Boccaccio and the medieval English poet Geoffrey Chaucer, whom Dryden considered the first great writer of English poetry. Dryden's effort to link the literature of England with the great traditions of the past was deeply appreciated by the reading public, and *Fables* was the book for which he was best remembered in the next century. Dryden's preface to the *Fables* is one of his finest critical essays. In it, he justifies his choice of literary works included in the *Fables* and evaluates the merits of each writer. After much comparing and contrasting, Dryden reaches the judgment that Chaucer is the greatest of all poets. Praising Chaucer, like Shakespeare, for his comprehensive nature, Dryden makes his famous statement on *The Canterbury Tales,* that "here is God's Plenty." Finally, by adding his own poems to the collection in *Fables,* Dryden plainly sees himself as Chaucer's heir in appropriating the best traditions that literature has to offer and creating new ones to the glory and honor of his country.

Dryden died in May 1700, just a few months after *Fables, Ancient and Modern* was published, and he was buried in the Poets' Corner of Westminster Abbey. Poetically gifted and keenly intellectual, Dryden's literary achievements dominated the period of the Restoration in every genre, and his place in English literary history is of the highest importance. A public poet, he wrote always for public occasions or performances and always with a sense of pride in his nation. In drama, his diverse body of works is the most impressive of the period. He excelled at every style of poetry at which he tried his hand: ode, lyric, heroic couplet, and verse satire. His critical writings form the foundation of the English canon in criticism. And his literary translations made the poetry of great classical and medieval authors accessible to his grateful contemporaries. As the eighteenth-century English critic Samuel Johnson said of Dryden's influence on English letters: "He found it brick, and left it marble."

PRIMARY WORKS

Play Productions

The Wild Gallant, revised from an older play, possibly by Richard Brome, London, Vere Street Theatre, February 5, 1663; *The Rival Ladies,* London, Theatre Royal, Bridges Street, possibly autumn 1663; *The Indian Queen,* by Dryden and Sir Robert Howard, London, Theatre Royal,

Bridges Street, January 1664; *The Indian Emperor*, London, Theatre Royal, Bridges Street, early 1665; *Secret Love*, London, Theatre Royal, Bridges Street, January 1667; *Sir Martin Mar-All*, by Dryden and William Cavendish, Duke of Newcastle, London, Lincoln's Inn Fields, August 15, 1667; *The Tempest*, revised from William Shakespeare's play by Dryden and William Davenant, London, Lincoln's Inn Fields, November 7, 1667; *An Evening's Love; or, The Mock Astrologer*, London, Theatre Royal, Bridges Street, June 12, 1668; *Tyrannic Love*, London, Theatre Royal, Bridges Street, June 24, 1669; *The Conquest of Granada*, Part 1, London, Theatre Royal, Bridges Street, December 1670; Part 2, January 1671; *Marriage A-la-Mode*, London, Theatre Royal, Bridges Street, probably late November or early December 1671; *The Assignation; or, Love in a Nunnery*, London, Lincoln's Inn Fields, early autumn 1672; *Amboyna*, London, Lincoln's Inn Fields, possibly February 1673; *Aureng-Zebe*, London, Theatre Royal, Drury Lane, November 17, 1675; *All for Love*, London, Theatre Royal, Drury Lane, probably December 12, 1677; *The Kind Keeper; or, Mr. Limberham*, London, Dorset Garden Theatre, March 11, 1678; *Oedipus*, by Dryden and Nathaniel Lee, London, Dorset Garden Theatre, autumn 1678; *Troilus and Cressida*, revised from Shakespeare's play, London, Dorset Garden Theatre, early months of 1679; *The Spanish Friar*, London, Dorset Garden Theatre, November 1, 1680; *The Duke of Guise*, by Dryden and Lee, London, Theatre Royal, Drury Lane, November 30, 1682; *Albion and Albanius*, opera with text by Dryden and music by Louis Grabu, London, Dorset Garden Theatre, June 3, 1685; *Don Sebastian*, London, Theatre Royal, Drury Lane, December 4, 1689; *Amphitryon*, London, Theatre Royal, Drury Lane, probably October 1690; *King Arthur*, opera with text by Dryden and music by Henry Purcell, London, Dorset Garden Theatre, early June 1691; *Cleomenes*, by Dryden and Thomas Southerne, London, Theatre Royal, Drury Lane, on or before April 16, 1692; *Love Triumphant*, London, Theatre Royal, Drury Lane, probably January 1694; "The Secular Masque," inserted into *The Pilgrim*, revised from John Fletcher's play by John Vanbrugh, London, Theatre Royal, Drury Lane, late April or early May 1700.

Books

Astraea Redux. A Poem On the Happy Restoration and Return Of His Sacred Majesty Charles the Second. London: printed by J. M. for Henry Herringman, 1660; *To His Sacred Majesty, A Panegyrick On His Coronation.* London: printed for Henry Herringman, 1661; *To My Lord Chancellor, Presented on New-years-day.* London: printed for Henry Herringman, 1662; *The Rival Ladies.* London: printed by William Wilson for Henry Herringman, 1664; *Annus Mirabilis: The Year of Wonders, 1666.* London: printed for Henry Herringman, 1667; *The Indian Emperour, or The Conquest of Mexico by the Spaniards.* London: printed by J. M. for H. Herringman, 1667; *Of Dramatick Poesie: An Essay.* London: printed for Henry Herringman, 1668; *Secret Love, or The Maiden Queen.* London: printed for Henry Herringman, 1668; *Sir Martin Mar-All, or The Feigned Innocence.* London: printed for H. Herringman, 1668; *The Wild Gallant.* London: printed by Thos. Newcomb for H. Herringman, 1669; *The Tempest, or The Enchanted Island*, by Dryden and William Davenant. London: printed for Henry Herringman, 1670; *Tyrannick Love, or the Royal Martyr.* London: printed for H. Herringman, 1670; *An Evening's Love, or The Mock Astrologer.* London: printed by T. N. for Henry Herringman, 1671; *The Conquest of Granada: In Two Parts.* London: printed by T. N. for Henry Herringman, 1672; *Marriage A-La-Mode.* London: printed by T. N. for Henry Herringman, 1673; *The Assignation: or, Love in a Nunnery.* London: printed by T. N. for Henry Herringman, 1673; *Amboyna.* London: printed by T. N. for Henry Herringman, 1673; *Notes and Observations on the Empress of Morocco*, by Dryden, John Crowne, and Thomas Shadwell. London: 1674; *Aureng-Zebe.* London: printed by T. N. for Henry Herringman, 1676; *The State of Innocence and Fall of Man.* London: printed by T. N. for Henry Herringman, 1677; *All for Love: or, The World Well Lost.* London: printed by Tho. Newcomb for Henry Herringman, 1678; *Oedipus*, by Dryden and Nathaniel Lee. London: printed for R. Bentley and M. Magnes, 1679; *Troilus and Cressida, or, Truth*

Found Too Late. London: printed for Jacob Tonson and Abel Swall, 1679; *The Kind Keeper; or, Mr. Limberham.* London: printed for R. Bentley and M. Magnes, 1680; *Absalom and Achitophel.* London: printed for J. T., 1681; *His Majesties Declaration Defended.* London: printed for T. Davies, 1681; *The Spanish Fryar, or The Double Discovery.* London: printed for Richard Tonson and Jacob Tonson, 1681; *The Medall. A Satyr against Sedition.* London: printed for Jacob Tonson, 1682; *Mac Flecknoe, or A Satyr Upon the True-Blew Protestant Poet, T. S.* London: printed for D. Green, 1682; *Religio Laici or A Laymans Faith.* London: printed for Jacob Tonson, 1682; *The Duke of Guise*, by Dryden and Lee. London: printed by T. H. for R. Bentley and J. Tonson, 1683; *The Vindication: or The Parallel of the French Holy League, and The English League and Covenant.* London: printed for Jacob Tonson, 1683; *Miscellany Poems.* London: printed for Jacob Tonson, 1684; *Threnodia Augustalis: A Funeral-Pindarique Poem Sacred to the Happy Memory of King Charles II.* London: printed for Jacob Tonson, 1685; *Albion and Albanius: An Opera.* London: printed for Jacob Tonson, 1685; *A Defence of the Papers Written by the Late King of Blessed Memory and Duchess of York.* London: printed for H. Hills, 1686; *The Hind and the Panther.* London: printed for Jacob Tonson, 1687; *A Song for St Cecilia's Day, 1687*, by Dryden with music by Giovanni Baptista Draghi. London: printed for T. Dring, 1687; *Britannia Rediviva: A Poem on the Birth of the Prince.* London: printed for J. Tonson, 1688; *Don Sebastian, King of Portugal.* London: printed for Jo. Hindmarsh, 1690; *Amphitryon; or The Two Socia's*, by Dryden with music by Henry Purcell. London: printed for J. Tonson and M. Tonson, 1690; *King Arthur: or The British Worthy*, by Dryden with music by Henry Purcell. London: printed for Jacob Tonson, 1691; *Eleonora: A Panegyrical Poem Dedicated to the Memory of the Late Countess of Abingdon.* London: printed for Jacob Tonson, 1692; *Cleomenes, The Spartan Heroe.* London: printed for Jacob Tonson, 1692; *Love Triumphant; or, Nature Will Prevail.* London: printed for Jacob Tonson, 1694; *An Ode, on the Death of Mr. Henry Purcell; Late Servant of His Majesty, and Organist of the Chapel Royal, and of St. Peter's Westminster.* London: printed by J. Heptinstall for Henry Playford, 1696; *Alexander's Feast; Or The Power of Musique. An Ode, In Honour of St. Cecilia's Day.* London: printed for Jacob Tonson, 1697.

Other Works

"Upon the Death of the Lord Hastings," in *Lachrymae Musarum: The Tears of the Muses: Exprest in Elegies; Written By divers persons of Nobility and Worth, Upon the death of the most hopefull, Henry Lord Hastings.* London: printed by Thomas Newcomb, 1649; "To his friend the Authour on his divine Epigrams," in *Sion and Parnassus, Or Epigrams On Severall texts of the Old and New Testament*, by John Hoddesdon. London: printed for R. Daniel for G. Eversden, 1650; "Heroique Stanzas, Consecrated to the Glorious Memory of his most Serene and renowned Highnesse Oliver Late Lord Protector of this Common-Wealth, &c.," in *Three Poems Upon the Death of his late Highnesse Oliver Lord Protector of England, Scotland, and Ireland.* London: printed by William Wilson, 1659; "To My Honored Friend, Sr Robert Howard, On his Excellent Poems," in *Poems*, by Sir Robert Howard. London: printed for Henry Herringman, 1660; "To My Honored Friend, Dr Charleton," in *Chorea Gigantum, or The most Famous Antiquity of Great-Britain, Vulgarly called Stone-Heng*, by Walter Charleton. London: printed for Henry Herringman, 1663; *The Indian-Queen*, by Dryden and Howard, in *Four New Plays, Viz: The Surprisal, The Committee, Comedies. The Indian-Queen, The Vestal-Virgin, Tragedies*, by Howard. London: printed for Henry Herringman, 1665; *Ovid's Epistles, Translated by Several Hands*, includes preface and translations of three epistles by Dryden. London: printed for Jacob Tonson, 1680; *The Second Part of Absalom and Achitophel*, by Nahum Tate, includes contributions by Dryden,. London: printed for Jacob Tonson, 1682; "The Life of Plutarch," in vol. 1 of *Plutarchs Lives, Translated from the Greek by Several Hands*, 5 vols. London: printed for Jacob Tonson, 1683; *The History of the League*, by Louis Maimbourg, trans. Dryden. London: printed by M. Flesher for Jacob Tonson, 1684; "To the Memory of Mr. Oldham," in *The Remains of Mr. John Oldham in Verse and Prose.* London: printed for Jo. Hindmarsh, 1684; *Sylvae; or, The*

Second Part of Poetical Miscellanies, includes preface and seventeen works by Dryden. London: printed for Jacob Tonson, 1685; "To the Pious Memory Of the Accomplisht Young Lady Mrs Anne Killigrew, Excellent in the two Sister-Arts of Poesie, and Painting. An Ode," in *Poems By Mrs. Anne Killigrew*. London: printed for Samuel Lowndes, 1686; *The Life of St. Francis Xavier, of the Society of Jesus*, by Dominique Bouhours, trans. Dryden. London: printed for Jacob Tonson, 1688; *The Satires of Decimus Junius Juvenalis. Translated into English Verse. By Mr. Dryden, and Several Other Eminent Hands . . . To which is Prefix'd a Discourse concerning the Original and Progress of Satire*. London: printed for Jacob Tonson, 1693; *Examen Poeticum: Being the Third Part of Miscellany Poems*, includes fifteen works by Dryden. London: printed by R. E. for Jacob Tonson, 1693; "A Character of Polybius and His Writings," in *The History of Polybius the Megalopolitan*, trans. Sir Henry Sheeres. London: printed for S. Briscoe, 1693; "To my Dear Friend Mr. Congreve, On His Comedy, call'd, The Double-Dealer," in *The Double-Dealer* by William Congreve. London: printed for Jacob Tonson, 1694; "To Sir Godfrey Kneller," in *The Annual Miscellany: for the Year 1694*. London: printed by R. E. for Jacob Tonson, 1694; "A Parallel, Of Poetry and Painting," in *De Arte Graphica*, by C. A. Du Fresnoy, trans. Dryden. London: printed by J. Heptinstall for W. Rogers, 1695; *The Works of Virgil: Containing His Pastorals, Georgics, And Aeneis*, trans. Dryden. London: printed for Jacob Tonson, 1697; *The Annals and History of Cornelius Tacitus: His Account of the Antient Germans And The Life of Agricola*, 3 vols., book 1 of vol. 1 trans. Dryden. London: printed for Matthew Gillyflower, 1698; "To My Friend, the Author," in *Beauty in Distress. A Tragedy*, by Peter Motteux. London: printed for Daniel Brown and Rich. Parker, 1698; *Fables Ancient and Modern; Translated into Verse, From Homer, Ovid, Boccace, & Chaucer; With Original Poems*, trans. Dryden. London: printed for Jacob Tonson, 1700; *The Pilgrim, A Comedy*, by John Fletcher, revised by John Vanbrugh, with prologue, epilogue, dialogue, and masque by Dryden. London: printed for Benjamin Tooke, 1700; "The Life of Lucian," in *The Works of Lucian, Translated from the Greek, by Several Eminent Hands, The First Volume*. London: printed for S. Briscoe, 1711.

Collections and Editions

The Works of John Dryden, 18 vols., ed. Walter Scott. London: William Miller, 1808. Rev. George Saintsbury. London: William Patterson, 1882–1893; *Essays of John Dryden*, ed. W. P. Ker. Oxford: Clarendon Press, 1926; *Dryden: The Dramatic Works*, 6 vols., ed. Montague Summers. London: Nonesuch Press, 1931; *The Letters of John Dryden: With Letters Addressed to Him*, ed. Charles E. Ward. Durham, NC: Duke University Press, 1942; *The Works of John Dryden*, ed. Edward Niles Hooker, H. T. Swedenberg et al. Berkeley: University of California Press, 1956–; *The Poems of John Dryden*, 4 vols., ed. James Kinsley. Oxford: Clarendon Press, 1958; *John Dryden: Of Dramatic Poesy and Other Critical Essays*, 2 vols., ed. George Watson. London: J. M. Dent, 1962; *Literary Criticism of John Dryden*, ed. Arthur C. Kirsch. Lincoln: University of Nebraska Press, 1967.

SECONDARY SOURCES

Aden, John M. *The Critical Opinions of John Dryden: A Dictionary*. Nashville, TN: Vanderbilt University Press, 1963; Barbeau, Anne T. *The Intellectual Design of John Dryden's Heroic Plays*. New Haven, CT: Yale University Press, 1970; Bredvold, Louis I. *The Intellectual Milieu of John Dryden*. Ann Arbor: University of Michigan Press, 1934; Bywaters, David. *Dryden in Revolutionary England*. Berkeley: University of California Press, 1991; Eliot, T. S. *John Dryden: The Poet, the Dramatist, the Critic*. New York: Holliday, 1932; Erskine-Hill, Howard. *Poetry and the Realm of Politics: Shakespeare to Dryden*. Oxford: Clarendon Press, 1996; Frost, William. *Dryden and the Art of Translation*. New Haven, CT: Yale University Press, 1955; ———. *John Dryden: Dramatist, Satirist, Translator*. New York: AMS Press, 1987; Hall, James M. *John Dryden: A Reference Guide*. Boston: Hall, 1984; Hammond, Paul. *John Dryden: A Literary Life*. London: Macmillan,

1991; Harth, Alan Fisher, and Ralph Cohen. *New Homage to John Dryden*. Los Angeles: Clark Library, 1983; Harth, Phillip. *Contexts of Dryden's Thought*. Chicago: University of Chicago Press, 1968; ———. *Pen for a Party: Dryden's Tory Propaganda in Its Contexts*. Princeton, NJ: Princeton University Press, 1993; Hopkins, David. *John Dryden*. Cambridge: Cambridge University Press, 1986; Hotson, Leslie. *The Commonwealth and Restoration Stage*. Cambridge, MA: Harvard University Press, 1928; Hughes, Derek. *Dryden's Heroic Plays*. London: Macmillan, 1981; Hume, Robert D. *The Development of English Drama in the late Seventeenth Century*. Oxford: Clarendon Press, 1976; ———. *Dryden's Criticism*. Ithaca, NY: Cornell University Press, 1970; Johnson, Samuel. "John Dryden." In *The Lives of the English Poets*, vol. 1, ed. George Birkbeck Hill. Oxford: Clarendon Press, 1905; King, Bruce. *Dryden's Major Plays*. Edinburgh: Oliver and Boyd, 1966; ———, ed. *Dryden's Mind and Art*. Edinburgh: Oliver and Boyd, 1969; Kinsley, James, and Helen Kinsley, eds. *Dryden: The Critical Heritage*. London: Routledge, 1971; Kirsch, Arthur C. *Dryden's Heroic Drama*. Princeton, NJ: Princeton University Press, 1965; ———, ed. *Literary Criticism of John Dryden*. Lincoln: University of Nebraska Press, 1966; Latt, David J., and Samuel Holt Monk. *John Dryden: A Survey and Bibliography of Critical Studies, 1895–1974*. Minneapolis: University of Minnesota Press, 1976; Macdonald, Hugh. *John Dryden: A Bibliography of Early Editions and Drydeniana*. Oxford: Oxford University Press, 1939; McFadden, George. *Dryden: The Public Writer, 1660–1685*. Princeton, NJ: Princeton University Press, 1978; Miner, Earl. *Dryden's Poetry*. Bloomington: Indiana University Press, 1967; ———, ed. *John Dryden*. Athens: Ohio University Press, 1972; ———. *The Restoration Mode from Milton to Dryden*. Princeton, NJ: Princeton University Press, 1974; Montgomery, Guy. *Concordance to the Poetical Works of John Dryden*. Berkeley: University of California Press, 1957; Moore, John Robert. "Political Allusions in Dryden's Later Plays." *PMLA* 73 (1958): 36–42; Osborn, James M. *John Dryden: Some Biographical Facts and Problems*, rev. ed. Gainesville: University Press of Florida, 1965; Pechter, Edward. *Dryden's Classical Theory of Literature*. London: Cambridge University Press, 1975; Roper, Alan. *Dryden's Poetic Kingdoms*. London: Routledge, 1965; Scott, Walter. "The Life of John Dryden." In *The Works of John Dryden*, vol. 1. London: William Miller, 1808 (published separately in 1826); Swedenberg, H. T., Jr., ed. *Essential Articles for the Study of John Dryden*. Hamden, CT: Archon, 1966; Ward, Charles E. *The Life of John Dryden*. Chapel Hill: University of North Carolina Press, 1961; Winn, James Anderson. *John Dryden and His World*. New Haven, CT: Yale University Press, 1987; Wykes, David. *A Preface to Dryden*. London: Longmans, 1977; Zamonski, John A. *An Annotated Bibliography of John Dryden: Texts and Studies, 1949–1973*. New York: Garland, 1975; Zwicker, Steven N. *Dryden's Political Poetry: The Typology of King and Nation*. Providence, RI: Brown University Press, 1972.

JENA TRAMMELL

MATTHEW ARNOLD
(December 24, 1822–April 15, 1888)

Duty to other human beings was paramount in Matthew Arnold's life and is constantly expressed in his poetry and criticism. Arnold's writings note problems, primarily social, and generally suggest ways to solve them. His criticism tends to be moralistic, and his poetry, while didactic, is also majestic, direct, and full of an unusual musical sadness. Fellowship and community spirit are prevailing topics in both his criticism and poetry and are seen as eroded by a fast-paced and arid modern life. The city of London is reflected as void of real humanity and also of the restorative elements found in the natural world. Arnold has often been noted for his optimism, but it is always undercut by melancholy. His was one of the great voices of the Victorian Age, particularly because he proclaimed both the good and the bad with great feeling and intellect. Classical scholarship was his forte, and it is reflected in his poetic subjects, as well as his essays stemming from Oxford lectures.

Arnold wrote only one Arthurian work, a poem titled "Tristan and Iseult," published in his collection called *Empedocles on Etna and Other Poems* (1852). Employing the ancient story in a manner similar to that of his contemporaries Alfred Tennyson, William Morris, and Algernon Swinburne, Arnold's poem is set in the medieval period, but is intended to criticize the social ills of Victorian society. Arnold's version is significant for two reasons: it is the first modern retelling of the Tristan legend, and the emphasis is not upon a great love story, but rather upon the problems caused by immoral love outside the domestic sphere.

Matthew Arnold was born on December 24, 1822, to Thomas and Mary (Penrose) Arnold at Laleham, near Staines, in Surrey. His lifelong penchant for the joys of writing, deep thought, and intelligent conversation are unsurprising given that his father was a clergyman and historian who became headmaster of Rugby. Thomas Arnold's efforts transformed Rugby into a public school of outstanding repute; Matthew Arnold became an Oxford professor of English and greatly supported the belief of his father that the masses needed to be educated out of their Philistine, middle-class responses to art, in particular to literature.

Arnold's own education began at the public school of Winchester, but he transferred to Rugby in 1837. While at Rugby he won a prize for the poem "Alaric at Rome." In October 1841 he entered Balliol College at Oxford, where he won the Newdigate Prize for "Cromwell, A Prize Poem" in 1843. During his years at Oxford, Arnold was a sociable young man, liking to talk long in a lively manner and dress fashionably. Arnold graduated in 1844 and was elected a fellow at Oriel College the next year. For the next few years he also taught at Rugby as an assistant master until, in 1847, he became the secretary of Lord Lansdowne, head of the committee of the Council on Education. Ultimately in 1851 Arnold was appointed Secretary of the Education Committee as a School Inspector. Checking school standards took up much of his time for the next thirty-five years.

Aside from the prize-winning poems, Arnold's known literary career did not begin in ernest until 1849, when *The Strayed Reveller and Other Poems* was published. The title poem is about a youth who drinks magical wine in the palace of Homer's Circe of the *Odyssey's* tenth book. The wine enables the youth to have a beautiful vision of the gods; also significant in this volume is "The Forsaken Merman," a poem based upon a Danish folk ballad about a human wife and mother who leaves her beautiful underwater world life, her merman husband, and their sea children to return to a gray and dull life on land. Critics were lukewarm about the volume by "A" and it was not reprinted after the first five hundred copies; however, only one of the twenty-seven poems in *The Strayed Reveler* was not placed by Arnold in later collections.

In June 1851 Arnold married Lucy Wightman and went on a honeymoon to Dover Beach (later the title of Arnold's most famous poem). The couple's first son, Thomas (Tommy), was born in July 1852. They had three other sons, Trevenen (Budge) in 1853; Richard (Dicky) in 1855; and Basil in 1868. Arnold outlived all of his sons. His daughters, Lucy born in 1858 and Nelly in 1861, both lived on after their father's death.

"Tristram and Iseult," Arnold's only Arthurian poem, is found in his next volume, *Empedocles on Etna, and Other Poems*, a work published in 1852. This collection features some of Arnold's best poetic works, including thirteen love poems and three lyrical poems after the title piece. "Tristram and Iseult" is the first English retelling of the tragic story in some four hundred years. The Tristram legends probably originated in the late eighth-century Pictish kingdom in Scotland. The original Tristram was most likely Drust, son of the Pictish king Talorc, who ruled Scotland around the year 740. From here, Tristram legends can be traced through Welsh, Cornish, and Breton sources. In one of her lays, Marie de France mentioned Tristram as an ideal lover, and Chrétien de Troyes also claimed to have written about the hero, although this work is no longer extant. The earliest surviving long poem about Tristram is a version by Thomas, who wrote at the Plantagenet Court in England around 1150. Thomas was followed by Eilhart von Oberge around 1170, and also by another Norman poet, Béroul, about 1190. Further, from Thomas's *Tristan*, a condensed version, *Sir Tristrem*, was composed in Middle English approximately a century later. Arnold had read Sir Thomas Malory's *Morte Darthur*, about one third of which was devoted to Trystrame and his two Isodes, but in a letter Arnold noted that the story had originally taken hold of him from an article in a French review on romance literature.

Arnold's basic plot has been traced to Thédore de la Villemarqué's "Les poèms gallois et les Romans de la Table-Ronde," which is only an outline, but the poem is also obviously indebted to Malory. In the original Tristram tale, Tristram wins the hand of the beautiful Iseult of Ireland for his uncle, King Marc of Cornwall. While Tristram and Iseult are en route to her wedding to Marc, they accidentally drink a magic potion created by Iseult's mother for the bride and the groom. The powerful drink was intended to ensure an enchanted and eternal love between the married couple. However, since Tristram drinks the potion instead of Marc, he constantly desires Iseult. The Irish princess continues to return Tristram's lust—even after she has married King Marc. When the lovers' liaisons are discovered by the king, Tristram flees to Brittany, where he marries Iseult of the White Hands, yet constantly pines for Iseult of Ireland. He seeks forgetfulness in knightly adventures—therefore becoming of greater renown—and eventually is mortally wounded. His wife tends his wounds, but Tristram sends for Iseult of Ireland. His wife tricks him into believing that his paramour is not coming and so he dies just as she arrives. Iseult of Ireland falls over the corpse, immediately dying of her grief. The lovers are buried together, leaving behind Iseult of the White Hands.

Arnold's conclusion is different from any other treatment of the tale because he leaves Iseult of Brittany with two children and spends the third canto of the poem explaining their life after the husband and father's death. In La Villemarquès's summary, when Iseult of Ireland is told that Tristram is dead, she runs madly through the streets, finds her dead lover, and dies upon his corpse. Malory, as almost an afterthought following the grail quest, significantly after his conclusion to the Trystrame section, eventually related Trystrame's death at the hands of Mark, and La Bealle Isolde's subsequent death. Neither of these authors mentioned Iseult of Brittany's (also called Iseult of the White Hands) existence after her husband's death, nor that the couple produced any offspring. Malory made it clear that the marriage of Trystrame and Isolde le Blaunche Maynys was never consummated. Arnold leaves the grieving wife with two small children to heighten the pathos.

Certainly the exotic atmosphere is entertaining, but Arthurian legends, even in the medieval period, were used to inspire rather than to amuse. Arnold, although his approach is more understated, echoes Alfred Tennyson's concern with lasciviousness in *Idylls of the King*. Arnold's position is moderate by comparison to Tennyson's attitude. Still, "Tristram and Iseult" reflects less the Christian didacticism of *The Idylls*' "The Last Tournament" (1872) and displays more simple familial concern. Arnold had little sympathy for the lovers and did not, as did Algernon Swinburne in a later work, *Tristram of Lyonesse* (1882), excuse their passion as fated or drug induced. His emphasis upon Iseult of Brittany as an abandoned wife and his invention of the couple's offspring appear intended to reflect the problems that an immoral love creates in the domestic sphere. In previous works, except for the *Idylls*, Tristram's adultery was largely ignored to glorify courtly love.

Arnold also uses the poem to attack his modern world as a place driven by foolish obsessions that gradually consume spirituality. The solution proposed seems to be a retreat into imagination and calming aesthetic pleasures. If individuals learn to distinguish universal themes in art, Arnold's theory may be that their own concerns will be deflected and thereby lessened in importance. As does the hectic pace of life, passion and melancholy, both cloud understanding of the value of real familial love. Further, the loss of creativity destroys spirituality, increasing a sense of confinement on earth and decreasing expectations of the afterlife. With a few small alterations, the long unused tale of Tristram and Iseult was resurrected as the ideal conveyor of Arnold's oft repeated message.

Particularly because Arnold left Iseult of Brittany in this quiet domestic situation, many critics have found the poem to be typical of the author's period. Commentators who attack the poem as being too Victorian and lacking a sufficient medieval atmosphere or attitude suggest that Arnold did not understand the real meaning of the story and that the poet wrote a domestic tragedy, rather than the high tragedy that he should have written. Arnold, like Tennyson, was not a medieval scholar and used his poetic imagination to speak to his own age. However, because much of the original charm of the Tristram legends is absent from the poem, those among Arnold's contemporary critics who knew the older material did not praise the work. Even those Victorian readers who knew little of medieval writing—and were, thus, unlikely to be bothered by modern elements—disliked the work because of its fragmented narration.

Part I, "Tristram," is 373 lines of mostly trochaic trimeter written in a ballad manner. Here the injured and delirious hero recalls the highlights of his love affair with Iseult of Ireland. His wife, who has been tenderly nursing his wound, watches and listens nearby. Part II, "Iseult of Ireland," is 193 lines of dramatic duet in quatrains of alternating trochaic and iambic pentameter, beginning as the lovers are reunited. Their stichomythic conversation ends with their deaths. Part III, "Iseult of Brittany," is 224 lines of quiet, mature heroic couplets that describe the life, one year after the lovers have died, of the widowed Iseult and her children. This innovative style, while interesting, makes the poem often confusing.

In addition to frequent mode shifts, from dramatic monologue to third person narrative to first person reverie, there are also many temporal juxtapositions. Inasmuch as Arnold wrote the first modern version, the love story of Tristram and Iseult was not well known in nineteenth-century England. Readers were likely to become frustrated when they attempted to understand the plot of "Tristram and Iseult," because it is not presented in a linear fashion. Arnold seems to have been purposefully obscure, because he may have been unsure of the details himself. Perhaps, however, the constant sequential disruption was intended to make the actual story less important than the codas at the end of each section, in which the narrator discusses small situational concerns in such a way that they become of universal importance. Arnold's poem shows little sympathy for Tristram's predicament. The poet's purpose is reflected in the narrator's coda about "how this fool passion gulls men potently" (III, 134). Arnold clearly did not consider this surrender to love to be ennobling. Further, the poem examines the conditions of life that deaden the human soul.

Iseult of Brittany's quiet life of seclusion was mentioned earlier as an ending that is unique to Arnold's version; even more startlingly different is Arnold's point of entry into the narrative. "Tristram and Iseult" opens with its hero weak, feverish, and ranting on his deathbed. All of the important, courageous, and gallant events of Tristram's early career are subordinated, while the poem concentrates on Tristram in middle age, a pathetic, "fever wasted" knight. A reader is immediately aware that this is not the same character who was glorified in medieval romances. Speaking excitedly, while in delirium, Tristram recounts four important episodes of his past life. These flashbacks, intermittently explicated by the narrator, serve to emphasize Tristram's degeneration through passion. The first two of these vividly recalled incidents concern his experiences with Iseult of Ireland, while the final two illustrate his haunting memories of the earlier love affair, after his marriage to Iseult of Brittany. Arnold subordinated these segments of Tristram's early life to expose the effects of his overwhelming passion.

The poem retains this feeling of distance, even through the seemingly unresolved conclusion. Arnold concentrated on the knight's "waning time," rather than "his resplendent prime" (I, 70, 71), to show that the brief joy of the Irish Iseult's love was not worth the price of a lifetime of banishment from Cornwall. Tristram, weak and pale, is unable to use his green hunter's dress and his golden harp, the two items that generally characterize this knight when he appeared in medieval romances; these items lie untouched on Tristram's bed, relinquished with his youth. His wife stands by the dying fire, watching and pitying Tristram, as the knight suffers the effects of a tyrannous and obsessive passion. Tristram does not realize that the Iseult he married is even in the room, and he compulsively recounts aspects of his earlier life: Iseult of Ireland asking Tristram to pledge her for courtesy with the drugged wine; the lovers discovered during a winter garden walk, and Tristram fleeing after one last kiss; the brave knight seeking to overcome his passion through challenges and, thereby, being wounded in King Arthur's war against Rome; and Tristram seeking refuge and solace in a forest, only to see Iseult of Ireland's face, when the moonlight shines upon the water of a spring. He has no thought of his wife and children. The narrator's enlargement upon Tristram's ranting is the bulk of Arnold's exposition in "Tristram and Iseult." Obviously, Arnold's omissions were intended to simplify the material and to focus attention upon Tristram in his last days, but a reader unfamiliar with the story would be likely to misunderstand exactly what is occurring.

Arnold devotes the second part of "Tristram and Iseult" to Iseult of Ireland. Just as Arnold invented Tristram's brown hair, he assigned raven locks and dark eyes to the Irish princess; this makes her a more perfect foil for Arnold's golden-haired Iseult of Brittany. The first Iseult is haughty, beautiful, and full of movement, while the second Iseult is sweet, pale, and static. Arnold did not overtly judge Iseult of Ireland, but simply showed the effects of the violent sexual passion that "consumed her beauty like a flame, / And dimmed it like the desert-blast" (II, 134–35). Marc's queen arrives at Tristram's bedside full of anguish as well as excuses for her late arrival. She announces that she has been detained in "royal state with Marc, my deep wronged husband" (II, 45). Tristram questions her fidelity since she has been with "silken courtiers whispering honeyed nothings" (II, 47). Iseult claims that she has been true to Tristram and equally miserable:

Ah, on which, if both our lots were balanced,
Was indeed the heaviest burden thrown—
Thee, a pining exile in thy forest,
Me, a smiling queen upon my thrown?
Vain and strange debate, where both have suffered,
Both have passed a youth consumed and sad,
Both have brought their anxious day to evening,
And now have short space for being glad! (II, 49–56)

Both lovers have been wretched while apart, and the reader remains uncertain about how much their passion stems from natural feelings of love, and how much is the effect of the magic potion. The lovers do indeed "have now short space for being glad" (II, 56); immediately after Iseult has comforted Tristram, he realizes that he is dying. Iseult, despite the immorality of their entire relationship or her pagan association with sorcery, demands that Tristram ask heaven for help: "Call on God and on the holy angels!" (II, 79). In the next line, Iseult, more characteristically, for one so lacking in Christian spirituality, utters an oath: "Christ, he is so pale" (II, 79). Tristram pleads with Iseult, asking that she not go far from his grave; with this for encouragement, Iseult kisses Tristram and dies with him.

The long-separated, middle-aged lovers have been wasted by passion, but are granted a final, tranquil moment in death. The proud, petulant, and imperious Irish Iseult is relieved of the stale court life in which she has been unable to hide her secret:

And the dames whispered scoffingly;
"Her moods, good lack, they pass like showers!
But yesternight and she would be
As pale and still as withered flowers,
And now tonight she laughs and speaks
And now has color in her cheeks;
Christ keep us from such fantasy!" (II, 124–30)

A great change comes over Cornwall's queen when she is relieved of the tormented passion that has consumed her life and looks. The narrator describes how this release returns her to her former beauty:

And though the bedclothes hide her face,
Yet it were lifted to the light,
The sweet expression of her brow
Would charm the gazer, till his thought
Erased the ravages of time,
Filled up the hollow cheek, and brought
A freshness back as of her prime—
So healing is her quiet now. (II, 136–43)

Iseult of Ireland becomes, with death, more like her formal rival Iseult of Brittany.

The narrator's first line, "What knight is this so weak and pale" (I, 9), unmistakably echoes Keats's "La Belle Dame sans Merci" (Carley, 2). This connection ends when Iseult of Ireland is destroyed along with her exhausted knight, unless the other Iseult is a Belle Dame, Part II is the most dramatic part of "Tristram and Iseult." Their bodies are taken by ship to Cornwall, where they are buried in state by King Marc, who now regrets having separated the lovers. The final section of the poem barely mentions the couple, but focuses upon the lonely life of Iseult of Brittany.

Arnold treated Iseult of Brittany with unprecedented expansiveness by devoting all of Part III of "Tristram and Iseult" to her life without her husband. The reader only once before saw her interact with Tristram, when he awakened from delirium to find that she had been in the chamber, listening to his excited talk about Iseult of Ireland. To her credit, Iseult of Brittany reacts as the perfect Patient Griselda by sympathetically regarding her husband:

Not with a look of wounded pride,
A look as if the heart complained—
Her look was like a sad embrace;
The gaze of one who can divine
A grief, and sympathize. (I, 320–24)

Iseult of the White Hands is much kinder to her husband in "Tristram and Iseult" than she is in most earlier sources.

Indeed, Arnold created an Iseult of Brittany devoid of treacherous intentions and one able to arouse the reader to sympathetic feeling. One pities the wife who loved and nursed her husband, bore his children, and yet had to endure his constant obsession with another woman. Iseult of Brittany is presented in the poem before her rival Iseult, and the wife is described by the narrator in words that would particularly appeal to a Victorian audience:

> Who is this snowdrop by the sea?———
> I know her by her mildness rare,
> Her snow-white hands, her golden hair;
> I know her by her rich silk dress,
> And her fragile loveliness—
> The sweetest Christian soul alive,
> Iseult of Brittany. (I, 49–55)

Further, the focus upon the long suffering wife, whose children are not of much importance to their father, ensures a reader's distaste for Tristram. Arnold, like Tennyson, did not intend for an adulterous love to be viewed as attractive. Swinburne is the only other poet to expand the wife's role, but his intent was to further glorify the lovers: his god of love reigns supreme in the universe and those who submit to it unconditionally achieve heroism and fame. In the third section, Iseult of Brittany becomes the central figure of Arnold's poem, and this character is likely to remain in a reader's memory and to be recalled as the most likable. Through the addition of details about her domestic life and activities with her children, Arnold made Iseult of Brittany much more substantial than her rival queen. Neither woman is perfect, but Iseult of Brittany is treated more sympathetically.

One year after the lovers' deaths, left with only her children and servants in the seaside castle, Iseult is lonely and languid. Iseult's only joy is playing on the heath with her children. The poem ends with the three walking among the hollies on a winter's day as Iseult tells her children "an old-world Breton history" (III, 37), the tale of Merlin and Vivian. This interpolated tale is puzzling because it is out of place, distracting, and a very strange conclusion to the poem. The story of Merlin's horrible fate does not seem a particularly appropriate topic to relate to small children, but entertaining youngsters was not Arnold's intention; the storytelling session is more a type of therapy for Iseult of Brittany. One is left with the feeling that passion creates a state of death-in-life. Applied to Arnold's characters, Merlin is Tristram and the fay Vivian seems, at first, to correspond with the enchanting Iseult of Ireland. However, because Arnold included few of Vivian's physical characteristics, the specific mention of her "white right hand" (III, 174) intentionally connects the character with Iseult of Brittany. This connection is strengthened when one remembers that the wife did, in effect, imprison Tristram through marriage and, thus, hasten his death by parting from his lover, his *raison d'être*.

Iseult's judgments on her marriage and her sorrow may well be transmuted into the aesthetic experience of storytelling. Arnold used Malory's darker view of Merlin's story and omitted La Villemarqué's more softened version, in which Vivian is eternally remorseful for the damage that she does to Merlin. Malory explained Nenyve's enchantment of Merlin by having his narrator report that "she was ever passinge wery of hym" (9126, bk. 4, chap. 1). Arnold again distinctly echoed Malory in the last line of "Tristram and Iseult," with Iseult's explanation of Vivian's treachery: "For she was weary of his love" (III, 224). After having a year to recall Tristram's limitations as a spouse, Arnold's Iseult may believe that she is well rid of a husband who was not of much use to her or their children. Iseult's passive life with Tristram gradually eroded any spirit she may have had before her marriage—leaving her trapped in a state like that of Merlin.

Perhaps Iseult's telling of this particular tale indicates her understanding of her own confined state, and suggests her possible future renewal, as well as the idea that she is now content to have lost Tristram. Arnold leaves Iseult of Brittany's feelings ambiguous. All that is certain is that her feelings of weary melancholy, bordering on ennui, are the results of Tristram's passion for another woman and his death. Grief would be acceptable, but Iseult's lack of vibrance, attitude of emptiness, and telling of the story of Merlin and Vivian are disconcerting.

Arnold used the power of artifice in an ancient tale to yield new meanings by enhancing his reader's understanding of contemporary life. The slow destructive power of the world is just as debilitating as the consuming force of passion. The poem's balanced opposition, shown in the contrast between two kinds of women and two kinds of love, is disturbing. Arnold revealed that this dichotomy can be neutralized through imaginative power combined with the serenity that this power can create. The poet's message may be that moderation and an understanding of the larger issues treated in the universal themes of art are the essential aspects of a fulfilling life. Love should not be a debilitating obsession or a force that gradually burns away all spirit, leaving only melancholy.

Arnold's next poetic volume after *Empedocles on Etna* was published the following year as simply *Poems* (1853). This book includes the well known "Preface" suggesting that literary criticism should be written primarily about how a piece morally improves or guides its readers. This very Victorian notion was Arnold's first foray into criticism and reflects his father's concern with improving the masses. The volume is also significant as the first issued under his full name rather than simply "A." The poems came from the earlier two volumes except for "Sohrab and Rustum" and "The Scholar Gipsy."

In 1855 *Poems, Second Series* was released. This volume included only one new poem, "Balder Dead." Despite being mocked by some reviewers as "Balder Dash," the poem was well reviewed. Balder is a character from Norse mythology who is killed through a trick and whom the gods try to bring back from the kingdom of the dead. After many years of working on it, Arnold released the *Tragedy of Merope*, which was published in 1857. It was a poem that Arnold hoped could be performed as a play, but it was very hard to read, much less act out. He had used his understanding of Sophocles to take this new direction, but the work was negatively reviewed.

His first critical work, *On Translating Homer* (1861), is composed of a series of lectures Arnold delivered at Oxford. He was always happy to speak of Homer's language and directness of thought, although Arnold never translated the Greek epic himself. Arnold's critical voice slowly developed from this point on. This early series is pedantic and conceited, but shows promise. His *Last Words on Translating Homer* (1862) was a response to criticism about his first work on Homer.

Essays in Criticism (1865) involves the work of Homer, but goes a step further by adding other pieces and a preface, "The Function of Criticism in the Present Time," which is still studied frequently today. Arnold wrote on Heine and Goethe and considered himself as working to liberate the Philistines of his country. To Arnold, it was seminal that mind and ideas should triumph over daily concerns.

Poetry was still written, but only criticism was published during this period. Finally, in *New Poems* (1867) Arnold repeated *Empedocles on Etna* and six other poems from his 1852 work. "Dover Beach" is the poem of greatest significance in this volume. The poem is about violence versus beauty and stems from his understanding of the biblical passage 1 John 4:7–10. In June 1867 *Essays on the Celtic Literature* was released. Celtic, Teutonic, and Norman elements of himself and of the British people are the subjects of the four lectures that became this book. Celtic literature was not Arnold's specialty, so he felt uncomfortable being considered an expert on the subject, unlike the excitement he felt when lecturing and publishing about Homer, whom he had studied extensively.

The publication of *Schools and Universities on the Continent* (1868) reminds one that Arnold made a living, not by his writing or lecturing, but as a school inspector. The job allowed him to travel and observe his countrymen. Most of his countrymen could not afford to educate their children nearly as well as those in other countries, especially Germany. The government policies that control education are most emphasized. *Culture and Anarchy* (1869) is the result of a lecture at Oxford about intellectual freedom. Arnold wanted idealistic thoughts to be available to all stemming from a feeling of freedom to be curious and ask questions.

Arnold turned his attention next to explaining various aspects of Christianity and its reflection of society. In 1870 *St. Paul and Protestants* was published; this stems from Arnold's ideas about culture mixed with biblical understanding and concerns with morality. Separation from the English Church by Protestant dissenters is also criticized as lacking public responsibility.

Bible in Literature and Dogma (1873) explains that anthropomorphism and miracles in the Bible must be ignored and the poetry of biblical passages embraced; allowing knowledge of an unknowable reality and an understanding of morality are the main significance. *God and the Bible* (1874) continues the exegetical disclosure of God's relationship with specific individuals. God is not a person, animal or thing that can be known as a talking, thinking being. The authenticity of John is questioned in this text as well. In *Last Essays in Church and Religion* (1878), Arnold re-examines the problems caused for believers by the miracles noted in the Bible.

In 1879 *Mixed Essays* was released and continued Arnold's pattern of including previously published works in a new collection. It is eclectic in subject and was a bit successful, perhaps because it was not completely concerned with biblical exegesis. The subjects were united in a playfully intellectually way. *Essays in Criticism: Second Series* (1881) was partly literary and continued his earlier work that was extremely successful, but the second *Essays* is unlike the first because of a variety of philosophical stances and the subjects. *Irish Essays* (1882) contains several new pieces and is about political problems in Ireland. Arnold's Celtic literature essays and concerns with Catholicism are reflected in the discussion of tyranny from England toward Ireland.

Discourses in America (1885) was an unexpected publication—Arnold had told reporters during his lecture tour in the United States that he would not write even an article about America. "A Word More about America" is an essay about civilization in England, Ireland, and America. He thought America had more social problems than the other two countries, but that the quality of life was still better anywhere besides America. These reflections continued in *Civilisation in the United States* (1888). The title work was the last essay he published in his lifetime. Arnold, always busy and hard working, died characteristically; while rushing to meet his daughter, he suffered a fatal heart attack. He fell in mid-stride chasing a horse-drawn carriage, leaving behind a collection of essays nearly finished.

Arnold's reputation as a great poet who spoke for the Victorian Age has only increased in significance. Currently, academics are not so interested in Arnold's didactic messages as they are about what Arnold's moralistic outcries say about his historical era. Further, current studies of literary criticism note Arnold's particular significance as the establishment of the *Apologia Critica* genre. This particular view of criticism begins with apologies for the author's critical views and his need to write them; it just assumes a reader's defensiveness about criticism as a lesser, secondary form of writing. Arnold encouraged the view that literary criticism is just as creative, artistic, and poetical as the texts it discusses. Contemporary scholars attribute the high value and heightened importance of literary criticism to Arnold's defense of the genre as equal to the primary text. This outlook revolutionized the world of arts and letters by making criticism a genre of equal standing with all other forms of literature.

PRIMARY WORKS

Alaric at Rome: A Prize Poem. Rugby: Combe & Crossley, 1840; *Cromwell: A Prize Poem.* Oxford: Vincent, 1843; *The Strayed Reveller and Other Poems.* London: Fellowes, 1849; *Empedocles on Etna and Other Poems.* London: Fellowes, 1852; *Poems.* London: Longman, Brown, Green & Longmans, 1853; *Poems, Second Series.* London: Longman, Brown, Green & Longmans, 1855; *Tragedy of Merope.* London: Longman, Brown, Green, Longmans & Roberts, 1857; *On Translating Homer.* London: Longman, Brown, Green, Longmans & Roberts, 1861; *Last Words on Translating Homer.* London: Longman, Green, Longmans & Roberts, 1862; *Essays in Criticism.* London and Cambridge: Macmillan, 1865; *Essays on the Study of Celtic Literature.* London and Cambridge: Macmillan, 1867; *New Poems.* London: Macmillan, 1867; *Schools and Universities on the Continent.* London: Macmillan, 1868; *Culture and Anarchy.* London: Smith, Elder, 1869; *St. Paul and Protestantism.* London: Smith, Elder, 1870; *A Bible-Reading for Schools.* London: Macmillan, 1872. Revised as *Isaiah XL-XLVI.* London: Macmillan, 1875; *Literature and Dogma.* London: Smith, Elder, 1873; *God and the Bible.* London: Smith, Elder, 1875; *Last Essays on Church and Religion.* London: Smith, Elder, 1878; *Poems of Wordsworth*, ed. Arnold. London: Macmillan, 1878; *The Six Chief Lives from Johnson's Lives of the Poets, with Macaulay's Life of Johnson.* 1878; *Mixed Essays.* London: Smith, Elder, 1879; *Passages from the Prose Writings of Matthew Arnold.* London: Smith, Elder, 1880; *Essays in Criticism: Second Series.* London: Macmillan, 1881; *Letters, Speeches, and Tracts on Irish Affairs by Edmund Burke*, ed. Arnold. London: Macmillan, 1881; *Poems of Byron*, ed. Arnold. London: Macmillan, 1881; *Irish Essays, and Others.* London: Smith, Elder, 1882; *Isaiah of Jerusalem in the Authorised Version with an Introduction, Correction, and Notes.* London: Macmillan, 1883; *Discourses in America.* London: Macmillan, 1885; *Elementary Education in Germany.* 1888; *Civilization in the United States: First and Last Impressions of America.* Boston: Cupples & Hurd, 1888; *Reports on Elementary Schools 1852–1882*, ed. Sir Francis Sandford. London: Macmillan, 1889; *Matthew Arnold's Note Books, with a preface by Mrs. Wodehouse.* London: Smith, Elder, 1902; *Essays on Criticism: Third Series*, ed. Edward J. O'Brien. Boston: Ball, 1910.

SECONDARY SOURCES

Barber, Richard, ed. *The Arthurian Legend.* London: Dorset, 1979; Baum, Paul F. *Ten Studies in the Poetry of Matthew Arnold.* Durham, NC: Duke University Press, 1958; Buckler, William E. *On the Poetry of Matthew Arnold.* New York: New York University Press, 1971; Buckley, Jerome Hamilton, and George Benjamin Woods, eds. *Poetry of the Victorian Period.* Atlanta: Scott, 1965; Carley, James P. *Matthew Arnold and William Morris.* Rochester, NY: Boydell, 1990; Culler, A. Dwight. *Imaginative Reason: The Poetry of Matthew Arnold.* New Haven, CT: Yale University Press, 1966; DeLaura, David J. "Matthew Arnold and the Nightmare of History." In *Victorian Papers*, 41–47. London: Edward Arnold, 1972; Loomis, Roger Sherman. *The Development of the Arthurian Romance.* New York: Norton, 1963; Roper, Alan H. "The Moral Landscape of Arnold's Poetry." *PMLA* 87 (1962): 289–96; Stange, G. Robert. *Matthew Arnold, the Poet as Humanist.* Princeton, NJ: Princeton University Press, 1967.

LAURA COONER LAMBDIN AND ROBERT THOMAS LAMBDIN

WILLIAM MORRIS
(March 24, 1834–October 3, 1896)

William Morris had a breadth that is recognized, a century later, as remarkable. He was poet, novelist, creator and translator of tales, artist and craftsman, designer, businessman, socialist, Marxist, preserver of churches, printer, illustrator, and collector of books and manuscripts. The list is impressive, but to each of area Morris brought a simple vision—in the face of exploitation and ugliness, he proclaimed fulfilment of labor and beauty in artifacts. In an aggressively masculine and naturalistic society, he developed a genre of romance and fantasy influencing many in the twentieth century, including Tolkien and C. S. Lewis. Morris, far from escapist, was a revolutionary. As Amanda Hodgson maintains, "for Morris romance provided not only a fictional satisfaction of his aesthetic and emotional desires, but a radically effective expression of his social and political views."

William Morris is a Janus figure. His critique of modern society led him back to a medieval world of fantasy, yet drove him forward to utopias of the future, and to a committed Marxist socialism. More radical than Marx, Morris was frustrated that Morris & Company, his family's business, produced luxury goods for the rich. Sharing much with the Pre-Raphaelite Brotherhood, his romances convey the tragic poignancy of love, made sharper by the unhappiness of his marriage. The eroticism of his language seems ill at ease with his own considerable sexual reticence. His delight in Arthurian legends, medieval fantasy, and science fiction appears anomalous set next to his earnest socialist praxis. Yet, at the intersection of all these dichotomies, we find the strange figure of Morris—exceptional artist and human being.

To the diverse areas in which he worked, Morris brought passion and obsessive skill. The influence of this complex artist and artisan continues to be profound, yet baffling. For example, his romantic vision seems far from modernism. Yet Jerome McGann argues that Morris is an essential context of modernism:

Much could and should be said about Morris and his work in a general way. Our interest in theory of art has been dominated for so long by the conceptual forms of Enlightenment and romantic thought that we have forgotten the revolutionary character of his basic insight: that if we wish to understand art and poetry we have to approach them as crafts, as practical forms of making.

For Morris, art is praxis, the poet a shaper of the world. Certainly, Morris has a seminal role in shaping the legends of Arthur. William Morris continues to challenge, although his very originality makes him hard to evaluate. Yet, as Fiona MacCarthy argues, "his highly original, painfully heroic progress through life impinges on us still, from old Socialists to new conservationists."

William Morris was born on March 24, 1834, in Walthamstow, Essex, the eldest son of William and Emma Shelton Morris. The family was of Welsh descent, and Morris had four sisters and four brothers. His father, a bill broker in Lombard Street, London, would travel daily by stagecoach to the city. Today, Walthamstow is highly urban, but in Morris's time it was a pleasant Essex village, a few miles from the beauty of Epping Forest. Although moving three times in Morris's childhood, the family were never far from this ancient forest, and it must have played an important part in shaping Morris's love for nature. When Morris was six, the family moved to Woodford Hall, a large house in fifty acres, next to the forest. There Morris and his brothers wandered, rode ponies, fished in the Roding River, or shot game. Sometimes, Morris would wear a suit of armor. Life at Woodford Hall seemed medieval: close to nature, the estate was virtually self sufficient. Morris's later quest for community—in the Court of Arthur, marriage, the arts and craft movement, or socialism—found its genesis in this home near historic Epping.

In 1847 Morris's father died, leaving the family well off. A few months later, young Morris went to school at Marlborough College, at this time in a period of chaos. Morris maintained that, apart from fighting, he learned "next to nothing." The neolithic monuments of Wiltshire did make an impression on him, as did a well-equipped library. Another sensibility, chapel at Marlborough, introduced Morris to the Oxford Movement—that religious revival begun in the 1830s by Newman, Keble, and Pusey. This influence was continued by the Reverend F. B. Guy, who later coached Morris for the Oxford entrance examination.

In 1853 Morris went to Exeter College, Oxford, becoming friends with Edward Burne-Jones. Although both young men originally intended to take holy orders, that was not to be. Great friends and collaborators, they found Oxford in transition. Only in 1844 had the railway reached the city; in many ways Oxford was still medieval. MacCarthy indicates that, "There was enough of the old city left intact for Morris to adopt it as the paradigm of the perfect medieval city." Oxford always retained a unique place in his emotions. Educationally, the University and Exeter College were far less satisfactory. Morris and Burne-Jones complained of the snobbery of Oxford life. At Exeter College, Morris read for a pass degree in "Greats" or classics, loathing the way the classics were taught. As before at school, Morris escaped into history, but less through academic study. More important was the ambiance of Oxford, the sense that its buildings—many from the fifteenth century—were organic, firmly rooted in their environment.

Early on, Morris became interested in the cult of Arthur, beginning to be a dominant cultural myth of the Victorians. In their first term, Morris would read out loud to Burne-Jones the poem "The Lady of Shalott" by Tennyson. For Morris, Burne-Jones, and others in the group known as the Brotherhood, the stories of Arthur became a quasi-religion, the chivalric code their rule of life. In the summers of 1854 and 1855, Morris visited the Cathedrals of Belgium and Northern France, being particularly impressed with Roen—like Oxford still largely a medieval city. After the 1855 visit, with Burne-Jones, the two men abandoned ideas of the ministry, instead choosing art— Burne-Jones as painter and Morris as architect. At some point, Morris lost his traditional Christian faith. Like Arnold's "Dover Beach" or Tennyson's "In Memoriam," Morris's journey is part of the complex secularization of mid-Victorian society. In 1855 Morris bought the 1817 Robert Southey edition of Malory's *Morte d'Arthur*, which quickly became a treasured book. After Tennyson's more diffident version of Arthur, Malory's explicit strength came as a shock and a revelation. MacCarthy suggests that, "The ambivalent splendor of Malory's Queen Guinevere, technically guilty but defying judgment, was a picture of womanhood that haunted and dazzled and bewildered William Morris. The Guinevere factor was a strong one in his life." That ambivalence is seen in his art and personal life.

Among his Oxford friends, Morris was becoming a caricature. With his unruly mop of hair, he was known as Topsy. Renowned for his larger than life persona, extravagant Morris stories circulated. More alarmingly, at times he would exhibit wild rages and irrational outbursts, about which there has been a conspiracy of silence. MacCarthy maintains that Morris did experience "a kind of seizure in which he partially lost consciousness." Yet she also points out that Morris uses rages or trances in his writing, perhaps suggesting prophetic or visionary power.

During 1856 the group of friends published a monthly magazine, the *Oxford and Cambridge Magazine*, initially edited and largely financed by Morris. His contributions included seven short romances, five poems, a love story, and an article in the style of Ruskin. Morris was finding his voice, "My work is the embodiment of dreams in one form or another." The contributors believed that, in the words of Godfrey Lushington, "the past, it is written, ever explains to us the present." On this point, Morris was somewhat ambivalent. Amanda Hodgson says,

> His early fiction and poetry seeks to create a sensually powerful romance world and large succeeds in the "embodiment," the making fictionally tangible, of fantasy. Yet unlike Stevenson and Haggard and his friends of the Oxford and Cambridge Magazine, he seems unconvinced about the usefulness of the dreams he is presenting with such vivid force.

In 1856 despite problems assenting to the Thirty-Nine Articles, Morris took his bachelor's degree. Initially articled to the Oxford architect, George Edmund Street, Morris was supervised by Street's senior clerk, Philip Webb, who became a close friend. What did Morris gain from his work with Street? With the architect barely a year, Morris still must have acquired much, though he never acknowledged Street's influence, finding the architect narrow and conservative. MacCarthy says, "Morris rejected Street as he had disowned his own father." Yet Street had a holistic view of architecture—concerned with painting, textiles, sculpture, and metalworking, for instance—and this comprehensive view had later echoes in the extraordinary breadth of Morris's craft.

In August 1856 Morris and Burne-Jones moved to Bloomsbury, London. After phenomenal growth earlier, London was now the greatest city in Europe. Inheriting his father's entrepreneurial skills, Morris would discover London the perfect arena for business success. Yet he found the problems of civilization writ large, and Morris was

ambivalent about the city. Cholera, smoke, sewage, and inadequate housing would provoke Morris's passionate denunciation. But London became and remained his city. Earlier in 1856, Morris had met the poet and Pre-Raphaelite painter Dante Gabriel Rossetti,
a fateful meeting. Rossetti, six years older than Morris, became, in MacCarthy's words,
"a combination of worldly mentor and the much older elder brother to Morris and
Burne-Jones." Under Rossetti's influence, Morris began to focus more on painting. Being
Morris, he also drew, carved, wrote, and illuminated manuscripts. In late 1857 he worked
with Rossetti, Burne-Jones, and others on the decoration of the new Oxford Union
debating hall. Worked in tempura, the murals illustrated scenes from Morte d'Arthur,
Morris choosing a rejected lover. However, because of inadequate preparation, within six
months the murals had deteriorated.

Earlier in 1857, Morris met "Janey," the beautiful, seventeen-year-old Jane Burden from
a poor Oxford family. Rossetti used her as a model for Guenevere: for the Pre-Raphaelites
her striking appearance became a quintessence of feminine beauty. Among these artists,
there was a predilection for working-class models, what MacCarthy calls "a chivalric drama
of finding and transforming." She suggests that "The Pygmalion factor cannot be
discounted in Morris's highly idealized and at times tormented relations with Janey."
Engaged in 1858, Morris and Burden married in 1859, when Morris was twenty-five.
Within three years, they had two daughters, Jenny and May. Neither Morris's family nor
Rossetti attended the wedding. It is not certain whether from the start Rossetti sabotaged
the marriage, but, as time went by, Rossetti and Janey spent much time together—not
always for artistic purposes. Morris seemed to have permitted the affair, but his motives are
unclear. It seems undeniable, however, that the poignant themes of unfulfilled love and
triangular relationships were constant in his art and experience.

The year before he married, in 1858, Morris published *The Defence of Guenevere and
Other Poems*, at his own expense. From the beginning, Morris joins his art and text
design since he chose, McGann points out, to put his first book "into the hands of one
of the very few fine-printing houses then operating in England." The poems in the book
are in three groups: four Arthurian poems, seven poems inspired by Froissart's
Chronicles, and nine dream-like poems. The first Arthurian poem, and title of the volume, is "The Defence of Guenevere." Like many before him, Morris used Malory's work
Morte d'Arthur to express his own poetic and moral ideas. As the Lambdins say, these
ideas "develop around the fine line between human love in its highest form and this same
love as it dissolves into sin." In the first words, Morris sets the tone:

> But, knowing now that they would have her speak,
> She threw her wet hair backward from her brow,
> Her hand close to her mouth touching her cheek. (1–3)

"But," the Lambdins point out, "defines the ambiguity of Guenevere's entire situation,
as well as her defense. The poem maintains a degree of uncertainty throughout about
Guenevere's degree of guilt and in which particular situations she actually committed
adultery." The language is sensual: her passion has undone her, yet her rhetoric seems
convincing. Is there an implicit challenge to Victorian hypocrisy? Carole Silver sees Guenevere's ambiguity within Morris himself, and his "genius is in his refusal to render a
smug verdict upon her. His testimony, as well as hers, is to the formidable power of
erotic passion which can dissolve all other values in it." The second poem, "King
Arthur's Tomb," also based on Malory, was suggested by a painting by Rossetti called

Arthur's Tomb (1854). The third poem, "Sir Galahad: A Christmas Mystery," delves into the psychic struggle of this favorite knight, on the longest night of the year, Galahad's dark night of the soul. The final Arthurian poem, "The Chapel at Lyoness," only ninety-two lines long, was first published in the *Oxford and Cambridge Magazine*. The scene in three voices, not found in Malory, merges flesh and spirit in a provocative way.

As the Lambdins conclude, "Morris's Arthurian poems reflect characters experiencing feelings of vacillation between sensual self-indulgence and spiritual puritanism. The poet seems to have been obsessed with the themes of immoral sexual desire and the guilt that accompanies it. The protagonists' problems largely remain unsolved, possibly suggesting Morris's understanding of the futility involved in opposing earthly to heavenly love."

Two other poems, "Praise of My Lady" and "Summer Dawn," seem inspired by his wife, Janey. A fragment exists, "The Maying of Guenevere," but Morris published nothing more in the Arthurian genre. He abandoned his planned Arthurian epic, probably dissuaded by the appearance in 1859 of Tennyson's hugely successful *Idylls of the King*. The critics and public did not welcome *The Defence of Guenevere and Other Poems*; the poems seemed dark and obscure, and not to Victorian taste. Today, many value the passion and youthful angst of these lyrical poems. Morris, however, was discouraged and for nine years published nothing.

In the meantime, he had built Red House, his home in Kent, designed in neo-Gothic style by his friend, Philip Webb. Finding nothing suitable in medieval-style furnishings, Morris began with friends to design his own. Thus in 1861, shortly after the birth of Jenny, their first daughter, the firm Morris, Marshall, Faulkner and Company was founded. Based in Bloomsbury and founded on Ruskin's principles, the firm was to revive older traditions of handcrafting artifacts—for homes, churches, and public buildings. The firm was a success, winning lucrative commissions, especially after the 1862 International Exhibition. The company became the focus of Morris's art and his designs included stained glass, furniture, wallpapers, carpets, and woven tapestries—all of a very high standard. Red House became a meeting place for Morris's circle, and May, Morris's second daughter, was born there in 1862. But in 1864 Morris became ill; the journey to Bloomsbury was too much. In 1865, therefore, the family relocated to Queen Square, Bloomsbury, living over the workshops.

In 1867 Morris published "The Life and Death of Jason: A Poem." It was originally to be part of much longer work, *The Earthly Paradise*, later published in three volumes in 1868–70. These long narrative poems were well received, giving Morris a considerable reputation as a poet. The style is medieval verse romance, the mood elegiac despair. The fall of Troy symbolized the decline of England and the loss of Eden. But Morris moves beyond elegy, as Silver says, "into a nihilistic statement of the meaninglessness of all things." These poems help to explain the link between the early romance and later socialism. The poems reject traditional Victorian answers for, in Silver's words, "in the despair and negation they voice lies the goad that will move Morris to embrace the stoic ethic of the North and to assert that men—through fellowship—must build their Eden in the ordinary world, the only paradise that they will ever find."

The years 1868 to 1875 were no Eden for Morris. Mackail's 1899 biography suppressed much, but it is certain that the tortuous relationship between Rossetti, Janey, and Morris, and Morris's love for Georgina Burne-Jones, the wife of his best friend, brought Morris pain and intense depression. In 1871 Morris and Rossetti became joint tenants of Kelmscott Manor, an Elizabethan manor on the upper Thames, where with Morris's acquiescence Rossetti and Janey could be together. Rossetti's health was now precarious, as was Janey's. Morris's "Love is Enough" (1873) expressed his emotional pain allegorically, and he continued to find consolation in work. In 1868 Morris met Eiríkr Magnússon and learned Icelandic. Together they published various translations from the Icelandic sagas. Morris made two journeys to Iceland, and wrote his own epic, *The Story of Sigurd the Volsung and the Fall of the Niblungs* (1876), acknowledged by the critics but never popular. It would be his last major work of poetry.

Late in 1876, Morris entered a new and political phase of his life. Two years before, he had reorganized the business as Morris and Company, learning traditional arts of dyeing and carpet weaving, and finally terminating the join tenancy of Kelmscott with Rossetti. Now, he worked against war with Russia, set up the Society for the Protection of Ancient Buildings in 1877, became treasurer to the National Liberal League in 1879, and became a socialist with the Democratic Federation in 1883. Although gradually becoming Marxist in his orientation, he felt the powers of reaction were too strong for a successful revolution, particularly after Bloody Sunday, November 13, 1887. Morris resumed his literary work with a historical romance, *A Dream of John Ball* (1888), a prose romance, *A Tale of the House of the Wolfings* (1889), and his quest romance, *The Well at the World's End* (1896)—forerunner of the stories of Charles Williams, Tolkien, and C. S. Lewis.

His "News from Nowhere," a dream of a future Communist England after the revolution, was published first in the Socialist Commonweal, then in book form in 1890. His final enterprise was the setting up of Kelmscott Press, designing both type and page, and producing some fifty-three fine works, including his own *The Story of the Glittering Plain* in 1891, and a magnificent edition of Chaucer in 1896 with woodcuts by Burne-Jones.

For some time, Morris had been an important collector of medieval manuscripts and early books, and both this activity and Kelmscott Press make Morris a major player in both fine printing and book collecting. Right to the end, he lectured on socialism, spoke on arts and crafts, and guided Morris and Company. This pace, however, could not be sustained by one man, and after 1891 his health deteriorated. On October 3, 1896, in Hammersmith, William Morris died. Three days later, he was buried in the churchyard at Kelmscott. MacCarthy has a moving account of his funeral, where many dichotomies of his life briefly came together. Initially, after his death, it was either as a designer or a socialist that Morris primarily was remembered. Then in 1955, *William Morris: Romantic to Revolutionary* by E. P. Thompson showed a more integrated Morris. Interest in this complex man has only increased since then. The struggles of William Morris—his search for genuine love and for a more just society—are consummated in his quest for an earthly paradise, a new Eden. His quest may still be ours.

PRIMARY WORKS

Books

The Defence of Guenevere, and Other Poems. London: Bell & Daldy, 1858; Boston: Roberts, 1875; *The Life and Death of Jason: A Poem*. London: Bell & Daldy, 1867; Boston: Roberts, 1867; revised as *The Life and Death of Jason*. London: Bell & Daldy, 1882; *The Earthly Paradise: A Poem*, 3 vols. London: Ellis, 1868–1870; Boston: Roberts, 1868–1870; *The Lovers of Gudrun: A Poem*. Boston: Roberts, 1870; *Love Is Enough; or, The Freeing of Pharamond: A Morality*. London: Ellis & White, 1873; Boston: Roberts, 1873; *The Story of Sigurd the Volsung and the Fall of the Niblungs*. London: Ellis & White, 1876; Boston: Roberts, 1876; *The Decorative Arts, Their Relation to Modern Life and Progress: An Address Delivered before the Trades Guild of*

Learning. London: Ellis & White, 1878; *Hopes and Fears for Art: Five Lectures Delivered in Birmingham, London, and Nottingham 1878-81.* London: Ellis & White, 1882; Boston: Roberts, 1882; *A Summary of the Principles of Socialism Written for the Democratic Federation,* by Morris and H. M. Hyndman. London: Modern Press, 1884; *Textile Fabrics: A Lecture.* London: Clowes, 1884; *Art and Socialism: A Lecture; and Watchman, What of the Night? The Aims and Ideas of the English Socialists of Today.* London: Reeves, 1884; *Chants for Socialists: No. 1. The Day Is Coming.* London: Reeves, 1884; *The Voice of Toil, All for the Cause: Two Chants for Socialists.* London: Justice Office, 1884; *The God of the Poor.* London: Justice Office, 1884; *Chants of Socialists.* London: Socialist League Office, 1885; republished as *Chants for Socialists.* New York: New Horizon, 1935; *The Socialist League: Constitution and Rules Adopted at the General Conference.* London: Socialist League Office, 1885; *Address to Trades' Unions.* London: Socialist League Office, 1885; *Useful Work v. Useless Toil.* London: Socialist League Office, 1885; *For Whom Shall We Vote? Addressed to the Working-Men Electors of Great Britain.* London: Commonweal Office, 1885; *What Socialists Want.* London: Hammersmith Branch of the Socialist League, 1885; *A Short Account of the Commune of Paris,* by Morris and E. Belfort Bax. London: Socialist League Office, 1886; *The Pilgrims of Hope: A Poem in Thirteen Books.* London: Forman, 1886; republished as *The Pilgrims of Hope: A Poem in XIII Books.* Portland, Maine: Mosher, 1901; *Alfred Linnell, Killed in Trafalgar Square, November 20, 1887.* London: Lambert, 1887; *The Aims of Art.* London: Commonweal Office, 1887; *The Tables Turned; or, Nupkins Awakened: A Socialist Interlude.* London: Commonweal Office, 1887; Athens: Ohio University Press, 1994; *Of the External Coverings of Roofs,* anonymous. London: Society for the Protection of Ancient Buildings, 1887?; *Signs of Change: Seven Lectures Delivered on Various Occasions.* London: Reeves & Turner, 1888; New York: Longmans, Green, 1896; *A Dream of John Ball, and A King's Lesson.* London: Reeves & Turner, 1888; East Aurora, NY: Roycroft, 1898; *A Tale of the House of the Wolfings and All the Kindreds of the Mark.* London: Reeves & Turner, 1889; Boston: Roberts, 1890; *The Roots of the Mountains, Wherein Is Told Somewhat of the Lives of the Men of Burgdale, Their Friends, Their Neighbours, Their Foemen and Their Fellows in Arms.* London: Reeves & Turner, 1890; New York: Longmans, Green, 1896; *Monopoly; or, How Labour Is Robbed.* London: Commonweal Office, 1890; *News from Nowhere; or, An Epoch of Rest: Being Some Chapters from a Utopian Romance.* Boston: Roberts, 1890; London: Reeves & Turner, 1891; *Statement of Principles of the Hammersmith Socialist Society,* anonymous. Hammersmith: Hammersmith Socialist Society, 1890; *The Story of Gunnlaug the Worm-Tongue.* London: Chiswick, 1890-1891; *The Story of the Glittering Plain, Which Has Been Also Called the Land of Living Men or the Acre of the Undying.* Hammersmith: Kelmscott, 1891; London: Reeves & Turner, 1891; Boston: Roberts, 1891; *Poems by the Way.* Hammersmith: Kelmscott, 1891; London: Reeves & Turner, 1891; Boston: Roberts, 1892; *Address on the Collection of Paintings of the English Pre-Raphaelite School.* Birmingham: Osborne, 1891; *Under an Elm-Tree; or, Thoughts in the Country-side.* Aberdeen: Leatham, 1891; Portland, Maine: Mosher, 1912; *The Reward of Labour: A Dialogue.* London: Hammersmith Socialist Society, 1892?; *Manifesto of English Socialists,* anonymous, by Morris, Hyndman, and Bernard Shaw. London: Twentieth Century, 1893; *Concerning Westminster Abbey,* anonymous. London: Women's Printing Society, 1893; *Socialism: Its Growth and Outcome,* by Morris and E. Belfort Bax. London: Swan Sonnenschein, 1893; *Help for the Miners: The Deeper Meaning of the Struggle.* London: Baines & Searsrook, 1893; *Gothic Architecture: A Lecture for the Arts and Crafts Exhibition Society.* Hammersmith: Kelmscott, 1893; *The Wood beyond the World.* Hammersmith: Kelmscott, 1894; Boston: Roberts, 1895; *The Why I Ams: Why I Am a Communist, with L. S. Bevington's Why I Am an Expropriationist.* London: Liberty, 1894; *Letters on Socialism.* London: Privately printed, 1894; *Child Christopher and Goldilind the Fair.* 2 vols., Hammersmith: Kelmscott, 1895; 1 vol., Portland, Maine: Mosher, 1900; *Gossip about an Old House on the Upper Thames.* Birmingham: Birmingham Guild of Handicraft, 1895; Flushing, NY: Hill, 1901; *The Well at the World's End: A Tale.* 1 vol., Hammersmith: Kelmscott, 1896; 2 vols., London, New York & Bombay: Longmans, Green, 1896; *How I Became a Socialist.* London: Twentieth Century, 1896; *Some*

German Woodcuts of the Fifteenth Century, ed. Sydney C. Cockerell. Hammersmith: Kelmscott, 1897; *The Water of the Wondrous Isles*. Hammersmith: Kelmscott, 1897; New York & London: Longmans, Green, 1897; *The Sundering Flood*. Hammersmith: Kelmscott, 1897; New York & London: Longmans, Green, 1898; *A Note by William Morris on His Aims in Founding the Kelmscott Press, Together with a Short Description of the Press by S. C. Cockerell, and an Annotated List of the Books Printed Thereat*. Hammersmith: Kelmscott, 1898; republished as *The Art and Craft of Printing ... a Note by William Morris on His Aims in Founding the Kelmscott Press, Together with a Short Description of the Press by S. C. Cockerell, and an Annotated List of the Books Printed Thereat*. New Rochelle, NY: Elston, 1902; *Address Delivered at the Distribution of Prizes to Students of the Birmingham Municipal School of Art on February 21, 1894*. London: Longmans, Green, 1898; *Art and the Beauty of the Earth*. London: Longmans, Green, 1898; *Some Hints on Pattern Designing*. London: Longmans, Green, 1899; *The Two Sides of the River, and Other Poems*. Portland, Maine: Mosher, 1899; *Architecture and History, and Westminster Abbey*. London: Longmans, Green, 1900; *Art and Its Producers, and the Arts and Crafts of Today*. London: Longmans, Green, 1901; *Architecture, Industry, and Wealth: Collected Papers*. London & New York: Longmans, Green, 1902; *A Dream*. Portland, Maine: Mosher, 1902; London: Thomson, 1904; *The Art of the People: An Address Delivered Before the Birmingham Society of Arts, February 19th, 1879*. Chicago: Seymour, 1902; *The Doom of King Acrisius*. New York: Russell, 1902; *Communism: A Lecture*, ed. Shaw. London: Fabian Society, 1903; *Summer Dawn*. London: Hodder & Stoughton, 1911; *Two Red Roses across the Moon*. London: Hodder & Stoughton, 1911; *Factory Work As It Is and Might Be: A Series of Four Papers*. New York: New York Labor News, 1922; *Some Thoughts on the Ornamented Mss. of the Middle Ages*. New York: Press of the Woolly Whale, 1934; *The Unpublished Lectures of William Morris*, ed. Eugene LeMire. Detroit: Wayne State University Press, 1969; *Icelandic Journals of William Morris*. Fontwell: Centaur, 1969; New York: Praeger, 1970; *Early Romances in Prose and Verse*, ed., with an introduction, by Peter Faulkner. London: J. M. Dent, 1973; *Political Writings of William Morris*, ed., with an introduction, by A. L. Morton. London: Lawrence & Wishart: New York: International Publishers; Berlin: Seven Seas, 1973; *The Story of Cupid and Psyche*. Cambridge: Rampant Lions, 1974; *A Book of Verse by William Morris Written in London 1870*. London: Scolar, 1980; New York: Potter, 1981; *Socialist Diary*, ed. Florence Boos. Iowa City: Windhover, 1981; *The Novel on Blue Paper*, ed. Penelope Fitzgerald. London: Journeyman Press, 1982; *William Morris's Socialist Diary*. London: History Workshop Journal, 1982; *The Juvenilia of William Morris*, ed. Boos. New York: William Morris Society, 1983; *How We Live and How We Might Live*. Lawrence, Kans.: Stamm, 1988; London: Socialist Party, 1990; *Love Poems*. Oxford: Poetry Press, 1990; *The Widow's House by the Great Water*. New York: William Morris Society, 1990; *The Designs of William Morris*. London: Phaidon, 1995; *A Factory As It Might Be*. Nottingham: Mushroom Bookshop, 1995; *The Sweet Days Die: Poems*. London: Pavilion, 1996.

Other Works

Grettis Saga: The Story of Grettir the Strong, trans. Morris and Eiríkr Magnússon. London: Ellis, 1869; republished as *The Story of Grettir the Strong*. London & New York: Longmans, Green, 1900; *Völsunga Saga: The Story of the Volsungs and Niblungs, with Certain Songs from the Elder Edda*, trans. Morris and Magnússon. London: Ellis, 1870; London & New York: Longmans, Green, 1901; *Three Northern Love Stories, and Other Tales*, trans. Morris and Magnússon. London: Ellis & White, 1875; London & New York: Longmans, Green, 1901; Publius Virgilius Maro, *The Aeneids of Virgil*. Boston: Roberts, 1875; London: Ellis & White, 1876; "The History of Pattern Designing" and "The Lesser Arts of Life," in *Lectures on Art Delivered in Support of the Society for the Protection of Ancient Buildings*, ed. J. H. Middleton. London: Macmillan, 1882; "Mural Decoration," by Morris and J. H. Middleton, in *Encyclopaedia Britannica*, ninth edition, vol. 17. Edinburgh: Black, 1884; New York: Allen, 1888, pp. 34-48; *The Manifesto of the Socialist League*, annotated by Morris. London: Socialist League Office, 1885; "The Labour Question from the Socialist Standpoint," in *The Claims of Labour: A Course of Lectures ... on*

Various Aspects of the Labour Problem, ed. James Oliphant. Edinburgh: Co-operative Printing, 1886; republished as *True and False Society*. London: Socialist League Office, 1888; Homer, *The Odyssey of Homer*, 2 vols. London: Reeves & Turner, 1887; New York: Longmans, Green, 1897; Frank Fairman, *The Principles of Socialism Made Plain*, preface by Morris. London: Reeves, 1888; *The Saga Library*, 6 vols., trans. Morris and Magnússon. London: Quaritch, 1891-1905; John Ruskin, *The Nature of Gothic*, preface by Morris. London: Allen, 1892; New York: Garland, 1977; Hugues de Tabarie, "The Ordination of Knighthood," trans. Morris from William Caxton's translation of *The Order of Chivalry*, 2 parts. London: Reeves & Turner, 1892–1893; Arts & Crafts Exhibition Society, *Arts and Crafts Essays*, preface and three articles by Morris. London: Rivington, Percival, 1893; New York: Scribners, 1893; Bartholomaeus Angelicus, *Medieval Lore: An Epitome of the Science ... and Myth of the Middle Age*, preface by Morris, ed. Robert Steele. London: Stock, 1893; Boston: Luce, 1907; republished as *Mediaeval Lore from Bartholomew Angelicus*. London: Chatto & Windus, 1905; King Florus, *The Tale of King Florus and the Fair Jehane*. Hammersmith: Kelmscott, 1893; Sir Thomas More, *Utopia*, foreword by Morris. London: Reeves & Turner, 1893; *Of the Friendship of Amis and Amile*. Hammersmith: Kelmscott, 1894; Emperor Constantius I, *The Tale of the Emperor Coustans, and of Over Sea*. Hammersmith: Kelmscott, 1894; John Mason Neale, *Good King Wenceslas: A Carol*, introduction by Morris. Birmingham: Cornish, 1895; *The Tale of Beowulf*, trans. Morris and A. J. Wyatt. Hammersmith: Kelmscott, 1895; republished as *The Tale of Beowulf, Sometime King of the Folk of the Weder Geats*. London & New York: Longmans, Green, 1898; *Old French Romances*. London: George Allen, 1896; New York: Scribners, 1896; Frækni Frithjófr, *The Story of Frithiof the Bold*. Portland, ME: Mosher, 1908; *The Story of Kormak, the Son of Ogmund*, trans. Morris and Magnússon, ed. Grace Calder. London: William Morris Society, 1970.

Papers

The majority of William Morris's manuscripts, letters, and other papers are in the British Library. Other significant collections include the Birmingham City Museum; the Bodleian Library; Cheltenham Art Gallery and Museum; the Fitzwilliam Museum, Cambridge; the National Art Library, Archive of Art and Design; the Victoria and Albert, London; and the William Morris Gallery, Walthamstow. Principal collections in the United States include the Beinecke Rare Book Room and Manuscript Library, Yale University; the Sanford and Helen Berger Collection in Carmel, California; the Henry E. Huntington Library, San Marino, California; the Pierpont Morgan Library, New York; the William R. Perkins Library, Duke University; and the Harry Ransom Humanities Research Center at the University of Texas, Austin. The International Institute of Social History, Amsterdam, holds an important collection.

Collections

The Collected Works of William Morris, ed. May Morris, 24 vols. London, New York, Bombay & Calcutta: Longmans, Green, 1910–1915; *The Letters of William Morris to His Family and Friends*, ed. Philip Henderson. London & New York: Longmans, Green, 1950; *William Morris: Artist, Writer, Socialist*, 2 vols., ed. May Morris. Oxford: Blackwell,. 1936; New York: Russell & Russell, 1966; *The Ideal Book: Essays and Lectures on the Arts of the Book*, ed. William S. Peterson. Berkeley: University of California Press, 1982; *The Collected Letters of William Morris*, ed. Norman Kelvin, vol. 1, 1848–1880. Princeton, NJ: Princeton University Press, 1984; vol. 2, part A, 1881–1884; vol. 2, part B, 1885–1888. Princeton, NJ: Princeton University Press, 1987.

SECONDARY SOURCES

Aho, Gary L. *William Morris: A Reference Guide*. Boston: G. K. Hall, 1985; *The Best Books in the Library of the Late William Morris*. London: Quaritch, 1897; Calhoun, Blue. *The Pastoral Vision of William Morris*. Athens: University of Georgia Press, 1975; Carter, Lin. *Imaginary Worlds*.

New York: Ballantine, 1973; *Catalogue of a Portion of the Valuable Collection of Manuscripts, Early Printed Books, etc., of the Late William Morris, of Kelmscott House, Hammersmith, Which Will Be Sold by Auction, by Messrs. Sotheby, Wilkinson & Hodge, Auctioneers . . . the 5th of December, 1898, and the Five Following Days.* London: Davy, 1898; *Catalogue of Manuscripts and Early Printed Books from the Libraries of William Morris, Richard Bennett, Bertram, fourth Earl of Ashburnham, and Other Sources Now Forming Portion of the Library of J. Pierpont Morgan,* 4 vols. London: Chiswick, 1906-1907; Faulkner, Peter. *Against the Age: An Introduction to William Morris.* London: Allen & Unwin, 1980; ———. *William Morris: The Critical Heritage.* London: Routledge & Kegan Paul, 1973; Faulkner, Peter, and Peter Preston. eds. *William Morris: Centenary Essays.* Papers from the Morris Centenary Conference organized by the William Morris Society at Exeter College Oxford, June 30–July 3, 1996. Exeter, UK: University of Exeter Press, 1999; Forman, H. Buxton. *The Books of William Morris Described, with Some Accounts of His Doings in Literature and in the Allied Crafts.* London: Hollings, 1897; Fredeman, William E. *Pre-Raphaelitism: A Bibliocritical Study.* Cambridge, MA: Harvard University Press, 1965; ———. "William Morris and His Circle: A Selective Bibliography of Publications." *Journals of the William Morris Society* 1 (Summer 1964): 23-33; *Journals of the William Morris Society* 2 (Spring 1966): 13–26; Goodwin, K. L. *A Preliminary Handlist of Manuscripts and Documents of William Morris.* London: William Morris Society, 1984; Grennan, Margaret R. *William Morris: Medievalist and Revolutionary.* New York: King's Crown Press, 1945; Harvey, Charles, and Jon Press. *Art, Enterprise, and Ethics: The Life and Works of William Morris.* London: Frank Cass, 1996; Henderson, Philip. *William Morris: His Life, Work, and Friends,* 2nd ed. Harmondsworth, UK: Penguin, 1973; Hodgson, Amanda. *The Romances of William Morris.* Cambridge: Cambridge University Press, 1987; Kirchhoff, Frederick. *William Morris.* Boston: Twayne, 1979; Lambdin, Laura Cooner, and Robert Thomas Lambdin. *Camelot in the Nineteenth Century: Arthurian Characters in the Poems of Tennyson, Arnold, Morris, and Swinburne.* Westport, CT: Greenwood, 2000; Latham, David, and Sheila Latham. *An Annotated Critical Bibliography of William Morris.* New York: St. Martin's Press, 1991; Lewis, C. S. "William Morris." In *Rehabilitations and Other Essays.* London: Oxford University Press, 1939. Reprint, New York: Folcroft, 1973; Lindsay, Jack. *William Morris: His Life and Work.* London: Constable, 1975; MacCarthy, Fiona. *William Morris: A Life for Our Time.* London: Faber & Faber, 1994; Mackail, John W. *The Life of William Morris,* 2 vols. London: Longmans, Green, 1899; Marshall, Roderick. *William Morris and His Earthly Paradises.* Tisbury, UK: Compton Russell, 1979; Mathews, Richard. *Worlds beyond the World: The Fantastic Vision of William Morris.* San Bernardino, CA: Borgo Press, 1978; McCann, Jerome. *Black Riders: The Visible Language of Modernism.* Princeton, NJ: Princeton University Press, 1993; Parry, Linda, ed. *Art and Kelmscott.* Woodbridge, UK: Boydell, 1996; ———. *William Morris.* London: Philip Wilson, in association with the Victoria and Albert Museum, 1996; Peterson, William S. *A Bibliography of the Kelmscott Press.* Oxford: Clarendon, 1984; Oberg, Charlotte H. *A Pagan Prophet: William Morris.* Charlottesville: University of Virginia Press, 1978; Scott, Temple, and J. H. Isaacs. *A Bibliography of the Works of William Morris.* London: Bell, 1897; Silver, Carole. *The Romance of William Morris.* Athens: Ohio University Press, 1982; Silver, Carole, and Joseph R. Dunlap, eds. *Studies in the Late Romances of William Morris.* New York: William Morris Society, 1976; Stansky, Peter. *William Morris.* Oxford: Oxford University Press, 1983; Thompson, E. P. *William Morris: Romantic to Revolutionary,* rev. ed. London: Merlin Press, 1977; Walsdorf, John J. *William Morris in Private Press and Limited Editions: A Descriptive Bibliography of Books by and about William Morris, 1891–1981.* Phoenix: Oryx Press, 1983.

RAYMOND M. VINCE

ALGERNON CHARLES SWINBURNE

(April 5, 1837–April 10, 1909)

theism and deviant sexual behavior are the most memorable characteristics of Algernon Charles Swinburne's literary works. With great delight Swinburne shocked and titillated his Victorian audiences by expounding views ridiculing devout Christianity and espousing the joys of sado-masochism. His poetry is of an exceptionally innovative, difficult, and advanced meter, but is primarily emotionally shallow. Elemental nature is of supreme importance, and the most a human being can hope for is a permanent merger with some part of it like the sea. As a writer seeking to share transcendent truths about human nature, Swinburne embodies a tragic, romantic voice to present views vacillating from traditional to radical. In criticism, Swinburne made astute observations after over or understating a work's merits; he either loved it or he hated it.

The underlying characteristics of Swinburne's Arthurian poetry are similar to those found in his other works. Perhaps attempting to reflect his ideologically rebellious opinions in a manner less offensive to Victorian readers, Swinburne often adopted a poetic stance outside his historical moment. Having spent many childhood years examining medieval manuscripts in the extensive family library, Swinburne was a medieval scholar well before he met Dante Gabriel Rossetti and William Morris at Oxford. The poet studied enough to understand the concepts of medieval Christianity, yet as an avowed iconoclastic atheist, he consistently developed medieval characters who are misguided in their adherence to Christian values or who trust in Love and Fate as supreme deities.

On April 5, 1837, Algernon Charles Swinburne was born to aristocratic parents, Charles Henry and Lady Jane Henrietta Hamilton Swinburne at Grosvenor Place, London. He was the first of six children born to the couple. Swinburne said that he was born nearly dead and not expected to live. The family spent much of Swinburne's youth on the Isle of Wight where they had ancestral homes. His grandfather was the third Earl of Ashburnham and his father was an admiral. His mother's family held land in the south of England, while his father's family was from the north. As high church Anglicans, the family insisted that all members have a detailed knowledge of the Scriptures. Although Swinburne grew up to be an atheist who delighted in ridiculing Christianity and especially Catholicism, his thorough knowledge of biblical exegesis is evident. Also apparent in his writings is his comprehensive understandings of classical, medieval, Renaissance, Enlightenment, and romantic texts. Swinburne was one of the best read men of the era because of the massive amount of time spent in his grandfather's extensive library.

Swinburne's favorite confidante growing up was his cousin Mary Gordon. When she married, he was broken hearted and never seemed to recover totally. She was unaware that his feelings for her went beyond familial love. Further, many may have found young Algernon Swinburne singularly unattractive with his bird-like movements, oddly shaped head, and tiny body. His shrill voice and nervous, jerking hands would hardly inspire romance. Swinburne was known through his life as having an extreme personality that matched his flaming red hair.

The boy was educated at home by tutors before leaving for Eton in 1849. During four years of schooling at Eton, he became devoted to the works of Victor Hugo and Walter Savage Landor. His parents left Swinburne in the care of his tutor James Leigh Joynes. Apparently he was whipped at Eton and so developed the flagellation mania that is so prevalent in his writing and was one of his favorite topics of conversation among friends. He left Eton in August of 1854 at age sixteen, a full two years before his graduation date, perhaps because of disciplinary problems, and was privately tutored by Rev. John Wilkinson. Swinburne was a poor student, preferring swimming and hiking to studying with his tutor. Of uncommon physical strength, Swinburne jumped at opportunities to try his endurance. In 1854 to test himself against a difficult environment, he climbed Culver Cliff, which was extremely dangerous. Swinburne enjoyed climbing and racing horses recklessly, both surprising given his small stature and apparent epilepsy. Also in 1854 Swinburne's father refused to allow him to enlist in the cavalry.

After some tutoring with Rev. Russell Woodford, Swinburne left for Balliol College at Oxford in 1856. He was tutored by Benjamin Jowett while at Balliol. He joined an undergraduate literary and discussion society called "Old Morality." This group published a journal called *Undergraduate Papers* that printed some of Swinburne's poems and essays. At Oxford he abandoned his devout Anglo-Catholic ways to worship Republicanism and art. Swinburne met the Pre-Raphaelites Dante Gabriel Rossetti, Edward Burne-Jones, and William Morris in November 1857 when they were painting Oxford's Union Hall. Although Swinburne left Oxford without a degree, lifetime friendships with Rossetti, Burne-Jones, and Morris ensued that influenced Swinburne's poetry as well as the patterns of his thoughts. The Pre-Raphaelite Brotherhood was devoted to aestheticism, beauty, love, and medievalism.

Swinburne's Arthuriana can be conveniently divided into three phases: the juvenilia composed between 1857 and 1859, the masterwork *Tristram of Lyonesse* (1882), and the relatively late piece, *The Tale of Balen* (1896). Although Swinburne wrote on many medieval topics, only seven of his poems are purely Arthurian. Rather than compose an entire Arthurian cycle as Tennyson did, Swinburne concentrated on the Arthurian characters and situations that could best reflect his particular philosophy: He took little interest in those characters who adopted strong Christian positions. The love of Tristram and Iseult, traditionally depicted in medieval works as the result of fate, with predetermined fortune symbolized in the love potion, is a narrative through which Swinburne could extol heroic individuals who accept their destiny despite the laws of God and man. The story of Balen, a knight who consistently acts in socially unacceptable ways that he nonetheless considers correct, and who is doomed by fate to cause grief in every situation, is another appropriate vehicle for Swinburne's fatalistic vision. Similarly, when Swinburne focused on such Arthurian characters as Arthur, Lancelot, and Ban, he chose only those portions of their lives that exposed the characters' acceptance of fate, love, or the laws of nature. Particularly in his mature works, the poet rarely deviated from the sources' medieval plots, except occasionally to tighten the structure, because he chose to develop only those stories that could be enhanced by the addition of philosophic sections reflecting his own beliefs. Swinburne responded to and amplified Arthurian material for some four decades; his thematic concerns worked well in the tragedies of Camelot, just as he had used them in various Hellenic narratives.

Swinburne arrived as an undergraduate at Oxford not only with a knowledge of the many fine illuminated manuscripts owned by his uncle, but also with a special appreciation for Sir Thomas Malory. The young man quickly became a disciple of Rossetti and Morris, who were obsessed with medievalism; it was a good match because Swinburne appears to have been reading medieval literature enthusiastically and extensively from childhood, even works in French and Italian, languages taught to him by his mother and her father. Between 1857 and 1859, Swinburne composed five short Arthurian poems (some were fragments), nearly all written in response to Morris's Arthurian works that were composed during the same period and published in *The Defence of Guenevere and Other Poems* (1859).

Swinburne drifted away from his Oxford studies once he met members of the Pre-Raphaelite Brotherhood who shared his passion for all things medieval. Although he hired a private tutor to live with him through the winter of 1859, Swinburne never returned to school. In 1859 he became interested in the doctrine of "art for art's sake" from the Pre-Raphaelite Brotherhood, and he took a trip to London to visit Rossetti. The attention given to poetry and new friends seems largely responsible for Swinburne's poor academic record. By 1860 Swinburne was a regular contributor of book reviews and political pieces for the *Spectator*, a popular weekly journal. Still, the medievalism of the Pre-Raphaelite Brotherhood was extremely appealing to a young man steeped in such lore, and Swinburne began his lifelong habit of explaining his personal philosophies within the context of Arthuriana. Swinburne's early Arthurian works are "Queen Yseult" (1857–1858), "King Ban" (1857), "The Day before the Trial" (1857–1858), "Lancelot" (1858), and "Joyeuse Garde" (1859).

Although Swinburne planned it in ten cantos, "Queen Yseult" remains an unfinished work in six cantos of irregular iambic tetrameter rhyming tercets. The first canto appeared in a volume of *Undergraduate Papers* in 1857, but the entire poem was not published until 1918. While Swinburne seems to have known the *Tristan* of Béroul and other French versions of the story from a compilation by Francisque Michel, he relied mostly on Sir Walter Scott's 1804 edition of the Middle English *Sir Tristrem* by Thomas of Ercildoune. Swinburne borrowed some details from Malory, and he was familiar with Arnold's "Tristram and Iseult" (1852), although "Queen Yseult" concerns the lovers in their early period and ends long before the portion of the story related by Arnold.

Morris, who had painted the story of Tristram and Iseult on the Oxford Union walls, apparently rekindled Swinburne's interest in the tale; however, Swinburne's first result was a slavish imitation of Morris's early unpublished work, rather than of those poems included in *The Defence of Guenevere and Other Poems* that inspired Swinburne's other short Arthurian poems. "Queen Yseult's" graphic, sensuous depictions of scenery and characters render it much more PreRaphaelite than medieval in tone. He began canto ix on November 19, 1857, nine days after meeting Morris and while it was envisioned ten cantos, the poem stops after the start of canto VII. Swinburne deliberately ignored much of the action and adventure described in *Sir Tristrem* and other sources, characteristically choosing instead to focus upon the love story of Tristram and Yseult. While the plot of "Queen Yseult" closely follows the outline of the medieval romance, Swinburne frequently deviates for extended, aesthetic descriptions that make his poem seem like a Pre-Raphaelite painting in words. Queen Yseult is repeatedly represented by "her golden hair cornripe" (canto I, 339). She is, in fact, indistinguishable from her tresses and is referred to as "Yseult queen, the hair of gold" (I, 333). Her hair "flowed and glowed" (195) in canto II, but becomes almost another character by the poem's end when the "weeping" (IV, 80) hair moves the saints to pity the queen.

Following a four-stanza introduction, the poem begins by describing another fair-haired woman, Tristram's mother Blaunchefiour, whose great love for Roland causes her to follow him to Ermonie. The travel is difficult, but Blaunchefiour, with typical courtly ethos, does not regret her decision to risk everything for love any more than her son does later:

> "Lo!" she said, "I lady free
> Took this man for lord of me
> Where the crowned saints might see." (I, 2224)

Most of the first canto is devoted to the love of Tristram's parents, their sad deaths, their son's revenge upon Moronde for those deaths, and the building of a tomb in their honor. The faithful and noble relationship of Blaunchefiour and Roland sets an example for Tristram and foreshadows his doom. At the canto's conclusion, Tristram arrives in Cornwall, is acknowledged by his uncle, King Mark, and is sent to capture the Irish Yseult's heart so that she may become Mark's queen.

Unlike his later work, *Tristram of Lyonesse*, "Queen Yseult" demonstrates Swinburne's inattention to details found in earlier versions of the romance. In this beginning section, the poet omitted Tristram's killing of Morhault, Irish Yseult's uncle, an act that gains the knight fame by allowing him to save Cornwall from monetary taxation and tributes of human lives. Further, Swinburne does not have Tristram arrive in Cornwall glorifying Yseult, so that his uncle will want her for his bride. Mark somehow already knows of and desires Yseult when Tristram arrives. This focus upon style rather than content continues throughout the poem and is especially evident in canto II, which begins with a discussion of Yseult's almost unworldly beauty. Tristram is instantly captivated (before the love potion is consumed) and, like a typical courtly lover, is prepared to die for her even though he feels unworthy of this sacrifice.

Hiding their passion from King Mark, Tristram and Yseult continue to meet after the wedding; the couple's most difficult and bloody liaison involves Yseult carrying Tristram upon her back to avoid two sets of footprints showing in the snowy, stoney path leading to her chamber. Yseult's wounds on her feet and her neck inspire "fierce and bitter kisses" (III, 138) from Tristram, and the pain catapults their lovemaking that evening to new heights. The reversal of sexual roles, with Yseult able to tolerate pain and carrying enormous weight and the sado-masochistic delight the couple feels are typical of Swinburne's writing that was most despised by his Victorian audience.

When Mark, "the king so lean and cold" (III, 153), is informed of the adulterous relationship between Tristram and Yseult, he orders Tristram to leave. Tristram passively accepts Yseult's order by immediately departing for Camelot. Canto IV concerns his visit to Arthur's court and his subsequent trip to Brittany. Guinevere's beauty reminds Tristram so much of Yseult's glorious looks that the good knight is plagued by memories of "the bitter love" (IV, 53) and wishes to escape these painful remembrances. In this canto, the typically compressed technique of the ballad style Swinburne was imitating is especially evident. No explanation is given of Tristram's destination; the knight simply lands in Brittany, a land ruled by the orphaned queen who, coincidentally, shares Tristram's lover's name. "For the love of her sweet name" (IV, 95), Tristram weds this second Iseult, but the marriage is unconsummated.

The loneliness of Yseult of Cornwall and her fears that Tristram is dead are the focus of canto 6. Her torment parallels Tristram's, but her sorrow is greater; not only must Yseult mourn the loss of her lover, but she also is faced with Mark's growing envy and hatred. Swinburne has consistently blackened the character of Mark until, in this last canto, the king appears as a cruel and vindictive drunkard. The poem ends abruptly with Yseult gloomily considering her diminishing beauty and Mark's hatred for her.

Swinburne's treatment of his subject in 1857 contains a hint of themes to be developed later in *Tristram of Lyonesse*, the poet's more mature approach to the Tristram and Iseult story. The early work contains many of the same social, psychological, and emotional entanglements, but they are not amplified by the long philosophic passages so prevalent in the later poem. Also, the ballad like diction, simple and frequently monosyllabic, contributes to the simple atmosphere "Queen Yseult," which often masks complex situations. Perhaps not yet capable of producing the ideological and ecstatic lyrical passages that dominate *Tristram of Lyonesse*, the young Swinburne first related the story with little artistic embellishment.

Swinburne's other early Arthurian works are much shorter than "Queen Yseult." "King Ban," published posthumously in 1915, is a melancholic, introspective 120-line fragment based loosely on the *Morte*. Unlike Malory's equivalent scene, however, Ban is not saved by King Arthur. Besieged by the forces of Claudas and betrayed by his own seneschal, Swinburne's Ban surveys the destruction of his kingdom and prays, like Christ, that he will not be forsaken. Ban waits in vain for Arthur to aid him. In the early chapters of the *Morte*, Ban is protected by the heroic young Arthur. However, in Swinburne's poem, Ban's personal reflections in his final soliloquy reflect a spirit crushed by the stark realization that he has been abandoned:

> Therefore I pray you, O God marvellous,
> See me how I am stricken among men,
> And how the lip I fed with plenteousness
> And cooled with wine of liberal courtesy
> Turns a snake's life to poison me and clings.... (116–20)

In "King Ban" are the ironic and muted seeds that are developed later in *Tristram of Lyonesse* and *The Tale of Balen* into a full blown challenging of the powers of Arthur and the Christian god.

In "The Day before the Trial," an apparently completed poem of forty-four lines, first published by George Lafourcade in 1928, Swinburne recast the scene of Morris's "The Defence of Guenevere," and portrayed Arthur's feelings about the accusations against his wife. Not the proud king of Malory's work, the Arthur of Swinburne's poem is filled with self-pity and anguish:

And I grow old waiting here,
Grow sick with pain of Guenevere,
My wife that loves not me. (4–6)

The entire poem is a melancholy soliloquy in which Arthur discusses not only his suspicions about his wife, but also his "dull hate of Launcelot" (28). Strangely, Arthur calls Launcelot "pure of sin" (30) and "clean as any maid" (31). The king compares himself unfavorably with his knight because, of the two, only Launcelot has been blessed from God. The poem ends with Arthur lamenting that he must endure the hateful glances of his wife who does not love him.

"And she loves not me" is a concluding line, again concerning Guenevere, spoken by the protagonist of "Lancelot." This poem, a dramatization in which Lancelot is visited by an angel who allows him a brief glimpse of the grail, is 325 lines long and was first printed for private circulation in 1915. "Lancelot" is similar to "The Day before the Trial" because it is written in the same verse form, and because it continues the story immediately after Guenevere's trial. In "Lancelot," the knight has rescued the queen before she was to be consumed by fire, and they now live together at Joyeuse Garde. With Lancelot's visitation by an angel and the emphasis on the grail quest, the poem is similar to Morris's "Sir Galahad, a Christmas Mystery." Lancelot's failure on the quest, caused by his sinful love of Guenevere, contrasts with his son Galahad's more successful adventures. "Lancelot" is also similar to Morris's "King Arthur's Tomb"; in both poems the atmosphere is hot and oppressive, the queen rejects Lancelot because she feels that the kingdom has been destroyed by their love, and Guenevere's ordeal has caused her beauty to fade.

The poem opens in autumn after Lancelot has searched in vain all summer for the grail. Exhausted by his long ride, the knight stops by a chapel and drifts into a somnolent state. After recalling his futile summer of searching, Lancelot is visited by an angel, who allows him a partial viewing of the grail, which is soon obstructed by a shadowy picture of Guenevere, standing under a tree. This vision of the woman who prevented Lancelot's success in his adventure provokes a prolonged and bitter self-examination by the knight. Ultimately, Lancelot seems more disappointed that Guenevere will not consent to be his queen than he is that he is unable fully to view the grail. As in a poem of the medieval dream-vision genre, this work's protagonist, in his altered state, is able accurately to understand the significance of his life. Lancelot contrasts the two most important features of his life, his love for the queen and the grail quest, and realizes that he will never be able to experience a full triumph in either area. Like Morris's Sir Galahad, Lancelot dramatizes in his sleep trance the struggle between earthly and spiritual love.

In Thomas Malory's *Morte d'Arthur*, Launcelot sees the grail as it heals a sick man. The vision leaves Launcelot unconscious, and upon his recovery, he is asked by a heavenly voice to leave that holy place. The knight realizes that his relationship with Guenevere has prevented him from responding more fully to the holy vessel: "And now I take uppon me the adventures to seke of holy thynges, now I se and undirstonde that myne olde synne hyndryth me and shamyth me, that I had no power to stirre nother speke whan the holy bloode appered before me" (896; bk. 13, chap. 19). Launcelot's newfound understanding causes him to repent to a holy man "how he had loved a quene unmesurabely and oute of mesure longe" (896; bk. 13, chap. 20), and to perform acts of penance. Later in the narrative, Launcelot attempts to enter a chamber in the Castle Carbenic wherein the grail shines. Because he has sinned for twenty-four years, his encounter with the grail leaves him unconscious for twenty-four days. When Launcelot awakens, he does not think of Guenevere, but is pleased that God has allowed him the vision: "Why have yee awaked me? For I was more at ease than I am now. A, Jesu Cryste, who myght be so blyssed that myght see opynly Thy grete mervayles of secretnesse there where no synner may be?" (1017; bk. 17, chap. 16). Obviously, Swinburne's conception of Lancelot is based less upon Malory's repentant knight than upon Morris's constantly devoted lover.

Swinburne's last short Arthurian poem, "Joyeuse Garde," was also directly inspired by Morris, in this case through an Oxford mural "How Sir Palomydes loved La Belle Iseult with exceeding great love, but how she loved him not but rather Sir Trystram." The poem expands an episode from the *Morte* in which Tristram and Iseult are reunited at Launcelot's castle. Swinburne's focus in this work, the satisfying lovemaking of the couple, is described in the sort of highly erotic terms Malory never attempted. These descriptions of carnal love would certainly have offended Victorian audiences but, like Swinburne's other short Arthurian works, this poem was published posthumously. A seventy-eight-line narrative fragment of iambic pentameter, the work was first printed for private circulation in *A Day of Lilies* (1918).

"Joyeuse Garde" may have been intended as a continuation of "Queen Yseult" because the meeting at Lancelot's castle is traditionally the next stage in the Tristram and Iseult narrative. "Queen Yseult" concluded with the lady's reflections about her abandonment by Tristram and her fear of Mark. "Joyeuse Garde" concentrates on the queen's joyous feelings about her reunion with her lover, but the celebration is marred by her anxiety about Mark's plotting:

> Men say the king
> Hath set keen spies about for many a mile,
> Quick hands to get them gold, sharp eyes to see
> Where your way swerves across them. This long while
> Hath Mark grown older with his hate of me,
> And now his hand for lust to smite at us
> Plucks the white hairs inside his beard that he
> This year made thicker. (48–55)

This concern about Mark's surveillance is, of course, a great obstacle to the lovers' meetings; yet traditionally the amount of ecstasy experienced by courtly lovers grows in proportion to the degree of danger their trysts generate. In "Joyeuse Garde," Yseult is perfectly able to relax in bed with her knight, despite the threat of Mark's spies. The sensuousness of descriptions here are meager compared to the explicitly erotic encounters the lovers enjoy in Tristram of Lyonesse.

While Swinburne's early Arthurian works have some merits, they are slight when compared to the poet's last two Arthurian poems. Significantly, Swinburne must have been dissatisfied with his youthful efforts, inasmuch as these five poems, with the exception of "Queen Yseult's" first canto, were all published posthumously; he never consented to widespread publication during his lifetime.

After these early poems, Swinburne set aside his Arthurian interests to write of other matters. In 1861, after Swinburne want on a solitary journey to Italy, his father agreed to let him move to London with an annual pension of two hundred pounds Soon after, Swinburne met Richard Burton, and his drinking bouts increased dramatically. After reviewing Victor Hugo's *Les Miserables*, Swinburne's long friendship with Hugo began. Also around this time, Swinburne began to read the works of the Marquis de Sade that so colored his thinking. The publication of *Atalanta* in 1865 brought Swinburne his first real success. Soon after he published *Chasteland* that received adverse criticism. The publication of *Poems and Ballads* in 1866 raised a critical storm, so Swinburne wrote *Notes on Poems and Reviews* the same year in defense of his work.

Constant writing enabled Swinburne to publish many collections of poems and essays during the ensuing years despite the turmoil of his personal life. The poems often contained a lurid and fevered sensuality for which Swinburne is best known. While the essays lavishly praise or roundly condemn other writers' literary achievements or are of political nature. Swinburne was not only interested in British government, but wrote persuasively concerning Italian, Irish, Turkish, and Russian affairs. He also wrote a plethora of letters, more than nineteen hundred of them, that reflect the themes of his writing such as sadism, political policies, and the beauty of the natural world and humanity.

After about 1867, Swinburne's drinking and the tirades it produced would have rendered a lesser artist unfit to write at all. He seems to have spent much of his time in brothels and pubs, generally feeling drunk and ill, completely dependent on his mother and his friend Walter Theodore Watts (later Watts-Dunton) to help him recuperate from his overindulgences. His notorious affair with Adah Isaacs Menken also began in 1867. By 1871 his excesses made him so ill that his father closed Swinburne's apartment and took him home.

By 1872 Swinburne and Rossetti had parted ways, the friendship destroyed by egos and Swinburne's refusal to accept Fanny Cornforth as Rossetti's companion after the death of his wife Elizabeth Siddal Rossetti in 1862. John Camden Hotten, an unsavory publisher who built his business upon pornographic books, encouraged Swinburne to be more bold in his writing; after many battles against paying Swinburne money owed for various publications, Hotten died suddenly in June 1873. Henceforth Swinburne's publisher was the reputable Andrew Chatto, chosen by his friend and solicitor, Watts-Dunton, who was such a help in Swinburne's later days toward keeping the poet somewhat on a respectable path. With the death of his father in March 1877, Swinburne's inheritance allowed him to afford life in London and unrestrained dissipation. Watts rescued Swinburne whose health was failing and took him to live at his home in Putney in June 1879. The move and solitude of "The Pines" also encouraged several publications, perhaps Swinburne's best work that his friend toned down whenever he perceived it to be overly erotic.

Whereas Swinburne's early Arthurian poems are marginal to his fame, *Tristram of Lyonesse* can be considered his magnum opus. The poem has been classified as an epic, but it is more lyrical than narrative with many nonnarrative, philosophical passages building to reflect one coherent ideology. The work is carefully constructed and full of important parallelism, such as the matching invocations to Love and Fate that open and close the poem. Parallelism, recurrent motifs, and the recapitulation of rhymes lend the poem a greatness beyond earlier versions. Swinburne's readers should approach *Tristram of Lyonesse* with a knowledge of major versions of the narrative. Confusing flashbacks, often even beginning mid-sentence, offer some exposition, but the disjunction they impose, particularly when added to long philosophical passages, makes a casual reading of this poem impossible.

For Victorian reviewers, Swinburne's unorthodox religious values, as exposed in this poem, were somewhat overshadowed by the work's blatant eroticism. Swinburne clearly intended to shock his audience, and it worked on the Victorians; however, modern audiences are more apt to be fascinated by Swinburne's addition of his own views concerning the meaning of human life to the ancient myth than they are likely to be horrified by the overt sexuality. The fatal passion of the medieval romance becomes, in Swinburne's poem, a celebration of human passion and sexual love. Because the poem shows Iseult learning to cherish Tristram's pantheistic philosophy, the work also seeks to erode the rock of Christianity. From its opening lines to its conclusion, *Tristram of Lyonesse* is about four lips that "become one burning mouth" (I, 136). Although this love is doomed and bleak, the lovers reach fulfillment with each other and with the universe of nature that surrounds and encourages them. Perhaps it is *because* the lovers are clearly fore-doomed that Swinburne could write so richly of their fulfillment. Tristram and Iseult are motivated by more than mere carnality; their sexuality merges with a transcendent spirituality that includes all of external nature.

The poet began the work *in medias res*, just before the lovers drink the magical wine. He ignored the early aspects of Tristram's life to concentrate on the development of the love story, as well as the joy and suffering it engenders. Although love brings pain to Tristram and Iseult, they, like all other men and women, are not free and can live fully only by accepting the experiences of desire. Whereas Tennyson's *Idylls* proposed personal restraint in favor of knightly responsibility, Swinburne glorifies a more hedonistic position. In *Tristram of Lyonesse* the philosophy for which Swinburne is most famous appears as clearly the lovers enjoy greater nobility and a more dignified end precisely because they completely indulge their desires. Swinburne chose to re-create the legend because he felt that it had been degraded by other writers of his era. Expressing in narrative form the metaphysics of love, Swinburne's poem employs the legend as an archetypal illustration of the human condition of perpetual passion. This condition, of course, suffers from mutability, but heroic men and women must accept transition by regarding it as part of a constantly changing yet changeless natural world.

None of Swinburne's many possible sources relates the legend in this manner. The poet reacted against Tennyson and Arnold, used Wagner and the German romantics, partially employed Scott's edition of Thomas's *Sir Tristrem* for plot structure, and borrowed heavily from Malory for details. However much of the outcome reflects debts to other sources, both medieval and modern; *Tristram of Lyonesse* is ultimately Swinburne's private mythology. The poet obviously read most of the Arthurian material available to him. However, the sheer abundance of the possible sources, coupled with the realization that Swinburne used the legend to express completely different views from his predecessors, makes of limited value a search for indebtedness.

In 1871 Swinburne published "Tristram and Iseult, Prelude to an Unpublished Poem." This "Prelude," a lyrical rhapsody on love's power, announces all the major themes of the fully developed poem, which was not published until 1882. The opening lines of the "Prelude" suggest, through their use of paradox and oxymoronic phrases, love's power as the force behind the action:

Love, that is first and last of all things made,
The light that has the living world for shade,
The spirit that for temporal veil has on
The souls of all men woven in unison. ("Prelude," Gosse and Wise, 14)

Through a catalog of constellations in which each monthly astrological sign represents a heroic and doomed love heroine such as Dido, Helen, or Francesca, love becomes linked with a natural cyclicity and interdependency that serves to guide the lives of all men. Iseult is part of April, and this is the only link in "Prelude" to the narrative portion of *Tristram of Lyonesse*. Like the story of Tristram and Iseult, and like all of human existence, the constellations change forever, but remain the same. All will one day pass from this world, so, as the "Prelude" suggests, it is best to live on earth to our fullest potential. The sungod, Love, is fed by the fame of tragic lovers who accepted their fate, and this deity's radiance is increased by those, like Swinburne, who gave a portion of their days to celebrate these heroic individuals. The jealous orthodox God may seem to doom these lovers unjustly, but he is shown to have no real power; he is unable to deprive any individual of the sleep that naturally follows an exemplary life, so each triumphant human being will eventually pass into a similar state of limbo. Therefore, according to Swinburne, it is best for one to accept completely his destiny so that he may be remembered as an example to future generations. The many ideas incorporated into the "Prelude" are more comprehensible in *Tristram of Lyonesse*, inasmuch as each separate episode in the poem is an example of a portion of Swinburne's rather difficult and involved philosophy. Tristram and Iseult function in the poem as models of lovers who survive the torments and navigate around the obstacles of the world to reach full consummation of love through a death that allows them fulfillment. The man-made concepts of God and time are Love's chief enemies, but they are powerless.

Tristram of Lyonesse, Swinburne's synthesis of passion, pantheism, and courtly love, appeared in its complete form of a prelude and nine cantos in 1882. Canto I, "The Sailing of the Swallow," begins with a description of the young, beautiful, and innocent Tristram and Iseult before they drink the wine. Iseult questions Tristram about the inhabitants of Camelot, and the knight's answers provide a background for the legend, as well as the framework for Swinburne's iconoclastic vision. Arthur's "sightless sin unknown" (I, 530) with his sister Morgause may be unforgivable by a wrathful god, but Tristram knows that men will remember the king for his greatness rather than for this one innocent and unfortunate act. Iseult does not understand why God should be less forgiving than his creatures on earth: "Great pity it is and strange it seems to me / God could not do them so much right as we, / Who slay not men for witless evil done" (I, 598–600). Thus begins the conflict of the two religious systems that are constantly opposed in the poem: orthodox Christianity versus the power of fate and love.

Canto II, "The Queen's Pleasance," introduces King Mark, "a swart lean man" with "cold unquiet eyes," who is "closemouthed, gauntcheeked, wan as a morning moon" (II, 6466). Iseult marries Mark, but substitutes her attendant Brangwain in the bridal bed. When Iseult slips between the sheets, replacing Brangwain at the light of dawn, Mark's musings concerning the wonder of his having lain with this ethereal woman are ironic. Iseult experiences carnal love with no man but the radiant sunworshipper, Tristram. Palamede, who kidnaps the Queen soon after the wedding, is also unable to touch Iseult, "for awe / Constrained him, and the might of love's high law" (II, 214–15).

Tristram takes Iseult deep into the woods, where they remain undisturbed for some time. The lovers experience a spiritual and physical fusion with each other, as well as a transcendental harmony with nature. Iseult, having learned well Tristram's philosophy, is the first to realize that this perfect time cannot last. She understands that the best solution to their dilemma is immediate death. Finally, the lovers are divided by Mark's discovery of their relationship. Tristram vows not to ask that his bitter fate be reversed. In the end, Tristram's lack of resistance proves the most practical course because fate is a benevolent deity who does not enforce punishment for joy and who allows a sleeping death, the only release from courtly love.

Fearing that the vindictive Christian god will punish Tristram with eternal damnation for his trysts with her, Mark's wife attempts to renounce her love for the knight. She prays that Tristram will forget her so that she will not see him in hell. Iseult refuses to repent of her adultery, knowing that the fires of hell will never be able to consume her great love. Then it is the turn of Iseult to rebuke the orthodox god for his lack of pity. Unfortunately, to pacify this vengeful god, Iseult offers, as the price for Tristram's salvation, to accept all the punishment for their sin upon herself. Iseult's feelings of desperation are dissolved not by mercy from god, but by a final meeting with her lover in the next canto, "Joyous Garde." Tristram's philosophical counsel encourages in Iseult a recognition of the didactic power of nature, and she is finally able to resign herself to fate. The fear of divine retribution dissolves when Iseult realizes that love leads one through death to peace. The poet of the impossibility of love's survival on earth, Swinburne consistently associated love with death.

In the next canto, "The Last Pilgrimage," the knight is revitalized when he swims in the sea and experiences communion with his true god, Love. The hero is reborn in this mystical fusion with the natural world, ready to face his final battle without fear. He does not have foreknowledge of his fate, but is prepared to accept his destiny. When Tristram receives a mortal wound, he and his wife are both pleased. The evocation of fate in the poem's final canto, "The Sailing of the Swan," echoes the glorification of love in "Prelude." While the poet claims that fate, the emissary of love, will overthrow the "miscreant" (IX, 90) Christian God, "the head of fear, the false high priest" (IX, 86), the reader is concerned for Tristram's safety and salvation. The knight lies dying under the bitter eyes of the white-handed Iseult. Indeed, Iseult of Brittany kills her husband with a word when she lies about the color of the boat's sail, and it seems that victory belongs to the wife and her vengeful God.

Iseult of Cornwall arrives too late, so a reunion on earth for the lovers is obstructed. However, the angry wife cannot prevent the couple's peaceful union after death. King Mark, having forgiven the lovers, builds a tomb to house their bodies; Swinburne deviates from his sources here when he allows the sea, an important image of eternity, to claim Tristram and Iseult forever. The waves erode the rock upon which Mark has built the chapel, allowing the lovers to be taken into the water, where they will share eternity with the transcendent forces of nature. Swinburne's message appears to be that those who submit to love as the supreme force in the universe will gain immortality, both through a peaceful union with spiritual, elemental nature and through the resurrection of their story by future generations.

During the latter years of his life, Swinburne became interested in children, especially in Bertie Mason, Watts-Dunton's five-year-old nephew who lived nearby. These poems after 1879 extol the sweetness of childhood and discuss none of the earlier interest in beating the wee ones until they bled. By now Swinburne was also much more conservative in his political views, most likely the influence of Watts-Dunton. Also, increasingly noticeable in his later work is a greater love of nature, especially the sea. Swinburne wrote much of his best material during this period.

In 1895, thirteen years after the publication of *Tristram of Lyonesse,* Swinburne began composing *The Tale of Balen* (1896). The poet again argues against a society dominated by the miseries produced by Christian doctrine. As the hero of Swinburne's final Arthurian work, Balen is the perfect representative to complete the poet's discussion of love and fate. Love in *The Tale of Balen,* befitting its feudal context, is rarely erotic, but rather fraternal or filial, with Balen's dedication to his fellow men always causing tragedy. Arthur's kingdom is shown to be infested with evil, even in its early days. Swinburne's most unoriginal Arthurian poem, *The Tale of Balen* is almost a paraphrase of the *Morte*'s discussion of this knight in Book Two, except that the poet makes Malory's plot seem less haphaz-ardly episodic through the addition of passages intended to increase a reader's under-standing of the role of fate in this knight's life. Swinburne's verbal fidelity to the *Morte* is also noticeable in his descriptive passages. The poem is divided into seven sections of nine-line iambic tetrameter stanzas. The short, balladic lines employ mostly monosyllabic words and frequent repetition.

Despite his nearly exact retelling of Malory's tale, Swinburne personalizes the narrative and adds passages that elevate Balen's tragic stature. Working to overturn the Victorian idealization of the "Golden Age" of Arthur, Swinburne emphasized Balen's agony, disap-pointment, and frustration in the world of Camelot. Because Balen was born in North-umbria (like Swinburne), he was able to provide a fresh perspective concerning courtly life. Swinburne's knight is a good, well-meaning man, completely unlike the wild and savage creature of Tennyson's "Balin and Balan." Tennyson's recreation of the story, with limited fidelity to medieval sources, prompted Swinburne's retelling. Swinburne was, of course, also attracted to Balen as a fatal character of great dignity able to represent a specifically Greek conception of the tragic human condition. Whereas Malory's Balan is a victim of his own rashness, Swinburne inserted unobtrusive references to fate and rein-forced aspects of Balen's innocent hubris to create a more tragic character. Swinburne's more deterministic version of the tale does not destroy its medieval spirit, but it does allow the poet to achieve the "tragic sublimity" at which he aimed.

Tightening the amorphous structure of the tale without altering Malory's perspective, Swinburne divided the story into separate parts and paralleled his hero's experiences with the rhythm of seasonal cycles. Like Tennyson's *Idylls*, Swinburne's poem concludes with its greatest of many tragedies taking place in winter. However, Swinburne uses the sea-sons in another way as well to suggest, as he did in *Tristram of Lyonesse,* the idea that na-ture and human life are a series of constant repetitions. Mutability is good and moves the hero toward his fulfillment in death, the complementary opposite of death.

The poem opens in spring, a season of gaiety and abandonment that mirrors Balen's youthful search for fame. Malory's tale begins in Arthur's court, but Swinburne allows the reader to enjoy the engaging Balen, "a northern child of earth and sea" (I, 14), before he is scarred by the corrupted world of Camelot. However, even in his early happy days, Balen has a suspicion of his tragic destiny:

> But always through the bounteous bloom
> The earth gives thanks if heaven illume
> His soul forefelt a shadow of doom,
> His heart forefelt a gloomier gloom
> Than closes all men's equal ways. (I, 2832)

Immediately upon his arrival at Camelot Balen's unfortunate fate begins when he kills one of King Arthur's despicable relatives and is sent to prison for six months. Malory did not explain the motivation behind the murder; Swinburne's Balen is provoked by insults to his homeland.

In the second part, which begins the four-part summer of Balen's life, the hero proves the wickedness of Arthur's court when he is the only knight pure enough to pull out the maiden's sword, Malison. Balen's refusal to return Malison, even though the maiden tells him that with it he will kill his best friend, reveals his stoic acceptance of fate: "What chance God sends, that chance I take" (II, 172).

To avenge the murder of his mother, Balen impetuously decapitates the Lady of the Lake and thus incurs Arthur's wrath. Unable to withstand his monarch's displeasure, Balen sets off to appease Arthur by performing heroic feats. First, however, at the start of the fourth part, Balen must defeat Launceor. Jealous of Balen's success in the sword challenge, Launceor wishes to murder Balen, and his desire is sanctioned by the king. Just as every seemingly innocent act of Balen's has terrible repercussions, his killing of Launceor directly causes another death: Launceor's paramour removes Balen's sword from her lover's body and commits suicide with it.

Although Balen appears to be a virtuous knight, the destruction he constantly causes seems demonic. His desire for fame and his allegiance to his feudal lord are laudatory, but Balen's courage always proves malevolent. Part 6 continues Balen's destiny with a new set of adventures that ultimately destroy three entire countries. Losing his weapon, Balen searches Pellam's castle until he discovers a golden spear. In attacking Pellam with this beautiful weapon, Balen strikes the dolorous stroke because this is the spear revered as the one that pierced the side of Christ. The corrupting of this relic, which was brought to England by Joseph of Arimathea, causes Pellam's castle to collapse and kill everyone inside except for Balen and Pellam. Further, Pellam's deep wound festers for twelve years (until Galahad heals it), and the surrounding lands are destroyed. Balen causes this destruction in the autumn of his life, but the worst is still to come. This knight's personal grief reaches its peak and its release in the winter, beginning in part 7.

Balen's dying vision underscores Swinburne's motif of natural cycles as perfect and unchanging. Because he has faced life and death stoically, Balen is granted a paradisiacal vision of his boyhood in Northumberland that "filled his death with joy" (VII, 576). As Merlin will later, Balen experiences final harmony with the transcendent forces of nature and expires peacefully.

With his conception of history as cyclical, Swinburne viewed the Middle Ages as filled with the same agonies to be discovered in any other period. The frustrating moral ambiguities experienced by Balen are never reconciled in the poem because these problems are eternal. The solution suggested, a return to natural primitivism, is clearly impossible in a world dominated by the laws of God and man, rather than those of nature.

Swinburne also wrote non-medieval fictional works, often sadistic and violent. The first two, both in 1860, were plays that were published with his father's money: *The Queen-Mother* takes place in 1572 in the court of Charles IX, showcasing the murder and sex themes Swinburne so enjoyed. The second play was called *Rosamund* and concerns King Henry's mistress. Neither work won critical acclaim. Living near Rosetti, Morris, and Burne-Jones after he left Oxford in 1869 produced an inroad to the celebrities of the day, such as John Ruskin, James McNeill Whistler, Robert Browning, and Alfred Tennyson. Swinburne was especially intimate with Rosetti and had been with him and his wife, Elizabeth Siddal Rosetti, on the night she died from an overdose of laudanum. After this, Swinburne and Rosetti lived together in Chelsea where they were creatures of extreme habits. Swinburne began regularly drinking to excess and exclaiming to all who would listen the joys of sado-masochism.

Several burlesques were written in the 1860s, but were published posthumously in 1964. Queen Victoria is satirized in *La Fille du Policeman*, a story, and in *La Soeurde de las Reine*, a poem. *A Year's Letters* and *Lesbia Brandon*, also published posthumously, concern the aristocratic world Swinburne knew well and mention his favorite topics: nature, flagellation, incest, adultery, and homosexuality. *Chasteland* was published in 1865 and was the first of three plays about the life of Mary Stuart. *Bothwell* (1874) and *Mary Stuart*

(1881) make up the rest of this grand and extensive trilogy about a strong and fatal queen. He wrote heavily in the time before chronic alcoholism blurred his abilities and he published three texts in 1865 and 1866: *Atalanta in Calydon*, *Chasteland*, and *Poems and Ballads*. Most of his writings outraged the Victorian public, as did his personal antics. Apparently, Swinburne drank each night until he passed out, and he claimed to have performed every possible lewd sexual act. However, because he bragged about his antics, it is difficult to differentiate fact from fiction.

William Blake (1868) shows a serious turn toward insightful criticism before Swinburne turned to writing two volumes of Republican lyrics, *Songs before Sunrise* (1871) and *Songs of Two Natures* (1875). His angry Republicanism is rescued by the overall theme that nature and humanity are one great spirit that longs to merge in all elements. *Essays and Studies* (1875) includes astute criticisms of early dramatists. Next came the lyrical poem *Erechtheus* (1876), which was well received. The work showcases Swinburne's depth as a classical scholar by describing the salvation of Athens through the noble sacrifice of a young virgin named Chthonia. The heroine accepts her death as the price for individual immortality; she will be remembered for freeing her people and thus live eternally as part of the social consciousness. *Poems and Ballads, Second Series*, was published in 1878 despite Swinburne's battles with deep depression stemming from loneliness, alcoholism, and illness. The volume features many of his finest poems.

Swinburne grew increasingly deaf and therefore increasingly dependent upon Watts-Dunton. By this time his reputation for frank discussions of deviant sexuality nearly overshadowed the public's acknowledgment of his lyrical gifts and the depth of his knowledge. Despite leaving Oxford without a degree, Swinburne has long been touted as one of the most learned English poets. The depth and breadth of history and literature from the ancient to modern times was easily accessed by his remarkable memory. Clearly indebted to Swinburne were Ezra Pound and James Joyce. "For if Swinburne proved nothing else, he aptly demonstrated that words have not only meanings, but sounds which may be combined into music and rhythm to achieve a higher meaning than any lexicographer can express or than any mere message-hunting reader of poetry can ever comprehend" (Cassidy, 162).

Just after the publication of *A Tale of Balen* in 1896, Swinburne was further weakened by two heavy blows: the deaths of his beloved mother and his friend Morris. At this time Swinburne moved permanently into the home of Theodore Watts-Dunton, lawyer and writer, to be away from the excesses of London that had so tempted and weakened him. Though Swinburne was gradually tamed into a man of normal, steady habits, his growing deafness made him much less social. He still wrote some poetry, but mostly Swinburne's last years were tranquil days of walks among the hawthorns and evenings reading Dickens aloud. Swinburne died at the home of Watts-Dunton on April 10, 1909, at the age of seventy-two after a cold became double pneumonia. Victorian prudery was thrust outside in Swinburne's work with sensual abandonment and nearly modern, frank appreciation for the body and senses. His complex poetry and criticism has not been as appreciated in the twenty-first century as in the one before it that was more sensitive to the innovativeness of his work.

PRIMARY WORKS

The Queen-Mother. Rosamund. Two Plays. London: Pickering, 1860; *Atalanta in Calydon.* London: Moxon, 1865; *Chasteland.* London: Moxon, 1865; *Poems and Ballads: First Series.* London:

Moxon, 1866; *A Song of Italy.* London: Hotten, 1867; *Songs before Sunrise.* London: Ellis, 1871; *Bothwell: A Tragedy.* London: Chatto & Windus, 1874; *Essays and Studies.* London: Chatto & Windus, 1875; *Poems and Ballads: Second Series.* London: Chatto & Windus, 1878; *Mary Stuart.* London: Chatto & Windus, 1881; *Tristram of Lyonesse.* London: Chatto & Windus, 1882; *Marino Faliero.* London: Chatto & Windus, 1885; *Astrophel and Other Poems.* London: Chatto & Windus, 1894; *The Tale of Balen.* London: Chatto & Windus, 1896; *A Channel Passage and Other Poems.* London: Chatto & Windus, 1904; *The Duke of Gandia.* London: Chatto & Windus, 1908; *King Ban.* London: Chatto & Windus, 1915; *Lesbia Brandon*, ed. Randolph Hughes. London: Falcon, 1952.

SECONDARY SOURCES

Cassidy, John A. *Algernon C. Swinburne.* New York: Twayne, 1964; Cochran, Rebecca. "An Assessment of Swinburne's Arthuriana." In *King Arthur Through the Ages*, eds. Valorie Lagorio and Mildred Leake Day, 62–80. New York: Garland, 1990; ———. "Swinburne's Conception of Hero in 'The Tale of Balen.'" *Arthurian Interpretations* 1 (1986): 47–53; Gitter, Elisabeth. "The Power of Women's Hair in Victorian Imagination." *PMLA* 99 (1984): 936–54; Harrison, Anthony. *Swinburne's Medievalism: A Study in Victorian Love Poetry.* Baton Rouge: Louisiana State University Press, 1988; Henderson, Philip. *Swinburne: Portrait of a Poet.* New York: Macmillan, 1974; Hyder, Clyde K. *Swinburne Replies.* Syracuse, NY: Syracuse University Press, 1966; Lambdin, Laura Cooner, and Robert Thomas Lambdin. *Camelot Revisited: Arthurian Characters in the Poems of Tennyson, Arnold, Morris, and Swinburne.* Westport, CT: Greenwood, 2000; McGann, Jerome J. *Swinburne: An Experiment in Criticism.* Chicago: University of Chicago Press, 1972; Miyoshi, Masao. "Narrative Sequence and the Moral System: Three Tristram Poems." *Victorian Newsletter* 35 (1969): 5–10; Rosenburg, John D. "Swinburne." *Victorian Studies* 9 (1967): 131–52; Staines, David. "Swinburne's Arthurian World." *Studia Neophilologica* 30 (1978): 53–70.

LAURA COONER LAMBDIN AND ROBERT THOMAS LAMBDIN

ALFRED, LORD TENNYSON

(August 6, 1809–October 6, 1892)

Alfred, Lord Tennyson is often recognized as the premier musician and symbolist among the Victorian poets. One of the most highly regarded authors of his age and one of its best represented figures in current scholarship, Tennyson renders timeless those conflicts and paradoxes considered central to the nineteenth century. The conflict between aesthetics and industrialization and the sense of abandonment that followed science into the religious psyche of the age are particularly emphasized in his work. Likewise, his work addresses gender issues central to the era of the rising suffrage movement. Tennyson's *The Princess*, for example, engages directly the emancipation and education of women. In other works, primarily in early poems such as "Mariana" and "The Lady of Shalott," Tennyson's treatment of gender surfaces as both product and sustainer of the sexist underpinnings of the age. Nevertheless, these works are generally recognized for their melliflous and imaginistic rendering of pervasive emotions. One of England's most popular poet laureates, Tennyson was the first English poet to be given a peerage "for services to literature." At times irascible and self-contradictory with regard to his artistic intentions and their critical reception, Tennyson invests his work with both the emotional extravagances of romanticism and the scientific engagement common to the Victorians. His interest in the Arthurian legends, an interest that spans the full spectrum of his career, thus finds expression in a particularly Tennysonian melding of romantic pathos and Victorian social concerns. Whether engaging the Mammonism engendered by industrialization or the falsely prophetic legacy of Camelot, Alfred Tennyson, perhaps chiefly among his peers, gives a voice to the central concerns of the nineteenth century.

Born at Somersby Rectory in Lincolnshire, on August 6, 1809, Alfred was the fourth of twelve children born to George and Elizabeth Tennyson: a displaced first son was forced into the clergy and the Pietist, famously beautiful daughter of the Louth Vicar. George Tennyson was widely read and a talented harpist; Elizabeth was fond of poetry, and the Tennyson children were encouraged from early youth to write, recite, and admire the musicality of verse. At age seven, after briefly attending a school in Holywell Glen, Alfred joined his two older brothers, Frederick and Charles, at the Louth Grammar School. At Louth, academic rigor was often enforced with fear and intimidation. Quite different from the gentle encouragement of his aesthetically inclined mother, such a means of promoting knowledge led the young Alfred to emotionally withdraw from his often brutal school masters and peers and seek communion with nature. Long an admirer of Byron, the young man who had memorized most of *Childe Harold's Pilgrimage* recalled his grandmother's recitations of "The Prisoner of Chillon" and projected emotional syllogisms onto the weed-strewn wall outside his window.

After leaving Louth to continue their studies at home, Alfred and his brother, Charles, began to hone their poetic talents under the strict tutelage of their father. By age twelve, Alfred had composed an epic of six thousand lines. Between 1823 and 1824, the year that brought the death of his beloved Byron, he composed *The Devil and the Lady*: a near complete Elizabethan comedy that juxtaposes the balanced wisdom of nature and the choleric, melancholy foibles to humanity. By the time Alfred was seventeen years old, he and Charles had compiled a collection of 102 works, *Poems by Two Brothers*, which was published in 1827 by Messrs. Their brother Frederick contributed four works to the collection, and the young poets received a sum of twenty pounds for the copyright. Life at the rectory soon deteriorated, however, as George Tennyson suffered from increasing bouts of epilepsy, violence, and depression. As their father began self-medicating with opium and alcohol, the Tennyson poets composed serials, collaborated on a romance, and exhausted their frustrations jousting in mock tournaments and waged wars as Napoleon and Wellington.

In November 1827, Alfred Tennyson matriculated at Trinity College, Cambridge. Unhappy and isolated during his freshman year, he met the dashing young idealist and poet, Arthur Hallam, in late 1828. This friendship was to prove enormous influence on Tennyson's evolving talent and lifelong sensibility. In 1829 Tennyson won the prestigious Chancellor's Medal for his poem "Timbuctoo" and, heralded by Hallam as the greatest poet of his generation, was invited to join the Cambridge Apostles, a club of young Cambridge intellectuals. Tennyson and his champion joined the other Apostles in debating issues central to science, politics, literature, philosophy, and theology. Energized by the rigorous intellectual debate and outpouring of creative support he found among the Apostles, a newly confident Tennyson wrote prolifically and honed his talents as a lyricist.

As he had previously with his brother Charles, Tennyson worked with Hallam toward a joint volume of poems. When Hallam was persuaded to withdraw from what his father saw as a premature publication venture, Tennyson's contribution appeared in 1830 as *Poems, Chiefly Lyrical*. That same year, Tennyson and Hallam undertook a journey to the Pyrenees to deliver money and instructions to Spanish insurgents, and much of Tennyson's 1832 volume, *Poems*, was inspired by their continental adventures. Hallam, frequently attending the poet on visits to Somersby, was soon betrothed to Tennyson's sister, Emily. It is in Hallam's review of *Poems, Chiefly Lyrical*, for *Englishman's Magazine* (August 1831) that Tennyson's facility as a symbolist is first, and perhaps best, proclaimed. Hallam addresses a convention he labels sympathy; Tennyson's particular talent for devising characters and settings around a pervasive sensation, such as despondency or expectation. Given the enormous influence Hallam had on the young Tennyson's social and psychological development, it is difficult to over-emphasize the impact of his support for the romantic and imagistic strains of the poet's early work.

The 1830s thus heralded a remarkably swift germination of Tennyson's muse, yet the growth of his talent was anything but unilateral. George Tennyson passed away in 1830, and Alfred returned to Somersby. Perhaps in nostalgic recollection of childhood jousts and his early attempt at the form, Tennyson revisited the possibility of writing an epic poem and began to consider working with an Arthurian themes. In doing so, he was forced to come to terms with the difficulty of modernizing such a subject without rendering it anachronistic and the attendant importance of form. Prior to a Victorian medievalism largely revived by Tennyson himself and the painters who immortalized his work, the nineteenth-century reading public was not receptive to an extended Arthurian work in poetic form. William Wordsworth, then poet laureate, had contemplated and rejected as vain folly the idea of reviving the Arthurian legends. Samuel Taylor Coleridge went so far as to dismiss Arthur as being completely foreign to the contemporary Englishman. Even Sir Walter Scott, the master of the historical romance whose 1813 "Bride of Triermain" features many of the Arthurian characters, dismissed as unapproachable a full treatment of the Arthurian legends. Nevertheless, Tennyson, back at Somersby with a talent and confidence nurtured by his friendship with Arthur Hallam, again turned his thoughts to Camelot.

In *Alfred Lord Tennyson: A Memoir by His Son* (subsequently cited as *Memoir*), the poet's son, named for the much beloved Arthur Hallam, describes three of his father's designs for an Arthurian work and attributes them to the early 1830s. Hallam Tennyson first quotes the fragment of an Arthurian epic found among his father's manuscripts and suggests that it is likely to have been sketched in 1833. He also notes that on October 1, 1869, the poet shared with T. J. Knowles an allegorical treatment of the Arthurian legend he had sketched out thirty to forty years earlier. In this version, Arthur was to have represented religious faith, Mordred was to have represented skepticism, Merlin was to have represented science, and the Round Table was to have represented liberal institutions. No doubt the debates held by the Apostles would have weighed heavily in such a work, had the poet's Arthurian designs been realized through this medium. Hallam Tennyson also suggests that at some point between the years of 1833 and 1840 his father was debating whether to treat the Arthurian legends in epic form or as a five-act musical mask—the idea of the latter destined to inspire much scoffing on the part of later critics. Setting aside the suitability of the form itself to the subject in question, it is not surprising that the man who was weaned on his father's music, who wrote his first dramatic piece by the time he was fifteen, and who closed his twilight years with the penning of seven more plays seriously considered the creation of a musical mask.

Tennyson's early navigation of the Arthurian legends reveals that he had not completely settled the issue of form. When the poet first began to explore the Arthurian theme, he did so in the familiar territory of the lyric mode. Although not published until the 1842 printing of *Poems*, Tennyson's "Sir Lancelot and Queen Guinevere: A Fragment" is described in *Memoir* as having been "partially if not wholly written in 1830." As the fragment nearly anticipates the verse form of the later lyric, it is not surprising that the poet was again working on it in 1833 as a companion piece to "The Lady of Shalott," the first published of his Arthurian poems. In a letter dated June 22, 1833, J. M. Kemble writes to W. B. Donne of Tennyson's "companion to 'The Lady of Shalott': a work in progress called the 'Ballad of Sir Lancelot.'" Kemble then expresses his bitter regret that he "had not the opportunity to take down what there is of it" and offers as a condolence "Sir L.'s song." Unpublished stanzas of "Sir Lancelot and Queen Guinevere" were circulated amongst Tennyson's peers at Cambridge and later adopted as verses within his "The Palace of Art" (1832) and *The Princess* (1847), yet critical attention directed toward the early fragment most often features its stylistic and thematic relationship with "The Lady of Shalott" (1832). The second poem provides a fuller view of the apocalyptic love introduced in the first, a view presented in stanzas, otherwise similar in form, embellished with fifth and ninth line refrains. Compare the first two stanzas of the 1842 "Sir Lancelot and Queen Guinevere":

> Like souls that balance joy and pain,
> With tears and smiles from heaven again
> The maiden Spring upon the plain
> Came in a sun-lit full of rain,
> In crystal vapour everywhere
> Blue isles of heaven laughed between,
> And far, in forest-deeps unseen,
> The topmost elm-tree gathered green
> From draughts of balmy air.
> Sometimes the linnet piped his song;
> Sometimes the throstle whistled strong;
> Sometimes the sparhawk, wheeled along,
> Hush'd all the groves from fear of wrong;
> By grassy capes with fuller sound
> In curves the yellow river ran,
> And drooping chestnut-buds began
> To spread into the perfect fan,
> Above the teeming ground. (1–18)

to the first two stanzas of 1832's "The Lady of Shalott":

> On either side the river lie
> Long fields of barley and rye,
> That clothe the wold and meet the sky
> And through the field the road runs by
> To many-towered Camelot;
> And up and down the people go,
> Gazing where the lilies blow
> Round an island there below,
> The island of Shalott.
> Willows whiten, aspens quiver,
> Little breezes dusk and shiver
> Through the wave that runs forever
> By the island in the river
> Flowing down to Camelot,
> Four gray walls, and four gray towers,
> Overlook a space of flowers,
> And the silent isle embowers
> The Lady of Shalott. (1–18)

The two selections, alike in form and meter, also share the Tennysonian quality famously cited by Arthur Hallam, and recognized by later critics, as sympathy. Both works open with an emotional syllogism: the germ of sympathy that provides the crux of both characterization and theme. With the opening of the fragment, we find the heady ripening of spring setting the context for the illicit passions of Lancelot and Guinevere. Likewise, the tower that entombs the Lady of Shalott dulls to distant echoes a crescendo of life and nature, and the isolation it enforces subdues the humanity of its inhabitant.

Just as "Sir Lancelot and Queen Guinevere: A Fragment" is considered a prelude to "The Lady of Shalott," the latter lyric is frequently upheld as an early draft of the later idyll "Elaine," even amidst celebrations of its individual merits. Aubre De Vere, for example, is quoted in Hallam Tennyson's *Memoir* as saying the lyric was "destined to reappear at the interval of many years in a nobler, ampler and richer form, but not one which challenged more vividly the youthful imagination." Although it is important to treat "The Lady of Shalott" in the context of Tennyson's *Idylls of the King*, it is equally important to treat it in the context of his early romanticism and as representative of the themes that pervade much of his career. This helps define our understanding of what it is to be Tennysonian, "The Lady of Shalott" remains the focus of considerable critical attention, and it is often suggested that no work did more to keep romanticism alive during the mid-nineteenth century. Nevertheless, the lyric is simultaneously credited with a duality that is both characteristically Victorian and categorically modern. Written, at least in part, by early October 1831, published in the 1832 *Poems*, and heavily revised for the two volume *Poems* of 1842, "The Lady of Shalott" features a tension between instinct and civilization culled from the nexus of romanticism and developed in epic proportions in the *Idylls*. Tennyson cited the Italian novella *Donna di Scalotta*, conjecturally dated 1321, as the source on which he based the Arthurian lyric, yet the poem is particularly indicative of the nineteenth-century cultural climate.

With the rise of romanticism, an obsession with breaking free of the shackles of neoclassicism became evident in a growing interest in demographics and a visible shift in the manner in which the middle and upper classes attired themselves. The romantics rushed headlong toward what they saw as a dawning new age, obsessed with separating themselves from their elitist predecessors. A period in which it was, to use William Wordsworth's signifiers, "bliss to be alive" and "very heaven" to be young, the romantic age might well have adopted "Make it new!" as a collective mantra. The Victorians were around when the novelty coveted by the Romantics became a reality, yet the awkward transition period that spanned the reign of Victoria Regina was a far cry from a Shelleyan utopia. When dawn broke, the Victorian period featured a rise of industrialization and empire building and a booming economy growing around a central nexus of cotton mills, coal mines, blast furnaces, and the exploited, landless wage earners who kept them running. England was producing more than half the world's industry, and Goldsmith's "deserted village" became a reality as a concomitant rise of the cities offered steady wages if not livable working conditions. In 1830, the same year that Tennyson published *Poems, Chiefly Lyrical*, the Liverpool and Manchester Railway was established. Six years later, one year before Victoria's ascent to the English throne, railway tracks spread through London. The Victorian culture may not have known the direction it was traveling, yet its awareness of the speed with which it traveled was pervasive. This awareness is reflected in the titles of many Victorian artistic products, such as Charles Dickens's *Great Expectations* and the Pre-Raphaelite journal, *The Germ*.

Published five years prior to the onset of Queen Victoria's reign, Tennyson's "Lady of Shalott" complicates an already problematic division between Romanticism and Victoriana, and it is not surprising that the work has enjoyed a central role in the cultural studies of both periods. In response to the German Naturphilosophie in the late 1700s, degeneration and extinction reached the foreground of early nineteenth century cultural consciousness. Well before the 1859 publication of Charles Darwin's *Origins of Species*, the reading public debated whether a god who seemed not to mourn the fall of the cave bear could be expected to immortalize the human soul. In response to the sense of abandonment that thus followed science into the religious psyche of the age, the romantic vale stepped into the vacuum left by a seemingly indifferent deity. Charles Lyell's apocalyptic three volume *Principles of Geology* exacerbated the tremors reverberating through the cultural psyche of the 1830s, and it is not surprising that one legacy the Romantics left to the Victorians is a sense that the artist would prove a spiritual and moral beacon in a largely destabilized age. Coupled with a new interest in demographics and a rise in periodical publication, this perception led early Victorian writers to a heightened concern with the present and future reception of their work.

The young Alfred Tennyson, not long removed from his isolated pre-Arthur Hallam days and painfully sensitive to criticism, was thus prompted by his culture to take particularly seriously his role as a poet. Correspondingly, his Lady of Shalott, entombed in a high gray tower, sits in the shadows and weaves a tapestry of all that she sees below. She thus experiences the whirl of commerce and industry only from the vantage point of one removed from it. Merely a seer and a recorder, it is solely through her art that she engages life. Through her, Tennyson illustrates the plight of the romantic vale. At the same time, his work reveals a dualism engendered by ambiguous Victorian progress and revisited by later modernism. When the Lady of Shalott, feared by a public that prefers to hear her ghostly songs from a distance, leaves the tower and offers her tapestry, her listeners cross themselves in fear. Thus is the poet torn between the necessarily distanced vantage point of the seer and an innate social impulse. Such duality also surfaces in a desire on the part of the audience to embrace faith in a poet prophet coupled with a simultaneous ignorance of an indifference toward the sacrifice demanded by the seer's role. The tension between private and social concerns, between aesthetic inertia and active engagement, proved central to the Victorian age and central to the poet who is often lauded for having well voiced the age's concerns.

Moreover, it is difficult to overemphasize the influence of Tennyson's poems of the 1830s on the small band of painters known as the Pre-Raphaelite Brotherhood. The imagistic details and sensuality of his landscapes, the romantic pathos of his subjects, and his mastery of sympathy combined to render this work particularly interesting to the revolutionary young men who viewed poetry and painting as sister arts and saw themselves as interpretive illustrators. Each of the Pre-Raphaelites painted Tennyson's "Lady of Shalott," and when Edward Moxon later published an 1857 volume of Tennyson's poetry, John Everett Millais, William Holman Hunt, and Dante Gabriel Rossetti contributed more than half of the volume's illustrations.

Compared to the earlier *Poems, Chiefly Lyrical*, the 1832 collection was not well received by the critical public, caught as it was in a backwash against the "Cockney School" with which it was linked. Particularly disturbing to the poet was John Wilson Croker's April 1833 review for *The Quarterly Review*. Croker's review was so vitriolic that Moxon exclaimed it would do the work of a hundred advertisements. Regardless, Tennyson is said to have never recovered from the anguish it brought him. Many critics have gone so far as to speculate that Croker's review was the catalyst behind the near decade long gap in the poet's publication history. Nevertheless, the less desirable reception of his work was not the greatest of the trials with which the poet had to contend in 1833.

Also in 1833, Alfred and his sister Emily were devastated by the unexpected loss of Arthur Hallam, who died in Vienna when a bout of apoplexy ruptured a blood vessel in his brain. Tennyson's "The Two Voices," originally titled "Thoughts of a Suicide," was thus begun during a period of pervasive grief. Such grief, the poet told his son, blotted all joy from his life and made him long for death, in spite of the duty he felt to try to alleviate Emily's suffering. Along with "The Two Voices," the poet began to jot down verses of what became the famous elegy, *In Memoriam: A. H. H.* Amongst these two expressions of mourning and melancholy, he composed the first draft of his third Arthurian lyric, "Morte d'Arthur." By 1834 he was copying out a complete version of the work. Nevertheless, the poem was not finished until 1842, when a two-volume edition of Tennyson's poems appeared. During the eight years between the poem's conclusion and its publication, the poet often read it aloud to friends, as he did his later monodrama, *Maud.* Edward Fitzgerald heard Tennyson read the poem aloud in 1835, and W. S. Landor was thus privileged in 1837. It is often suggested that "Morte d'Arthur," the chronicle of a mythic king who eternally exists in the realm of idealization, reflects the poet's attempt to objectify his grief and preserve the memory of Arthur Hallam. Thus, it is not surprising that the work was not subjected to publication and critical review until 1842. When the word did appear, it was received in such a fashion as to validate the poet's early hesitancy. "Sir Galahad," written by September 19, 1834, was likewise published in 1842. Many critics have suggested that this poem was written as a counterpart to "St. Agnes." Like "The Lady of Shalott," "Sir Galahad" is often upheld as a precursor to a later idyll; in this case, it is "The Holy Grail."

Although the period between 1833 and 1842 marked a lull in Tennyson's publication history, it was by no means an unproductive period for him. After the death of Arthur Hallam, Tennyson began revising his published poems and composing new ones. The lack of their public presentation represents the poet's conscious unwillingness to subject his work to critical scorn rather than a period of stasis engendered by mourning. Such is evident in an undated 1835 letter in which the poet tells James Spedding that he has learned of John Stuart Mill's intention to praise his work in a forthcoming edition of *The London Review.* In this letter, the poet declares a desire that someone share with Mill his wish to completely avoid "being dragged in front of the reading public at present."

Tennyson is justifiably notorious for his sensitivity to criticism. With this in mind, critics are inclined to agree that Tennyson's eventual decision to publish "Morte d'Arthur" reflects an attempt to gauge the reception of his audience to a potential Arthurian epic. "Morte d'Arthur" is the last of the lyrics with which Tennyson began his foray into Arthurian them and the first of these to find its way into the zenith of his Arthurian designs: *Idylls of the King.* Nevertheless its 1842 publication did not herald the swift ascent of an extended Arthurian masterpiece, for its audience proved no more receptive to the Arthurian theme than it had in the 1830s. Attempting to ward off much dreaded claims of irrelevance, Tennyson published "Morte d'Arthur" within a framing poem titled "The Epic." He thus set the poem in the context of a Christmas party at which a poet recites the sole remaining selection of a twelve-book Arthurian epic he tossed in a fire. Tennyson's attempt to render the work contextually modern did not yield the results for which he had hoped. "Morte d'Arthur," in spite of its frame poem, was largely viewed by its Victorian audience as an exercise in irrelevance. John Sterling, in a September 1842 review for *The Quarterly Review* voices popular consensus in describing the poem as a "mere ingenious exercise of fancy," As a whole, the 1842 collection was well received, but the first of Tennyson's *Idylls* floundered. In response, Tennyson, with characteristic sensitivity, let "Morte d'Arthur" languish for twenty-seven years before he added it complete to the second quartette of *Idylls*, which is titled *The Holy Grail, etc.* Years later, he spoke to William Arlington of Sterling's review and affirmed that it delayed his intended work on a twelve-book Arthurian epic. Nevertheless, Tennyson did continue to develop his Arthurian masterpiece, albeit at a slower pace than which he had initially imagined.

On October 3, 1859, the poet wrote to his friend the Duke of Argyll that many years ago he composed "Lancelot's Quest of the Grail," a work which has slipped from his memory before he wrote it down, and we know that in 1843 the poet began working on "Merlin and Vivien," then titled "Nimüe." However, Tennyson's Arthurian designs did not fully bloom until 1899, when *Idylls of the King* was published complete. Begun in 1842 with "Morte d'Arthur" and concluded with the 1886 "Balin and Balan," the development and publication history of Tennyson's *Idylls of the King* illustrate two central aspects to the poet's muse: his infamous sensitivity to criticism and his tendency to think in terms of duality and sharp contrasts.

In *Idylls of the King*, Tennyson returns to the duality that characterizes his presentation of the romantic vale. In this extended treatment, however, the Tennysonian axis of duality moves from the divided sensibility of the human psyche, through the divided loyalty of an entire culture, to the ambiguous value of ideals and absolutes. Rather than the product of a culture in which idealism is premature, Tennyson's ill-fated Camelot is the work of individuals who pledge themselves entirely to problematic ideals. Hence, the work reflects Tennyson's awareness of the ambiguity behind the Victorians obsession with progress. Such is a statement the poet also features in his 1855 monodrama, *Maud*, a portrait of society in which idealism itself becomes the agent of Mammonism and self-deception. Ever a perspicacious poet, Tennyson was all too aware of the high price paid for the economic, industrial, and scientific achievements of his day. Therefore, as Victorian London presented a facade of economic growth behind which lurked exploited workers, adulterated foodstuffs, and deplorable living conditions, Tennyson's Camelot is a golden frieze beneath which lurks a destructive idealization of earthly love and an all-consuming religious fervor. Individually indicative of specific points in his career, taken as a whole, Tennyson's *Idylls* serve a two-fold purpose. As a collective Arthurian epic, they feature both the evil that lurks behind appearance and the folly of chasing pure ideals while scorning the compromised form in which they enter the realm of human comprehension. An idyll is defined as a "little picture" of a character or mood that is colored by a single dominant emotion: the textual equivalent of the vignette and a form that lends itself well to allegory. As a master of sympathy and imagery and a poet attempting to modernize what was seen as a too distant subject, Tennyson well selected the idyll form for his Arthurian epic. Nevertheless, the work evolved slowly, often overshadowed by negative criticism and alternately inspired and stalled by publications to which the public was more receptive.

The first obstacle set against the publication of the collective *Idylls* was the hostile critical reaction to their first installment: the ill-fated 1842 "Morte d'Arthur." After the publication of the lyric, Tennyson's characteristic sensitivity dulled his relationship with his publishers but not his interest in the Arthurian legends. In 1843, just one year after the lyric was charged with irrelevance, the poet undertook a journey to Ireland and wrote a few lines of what would later become the idyll "Nimüe." This was the same year in which Tennyson lost most of his fortune in a woodcarving scheme he undertook with Matthew Allen, and the poet's despondency and anxiety pervade the consciousness of the old wizard who falls prey to a seductive enchantress. Tennyson's financial distress was somewhat relieved in 1835, when friends secured for him a civil list pension, the acceptance of which he rationalized by reminding himself it was provided without his having requested it.

In November 1847 Tennyson published *The Princess: A Medley*, and a favorable critical response to this extended idyll encouraged him to refocus his attention on his Arthurian designs. Because his audience had proved receptive to work on female emancipation set in a context of knights, it seemed an opportune moment to resume work on the Arthurian *Idylls*. The reception of *The Princess* thus played a large role in the germination of Tennyson's *Idylls*. The following year, to further inspire his Arthurian visions and simultaneously avoid unwelcome social engagements, Tennyson opted to visit the ruined castle of Tintagel, King Arthur's Stone near Slaughter Bridge, and Land's End at the tip of Cornwall. In *Alfred Tennyson*, Charles Tennyson describes this impetus behind the poet's revived interest in Camelot and adds to it a somewhat less noble point of inspiration:

> The success of *The Princess* had made him feel that his powers were now at last adequate for his long-cherished project, and perhaps he was also stimulated by the news that the old enemy, Bulwer Lytton, was bringing out an epic poem on the subject which he intended to be his masterpiece.

Lytton had previously suggested that Tennyson's work best suits an audience of schoolgirls and Oxford Dons, and it is not hard to believe that the sensitive poet responded in an equally cantankerous fashion. During his 1848 sojourn, the poet was further encouraged by a visit with Stephen Hawker, the lively scholar, poet, and Morwenstow vicar. Not knowing whom he addressed, Hawker spoke with the poet of King Arthur and Cornwall and recited fondly the section of "Morte D'Arthur" in which Excalibur is returned to the Lady of the Lake. Upon discovering the identity of his guest, the delighted vicar bestowed upon him an extensive collection of Arthurian books and manuscripts. On the way home, Tennyson once again directed his attention to the seduction of Merlin.

The 1850s mark Tennyson's preoccupation with two of his most extensive works: the elegy for which he is best known and was named poet laureate and the masterpieces he considered the zenith of his career, *In Memoriam* and *Maud*. They also mark his transition from bachelorhood to married life. In 1853, after marrying Emily Sellwood, whom he had met in 1836, Tennyson relocated to Farringford, an estate on the Isle of Wight. In spite of the many changes and challenges heralded by the 1850s, the poet did not completely abandon his Arthurian designs. In a February 7, 1852, edition of *The Examiner*, he published two poems under the pseudonym "Merlin." By March 1856, the poet had completed a draft of "Nimüe," the idyll named for the sorceress who seduces Merlin. Edward Burne-Jones, an associate of the Pre-Raphaelite Brotherhood, later suggested that Tennyson rename the title character Vivien and leave the name Nimüe to Malory's Arthurian enchantress. Such a shift is contextually justified, for Tennyson's Vivien bears little similarity to Malory's Nimüe. Although early critics were apt to draw similarities between the two enchantresses, Tennyson's wily Vivien is much more morally culpable than Malory's Nimüe, who is brought to Camelot against her will and who has to enchant a besotted Merlin in order to escape his unwelcome lascivious advances. Moreover, Nimüe twice saves the life of Arthur and once saves the life of his queen, while Vivien gleefully reveals the secret love of Lancelot and Guinevere to the treacherous Mordred. A more likely predecessor, the Vivien found in Lady Charlotte Guest's *Mabinogion* is a wily seductress who flatters Marlin, cajoles from him a magic charm, and then encloses him in an impregnable tower.

Tennyson's next Arthurian idyll also shows the influence of *Mabinogion*, but with this work the poet, with characteristic dualism, revives a character that is antithetical to his previous Vivien. Whereas his Eve-like Vivien is often decried by feminist critics as exemplifying a misogynistic fear of women, Enid is often decried as an equally misogynistic icon of femininity that allows herself to be emotionally battered by a jealous, paranoid husband. Perhaps encouraged by the public response to *Maud*, a work enormously popular with the public, however heatedly debated by critics, Tennyson began working on "Enid" on April 16, 1856, less than a month after he finished "Nimüe." Motivated by the poet's desire to gather impressions for an Enid idyll, the Tennyson family spent July and August in Wales. The tempestuous weather surrounding the peaks of Calder Idris and the torrential pools of Dolgelly provided the anticipated inspiration, and Tennyson returned to Farringford refreshed and eager to write. By October 17, he had completed enough of the work to read it aloud to friends, and, according to his son's *Memoir*, he was working on it again on November 11. By May 1857, it was complete.

Also in May 1857, the idylls "Nimüe" and "Enid" were typeset and bound together in a trail book titles *Enid and Nimüe: the True and the False*. As noted in John Pfordresher's *Valorium Edition of* The Idylls of the King, Tennyson told F. T. Palgrave that he had planned on publishing the two poems alone but ultimately decided against doing so after a negative comment made about "Nimüe" led him to recall the trial book after six copies had been produced. Thus, Tennyson's infamous sensitivity to criticism once again influenced the evolution of his Arthurian designs.

In 1870 "Enid" was retitled "Geraint and Enid," and in 1873 it was split into parts one and two. The first part features Geraint's pursuit of a knight who has besmirched the good name of Guinevere, his subsequent defeat of the knight, restoration of the knight's property to the rightful owner, and marriage to the benefactor's daughter, Enid. In the second segment, Geraint becomes irrationally obsessed with his wife's fidelity and forces her to undergo humiliating tests of loyalty until he finally find his faith in her restored. In 1886 the two parts were titled "The Marriage of Geraint and Enid," and "Geraint and Enid," respectively.

According to a July 9, 1857, entry in Emily Tennyson's journal, Tennyson had recently presented his wife with the lines, "But hither shall I never come again / Never lie by thy side; see them no more, / Farewell," which form the nucleus of what became the idyll "Guinevere." By March 15, 1858, he had composed the complete idyll. Tennyson's Guinevere is an amalgamation of his Enid, his Lady of Shalott, and his Vivien. In being true to Lancelot and to love, she must be false to Arthur. It is this dubious purity of intent, which she shares with Enid and Elaine, that evokes the destructive power she shares with Vivien. A penitent sinner who eventually becomes abbess of Almesbury nunnery, she nevertheless parts from Lancelot in response to the power of scandal rather than the imposition of conscience. Guinevere attributes her adulterous love to Arthur's Godlike inapproachability and Lancelot's warmth and color, the same warmth and color that leads the "Lady of Shalott" of the 1833 *Poems* to quit her shadowed tower cell and sacrifice herself for love. However, Guinevere's idealistic and rash investment in earthly love evokes the destruction of Camelot, whereas the sacrifice of Elaine is answered with muted prayer and offhand notations of her beauty. In consequence, if not in intent, Tennyson's Guinevere is more Vivien than Elaine.

Tennyson's Elaine, an extension of his earlier Lady of Shalott, again took center stage when the poet began constructing the fifth idyll. By mid-June 1858, Tennyson had a plan for "The Maid of Astolat," to which he devoted his attention during a July visit to Little Holland House in Kensington. From there, the poet undertook a journey to Norway, and the smoky crests of a seething ocean storm inspired him to pen the famous passage in which a flood of knights, "As a wild wave in the wide North-sea," overcomes Lancelot and his charger. By February 4, 1859, the idyll was nearly complete. In the third proof it became "Elaine," and in 1870 it was retitled "Lancelot and Elaine." In this idyll, the erotomaniac heroine of the 1830s resurfaces, and an idealization of love once again proves fatal. Elaine is too Victorian to explicitly reveal her love for Lancelot and too idealistic to accept a revelation of Lancelot's love for his queen. Her love serves the purpose of featuring the mutually destructive power of adultery and idealism wield over the innocent.

By July 1859, Tennyson had compiled "Nimüe," "Enid," "Guinevere," and "Elaine" in a second trial book of idylls. The poet originally planned on calling the quintet *The True and the False: Four Idylls of the King*, but, as Thomas Wise suggests in his 1908 *Bibliography of the Writings of Alfred Lord Tennyson*, the 1859 publication of Lena Eden's novel *False and True* led the poet to retitle his collection *The Idylls of the King*. Within one week of its publication, the Moxon collection of the first four idylls sold more than ten thousand copies. Contrasting the reception of the ill-fated "Morte d'Arthur," the collection was well received by many of the poet's contemporaries. In a July 1859 review for *The Edinburgh Review*, Coventry Patmore voices the opinion that "no language has surpassed in epic dignity the English of these poems." Walter Bagehot, in an October 9 review in *National Review*, compares Tennyson to Keats, Wordsworth, and Shelley and lauds him for revealing, with greater success than the aforementioned, "a general picture of human life." In an October 1859 review for *Quarterly Review*, William Gladstone, who singles out *Maud* for strident criticism, simultaneously praises Tennyson's *Idylls* and *In Memoriam*, In an October 16, 1859, letter, W. M. Thackeray, one of the age's masters of cynicism and social satire, affirms that the *Idylls* gave him a sense of delight he had not felt since his childhood reading of *Arabian Knights*. Among the four idylls, the work least admired by Victorian critics was "Vivien," a product and sustainer of Victorian reticence about female sexuality and a departure from the characteristically Tennysonian portrait of femininity. The more liberal-minded of Tennyson's friends, however, pronounced the work a favorite.

On December 14, 1859, the prince consort died. Upon hearing of his death, Tennyson dedicated the *Idylls* to him and sent the dedication to Princess Alice with his condolences. The dedication was printed and sent free of charge to individuals who had purchased the 1859 collection. It was later added to the fourth edition of the work, which appeared in a slightly revised form in 1862. The queen, who was also much consoled by Tennyson's *In Memoriam*, was moved by the gesture and consequently invited the poet to visit her in the spring at Osborne, her Isle of Wight estate. Before the end of the year, a second edition of the *Idylls* was in press, and the proceeds from the work had surpassed even those of *Maud*, which generated the funds with which Tennyson purchased Farringford, his Isle of Wight estate.

An interesting consequence of the popularity of the 1859 volume was Tennyson's growing struggle to maintain his privacy. The poet who once scorned Byron for having courted the public eye now found himself having to sneak to a secret staircase in order to escape unwelcome visitors. When Tennyson made his way to Osborne, he lightheartedly noted that a sentry, akin to those guarding the queen, was precisely what he needed at Farringford. His reclusive behavior and his visit with the queen only served to heighten public interest and speculation. Relentlessly pursued by autograph hunters, Tennyson remarked that great men are akin to pigs in the desire of the public to rip them apart. In 1864 his *Enoch Arden, and Other Poems* brought more success, selling more than sixty thousand copies and earning him the title "poet of the people." Thus, it is not surprising that by March 1868 the poet was working on "The Holy Grail," a subject he had previously rejected, in spite of the recommendations of Macauley and other peers. Tennyson had dismissed the subject out of fear that it would be met with the charges of irrelevance that overshadowed his earlier "Morte d'Arthur." The support of the queen and the success of *Enoch Arden* and the 1859 and 1860 *Idylls* perhaps assuaged that fear.

In spite of his initial trepidation, Tennyson viewed "The Holy Grail," originally sketched out in prose form, as one of his most imaginative poems and one in which he expressed particularly well in his impression of the "reality of the unseen." Such primacy of the spiritual and the real over material and the visible is made explicit in three of Arthur's lines, which the poet saw as the spiritual nexus of his *Idylls*: "In moments when he feels he cannot die, / And knows himself no vision to himself, / Nor the High God a vision." In the wake of the apocalyptic visions of German *Naturphilosophie* and the doom laden speculations of British geology, such de-emphasizing of the human husk and amplification of the soul was precisely the message necessitated by the religious and scientific backdrop of the age. It is the ambiguous if not ironic rendering of this balance, featured at the conclusion of *Maud*, that led the poet's detractors to scorn the earlier work. Thus, many of Tennyson's readers were more than ready to see the "poet of the people" turn from what they perceived as morbid, jingoistic, and doom-laden speculation to a less accusatory, less ambiguous tale of morality. Unlike that of the 1830s, Tennyson's 1860s audience was more than ready for "The Holy Grail." Such is likewise evident in the increasing popularity of the Arthurian legends. In 1858 William Morris had published two poems in which Galahad plays a central role. That same year, an anonymous author had published the extensive poem, *Arthur's Knights, an Adventure from the Legend of the Sangrale*. In 1864 F. J. Furnivall had edited Walter Map's *Le Quest del San Graael*.

Tennyson was particularly eager to explore the previously shunned subject of the Holy Grail, and it is said that the resulting idyll was composed, in a whirl of inspiration, in less than a week. Rather than a second "exercise in irrelevance," "The Holy Grail" proved anything but anachronistic. Composed in the wake of Charles Darwin's *Origin of Species*, the idyll is particularly Victorian in its questioning of orthodoxy and spiritual absolutism. Here, the poet presents spiritual obsession as a detrimental force on par with sexual obsession. This comparison is made explicitly clear when a nun in a state of erotic ecstasy is transfixed by the red hue of the grail, which Sir Galahad associates with the blood of Christ. Such ties between spirituality and eroticism are characteristically Victorian, for the Pre-Raphaelites and their imitators had earlier constructed an entire movement around the connection, immortalizing such subjects as nuns rapt with passion flowers and saints captured in moments of erotic ecstasy. After concluding "The Holy Grail," his inspiration increasing rather than deflating, the poet decided to withhold the poem until he could complete three or four more idylls and present them as a unit. Thus, he immediately began working on "The Birth of Arthur," which we now know as "The Coming of Arthur."

By late February 1869, Tennyson had composed most of "The Birth of Arthur," which is credited with the influence of Geoffrey of Monmouth's *Historia Britonum*. In

"The Birth of Arthur," the poet ties the ascent of the young King Arthur to that of the human race: an ascent from the beast, to the heathen, and on to the knight of post-Rome civilization. Characteristically Victorian, the ascent is complicated, for Arthur's birth and station are as ambiguous as the position of the human being in the age of Lyell and Darwin. On May 7, Tennyson added the dream that finally persuades Leodogran to allow his daughter Guinevere to marry Arthur, underscoring the instability of the ascent and the ambiguity of the ideal. As Leodogran dreams of a far too absolute triumph of spirit over sense, Arthur imagines in Guinevere the alliance that will engender a ubiquitous harmony, and perfect unification under Arthur is a dream so absolute it cannot help but dissolve into a nightmare.

By mid-May of the same year, the poet began reading drafts of "Sir Pelleas" to his wife, developing and sharing a vision he first contemplated nearly ten years earlier after reading aloud Malory's "Sir Pelleas and Etarre." A dark reversal of the skeptical protagonist of "Enid," Pelleas reads his own idealism and purity into all those who surround him. Thus, his idealism blinds him to the machinations of his wife and engenders his fall from genuine courtesy to superficial courtliness. Like Leodogran and Arthur, he commits himself to an ambiguous, if not dubious, compromise between vision and reality. After the "Sir Pelleas" idyll, Tennyson directed his attention to revising "Morte d'Arthur," to which he added one hundred and eight lines. By November 1869, proofs of the four idylls had been sent to Strahan. In order to take advantage of the Christmas market, in spite of the fact that the title page is dated 1870, the revised "Passing of Arthur" was published in December, along with the three new idylls, as *The Holy Grail, and Other Poems*. Included with the front matter of the 1869 volume is the inscription:

These four "Idylls of the King" are printed in their present form for the convenience of those who possess the former volume. The whole series should be read, and is today published, in the following order:

THE COMING OF ARTHUR

The Round Table.
GERAINT AND ENID.
MERLIN AND VIVIEN.
LANCELOT AND ELAINE.
THE HOLY GRAIL.
PELLEAS AND ETARRE.
GUINEVERE.

THE PASSING OF ARTHUR*
*This last, the earliest written of the poems, is here connected with the rest in accordance with an early project of the author['s].

Almost simultaneously, the publisher compiled all eight idylls under the title *Idylls of the King*. This compilation appeared in January of the following year.

With the publication of the set of eight idylls, charges of irrelevancy or impropriety leveled at the individual poems largely gave way to a favorable critique of the collective *Idylls*. For example, R. H. Hutton, in a December 1873 edition of *Macmillan's Magazine*, praised the grand scope of the collected idylls, as did a May 1873 article in *Contemporary Review*. A Philadelphia literary society named itself in honor of Tennyson and adopted as its motto the apophthegm that adorns the entrance to the poet's Isle of Wight estate: "Y Gwir yn erbyn byd" ("The truth against the world"). In spite of its popularity, the collection was not entirely without detractors. For example, the moral agenda that saved the work from the same critical fate as the original "Morte d'Arthur" also inspired a critical backlash on the part of those who were sympathetic to the ideals of the aesthetic movement. Tennyson responded to such detractors with the famous epigram, "Art for Art's Sake":

Art for Art's sake! Hail, truest Lord of Hell!
Hail, Genius, blaster of Moral Will!
The Filthiest of all paintings painted well
is mightier than the purest painted well,
So prone are we that broad way to Hell.... (l, 105)

Tennyson thus expresses his opinion that the innate morality of English poetry is being sullied by the Art for Art's Sake movement, rendering it another casualty of the divided Victorian cultural psyche. It was no doubt immensely gratifying to Tennyson that James Spedding responded to "The Holy Grail" by suggesting the poet next focus his narrative prowess to the tale of Job. Spedding's suggestion was well made, for the tale of Job, grounded in sublimity, pathos, and conflict between morality, selflessness, and gratification, is characteristically Tennysonian in its duality and potentially dramatic imagism.

With the onset of the 1870s, Tennyson's career took another direction. In 1875 the poet completed the play *Queen Mary*, which heralded a seventeen-year dramatic period in which he composed seven plays. Nevertheless, Tennyson's growing interest in the stage did not stall his exploration of the Arthurian legends. In 1871 Strahan released the miniature edition of Tennyson's works, which contains all of the idylls written to date and changes the titles of "Enid," "Vivien," and "Elaine" to those by which the idylls are currently known. By November of the same year, Tennyson was working on "The Last Tournament," a few lines of which he had composed in July 1866. In this idyll, Tennyson presents a swan song for chivalric nobility and strength. As his Tristram plummets toward a bondage greater than his chivalric vows, Lancelot is bewildered by an innocence of which he is not capable, and the Round Table of the North, a meeting ground for vice and corruption, proves less false to itself than Arthur's Camelot. In "The Last Tournament," the champion of human redemption goes by the name Dagonet and walks the earth in the guise of a fool. By May 1871, "The Last Tournament" was finished, and in December it was published in *The Contemporary Review*.

By September 1872, Tennyson had completed "Sir Gareth," the idyll he had started working on in October 1869 and set aside to work on "The Last Tournament." The characteristic Tennysonian duality necessitated the addition of this particular idyll, for it is the only idyll that features a hero who is true to the ideals of Camelot: a position needed to counteract the bleak underpinnings of "Pelleas and Etarre" and "The Last Tournament." Gareth thus epitomizes blended innocence and maturity. He lacks neither humility nor virtue, and he serves Arthur to serve the will of God, rather than to glorify humanity by following rigid human ideals. It is thus his innate worth that subdues the proud condescension of Lynette, rather than his lineage. Because Gareth does not seek validation through glory, because he views the world through the lens of a modest yet mature hopefulness, he is not undone by the rigid idealism that consumes his peers. In December 1872, "The Last Tournament" and "Gareth and Lynette" were published together as *Gareth and Lynette, etc.* As the compilation went to press, Tennyson immediately began working on the 1873 Strahan's library edition of his works to date, seizing the opportunity to revise his idylls and add them to an epilogue addressed to Queen Victoria. Victoria responded to the gesture with an invitation to visit the mausoleum of the departed Albert: the "white flower of a blameless life."

When Tennyson published *Gareth and Lynette, etc.*, he imagined his Arthurian epic complete. However, he later acted on an impression that an introduction to "Merlin and Vivien" was needed. Thus, he compiled "Balin and Balan," which he had begun composing in the early 1870s after he completed "Gareth and Lynette." Like the previous idylls, "Balin and Balan" illustrates the disastrous consequences of both idealism and the neglect of it. Balin is rescued from his less civilized animal impulses by the supposed civility of Camelot and a misguided idealization of the queen, Balan's rigid idealism sends him on a quest to slay the demon of the woods and thus leads him to murder, and be murdered by, his newly disillusioned and maddened brother. Their mutual fall reflects the paradox that all-consuming passions are destructive both in themselves and in their total annihilation. In November 1885, "Balin and Balan" was published in *Tiresias and Other Poems* and subtitled "An Introduction to 'Merlin and Vivien.'" Critical reaction to the collection was largely favorable. The new miniature edition of the *Idylls of the King*, published in 1886, was the first edition to include all of the idylls, from "The Passing of Arthur" to "Balin and Balan," yet the final version of the *Idylls* did not appear until after the poet's death. In 1891 the Tennyson had asked his son to add a line, describing Arthur Hallam as "Ideal manhood closed in real man," to the "Epilogue" to the *Idylls*, and his request was honored in the deluxe edition of 1899.

Critical evaluation of Tennyson's Arthurian epic, like the work's publication history, has been anything but unilateral. The poet's contemporaries primarily dedicated their critical attention to evaluating the epic's moral vision, literary heritage, and allegorical structure. Such themes remained popular points of evaluation in the early twentieth century. Although popular with the new critics, Tennyson's *Idylls* fell somewhat out of fashion with the onset of modernism, a position redeemed only slightly by recent wew historicist examinations of its female protagonists. Harold Littledale's *Essays on Lord Tennyson's "Idylls of the King"* is considered one of the most important nineteenth-century introductions to the *Idylls*, and the first sustained book-length study of the *Idylls* was Richard Jones's 1895 *The Growth of the "Idylls of the King."* In 1936 Sir Charles Tennyson did much to enhance our understanding of the epic when he published "Some Manuscripts of the *Idylls of the King*," which treats the idylls in the order of their publication. However, many post-World War I critics dismissed Tennyson's *Idylls* as intellectually insincere, a charge they also leveled against his *Maud*. John Rosenberg perhaps best summarizes the modernists's reaction to the epic in his 1973 study, *The Fall of Camelot: A Study of Tennyson's "Idylls of the King."* Rosenberg notes that the epic "was their culture's bones" and that it "came to them wrapped on precisely the kind of repugnant piety that made its rejection a mark of one's coming of age." Regardless, one cannot deny the irony behind their dismissal of the work, given the central duality at the heart of modernism. Just as the *Idylls* feature a central paradox of golden dreams, dark realities, striving, and doubt, modernism presents archetypes in fragmented form and features heroes who seek relief from spiritual starvation in the banalities of life. In the 1940s and 1950s, critics largely returned to the issue that captivated Tennyson's peers and investigated links between the *Idylls* and the sources that inspired them. David Staines's 1983 *Tennyson's Camelot: The Idylls of the King and its Medieval Sources* is an example of such readings. In 1973 John Pfordresher add to the aforementioned *A Variorum Edition of Tennyson's Idylls of the King*, which contains the exhaustive collection of the work's varied manuscripts and printing proofs. Elliot Gilbert's "The Female King: Tennyson's Arthurian Apocalypse," published in and October 1983 edition of *PMLA*, is an excellent example of the provocative bender studies favored by Tennyson's new historicist critics.

The question of unity has played a particularly central role in the critical reception of Tennyson's *Idylls of the King*, and the compilation's extended and sporadic composition history has no doubt played a large role in that debate. Critics have long debated the merits of classifying *Idylls as* a tapestry of twelve loosely interwoven tales or as a richly layered organic whole. In the frame poem in which the early version of "Morte d'Arthur" is set, the speaker refers to his poem as one section of an Arthurian "epic" he can cast into the fire, but is this description indicative of the larger frame in which Tennyson himself intended to place "Morte d'Arthur"? Critics who favor a unified perception of the work have often seen the allegorical function of the *Idylls* as its unifying feature, yet this interpretation is problematic. Tennyson himself is infamously self-contradictory in discussing his own work, and his comments on the form of the *Idylls* are characteristically divided. James Knowle's January 1893 article in *The Nineteenth Century*, quotes the poet as affirming: "By King Arthur I always meant the soul, and by the round table the passions and capacities of a man." Moreover, the *Idylls'* epilogue, "To the Queen," asks that Queen Victoria accept Tennyson's "old imperfect tale" as "New-Old, and shadowing Sense at war with Soul" rather than as a tale of the king whose name pervades the land itself and renders immortal the work of Geoffrey and Malory. Interestingly, the poet also complained that his critics were reading his work too allegorically. Hallam Tennyson's *Memoir* quotes the poet as exclaiming:

> They have taken my hobby, and ridden it too hard, and have explained some things too allegorically, although there is an allegorical or perhaps a parabolic drift in the poem. . . . Of course Camelot for instance, a city of shadowy places, is everywhere symbolic of the gradual growth of human beliefs and institutions, and of the spiritual development of man. Yet there is no single fact or incident in the "Idylls," however seemingly mystical, which cannot be explained as without any mystery or allegory whatever.

"Merlin and Vivien" and "The Holy Grail" are more explicitly allegorical than most of the idylls, and "The Coming of Arthur" and "The Passing of Arthur" are presented in a more archaic style than the other idylls, which emphasizes the cyclical nature of the work. Nevertheless, the question of unity is likely to retain a central role in the critical exploration of Tennyson's most extensive Arthurian design, and the poet's own comments on the subject do much to complicate the issue.

Written in August 1889 and published the same year as *Demeter and Other Poems*, "Merlin and the Gleam" is the first Arthurian work Tennyson published after concluding the *Idylls* and the last Arthurian work of his career. It also represents the author's twilight examination of his life's literary achievements: one of his most explicitly and unapologetically autobiographical undertakings. Tennyson explores the gleam sought by Merlin as a material counterpart to the higher poetic imagination. He thus treats the Arthurian subject without reference to the *Idylls*, returning instead to the theme of his earlier "Ulysses."

Through the old wizard, whose journey in pursuit of the gleam parallels the closing of an age, the poet unfurls a swan song for the Victorian cultural psyche, tensed between faith and progress. Now at the close of his life, Tennyson bequeaths his position as recorder of that tension to the young mariner and his companions, who must follow the gleam "ere it vanishes / Over the margin." On October 6, 1892, Tennyson quietly passed away at Aldworth House, Surrey. He was buried in the Poets' Corner of Westminster Abbey, along with the copy of Shakespeare's *Cymbaline* he had been reading the evening before his death.

Tennyson is a poet whose work has always inspired heated debate. With the singular style that is simultaneously lauded and dismissed for its imagism and lyricism, his work garners a full spectrum of response, excluding the middle ground of indifference. As successive generations attempt to define Tennyson's contribution to English literature, the variety of their analyses will remain a tribute to the intrinsic richness of their subject. When directing their attention to the poet's Arthurian designs, Tennyson's readers will engage a bumpy career length progression through romanticism, medievalism, and Victoriana. Moreover, they will have to come to terms with the poet's comments on his own work, comments that are often puzzling and contradictory. With such in mind, it is perhaps Tennyson's twilight assessment of his *Idylls*, as quoted in Hallam Tennyson's *Memoir*, that best describes the impact of his career as a while:

> Birth is a mystery and death is a mystery, and in the midst lies the tableland of life, and its struggles and performances. It is not the history of one man or of one generation but of a whole cycle of generations.

PRIMARY WORKS

Poems by Two Brothers, by Alfred and Charles Tennyson. London: Messrs, 1827; *Poems, Chiefly Lyrical*. London, Effingham Wilson, 1830; *Poems*. London; Moxon, 1833; *Poems*, 2 vols. London: Moxon, 1842; *Enid and Nimüe: the True and the False*. London: Moxon, 1857; *Idylls of the King*. London: Moxon, 1859; *Enoch Ardern, and Other Poems*. London: Moxon, 1864; *"The Holy Grail," and Other Poems*. London: Strahan, 1869; *Idylls of the King*. London: Strahan, 1870 [i.e., 1869]; "The Last Tournament." *Contemporary Review*. December 1871; *The Last Tournament*. London: Strahan, 1871; *Gareth and Lynette, etc*. London: Strahan, 1872; *The Works of Alfred Tennyson*, Library Edition, 7 vols. London: Strahan, 1872; *The Passing of Arthur*. London: Macmillan, 1884; *Tiresias and Other Poems*. London: Macmillan, 1885; *Idylls of the King*, New Miniature Edition, 10 vols. London: Macmillan: 1886; *Demeter and Other Poems*. London: Macmillan, 1869; *Works of Alfred Lord Tennyson*, Deluxe Editions, 12 vols. London: Macmillan, 1899.

Papers

Major collections of Tennyson's manuscripts are housed at Trinity College, Cambridge; Houghton Library, Harvard University; The New York Public Library; the British Museum; and the Tennyson Research Center, Lincoln.

Collections

Poems. London: Moxon, 1857; *Idylls of the King: Enid, Elaine, Vivian, Guenevere, with designs by Gustave Doré*. London: Moxon, 1867; *The Complete Works of Alfred Tennyson*, Miniature Edition. London: Strahan, 1871; *The Works of Alfred, Lord Tennyson*, Eversley Edition, 9 vols. 1907; *The Poems of Tennyson*, 3 vols., ed. Christopher Ricks. London: Longman, 1969; *Variorum Edition* of *Tennyson's Idylls of the King*, ed. John Pfordresher. New York: Columbia University Press, 1973; *The Letters of Alfred Tennyson*, 3 vols., ed. Cecil Lang and Edgar Shannon. Vol. 1, 1821–1850. Cambridge, MA: Harvard University Press, 1981. Vol. 2, 1851–1870. Cambridge, MA: Harvard University Press, 1987. Vol. 3, 1871–1892. Oxford: Clarendon, 1990.

SECONDARY SOURCES

Beetz, Kirk. *Tennyson: A Bibliography, 1827–1982*. Metuchen, NJ: Scarecrow, 1984; Elsdale, Henry. *Studies in the Idylls*. London: King, 1878; Gray, J. M. *Thro' the Vision of the Night: A Study of Source, Evolution, and Structure in Tennyson's "Idylls of the King."* Montreal: McGill-Queens University Press, 1980; Jones, Richard. *The Growth of the "Idylls of the King."* Philadelphia: Lippincott, 1895; Knowles, T. J. "Aspects of Tennyson II: A Personal Remembrance." *The Nineteenth Century* (January 1893): 5; Littledale, Harold. *Essays on Lord Tennyson's "Idylls of the King."* London: Macmillan, 1893; Martin, Robert. *Tennyson: The Unquiet Heart*. London: Faber, 1980; Reed, John. *Perception and Design in Tennyson's "Idylls of the King."* Athens: Ohio University Press, 1969; Rosenberg, John. *The Fall of Camelot: A Study of Tennyson's "Idylls of the King."* Cambridge, MA: Harvard University Press, 1973; Ryals, Clyde de la. *From the Great Deep: Essays on "Idylls of the King."* Athens: Ohio University Press, 1967; Tennyson, Charles. *Alfred Tennyson*. New York: Macmillan, 1949; Tennyson, H. *Alfred Lord Tennyson: A Memoir by His Son*. London: Macmillan, 1897; Wise, Thomas. *Bibliography of the Writings of Alfred Lord Tennyson*, 2 vols. London: printed by R. Clay, 1908.

PRISCILLA GLANVILLE

MARK TWAIN
(November 30, 1835–April 21, 1910)

With the possible exception of T. S. Eliot's *The Wasteland*, Mark Twain's *A Connecticut Yankee in King Arthur's Court* (1889) is arguably the best known American work derived from Arthurian legends. Its immediate inspiration was Sir Thomas Malory's *Morte d'Arthur* (completed 1469–1470, first published in 1485). Although most of the story of Hank Morgan, a Connecticut factory worker who is knocked unconscious and wakes to find himself in sixth-century Britain, is Twain's own, he drew upon Malory's work for themes (Lancelet's love for Guenevere, the grail quest), the names of the Arthurian characters, and for some extensive quotations. Some of the latter were intended to ridicule Malory's style, as in the long-winded accounts Hank's love Sandy gives of the adventures of Arthur's knights, others to show reverence for Malory's book, as in, for example, the final newspaper account of the fall of Arthur, taken from the final pages of *Morte Darthur*.

Twain became acquainted with Malory's work through Sidney Lanier's expurgated abridgment for children, *The Boy's King Arthur*, which the Clemens family purchased in 1880. He decided to write a book on an Arthurian subject a few years later when in the fall of 1884 he was on a lecture tour with George Washington Cable. Because of Cable's recommendation, Twain bought a copy of Edward Strachey's Globe edition of Malory on December 6 of that year. In a letter to his daughter Susy he described it as "the quaintest and sweetest of all books ... full of the absolute English of 400 years ago." At about that time he wrote a *Notebook* entry about the difficulties a knight would have wearing a suit of armor, and this entry offers the first indication that Twain was planning to write an Arthurian novel.

Connecticut Yankee was not the only work that he wrote that involved medieval or early modern settings: he had previously published his "Awful, Terrible, Medieval

(Samuel Langhorne Clemens)

Romance" in *The Express* (1870; reprinted in *Mark Twain's (Burlesque) Autobiography and First Romance* in 1871 and in *Mark Twain's Sketches, New and Old* in 1875); "'1601' Conversation, As It Was by the Social Fireside in the Time of the Tudors" (1880); and *The Prince and the Pauper* (1881), set in sixteenth-century England. Several years after *Connecticut Yankee* he wrote a serious biography of Joan of Arc, *Personal Recollections of Joan of Arc by the Sieur Louis de Conte* (1896).

In writing an often comic and irreverent version of the Arthurian stories, Twain used material that had been revered in both Britain and the United States since the rediscovery of Malory in the early nineteenth century. The reverence that some had for Malory's book can be gauged by Dante Gabriel Rosetti's description of it as one of the two greatest books ever written, the other being the Bible. The Arthurian legends and the chivalric values associated with it had been idealized and popularized by Tennyson's *Idylls of the King* and the work of other Victorian writers and artists, notably the Pre-Raphaelites, who looked upon the Middle Ages as a simpler time that had been uncorrupted by the Industrial Revolution. Although in the United States Edgar Fawcett and Oscar Fay Adams had parodied the legend in 1885 and 1886, Ralph Waldo Emerson's "Merlin" poems (1846) and James Russell Lowell's "The Vision of Sir Launfal" (1848) had treated it seriously. Lanier's *The Boy's King Arthur* was published to teach the ideals of chivalry to American youth after the Civil War had destroyed what to many was a chivalric society in the southern United States.

Connecticut Yankee is a reaction against the idealization of the Middle Ages in nineteenth-century literature and the idealization of life in medieval romances that overlooked ugliness and concentrated instead on what Erich Auerbach would describe as the "colorful surface" of reality. Thus, Twain's description of Camelot as a place with "muck and swine, and naked brats, and joyous dogs, and shabby huts" reflects both a realist's picture of what a medieval town would look like, as well as reaction against Mallory's failure to give much physical description at all or Tennyson's idealized description of Camelot in his "Gareth and Lynette" as a "city ... built / To music."

Moreover, Twain, born in 1835 in Florida, Missouri, to John Marshall and Jane Lampton Clemens and moving in 1839 with his family to Hannibal, Missouri, grew up in a border state where, in the years before and during the Civil War, there was much sympathy for the South. Works like *Life on the Mississippi* (1883) and *Huckleberry Finn* (1884) indicate that he recalled the pre-Civil War South with a more jaundiced eye than Lanier did. In fact, in *Life on the Mississippi* Twain described the people of the South as having been "run ... mad" by the medieval romances of Sir Walter Scott and observed that "the South has not yet recovered from the debilitating influence of his books." The fact that Twain anachronistically added slavery to the sixth-century Britain of his novel has suggested parallels between the pre–Civil War American South and the Britain of Twain's novel. Moreover, Twain's medieval Britain, like the South he remembered, at the beginning of the book is an agrarian society that becomes, like the post–Civil War South, industrialized, and both societies are destroyed by civil war.

The Clemens family had moved to Hannibal after series of business failures. The family was not affluent, and his father had to sell property and furniture in order to pay debts. Jane Clemens took in boarders to help make ends meet. Twain's formal schooling began in Hannibal in 1840, where his family paid for him to attend four different schools until 1849, when his formal schooling ended. His father died in 1847, and his mother, no longer able to afford to send him to school, apprenticed him to a printer, where he began working as an after-school printer's devil in 1848 and then became a full-time apprentice after leaving school. He left the apprenticeship in 1851 to begin working for his brother Orion, who had purchased the weekly *Hannibal Journal*. Beginning in 1853, he worked for a few years as an itinerant typesetter in St. Louis, New York, and Philadelphia, as well as in Keokuk, Iowa, for another newspaper Orion had purchased. His early experiences working and writing for newspapers are reflected in *Connecticut Yankee* in the passages concerning Hank Morgan's establishment of a newspaper in medieval Britain.

In 1856, after working as printer in Cincinnati, Ohio, he became an apprentice to a steamboat pilot, and in 1861 moved to Nevada with Orion, who had taken a position as secretary to the new territorial government. There Samuel Clemens worked first at gold and silver prospecting and then beginning in 1862 as a reporter for a Virginia City paper, the *Territorial Enterprise*. While working for the *Enterprise* he wrote short sketches for the paper and in February 1863 first used the pseudonym Mark Twain for short sketches he wrote. By 1866 he had become a traveling correspondent for the San Francisco *Alta California*, a position that took him on his first trip to Europe and the Middle East in 1867, a journey that provided material for his first successful book *Innocents Abroad* (1869). In 1867 he also met his future wife, Olivia Langdon, in New York City, and they were married three years later. Their son, Langdon, was born prematurely in 1870 and died in 1872, a few months after the birth of their first daughter Olivia (Susy). They had two other daughters, Clara, born in 1874, and Jane, in 1880. The family lived in Elmira, New York, and then Nook Farm, Hartford, Connecticut (1871). In 1874 they moved into their home in Hartford, the town which would also be the home of Hank Morgan, the Connecticut Yankee. In 1884 Twain began a publishing company in Hartford, to be managed by Charles Webster and named Charles Webster & Co. This firm would publish *Huckleberry Finn* (1885), and after the firm ran into financial difficulties, Twain hoped that *Connecticut Yankee* would help make the company solvent.

Although *Connecticut Yankee* was in part a reaction against Mathew Arnold's condescending, critical view of America in his essay "Civilization in the United States" (April 1888), much of the book had been written by the time Arnold's essay appeared, and Twain had developed views critical of England long before that. Although he might have once been described as an Anglophile because of the favorable impression he had had of England during his visits there in 1872 and 1873–1874, by late 1884, when he began thinking of writing a novel set in medieval England, his views had changed. In a *Notebook* entry of 1879 he observes that while the English like and respect American individuals, their newspapers "scoff at America or contemptuously ignore her." He believed that "the English nation despises America and Americans." and added, "We shall presently be indifferent to being looked down upon by a nation no bigger and no better than our own." Twain originally planned to include in *Connecticut Yankee* an appendix that would show the depravity of English civilization prior to the nineteenth century. *Notebook* entries that he made while writing *Connecticut Yankee* in 1888 and 1889 indicate his contempt for the British class system and the "kingly office." which is "no more entitled to respect than is the flag of a pirate."

Scholars generally accept Howard Baetzhold's argument that Twain composed *Connecticut Yankee* in five stages and that his conception of the book changed as he was writing it. A work that began as a burlesque evolved into a serious critique of problems of society—American as well as British and European—and of human nature. He did not return to the earlier comic chapters to make them consistent with the later ones.

The first stage was the *Notebook* entry concerning difficulties a knight would have wearing armor, written in December 1884 at about the time he had purchased his copy of *Morte Darthur*. This entry indicates that he was thinking of writing a burlesque that would make the age of chivalry, which many in the nineteenth century had idealized, look absurd. The knight would have no pockets in the armor; he would have "no way to manage certain requirements of nature"; he would be unable to scratch or blow his nose on a handkerchief or use his iron sleeve; he would get hot in the sun and freeze in winter; and he would be in danger of being struck by lightning.

The second stage consisted of *Notebook* entries written in 1885 that Twain later incorporated into the book: a notation that the country has been placed under an interdict, which suggests a conflict with the established church; the idea of having his protagonist fall in love with an Arthurian heroine, for whom he longs after he returns to the nineteenth century; a battle between a modern army with Gatling guns and medieval knights, which may have led Twain to make his chief character the foreman at the Colt arms factory at Hartford.

The third stage was the composition, probably in January and February 1886 of the preface and the first three chapters. Twain read from these on November 11, 1886, at a social event on Governor's Island in New York Bay before General W. T. Sherman and other members of the Military Service Institution, their wives, and guests. *The New York Sun, The New York Herald,* and *The New York World* gave accounts of his remarks the following day, and at this point the hero was named Sir Robert Smith or Sir Bob Smith. These opening chapters otherwise appear to be essentially as they are in the final version of the book. At this point, the story was still a burlesque, with no sign of its being concerned with satire or politics. The narrator is a shrewd rustic Yankee who hopes to get power though technological know-how and the training he had received, not at college, but at the Colt factory.

In a letter dated November 16, 1886, Twain referred to his novel and promised his friend Mrs. Mary Mason Fairbanks that he would "leave unsmirched & unbelittled the great & beautiful characters drawn by the master hand of old Malory." He told her that Arthur would "keep his sweetness & his purity" and that he would "grieve . . . if the final disruption of the Round Table, & the extinction of its old tender & gracious friendships, & that last battle . . . should lose their pathos & their tears through my handling." Twain's thoughts on how to develop the story, however, changed during the next few years, and if he had originally intended to treat the story of the downfall of Arthur's kingdom with reverence, by the time he was finished he had changed his mind, and he had indeed besmirched many of the characters. (The final battle, for example, is caused by Mordred and Agravaine's calling Arthur's attention to Lancelot's affair with Guenevere because they were angry that Lancelot had "skinned them alive" in a stock deal.)

After setting the manuscript aside for about a year, during summer 1887 (the fourth stage of composition), he wrote chapters IV–IX and XI–XX. In chapters IV–IX the Yankee gains power, wishes to make money, and becomes known as "The Boss." Chapters XI–XX expand Twain's original *Notebook* entry about the difficulties a knight would have wearing armor into a journey with Sandy to a pigsty. His contempt for European institutions like the class system led to this episode, in which Sandy leads the Yankee on a quest to rescue forty-five princesses and noble ladies imprisoned in an enchanted castle. The ladies turn out to be pigs and the enchanted castle a pigsty, and in an episode that Smith calls a "brilliant inversion of the Don Quixote-Sancho Panza relationship" (inverted because in this case the knight Hank sees the pigs for what they are and the Sancho character, Sandy, is the one who is deluded), the pigs must be addressed as "my lady" and "your highness." He also introduced in these chapters serious concerns about the evils of feudal laws and institutions through scenes that showed the suffering of the peasants. In August 1887 Twain indicated that he was concerned about the "funereal" tone that was beginning to appear in the book.

Much of this funereal tone reflects Twain's reading when he was writing *Connecticut Yankee*. During the summer 1885 he read W. E. H. Lecky's *History of the Rise and Influence of the Spirit of Rationalism in Europe* (1865), which probably suggested to Twain the theme of contrasting science and magic in *Connecticut Yankee* and much of the criticism of the Church. In 1886 and 1887 he read the London printer George Standring's *The People's History of the English Aristocracy*, which criticized the British acceptance of an aristocracy based upon birth. He was also offended by reports in June 1887 of Queen Victoria's Jubilee and the appearance of much of the royalty of Europe in Britain to help celebrate it. After having first read Carlyle's *The French Revolution* in 1871, he reread it during the summer of 1887 when he was writing *Connecticut Yankee* and found that he sided this time with the radicals. His accounts of slavery in Britain were influenced by George F. Kennan's articles in *The Century Magazine* on Siberian slave labor (1888), and he attended one of Kennan's lectures on Siberia at the Lowell Institute in Boston sometime during the first three months of 1889 as well. During that period he also read *Slavery in the United States: A Narrative of the Life and Adventures of Charles Ball, A Black Man* (1836). Other influences were Macaulay's *The History of England* (1848, 1855) and Lecky's *A History of England in the Eighteenth Century* (1878) and his *History of European Morals from Augustus to Charlemagne* (1869).

Critics have found the book uneven, in part because Twain began writing the early chapters as a burlesque, then turned to more serious issues, but left, for the most part, the early material unrevised. The Yankee dreams of doing good for the people of Britain, of giving them a "new deal" (a term that Franklin D. Roosevelt borrowed from the book) by allowing them to advance through their own talents, by establishing schools and colleges for them, and by giving them modern conveniences ranging from soap and tobacco to railroads and telephones. The book shows Twain's acceptance of eighteenth- and nineteenth-century optimism, democracy, and faith in technology on the one hand and his pessimistic view of human nature on the other. It attacks much that he disliked about Britain and Europe, such as the aristocracy based on birth and established churches, and it reflects the anti-Catholicism of Twain and much of nineteenth-century America. The church opposes Hank's efforts to enlighten an oppressed people, and its priests conspire against him. Some of the problems with British society that Twain was attacking in the book such as the granting of military commissions because of birth rather than merit and misuse of legal power were ones also of concern to British liberals of the time. For all of the book's criticism of Britain and the Middle Ages, at the end Hank Morgan dies longing for his beloved Sandy and their child, Hello Central, an ending that possibly reflects Twain's nostalgia for an earlier time.

In the final stage, from July 1888 through May 1889, he wrote chapter X and chapters XXI–XLIV and the two postscripts. He wrote almost all of chapter X, which tells of the Yankee's setting up industries in the kingdom, a theme that is important to the end of the book, and chapters XXI–XXXVI while he and his family were staying at Quarry Farm, near Elmira, New York, the home of Livy Clemens's foster sister Susan Crane and her husband, Theodore. By late summer 1888, Theodore had suffered a paralytic stroke while the Clemenses were staying with them, and Livy was helping care for him. In the fall they took him to their Hartford home for medical treatment. The strain of the nursing care caused Livy to contract a disease of the eyes that made her unable to read for weeks. To make matters worse, Twain was haunted during this period by fears of failure and anxiety over not having produced a significant book since the publication of *Huckleberry Finn* four years earlier.

Twain was having other serious problems during the final stage of writing. His publishing business was close to failure: it had not produced a successful book in years, and to make matters worse, a bookkeeper had embezzled twenty-five thousand dollars. One reason he had for writing *Connecticut Yankee* was his company's need for a successful book if it were to survive. Twain had also invested heavily in a typesetter that a Hartford machinist James W. Paige was developing. Twain believed Paige's claim that the machine would do the work of six men and revolutionize publishing. After an initial investment of two thousand dollars in 1880, within five years he had bought half-ownership for thirty thousand dollars; and believing it would make him a multi-millionaire and that he would no longer have to write for a living, he continued to pour money into it. He was having to take some three thousand to five thousand dollars a month out of his publishing company to meet the expenses of producing the machine. He hoped desperately for the completion of the typesetter at the same time as the completion of *Connecticut Yankee* and was repeatedly disappointed by delays in the production of the machine. The financial strain made this a period of frustration and anxiety for him. The machine was eventually a failure, and Twain lost about two hundred thousand dollars in the venture. This period marks the beginning of serious financial problems, which would necessitate the family's move to Europe in 1891, where they would live for nearly nine years in order to save money.

The final chapters, which show that technology can also be dangerous, probably reflect Twain's own disillusionment with technological progress. *Connecticut Yankee* concludes with the battle of the sand belt, which results in twenty-five thousand rotting corpses of knights who have been killed by the Yankee's Gatling guns and electrically charged fences. The scene dwarfs the slaughter possible in the Middle Ages and to many readers foreshadows the destruction of twentieth-century warfare.

Twain's attitude toward his hero also appears to have changed as he wrote the book. At the outset the narrator is a working-class Yankee, the practical man who gets things done and who has little use for European culture. However, though starting out as an idealist who hopes to reform British society, by the end of the book, he becomes a menace, one who has disdain for those he supposedly wanted to help and who is more ruthless than those of medieval Britain whose power he attacked. At some point too, Twain decided to change the name of the hero, a change that appears to reflect his developing concept of the Yankee. In the draft read before the Military Service Institute in November 1886, the hero had been named Robert or Bob Smith. But Twain's notes indicate that he changed this first to Hank Smith and then to Hank Morgan, a name that critics suggested sounded like sinister figures ranging from the British pirate Henry Morgan, to the wicked Arthurian character Morgan le Fay to the American financier J. P. Morgan. The title Hank assumes—"The Boss"—indeed sounds American, but would have connoted Boss Tweed of Tammany Hall, whose name had become a synonym for political corruption.

Thus, a book that began as a burlesque of medieval romance and a satire on British customs became a critique of much that nineteenth-century America, and Twain himself, had valued. It reflects Twain's concern and ambivalence about industrialization and American society, and such problems as the power of labor unions on the one hand and of monopolies and trusts on the other. In *Connecticut Yankee* belief in progress becomes an illusion, and Arthurian society is ultimately destroyed. While *Connecticut Yankee*, in its account of the contrasting civilizations of Europe and the United States, has affinities with Twain's travel literature, such as *The Innocents Abroad* (1869), its contempt for and distrust of people and its portrait of them as being bound by superstitions and prejudices have affinity with Twain's later pessimistic works like *Pudd'nhead Wilson* (1894) and *The Mysterious Stranger* (published in 1916, after Twain's death) and, to some extent, with the novel that preceded it, *Huckleberry Finn* (1885).

Twain completed the novel by mid-April or mid-May 1889. He sent the manuscript to the poet and critic Edmund C. Stedman. In a report issued on July 7, Stedman made suggestions for changes for consistency of tone and a few concerning propriety, but he praised its "magnificently riotous & rollicking imagination & humor." Comparing it to Twain's earlier historical work, *The Prince and the Pauper*, Stedman said the earlier book "was checkers: this is chess." Stedman was, however, also aware that some would be offended by the book's condemnation of injustices in society and the church. Twain, at his wife's urging, sent it to his friend, author William Dean Howells, in August for further suggestions. As *Connecticut Yankee* became more serious, he thought for a time that he would not publish it at all, and after he decided to go on with it, in a letter to Howells on August 24, 1889, he expressed concern about how critics would respond to it: "I'm not writing for those parties who miscall themselves critics, and I don't care to have them paw the book at all." It would be his "swan-song." his "retirement from literature permanently." For advance publicity, sales prospectuses and circulars describing *Connecticut Yankee* as "a keen and powerful satire on English nobility and royalty, a book that appeals to all true Americans" were sent to agents and prospective buyers in October, and a ten-page excerpt appeared in *The Century Magazine* in November. It was published on December 10, 1889, by Twain's publishing house, Charles L. Webster & Co., and shortly thereafter by Chatto & Windus in London.

Important to the first American and British editions of *Connecticut Yankee* were the 220 illustrations that Daniel Carter Beard (1850–1941) provided. These introduced themes that were not even hinted at in the book, but which made its contemporary relevance more explicit. They delighted Twain. One of the illustrations, for example, presents three scenes: a medieval king and his serf, a plantation owner and a black slave, and a capitalist and one of his factory workers. Beard also drew caricatures of public and historical figures for some of the characters. Merlin, presented by Twain as a "cheap old humbug" and a bore whose oft-repeated tale of Arthur receiving Excalibur from the Lady of the Lake puts his audience to sleep, appears in Beard's illustrations as Tennyson. In the story of the enchanted pigs, the "troublesomest old sow of the lot," depicted with a crown on her head and a diamond ring in her nose, resembles Queen Victoria. The Prince of Wales, the Duke of Clarence, and Kaiser Wilhelm II appear as a trio of "Chuckleheads." Twain described the illustrations as "charming & beautiful" and considered himself lucky to have Beard as his illustrator. Beard's cover design and spine of the book were controversial since he omitted "Connecticut" and gave the book the title *A Yankee in King Arthur's Court*, not to be confused with the title of the British edition, *A Yankee at the Court of King Arthur*. In his autobiography Beard indicated that "the illustrations which so pleased Clemens and delighted people all over the world grievously offended some big advertisers." notably because of some that attacked the Roman Catholic Church. The illustrations were removed from later editions, and according to Beard, his work was "boycotted for many years" by most of the prominent magazines, and, for a time, he "went practically broke."

About a month before the book was published, an article appeared in the November 4 issue of the *New York World* reporting that some people in Philadelphia were charging Twain with plagiarizing the idea for the Yankee's visit to Arthur's Britain. Although other books published shortly before *Connecticut Yankee* were concerned with contemporary people having to confront earlier civilizations (H. Rider Haggard's *King Solomon's Mines* [1885] and *She* [1887]) or with examination of an earlier period from the vantage point of a later (Edward Bellamy's *Looking Backward* [1887]), there were closer parallels to *Connecticut Yankee* in a story published several years earlier. The Philadelphia humorist Charles Heber Clark, who wrote under the name Max Adeler, published a story "Professor Baffin's Adventures" in 1880 and 1881 and republished it again in 1882 as "The Fortunate Island" and again in an abridged version in 1883. In this story, a shipwrecked sociologist, Professor Baffin, discovers a floating island that had broken away from England in King Arthur's days. Like Hank Morgan he attempts to change the society and uses modern inventions to demonstrate the superiority of nineteenth-century civilization. Twain responded to the charges of plagiarism in an article in *The New York World* on January 12, 1890, and dismissed the similarities as coincidental. He did not, however, mention the name of the story and appears to have assumed the charges were about another Adeler story, "An Old Fogey," that had minor similarities to *Connecticut Yankee*. No one has proven that Twain had read Adeler's story, but the correspondences suggest that Adeler's work could have given Twain the idea for *Connecticut Yankee*.

The day the book was published, an interview with Twain appeared in *The New York Times*. In the interview, Twain emphasized the criticism of Britain in the book, although he also praised Dan Beard's caricature of Jay Gould, a contemporary American robber baron, as a slave driver, and this should have alerted readers to the book's relevance to the United States as well. In the interview he emphasized the contemporary relevance of the book in other ways as well: the time was ripe for the book, he maintained, because it suggested the abolition of the monarchy, and Brazil had deposed her emperor, and Portugal and Australia were supposedly about to establish republics. He spoke too of the importance of maintaining a national American literature. Americans, he argued, are overly influenced by foreign literatures, but Americans can not get their views published in Britain: "But if I were to go to England and write down what I think of their monarchical shams, pour out my utter contempt for their pitiful lords and dukes, and preach my sermon, I would not be able to get my views published." He complained about having to "modify and modify my book to suit the English publishers' taste until I really cannot cut it any more." Half his preface was gone from the English edition, he complained, because of "a little playful remark of mine about the divine right of kings." In fact, Andrew Chatto, the English publisher, does not appear to have insisted on changes; suggestions for toning down the introduction to the English edition seem to have come from Twain's own publishing house, Webster & Co., and from Twain himself.

Connecticut Yankee was reviewed at least eleven times in the United States and another eleven in England and once in Australia. In an unsigned review in *The Boston Sunday Herald* (December 15, 1889), Sylvester Baxter (who had agreed to review the book favorably before it was published) observed that the "pages are eloquent with a true American love of freedom, a sympathy with the rights of the common people, and an indignant hatred of oppression of the poor, the lowly and the weak, by the rich, the powerful and the proud." Twain's friend William Dean Howells, in an review in *Harper's Magazine* (January 1890), while noting Twain's "blasting contempt of monarchy and aristocracy," saw parallels between the exploitation of laborers in Arthur's time and those in contemporary

America and observed that Twain's Arthur "has his moments of being as fine and high as the Arthur of Lord Tennyson." Not all American reviewers acted favorably to it: the reviewer in the *Boston Literary World* (February 15, 1890), for example, described it as a "tiresome travesty." British reviewers generally condemned the book. An article in the *Pall Mall Gazette* (December 21, 1889) criticized Twain for using his "undoubted genius" to "vulgarize and defile the Arthurian legend." The *London Daily Telegraph* (January 13, 1890) complained that the book "tries to deface our moral and literary currency by bruising and soiling the image of King Arthur." Its attack on the ideals of King Arthur is "a coarse pandering to that passion for irreverence which is at the basis of a great deal of Yankee wit." Similarly in an article on February 28, 1890, in the *Pall Mall Gazette*, Reginald Brett complained that Twain might have criticized the United States and "leave to us for a short while longer our ideals." a point of view that overlooked the extensive criticism of the United States that the book offered.

Although in a letter of August 15, 1887, to his American publisher, Twain had expressed the hope that he was writing what would be "a 100,000-copy book." its sales were disappointing. It sold only twenty-four thousand copies within six months in the United States, and Webster & Co. was having such financial problems that it was unable to pay Twain anything. It sold poorly in Britain as well, and the British objections to it, probably exacerbated by Beard's illustrations showing Tennyson as Merlin and Queen Victoria as a troublesome old sow, also hurt the sales of Twain's other books there.

The book has been adapted several times for stage and screen, and the adaptations have generally emphasized the comic elements. Twain commissioned a friend Howard Taylor to write a dramatic version of the book, but in a letter to his daughter Clara dated July 21, 1890, he said that Taylor's four-hour reading of the play to him had "bored the very soul out of me" and complained that the play "captured but one side of the Yankee's character—his animal side, his circus side"; Hank had become "a mere boisterous clown." Richard Rogers and Lorenz Hart produced a successful musical version for the stage in 1927 and revised it for a new production in 1943 that was relevant to the war years: the Yankee became an officer in the Navy. Motion picture adaptations of *Connecticut Yankee* appeared in 1921, 1931 (with Will Rogers), 1949 (a musical with Bing Crosby), and 1995 (now entitled "A Young Connecticut Yankee at King Arthur's Court" or "A Kid in King Arthur's Court"). At least nine television productions include versions from the early days of television drama—Studio One in 1952 and Kraft Television Theater in 1954—and productions in 1978 and 1989, with the chief character in the latter being a young African-American girl. Other variants include "A Tennessee Rebel in King Arthur's Court" (a 1960 television version with Tennessee Ernie Ford) and a Disney movie (with live actors) "The Spaceman and King Arthur" (1982; also known as "Unidentified Flying Oddball"). Twain's book also inspired Chuck Jones's highly regarded animated version for television, *A Connecticut Rabbit in King Arthur's Court* (1978; released for video as *Bugs Bunny in King Arthur's Court*).

PRIMARY WORKS

The Innocents Abroad, or the New Pilgrims' Progress. Hartford, CT: American Publishing, 1869; republished in two volumes as *The Innocents Abroad* and *The New Pilgrims Progress*. London: Hotten, 1870; "Awful, Terrible Medieval Romance." *Mark Twain's. Burlesque Autobiography and First Romance*. New York: Sheldon, 1871; London: Hotten, 1871, reprinted from *The Express*. 1870 and later published as "A Medieval Romance." *Mark Twain's Sketches, New and*

Old. Hartford, CT: American Publishing, 1875; *"1601" Conversation, As It Was by the Social Fireside, in the Time of the Tudors*. Cleveland, 1880; *The Prince and the Pauper*. London: Chatto & Windus, 1882; Boston: Osgood, 1882; *Life on the Mississippi*. London: Chatto & Windus, 1883; Hartford, CT: Osgood, 1883; *The Adventures of Huckleberry Finn*. London: Chatto & Windus, 1884; *Adventures of Huckleberry Finn*. New York: Webster, 1885; *A Connecticut Yankee in King Arthur's Court*. New York: Charles L. Webster, 1889; republished in England as *A Yankee at the Court of King Arthur*. London: Chatto & Windus, 1889; "Mark Twain and His Book" (interview), *New York Times*, December 10, 1889, 5; *Pudd'nhead Wilson, A Tale*. London: Chatto &Windus, 1894; *The Tragedy of Pudd'nhead Wilson and the comedy of Those Extraordinary Twins*. Hartford, Conn.: American Publishing, 1894; *Personal Recollections of Joan of Arc by the Sieur Louis de Conte*. New York: Harper, 1896; London: Chatto & Windus, 1896; *The Mysterious Stranger, a Romance*, ed. Albert Bigelow Paine and Frederick A. Duneka. New York & London: Harper, 1916; augmented edition *The Mysterious Stranger and Other Stories*, ed. Paine. New York & London: Harper, 1922; *Mark Twain's Letters*, arranged with comment by Albert Bigelow Paine. New York: Harper & Brothers, 1917; *Mark Twain's Notebook*, ed. Albert Bigelow Paine. New York: Harper & Brothers, 1935; *Mark Twain to Mrs. Fairbanks*, ed. Dixon Wecter. San Marino, CA: Huntington Library, 1949; *Mark Twain-Howells Letters*, 2 vols., ed. Henry Nash Smith and William M. Gibson. Cambridge, MA: Harvard University Press, 1960; *Mark Twain's Letters to His Publishers, 1867–1894*, ed. Hamlin Hill. Berkeley: University of California Press, 1967; *Mark Twain's Notebooks & Journals*. Vol. 2, 1877–1883, ed. Frederick Anderson and Bernard L. Stein. Berkeley: University of California Press, 1975. Vol. 3, 1883–1891, ed. Robert Pack Browning, Michael B. Frank, and Lin Salamo. Berkeley: University of California Press, 1979.

Editions

A Connecticut Yankee in King Arthur's Court. New York: Harper & Row, 1917; *A Connecticut Yankee in King Arthur's Court*. New York: Modern Library, 1949; *A Connecticut Yankee in King Arthur's Court: A Facsimile of the First Edition*, introduction and bibliography by Hamlin Hill. San Francisco: Chandler, 1963; *A Connecticut Yankee in King Arthur's Court*, ed. Bernard L. Stein, introduction by Henry Nash Smith. Published for the Iowa Center for Textual Studies by the University of California Press. Berkeley: University of California Press, 1979; *A Connecticut Yankee in King Arthur's Court: An Authoritative Text, Backgrounds and Sources, Composition and Publication*, ed. Allison R. Ensor. New York: Norton, 1982; *Historical Romances: The Prince and the Pauper, A Connecticut Yankee in King Arthur's Court, Personal Recollections of Joan of Arc*. New York: Library of America, 1994; *A Connecticut Yankee in King Arthur's Court*, foreword by Shelley Fisher Fishkin, introduction by Kurt Vonnegut, Jr., and afterword by Louis J. Budd, illustrations by Daniel Carter Beard. The Oxford Mark Twain. New York: Oxford University Press, 1996; *A Connecticut Yankee in King Arthur's Court*. Illustrations by Daniel Carter Beard. New York: Modern Library, 2001; *A Connecticut Yankee in King Arthur's Court*, ed. Bernard L. Stein, illustrations by Daniel Carter Beard. Berkeley: University of California Press, 2002.

Papers

The major collections of Clemens's papers are at the Bancroft Library, University of California at Berkeley; the Beinecke Library, Yale University; The New York Public Library; the Mark Twain Memorial and Stowe-Day Foundation, Hartford, Connecticut; the Library of Congress; The Houghton Library, Harvard University; the Buffalo and Erie County Public Library; The Harry Ransom Humanities Research Center, University of Texas, Austin; the Mark Twain Museum, Hannibal, Missouri; the Vassar College Library; the Alderman Library, University of Virginia; the Center for Mark Twain Studies at Quarry Farm, Elmira College, New York.

SECONDARY SOURCES

Anderson, Frederick, ed. *Mark Twain: The Critical Heritage*. New York: Barnes & Noble, 1971; Auerbach, Erich. *Mimesis: The Representation of Reality in Western Literature*, trans. Willard Trask. Princeton, NJ: Princeton University Press, 1953. Reprint, New York: Doubleday Anchor Books, 1957; Baetzhold, Howard G. "'The Autobiography of Sir Robert Smith of Camelot': Mark Twain's Original Plan for *A Connecticut Yankee*." *American Literature* 32 (1960–1961): 456–61; ———. "The Course of Composition of *A Connecticut Yankee*: A Reinterpretation." *American Literature* 33 (1961–1962): 195–214; ———. "Mark Twain: England's Advocate." *American Literature* 28 (1956–1957): 328–46; ———. *Mark Twain and John Bull: The British Connection*. Bloomington: Indiana University Press, 1970; ———. "'Well, My Book Is Written—Let It Go . . .': The Making of *A Connecticut Yankee in King Arthur's Court*." In *Biographies of Books: The Compositional Histories of Notable American Writings*, ed. James Barbour and Tom Quirk, 41–77.Columbia: University of Missouri Press, 1996; Beard, Dan. *Hardly a Man Is Now Alive: The Autobiography of Dan Beard*. New York: Doubleday, 1939; Bellamy, Gladys. *Mark Twain as a Literary Artist*. Norman: University of Oklahoma Press, 1950; Chandler, Alice. *A Dream of Order: The Medieval Ideal in Nineteenth-Century English Literature*. Lincoln: University of Nebraska Press, 1970; Clemens, Clara. *My Father, Mark Twain*. New York: Harper, 1931; David, Beverly R. "The Unexpurgated *A Connecticut Yankee*: Mark Twain and His Illustrator, Daniel Carter Beard." *Prospects* 1 (1975): 98–117; David, Beverly R., and Ray Sapirstein. "Reading the Illustrations in *A Connecticut Yankee*." In *A Connecticut Yankee in King Arthur's Court*. New York; Oxford University Press, 1996; Emerson, Everett. *The Authentic Mark Twain: A Literary Biography of Samuel L. Clemens*. Philadelphia: University of Pennsylvania Press, 1984; ———. *Mark Twain: A Literary Life*. Philadelphia: University of Pennsylvania Press, 2000; Foster, Edward. "*A Connecticut Yankee* Anticipated by Max Adeler's *Fortunate Island*." *Ball State University Forum* 9, no. 4 (1968): 73–76; Fulton, Joe B. *Mark Twain in the Margins: The Quarry Farm Marginalia and "A Connecticut Yankee in King Arthur's Court."* Studies in American Literary Realism and Naturalism. Tuscaloosa: University of Alabama Press, 2000; Girouard, Mark. *The Return to Camelot: Chivalry and the English Gentleman*. New Haven, CT: Yale University Press, 1981; Goodman, Jennifer R. *The Legend of Arthur in British and American Literature*. Boston: Twayne, 1988; Gribben, Alan. "'The Master Hand of Old Malory': Mark Twain's Acquaintance with *Le Morte d'Arthur*." *English Language Notes* 16 (1978): 32–40; Hansen, Chadwick. "The Once and Future Boss: Mark Twain's Yankee." *Nineteenth-Century Fiction* 28 (1973): 62–73; Harnsberger, Caroline Thomas. *Mark Twain, Family Man*. New York: Citadel Press, 1960; Hoben, John B. "Mark Twain's *A Connecticut Yankee*: A Genetic Study." *American Literature* 18 (1946–1947): 197–218; Holmes, Charles S. "*A Connecticut Yankee in King Arthur's Court*: Mark Twain's Fable of Uncertainty." *South Atlantic Quarterly* 61 (1962): 462–72; Kaplan, Justin. *Mark Twain and His World*. New York: Simon and Schuster, 1974; ———. *Mr. Clemens and Mark Twain: A Biography*. New York: Simon and Schuster, 1966; Kennedy, Edward Donald. "Introduction." In *King Arthur: A Casebook*. New York: Garland, 1996. Reprint, New York: Routledge, 2002; Ketterer, David. "'The Fortunate Island' by Max Adeler: Its Publication History and *A Connecticut Yankee*." *Mark Twain Journal* 29, no. 2 (1991): 28–32; ———. "'Professor Baffin's Adventures' by Max Adeler: The Inspiration for *A Connecticut Yankee in King Arthur's Court*?" *Mark Twain Journal* 24, no. 1 (1986): 24–34; Knight, Stephen. *Arthurian Literature and Society*. New York: St. Martin's Press, 1983; Kordecki, Lesley C. "Twain's Critique of Malory's Romance: *Forma tractandi* and *A Connecticut Yankee*." *Nineteenth-Century Literature* 41 (1986): 329–48; Kruse, Horst H. "Literary Old Offenders: Mark Twain, John Quill, Max Adeler, and Their Plagiarism Duels." *Mark Twain Journal* 29, no. 2 (1991): 10–27; ———. "Mark Twain's *A Connecticut Yankee*: Reconsiderations and Revisions." *American Literature* 62 (1990): 464–83; Lupack, Alan. "A Bibliography of Critical Studies of Mark Twain's *A Connecticut Yankee in King Arthur's Court*," updated by Anne Zanzuchi. An *Arthuriana*/Camelot Project Bibliography, available at http://www.lib.

rochester.edu/camelot/acpbibs/twainbib.htm; ———. "The Figure of King Arthur in America." In *King Arthur's Modern Return*, ed. Debra N. Mancoff. New York: Garland, 1998; Lupack, Alan, and Barbara Tepa Lupack. *King Arthur in America*. Cambridge: D. S. Brewer, 1999; Miller, Robert Keith. *Mark Twain*. New York: Frederick Ungar, 1983; Rasmussen, R. Kent. *Mark Twain A to Z: The Essential Reference to His Life and Writings*. New York: Facts on File, 1995; Smith, Henry Nash. *Mark Twain: The Development of a Writer*. Cambridge, MA: Belknap Press, 1962; ———. *Mark Twain's Fable of Progress: Political and Economic Ideas in "A Connecticut Yankee."* New Brunswick, NJ: Rutgers University Press, 1964; Taylor, Beverly, and Elisabeth Brewer. *The Return of King Arthur: British and American Arthurian Literature since 1900 [i.e., 1800]*. Cambridge: D. S. Brewer, 1983; Ward, Geoffrey C., and Dayton Duncan. *Mark Twain*, based on a documentary film directed by Ken Burns. New York: Alfred A. Knopf, 2001; Welland, Dennis. *Mark Twain in England*. London: Chatto & Windus, 1978; Williams, James D. "Revision and Intention in Mark Twain's *Connecticut Yankee*." *American Literature* 36 (1964–1965): 288–97; Wilson, Robert H. "Malory in the *Connecticut Yankee*." *University of Texas Studies in English* 27 (1948): 188–205.

EDWARD DONALD KENNEDY

EDWIN ARLINGTON ROBINSON

(December 22, 1869–April 6, 1935)

Many people are familiar with Edwin Arlington Robinson through two of his frequently anthologized poems: "Richard Cory" (the man who was admired about the town, yet who "one calm summer night,/Went home and put a bullet through his head" [15–16]), which is occasionally set in contrast with songwriter Paul Simon's version of the same story, and, less frequently, "Miniver Cheevy" (the man who "loved the days of old" [5] and "dreamed of Thebes and Camelot" [11]). But this Maine poet also published three poems significant to Arthurian studies: *Merlin* (1915), *Lancelot* (1920), and *Tristram* (1927). The final poem in the trilogy became a national bestseller, largely because the Literary Guild of America selected it as a monthly selection, and won the author his third Pulitzer Prize.

The critics seem to agree that Robinson's poetry, in general, reflects what his contemporary biographer Mark Van Doren refers to as his "brooding over the fundamental perplexities of a life wherein most good things are fragile and soon gone" (25). Robinson achieves this mood in his writing by focusing on individuals and their relationships with each other and with society instead of writing about other themes that were more common in the late nineteenth and early twentieth centuries. Blending the poetry of England and New England, the romantics and the realists, Robinson generally provides a transition between those periods. In his *Critical Introduction* (1968) to the poet, Wallace Anderson specifically describes Robinson as providing a transition between the great Civil War poets, which include Henry Wadsworth Longfellow, Ralph Waldo Emerson, and Walt Whitman (all of whom, Anderson observes, were dead by 1892, when Robinson was first being published) and the new poets of the twentieth century—poets such as Carl Sandburg, Edgar Lee Masters, T. S. Eliot, Robert Frost, and William Carlos Williams. According to Robinson's contemporary, Ben Ray Redman, in his 1928 book on the author, Robinson debuted during what can be seen, in retrospect, as basically "a barren period" between these two groups of writers (31), while Edwin Fussell writing in

1954 about *The Literary Background of a Traditional Poet* sees Robinson as having been "a forerunner" to greater poets such as Eliot and Ezra Pound (2). In a manner similar to Frost, yet quite unlike other twentieth-century poets, Robinson was most comfortable putting his insights regarding modern people and modern life into traditional verse forms like the sonnet and the ballad. For his longer poems, however, Redman observes, Robinson writes quite comfortably in "English heroic blank verse" (85), a format certainly appropriate for the trilogy. On the occasion of Robinson's fiftieth birthday, *The Outlook* summed up his contribution to literature by observing that he "breaks away from those worn-out symbols of expression which have lost the power to transmit thought and emotion to the modern mind" (quoted in Anderson, 20). In the process, Robinson leads the way to a new consideration of the human condition, which is a prevalent thread in Robinson's poetry.

Edwin Arlington Robinson was born December 22, 1869, to Edward and Mary Elizabeth Palmer Robinson of Head Tide, Maine, one of three boys. The following year the family moved to Gardiner, Maine, where Robinson spent the next twenty-seven years of his life. When he was seventeen, he was introduced to English blank verse at a poetry club sponsored by Caroline Davenport Swan. Three years later, March 29, 1890, Robinson saw his first poem, "Thalia," published in *The Reporter Monthly* of Gardiner. In 1897, after a brief period at Harvard as a special student, he moved to New York, where his first collection of poems, *The Children of the Night* (which includes "Richard Cory"), was published. Later, in 1905, President Theodore Roosevelt wrote a review of the book, which appeared in the August 12 issue of *The Outlook* and led to the book's being reprinted that October. Another result of Roosevelt's attention to the poet was a job given to Robinson as an agent in the New York Custom House, a position he held until 1909 when Roosevelt left office. From 1906 to 1913, Robinson took a break from writing poetry to focus on writing prose plays. His return to poetry resulted in the 1916 publication of *The Man Against the Sky* collection and the first real critical acceptance of his work, which culminated in *The New York Times Review of Books*'s salutation of his fiftieth birthday in its December 21, 1919, issue.

Meanwhile, in 1917 Robinson published the first work in his Arthurian trilogy—*Merlin*. The story of *Merlin* opens with a rumor that Merlin, after having been gone for ten years, has returned from his adventure with Vivian at Broceliande in Brittany, a place where Merlin had previously foretold that he would be buried alive. So Gawaine and Dagonet feel that his return does not bode well for Camelot. Part II reveals the current situation at Camelot: the queen has gone to the nunnery, Lancelot has disappeared, and the king is now wasting away, a shadow of his former self. Everything has happened just as Merlin had prophesied it would. Sir Kay reveals that Modred and Agravaine have been stirring things up. Part III presents a lonely Arthur who is pacing the floor when Merlin arrives. Arthur tries to talk Merlin out of returning to Brittany and Vivian. Merlin, however, turns the talk back to Arthur, warning him to beware of fawning enemies and to see to the health of the kingdom lest he lose that kingdom. He reminds Arthur that it is impossible to undo what has been done (Lancelot and Guinevere); instead, the king must focus on the perilous siege that is to come. After Merlin heads off to bed, Arthur is alone with his thoughts and his memories in the cold hours before dawn.

Arthur finally realizes in Part IV that Vivian means more to Merlin that he does. Conversely, Vivian fears the lure of Camelot will keep Merlin from returning to her. But Merlin does return to her, and he remembers back ten years to his first arrival at her gate: Broceliande is a beautiful place in the springtime, filled with cherry blossoms; Vivian, fittingly dressed all in green, invites him into her home so that he might teach her all he knows. Part V continues the memory of Merlin's sojourn at Broceliande. They stay there alone in their happiness, teacher and pupil (in some ways, at times, trading those roles), for ten years, until Dagonet comes at the king's request to bring Merlin back to Camelot. Part VI brings the story back to the present, as Merlin shares with Vivian information about his trip to Camelot. Vivian worries he will find life too boring with her; Merlin, in contrast, finds he is miserable unless she is near him. With time, however, he becomes more melancholy, so Vivian asks for a story, and he tells Arthur's story emphasizing the transgression that was tearing the kingdom apart. Vivian responds coldly to the story, dismissing Merlin's message, causing a distraught Merlin to see another side of her. He finally realizes that he is too old for Vivian, and he must leave her although he loves her still. He must return to Camelot.

The final section of the poem takes the action back near Camelot at Merlin's Rock. Bedivere tries to convince Gawaine to change the king's mind about Lancelot, but Gawaine cannot forgive Lancelot for slaying Gawaine's two brothers and stands firm in his desire for revenge. Dagonet arrives at the rock as Gawaine and Bedivere head off for the court, and he ruminates on what might have been. Merlin walks up and startles him, having passed Gawaine and Bedivere unrecognized. Merlin and Dagonet speak of what has passed, of the knights who have unsuccessfully sought the grail, of the events that have happened since those few returned. Finally, as the sun sets and the wind begins rising, they slowly make their way down the hill to the darkness that was Camelot.

Merlin was followed in 1920 by the second volume of the trilogy—*Lancelot,* which fills in some of the background of the action depicted in the first volume. *Lancelot* opens with Gawaine and Lancelot in the king's garden talking about Lancelot's pending trip south. Merlin has already left the kingdom for his adventure with Vivian at Broceliande. The knights have returned from their quest for the Holy Grail; apparently, at this point only Gawaine has actually seen anything. Lancelot reveals that he is not leaving Camelot because of Gawaine, but because of Modred and Agravaine, who have been spreading stories about the court. Guinevere arrives, and Gawaine leaves them alone to say their good-byes. Part II depicts Guinevere and Lancelot in a heart-wrenching discussion of their situation. Guinevere vows that she will never become a curse on Lancelot or his conscious, nor a burden for him to bear. She kisses Lancelot, informs him the king is off that evening to go hunting, and asks if he would come to her that evening; then she disappears. Part III reveals Lancelot alone, filled with regret and remorse for all that has happened. He finally realizes that exile is the only viable option remaining for him, so he starts to leave Camelot but hesitates, after seeing visions of Galahad and Guinevere.

In Part IV the king, feigning illness, returns to Camelot. Bedivere and Gawaine join him in his inner chamber for the rest of the night. As morning nears, Gawaine laments his missed opportunity to persuade Lancelot to leave the evening before while he and Lancelot had been talking in the garden. When Arthur recognizes his knights' concern for him, he tries to reassure them, conceding that Merlin had been right about the queen. He also acknowledges the appropriate punishment under the laws he had made requires that the queen be burned at the stake. The story continues in Part V as Gawaine listens trembling while the king breaks down in pain. The loud noise of battle fills the halls, coming nearer to the room where they wait. Sir Lucan bursts in with the news that Lancelot has just rescued the queen from the fire. Arthur sends the others away, leaving him and Gawaine alone. Arthur has a vision of Guinevere and Lancelot safe at Joyous Gard, giving him a moment of thankfulness that she escaped. As his attention returns to Gawaine, Arthur recognizes the Round Table is now a wreck.

Angry at the death of his brothers, Gawaine goads Arthur to attack Joyous Gard in Part VI, insisting there can be no peace until either Gawaine, Lancelot, or Arthur is dead. On the ramparts of Joyous Gard, Bors questions Lancelot as they look down on the resulting carnage, asking how long he will let the battle continue when he should be out seeking "The Light" (403) that is neither Rome nor Camelot. Bors leaves and Guinevere comes up; Lancelot asks her if they can be happy if he were to kill both Arthur and Gawaine. She responds that he could easily end the carnage if he would just signal for peace, and she questions why he does not do so before more men are slain. The next day dawns with a downpour that cleanses the battlefield; Arthur's army is gone, replaced by three people who approach the gate. One of them is the bishop of Rochester, who brings a letter from the king requesting the return of the queen within the next week; if she returns, the king will be merciful. When Lancelot informs Guinevere she will be returning to Camelot, she faints.

It is still raining as Part VII begins. Lancelot sits alone with his thoughts, including the fact that he let Gawaine and the king live, although many others died in the process. Lancelot now fears Modred most of all and regrets that he did not (or was not able to) slay him. When Guinevere joins him by the fire, he tries to reassure her. Instead she chastises him for rescuing her from the fire in the first place; if he had let things be, all the troubles would now be over. Lancelot finally recognizes that all that has happened, all the deaths, all the desperation, has occurred because their "world is dying, / As Merlin said it would" (416). Although Guinevere admits she could never return to Camelot and Arthur after all that has happened, in seven days, Lancelot brings her back to Camelot, then leaves. Gawaine, however, still seeks revenge; so when Lancelot and his group of knights set sail for Bayonne, the king's army led by Gawaine soon follows. This action sets the stage for Part VIII, which opens with war once again waging outside Benwick, where Lancelot has repaired. Suddenly the siege stops—the king and Gawaine have called off the battle, because the army needs to return to Camelot; Modred has seized his opportunity to make trouble while they have been gone. Lancelot goes to see Gawaine, who has been mortally wounded in their last battle. Gawaine is lamenting the way things have turned out, revealing that the queen is hiding in London in the Tower because things have become so bad back in Britain. Lancelot tries to calm him and stays with Gawaine until he dies.

In the final section, Lancelot takes what is left of his army and heads for the white cliffs of Dover to help the king one last time, but they arrive too late. Modred and Arthur have slain each other in their battle, and the lone survivor, Bedivere, has slipped away to some far-off hermitage and his eventual death. So Lancelot rides off into the west, with only his memories surrounding him, seeking Guinevere, who has taken refuge in the west with the nuns of Almesbury. Guinevere asks his forgiveness for coming between him and the Light, and sends him on his way. Dazed, he leaves her, stopping to watch some reapers at work. Gazing down at the new world before him that was so different from the world he had known, he finally rides off into the night, "led by the living Voice / That would not give him peace . . . / out of a world / That was not his, or the King's" (448). The poem ends with Lancelot disappearing into the darkness out of which "came the Light" (449).

The poet himself indicated that he had written *Merlin* in anticipation of *Lancelot,* intending the former to complement the incompleteness of the latter; therefore, he advocated that the two poems be read together in order for the reader to possess the same power as the seer. Readers found it easier to do so when both poems were published in

1921 in *Collected Poems*, which includes *The Man Against the Sky, The Children of the Night, Captain Craig, The Town Down the River, The Three Taverns* and *Avon's Harvest* as well as *Merlin* and *Lancelot*. In 1922 Robinson received the Pulitzer Prize for this volume of *Collected Poems*; this same year Yale awarded him an honorary doctorate of literature degree. His success was repeated in 1924, when he received his second Pulitzer Prize for *The Man Who Died Twice,* then another doctorate of literature degree from Bowdoin in 1925.

His third Pulitzer Prize was awarded in 1927 for *Tristram,* his only book to become a national bestseller. *Tristram,* the third poem in the Arthurian trilogy, opens in Brittany, where we learn that Isolt of Brittany, now eighteen years old, loves Tristram. But Tristram loves Isolt of Ireland, who in Part II of the poem is forced to marry his uncle, King Mark of Cornwall, for an alliance. Just after the wedding at Tintagel, Tristram and Isolt of Ireland confess their love for each in Part III. Andred, however, overhears their tryst; Tristram chases after him and throws him over the parapet onto the rocks of Cornwall's bay, although Andred survives to cause more trouble later. When King Mark learns of his nephew's treachery, he banishes Tristram from Cornwall.

With Gouvernail's assistance, Tristram escapes from Cornwall, only to fall ill in Part IV from traveling in the cold and rainy weather. He ends up in Queen Morgan's home, where she nurses him back to health. When he is better, he leaves with Gouvernail and slowly makes his way back to Brittany, arriving there just in time to save the country from Griffon, "the giant scourge of Brittany" (84) in Part V. While recovering in Brittany from his battle wounds, Tristram feels compassion for this other Isolt and eventually marries her. They live together happily for two years until one of King Arthur's barges comes sailing in from the north. The barge is carrying Gawaine, who has come to invite Tristram to Camelot so Arthur can make him a knight of the Round Table. In Part VI while they are waiting to sail, Gawaine becomes enamored of Isolt's fairness and innocence. Isolt realizes that this trip, which is so important to her husband, will ultimately mean his death at King Mark's hands. Gawaine tries to allay her fears by assuring her that Mark is currently in prison for his attempt to send Tristram to fight the Saracens and be killed. Gawaine and Tristram eventually set sail for Camelot, with a first stop at Joyous Gard, Lancelot's home.

Meanwhile, in Part VII, Isolt of Ireland has become more disappointed with her marriage to Mark, and she travels with Guinevere to Joyous Gard, where Isolt catches up with Tristram. Their time apart melts away; it is as if they had never been separated. They spend several months together happily before Gawaine returns in Part VIII with the news that Mark has escaped. Mark captures his queen and sets sail with her to Cornwall. Tristram falls into a mad fit that lasts a week before Gawaine travels on to Camelot with Brangwaine. Tristram remains at Joyous Gard for another month waiting for word about Isolt in Cornwall, when a letter arrives for him from Morgan, who encourages him to return to Cornwall to save Isolt, whose health has been foundering since her abduction. He returns to Cornwall, finds Isolt and then is discovered lying in her arms by Andred who stabs them both with a knife. Mark walks in with Gouvernail, scrutinizes the scene, starts to strangle Andred for his deed, then finds the knife and heaves it over the parapet into the sea. The scene of the final section then shifts back to Brittany and the other Isolt. Gouvernail arrives with the news of Tristram's death, confirming what in her heart she had always known would happen. The story ends with her standing alone on the edge of the water watching the white birds flying while the sunlight flashes white on the sea.

The final section of Robinson's life was much less dramatic. The National Institute of Arts and Letters awarded Robinson a gold medal in 1929, his last major recognition, as the poems published after *Tristram* were not well received. An exception can be found in Redman's 1928 biography of the poet, in which Redman describes Robinson's poetry as altering reality from what is beautiful into what is bizarre. Robinson applies this principle of transmutation to all of his works, including those dealing with the Arthurian legend in which, according to Redman, he accurately depicts human types, much as "a shrewd doctor of souls, a sharp psychologist" would as he transports his characters into a territory he has created, setting them down "within the confines of his own subjective universe . . . in a world fraught with infinite suggestions and myriad romantic implications" (25). According to Redman, Robinson developed "an indirect, oblique approach that has since become as characteristic of him as his signature; a technique of poetic narration, description or dramatization not dissimilar to the method that Conrad elaborated in prose" (40). This indirect method using understatement instead of overstatement creates, for most twentieth-century critics, "the drama and the haunting atmosphere which pervades the whole" and gives Robinson's poetry its relevance (41). Robinson died in April 1935 from cancer, bringing a long and significant career to a close.

Significant critical reception of Robinson's Arthurian literature did not begin until about twenty years after his death. While examining *The Literary Background of a Traditional Poet* in 1954, Edwin Fussell finds similarities to Shakespeare in passages in Robinson's poems: for example, *Merlin* echoes *Hamlet*'s rejoinder to Horatio ("There are more things in heaven and earth, Horatio / Than are dreamt of in your philosophy"), while Fussell locates for the reader several passages from *King Lear* that are blended in *Lancelot* (60–62). Coincidentally, in "Three Reviews," Conrad Aiken describes Robinson as having the eye of a dramatist in his use of action while also seeing evidence of Henry James's style in Robinson's characterizations, although Aiken also describes Robinson's heroes as thinkers and feelers, not "men of action" like they would be in James's stories (27). In addition, Fussell subsequently observes that "Miltonic devices and patterns" appear along with the Shakespearean stylistic influences in *Tristram* (69), while classical allusions pervade all three poems. In a simpler analysis in his 1968 biography of the poet, Hoyt Franchere simply notes that *Merlin* and *Tristram* contain "many lyrical passages" (94), which would connect the poet to his predecessors.

Looking beyond the background of and influences on the poems, Fussell observes that Robinson's poetry primarily "deals with the opposition of what are supposed to be masculine and feminine characteristics; the real concern is symbolic, with the feminine nature symbolizing a wide range of attitudes, sympathy, tenderness, humility, sacrifice, selflessness, imagination, charm" (75). For example, in *Merlin,* Robinson creates a "woman, who, together with the light that Galahad found, is yet to light the world" (*Collected Poems*, 307); Fussell notes that Robinson always indicated that he intended this statement from the poem be taken "quite literally" (75). In "Three Reviews," Aiken comments that Robinson "particularly excels in his portraits of women" (26). Expanding on this idea, Nathan Comfort Starr's 1969 essay on "The Transformation of Merlin" addresses the originality of Vivian as "a believable and intelligently conceived woman," not at all comparable to Alfred, Lord Tennyson's "vulgar wanton" or Sir Thomas Malory's "ambitious amateur in magic," but a capable, even fascinating individual who actually is seeking Merlin's wisdom instead of his incantations (106); this change in the traditional perspective makes their relationship even more authentic thereby removing the mythology that had previously underscored the legend. In return for Merlin's knowledge, Starr logically asserts, Vivian provides the magician with the intellectual stimulation he has been craving, making the portrayal of their relationship more innovative and dynamic than previous depictions had been.

Starr is not the only critic to be impressed with the poet's innovations in *Merlin*. In his 1967 book titled *A Poetry of the Act*, W. R. Robinson describes Robinson's poetic vision as one centered on man's inability to really understand the events going on around him. The poet strives to create a new relationship between the mind and the soul when he has the protagonist of *Merlin* say, "I saw too much when I saw Camelot . . . / On Fate there is no vengeance, even for God" (297). According to Robinson the critic, Merlin possesses "a seer's power to know; but to know, finally and completely, is to understand that one is not outside of, but inextricably involved in, what is. The seer sees only what fate permits him to see and is just another instrument in the unfathomable progression and reach of events" (68–69). Merlin, who had believed he stood safely outside life, aloofly surveying it, finally realizes in the end, according to the critic, that "he has been caught in the web from the very beginning. He has been fate and time's fool, a tool of reality" (69). These observations would mesh with what Robinson the poet saw as the role of Merlin the character and *Merlin* the poem, which he specifically said he wrote in anticipation of *Lancelot,* intending the former to complement the incompleteness of the latter; when taken together the two books provide the reader with the same power as the seer.

Understanding and analyzing Robinson's characters becomes important to the critics of his poetry, since so many of Robinson's other poems deal with telling stories about characters he has met; this type of analysis is key in the Arthurian poems because of the poems' focus on relating the motivations of the characters for their well-known actions. Ellsworth Barnard's *Critical Study* (1977) of Robinson commends the uniqueness of the poet's Arthurian characters, especially when those characters are compared with medieval models upon which they are based. The most significant difference is that Robinson's characters are not static; they change in response to both their circumstances and the events in which they find themselves entangled. In the 1973 article "A Grave and Solitary Voice," Irving Howe describes both of the poems *Merlin* and *Lancelot* as portraying "profound explorations of human suffering," thereby providing what he sees as a sharp contrast to Tennyson's *Idylls of the Kings*, which Howe envisions as "mainly a pictorial representation of waxen figures, beautiful in the way a tapestry might be but not very gripping as drama" (125). According to Howe, Robinson's Guinevere and Lancelot differ significantly from Tennyson's characters by being "errant human beings separated from us only by costume and time; his Merlin is an aging man of worldly power and some wisdom who finds himself drawn to the temptations of private life" (125).

In fact, the general critical consensus today praises the contemporariness of the characters in the Arthurian poems to Robinson's time. For example, in his 1968 biography of the poet, Franchere acknowledges the deep effect World War I had on the poet. Robinson apparently considered the war to be "the beginning of the end for a civilization" (119); the critics overall agree that idea definitely appears as one of the major themes underlying the poems in the trilogy. In his 1985 article "*Merlin*: E. A. Robinson's Debt to Emerson," Owen Gilman describes Robinson as striving "to broaden the context of life" for a generation weary, even hopeless, after confronting the horrors of war (140). Along with Gilman, Louis Coxe, who wrote about Robinson in *The Life of Poetry* (1969), also finds "the Emersonian ambience" in Robinson's poems as the poet "conveys a sense of authenticity, of plain wisdom about things that matter" (11, 12–13); this is true even in his storytelling about events from the distant past. Starr echoes these assessments in his 1969 article about "The Transformation of Merlin" while describing Robinson's characters as "moderns ... easily recognizable as parts of our own experience" (112), indicating readers can still connect to the poems and their characters two and a half wars later.

Providing contrast to the prevailing point of view regarding Robinson's poetry, or at least his Arthurian poems, in his 1984 article titled "The Idealist *in Extremis*" Hyatt H. Waggoner sees the Arthurian legend poems as being the worst examples of the Robinson canon, although he concedes the poet "does bring grief and despair to quintessential expression in the concluding lines of *Tristram*" (94), which leaves Isolt of Brittany staring out at the sea. Waggoner considers Robinson's Arthurian poems as obscure, wordy, and tedious, an evaluation with which James Dickey, who finds Robinson's writing in severe need of editing, would concur. Waggoner describes the poet's technique as "playing solitaire and hoping the game might last as long as possible ... using words in these poems not to reveal but to delay or obscure meaning" (94), making the poems, at least for Waggoner, "'realistic' without seeming 'real'" (97). This point of view regarding Robinson, however, appears to be in the minority.

More often the critics of the latter part of the twentieth century spend their time examining the many themes found in the poems. In his 1964 article "A Poet of Continuing Relevance," Denis Donoghue notes that Robinson also "put great stock in the idea of vision and action"; in fact, he finds that another major theme in the poems is "the disproportion between the two, the gap between what one can see and what one can realize in action" (30). According to Donoghue, Robinson pushes the reader to recognize this dichotomy and its significance in order to understand the poems. As an example, in *Merlin* Vivian says, "Like you, I saw too much; and unlike you / I made no kingdom out of what I saw." Donoghue sums up this passage with an observation that the people in these poems ultimately end up frustrated because they "see too much, or else they see it too late [and] vision and action do not synchronize" (30). The critic W. R. Robinson sees this dichotomy as part of the age-old "antagonism between the mystical inner reality and society" (83), which appears most clearly in a general form at the end of *Lancelot* where the antagonism includes personal as well as group relationships as Lancelot, in the last ten lines of the poem, rides out of the world. This image is evocative of Robinson's image of man as "alienated" from the rest of society (an image that the poet had earlier compressed into "Richard Cory").

For Robinson, however, man is not always alienated, and another of the major concerns in his Arthurian poems reflects the relationship between man and woman that some of the critics see as reflecting events occurring in the poet's own life, as his love was frequently unrequited. The romantic relationship takes on varying forms in the three poems. For instance, according to the critic W. R. Robinson, in *Tristram*, "love is not passionately proclaimed but cautiously assessed" (137), as the poet explores the effects of a love triangle between Tristram and the two Isolts. In fact, as Donoghue notes, in these long narratives "love is often a cross for hero and heroine to bear, but it is sometimes more than that" (39). For example, in *Tristram*, Donoghue explains that when Isolt "speaks of her love [as], 'larger than all time and all places,' she contrasts it with the normal temporal loves in which the violence is subdued to a puny order" (40). Donoghue sees this contrast as Isolt's theme, one version of Robinson's formula that "cut[s] down to size the passions ... and their justification" (40).

This kind of representation of passion, according to Donoghue, is where Robinson at his thematic best can be found—in his dramatization of the problems of personal ethics, which some poets see "as the conflict between reason and passion, others as that between authority and the self" (40). Robinson's long poems offer to the reader a kind of resolution of these conflicts. First, as Donoghue reminds his readers, *Merlin* ends with the darkness descending over Camelot; into that darkness comes Merlin's vision of "two fires that are to light the world" (314). Then *Lancelot* ends with the hero conflicted about his destiny, since Guinevere has refused to go with him, and he is no longer certain he will ever find the Grail, yet he eventually rides off alone seeking the light. Finally, in *Tristram* Isolt lives alone with her dreams after the hero's death. According to Donoghue, "in the short poems, the poems of circumstance, there was often no way out. The Arthurian legends, halfway between time and eternity, gave him a visionary gleam that he could not find on earth and would not posit there. That was why he needed them" (52). And that is why readers still read them.

Although Robinson's subject matter and philosophical stance is considerably different from his predecessors', his form is persistently traditional. Critic Nancy Carol Joyner, among others, considers him in her 1980 article "What Ever Happened to *Tristram*?" as one of America's greatest practitioners of both the sonnet and the dramatic monologue, the dominant verse forms of his shorter poems. Critics in general see Robinson's poetry, as Redman so eloquently explains, as "the product of a thoughtful, enveloping, deeply penetrating mind, that must at times achieve expression in unfamiliar terms and patterns, because it has traveled much alone" (95). In all of his poems, both the long and the short, but especially in the poems considered here, Robinson creates biographies, delving into the soul of his characters as he attempts to bond them to his readers by using both humor and sympathy in his portrayals of those characters. In the process, he interprets existence, presents relationships of human beings with others and with the universe, all while expressing himself using poetic language that puts him on a level with his contemporaries and his predecessors. Redman sums up Robinson's significance and influence by describing him as "less egocentric and less subjective that any other poet of his generation," then going on to assert that "he has, more truly than any other, given us a whole world of his own making" (95), which makes Robinson a poet worthy of consideration in the twenty-first century.

PRIMARY WORKS

"Thalia." *The Reporter Monthly*, March 29, 1890; Virgil, "The Galley Race." from Book V of the *Aeneid*, trans. Robinson. *The Reporter Monthly*, May 31, 1890; Five poems. *The Harvard Advocate*, 1891–1893; *The Torrent and the Night Before*. Cambridge, MA: privately printed, 1896; *The Children of the Night*. Boston: Richard J. Badger, 1897; *Captain Craig*. New York: Houghton Mifflin, 1902; London: A. P. Watt, 1902; *The Town Down the River*. New York: Scribner, 1910; *Van Zorn*. New York: Macmillan, 1914; *The Porcupine*. New York: Macmillan, 1915; *The Man Against the Sky*. New York: Macmillan, 1916; *Merlin*. New York: Macmillan, 1917; *Lancelot*. New York: Thomas Seltzer, 1920; *The Three Taverns*. New York: Macmillan, 1920; *Avon's Harvest*. New York: Macmillan, 1921; *Roman Bartholow*. New York: Macmillan, 1923; London: Cecil Palmer, 1923; *The Man Who Died Twice*. New York: Macmillan, 1924; London: Cecil Palmer, 1923; *Dionysius in Doubt*. New York: Macmillan, 1925; *Tristram*. New York: Macmillan, 1927; London: Gollancz, 1928; *Fortunatus*. Reno, NV: Slide Mountain Press, 1928; *Sonnets: 1889–1927*. New York: Crosby Gaige 1928; *Cavender's House*. New York: Macmillan, 1929; London: Hogarth Press, 1930; *The Glory of the Nightingales*. New York: Macmillan, 1930; *Matthias at the Door*. New York: Macmillan, 1931; *Nicodemus*. New York: Macmillan, 1932; *Talifer*. New York: Macmillan, 1933; *Amaranth*. New York: Macmillan, 1934; *King Jasper*. New York: Macmillan, 1935.

Collections

The Children of the Night, 2nd ed. New York: Scribner, 1905; *Captain Craig*, rev ed.. New York: Macmillan, 1915; *Collected Poems*. New York: Macmillan, 1921 [i.e., 1920]; London: Cecil Palmer, 1922; *Collected Poems*, 5 vols. Cambridge, MA: Dunster House, 1927; *Collected Poems*. New York: Macmillan, 1930; *Selected Poems*. New York: Macmillan, 1931; *Untriangulated Stars: Letters to Harry de Forest Smith, 1890–1905*, ed. Denham Sutcliffe. Cambridge, MA: Harvard University Press, 1947; *Selected Letters of Edwin Arlington Robinson*, ed. Ridgely Torrence. New York: Macmillan, 1948; *Selected Early Poems and Letters,* ed. Charles T. Davis. New York: Holt, Rinehart and Winston, 1960; *Edwin Arlington Robinson's Letters to Edith Brower*, ed. Richard Cary. Cambridge, MA: Harvard University Press, 1968; *Uncollected Poems and Prose,* ed. Richard Cary. Waterville, ME: Colby College Press, 1975.

Papers

Substantial holdings of Robinson papers are in the Colby College Library, the Houghton Library at Harvard University, the New York Public Library, and the Library of Congress.

SECONDARY SOURCES

Aiken, Conrad. "Three Reviews." In *Edwin Arlington Robinson: A Collection of Critical Essays,* ed. Francis Murphy, 15–28. Englewood Cliffs, NJ: Prentice Hall, 1970. (Reprint of "Three Essays on Robinson" from Aiken's *A Reviewer's ABC*, published in 1958.) Anderson, Wallace L. *Edwin Arlington Robinson: A Critical Introduction.* Cambridge, MA: Harvard University Press, 1968; Barnard, Ellsworth. *Edwin Arlington Robinson: A Critical Study.* New York: Octagon, 1977; Berman, Ruth. "E. A. Robinson and Merlin's Gleam." *Eildon Tree: A Journal of Fantasy* 1, no. 2 (1976): 16–19; Bloom, Harold, ed. *Modern Critical Views: Edwin Arlington Robinson.* New York: Chelsea House, 1988; Clark, S. L., and Julian N. Wasserman. " 'Time Is a Casket': Love and Temporality in Robinson's *Tristram.*" *Colby Library Quarterly* 17, no. 2 (1981): 112–16; Cochran, Rebecca. "Edwin Arlington Robinson's Arthurian Poems: Studies in Medievalisms?" *Arthurian Interpretations* 3, no. 1 (1988): 49–60; ———. "Edwin Arlington Robinson's Morgan le Fay: Victim or Victimizer?" *Platte Valley Review* 19, no. 2 (1991): 54–60; Cox, Don Richard. "The Vision of Robinson's *Merlin.*" *Colby Library Quarterly* 10, no. 8 (1974): 495–504; Coxe, Louis. *Edwin Arlington Robinson: The Life of Poetry.* New York: Pegasus, 1969; Dickey, James. "Edwin Arlington Robinson: The Many Truths." In *Selected Poems,* ed. Morton Dauwen Zabel, xi–xxvii. New York: Macmillan, 1965. (Reprinted in *Edwin Arlington Robinson: A Collection of Critical Essays,* ed. Francis Murphy, published in 1970.) Domina, Lyle. "Fate, Tragedy, and Pessimism in Robinson's *Merlin.*" *Colby Library Quarterly* 8, no. 4 (1969): 471–78; Donoghue, Denis. "A Poet of Continuing Relevance." In *Connoisseurs of Chaos.* New York: Columbia University Press, 1964. (Reprinted in *Modern Critical Views: Edwin Arlington Robinson,* ed. Harold Bloom, published in 1988.) Doren, Mark Van. *Edwin Arlington Robinson.* New York: Literary Guild, 1927; Dunn, N. E. " 'Wreck and Yesterday': The Meaning of Failure in *Lancelot.*" *Colby Library Quarterly* 9, no. 7 (1971): 349–56; Fisher, John Hurt. "Edwin Arlington Robinson and Arthurian Tradition." In *Studies in Language and Literature in Honour of Margaret Schlauch,* 117–131. Warsaw: Polish Scientific Publishers, 1966; Franchere, Hoyt C. *Edwin Arlington Robinson.* New York: Twayne, 1968; Fussell, Edwin S. *Edwin Arlington Robinson: The Literary Background of a Traditional Poet.* Berkeley: University of California Press, 1954; Gilman, Owen W., Jr. "*Merlin*: E. A. Robinson's Debt to Emerson." *Colby Library Quarterly* 21, no. 3 (1985): 134–41; Hagedorn, Hermann. *Edwin Arlington Robinson: A Biography.* New York: Macmillan, 1936; Hogan, Charles Beecher. *A Bibliography of Edwin Arlington Robinson.* New Haven, CT: Yale University Press, 1936; Howe, Irving. "A Grave and Solitary Voice." In *The Critical Point: On Literature and Culture.* New York: Horizon Press, 1973. (Reprinted in *Modern Critical Views: Edwin Arlington Robinson,* ed. Harold Bloom, published in 1988.) Joyner, Nancy Carol. *Edwin Arlington Robinson: A Reference Guide*. Boston: G. K. Hall, 1978; ———. "What Ever Happened to *Tristram?*" *Colby Library Quarterly* 16, no. 2 (1980): 118–131; Kinneavy, Gerald B. "Time, Space, and Vision in E. A. Robinson's *Tristram*." *Language Quarterly* 25, nos. 3-4 (1987): 35–39; Lagorio, Valerie M. "Edwin Arlington Robinson: Arthurian Pacifist." In *King Arthur Through the Ages*, ed. Valerie M. Lagorio and Mildred Leake Day, 165–79. New York: Garland, 1990; McCoy, Dorothy Schuchman. "The Arthurian Strain in Early Twentieth-Century Literature: Cabell, T. S. Eliot, and E. A. Robinson." *West Virginia University Philological Papers* 28 (1982): 95–104; Miles, Josephine. "Robinson's Inner Fire." In *Edwin Arlington Robinson: A Collection of Critical Essays,* ed. Francis Murphy, 110–16. Englewood Cliffs, NJ: Prentice Hall, 1970; Morris, Celia. "Robinson's Camelot: Renunciation as Drama." *Colby Library Quarterly* 9 (1972): 468–81; Morris, Lloyd. *The Poetry of Edwin Arlington Robinson: An Essay in Appreciation*. New York: Haskell House, 1969; Murphy, Francis, ed. *Edwin Arlington Robinson: A Collection of Critical Essays*. Englewood Cliffs, NJ: Prentice Hall, 1970; Neff, Emery. *Edwin Arlington Robinson*. New York: Sloane, 1948; Perrine, Laurence. "The Sources of Robinson's Arthurian Poems and His Opinions of Other Treatments." *Colby Library Quarterly* 10, no. 6 (1974): 336–46; ———. "The Sources of Robinson's *Merlin*." *American Literature* 44 (1972): 313–21; Redman, Ben Ray. *Edwin Arlington Robinson*. New York: McBride, 1928; Robinson, W. R. *Edwin Arlington Robinson: A Poetry of the Act*. Cleveland: Press of Western Reserve University, 1967; Sampley, Arthur M. "The Power or the Glory: The Dilemma of Edwin Arlington Robinson." *Colby Library Quarterly* 9, no. 7 (1971): 357–66; Smith, Chard Powers. *Where the Light Falls: A Portrait of Edwin Arlington Robinson*. New York: Macmillan, 1965; Starr, Nathan Comfort. "Edwin Arlington Robinson's Arthurian Heroines: Vivian, Guinevere, and the Two Isolts." *Philological Quarterly* 56 (1977): 253–58; ———. "The Transformation of Merlin." In *Edwin Arlington Robinson: Centenary Essays,* ed. Ellsworth Barnard. Athens: University of Georgia Press, 1969. (Reprinted in *Modern Critical Views: Edwin Arlington Robinson,* ed. Harold Bloom, published in 1988.) Waggoner, Hyatt H. "The Idealist *in Extremis*." In *American Poets: From the Puritans to the Present*. Baton Rouge: Louisiana State University Press, 1984. (Reprinted in *Modern Critical Views: Edwin Arlington Robinson,* ed. Harold Bloom, published in 1988.) White, William. *Edwin Arlington Robinson: A Supplementary Bibliography*. Kent, OH: Kent State University Press, 1971.

PEGGY J. HUEY

T(HOMAS) S(TEARNS) ELIOT

(September 26, 1888–January 4, 1965)

Thomas Stearns Eliot, an American expatriate living in London, was a prolific writer of poetry, drama, prose literature, and social criticism. His influence upon poetry is of immense import because his experimental forms and styles forever altered the ways that texts are both written and understood. In terms of literature, he was the at the forefront of the modernist movement, and in 1948, Eliot was awarded the Nobel Prize for literature. He is most noted for composing *The Waste Land* (1922), a description of cultural and spiritual crisis, reflected through fragmentation and discontinuity.

Eliot's *The Waste Land* is significant to Arthuriana because it employs the grail story of the maimed Fisher King to portray modern civilization's lack of spirituality and community. Human relationships are sterile, reflecting the wound that leaves the Fisher King and his lands infertile and blighted. *The Waste Land* is Eliot's response to the First World War and the mood of post-war Europe.

Thomas Stearns Eliot was born in St. Louis, Missouri, on September 26, 1888. He was youngest of seven children born to a distinguished family of New England origin. His kin include the Reverend William Greenleaf Eliot, founder of Washington University in St. Louis, and on his mother's side, Isaac Stearns, one of the original settlers of Massachusetts Bay Colony. Eliot's father was a prosperous industrialist and his mother wrote, among other things, a biography of William Greenleaf Eliot. Educated as a boy at Smith Academy in St. Louis and the Milton Academy in Massachusetts, Eliot then attended Harvard, where he contributed poetry to the *Harvard Advocate*. While enrolled there, he spent a year in France, frequently attending lectures at the Sorbonne. When Eliot returned to Harvard, he completed a dissertation on the English idealist philosopher F. H. Bradley. He also studied Sanskrit and Buddhism.

In 1914 Eliot relocated to London, where he started, with his close friend Ezra Pound, to reform poetic diction. Pound would be among those who were responsible for encouraging Eliot to publish his poetry, including importantly *The Love Song of J. Alfred*

Prufrock in *Poetry,* a Chicago publication, in 1915. In his early poems Eliot opted not to begin with a theme but with a fragmented motif or a poetic rhythm.

Pound later was responsible for Eliot's meeting with Harriet Weaver, who published Eliot's first full volume of verse in 1917, *Prufrock and Other Observations.* However, his career did not initially take off, so Eliot was forced to teach for a year at Highgate Junior School in London. This proved a futile effort, and he then took employment as a clerk at Lloyds Bank. From 1917 to 1919, Eliot was an assistant editor of the journal the *Egoist;* also, beginning in 1919 he was a regular contributor to the *Times Literary Supplement.* He wanted to participate in World War I, but he was refused entrance into the United States Navy in 1918. In 1920 his second book, *Ara Vos Prec,* was hand-printed by Virginia and Leonard Woolf at the Hogath Press.

Eliot longed for poetry to be impersonal and free from the chains of the romantic practices that he believed had bound it for too many years. He proposed this idea in "Tradition and the Individual Talent," noting that an artist's progress is a continual changing steeped in self-sacrifice, often coming at the cost of his personality. Thus, Eliot was able to draw a link between art and science, especially in terms of depersonalization. Eliot's reputation soon grew to that of a grand literary critic. Three of his collections of essays, *The Sacred Wood* (1920), *The Use of Poetry and the Use of Criticism* (1933), and *The Classics and the Man of Letters* (1942), established his reputation as a critic. This esteem allowed Eliot to have enormous impact on contemporary literary taste. Previously, in 1922, Eliot had started *Criterion,* a quarterly review that he edited until publication stopped at the onset of World War II. In 1925 Eliot began working at the publishing house of Faber and Gwyer, which would later become Faber and Faber, the house that published the bulk of his work. Eliot eventually became one of Faber's directors.

During his lifetime, Eliot published some six hundred articles and reviews. He was especially keen on literary criticism, which he thought should be for the clarification of works of art and what he perceived as the correction of taste. Among Eliot's favorites were the seventeenth-century metaphysical poets, especially John Donne, Crashaw, Vaughan, Lord Herbert, and Cowley. It was his hope that a movement a là the Pre-Raphaelites could be established for his icons. However he also exposed the difficulty of defining metaphysical poetry and discerning metaphysical poets. He was moved by the works of this time because they were a mixture of both intellect and passion, two elements missing from much of the modern material Eliot read. In the essay "Religion and Literature" (1935) Eliot expressed that literary criticism should be presented from a definite ethical and theological standpoint.

In 1915, Eliot married ballet dancer Vivienne Haigh-Wood; this turned out to be a serious mismatch. Haigh-Wood was gregarious; she was passionate about life and lived it to the fullest. However, she had a serious hormonal imbalance; when her menstrual period arrived, she experienced incredible mood fluctuations, as well as crippling cramps. Finally she was diagnosed as having hysteria, a malady causing her to be confined in mental institutions from 1930 until her death in 1947. Eliot refused to share a bed with Vivienne. She, in turn, began a tempestuous affair with Bertrand Russell. Eliot next married his secretary, Valerie Fletcher; again the relationship failed. Eliot's lack of success with women has caused conjecture that he may have been homosexual.

In 1922 Eliot published his most famous work, *The Waste Land*, a fragmented poem in five parts. Its innovative style reflects both Eliot's enervation following a mental breakdown and his perception of Europe's attitude following World War I. Spiritually empty himself, Eliot wrote a draft of *The Waste Land* in autumn of 1921 and gave it to his friend and fellow writer, Ezra Pound, in Paris. Editing via Pound's suggestions, Eliot cut the work in half and published the poem in a magazine of which he was the editor, *The Criterion*. The startling techniques bewildered many early readers, but the poem ultimately won acclaim and has been imitated repeatedly.

The poem's five sections feel disjointed, as though they were written by different people—but combine to produce a picture or mood. A variety of styles—dramatic, intellectual, formal, conversational, arch, humorous, and satirical—build to produce an effect of people transfixed in a meaningless life-in-death existence. Sophisticated characters, complicated social behavior and urban landscapes are critically observed to reflect a general cultural decadence. Unromantic in subject, the pictures drawn are of people, buildings, and streets, rather than fields, streams, and flowers. Lovers are disillusioned, unsuccessful, and stifled by propriety. They have limited compassion for one another because the overall image is of selfish people, rotting civilization, and corrupt institutions. The church is barely alive and inconsequential in this land where money rules.

The poem has no real chronology nor normal cohesion because it is a series of images requiring the reader to work at building a whole understanding. Probably examination by sections is most effective. Part I, "The Burial of the Dead," shows a painful blossoming in spring of lilacs then hyacinths, pretty flowers that make the Waste Land look even bleaker. The voice of the Countess Marie describes her dried up life of fragmented memories. The section includes lines in German from a sailor in Wagner's *Tristan and Isolde* who says, "The wind blows freshly to the homeland. My Irish child, where do you linger?" The crowd of people in London are like dead things with no reason to stay. Madame Sosostris, the ill, card reading clairvoyant belongs in that land of desolation and suspicion. The city is London, but it might be any soulless, modern place. A crowd crossing London Bridge is hopeless and undone by death and negativity. They reside in Limbo, aware of their loss of grace.

In Part II, "A Game of Chess," is the unredeemed Waste Land void of spring and trapped in stale interiors. A bored woman and her male companion tolerate each other's company and are aware of the burning desert sun of the Waste Land even within their splendid surroundings. This scene is followed by an equally disturbing conversation inside a bar. Lil, who has had five children and a recent abortion, is told by the barmaid to smarten herself up because her husband is coming back from the war. The wife is expected to show her husband a "good time," which seems futile given her recent abortion. Life is an empty void in both scenes.

Part III, "The Fire Sermon," involves a mixture of quotations and personalities who converge in Tiresias, the genderless, blind seer of *Oedipus*. Images of the beautiful and fruitful old Thames River are juxtaposed with the dirty, trash filled Thames as it is in modern times. A typist is passionlessly seduced by a real estate agent in a meaningless, dull sexual act. The process is automatic and lacking in human feeling. References to St. Augustine and Buddha, both of whom extolled spirit over flesh, suggest a manner of atonement.

"Death by Water," the fourth section, marks a death that must precede any hope of regeneration. Dreamlike closeups of the Waste Land pass quickly. People, stores, and a prison are all parts of the arid, barren land. There is no water, only thunder. Images become a nightmarish juble of cities breaking up, whistling bats, and a woman using her hair like strings on a violin.

Part V, "What the Thunder Said," moves us through the rocky sterile ground, where thunder is unaccompanied by rain, to a traveler who feels mysteriously compassionate. A derelict chapel appears with a crowing cock, a symbol of Christ, on the roof. The thunder tells us in Sanskrit words about encouraging sympathy and self-control, ways of escaping the self to achieve freedom, gaiety, or delight. The final statement of the thunder is "shanti," the formal ending of a sacred Hindu writing meaning "The peace which passes understanding."

The degeneracy of human nature is repeatedly experienced in the *Waste Land*, particularly regarding the loss of sacredness in love and in the sexual act. Also gone is the all encompassing, divine love of God. It is these three problems that explain the poem's link to its own title and to the medieval Fisher King. Probably of Celtic origin but introduced in the poetic French romance of Chretien de Troye's *Perceval*, the Waste Land is a condition relating the fertility of the land to the health of its ruler. The land cannot be restored until the Fisher King's condition, usually a maiming of the genitals, is cured. The sexual waste land condition also perpetrates unnecessary wars, lost battles, and excessive crime. The wound is the condition, but the troubles are caused by a hero who refuses to acknowledge the crisis and thereby solve it. Chrétien's hero, Perceval, has been told that he sounds ignorant when he speaks, so he considers but does not *ask* the correct questions when he goes to the grail castle. Had Perceval asked why the lance bleeds and who is fed by the grail, the land would have been regenerated, and the Fisher King healed. This explains Eliot's other use of the Waste Land theme: loss of modern community spirit and inability to care deeply about the well being of fellow man.

Originally a Christian story, the Fisher King is Bron, Joseph of Arimethea's brother-in-law, who is a rich fisher and who catches the fish for the grail table. God had told Joseph to find a table like the one from the Last Supper with seats for thirteen, to sit by the rich fisher Bron, and to set the grail on the board. In medieval works, Bron turns into the maimed Fisher King at whose table sit twelve knights who are one hundred years old but look younger. The grail feeds them what they most desire and, although they have been there for years, they feel as though they have just arrived. In legend, the grail is the vessel used by Jesus at the Last Supper and employed later by Joseph of Arimethea to collect Christ's blood. The Fisher King is traditionally fed from it meals that are always communion wafers. A beautiful maiden delivers the grail to the Fisher King and Perceval watches her walk through the castle. He longs to ask her whom she feeds but fears showing himself to be an ignorant country boy. So holy are the man and the mass wafers that the grail has been employed in this manner for many years. The holiness of feeding, supplying, and serving works well with *The Waste Land*'s thunder and Sanskrit message about community spirit and the oneness of all.

The Fisher King's people did not allow the king to run or ride a horse because to worsen his condition would mean their certain death for they understand that the ruler, the land, and the folk are all one, a lesson lost in the modern world. The Fisher King, therefore, is often found lying in a garden, reminding us of the two frightening garden scenes at the beginning of *The Waste Land*. A purified knight is the sick king's only hope for rebirth. The holy, bejeweled relic has kept him alive by dispensing the Catholic Mass's body of Christ but it can not cure the wound between the king's thighs, nor can the grail alone disenchant the land of its curse. For Eliot, the modern world is devoid of real Christianity or any deep spiritual values that could improve its bloated, yet dried out, condition. There are glimmers of faith or hope for redemption from this constant wry despair in Part V, but generally the unfeeling, decayed, amoral society remains unconscious of its state.

The sympathetic relationship between the health of the Fisher King and the well being of his domain is perfect for Eliot's conception of the blighted landscape as a reflection of ruined mankind. Traditionally in the Fisher King's land, no sown seed grows, no grass or trees are green, no animals grow or reproduce, no fish swim in the water, and no maiden finds a husband nor bears a child. In the concrete jungle of London, a rare flower is cause for sorrow because it serves as a reminder of growth possibilities; the Thames River is filled with trash rather than fish; the sexual acts are empty and lead to abortion.

In medieval tradition the land is laid waste and the leader hurt by a ridiculous and destructive battle ending with a dolorous stroke. Eliot uses this to express the world war, which destroyed land, property, and souls. This violent upheaval upset Europeans who now can find no relief from the destruction because whether they are aware of it or not, the state of the environment and the responses of their souls are one blighted and burned out mess. Civilization can never understand its current condition, nor has any recent culture discerned completely the link of man, society, and the universe despite teachings of the world's religions. To make the people vigorous and productive again, their connections to the other parts must be repaired, a seemingly impossible task.

The Isle of Britain is a sterile waste land in the early medieval Fisher King accounts because of a war wound, and *The Waste Land* shows modern England in the same dismal state of calamity after the war: women lose infants in the womb; men have no faith or vitality; plants, animals, and water lack their normal regenerative powers. The arid desert of his feudal kingdom and the Fisher King's emasculating war wounds or castration remain uncured in legend, just as the sterile modern world has little hope of improvement. The soul in despair, struggling for redemption, cannot know the correct question to ask for relief from spiritual drought. Eliot's *Waste Land* has no resolution at the end, just a cacophony of religious sentiments that are more noise than meaning. Controversy surrounded the poem's publication not just because of its depressing message, but because it broke critical modes with its confusing narrative sequence and condensed form of expression.

In 1927 Eliot became a British citizen and also joined the Church of England. His movement towards a brand of High Anglicanism can be followed in his poetry, starting with "The Hollow Men" (1925) and moving to the intense visions in *Four Quartets* (1943), which consists of "Burnt Norton" (1935), "East Coker" (1936), "The Dry Salvages" (1936) and "Little Gidding" (1936). These works contain distinct references to Eliot's experiences in World War I when he labored as a watchman checking for fires during bombing raids. These versatile quartets represent not only the four seasons, but they also demonstrate the four elements. Critics perceive this poem as expressing a philosophical view about time's losses and gains.

Eliot also experimented with other works, including poetic dramas. His dramatic verse's diction slowly moved from the spoken vernacular to regular prose. *Murder in the Cathedral* (1935), perhaps his most famous play, was written for a church performance concerning the martyrdom of St. Thomas à Beckett. Another of his plays, *The Family Reunion* (1939), demonstrates a theme of contemporary life; the work is interesting because Eliot tried to find a rhythm close to contemporary speech, much the same way as Shakespeare relied upon iambic pentameter. His play *The Cocktail Party* (1950) is rooted in the classics; it was partly based on Euripides's *Alcestis*. Here we see Eliot's maturity as a dramatist, as he takes greater liberties with ordinary colloquial speech in the work. Eliot felt that it was important to mix genres when composing his dramas. His ideal play would be a poetic piece paralleling the audience members' lives. He felt that many of the plays being passed on to the public were shallow and superficial because the reality ended when they left the theater. Thus those who took the audience into imaginary worlds totally unlike their own were creating useless, unreal atmospheres. Eliot believed that he and other dramatists should show their audiences that the theater was indeed poetic and that the poetry imitates real life. Thus, regular folk should realize that every time they speak, they have the opportunity to be poetic. This would eliminate the need for an artificial escape, and their sad, dreary existences would be given some meaning.

It is surprising, given Eliot's serious reflections of life, that he was a jolly joker who loved to pull pranks on his friends and relations. Many an unsuspecting guest of his would be seated in chairs that secretly held whoopee cushions; Eliot also loved to offer them exploding cigars. Thus, he was thrilled to discover that Groucho Marx, the great American comedian, was his enormous fan. The two became fast friends and communicated rather often. In 1964 Eliot wrote to Groucho, wryly commenting on how Marx was quoted in the newspaper as saying that, because he (Marx) came to London specifically to see Eliot, the poet's credit line in the neighborhood, and particularly with the greengrocer across the street, increased greatly.

In 1939 Eliot published *Old Possum's Book of Practical Cats*. This work was a departure from the staid overwhelming sadness of his earlier poems and would years later achieve a huge following after it was successfully adapted into the musical *Cats*. These poems were set to music in their originally published form with only a few minor revisions of tense or pronouns, although eight lines were added to "The Song of the Jellicos." Some of the lyrics were discovered among the unpublished writings of Eliot. Most notably "The Marching Song of the Pollicle Dogs and the story of Grizabella." From the "Prufrock" period were taken many lines included in "Memory."

Following a prolific career, Eliot died in London on January 4, 1965. Late in his life his renown was overshadowed by accusations that he was really an intolerant cretin. He was accused of everything from racism, to misogyny, fascism, emotional coldness, and anti-Semitism; this made it hard for many readers to appreciate his works. He has not been regarded as a Communist, and there is very little evidence linking him to this brand of politics; however, many do find hints of Eliot's anti-Semitism, like in the poem "Burbank With a Baedeker: Bleistein With a Cigar." Again this may be a subtext, but never the center of his thoughts nor point of his message. However, the poem did not help him in terms of notoriety. Perhaps Eliot was parodying anti-Semitism or made a statement on misreading Dante, but this seems highly unlikely given his keen knowledge of subjects. Regardless, T. S. Eliot proved himself time and again to be a man of immense talents. His contributions to literature are staggering, with Arthuriana he followed the Victorian tradition of using the old material as a thin veneer for social criticism.

PRIMARY WORKS

Prufrock and Other Observations. London: The Egoist, 1917; *Ezra Pound: His Metric and Poetry*. New York: Knopf, 1918; *Poems*. Richmond: Hogarth Press, 1919; *Ara Vos Prec*. London: Ovid, 1920; *The Sacred Wood: Essays on Poetry and Criticism*. London: Methuen, 1921; *The Waste Land*. New York: Boni & Liveright, 1922; *Homage to John Dryden: Three Essays on Poetry of the Seventeenth Century*. London: Hogarth, 1924; *Poems 1909–1925*. London: Faber & Gwyer, 1925; *Journey of the Magi*. London: Faber & Gwyer, 1927; *Shakespeare and the Stoicism of Seneca*. London: Oxford University Press, 1927; *A Song for Simeon*. London: Faber & Gwyer, 1928; *For Lancelot Andrews: Essays on Style and Order*. London: Faber & Gwyer; *Dante*. London: Faber & Faber, 1929; *Animula*. London: Faber & Faber, 1929; *Ash-Wednesday*. New York: Fountain, 1930; *Marina*. London: Faber & Faber, 1930; *Thoughts after Lambeth*.

London: Faber & Faber, 1930; *Triumphal March*. London: Faber & Faber, 1931; *Charles Whibley: A Memoir*. London: Oxford University Press, 1931; *Selected Essays: 1917–1932*. London: Faber & Faber, 1932; *John Dryden: The Poet, The Dramatist, The Critic*. New York: Holliday, 1932; *Sweeney Agonistes: Fragments of an Aristophonic Melodrama*. London: Faber & Faber, 1932; *The Use of Poetry and the Use of Criticism: Studies in the Relationship of Criticism to Poetry in England*. London: Faber & Faber, 1933; *After Strange Gods: A Primer of Modern Heresy*. London: Faber & Faber, 1934; *The Rock: A Pageant Play*. London: Faber & Faber, 1934; *Elizabethan Essays*. London: Faber & Faber, 1934; *Words for Music*. Bryn Mawr, PA: Privately printed, 1934; *Murder in the Cathedral*, complete edition. London: Faber & Faber, 1935; *Two Poems*. Cambridge: Cambridge University Press, 1935; *Essays Ancient and Modern*. London: Faber & Faber, 1936; *Collected Poems 1909-1935*. London: Faber & Faber, 1936; *The Family Reunion*. London: Faber & Faber, 1939; *Old Possum's Book of Practical Cats*. London: Faber & Faber, 1939; *The Idea of a Christian Society*. London: Faber & Faber, 1939; *The Waste Land and Other Poems*. London: Faber & Faber, 1940; *East Coker*. London: Faber & Faber, 1940; *Burnt Norton*. London: Faber & Faber, 1941; *Points of View*, ed. John Hayward. London: Faber & Faber, 1941; *The Dry Salvages*. London: Faber & Faber, 1941; *The Classics and the Man of Letters*. London: Oxford University Press, 1942; *Little Gidding*. London: Faber & Faber, 1942; *Four Quartets*. New York: Harcourt, 1943; *Reunion by Destruction*. London: Pax House, 1943; *What Is a Classic?* London: Faber & Faber, 1945; *Die Einheit der Europäischen Kultur*. Berlin: Carl Habel, 1946; *A Practical Possum*. Cambridge, MA: Harvard Printing Office, 1947; *On Poetry*. Concord, MA: Concord Academy, 1947; *Milton*. London: Cumberlage, 1947; *A Sermon*. Cambridge: Cambridge University Press, 1948; *Selected Poems*. Harmondsworth: Penguin, 1948; *Notes Towards the Definition of Culture*. London: Faber & Faber, 1948; *From Poe to Valéry*. New York: Harcourt, 1948; *The Undergraduate Poems of T. S. Eliot*, unauthorized publication. Cambridge, MA, 1949; *The Aims of Poetic Drama*. London: Poet's Theatre Guild, 1949; *The Cocktail Party*. London: Faber & Faber, 1950; *Poems Written in Early Youth*. Stockholm: Privately printed, 1950; *Poetry and Drama*. Cambridge, MA: Harvard University Press, 1951; *The Film of Murder in the Cathedral* by T. S. Eliot and George Hoellering. London: Faber & Faber, 1952; *The Value and Use of Cathedrals in England Today*. Chichester: Friends of Chichester Cathedral, 1952; *An Address to the Members of the London Library*. London: London Library, 1952; *The Complete Poems and Plays*. New York: Harcourt, 1952; *Selected Prose*, ed. Hayward. London: Penguin; *American Literature and American Language*. St. Louis: Department of English, Washington University, 1953; *The Three Voices of Poetry*. Cambridge: Cambridge University Press, 1953; *The Confidential Clerk*. London: Faber & Faber, 1954; *Religious Drama: Medieval and Modern*. New York: House of Books, 1954; *The Cultivation of Christmas Trees*. London: Faber & Faber, 1954; *The Literature of Politics*. London: Conservative Political Centre, 1955; *The Frontiers of Criticism*. Minneapolis: University of Minnesota Press, 1956; *On Poetry and Poets*. London: Faber & Faber, 1957; *The Elder Statesman*. London: Faber & Faber, 1959; *Geoffrey Faber 1889-1961*. London: Faber & Faber, 1961; *Collected Plays*. London: Faber & Faber, 1962; *George Herbert*. London: Longmans, 1962; *Collected Poems 1909-1962*. London: Faber & Faber, 1963; *Knowledge and Experience in the Philosophy of F. H. Bradley*. London: Faber & Faber, 1964; *To Criticize the Critic and Other Writings*. London: Faber & Faber, 1965; *The Waste Land: A Facsimile and Transcript of the Original Drafts Including the Annotations of Ezra Pound*, ed. Valerie Eliot. London: Faber & Faber, 1971; *Selected Prose of T. S. Eliot*, ed. Frank Kermode. London: Faber, 1975.

SECONDARY SOURCES

Ackroyd, Peter. *T. S. Eliot: A Life*. New York: Simon and Schuster, 1984; Bloom, Harold. *T. S. Eliot: Comprehensive Research and Study Guide*. London: Chelsea House, 1998; ———. *T. S. Eliot's The Waste Land*. New York: Chelsea House, 1988; Brooker, Jewel Spears. *T. S. Eliot and Our Turning World*. New York: Macmillan, 2001; Brooker, Jewel Spears, and Joseph Bentley.

Reading "The Waste Land": Modernism and the Limits of Interpretation. Boston: University of Massachusetts Press, 1990; Bush, Ronald. *T. S. Eliot: The Modernist in History.* Cambridge: Cambridge University Press, 1991; Cooper, John Xiros. *T. S. Eliot and the Ideology of Four Quartets.* Cambridge: Cambridge University Press, 1996; Crawford, Robert. *The Savage and the City in the Work of T. S. Eliot.* Oxford: Oxford University Press, 1991; Ellman, Maud. *The Poetics of Impersonality: T. S. Eliot and Ezra Pound.* Cambridge, MA: Harvard University Press, 1987; Frye, Northrup. *T. S. Eliot: An Introduction.* Chicago: University of Chicago Press, 1981; Gordon, Lyndall. *Eliot's Early Years.* London: Oxford University Press, 1977; ———. *T. S. Eliot: An Imperfect Life.* New York: Norton, 2000; Grant, Michael. ed. *T. S. Eliot: The Critical Heritage.* New York: Routledge, 1982; Jain, Manju. *A Critical Reading of the Selected Poems of T. S. Eliot.* Oxford: Oxford University Press, 2002; Jay, Gregory S. *T. S. Eliot and the Poetics of Literary History.* Baton Rouge: Louisiana State University Press, 1983; Julius, Anthony. *T. S. Eliot: Anti-Semitism and Literary Form.* Cambridge: Cambridge University Press, 1996; Martin, Mildred. *A Half-Century of Eliot Criticism.* New York: Associated University Presses, 1979; Menand, Louis. *Discovering Modernism: T. S. Eliot and His Context.* Oxford: Oxford University Press, 2003; Moody, Anthony David. *Thomas Stearns Eliot, Poet.* Cambridge: Cambridge University Press, 1979; Perl, Jeffrey M. *Skepticism and Modern Enmity: Before and After Eliot.* Baltimore: Johns Hopkins University Press, 1989; Riquelme, Paul. *Harmony of Dissonances: T. S. Eliot, Romanticism, and Imagination.* Baltimore: Johns Hopkins University Press, 1991; Schuchard, Ronald. *Eliot's Dark Angel: Intersections of Life and Art.* Oxford: Oxford University Press, 1999; Schwartz, Sanford. *The Matrix of Modernism: Pound, Eliot, and Early Twentieth-Century Thought.* Princeton, NJ: Princeton University Press, 1985; Sigg, Eric. *The American T. S. Eliot: A Study of the Early Writings.* Cambridge: Cambridge University Press, 1989; Smith, Grover Cleveland. *T. S. Eliot and the Use of Memory.* Lewisburg, PA: Bucknell University Press, 1996; Southam, B. C. *A Guide to the Selected Poems of T. S. Eliot.* New York: Harvest Books, 1996; Spender, Stephen. *T. S. Eliot.* New York: Viking Press, 1976; Watkins, Floyd C. *The Flesh and the Word: Eliot, Hemingway, Faulkner.* Nashville, TN: Vanderbilt University Press, 1971; Welshimer, Linda Wagner, ed. *T. S. Eliot: A Collection of Criticism.* New York: McGraw-Hill, 1974; Williamson, George. *A Reader's Guide to T. S. Eliot: A Poem-by-Poem Analysis.* Syracuse, NY: Syracuse University Press, 1998.

ROBERT THOMAS LAMBDIN AND LAURA COONER LAMBDIN

C(LIVE) S(TAPLES) LEWIS
(November 29, 1898–November 22, 1963)

C. S. Lewis was an academic lecturer, a Christian apologist, a novelist for both adults and children, and a literary critic. He was also, however, a creator and student of myth. Lewis frankly acknowledged his love of and creative debt to Irish, Greek, and Norse myth but was less forthcoming about his interest in and debt to the myth of King Arthur. Nevertheless, Lewis's consistent fascination with and desire to respond to the myth of King Arthur emerges in his spiritual autobiography *Surprised by Joy*, personal letters, scholarly writing, and fiction. Although it was just one of several mythical influences on Lewis as a writer, the myth of King Arthur was a powerful source of inspiration for Lewis's poetry and fiction. In addition, Lewis's Arthurian works constitute a noteworthy contribution to the tradition of Arthurian literature.

Clive Staples ("Jack") Lewis was born in Belfast, Northern Ireland on November 29, 1898. His mother Florence ("Flora") Hamilton Lewis was a member of an established Irish family. She was a mathematician who took her first degree in mathematics at Queen's College Belfast, and then earned first-class honors in logic and second-class honors in geometry and algebra. She instilled in her younger son a love of studying languages as she supervised his first lessons in French and Latin. Jack's father, Albert Lewis, was a solicitor of Welsh extraction who was one of the first working professionals in his family. C. S. Lewis, along with his older brother Major Warren ("Warnie") Hamilton Lewis, grew up in a house filled with books and had a happy early childhood. Lewis states in *Surprised by Joy*—which covers events up to the point of his conversion to Christianity at the age of thirty-one—how he was blessed with "good parents, good food, and a garden," his nurse Lizzie Endicott's wisdom that social class does not correlate directly with moral virtue, and Warnie's intimate friendship. That friendship sparked their childhood make-believe worlds of India (Warnie's realm) and Animal-Land (Jack's). Nevertheless, Lewis's early childhood lacked two elements that became crucial to him as an adult: beauty and genuine faith in God.

Lewis began to write stories before the age of six. In his autobiography, he says these stories combined "dressed animals" and "knights-in-armour"—his "two chief literary pleasures" as a child. He goes on to describe his illustrations for these stories as possessing perspective and motion, but not beauty. When he was a child, beauty resided for Lewis not in daily life, but in the toy garden his brother made and the distant Castlereagh Hills that taught him to long for something outside of himself. Lewis's Protestant father exposed him to the "charm of tradition and the verbal beauty of the Bible and Prayer Book," but he did not instill in his younger son a connection to faith.

According to his biographers Roger Lancelyn Green and Walter Hooper, Lewis's romantic sensibilities began to develop following his contact with *A Connecticut Yankee in King Arthur's Court*. Of *Connecticut Yankee* Lewis says in *Surprised by Joy* that, although he disliked Mark Twain's book as an adult and did not reread it, it offered to him his only access to the Arthurian story at a young age. Having read Twain's novel as a boy, he absorbed its romantic elements rather than its ironic presentation of the romantic ideals of the Middle Ages. *Connecticut Yankee*, along with Sir Arthur Conan Doyle's *Sir Nigel*, helped to introduce Lewis to the concept of chivalry. More influential than these literary forces, however, were the *Strand* serials written by E. Nesbit—especially *The Story of the Amulet* (May 1905–April 1906). *The Story of the Amulet* gave Lewis access to the darkness and mystery of the ancient world while the books of Beatrix Potter gave him access to beauty.

On August 23, 1908, Flora Hamilton Lewis died of cancer. Losing his mother at the age of nine deeply affected young Lewis, causing him to cling to Warnie for the love and support their father was unable to give. Another result of his mother's illness and death was that Lewis failed to connect with God. He explains in *Surprised by Joy* that he had tried to will himself into believing that his prayers for his mother's recovery would work, but her death left him as spiritually lost as he was before: "The thing hadn't worked, but I was used to things not working, and I thought no more about it. I think the truth is that the belief into which I had hypnotized myself was itself too irreligious for its failure to cause any religious revolution. I had approached God, or my idea of God, without love, without awe, even without fear." Sadly, Albert Lewis became a distant parent after his wife's death, partially because he worried about the possibility of ending up destitute despite his evident professional success. These unfounded concerns about family finances did not, however, keep Albert Lewis from generously supporting his younger son during his years at Oxford prior to gaining his first academic appointment in 1925.

Albert Lewis sent his son away to the Wynyard School in Hertfordshire to further his education, but the boy who felt that he had lost "all settled happiness, all that was tranquil and reliable" experienced only intellectual boredom and fear of being beaten by his teachers. He did, however, form friendships with a few of the boys who remained at the school in its waning years. He also "began seriously to pray and to read [his] Bible and to attempt to obey [his] conscience" because at Wynyard he "heard the doctrines of Christianity . . . taught by men who obviously believed them." As he experienced this beginning of a spiritual life, Lewis discovered the science fiction of H. G. Wells, which stimulated the sensibility that later produced the Ransom Trilogy. Lewis described his space trilogy as "planetary romances" that exorcised his "fierce curiosity" about other worlds.

In the fall of 1910, Lewis enrolled at Campbell College—a Belfast school where he began to enjoy his studies. Here he "rubbed shoulders with farmers' sons" and read Matthew Arnold's poems. Arnold gave Lewis access to "a passionate, silent gazing at things a long way off" as well as to the "grave melancholy" of Iranian epic through his retelling of the tale of Sohrab and Rostam. After one term at Campbell, however, Lewis took ill and spent "a blessed six weeks at home" during which he "could read, write, and draw to [his] heart's content." This solitude with books became Lewis's preferred mode for the rest of his life. In January 1911, he went to Cherbourg preparatory school in Malvern, England, where he began to study Latin and English more seriously and where he decided to reject Christianity. Lewis explains in *Surprised by Joy* that as an adolescent, "[He] began to labor very hard to make [himself] into a fop, a cad, and a snob." During this same period, though, Lewis encountered Northernness in the form of *Siegfried and the Twilight of the Gods*—a book that reacquainted him with the desire for that something outside himself he later termed Joy. This encounter with Northernness Lewis later saw as preparation for true worship: "Sometimes I can almost think that I was sent back to the false gods there to acquire some capacity for worship against the day when the true God should recall me to Himself." During this period, he built upon his earlier childhood writings about Animal-Land and his brother Warnie's about India, transforming these imaginary places into a single land called Boxen. Although Lewis later made a sharp distinction between the creations of his childhood and those of his adult career, his gift for imagining talking creatures with rich histories is evident even in his earliest tales.

During his years at Malvern College (fall 1913–1916), Lewis got drawn into serving the Bloods—boys with athletic skill, good looks, and personality—while trying to keep up with his advanced-level academic work. He did, nevertheless, benefit from his formmaster's "perfect courtesy" and love of savoring of "the right sensuality of poetry" as well as from his own discovery of John Milton, W. B. Yeats, and a book on Celtic mythology at the school's library. At this time Lewis wrote a Norse-content Greek-style tragedy called *Loki Bound*—dramatizing his oppression by the Bloods. Lewis describes his spiritual confusion while at Malvern in *Surprised by Joy*: "I maintained that God did not exist. I was also very angry with God for not existing. I was equally angry with Him for creating the world." In April 1914 Lewis became a friend of Arthur Greeves because of their shared love of Norse mythology. In the winter of 1914–1915, Lewis went to study with W. T. Kirkpatrick (1848–1921) who taught him to argue logically and to read French, German, Greek, Italian, and Latin. Of all the literature he read and translated with Kirkpatrick, Homer's *Odyssey* enraptured Lewis with "the music of the thing and the clear, bitter brightness that lives in almost every formula." During the 1910s, Lewis struggled "to get the comforts of both a materialist and of a spiritualist philosophy without the rigors of either" until he rediscovered "Holiness" by reading George MacDonald's *Phantastes, a Faerie Romance for Men and Women*. According to Lewis's introduction to selections from MacDonald, this "baptism of his imagination" prepared him for his later conversion.

In December 1916 Lewis won a scholarship to University College at Oxford and attended from April to September 1917. In June 1917 Lewis volunteered for military service—despite his exemption as an Irishman. After reaching the front lines on his nineteenth birthday, he was wounded on April 15, 1918, during the Battle of Arras. After recuperating, he returned to duty near Andover, England, before his discharge in December 1918. His roommate at officer's training camp, Edward Francis Courtenay "Paddy" Moore (1898–1918), was killed in battle. Paddy Moore's death called Lewis to honor the pact the two young men had made to care for the other's parent should he die in the war. Consequently, while he was still a student at Oxford, Lewis took up residence with his friend's mother, Mrs. Janie King Askins "Minto" Moore (1872–1951) and her daughter Maureen. Although A. N. Wilson speculates that Lewis had an affair with Mrs. Moore from the summer of 1918 onwards, other Lewis scholars tend to assume that Moore was merely a mother-figure to Lewis. However, the exact nature of their relationship is unknown. What is known is that, after sharing a rented house with the Moores from June 1921 onward, Lewis bought a house called The Kilns jointly with Mrs. Moore and his brother Warnie, and then pursued his degree at Oxford. Despite living in a household that was not conducive to scholarly pursuits, Lewis's studies yielded impressive results: a first in honor Moderations (Greek and Latin literature) in 1920, a first in Greats (classics and philosophy) in 1922, and a first in English language and literature in 1923.

Two of Lewis's early compositions were influenced by the myth of King Arthur. The first was *The Quest of Bleheris*, a prose romance he left unfinished before departing for Oxford in 1917. It survives in manuscript form at Oxford's Bodleian Library. Lewis discussed his struggle to write *The Quest of Bleheris* in a dozen letters addressed to Arthur Greeves. In a letter dated October 12, 1916, he set the work aside with this comment: "As to Bleheris, he is dead and I shan't trouble his grave." The second composition inspired by Arthurian literature was a long narrative poem about Merlin and Nimue on which Lewis worked periodically from 1919 to 1922. Lewis shared with Arthur Greeves both his enthusiasm for the project during the poem's composition in stanzaic verse, in a letter of September 18, 1919, and his feeling that "there must be some good in a subject which drags me back to itself so often," in a letter of April 11, 1920. Don W. King notes that Lewis completed a version of the poem, probably in blank verse, and submitted it to the *London Mercury* on May 3, 1922. The poem, however, was rejected and is now lost.

After serving as a philosophy tutor for the 1924–25 academic year, Lewis was elected a fellow of Magdalen College, Oxford, where he was a tutor in English language and literature for the next twenty-nine years. In May 1926 he met J. R. R. Tolkien for the first time, soon becoming Tolkien's close friend despite his initial dislike of the philologist. Lewis later claimed that Tolkien helped him to get over his prejudices against both Roman Catholics and philologists. With his friend as a significant source of inspiration, Lewis became a theist in 1929: "In the Trinity Term of 1929 I gave in, and admitted that God was God, and knelt and prayed: perhaps, that night, the most dejected and reluctant convert in all England." Then, on September 28, 1931, Lewis became a Christian after a long discussion with Tolkien and Hugo Dyson. While traveling a short distance in the side-car of his brother's motorcycle, the conversion occurred: "When we set out I did not believe that Jesus Christ is the Son of God, and when we reached the zoo I did. Yet I had not exactly spent the journey in thought . . . It was more like when a man, after long sleep, still lying motionless in bed, becomes aware that he is now awake." In a letter to Arthur Greeves dated October 11, 1931, Lewis explained that he now understood "the story of Christ" to be "God's myth":

> "Now the story of Christ is simply a true myth . . . Pagan stories are God expressing Himself through the minds of poets, using such images as He found there, while Christianity is God expressing Himself through what we call 'real things'. . . the actual incarnation, crucifixion, and resurrection."

Following his conversion, Lewis continued to draw upon several mythologies because he believed that all myths could lead a person to God.

Still, the myth of King Arthur attracted Lewis throughout his life, perhaps because it combined the Christian myth with Celtic mythology. Lewis's letters document how he sought out and read several versions of the Arthurian legend in translation: Geoffrey of Monmouth's *History of the Kings of Britain* (written c. 1136–1138), the Arthurian portions of both Wace's *Roman de Brut* (c. 1155) and Lawman's *Brut* (c. 1200), the French prose *Merlin* and *Quest of the Holy Grail* (written c. 1215–1235), and the English poem *Sir Gawain and the Green Knight* (written c. 1375). He also read Sir Thomas Malory's *Le Morte Darthur* (written 1469–1471) in Eugène Vinaver's three-volume edition, Charles Williams's *Taleissin through Logres* and *The Region of the Summer Stars*, and at least the first part of T. H. White's Arthuriad (published in 1958 as *The Once and Future King*)— the first three parts of which were published between 1938 and 1940. A letter of Lewis's to Brother George Every, dated December 11, 1940, and expressing his strong disapproval of White's "vulgar" humor in "The Sword in the Stone," confirms that he read at least the first part of this modern Arthuriad with interest.

In the early 1930s, Lewis began a poem called "Launcelot." It survives as a fragment of nearly three hundred lines of Alexandrine couplets. The small body of criticism about this poem notes both the strong influence upon it of Malory's *Morte Darthur* and the lesser influences of Tennyson's *Idylls of the King* and the Arthurian works of Charles Williams. "Launcelot" begins by describing Arthur's court as it suffers the painfully slow passing of time during the two years the Grail knights are absent from the City of Legions. Like Tennyson, Lewis defines the time of the quest as bringing salvation to a few men while Arthurian society suffers devastation. Guinever's hope that Arthur's knights will return contrasts with Lucan's repetition of King Pelles's prophecy that the grail quest will result in Arthur's defeat at the hands of the Picts. After the return of the defeated and demoralized Gawain during the winter, the spring brings further devastation to the court: "The home-coming of heroes from the Quest, by two's / And three's, unlike their expectations, without news, / A dim disquiet of defeated men" (51–53). Then, after two full years, Launcelot returns—another haunted man who has failed on the quest. Although he is unwilling, at first, to communicate with his lover queen Guinever, he finally tells her of his spiritual failure and his encounters with two women.

In this account, Launcelot describes how his wanderings take him to a wasteland where he finds a hermit who explains that nine realms will continue in their "distress" (153) until the Good Knight asks why the Fisher King lies sick. Although Lewis could have derived this plot detail from either T. S. Eliot's *The Waste Land* or Sir James George Frazer's *The Golden Bough*, the motif of the knight having to ask about the sick king originated with Chrétien de Troyes's late twelfth-century romance *Perceval*. Next Launcelot rides to a green valley where he meets a damsel. She tells him that the tomb over which she watches will house the bodies of the three best Christian knights. When Launcelot asks her "half ashamed" (213) who they are, he receives the answer of "a disembodied voice" (218): the tomb is for Bors, Percivale, and Galahad "but not / For the Knight recreant of the Lake, for Launcelot!" (220–21). The hero then rides to the "Castle Mortal" or palace of earthly pleasure, where he meets its queen who looks "somewhat" like both Morgan and Guinever.

This queen embodies the moral dangers of pursuing earthly pleasures such as women and strong wine. She shows Launcelot three coffins, the heads of which "passed beneath three arches in the wall" (275). When the queen announces that the three best earthly knights will lie in her house, and Launcelot hesitates to name them, she identifies them as Sir Lamorake, Sir Tristram, and Launcelot du Lake (279–85). The queen explains that when the three knights lie in these beds, she will behead them and thus keep "their sweetness" for herself while denying it to Morgan, Guinever, Nimue, Isoud, and Elaine

(297–99). Her final statement, that she will "Keep those bright heads and comb their hair and make them lie / Between my breasts and worship them until I die," disturbs Sir Launcelot. Although the fragment ends here, it reflects the stark contrast between the sinful Launcelot and the holy Perceval, Bors, and Galahad present in the thirteenth-century *Quest of the Holy Grail* and in Malory's translation of it. It also evokes the nightmarish quality of the quest sequence in Tennyson's *Idylls of the King* and reinterprets Malory's episode involving the necrophilic Hallewes who wants to possess Lancelot's dead body. Despite these points of contact with previous versions of the Arthurian myth, commentators on "Launcelot" agree that Lewis offers an original version of it through this poem.

According to A. N. Wilson, Lewis's "full conversion to Christianity released in him a literary flow which ceased only with his death. From then on, works of scholarship, fantasy, literary appreciation, and apologetics poured from his ever fertile brain." Shortly after his conversion, Lewis began writing *A Pilgrim's Regress* in the spring of 1932. He published it in 1933 after reading it aloud to Tolkien during its composition. By retelling John Bunyan's *Pilgrim's Progress*, Lewis demonstrated the dangers of the intellectual sins that separate the pilgrim John from his God until he seeks and receives spiritual aid. Once he asks for help, History, Reason, and Mother Kirk lead John to his Landlord's house. Also in 1933 "The Inklings"—an informal group of male friends that included Charles Williams, Warren Lewis, and Hugo Dyson—formed around Lewis and Tolkien. Its members argued about ideas, read their works aloud, and continued to hold formal meetings until 1949. Frequent informal meetings of Lewis and his friends continued long after that. According to A. N. Wilson, Lewis's spiritual practice—founded on the principle of obedience—took the form of attending his college chapel on weekdays and his parish Church on Sundays, despite his dislike of rituals such as taking a palm on Palm Sunday and of hymns. In 1936 Lewis published *The Allegory of Love: A Study in Medieval Tradition*, a history of the development of both the romantic conception of love and the love allegory in the West from Ovid to Spenser, which he had been writing since 1925. The manuscript for this book was given to Charles Williams, whose *The Place of the Lion* Lewis was reading at the time. After Lewis wrote to Williams to praise *The Place of the Lion*, the two became close friends and fellow Inklings. This book centers on the Lion of Strength that A. N. Wilson believes inspired Lewis's creation of Aslan in the Narnia series. *The Allegory of Love* won Lewis The Gollancz Prize for Literature in 1937 and, along with *English Literature in the Sixteenth Century* (1954), made Lewis one of the revivers of historicist literary criticism.

Also during 1936, Tolkien and Lewis made a pact requiring Lewis to write a book about space travel—*Out of the Silent Planet*—and Tolkien to write a book about time travel, the fragmentary *The Lost Road*. Lewis did not begin *Out of the Silent Planet* with a plan for a trilogy. Published in 1938, *Out of the Silent Planet* tells of how Dr. Elwin Ransom—a philologist don from Cambridge University, not unlike Tolkien—travels to the planet Malacandra as the kidnapping victim of Dick Devine and Professor Edward Weston, who plan to sacrifice him to the ruler of the planet. Ransom escapes and discovers that the three races of Malacandrian beings are good-hearted and civilized. Unlike many of his predecessors in the genre of science fiction, Lewis chose not to demonize the Martians and other species that would later appear in his trilogy. Green and Hooper note that "Certainly some readers of *Out of the Silent Planet* enjoyed it in spite of its Christian background, some because of it—and many without realizing it at all." In 1948 this novel received high praise from Marjorie Nicolson: "Mr Lewis has created *myth* itself."

Lewis became a public scholar during the late 1930s and 1940s. He communicated with the public through newspapers, radio broadcasts, and books aimed at a general audience. In 1940 Lewis published *The Problem of Pain*, a brief book that tries to solve the intellectual problem human and animal suffering poses. In it he observes that "when pain is to be borne, a little courage helps much more than much knowledge, a little human sympathy more than much courage, and the least tincture of love of God more than all." In 1941 Lewis published thirty-one Screwtape letters in *The Guardian* in weekly installments between May 2 and November 28. Although Lewis received payments of two pounds per letter, he donated the money to charity. These letters record the advice and warning of Uncle Screwtape to his nephew Wormwood, a devil-in-training. Wormwood fails to ensnare the soul of a young man who manages to become a Christian, fall in love with a Christian woman, die in an air raid, and receive God's welcome in Heaven. *The Screwtape Letters* were Lewis's most popular works after The Chronicles of Narnia. Continuing his life as a public scholar, in August 1941 Lewis gave four live radio talks on BBC radio he titled "Right and Wrong" and then went on the air again to answer questions from listeners. In January and February 1942, Lewis delivered five radio talks on Sunday evenings about "What Christians Believe" and then from September 20 to November 8 gave a series of talks he called "Christian Behaviour." In that same year, Lewis published *A Preface to Paradise Lost*, analysis he had originally presented as the Ballard Matthews lectures. The book is an attempt to defend Milton's choice of the epic form and to refocus Milton studies on the nature of man and of joy rather than on Milton's poetics.

In 1943 Lewis delivered the Riddell Memorial Lectures, later published as *The Abolition of Man*, in which he explains to a general audience that values such as goodness and beauty are objective. Both this work and his Ransom trilogy reflect Lewis's fear, spelled out in a July 30, 1954, letter to William L. Kintner, that "modern industrialism, scientism and totalitarian politics" would defeat "Nature." In a letter dated August 9, 1939, Lewis noted that modern man's belief in "a 'scientific' hope of defeating death" was "a real rival to Christianity." From February 22 to April 4, 1944, Lewis gave a series of radio talks known as "Beyond Personality," which then joined his earlier broadcasts to form the text of the book *Mere Christianity* in 1952. *Mere Christianity* makes this argument: moral law exists, people disobey it, and without some hope of atonement for sins modern life will drive them to despair. From November 10 to April 14, 1945, Lewis published *The Great Divorce* in weekly installments in *The Guardian*. This book presents Lewis as the narrator of a dream in which he tours hell and heaven, arguing for the plausibility of their existence and suggesting that those who are in hell have chosen to be there. This work led him to write another book on theology for the general reader titled *Miracles: A Preliminary Study*. Published in 1947, this book argues that naturalism—the belief that the real consists only of that which is empirically verifiable—presupposes that the search for miracles is ridiculous. In contrast, supernaturalism, which is based upon a belief in God and supernatural phenomena, makes belief in miracles logical.

During the period of his radio broadcasts, Lewis finished his Ransom trilogy. In 1943 he published *Perelandra*, the second installment, which reflects Lewis's scholarly interest in Milton's *Paradise Lost*. While Thulcandra (Earth) is embroiled in World War II, Lewis's Perelandra (Venus) offers paradise: it is an un-fallen natural world giving to the Green Lady—the first woman of that world—a second chance at the sinless perfection offered to Eve on earth. Professor Weston pursues Ransom to Perelandra, and then tries to coerce the Green Lady into disobeying Maleldil (God). Ransom prevents the demon-possessed Weston from achieving his goal first through an argument with both him and the Green Lady, and finally through a physical fight in which Ransom defeats Weston but receives a wound on the heel from which he can never be made whole. Ransom's wound transforms him into a Fisher King, a name he assumes in *That Hideous Strength*, and signifies that he is a Christ figure. The novel ends celebrating the "Great Dance" of the universe that connects human life with all other life. Lewis continued his exploration of evil in the third and final installment in the space trilogy, set several years later. In 1945, the year in which he lost his close friend Charles Williams, Lewis published *That Hideous Strength*.

In this novel, Lewis has Ransom back on Thulcandra to battle evil, drawing upon both Arthurian mythology and biblical episodes such as the building of the Tower of Babel and the destruction of Sodom and Gomorrah. Lewis sets this final battle for the soul of humanity at Edgestow, a small university town that Green and Hooper say suffers the spiritual and environmental desolation Lewis feared Oxford would suffer following the controversial "founding of the atomic factory of Harwell," only fifteen miles away. Just after World War II, the N.I.C.E. (National Institute for Co-ordinated Experiments) infiltrates and takes over the university in order to gain access to the wood on its grounds. In this wood, Merlin lies in a deep trance that prevents him from aging. The technocrats at N.I.C.E. manage to flatter a young academic, Mark Studdock, into writing propaganda for them, isolating him from his considerably more spiritual wife Jane. Jane is struggling to finish her doctoral thesis, but she gradually learns that her strange dreams are actually products of her second sight. This gift draws Jane into contact with Ransom and his companions, and it enables her to help the group locate Merlin and track the N.I.C.E.'s "progress." Merlin's ancient wisdom empowers him to orchestrate an appropriate end for the Institute's members. Since these evil technocrats have corrupted language—causing men to commit evil acts and to destroy the order of nature—Merlin brings down the curse of Babel upon them, leaving them lost in the verbal chaos that destroys them. Lewis's nightmarish Earth has lost its connection with Deep Heaven's beatific language and worlds, despite the presence of Ransom as a Christ figure, Fisher King, and Arthurian king—the Pendragon of Logres. Lewis demonstrates this lack of connection with the sacred through Jane and Mark's marriage, which reflects the emotional and moral emptiness Lewis feared could result if technology overwhelmed nature. Lewis uses the mythical geography of Logres, like that in the works of Charles Williams, to present an image of an unfallen old Britain that contrasts sharply with fallen, post-World War II Britain. By returning this young married couple to a state of love and fertility, Lewis explores both modern gender roles and the institution of marriage.

Although his friend Tolkien attained one of the Merton chairs in 1945, Lewis was passed over for the Merton Professorship in English at Oxford in 1947–1948. This disappointment typified his academic career in which he struggled for recognition at Oxford at least in part because of his popularity outside of the academy. Nevertheless, Lewis received an honorary doctorate of divinity from the University of St. Andrews in 1946 and continued to pursue a wide range of writing projects. His next Arthurian project was his 1947 exchange of letters with his friend Owen Barfield, later published as *Mark vs. Tristram: Correspondence between C. S. Lewis and Owen Barfield*. Through these letters, they created an imaginary version of the legal proceedings that Sir Thomas Malory's King Mark might have initiated against his wife's lover, Tristram. Lewis's participation in this Arthurian exchange with a friend is consistent with his lifelong correspondence with Arthur Greeves, whom he addressed as Galahad in dozens of letters written between

1915 and 1918 and with whom he exulted over Norse and Arthurian myth. As Hooper notes in his introduction to *Mark vs. Tristram*, this exchange with Barfield grew out of Lewis's concern over Eugène Vinaver's 1947 edition of Malory's *Le Morte Darthur* (an edition Lewis anonymously reviewed for *The Times Literary Supplement* that same year in an essay later reprinted in *Studies in Medieval and Renaissance Literature*). The *Times* had encouraged literary critics to attack Malory because he was convicted of crimes ranging from cattle theft, extortion, and sacrilegious theft to attempted murder and rape. In response, Lewis asked whether Malory's behavior could be categorized as "unknightly"—since (as Lewis observed in the *TLS* review) what the Middle Ages called rape modern people might call abduction, and honor could have required acts of theft and extortion—and whether the medieval lawyers, whose accounts were fuelling the modern attacks on Malory, might have had political motives for branding Malory a criminal. These questions spurred Lewis to conclude, "how different such nobility may be from the virtues of the law-abiding citizen will appear if we imagine the life of Sir Tristram as it would be presented to us by King Mark's solicitors."

In response to Lewis's assertion, Barfield's first letter outlines Tristram's crimes of seducing the fiancée of King Mark of Cornwall (Isode) while escorting her across the Irish Channel, and of carrying on an affair with her. The letter requests compensation for King Mark in light of Tristram's violations of filial and feudal loyalty. Lewis's response on behalf of Tristram's lawyers, Blaise and Merlin, dismisses the first letter. It then notifies Barfield and Barfield of the witnesses ready to testify that Tristram committed no wrong as well as of Tristram's eagerness to settle the issue by combat on the strength of his encounters with twenty-five previous opponents, all deceased. Barfield's next letter refers the legal dispute to arbitration by King Arthur while the one following it demands "a full and complete *Retractio* of all the works of the flesh" on the model of the retraction for the case of *Arthur v. Lancelot*. Lewis then offers a final letter in pseudo-Malorian English. In it he notes that Tristram has returned home and met with Kay who has recorded Tristram's denial of any communication with Barfield and Barfield. Then, as Maistre Bleyse, Lewis further obscures the legal issue by reporting that Merlin has transformed him into an ass and partially retransformed him—leaving him with an ass's ears and hooves. Lewis ends by implying that Merlin could likewise transform others. This work reflects Lewis's imaginative engagement with Malory's *Le Morte Darthur*, particularly the moral issues the medieval work raises for modern people. As Michael Harry Blechner has noted, by creating a pattern in these letters in which both Tristram and Merlin win through implied physical threat of others, Lewis highlights a key issue in Malory: rule by force as opposed to rule by law. This issue had powerful resonance for Lewis's post-World War II audience. Lewis's engagement with *Le Morte Darthur* as a creative writer paralleled his engagement with it as a literary critic who (in the review that later became part of the volume *Studies in Medieval and Renaissance Literature*) defended Malory's varying degree of originality as he translates his sources, William Caxton's editing of Malory's Roman War sequence, and Eugène Vinaver's edition of Malory's text, which he called "extraordinarily interesting."

In 1948 Lewis used his popularity in the United States to publish two unfinished works by his friend Charles Williams, under the title *Arthurian Torso*. Lewis did so because he did not want the wisdom in Williams's Arthuriad to be lost. This book contains Williams's unfinished cycle of lyric poems that presents his version of the Arthurian legend (*Taliessin Through Logres* and *The Region of the Summer Stars*), Williams's unfinished prose account of King Arthur's development as a literary figure, and Lewis's commentary explicating these two fragmentary works. In his hundred-page commentary "Williams and the Arthuriad," Lewis first discusses his friend's eighty-five-page literary history of "The Figure of Arthur," then defends both the content and style of Williams's Arthurian poetry. In the pages he allots to the prose work, Lewis offers his hypothetical list of contents for Williams's book although some evidence in the text works against it. He then summarizes his friend's commentary on Tennyson's *Idylls of the King* and concludes by defining Williams as a thoughtful literary critic whose prose work disentangles the threads of the Arthurian myth while creating an original version of it. Lewis then offers a suggested order for reading the poems and explicates each poem thoroughly— trying to defend as engaging the complex content of his friend's lyric poetry. Lewis not only defends Williams against possible charges of obscurity but also praises the beauty and sensory appeal of his verse despite its occasional stylistic problems. Lewis pays homage to his friend's mainstream Christian theology, use and revision of the romantic sensibility, and revision of Arthurian material that draws meaningfully upon medieval sources. Williams finally earns Lewis's praise because his poetry reflects modern concerns as well as a full understanding of the values of the medieval works upon which he based his cycle of lyric poems, particularly the Welsh *Mabinogion* and Malory's *Le Morte Darthur*. *Arthurian Torso* was the last of Lewis's Arthurian projects.

In 1950 Lewis published his first Chronicle of Narnia *The Lion, the Witch and the Wardrobe*. This novel introduces readers to Peter, Susan, Edmund, and Lucy Pevensie, children who enter Narnia through the wardrobe in Professor Kirke's house and befriend several Talking Beasts. Edmund's betrayal of Aslan results in the Great Lion's death, resurrection, and final defeat of the witch Jadis. In 1951, the year of Mrs. Moore's death on January 12, Lewis published his second Narnia story. In *Prince Caspian*, the four Pevensie children return to Narnia, helping Caspian—the true heir to the throne—defeat his tyrant, Uncle Miraz, who has seized power and suppressed the Old Narnians loyal to Aslan. In 1952 Lewis published *The Voyage of the "Dawn Treader."* In this novel, Lucy and Edmund Pevensie enter Narnia with their cousin Eustace Scrubb through a painting of a ship. They join King Caspian's quest to seek the seven nobles the dead King Miraz sent to the east. In the course of this adventure, Eustace becomes a much nicer child after Aslan first strips off the dragon skin in which the boy suddenly finds himself and then baptizes him. Lucy, however, remains steadfast in her faith and good behavior despite the temptations of a magical book. *The Voyage of the "Dawn Treader"* ends with the children reaching the end of the Narnian world and witnessing the departure of Reepicheep, the chivalric mouse, who joins his lord in Aslan's country.

Shortly after publishing *Mere Christianity*, in September 1952, Lewis met Joy Davidman (April 18, 1915–July 13, 1960), who was fifteen years his junior. Davidman, an American poet and novelist whose intellectual vitality and candor won her Lewis's friendship, had abandoned Marxism for Christianity in the late 1940s. Her conversion, according to A. N. Wilson, occurred after she discovered her husband Bill Gresham's most recent affair. Green and Hooper, in contrast, claim that both Joy and her husband converted "in part due to Lewis's books." Wilson describes how quickly Lewis became fond of Davidman, as well as how she moved to Oxford with her sons, with Lewis paying both her rent and her sons' tuition, only a year after her divorce in August 1954.

In 1953 Lewis published *The Silver Chair* and in 1954 *The Horse and His Boy*. In *The Silver Chair*, Eustace Scrubb returns to Narnia with classmate Jill Pole to help Prince Rilian, son of Caspian. With the help of Puddleglum the Marshwiggle, the children behead the Queen of Underland who had murdered Rilian's mother. *The Horse and His*

Boy concerns the adventures of Cor, a lost son of King Lune of Archenland, and of Aravis, a member of the Calormene nobility. Cor has been raised by adoptive parents ignorant of his royal parentage while Aravis is fleeing an arranged marriage. At the instigation of talking horses, the children travel to Narnia and foil the plot of Prince Rabadash to conquer both Narnia and Archenland. They later marry and become king and queen of Archenland after the death of Cor's father.

In June 1954 Lewis left Oxford to accept the chair of Medieval and Renaissance Literature at Magdalene College, Cambridge. Although Lewis had mixed feelings about leaving his long-time academic home, Cambridge offered Lewis the type of position that had always eluded him, and taking that position did not require Lewis to give up living at Oxford on weekends and during vacations. Lewis finally had a position comparable to Tolkien's as the Rawlingson and Bosworth Professor of Anglo-Saxon, and that fact kept him loyal to Cambridge despite Oxford's efforts to give him the Merton chair. Also in this year, Lewis published *English Literature in the Sixteenth Century*, a volume he wrote between 1938 and 1954 that received critical acclaim. This book provides an historical account of the literature of the period while cautioning the reader against trying to fit the past into neat patterns. The book's introduction discusses how the new empiricism had transformed the concept of magic and explains how a scientist can also be a magician. Lewis explored these themes further in *The Discarded Image: An Introduction to Medieval and Renaissance Literature*, published in 1964. In this book, Lewis explicates and celebrates the medieval worldview while contrasting it with the modern one. *The Discarded Image* gives to the reader both information and an invitation "to enter more fully into the consciousness of our ancestors."

In 1955 Lewis published *The Magician's Nephew*, in which he explains the origins of Narnia, the wardrobe, and the central role in the Narnian tales of Professor Digory Kirke (whose childhood is the focus of the book). This novel gave Lewis the means to revise his mother's death, through Digory's use of a magic apple to heal his sick mother, and to retell the story of Genesis through Aslan's singing Narnia into existence. As Joe R. Christopher has noted in his Twayne series volume *C. S. Lewis*, Lewis's retelling not only puts into action the statement in the Gospel of John 1:3 that the Divine Word made all things, but also echoes Tolkien's account in *The Silmarillion* of Ilúvatar (God) and the Ainur (angels) singing the world into existence. In 1955 Lewis also published his spiritual autobiography *Surprised by Joy*. It describes his struggle to reconcile the wonder of myth with the rationalism his education encouraged and to find Joy—a feeling of inconsolable longing he first experienced as a child. This feeling, however, was finally much less important than his ultimate union with God. *Surprised by Joy* also details Lewis's experiences at various schools, at Oxford, and at the front line in France during World War I.

On April 23, 1955, Lewis entered into a civil marriage with Joy Davidman at the Oxford Registry Office so that she could remain in England as a citizen. Lewis soon fell in love with Davidman, however, and in December an Anglican marriage ceremony was performed at her bedside in Wingfield Hospital. When she was undergoing treatment for bone cancer, Lewis prayed that her illness be transferred to him, and when it appeared that Davidman would die, the priest who had married them laid hands upon her. When her cancer went into remission in the summer 1958, Davidman believed that the priest had cured her. Despite the happiness Lewis and his wife experienced in their marriage, their union alienated Tolkien.

In 1956 Lewis published both *The Last Battle* and *Till We Have Faces: A Myth Retold*. *The Last Battle*, using imagery derived partially from the Book of Revelation, completes the Narnian series with Aslan bringing the world of Narnia to its end. This vision of the end of the world eventually leads the children to their own revelation: they have all died in a train crash and will now enter a heaven that is the Platonic form of England. The closing scenes present Aslan taking his true form and the children who have served him entering into perfect joy. *Till We Have Faces* was Lewis's last novel. At the time of its publication, it got mixed reviews because its mood differed greatly from that of his previous novels, but some critics think it is his best. According to Green and Hooper, Lewis "liked *Perelandra* best of all his works of fiction, though he considered *Till We Have Faces* his masterpiece in this kind." In a 1956 letter published in *Letters to an American Lady*, Lewis boasted about his achievement in *Till We Have Faces*: he had "lived in the mind of an *ugly* woman for a whole book," and he was pleased that "All female readers so far have approved the feminine psychology of it: i.e. no masculine note intrudes." The novel retells the Cupid and Psyche myth from the point of view of Psyche's physically and spiritually ugly sister Orual, and it demonstrates Lewis's belief that paganism offers access to the beauty that is God. After causing her sister Psyche to disobey her divine husband Cupid and consequently suffer the punishment of wandering the earth doing impossible tasks, Orual realizes that she loves too possessively and thereby causes harm to those she holds dear. By substituting for and suffering for Psyche, Orual not only relieves her sister's pain, but also purges herself of jealous and possessive love, finally becoming a whole person who is beautiful.

On August 19 and 20, 1958, Lewis recorded ten talks on *The Four Loves* in London. He was also elected an honorary fellow of University College, Oxford and published *Reflections on the Psalms* that same year. *Reflections on the Psalms* reveals Lewis's approach to reading scripture—one that explores both the theological meanings and literary contexts of the sacred text. This work earned Lewis membership on the committee the Convocations of Canterbury and York appointed to revise the psalms for the Church of England. This committee produced *The Revised Psalter*, published in 1966. It also earned Lewis an invitation to broadcast his reflections on the four Loves—Storge (affection), Philia (friendship), Eros (sexual love), and Agape (charity or divine love)—on American radio. In these talks, he stressed that recognizing the unique character of each type of love made it possible to make human love resemble divine love. These talks were later broadcast in late 1958, but only to a limited audience because of the Episcopal Church's concerns about Lewis's frank discussion of sex in speaking of Eros. During 1959 Lewis rewrote these talks to form the manuscript of his book titled *The Four Loves*, and he published it in spring 1960. Also in 1960, after learning that Joy's cancer had returned, Lewis took her on a trip to Greece in April, accompanied by his future biographer Roger Lancelyn Green and Green's wife. Helen Joy Davidman Lewis died on July 13, 1960.

In 1961 Lewis published *Studies in Words*. *Studies in Words* grew out of lectures Lewis had given at Cambridge demonstrating that how words change over time reveals the history of ideas. Also in 1961, Lewis (under the pseudonym N. W. Clerk) published *A Grief Observed*, reflecting on his suffering following his wife's death. In that same year, he published *An Experiment in Criticism* in which he argues that it is more important to distinguish between good and bad readers than between good and bad books. According to Lewis, good reading is like loving, acting morally, and gaining knowledge: it is entering the author's world while still remaining oneself. Therefore, he argues that literary critics may praise a work's merits but may attack it only when they have considerable evidence of deficiency. In 1962 Lewis published *They Asked for a Paper: Papers and Addresses*. This collection of literary and theological essays reprints some material from *Transpositions and*

Other Addresses and includes "Psychoanalysis and Literary Criticism," "On Obstinacy in Belief," "The Weight of Glory," and "Hamlet: The Prince or the Poem?" After resigning his position at Cambridge in summer 1963 because of heart and bladder problems, Lewis was elected an honorary fellow of Magdalene College, Cambridge. Lewis enjoyed his final months, spending time with his favorite books and with his brother who had returned to The Kilns to care for him. C. S. Lewis died in 1963, one week before his sixty-fifth birthday, at his home on November 22. Lewis was buried on November 26, 1963, at Holy Trinity Church in Oxford.

Assessment of Lewis's Arthurian works has not been a major focus of scholarly investigations of his writings. Analysis of his contributions to the romance tradition—*Launcelot*, *The Quest of Bleheris*, and *Nimue*—has occurred mainly as part of recent investigations of Lewis's career as a poet. Many critics have discussed the Arthurian material in *That Hideous Strength*, tracing the medieval and modern Arthurian sources of Lewis's portrayal of Merlin and Arthur Ransom. Readers will find, however, relatively few resources available regarding the influence of the Arthurian myth on Lewis's other works. The reason for this is that Lewis critics have tended to focus either on the Christian content of his writings or on his artistic achievements as a writer of verse, fiction, and theology.

Nevertheless, the Arthurian myth was one of the myths that shaped Lewis's imagination and provided a source for his imagery and characters. Reading medieval and modern Arthurian literature inspired a prose romance (*The Quest of Bleheris*), a long narrative poem about Merlin and Nimue, an unfinished but original poem (*Launcelot*), a science-fiction novel (*That Hideous Strength*), a set of letters (*Mark vs. Tristram*), and scholarly analysis of both the Arthurian works of Charles Williams and *Le Morte Darthur* of Sir Thomas Malory. Lewis's body of Arthurian verse, prose, and scholarship attests to his sustained interest in the Arthurian myth—as do his letters to Arthur Greeves and other friends. Admittedly, Lewis's strong and consistent interest in the myth of King Arthur did not produce a high-profile work like T. H. White's *The Once and Future King*, but it did produce several works of note to today's readers of Arthuriana. Because this myth engaged Lewis consistently and powerfully, it enabled him to make a substantial contribution to both the tradition of Arthurian literature and the scholarly investigation of that tradition.

Author's Note: I would like to acknowledge Andrew Lazo of Rice University for his editorial and bibliographical assistance.

PRIMARY WORKS

Spirits in Bondage: A Cycle of Lyrics [as Clive Hamilton]. London: Heinemann, 1919. With a Preface by Walter Hooper. San Diego: Harcourt Brace Jovanovich, 1984; *Dymer* [as Clive Hamilton]. London: Dent, 1926; New York: E. P. Dutton, 1926; *The Pilgrim's Regress: An Allegorical Apology for Christianity, Reason and Romanticism*. London: J. M. Dent and Sons, Ltd., 1933; New York: Sheed and Ward, 1935. Reprinted with a new preface. London: Bles, 1943. Paperback edition including Lewis's Afterword to the third edition. Grand Rapids, MI: Eerdmans, 1992; *The Allegory of Love: A Study in Medieval Tradition*. Oxford: Clarendon, 1936; New York: Oxford University Press, 1960; *Out of the Silent Planet*. London: Bodley Head, 1938; New York: Macmillan, 1943; *Rehabilitations and Other Essays*. London: Oxford University Press; New York: Oxford University Press, 1939; *The Personal Heresy: A Controversy with E. M. W. Tillyard*. London: Oxford University Press; New York: Oxford University Press, 1939; *The Problem of Pain*. London: Centenary, 1940; New York: Macmillan, 1943; *A Preface to Paradise Lost: Being the Ballard Matthews Lectures Delivered at University College, North Wales, 1941*.

London: Oxford University Press, 1942; New York: Oxford University Press, 1942. Revised and enlarged edition. London: Oxford University Press, 1960; New York: Oxford University Press, 1961; *Broadcast Talks: Reprinted with some alterations from two series of Broadcast Talks. "Right and Wrong: A Clue to the Meaning of the Universe" and "What Christians Believe" given in 1941 and 1942*; U.S. title *The Case for Christianity*. London: Bles, 1942. Republished as *The Case for Christianity*. New York: Macmillan, 1943; *The Screwtape Letters*. London: Bles, 1942; New York: Macmillan, 1943. Reprinted with additional material as *The Screwtape Letters and Screwtape Proposes a Toast*. London: Bles, 1961, and New York: Macmillan, 1962. With further additional material as *The Screwtape Letters and Screwtape Proposes a Toast*. New York: Macmillan, 1982; *Christian Behaviour: A Further Series of Broadcast Talks*. London: Bles, 1943; New York: Macmillan, 1944; *Perelandra: A Novel*. London: John Lane The Bodley Head, 1943; New York: Macmillan, 1944. Reprinted as *Voyage to Venus*. London: Pan Books, 1953. Reprinted as *Perelandra: World of the New Temptation*. New York: Macmillan, 1965; *Beyond Personality: The Christian Idea of God*. London: Bles, 1944; New York: Macmillan, 1945; *English Literature in the Sixteenth Century Excluding Drama, the Completion of "The Clark Lectures." Trinity College*. Cambridge: Cambridge University Press, 1944. Reprinted as *The Oxford History of English Literature*, Vol. III. Oxford: Clarendon, 1954; New York: Oxford University Press, 1954. Reissued as Volume IV, *Poetry and Prose in the Sixteenth Century*. Oxford: Oxford University Press; New York: Oxford University Press, 1990; *That Hideous Strength: A Modern Fairy-Tale for Grown-Ups*. London: John Lane, 1945; New York: Macmillan, 1946. Reprinted as *The Interplanetary Adventures of Dr. Ransom*. New York: Macmillan, 1946. Abridged by the author as *The Tortured Planet*. New York: Avon, 1946. Reprinted as *That Hideous Strength*. London: Pan Books, 1955; *The Great Divorce: A Dream*. London: Bles, 1945; New York: Macmillan, 1946. Originally published as a series in *The Guardian* in 1944; *George MacDonald: An Anthology*. London: Bles, 1946; New York: Macmillan, 1947; *Essays Presented to Charles Williams*. London: Oxford University Press; New York: Oxford University Press, 1947; *Miracles: A Preliminary Study*. London: Bles, 1947; New York: Macmillan, 1947. Revised edition. London: Collins Fontana, 1960; *Arthurian Torso: Containing the Posthumous Fragment of The Figure of Arthur by Charles Williams and A Commentary on The Arthurian Poems of Charles Williams by C. S. Lewis*. London: Oxford University Press, 1948; New York: Oxford University Press, 1948; *Transposition and Other Addresses*. London: Bles, 1949. U.S. title *The Weight of Glory and Other Addresses*. New York: Macmillan, 1949. Revised and expanded U.S. edition, ed. Walter Hooper. New York: Macmillan, 1980; *The Lion, the Witch and the Wardrobe: A Story for Children*. London: Bles, 1950; New York: Macmillan, 1950; *Prince Caspian: The Return to Narnia*. London: Bles, 1951; New York: Macmillan, 1951; *Mere Christianity*, revised and enlarged edition of *Broadcast Talks*. U.S. title *The Case for Christianity* [1942], *Christian Behaviour* [1943], and *Beyond Personality* [1944]. London: Bles, 1952; New York: Macmillan, 1952; *The Voyage of the "Dawn Treader."* London: Bles, 1952; New York: Macmillan, 1952; *The Silver Chair*. London: Bles, 1953; New York: Macmillan, 1953; *The Horse and His Boy*. London: Bles, 1954; New York: Macmillan, 1954; *The Magician's Nephew*. London: Bodley Head, 1955; New York: Macmillan, 1954; *Surprised by Joy: The Shape of My Early Life*. London: Bles, 1955; New York: Harcourt, Brace 1956; *The Last Battle: A Story for Children*. London: Bodley Head, 1956. U.S. title *The Last Battle*. New York: Macmillan, 1956; *Till We Have Faces: A Myth Retold*. London: Bles, 1956; San Diego: Harcourt, Brace, 1957; *Reflections on the Psalms*. London: Bles, 1958; New York: Harcourt, Brace & World, 1958; *Studies in Words*. Cambridge: Cambridge University Press, 1960; New York: Cambridge University Press, 1990; *The Four Loves*. London: Bles, 1960; New York: Harcourt, Brace, & World, 1960; *A Grief Observed* [as N. W. Clerk]. London: Faber & Faber, 1961; Greenwich, CT: Seabury Press, 1963; *They Asked for a Paper: Papers and Addresses*. London: Bles, 1962; *Beyond the Bright Blur* taken from *Letters to Malcolm: Chiefly on Prayer* chapters 15–17 and published in a limited edition. New York: Harcourt, Brace & World, 1963; *Letters to Malcolm: Chiefly on Prayer*. London: Bles, 1964; New York: Harcourt, Brace & World, 1964; *Poems*, ed. Walter Hooper. London: Bles, 1964; New York: Harcourt,

Brace & World, 1965; *The Discarded Image: An Introduction to Medieval and Renaissance Literature*. Cambridge: Cambridge University Press, 1964; *Letters of C. S. Lewis*, ed. W. H. Lewis. London: Bles, 1966; New York: Harcourt, Brace & World, 1966. Revised and enlarged edition. Ed. Walter Hooper. London: Collins, 1988; *Of Other Worlds: Essays and Stories*, ed. Walter Hooper. London: Bles, 1966; New York: Harcourt, Brace & World, 1967; *Studies in Medieval and Renaissance Literature*, ed. Walter Hooper. Cambridge: Cambridge University Press, 1966; New York: Cambridge University Press, 1979; *The Revised Psalter: Pointed for Use with Anglican Chants*. London: Cambridge University Press, 1966; *Christian Reflections*, ed. Walter Hooper. London: Bles, 1967; Grand Rapids, MI: Eerdmans, 1967; *Mark vs. Tristram: Correspondence Between C. S. Lewis and Owen Barfield*, ed. Walter Hooper. Cambridge, MA: Lowell House Printers, 1967; *Spenser's Images of Life*, ed. Alastair Fowler. Cambridge: Cambridge University Press, 1967; *A Mind Awake: An Anthology of C. S. Lewis*, ed. Clyde S. Kilby. London: Bles, 1968; New York: Harcourt, Brace & World, 1969; *C. S. Lewis: Letters to an American Lady [Mary Willis Shelburne]*, ed. Clyde S. Kilby. London: Hodder and Stoughton, 1969; Grand Rapids, MI: Eerdmans, 1967; *Narrative Poems*, ed. with a preface by Walter Hooper. London: Bles, 1969; New York: Harcourt Brace Jovanovich, 1972; *Selected Literary Essays*, ed. with a preface by Walter Hooper. London: Cambridge University Press, 1969; New York: Cambridge University Press, 1979; *God in the Dock: Essays on Theology and Ethics*, ed. with a preface by Walter Hooper. Grand Rapids, MI: Eerdmans, 1970. Republished in United Kingdom as *Undeceptions: Essays on Theology and Ethics*, ed. Walter Hooper. London: Bles, 1971; *Fern-Seed and Elephants and Other Essays on Christianity*, Ed. with a preface by Walter Hooper. London: Fontana, 1975; *The Dark Tower and Other Stories*, ed. with a preface by Walter Hooper. London: Collins, 1977; New York: Harcourt Brace Jovanovich, 1977; *The Joyful Christian: 127 Readings from C. S. Lewis*, ed. Henry William Griffin. New York: Macmillan, 1977; *They Stand Together: The Letters of C. S. Lewis to Arthur Greeves. 1914-1963*, ed. Walter Hooper. London: Collins, 1979; New York: Macmillan, 1979; *The World's Last Night and Other Essays*. New York: Harcourt, Brace, & World, 1960. Revised and expanded edition. New York: Macmillan, 1980; *The Visionary Christian: 131 Readings from C. S. Lewis*, Ed. Chad Walsh. New York: Macmillan, 1981; *Of This and Other Worlds*, ed. Walter Hooper. London: Collins, 1982. U.S. title *On Stories: and Other Essays on Literature*, ed. Walter Hooper. New York: Harcourt Brace Jovanovich, 1982; *The Business of Heaven: Daily Readings from C. S. Lewis*, ed. Walter Hooper. London: Collins Fount, 1984; San Diego: Harcourt Brace Jovanovich, 1984; *Boxen: The Imaginary World of the Young C. S. Lewis*, ed. Walter Hooper. London: Collins, 1985 and San Diego: Harcourt Brace Jovanovich, 1985; *C. S. Lewis: Letters to Children*, eds. Lyle W. Dorsett and Marjorie Lamp Mead with a forward by Douglas H. Gresham. London: Collins, 1985; New York: Macmillan Publishing Company, 1985; *First and Second Things: Essays on Theology and Ethics*. excerpts from *God in the Dock*, ed. with a preface by Walter Hooper. London: Collins, 1985; *Present Concerns*, ed. Walter Hooper. London: Collins Fount, 1986; San Diego: Harcourt Brace Jovanovich, 1987; *Timeless at Heart: Essays on Theology*, ed. Walter Hooper. London: Fount, 1987; "Launcelot." In *"Arthur, the Greatest King": An Anthology of Modern Arthurian Poems*, ed. Alan Lupack, 189–96. New York: Garland, 1988; *Letters: C. S. Lewis [and] Don Giovanni Calabria: A Study in Friendship*, ed. and trans. Martin Moynihan. London: Collins, 1988; Ann Arbor, MI: Servant Books, 1988; *The Essential C. S. Lewis*, ed. and with an introduction by Lyle W. Dorsett. New York: Macmillan, 1988; *The Quotable Lewis*, eds. Wayne Martindale and Jerry Root. Wheaton, IL: Tyndale House Publishers, 1989; *Christian Reunion and Other Essays*, ed. Walter Hooper. London: Collins Fount, 1990; *All My Road Before Me: The Diary of C. S. Lewis, 1922–1927*, ed. Walter Hooper. London: Fount. HarperCollins, 1991; San Diego: Harcourt Brace Jovanovich, 1991; *An Experiment in Criticism*. Cambridge: Cambridge University Press, 1961; New York: Cambridge University Press, 1992; *Daily Readings with C. S. Lewis*, ed. Walter Hooper. London: HarperCollins, 1992. Reissued as *C. S. Lewis: Readings for Meditation and Reflection*, ed. Walter Hooper. London: Fount. HarperCollins, 1995; San Francisco: HarperSanFrancisco, 1996; *The Collected Poems of C. S. Lewis*, ed. Walter Hooper. London:

Fount HarperCollins, 1994; *The Shadowlands of C. S. Lewis: The Man Behind the Movie, Selections from the Writings of C. S. Lewis*, ed. Peter Kreeft. San Francisco: Ignatius Press, 1994; *Essay Collection and Other Short Pieces*, ed. Lesley Walmsley. London: HarperCollins, 2000; *The Chronicles of Narnia: Full-Color Collector's Edition*. New York: Harper Trophy, 2000; *The Collected Letters of C. S. Lewis*, ed. Walter Hooper. Vol. 1, *Family Letters, 1905–1931*. London: HarperCollins, 2000; San Francisco: HarperSanFrancisco, 2000. Vol. 2, *Books, Broadcasts, and the War, 1931–1949*. London: HarperCollins, 2004; San Francisco: HarperSanFrancisco, 2004; *From Narnia to A Space Odyssey: The War of Ideas between Arthur C. Clarke and C. S. Lewis*, ed. Ryder W. Miller. New York: ibooks, 2003; *The Lewis Papers*, ed. W. H. Lewis. Eleven volumes of mostly unpublished material at the Marion E. Wade Center, Wheaton College, Wheaton, Illinois, with a copy at Oxford's Bodleian Library.

SECONDARY SOURCES

Blechner, Michael Harry. "Tristan in Letters: Malory, C. S. Lewis, Updike." *Tristania* 6, no. 1 (1980): 30–37; Carpenter, Humphrey. *The Inklings: C. S. Lewis, J. R. R. Tolkien, Charles Williams, and Their Friends*. London: Allen and Unwin, 1978; Christopher, Joe R. *C. S. Lewis*. Boston: Twayne, 1987; Christopher, Joe R., and Joan K. Ostling. *C. S. Lewis: An Annotated Checklist of Writings about Him and His Works*. Kent, OH: Kent State University Press, 1974; Green, Robert Lancelyn, and Walter Hooper. *C. S. Lewis: A Biography*, rev. ed. San Diego: Harcourt Brace, 1994; Hooper, Walter. *C. S. Lewis: A Companion and Guide*. New York: HarperCollins, 1996; ———. "Introduction." In *Mark vs. Tristram: Correspondence between C. S. Lewis and Owen Barfield*, ed. Walter Hooper. Oxford: Oxford University C. S. Lewis Society, 1990; ———. *Through Joy and Beyond: A Pictorial Biography of C. S. Lewis*. New York: Macmillan, 1982; King, Don W. *C. S. Lewis, Poet: The Legacy of His Poetic Impulse*. Kent, OH: Kent State University Press, 2001; Lacy, Norris J., ed. *Lancelot-Grail: The Old French Arthurian Vulgate and Post-Vulgate in Translation*, 5 vols. New York: Garland, 1993–1996; Lowenberg, Susan. *C. S. Lewis: A Reference Guide, 1972–1988*. New York: G. K. Hall, 1993; Malory, Sir Thomas. *The Works of Sir Thomas Malory*, ed. Eugène Vinaver and rev. P. J. C. Field, 3rd ed., 3 vols. Oxford: Clarendon Press, 1990; Nicolson, Marjorie. *Voyages to the Moon*. New York: Macmillan, 1948; Pauphilet, Albert, ed. *La Queste del Saint Graal: Roman du XIIIe Siècle*. Paris: Champion, 1923; Sayer, George. *Jack: C. S. Lewis and His Times*. San Francisco: Harper and Row, 1988; Tennyson, Alfred Lord. *The Idylls of The King*, ed. J. M. Gray. New Haven, CT: Yale University Press, 1983; Tolkien, J. R. R. *The Silmarillion*, ed. Christopher Tolkien. Boston: Houghton Mifflin, 1977; Twain, Mark. *A Connecticut Yankee in King Arthur's Court*, ed. M. Thomas Inge. Oxford: Oxford University Press, 1997; White, Michael. *C. S. Lewis: A Life*. New York: Carroll & Graf, 2004; White, T. H. *The Once and Future King*. New York: Putnam, 1958; Williams, Charles. *The Place of the Lion*. New York: Pellegrini & Cudahy, 1951; Wilson, A. N. *C. S. Lewis: A Biography*. New York: Norton, 1990.

FIONA TOLHURST

JOHN STEINBECK

(February 27, 1902–December 20, 1968)

Some people consider John Steinbeck to be one of the seminal writers in American literature of the twentieth century. He was certainly one of the more popular authors with the reading public if not with all of the literary critics. His most influential books concern the plight and sufferings of the common people: for example, the "Okies" of *The Grapes of Wrath* (1939) or the itinerant ranch hands in *Of Mice and Men* (1937). In all of his stories, according to Robert Murray Davis in his introduction to the 1972 collection of critical essays on the author, a "fictional world which ... is, paradoxically, interesting to his readers because it includes actions and sensations they recognize and which few other writers give them" (10). This distinctive writing style resulted in him winning the O. Henry Prize for "The Murder" in 1934, then being awarded Gold Medals from the Commonwealth Club of California for *Tortilla Flat* in 1935 and *In Dubious Battle* in 1936, the New York Drama Critics' Circle Silver Plaque in 1937 for *Of Mice and Men*, and a Pulitzer Prize for *The Grapes of Wrath* in 1940. The accolades for his work culminated in the Nobel Prize for literature in 1962.

John Ernst Steinbeck was born in Salinas, California, on February 27, 1902, to John Ernst and Olive Hamilton Steinbeck. In 1919 he graduated from Salinas High School; a year later, he enrolled at Stanford University as an English major, attending intermittently until 1925 when he left without receiving a degree. That year he sailed through the Panama Canal to New York City, where he briefly worked as a reporter for the *American*, William Randolph Hearst's morning newspaper. In 1929, his first novel *Cup of Gold*, a historical novel that loosely reflects the author's interest in the Arthurian grail legends, was published. The novel tells of Henry Morgan's evolution into a buccaneer as he captures Panama, referred to as the Cup of Gold, wresting it from the hands of the Spanish while searching for a beautiful woman everyone calls La Santa Roja (The Red Saint), but whom Morgan describes as being "the harbor of all [his] questing" (149).

When he finally finds her, he realizes she is not the woman of his dreams, so he ransoms her back to her husband and returns to England as a hero with his newfound fortune.

The year after *Cup of Gold* was published, on January 14, Steinbeck married Carol Henning of San Jose, California. That same year he became a client of literary agents Mavis McIntosh and Elizabeth Otis, beginning a relationship that continued for the remainder of his life; meanwhile, in Monterey, California, he met marine biologist, philosopher, and ecologist Edward F. Ricketts, who would have a significant influence on Steinbeck's thinking and writing.

The next decade of Steinbeck's life was filled with many highs, and only a few lows. In 1934 Steinbeck's short story "The Murder" was selected for the O. Henry Prize. That same year, Steinbeck's mother died (followed by his father two years later) and he connected with Pascal Covici, who became his lifelong editor.

The following year, Steinbeck's novel *Tortilla Flat*, which patently imitates the Arthurian legends, won the annual Commonwealth Club of California award for the best novel by a state resident. *Tortilla Flat*, whose chapters have descriptive titles right out of Malory (for example, "How three sinful men, through contrition, attained peace. How Danny's Friends swore comradeship," the title of Chapter VI), presents the tale of Danny and his friends, the *paisanos*, who gather at his house, which sits on a hillside above Monterey. The story begins when Danny returns home from World War I and finds himself the owner of two houses inherited from his grandfather. He lives in one of the houses, drawing his mixed-blood friends to join him for the camaraderie, while renting out the other one for some income, although he collects little rent before the second house burns down. The *paisanos* have many adventures together, including discovering a buried geodetic survey marker, before Danny dies. In sorrow after his funeral, his friends burn down the remaining house as their way of honoring their friendship.

Changing his focus while working for the *San Francisco News* in 1936, Steinbeck wrote "The Harvest Gypsies," reporting the horrific conditions in migrant workers' camps. In 1937 he published *Of Mice and Men*; the play version of the story, which premiered at the Music Box Theatre in New York November 23, 1937, won the New York Drama Critics' Circle Award while the author was chosen one of the ten outstanding young men of the year. Two years later, Steinbeck's novel *The Grapes of Wrath*, with its acknowledged Biblical imagery, won the Pulitzer Prize and the author was elected to the National Institute of Arts and Letters. Steinbeck completed the decade by seeing both *Of Mice and Men* and *The Grapes of Wrath* made into critically acclaimed movies: the former starring Lon Chaney, Jr., and Burgess Meredith; the latter starring Henry Fonda with an Oscar-winning performance by Jane Darwell as the family matriarch.

In 1941 Steinbeck and Ed Ricketts published the nonfiction record of their marine-life collecting trip, *Sea of Cortez*, the work which, according to Charles Shively in *John Steinbeck: From the Tide Pool to the Loyal Community*, finally reveals "the full extent of the holistic world-view which he had developed as the base for his fiction of the 1930's" (25). Shively goes on to summarize Steinbeck's viewpoint as the "belief that all living things are inherently related into a Whole" (25). The next year Steinbeck's attention turned to the war in Europe; *The Moon Is Down*, a story about the Nazi invasion of Norway, appeared as both a novel and a play, with a film version following in 1943. In addition, Steinbeck wrote *Bombs Away: The Story of a Bomber Team*, a propaganda novel for the Army Air Corps, at the direction of President Franklin Roosevelt, who, as Warren French explains in *John Steinbeck's Fiction Revisited*, wanted "a morale-boosting work to acquaint Americans with the training of a bomber crew" (91). Steinbeck went on from this project to develop a story for an Alfred Hitchcock project, *Lifeboat;* however, creative differences between the writer and the director caused Steinbeck to remove himself from the project.

Meanwhile, changes were happening in the author's personal life. In 1942 Steinbeck divorced Carol Henning, his wife of approximately twelve years. The following year, he married Gwyndolen Conger; then he traveled to Europe as a war correspondent for the *New York Herald Tribune.* The Steinbecks had two children, Thomas, born in 1944, and John IV, in 1946, before they divorced in 1948. That same year he lost his best friend Ed Ricketts in a car-train accident; both Ricketts and their friendship would be immortalized in 1951 in Steinbeck's preface to the *Log from the Sea of Cortez,* his narrative of their 1940 trip together. Two years after his divorce from Gwendolyn, Steinbeck married Elaine Scott, with whom he spent the remainder of his life.

Turning attention to the author's work after the war, *Cannery Row* was published in 1945 along with *The Red Pony,* a story cycle in four parts that had previously appeared in segments in various periodicals such as *North American Review* and *Harper's,* as well as in an earlier version consisting of only three parts. These two popular novels were followed in 1947 by *The Wayward Bus,* which became, according to movie critic Leonard Maltin, an uninspired movie in 1957, and *The Pearl,* which was filmed in Mexico in 1948. Praise for Steinbeck as an author resulted in his being elected to the American Academy of Letters in 1948, the same year he published *A Russian Journal,* a travel report from his trip with photographer Robert Capa. Two years later, Steinbeck experimented with a novelette and a play presenting the idea, according to French in his 1994 book on the author, that "everyone is responsible for the world's children" (112); this work, *Burning Bright,* was not very well received in either form. He redeemed himself two years after that with the publication of *East of Eden,* which would become a four-star film in 1955 showcasing James Dean's debut and netting an Oscar for Jo Van Fleet as the mother. That novel was followed in 1954 by a kind of a sequel to *Cannery Row, Sweet Thursday,* which Richard Rodgers and Oscar Hammerstein turned into a musical called *Pipe Dream* in 1955, fulfilling, according to French, a lifelong dream to create a musical similar to Frank Loesser's *Guys and Dolls,* but disappointing Steinbeck with the end product.

Sweet Thursday ended Steinbeck's fascination with California as a setting for his stories. His next novel, *The Short Reign of Pippin IV* (1957), about one of Charlemagne's descendants, was set in Paris where the Steinbecks had spent the summer of 1954. *Pippin* was finally followed in 1961 by Steinbeck's last completed novel, *The Winter of Our Discontent,* set on Long Island, where Steinbeck himself had settled in 1955 (in Sag Harbor). For all of his work to this point, Steinbeck was awarded the Nobel Prize for literature in 1962. The time in between the publication of these two final novels was largely taken up with the background research Steinbeck did in preparation for his translation of Sir Thomas Malory's *Le morte d'Arthur (The Death of Arthur),* which was unfinished at the time of his death. According to a letter dated August 5, 1965, that he wrote to Carlton A. Sheffield collected in *A Life in Letters,* the preparation work for the translation did inspire Steinbeck to inscribe the last words of Lancelot to Guinevere ("Ladye, I take reccorde of God, in thee I have myn erthly joye" [829]) into a stepping stone that he had placed near a swimming pool he had built for his wife.

In the last years of his life, Steinbeck focused on his nonfiction, completing in 1962 *Travels with Charley in Search of America,* about a trip he had taken with his dog in autumn 1960. He spent 1963 touring Europe with playwright Edward Albee as part of the Department of State's cultural exchange program; Lyndon B. Johnson presented him with the Presidential Medal of Freedom in 1964 for his efforts with the program. In 1965 he began a series of columns for weekend editions of *Newsday*, which he called "Letters to Alicia" reporting his adventures in various places he visited, including Europe and Vietnam. His final completed new effort was *America and Americans* in 1966, a collection of essays presenting his reflections on photographs depicting the diversity that is America. In his book on *The King Arthur Myth in Modern American Literature*, Andrew Mathis observes that "the various essays often bear no relationship to the montage of photographs . . . , but they contain many of the themes that Steinbeck had been developing over his entire career" (102). Just before his death, Steinbeck prepared for publication his 1952 diary that he had kept while writing *East of Eden;* this format was repeated in 1989 using the diary he had kept in 1938 while writing *The Grapes of Wrath*. John Steinbeck died in New York City, December 20, 1968, and was buried in Salinas, California, current home of the National Steinbeck Center.

As John Steinbeck himself observed in a 1959 letter to director Elia Kazan, "a writer sets down what has impressed him . . . at an early age" (*Letters*, 630). For Steinbeck, that clearly was the story of King Arthur and his knights. As Andrew Mathis observes in *The King Arthur Myth in American Literature* (2002), "Steinbeck relied on Camelot for his inspiration even more than on the Bible or classical mythology" that his contemporaries William Faulkner and T. S. Eliot favored (25). Mathis believes Steinbeck relied on Arthurian imagery because the author found the idealized chivalry of Malory no longer attainable, especially in a world that had been devastated by two world wars. Overt Arthurian imagery in Steinbeck's work begins with his first novel, *City of Gold*, about the life and adventures of privateer Henry Morgan, in which he depicts what Alan and Barbara Lupack describe in their chapter on "Steinbeck and the Arthurian Legend" in their 1999 book *King Arthur in America* as "a rather unusual quest for the Grail" (183)—in this instance, the "Grail" is represented dually by a woman referred to as "La Santa Roja" (the Red Saint) and the province of Panama where she resides instead of the conventional cup. The imagery continues quite overtly through *Tortilla Flat*, to which, as Arthur Kinney reminds readers in his 1965 article "The Arthurian Cycle in *Tortilla Flat*" for *Modern Fiction Studies*, Steinbeck appended a preface specifically drawing analogies to the Round Table legends when he discovered people did not make the connection on their own, even after he titled his chapters according to the style of Malory (for example, Chapter XIII is "How Danny's Friends threw themselves to the aid of a distressed lady"). The critics by and large agree that the final appearance of Arthurian imagery is in his last completed work, *The Winter of Our Discontent*, in which the novel's hero, Ethan Allen Hawley, according to Scott Earle's 2000 analysis of "Ethan as Lancelot" for the *Steinbeck Yearbook*, can be clearly perceived as a quester with his Knight Templar plumed hat and his Holy Grail-like talisman. However, the Lupacks also find general Arthurian references in less often considered works like *In Dubious Battle, Of Mice and Men*, and *Sweet Thursday*, while Mimi Reisel Gladstein finds them also in the final work published during Steinbeck's lifetime, *America and Americans*.

Steinbeck's reliance on Camelot ultimately reaches its pinnacle in his uncompleted "translation" of Sir Thomas Malory's *Le morte d'Arthur*, published eight years after the author's death through the efforts of Steinbeck's longtime friend and editor, Chase Horton. Working with Malory's translation of the original French stories, Steinbeck attempted to render Malory's fifteenth-century English into twentieth-century vernacular. Steinbeck was able to use the Winchester manuscript instead of the traditional Caxton version of Malory because of the support of Eugène Vinaver of the University of Manchester, who had been working with that manuscript on his own adaptation of the tales first published in 1956. When *The Acts of King Arthur and his Noble Knights* first appeared, G. A. Masterton, writing a review for the October 15, 1976, issue of *Library Journal,* deemed the novel less effective than the letters about the project that accompany it. In contrast, Cynthia Johnson, writing a review for the April 1977 issue of the *School Library Journal,* offered the opinion that "Steinbeck has rendered a great legend intelligible and intriguing to a modern, non-academic audience" (84).

The first chapter of the book "Merlin" introduces Arthur's story from his inception through his battles to unite the kingdom after drawing the sword from the stone. When King Lodegrance of Camylarde is attacked, Arthur goes to his rescue and meets the king's daughter, Guinevere, who will become Arthur's queen. Soon afterwards, Arthur travels to Caerleon, where Margause, the wife of rebellion leader King Lot, visits him and conceives the child who will be Sir Mordred. When Arthur destroys his sword during a fight with King Pellinore, Merlin leads him to a nearby lake in the middle of which an arm holds a sword by its magical scabbard, which is given to Arthur in exchange for a favor to be named. Arthur returns to Caerleon, learns the child who will cause him trouble was born on May Day and orders "that any male child born on May Day must be sent to the king on pain of death" (47). All of the babies are placed in a little ship and sent out to sea unattended. One baby falls off and is rescued by a peasant living near the shore, ending the first chapter.

Chapter Two, "The Knight with the Two Swords," offers the story of Balin and Balan and their quest for the Lady Lyle of Avalon, who arrives at court wearing a noble sword until an honorable knight takes it from her. Balin is able to draw it, but he refuses to return it to her even though she warns him that the sword will destroy him. The Lady of the Lake arrives and reveals the name of the sword she had given Arthur—Excalibur, which "means Cut Steel" (54). She has come to claim her payment for her gift of the sword—the head of the lady who brought the sword and the knight who drew the sword. When Balin sees her, he recognizes her as the person responsible for his mother's death three years earlier, and he slays her, upsetting Arthur because she was at court under his protection. To atone for his act, Balin sets off on several quests that are detailed in the chapter. Finally, Balin arrives at a castle, which has as its custom that any stranger must joust with a knight guarding a nearby island. After they trick him into carrying a larger shield, Balin goes into battle with the knight, who turns out to be his brother Balin; they slay each other, ending their story.

Chapter Three presents "The Wedding of King Arthur." To ensure the succession to the crown, Arthur decides to take as his wife Guinevere, the daughter of King Lodegrance of Camylarde, to whom his father, Uther, had given as a gift a great round table. Merlin warns Arthur this wedding will mean inevitable problems, yet Arthur will not be swayed and sends Merlin to make the request. Lodegrance not only sends his daughter, but he also includes the round table, which seats 150, and one hundred knights to serve the king. Arthur sends Merlin out to find the best knights to complete the table, but he can only find twenty-eight. In honor of the wedding, Arthur agrees to make a knight of Gawain, Margause's son, and Torre, King Pellinore's son. During the feast after the wedding ceremony at St. Stephen's Church, a white stag pursued by a white hound bursts into the hall, followed by a lady on a white palfrey, then an armed knight on a warhorse who grabs the lady and rides away. Citing "the law of quest" (82), Arthur sends Gawain with his brother Gaheris as his squire out to find the stag, Torre to find the dog, and Pellinore to find the knight and the lady and return them to the feast. Their separate adventures are detailed with varying degrees of success before the knights return to the king's court.

Chapter Four acquaints us with "The Death of Merlin." When Pellinore brought Nyneve back to Arthur's court after the previous adventure, Merlin saw her and "his desire overcame his years and knowledge" (99). Before they leave the court together, Merlin warns Arthur to guard carefully both Excalibur and its scabbard, because someone Arthur trusts will steal them both. Meanwhile, Nyneve has been getting Merlin to reveal to her his knowledge of magic; he finally, foolishly, teaches her those spells that cannot be broken, which proves to be his undoing when she imprisons him in a cave she magically carves in the cliffs of Cornwall. Back at Cardolle, where Arthur has moved his court, the king faces an attack by the Kings of Denmark, Ireland, Vale, Sorleyse, and the Isle of Longtaynse, who have joined forces against England. With Guinevere by his side, Arthur sets out with a small band of followers, who are attacked in the night before reinforcements can arrive. Arthur and Guinevere are escaping with Sir Kay, Sir Gawain, and Sir Gryfflet when they meet the five kings out riding alone. The four men attack the five kings and slay them all, then with the few followers remaining destroy the last of the invaders. Arthur replaces the fallen knights with Uryens, Gawain, Gryfflet, Kay, and Torre, among others.

In Chapter Five, attention turns to "Morgan le Fay," Arthur's cruel and ambitious half sister who plots the murder of the king. Using her magical arts, she fashions a sword identical in appearance to Excalibur, then switches the swords. She gives the real sword to Sir Accolon of Gaul, a knight she has enchanted to perform her bidding. Morgan arranges for the king to be captured by Sir Damas, a cowardly knight who forces Arthur to fight as his champion against Accolon. During the fight, Arthur is severely damaged by his own sword and, of course, can inflict no damage with the sword he wields. Nyneve arrives barely in time to cast a spell forcing Excalibur back into Arthur's hand, allowing him to defeat Accolon. Sure that her plan has succeeded, Morgan goes to kill her husband Uryens while he sleeps; when their son Ewain stops her, she claims to have been enchanted by an evil spirit. She slips out of Camelot just before Arthur arrives and quickly returns "to her lands in the country of Gore" (123) to strengthen them against a possible retaliation by Arthur.

Chapter Six puts forward the adventures of "Gawain, Ewain and Marhalt." To atone for her earlier misdeeds, Morgan le Fay sends a damsel to court with a beautiful cloak Morgan had prepared for the king. Luckily, Nyneve persuades Arthur to have the girl try it on first, because the cloak is impregnated with poison. Now that Arthur is unsure whom he can trust, he insists that Ewain, Morgan's son, leave the court. To prove his loyalty to the king, Ewain decides to go on a quest and his cousin Gawain elects to accompany him. Before long, they encounter Sir Marhalt, a son of the King of Ireland, who joins them on their journey, which begins in "a great and mysterious wood called the Forest of Arroy" (135). In the forest, they find three ladies sitting near a spring. Each of the ladies joins one of the knights on separate quests, with all agreeing to return to the spring in one year, which they do. The three knights then return to King Arthur's court with their stories of their deeds to tell.

The final and longest chapter relates "The Noble Tale of Sir Lancelot of the Lake." Peace now reigns in Arthur's kingdom, causing its own kind of trouble. To keep his knights in shape, Arthur holds several tournaments; Lancelot quickly is revealed as the best, unbeatable in every contest, which soon bores him. Guinevere recognizes his resultant restlessness and proposes that Arthur create a new corps of knights who would become instruments "of the King's Justice" (210), roving the kingdom and righting wrongs. She pairs up Lancelot, the best knight, with his lazy nephew Lyonel who, it is hoped, will learn something from the experience. The knights set off with their squires, though they are soon separated. Lyonel is captured and carried off by Sir Tarquin while Morgan drugs Lancelot to enable four queens to transport him to Maiden's Castle, where they imprison him. After escaping and rescuing his nephew, then having several more adventures and encounters with various knights, Lancelot returns to court for Whitsun-tide. All of the knights are at court relating their adventures, which tires Lancelot, so he asks to be excused to tend to his wounds. Arthur takes him into the tower, where the queen was waiting. Discussing the degree of embellishment occurring in the stories being related below, the queen asks if he truly rescued all the damsels reported, and if he loved any of them. He acknowledged he was happy being sheltered by his courtly vow to love only her. However, as he departs for his bed, Guinevere stops him and leads him to her chamber, where the tale ends with their passionate kiss.

Criticism of Steinbeck's work frequently tends to focus on the individual chapters instead of the work as a whole. For example, the episode focused on critically in the first chapter, which is titled "Merlin," occurs at the end of the chapter, with its retelling of the story of Herod as "human experience . . . a version of 'Power corrupts'" (*Acts*, 344), as Steinbeck explains in a 1959 letter to his literary agent Elizabeth Otis and his editor Chase Horton. In a 1959 letter to Kazan, Steinbeck remarks "there is nothing nastier in literature than Arthur's murder of the children because one of them might grow up to kill him" (*Letters*, 630–31). Marie Nelson, in her 2001 article about the episode in works by Steinbeck, Mary Stewart, and T. H. White, observed that "Steinbeck directly indicts King Arthur as a murderer of children" with the language he uses to describe the king throughout the passage (268)—adjectival phrases such as "incestuous shame," "cruel and cowardly plan," "shamed and evil eyes" (*Acts*, 47), which certainly darken this telling of the story.

The depiction of knightly and kingly "virtue" in the first chapter is contrasted by Stein-beck's portrayal of various characters in subsequent adventures; for example, Mary C. Wil-liams addresses the "Lessons from Ladies in Steinbeck's 'Gawain, Ewain, and Marhalt'," the sixth chapter of the book, in her 1984 article in *Avalon to Camelot*. She considers the author as trying to improve upon Malory's depiction of female characters with this story, trying to expose a medieval woman's life to twentieth-century readers, an intention the author himself made clear in a letter dated July 11, 1958, to his agent, Elizabeth Otis, and editor, Chase Horton (*Acts*, 322). Williams also posits that, with his depiction of Lady Lyne (the oldest of the three ladies of the tale), Steinbeck was attempting to create "a role in the Arthurian world for his tomboy sister Mary, to whom *The Acts* is dedicated" (40). The portrayal of ladies in this episode is in marked contrast to Steinbeck's dramatization of Morgan le Fay who, according to Laura Hodges's 1992 article for *Quondam et Futurus: A Journal of Arthurian Interpretations* titled "Steinbeck's Adaptation of Malory's Launcelot: A Triumph of Realism over Supernaturalism," "seeks the political power she might have had, had she been a duke's son instead of a daughter," using "magic" as "her means to power" (72). A May 1959 letter to Vinaver reveals Steinbeck's fascination with Morgan and her plot against the king, a fascination based in part upon where she had learned her necro-mancy—in a nunnery, which he deemed a fitting place to develop witches with all of the "lone, unfulfilled women living together" (*Letters*, 638).

In Hodges's 1990 consideration of "Steinbeck's Dream Sequence in *The Acts of King Arthur and His Noble Knights*" for the journal *Arthurian Interpretations*, after listing a significant number of dream visions that occur in the original Malory, she observes that Steinbeck follows the precise format of the medieval dream vision as described by Macrobius while analyzing the dream of Scipio in his medieval commentary on the topic. In the dream vision format, Hodges explains, "a dream is the perfect vehicle for portraying a spiritual crisis ... that, within the dream, is ultimately resolved" (36), as it is for Lancelot in the final episode in Steinbeck's translation, "The Noble Tale of Sir Lancelot of the Lake." Lancelot's crisis is centered in his struggle to live up to the codes of love and chivalry by which he has been living, a struggle, Hodges reminds readers, brought to the forefront by his conversation with his nephew Lyonel. Andrew Welsh's 1991 article for *Philological Quarterly*, "Lancelot at the Crossroads in Malory and Steinbeck," analyzes this episode, seeing Lancelot as forced by his adventure with the four queens into finally making his choice for the fifth queen, Guinevere. For John Ditsky, writing in "The Friend at the Round Table: A Note on Steinbeck's Acts," a 1978 article for *American Literature*, the depiction of Lancelot in this entire episode turns what "had been simply a readable and competent rendering into modern English of a classic work into a piece of imaginative fiction which ... contains ... some of Steinbeck's finest writing" (635). In the 1992 article for the journal *Quondam et Futurus*, Hodges considers "Steinbeck's Adaptation of Malory's Launcelot," concluding that for Steinbeck, Lancelot "is isolated by greatness ... a valiant, but fallible and lonely man" (69). Hodges emphasizes that Steinbeck's stress on providing motivation for his character's actions reaches its zenith in Lancelot's tale, reconsidering an earlier article on "Arthur, Lancelot, and the Psychodrama of Steinbeck" that she wrote in 1980 for *Steinbeck Quarterly*. Comparing the psychodrama, which like the dream vision provides a cathartic relief to an inner conflict, to an allegory, Hodges describes Arthur as a "man at an egotistic and immature stage of his life" while Lancelot "illustrates man in his maturity" (72).

Continuing her analysis of the character of Arthur, Hodges observes that Steinbeck's "emphasis in *Acts* is on Arthur the man. He is seen to be an imperfect king because he is an immature man, lacking self-control, goodness, and wisdom" (74), characteristics ultimately "responsible for the destruction of the round table" (75). Within Steinbeck's psychodrama, symbolic characters portray "the universal conflict within each individual of the desires for power, for peace, for love, and for perfection" (79), amplifying the medieval tradition to reveal twentieth century foibles. In contrast, considering the work as a whole, Scott Earle observes, in his 2000 article for the *Steinbeck Yearbook*, "Ethan as Lancelot: *The Winter of Our Discontent* and the Arthurian Code," that "one is struck by the translation's early fidelity and its later artistic license" (79). Later in the article, Earle also notes that "Lancelot and the other knights of Arthur's court live and fight within a Christian context; faith in God is as natural for them as breathing and lets them access a remarkable reservoir of strength" (83), adequately summing up Steinbeck's ultimate plan for the text.

Believing that, according to a June 27, 1958, letter to Professor and Mrs. Eugène Vinaver, the twentieth century "has more parallels with the fifteenth century than ... the nineteenth century did" (*Letters*, 592), in *The Acts of King Arthur and His Noble Knights* Steinbeck created an intriguing work that most people regret he did not finish. According to Steinbeck's friend Webster Street, who presented a paper on the man and his work at the 1970 Steinbeck Conference, "in writing *Tortilla Flat*, John firmly believed he was writing folklore" (38), and that interest in folklore became clearest in *The Acts*. His use of nature as a theme is frequently compared to William Faulkner, while other critics, like Charles Shively in his paper for that same conference, see him as continuing the vein of American philosophical thought descending from Ralph Waldo Emerson and Walt

Whitman. Summing up the importance of *The Acts* in "A Note on John Steinbeck in King Arthur's Court" for *The Arthurian Myth of Quest and Magic*, a 1993 "Festschrift in Honor of Lavon B. Fulwiler," Bob Dowell observes that "the seven completed tales come to life in the lucid Steinbeck style offering a pleasurable feast for the reader" who is hungry for a twentieth-century glimpse of Arthurian life (72).

PRIMARY WORKS

"The Gifts of Iban" (as John Stern). *The Smoker's Companion* (1927); *Cup of Gold*. New York: Robert M. McBride, 1929; London: Heinemann, 1937; *The Pastures of Heaven*. New York: World Publishing Co., 1932; London: Allan, 1933; *To a God Unknown*. New York: Robert O. Ballou, 1933; London: Heinemann, 1935; *Tortilla Flat*. New York: Covici-Friede, 1935; London: Heinemann, 1935; *In Dubious Battle*. New York: Modern Library, 1936; London: Heinemann, 1936; *The Harvest Gypsies: on the Road to the Grapes of Wrath*. San Bernardino, CA: Borgo Press, 1936; *The Red Pony*. New York: Covici-Friede, 1937; enlarged edition, New York: Viking, 1945; London: Heinemann, 1949; *Of Mice and Men*. New York: Covici-Friede, 1937; London: Heinemann, 1937; *Of Mice and Men: A Play in Three Acts*, by Steinbeck and George S. Kaufman. New York: Covici-Friede, 1937; *The Long Valley*. New York: Viking Penguin, 1938; London: Heinemann, 1939; *The Grapes of Wrath*. New York: Viking, 1939; London: Heinemann, 1939; *The Forgotten Village*. New York: Viking, 1941; *The Sea of Cortez: A Leisurely Journal of Travel and Research*, by Steinbeck and Edward F. *Ricketts*. New York: Viking, 1941. Republished, with "About Ed Ricketts." by Steinbeck, as *The Log from the Sea of Cortez*. New York: Viking Penguin, 1951; London: Heinemann, 1958; "How Edith McGillcuddy Met R. L. Stevenson." *Harper*, 183 (August 1941): 252–58; reprinted in *Senior Scholastic* 44 (April 24, 1944): 21–22; *Bombs Away: The Story of a Bombing Team*. New York: Viking, 1942; *The Moon is Down*. New York: SunDial Press, 1942; London: Heinemann, 1942; *The Moon is Down: A Play in Two Parts*. New York: Dramatists Play Service, 1942; London: English Theatre Guild, 1943; *Cannery Row*. New York: Viking Penguin, 1945; London: Heinemann, 1945; "The Pearl of the World." *Woman's Home Companion* 72 (December 1945) 17–19; *The Pearl*. New York: Viking, 1947; London: Heinemann, 1948; *The Wayward Bus*. New York: Viking, 1947; London: Heinemann, 1947; "The Time the Wolves Ate the Vice-Principal." *The Magazine of the Year* 1, no. 1 (March 1947): 26–27; *A Russian Journal*. New York: Viking, 1948; London: Heinemann, 1949; "Miracle of Tepayac." *Collier's* 122 (December 25, 1948): 22–23; *Burning Bright: A Play in Story Form*. New York: Viking, 1950; London: Heinemann, 1951; *Burning Bright: A Play in Three Acts*. New York: Dramatists Play Service, 1951; *East of Eden*. New York: Viking Penguin, 1952; London: Heinemann, 1952; "Sons of Cyrus Trask." *Collier's* 130 (July 12, 1952): 14–15; *Sweet Thursday*. New York: Viking, 1954; London: Heinemann, 1954; "How Mr. Hogan Robbed a Bank." *Atlantic Monthly* 197 (March 1956): 58–61; *The Short Reign of Pippin IV*. New York: Viking, 1957; London: Heinemann, 1957; *The Winter of Our Discontent*. New York: Viking Penguin, 1961; London: Heinemann, 1961; "The Black Man's Ironic Burden." Reprinted in *Negro History Bulletin* 24 (April 1961): 146; *Travels with Charley in Search of America*. New York: Viking Penguin, 1962; London: Heinemann, 1962; "Letters to Alicia" (1965–1967) reports from Europe and Vietnam for weekend editions of *Newsday*; *America and Americans*. New York: Viking Penguin, 1966; London: Heinemann, 1966; *The Acts of King Arthur and His Men*, ed. Horton Chase. New York: Farrar, Straus & Giroux, 1976: London: Heinemann, 1976; *The Uncollected Stories of John Steinbeck*, ed. Kiyoshi Nakayama. Tokyo: Nanún-do, 1986; *Conversations with John Steinbeck*, ed. Thomas Fensch. Jackson: University of Mississippi Press, 1988; *John Steinbeck on Writing*, ed. Tetsumaro Hayaski, Steinbeck Essay Series, no. 2. Muncie, IN: Steinbeck Research Institute, Ball State University, 1988; *Working Days: The Journal of "The Grapes of Wrath."* ed. Robert DeMott. New York: Viking, 1989.

Play Productions and Produced Scripts

Of Mice and Men, New York, The Music Box Theatre, November 23, 1937; *The Forgotten Village*, motion picture, Pan American Films, directed by Herman Kline, 1940; *Tortilla Flat*, motion picture, M-G-M, directed by Victor Fleming, 1942; *The Moon is Down*, New York, Martin Beck, April 18, 1942; *The Moon Is Down*, motion picture, 20th Century Fox, directed by Irving Pichel, 1943; *La Perla. The Pearl*, motion picture, RKO/Aguila-Films Asociados, directed by Emilio Fernandez in Spanish, 1948; *The Red Pony*, motion picture, Republic, directed by Lewis Milestone, 1949; remade as television movie directed by Robert Totten, 1973; *Viva Zapata!*, motion picture, 20th Century Fox, directed by Elia Kazan, 1950; *Burning Bright*, New York, Broadhurst Theatre, October 18, 1950; *Pipe Dream*, New York, Sam S. Shubert Theatre, November 30, 1955. Music by Richard Rodgers and Oscar Hammerstein based on *Sweet Thursday*; *The Wayward Bus*, motion picture, 20th Century Fox, directed by Victor Vicas, 1957.

Collections

Their Blood Is Strong. Pamphlet version of *San Francisco News* articles. San Francisco: Simon J. Lubin Society of California, 1938; *The Portable Steinbeck, Selected by Pascal Covici*, with an introduction by Lewis Gannett. New York: Viking, 1946. Republished, with an introduction by Pascal Covici, Jr. New York: Viking, 1971; Harmondsworth, UK: Penguin, 1976; *The Short Novels of John Steinbeck*. New York: Viking, 1953; *Once There Was a War*. Collection of war dispatches. New York: Viking Penguin, 1958; *Journal of a Novel: The "East of Eden" Letters*. New York: Viking, 1969; *Steinbeck: A Life in Letters*, ed. Elaine Steinbeck and Robert Walsten. New York: Viking, 1975; *Novels and Stories, 1932–1937*. New York: Library of America, 1994; *Novels, 1942–1952*. New York: Library of America, 2001.

Papers

The largest collections of John Steinbeck's letters, manuscripts, and related materials are held by the Department of Special Collections at Green Library, Stanford University; and by the Harry Ransom Humanities Research Center at the University of Texas at Austin. Other significant collections of Steinbeck material are held by the Martha Heasley Cox Center for Steinbeck Studies at San Jose University; Columbia University; the University of California, Berkeley; Ball State University; and the National Steinbeck Center in Salinas, California.

SECONDARY SOURCES

Beebe, Maurice, and Jackson R. Bryer. "Criticism of John Steinbeck: A Selected Checklist." *Modern Fiction Studies* 11 (Spring 1954): 90–103; Benson, Jackson J. *The True Adventures of John Steinbeck, Writer*. New York: Viking, 1984. Republished as *John Steinbeck, Writer: A Biography*. New York: Penguin, 1990; Benson, Jackson J., ed. *The Short Novels of John Steinbeck: Critical Essays with a Checklist to Steinbeck Criticism*. Durham, NC: Duke University Press, 1990; Davis, Robert Murray, ed. *Steinbeck: A Collection of Critical Essays*. Englewood Cliffs, NJ: Prentice Hall, 1972; Ditsky, John. "The Friend at the Round Table: A Note on Steinbeck's *Acts*." *American Literature* 49, no. 4 (1978): 633–35; Dowell, Bob. "A Note on John Steinbeck in King Arthur's Court." In *The Arthurian Myth of Quest and Magic: A Festschrift in Honor of Lavon B. Fulwiler*, ed. William E. Tanner, 71–74. Dallas: Caxton's Modern Arts Press, 1993; Earle, Scott. "Ethan as Lancelot: *The Winter of Our Discontent* and the Arthurian Cycle." *Steinbeck Yearbook* 1 (2000): 77–92; French, Warren. "End of a Dream." In *Steinbeck: A Collection of Critical Essays*, ed. Robert Murray Davis, 63–69. Englewood Cliffs, NJ: Prentice Hall, 1972. (Reprint from French's *John Steinbeck*, published in 1961.) ———. *John Steinbeck's Fiction Revisited*. New York: Twayne, 1994; Gladstein, Mimi Reisel. "*America and Americans*: The Arthurian Consummation." In *After Grapes of Wrath: Essays on John Steinbeck in Honor of*

Tetsumaro Hayashi, 228–37. Athens: Ohio University Press, 1995; Goldstone, Adrian Homer, and John R. Payne. *John Steinbeck: A Bibliographical Catalogue of the Adrian H. Goldstone Collection.* Austin: Humanities Research Center, University of Texas, 1974; Hayashi, Tetsumaro. *A New Steinbeck Bibliography, 1929–1971.* Metuchen, NJ: Scarecrow Press, 1973; ———. *A New Steinbeck Bibliography, 1971–1981.* Metuchen, NJ: Scarecrow Press, 1983; Hayashi, Tetsumaro, ed. *A Handbook for Steinbeck Collectors, Librarians, and Scholars.* Steinbeck Monograph Series, no. 11. Muncie, IN: John Steinbeck Society of America, Department of English, Ball State University, 1981; Hayashi, Tetsumaro, and Thomas J. Moore. "Cumulative Index to Volumes XI–XX (1978–1987)." Steinbeck Bibliography Series, no. 2. *Steinbeck Quarterly* 22 (1989); Heavilin, Barbara A. "Steinbeck's American Arthuriad: Ethan Allen Hawley as Lancelot Grotesque." *Steinbeck Yearbook* 1 (2000): 145 57; Hodges, Laura F. "Arthur, Lancelot, and the Psychodrama of Steinbeck." *Steinbeck Quarterly* 13 (1980): 71–79; ———. "Steinbeck's Adaptation of Malory's Launcelot: A Triumph of Realism over Supernaturalism." *Quondam et Futurus: A Journal of Arthurian Interpretations* 2, no. 1 (1992): 69–81; ———. "Steinbeck's Dream Sequence in *The Acts of King Arthur and His Noble Knights.*" *Arthurian Interpretations* 4, no. 2 (1990): 35–49; Johnson, Cynthia. "Review of *The Acts of King Arthur and His Noble Knights*, by John Steinbeck." *School Library Journal* 23, no. 8 (1977): 84; Kiernan, Thomas. *The Intricate Music: A Biography of John Steinbeck.* Boston: Little, Brown, 1979; Kinney, Arthur F. "The Arthurian Cycle in *Tortilla Flat.*" *Modern Fiction Studies* 11, no. 1 (1965): 11–20. (Reprinted in *Steinbeck: A Collection of Critical Essays*, ed. Robert Murray Davis, published in 1972.) Lupack, Alan, and Barbara Tepa Lupack. "Steinbeck and the Arthurian Legend." In *King Arthur in America*, 183–209. New York: Brewer, 1999; Maltin, Leonard. *Leonard Maltin's Movie and Video Guide*, 1996 ed. New York: Penguin, 1995; Materton, G. A. "Review of *The Acts of King Arthur and His Noble Knights*, by John Steinbeck." *Library Journal* 101, no. 18 (1976): 2178; Mathis, Andrew E. *The King Arthur Myth in Modern American Literature.* Jefferson, NC: McFarland, 2002; Meyer, Michael J. *The Hayashi Steinbeck Bibliography, 1982–1996.* Lanham, MD: Scarecrow Press, 1998; Nelson, Marie. "King Arthur and the Massacre of the May Day Babies: A Story Told by Sir Thomas Malory, Later Retold by John Steinbeck, Mary Stewart, and T. H. White." *Journal of the Fantastic in the Arts* 11, no. 2 (2001): 266–81; O'Connor, Richard. *John Steinbeck.* New York: McGraw-Hill, 1970; Parini, Jay. *John Steinbeck: A Biography.* New York: Holt, 1995; Shively, Charles. "John Steinbeck: From the Tide Pool to the Loyal Community." In *Steinbeck: The Man and His Work*, ed. Richard Astro and Tetsumaro Hayashi, 25–34. Corvallis: Oregon State University Press, 1971; Siefker, Donald L. "Cumulative Index to Volumes I–X (1968–1977)." *Steinbeck Quarterly* 11 (1978); Simmonds, Roy. *John Steinbeck: The War Years, 1939–1945.* Lewisburg, PA: Bucknell University Press, 1996; Steinbeck John, IV, and Nancy Steinbeck. *The Other Side of Eden: Life with John Steinbeck.* Amherst, NY: Prometheus Books, 2001; Street, Webster. "Steinbeck: The Man and His Work." In *Steinbeck: The Man and His Work*, ed. Richard Astro and Tetsumaro Hayashi, 35–41. Corvallis: Oregon State University Press, 1971; Thomas, Jimmie Elaine. "The Once and Present King: A Study of the World View Revealed in Contemporary Arthurian Adaptations." Ph.D. dissertation, University of Arkansas, 1982. Abstract in *Dissertation Abstracts International* 43 (1983): 3316A; Valjean, Nelson. *John Steinbeck: The Errant Knight.* San Francisco: Chronicle Books, 1975; Welsh, Andrew. "Lancelot at the Crossroads in Malory and Steinbeck." *Philological Quarterly* 70 (1991): 485–502; Williams, Mary C. "Lessons from Ladies in Steinbeck's 'Gawain, Ewain, and Marhalt.'" *Avalon to Camelot* 1, no. 4 (1984): 40–41.

PEGGY J. HUEY

T(ERENCE) H(ANBURY) WHITE

(May 29, 1906–January 17, 1964)

Born in Mumbai (then Bombay), India, on May 29, 1906, Terence Hanbury White became known for his inspired retellings of Arthurian legend beginning with *The Sword in the Stone* (1939), and he is probably the main articulator of Arthurian fantasy literature in the mid-twentieth century. White's engagement with the Arthurian materials culminated in *The Once and Future King* (1958), a tetralogy which reedited and brought together *The Sword in the Stone, The Queen of Air and Darkness, The Ill-Made Knight*, and *The Candle in the Wind*. White's love for the Middle Ages and his creative revisions and extensions of the myths not only rekindled popular enthusiasm for the world of King Arthur, but also inspired other writers, dramatists, and film producers to take up the Arthurian materials.

White's life was quite painful, especially his early years in India. His family was supremely dysfunctional. White's father, Garrick, a district superintendent of police, was part of the colonial apparatus in India. White's mother, Constance Aston, married the first man who proposed marriage as a means of spiting her parents, bore a child after eighteen months of marriage, and shortly thereafter ended all sexual relations with her husband. Garrick White turned to alcohol while Constance became excessively devoted to her pet dogs. Garrick sought revenge by shooting his canine rivals (Warner, 27).

According to White, "My parents loathed each other." Even more graphic is the oft-cited passage, "I am told that my father and mother were to be found wrestling with a pistol, one on either side of my cot, each claiming that he or she was going to shoot the other, and himself or herself, but in any case, beginning with me" (Warner, 23). Although he was permanently alienated from his father, White's most traumatically failed relations were with his mother, whose unrelenting domination is directly reflected in White's most persistent theme, "the evil of attempting to possess or manipulate another person" (Kellman, 3). Indeed, according to Warner, Constance White was famously possessive, once in a fit of jealousy dismissing an Indian servant for whom young White showed affection. At the same time, this always-demanding mother found it hard if not impossible to give any love to her son. One measure of Constance's self-preoccupation is the fact that "Beyond a few brief references to 'my infant' there are only three mentions of the child" in an entire manuscript of Constance's reminiscences of her life in India (Warner, 27). White's own assessment is even more damning. He wrote in his diary: "It was my love that she extracted, not hers that she gave. I've always thought she was sexually frigid, which was maybe why she thrashed it out of me. Anyway, she managed to bitch up my loving women" (Warner, 28). Indeed, of the very few women to whom White was ever attracted, all were "hopelessly unavailable" (including a barmaid he courted as therapy for his homosexuality; Warner, 82).

In 1911, when he was five, White's parents took him to live in England, where he enjoyed relatively happy years living with his grandmother, until he went at the age of fourteen to Cheltenham College, a school for military officers that adhered to the "theory that education must be harassing and the harassing must be systematically applied" (Warner, 30). Discipline at Cheltenham was physical, in the form of canings delivered by prefects. Homosexuality, whether consensual or forced, was widespread. White credits the canings at Cheltenham as the source of his own sado-masochism, a quality he later transfers to Lancelot (Warner, 148–49). The brutality of White's military warriors may reflect some of White's Cheltenham experiences. White describes his reckless driving, flying lessons, and frantic outdoorsmanship as "compensating for my sense of inferiority, my sense of danger, my sense of disaster" (Warner, 25). Not surprisingly, White was a great admirer of T. E. Lawrence in whom one finds many of the same haunting qualities and compensations. Lancelot seems to combine them both as well (Kellman, 120).

In 1923 his parents proceeded towards an inevitable, although long-delayed divorce. White spent 1925–1929 at Queens College, Cambridge. There he became "Tim," a lifelong renaming, and made several friendships that were to last most of his life, although these were friendships on White's terms. White and David Garnett found their friendship "better when apart" (Warner, 86). White's most enduring friendships seem anchored in correspondence, where feelings and ideas could be expressed safely at a remove, especially from White's "psychological sadism." In fact, White was said to have "often hurt the people he loved most" (Kellman, 3). Nevertheless, Cambridge probably offered White his first real feeling of community, an element essential in any retelling of the legend of Arthur. At Cambridge White formed his lasting friendship with tutor L. J. Potts, again a friendship bolstered by separation and correspondence. In his second year, White contracted tuberculosis, and with the help of funds provided by his instructors, in 1928 he went to convalesce in Italy. Such illness may well have added to his already strong sense of doom and lack of control (Warner, 38).

In Italy, White wrote his first novel, *They Winter Abroad* (1932), a non-Arthurian work described as nearly plotless (Crane, 42). More importantly, during his time in Italy, White tried to confront his homosexuality. With the same cold thoroughness that he later used in outlining his characters, White drew up a list of the problems to be faced living with his newly recognized sexual orientation, including the self-posed question, "What makes the homosexual's life inevitably more tragic than the great percentage of normal people's?" (Warner, 42).

Graduating from Cambridge in 1928, White began another important phase of his life, his career as a teacher. White's first teaching position was as an assistant master at St. David's, a preparatory school at Reigate, which he left after two years to become head of the Department of English at Stowe (1930–1936), where he was much more successful.

During his time at St. David's and Stowe, White wrote several semisuccessful novels, causing a minor stir when a Stowe student's father identified White as author of several of the "racier" ones (Crane, 20). While at Stowe, he began to weary of teaching. Additionally, he started intensive psychoanalysis to "cure" his homosexuality, a revealing formulation of self-loathing (Warner, 82–83). White developed a keen interest in psychology, both Freudian and what Kellman terms "more than a passing interest in the Jungian unconscious of a race" (81). White's life and interests prefigure his Arthurian epic. Although certainly not the first to do so, White will endow his characters with fully developed psychologies that clearly reflect early twentieth century psychoanalytic theories and doctrines, especially along rather Freudian lines in regard to childhood development. Just as White felt in his own childhood lay the keys to his own psychological makeup, so it became necessary to explore, in this case create, the childhood of Arthur that, in his own words, became the necessary "prelude to Malory."

This period of psychoanalysis, just before White's writing of *The Sword in the Stone*, is also the period of White the sportsman. He took up riding to the hounds, participated in reckless adventurism, and nearly blinded himself when he crashed his Bentley. White also learned to fly to confront his fear of falling from great heights. He produced *England Have My Bones*, a compendium of pieces on outdoor activities, including hunting and fishing that disclose a sense of the naturalism that was to be the core of *The Sword in the Stone*. The publication of *England Have My Bones* (1936) allowed White to retire from teaching, especially after he managed to acquire permission to take up residence in a gamekeeper's cottage in Stowe.

It was while living in this cottage that White rediscovered Thomas Malory's *Morte d'Arthur*, the fifteenth-century account of "The Matter of Britain"—the legends and tales surrounding the figure of King Arthur. "Do you remember I once wrote a thesis on the Morte d'Arthur?" White wrote in a very important letter to Potts.

> Naturally I did not read Malory when writing the thesis on him, but one night last autumn I got desperate among my books and picked him up in lack of anything else. Then I was thrilled and astonished to find (a) that the thing was a perfect tragedy, with a beginning, a middle, and an end implicit in the beginning, and (b) that the characters were real people with recognizable reactions which could be forecast. Anyway, I somehow started writing a book. It is not a satire. Indeed, I am afraid it is rather warm-hearted—mainly about birds and beasts. It seems impossible to determine whether it is for grown-ups or children. It is more or less a kind of wish-fulfillment of the things I should like to have happened to me when I was a boy. (Warner, 98)

White's rediscovery of Malory along with his encounter with psychoanalysis set the stage for White's epiphany of the tragic nature of Malory's "real people" and what would be the most productive period of White's career as a writer. White's recognition of Mallory as a "perfect tragedy" was the means by which he raised himself out of a deep depression, and rescued himself from writing solid but not great fiction. This very recognition of tragedy where before he had seen none allowed White to produce *The Sword in the Stone*, a work founded on the philosophical question of free will vs. predestination.

A number of commentators have linked White's personal and interior world with his Arthurian narratives. Several reviewers have felt the presence of White in his works. "The character of the author himself—headstrong, eccentric, humorous, and kind" is "woven into his descriptions of people and places" (*Chicago Sunday Tribune*, July 5, 1959). In the *Times Literary Supplement*, Siriol Hugh-Jones claimed to "recognize more than a little of T. H. White's dual nature" as both teacher and learner in the characters of both Lancelot and Merlyn (ix).

The most lasting and significant work done on White is his biography by Sylvia Townsend Warner (1967). Where White acknowledged that the idyllic childhood of Wart in *The Sword in the Stone* constitutes "a wish-fulfillment of the things I should like to have happened to me when I was a boy," Warner elaborates this into the assertion that "*The Sword in the Stone* had allowed him two wish fulfillments. He gave himself a daunt-less, motherless boyhood; he also gave himself an ideal old age, free from care and the contradiction of circumstances, practising an enlightened system of education on a cho-sen pupil, embellished with an enchanter's hat, omniscient, unconstrainable and with a sink where the crockery washed itself up" (Warner, 99).

While Warner remains the primary sourcebook of virtually all that has been written about White, she has been severely scolded by Sven Eric Molin. Molin acknowledges that Warner's book on White "has considerable merit," but points out that "[f]ully half of the book is quotations" (144). "Miss Warner," complains Molin, "leaves [White] in a vacuum from the world in which he lived and wrote" (147). Molin is certain that White's books are "highly autobiographical" while at the same time being "highly reti-cent" (144). Molin does not say that he knew White, but he implies substantial familiar-ity with White's hidden sides—sides which White may have worked into his fictions.

Molin says that "a journal of his sexual life ... is still to come," a journal that he claims White compiled "in hope that a case history will ameliorate the social life of the homosexual" (146). Warner says, however, that the "sexual autobiography for the benefit of other poor devils was not written. But between 1957 and 1961 he kept an intimate re-cord of his own poor devil state. He considered this the most important of his books ("It has cost more") and made a special bequest to it with the hope that its publication (at a date when it could no longer distress those it concerned) might contribute to a more enlightened and merciful outlook on sexual aberrants" (Warner, 83 n.).

After completing the first part of his tetralogy in the English countryside at Stowe cot-tage, White moved to the country of the Gaels, Ireland, where he remained, never quite assimilated, for six years working on *The Ill-Made Knight*, a dramatic version of *The Can-dle in the Wind*, and what was to become *The Book of Merlyn*. One detects a rather colo-nial attitude towards the Irish not only in, say, the passages devoted to the Irish "saint" in *The Witch in the Wood*, but in much of White's correspondence as well (See *Letters*, 102; Crane, 98). For their parts, despite his early efforts to develop the Gael in himself, even his longtime Irish hosts never completely accepted White, and he was eventually suspected of being a British spy. In fact, White's hosts at Doolistown, the McDonaghs, like many of their countrymen, were so offended at White's portrayal of Irish superstition in *The Elephant and The Kangaroo* (1946) that the book's publication generated a perma-nent rift between them (Warner, 241).

White's greatest advancement of Arthurian material was his filling in the missing childhoods not only of Arthur, but also of Lancelot and of the troubled "Orkneys" (Gawain, Gareth, Gaheris, Agravaine) as well as Mordred. Readers of *The Sword in the Stone* will recognize that the first step to creating Wart's idyllic childhood, so antithetical to White's, was the removal of parents—perhaps the central wish in White's "wish fulfill-ment." Similarly, White's Lancelot is without parents, although "Uncle Dap" schools him. The Orkneys, who do have parents, suffer the outrages of White's youth. In essence, the four sons of Lot form their own dysfunctional family, without parents. Lot is a relatively weak and disposable figure much like Garrick White. Their mother, Morgause, is utterly self-absorbed, completely unloving. There is something pathetic, if not profoundly disturbing, about the conclusion the tetrology's second book as we see the Orkney children "praying that they might be true to their loving mother—that they might be worthy of the Cornwall feud which she had taught them." Morgause produces in her children many of the qualities (sadism, masochism) that White loathed in himself and blamed his mother for and Morgause overwhelmed and nearly destroyed *The Witch in the Wood* until (in the final edit of the manuscript) editors and friends helped him pare down her role. In fact, White's editors found it impossible to publish the book until her malignant presence was repressed. The traditional absence of Arthur's parents may, in fact, have drawn White to Arthur. Perhaps the collapsed marriage of Arthur as well as the elements of thwarted obsessive love likewise attracted White to what he referred to as the Arthurian "tragedy." A man who could at the end of his life write to his friend David Garnett, "It has been my hideous fate to be born with an infinite capacity for love and joy with no hope of using them" (Warner, 277–78), certainly must have been drawn to Lancelot and would, no doubt, have portrayed the conflicted lover as White did in *The Ill-Made Knight*.

White's "preface to Malory," *The Sword in the Stone*, reflects White's wide range of reading and firsthand outdoor lore gained during his athletic period at Stowe. Mixed in with observations about the language of birds, hunting lore, and natural history, there is broad satire of medieval culture (jousts, questing, and chivalry) and of human nature, both medieval and modern. One feels within the novel the reflected energy of White's recent exploits (flying, riding to the hounds) and a freshness of observation based on his own attempts at archery and, especially, falconry.

The powerful description of the hunt in Chapter 16 obviously owes much to White's outdoor adventures in *England Have My Bones*. The passage describing the death of a hunting hound is one of the most genuinely poignant in White, reflecting his famous attachment to "Brownie" his Irish setter. Although humor is found throughout, the broadest satire, bordering on slapstick, is found in the passages describing the redoubtable but flummoxed Pellinore and his comic antics with his friend and rival Sir Grummore in Chapter 7. The Robin Hood, or "Robin Wood," adventure is a representation of White's keen wit and verbal dexterity. Much of this energy and humor comes from relative freedom White has in telling a history that has largely been untold, namely the history of Arthur's childhood. Even the obligatory Uther/Ygraine tale (and hence the roots of the "tragedy") has been held in abeyance for a later volume. With so few narrative obligations from other writers in the tradition, White's hand was free to apply whatever insights his recent forays into analysis had yielded about the nature of childhood and education.

Adding to the generally light tone of this idyllic wish fulfillment is White's deliberately anachronistic style. Stating that Malory was a fifteenth-century writer trying to write from both a fifteenth- and a fifth-century points of view (Warner, 135), White attempted to write as a twentieth-century writer looking through Malory's eyes about Malory's own time and the Arthurian past. The result of this temporal stew is a continual set of chronological incongruities that is the source of much of the novel's gentle humor and wit.

At the center of the book is Merlyn whose process of living backward allows the sort of anachronistic sport that Twain explored in *Connecticut Yankee*. Acting as Wart's mentor, Merlyn comprises "the most complete self-portrait White . . . put in any book" down to his beard, knitting, irascible temperament, and ideas (Kellman, 97).

With so much of the novel as projection/wish fulfillment, it is not surprising that the bulk of Arthur's education is achieved by a similar means of imaginative self-projection—in Wart's case by assuming the role of the various animals that inhabit his medieval world. As a fish in the moat, Wart learns about power from Mr. Pike. From his encounter with a hedgehog, he learns mercy; from a badger he learns a creation myth, which speaks to the problem of free will. In revising the tale of Wart's education as part of *The Once and Future King*, White added two additional animal adventures. From his encounter with the ants, Wart learns about fascism and from the geese about freedom from boundaries, which are the causes of human wars. In the end, having told a tale of himself as both child (Wart) and adult (Merlyn), White has created something of a hybrid, not quite children's book, not quite adult fiction.

The Once and Future King has been described as a book that matures along with its protagonist. The second book in the series, *The Witch in the Wood* (edited and renamed *The Queen of The Air and Dark* in *The Once and Future King*), where Wart has left the world of Merlyn's enchanted forest, gave White his most difficulty. Certainly the second volume is a beginning of loss of innocence and freedom on Arthur's part. No doubt, that reflects part of the loss of artistic freedom on the part of the author who is no longer free to fill in blank spaces of the legend, but must follow plot, including elements such as the Uther/Ygraine liaison that were deferred/repressed from the previous chapter.

Part of the problem in the second book is that it reflects the difficulties of its conflicted author. There one finds an unsettling mixture of philosophy, still broader slapstick than that in *Sword*, and a psychological terror/sadism that arises directly out of White's troubled childhood. As the "Witch" in the title suggests, the second of White's Arthurian works is dominated by Morgause. The book opens with a rather naive and innocent recounting of the "ancient wrong" in the begetting of Arthur as told by the young and still largely innocent sons of King Lot. The children's natural affection for their mother becomes a source of horror as they realize that they are victims of an utterly unloving self-preoccupied mother incapable of even the simplest return of affection. The poisonous quest for maternal affection reaches its height in one of White's most powerful displays of writing—the horrific hunting, capture, and mutilation of a unicorn by emotionally starved sons who hope to win their mother's attention. The pure sadism of Agravaine and the utter indifference of Morgause are simultaneously repulsive and fascinating. By book's end, one sees Morgause equipped with a spancel, a coil of human skin, as a magic talisman whereby she manipulates Arthur into siring Mordred so that his (and the kingdom's) fate is sealed. Tragedy is irrevocably begun.

Set in counterpoint to the Gaels's murder and mutilation of the human and the magical are Arthur's moral debates with Merlyn over the nature of war, the victimization of the lower classes at the hands of the nobles, and even a slightly Tennysonian sense of Arthur's "purpose." There is a powerful scene wherein Arthur, standing on a parapet, muses that he could kill a peasant working below by dropping a large stone from such a great height and that no one would charge him since he is king.

Far more jarring than these philosophical debates of might and right is the comic relief supplied by the arrival of Pellinore and Grummore at the home of Morgause. Pellinore having fallen in love with Queen of Flanders's daughter, affectionately known as "Piggy," has abandoned the questing beast. When the questing beast turns up, a plan to lure the beast away using a two man questing beast costume goes comically awry when the real beast falls hopelessly in love with the fake one, thus trapping Pellinore and Grummore as the object of the beast's unwanted advances. Eventually all is set right; Pellinore finds his lost love, and the beast watches over Pellinore in case things do not work out with Piggy. In fact, White was repeatedly advised to trim and soften material devoted to Morgause. By the time White reedited the tale for *The Once and Future King*, three-quarters of material about Morgause was eliminated, but her portrait is still one of the most overpowering and sinister in the entire tradition.

The third and longest book in the tetralogy, *The Ill-Made Knight*, demonstrates White's greatest conformity to Malory's plot elements, and yet it also presents one of White's most radical departures in characterization. Although White takes Lancelot through the host of traditional wars and rescues—the war with the Roman Emperor, the rescue of Guenivere from Maliagrance, to name a few—it is the psychological tension in Lancelot that really carries the book. Following Malory, White begins to make Lancelot the real focus of his Arthurian epic.

White produces a Lancelot whose sexuality is in question. White was attracted to the theme of forbidden love inherent in the Arthurian tragedy. But there is far more than that. Clearly Lancelot's first attraction, love, for Arthur is at least mildly homoerotic. One senses genuine feelings of betrayal when he learns of Arthur's betrothal to Guenivere. Much of Lancelot's self-loathing and complex psychology clearly emerge from White's own self-exploration and analysis. "The fellow's character I understand already: it is my own" (Warner, 150). White's correspondence yields a good deal about his concept of this character who, against tradition, he describes as ugly with a strong sense of inferiority. In White's hands, Lancelot's famous gallantry is a desperate attempt to contain his fundamental "sadism." Lancelot is as fearful as White who similarly turned to athleticism and dangerous outdoor activities as constant means of testing himself, and possibly his "manhood."

Arguably *Le Morte D'Arthur* is really the story of the agony, or *sparagmos*, of Lancelot rather than of Arthur, much as the *Iliad* is really the story of the anger of Achilles rather than merely a chronicle of the Trojan War. White's genius was to make Lancelot ugly, a creature of self-doubt and self-loathing—a person of character by virtue of a life-long struggle to keep what he felt to be his true character in check, a struggle that mirrors White's struggle with his own homosexuality. White chose to keep himself in check by living an asexual life. For White, as with Lancelot, the result was a life of failed or stunted emotion. This third book begins with a young Lancelot who seems much like the young White at Cheltenham. The adolescent Lancelot is driven to excel as the best knight in the world reflecting White's own self-assessment of his physical exploits as a means of containing his fear and self-doubt. Arriving at Camelot with a crush on Arthur, Lancelot becomes jealous of Guenivere, his inability to address the Queen or other women reflecting White's own stunted relations and difficulties addressing women.

Significantly, when White went to write Guenivere, he had no more idea of how to approach her than did Lancelot. Having made Morgause the villain of the work, he realized he could not have a second female villain, and so he turned to Ray Garnett, explaining to her that he simply could not portray women. On her advice, White turned to Russian novelists to find literary models for women because he could not find them in real life (Warner, 156). White's journals and letters are particularly revealing as he writes out a character analysis of Guenivere (Warner, 150–52), just as methodically as he listed problems of his own sexuality years earlier. Despite his proclaimed sympathy for Guenivere, the queen is still often unsympathetic, but because of White's struggles to understand her (and her gender), she is psychologically complex in a way that predecessors have often not been. Chapters 16 and 33 of *The Ill-Made Knight* do provide excellent psychoanalysis of the queen and her complex motives. Lancelot, too, has a fully realized psychology, with depth that is as real as White's own struggles. White's years of attempting self-understanding yield power to Chapter 10 where the narrator explains roots of Lancelot's self-image. White is especially adept at revealing the complexities and contradictions of Lancelot's spiritual life, particularly his desire/need to produce a miracle. It is a desire that is poignantly realized at the very end of the book in Chapter 45. By then, though, it is too late.

As White remarked in his letters, the inclusion of God made the Arthur-Lancelot-Guenivere triangle into a quadrilateral. In the previous century, Tennyson had tried the same geometry, with Arthur and God as successful union, but with far less artistic success and none of the pathos of Lancelot's final miracle (Warner, 150).

For her part, Elaine remains largely long-suffering but also largely unsympathetic. Elizabeth Brewer's account of White's difficulty with the "two Elaines" is particularly revelatory of White's struggle with female characters (95–98). White's treatment of Galahad, on the other hand, is marvelously modern, rejecting his sainthood for an off-putting religious fanaticism. One sees Galahad as a child rejecting a jousting toy and being almost autistically preoccupied with his doll which he incessantly calls "holy, holy." While White closely follows the traditional storyline of Lancelot's adventures, the complexity of Lancelot's religious psychology made the grail story extremely problematical, especially since White is particularly unsympathetic to those who by tradition achieve the grail. Lancelot is the hero here, and precisely for the reasons that he did not achieve the grail. As he wrote to his friend Garnett, White found a solution in telling the grail tales indirectly. For White, the grail quest is a means of chronicling the diminishment of the court and "the declining rhythm in righteousness of [Arthur's] cause" (Kellman, 117).

The final part of the tetralogy is *The Candle in the Wind*. Originally written as a play and then converted to novel form, this fourth book, while closely following the narrative lines laid down by Malory, relies heavily on dialogue. Predictably, White's additions are projections of his internal struggles, this time as a result of his complex feelings about World War II. The Growth of Mordred's "Thrashers" with their massacres of Jews clearly parallels the rise of the brutish Nazi party (Brewer, 108–9). White, reflecting the paternalism for the masses that pervades much of *The Once and Future King*, understands the way the common people are misled. Arthur is allowed to speak for justice; Mordred for Iago-like evil. It is not a particular grudge that Mordred has against Arthur; what motivates Mordred is the malignancy from being raised by Morgause.

Of particular interest is White's handling of Gawain who, though rather thick, is the best of the Orkneys. Having long since spelled out the psychological drives of the other characters, White does a particularly good job of rendering Gawain's finest hour, his refusal to be a part of the execution of the queen, Gawain's subsequent madness and agony over the killing of his younger brothers, and his final recognition that his insistence on the feud of Lancelot has led to the destruction of the kingdom. It is a fine Greek tragedy within a tragedy that adds to the sense of loss over the failure of Camelot. The book ends with White explaining the nature of tragedy and a well-wrought summary of Arthur's career with White raising the question of exactly who is to blame here. The fates? The people? Their leaders? White cannot bring himself to portray the end of Arthur. The book closes with remarkable dialogue between Arthur and a page, a final act of noble generosity and a note of hope that his hero will be remembered.

In 1944 White began to conceive of his Arthurian narratives not as a series of novels but as a single epic, a Malorian "novel" composed of books which while seemingly separate formed a cohesive whole. He suggested that his publisher, Collins, reissue the first three books along with what he proposed to be the final two books. Collins balked, rejecting the fifth book entirely and declining even the tetralogy on the grounds that a paper shortage precluded publication. Eventually White received permission to publish the new tetralogy with revised versions of the earlier books under the title of *The Once and Future King.* This reworking of his Arthurian vision again owes much to the pattern of trauma and projection that engendered the earlier work. This time the trauma was White's internal conflict over his military obligations in World War II. An Englishman, safely ensconced in Ireland for much of the war, White continually fretted about his duty to join the fight against fascism which he rejected out of hand. His correspondence reveals motives both petty and altruistic. At times he states his willingness to serve, but at other times he goes so far as to consider the effect that his absence would have on his set-ter, Brownie. Once he declared that it was a greater service to Britain to finish his Arthur-ian epic than to join the war effort. During this period, he discovered that Malory and his own retelling of Malory were really about finding the "antidote to war" (Warner, 180). Perhaps his conflicts about military service are rooted in his traumatic experiences at Cheltenham. Whether this was a genuine discovery or an epiphany of convenience, it is hard to tell, but the result was a rewriting of the earlier works, the inclusion of material consonant with his view of warfare in general, and insertion of anti-fascist material from the rejected fifth book, namely the encounter with the fascist ants.

The material for the fifth book remained in White's papers and was eventually depos-ited at the University of Texas at Austin until discovered and published posthumously in 1977 as *The Book of Merlyn.* In general, touted as Arthur's return to the animals and the lessons of *The Sword and the Stone,* the fifth book is anything but a return to his first Arthurian work in either tone or artistry. Lacking both the charm and literary power of the tetralogy, *The Book of Merlyn* is a tangled, often haranguing, and sometimes tiresome "meditation" on the violence of man, or *homo ferocious* as humankind is dubbed in the novel. Here White takes what have been termed "Hobbesian conclusions about the na-ture of man" along with a rather "Schopenhaurian view of the evil of the will to survive and perpetuate the species" (Kellman, 4) to their fullest extreme. In the end, this final volume only validates White's publisher's earlier rejection of the material as a poor coda for the powerful, humorous and often lyrical *The Once and Future King.*

With the publication of *The Once and Future King,* White's reputation, already estab-lished, was assured. Although he continued to write non-Arthurian material, his career had, in essence, peaked. The latter years saw a decline in his health and considerable per-sonal anguish about the decline of his ability as a writer. Two events in White's later years, offshoots of *The Once and Future King,* did serve to cement White's reputation in the public imagination. Fittingly, they represented the conflicted nature of the writer, himself.

The first was the long delayed production by Disney in 1963 of an animated version of *The Sword in the Stone.* While this rather well done film continues to be a perennial favorite among children, its success may have impeded White's reputation among the growing ranks of Arthurian scholars in the late twentieth century. Over the years, several canonical adult books—*Gulliver's Travels, Huck Finn*—have been mistakenly identified or classified as children's fare—usually with doubtful results. When such works are "adapted" for younger audiences, the reading public and certainly scholars are certainly aware of the nature of the original work. This has not always been the case with White. Too many readers, including Arthurians, seem, on the basis of their familiarity with the

Disney cartoon, completely unaware of the adult nature of *The Once and Future King*. The novel, often thought of merely as "the source of *The Sword in the Stone*," probably seems too long for children and too childish for adults, especially by those for whom "*The Sword and the Stone*" refers to the movie.

Remarkably, the second popularization of White's work, the enduring musical *Camelot*, has complicated the matter of his reception even further. The Lerner and Loewe musical was clearly promoted as an adaptation of White's *The Once and Future King*. Perhaps as a result of expectations based on the musical genre, audiences found the 1960 production far too dark and disturbing, and it received mixed reviews from critics. Seven years later after the assassination of John Kennedy, the country was in a darker and, hence, more receptive mood, and the cinematic version of the musical received a much better reception. The musical, like the Disney film, remains popular, but one often senses that fans of the musical frequently do not know its source and assume it to be taken from the legend in general rather than a specific adaptation. Curiously, while White, himself may no longer be as well known as in his heyday, his influence can be detected in a number of places. While it is *de rigueur* for Arthurian films to append "based on the *Le Morte D'Arthur* of Sir Thomas Malory" to their closing credits, a number of films— Boorman's *Excalibur*, included—seem to have borrowed elements from White, especially in their portrayals of Merlin. More tellingly, it is arguable that Marion Zimmer Bradley's influential feminist retelling of the Arthurian saga, *The Mists of Avalon*, relies heavily on the horrific Morgause created by White.

Kellman observed in 1988 that White's work, especially his Arthurian materials, had been "curiously neglected" (2) with only one major academic study of White at that time. At of the beginning of the twenty-first century, that neglect has largely continued. Articles have been, comparatively speaking, somewhat scarce. White has been the subject of a few dissertations, but these have remained largely unpublished. The reasons for this critical neglect are not difficult to discern. Almost everything that has been written on White has been strongly based on biography. White was, in fact, blessed with a remarkably thorough and devoted biographer, Sylvia Townsend Warner, whose work has been the basis of virtually everything that has since been written. White also commented extensively on his own work in his voluminous correspondence and seemed to leave few stones unturned for formalist critics in search of an unexplained crux. Additionally, the prominence of *The Sword in the Stone* via Disney has probably misrepresented the bulk of the novel to potential critics, who, expecting little there, have ironically sought more complex and "adult" characters in works such as *The Mists of Avalon*. Finally, many critics have in passing noted the exasperating contradictions in White, contradictions that have, no doubt, forced structuralist critics wishing to write about the Aristotelian unities to look elsewhere in the Arthurian canon. Indeed, Kellman, sees in White's works "an Einsteinian view of the unity of time and space, making it truly epic in the Joycean sense, partially revelatory of the author's own personality" (88). Ironically, such "Einsteinian" sensibilities as well as his endless contradictions may bode well for White's critical future. White, if turned to, may likewise be a fertile field for psychologically based criticism, of the Freudian and especially Lacanian varieties. Gender studies may also find White an apt subject of study, especially in White's construction of Morgause and his candid correspondence about his difficulties in "drawing women." Queer Studies have much to offer in untangling the complex web of relationships cast by White. So, too, post-colonial approaches may well prove profitable in understanding White as another wounded child of the British Empire.

PRIMARY WORKS

Loved Helen and Other Poems. London: Chatto & Windus, 1929; *They Winter Abroad,* as James Aston. London: Chatto & Windus, 1932; *Earth Stopped or, Mr. Marx's Sporting Tour.* London: Collins, 1934; *Gone to Ground or the Sporting Decameron.* 1935; *England Have My Bones.* London: Macmillan, 1936; *Burke's Steerage or, The Amateur Gentleman's Introduction to Noble Sports and Pastimes.* London: Collins, 1938; New York: G. P. Putnam's Sons, 1939; *The Sword in the Stone,* illustrated by White, with endpapers by Robert Lawson. London: Collins, 1938; New York: G. P. Putnam's Sons, 1939; *The Witch in the Wood,* illustrated by White. New York: G. P. Putnam's Sons, 1939; London: Collins, 1940; revised edition published as *The Queen of Air and Darkness* in *The Once and Future King.* New York: G. P. Putnam's Sons, 1958; *The Ill-Made Knight,* illustrated by White. New York: G. P. Putnam's Sons, 1940; London: Collins, 1941; *Mistress Masham's Repose.* New York: G. P. Putnam's Sons, 1946; London: Jonathan Cape, 1947; *The Elephant and the Kangaroo.* New York: G. P. Putnam's Sons, 1947; London: Jonathan Cape, 1948; *The Age of Scandal, An Excursion through a Minor Period.* London: Jonathan Cape, 1950; *The Goshawk.* New York: G. P. Putnam's Sons, 1952; London: Jonathan Cape, 1951; *The Scandalmonger.* New York: Putnam, 1952; *The Book of Beasts: Being a Translation from a Latin Bestiary of the Twelfth Century Made and Edited by T. H. White.* London: Jonathan Cape, 1954; New York: Putnam, 1955; *The Best of Friends: Further Letters to Sydney Carlyle Cockerell,* ed. Viola Meynell. London: Rupert Hart-Davis, 1956; *The Master.* Jonathan Cape, London, 1957; New York: G. P. Putnam's Sons, 1957; *The Once and Future King,* a tetralogy composed of *The Sword in the Stone, The Queen of Air and Darkness, The Ill-Made Knight,* and *The Candle in the Wind,* previously unpublished. New York: G. P. Putnam's Sons, 1958; *The Godstone and the Blackymor,* illustrated by Edward Ardizzone. New York: G. P. Putnam's Sons, 1959; *America at Last: The American Journal of T. H. White.* New York: Putnam, 1965; *The White/Garnett Letters,* ed. David Garnett. New York: Viking, 1968; *The Book of Merlyn: The Unpublished Conclusion to The Once and Future King,* prologue by Sylvia Townsend Warner, illustrated by Trevor Stubley. Austin: University of Texas Press, 1977; *Darkness at Pemberley.* New York: Dover, 1978; *The Maharajah & Other Stories.* New York: Putnam, 1981; *Letters to a Friend: The Correspondence between T. H. White and L. J. Potts,* ed. François Gallix. New York: Putnam, 1982; *A Joy Proposed: Poems,* written with Kurth Sprague. Athens: University of Georgia Press, 1983.

SECONDARY SOURCES

Adderley, C. M. "The Best Thing for Being Sad: Education and Educators in T. H. White's *Once and Future King.*" *Quondam et Futurus: A Journal of Arthurian Interpretations* 2 (Spring 1992): 55–68; Blake, Andrew. "T. H. White, Arnold Bax, and the Alternative History of Britain." In *Impossibility Fiction: Alternativity, Extrapolation, Speculation,* ed. Derek Littlewood and Peter Stockwell, 25–36. Amsterdam: Rodopi, 1996; Brewer, Elisabeth. "Some Comments on 'T. H. White, Pacifism, and Violence.'" *Connotations: A Journal for Critical Debate* 7 (1997): 128–34; ———. *T. H. White's "Once and Future King."* Rochester, NY: D. S. Brewer, 1993; Chapman, Susan Elizabeth. "A Study of the Genre of T. H. White's Arthurian Books." *Dissertation Abstracts International* 50 (1990): 2903A; Clute, John. "T. H. White." in *Supernatural Fiction Writers: Fantasy and Horror.* Vol. 2, *A. E. Coppard to Roger Zelazny,* ed. Everett Franklin Bleiler, 651–57. New York: Scribner's, 1985; Crane, John K. *T. H. White.* New York: Twayne, 1974; Gallix, François. "*T. H. White: An Annotated Bibliography.* New York: Garland, 1986; ———. "T. H. White and the Legend of King Arthur: From Animal Fantasy to Political Morality." In *King Arthur: A Casebook,* ed. Edward Donald Kennedy, 281–311. New York: Garland, 1996; Grellner, Alice. "Two Films That Sparkle: *The Sword in the Stone* and *Camelot.*" In *Cinema Arthuriana,* ed. Kevin J. Harty, 159–62. New York: Garland, 1991; Hadfield, Andrew. "T. H. White, Pacifism, and Violence: The Once and Future Nation." *Connotations: A Journal for*

Critical Debate 6 (1996): 207–26; Herman, Harold J. "Teaching White, Stewart, and Berger." In *Approaches to Teaching the Arthurian Tradition*, eds. Maureen Fries and Jeanie Watson, 113–17. New York: Modern Language Association, 1992; Hugh-Jones, Siriol. "A Visible Export: T. H. White—Merlyn's Latest Pupil." *Times Literary Supplement*, August 7, 1959, ix; Kellman, Martin. *T. H. White and the Matter of Britain: A Literary Overview*. Studies in the Historical Novel, vol. 2. Lewiston, NY: Mellen, 1988; ———. "T. H. White's Merlyn: A Flawed Prophet." In *Comparative Studies of Merlin from the Vedas to C. G. Jung*, ed. James Gollnick, 55–61. Lewiston, NY: Mellen, 1992; Kertzer, Adrienne. "T. H. White's *The Sword in the Stone*: Education and the Child Reader." In *Touchstones: Reflections on the Best in Children's Literature*, vol. 1, ed. Jill P. May, 281–90. West Lafayette, IN: Children's Literature Association, 1985; Lindley, Angela. "Biography and the Critical Reception of T. H. White's 'The Once and Future King.'" *Dissertations Abstracts International* 50 (1990): 3717A; Lupack, Alan. "*The Once and Future King*: The Book That Grows Up." *Arthuriana* 11 (Fall 2001): 103–14; Macdonald, Alan. "A Lost Story of Perversion: T. H. White's 'The Witch in the Wood.'" *Library Chronicle of the University of Texas* 23 (1993): 106–29; Molin, Sven Eric. "Appraisals: T. H. White, 1906–1964." *Journal of Irish Literature* 2 (1973): 142–50; Nellis, Marilyn K. "Anachronistic Humor in Two Arthurian Romances of Education: *To the Chapel Perilous* and *The Sword and the Stone*." *Studies in Medievalism* 2 (Fall 1983): 57–77; Nelson, Marie. "T. H. White: Master of Transformation." *Neophilologus* 85 (2001): 309–21; ———. "T. H. White: The Poet Behind the Fiction." *Neophilologus* 83 (1999): 653–59; Ross, Meredith Jane. "The Sublime to the Ridiculous: The Restructuring of Arthurian Materials in Selected Modern Novels." *Dissertations Abstracts International* 46 (1986): 3717A; Serrano, Amanda. "T. H. White's Defence of Guenever: Portrait of a 'Real' Person." *Mythlore: A Journal of J. R. R. Tolkien, C. S. Lewis, Charles Williams, and the Genres of Myth and Fantasy* (Summer 1995): 9–13; Smith, Evans Lansing. "The Narrative Structure of T. H. White's *The Once and Future King*." *Quondam et Futurus: A Journal of Arthurian Interpretations* 1 (Winter 1991): 39–52; Thomas, Jimmie Elaine. "The Once and Present King: A Study of the World View Revealed in Contemporary Arthurian Adaptations." *Dissertations Abstracts International* 43 (1983): 3316A; Warner, Sylvia Townsend. *T. H. White: A Biography*. London: Cape, Chatto & Windus, 1967.

MARCUS A. J. SMITH AND JULIAN N. WASSERMAN

WALKER PERCY

(May 28, 1916–May 10, 1990)

Given his relatively long and event-filled life and career, this article can only provide a cursory look at Walker Percy. The major elements of Percy's personal history have here been pulled largely from Patrick S. Samway's *Walker Percy: A Life*, which is a reliable and highly detailed must read for the serious student of Percy's life and writing. Additionally, the select general bibliography provided here is a good starting point for the study of a writer whose perspectives, both in his fiction and nonfiction, boldly grappled with the most complex issues in modern science and the most profound reflections in modern and post-modern philosophy. Here we will take a brief look at Percy's life and then identify how his personal experiences and his writing specifically led him to be placed in this anthology of Arthurian authors. With passing respect paid to the many profound spiritual themes in Percy's work, our main concern here is on the Arthurian elements of Percy's writing, but again only on a summary level. A more focused bibliography has been provided for specialists on the esoteric connections between Percy and the medieval elements of his writing.

Aside from the novel, *Lancelot*, it is not immediately visible how or why Walker Percy would be considered uniquely Arthurian or, given Percy's preoccupation with modern existentialist philosophy, why the writer merits inclusion in this particular canon of authors. Unlike a number of writers included in this volume, Percy hardly celebrates Arthurian themes or values in his fiction. His characters may identify sporadically with the chivalric ideals of yore, but they are helplessly thwarted by the distresses of modernity in any effort to champion these ideals. Percy's narrators are usually in search for amorphous meanings—often this search includes travel—but Percy's characters are hardly grand or Wagnerian in their quests, nor are they seeking something as symbolically concrete and spiritually appeasing as the Holy Grail. Indeed his fiction typically features a philosophically and spiritually vexed, even befuddled or insane, hero (or nonhero) who is often lulled into ironic reflections accompanied by strange or even violent results while trying to sort out the tragicomic complexities of modern or post-modern existence.

Yet taken as a whole, Percy's work is profoundly Arthurian in that it exposes features of the modern world that do not hold up to the heroic, the sacrosanct, or the romantic. Many young readers during Percy's own youth would have come across the Arthurian legend, not through Malory, but through more recent and idyllic treatments of the material during the nineteenth century, chiefly in Sir Walter Scott and in Alfred, Lord Tennyson. Probably more through such sources than directly through Malory or other ancient works, Arthurian ideals or lack thereof are prominently enmeshed in Percy's work. Percy's *Lancelot* is of course the most overtly suggestive of Arthurian influence, but other titles— *The Last Gentleman, Love in the Ruins, The Second Coming*—usher the old tradition to the fore by highlighting the absence of Arthurian standards in the modern world.

Medievalism, particularly Arthurian heroic ideals and the loss of the same, can be located in the cultural sentiments of the late-nineteenth- and early-twentieth-century Southern classes to which Percy belonged. If one places personal disaster next to the martial or heroic conflicts of old, if one compares and contrasts dislocation and travel to the spiritual quests of Arthurian knights, and if the pursuit of love, and the disappointments that result from such activity, can be viewed in relation to rituals of medieval courtly romance, then one may draw comparisons, or at least viable juxtapositions, between the Arthurian legend and Percy's own life and work.

Percy was born on May 28, 1916, in Birmingham, Alabama, to LeRoy Pratt Percy and Mattie Sue Phinizy Percy. On both sides Percy descended from well-established, Southern gentry. The Birmingham Percys had been on the rise for two generations, aided, no doubt, by Birmingham's growing steel industry. Percy's father, LeRoy Pratt, was apparently bright and appropriately well rounded. While at prep school at the Lawrenceville School he edited the yearbook, he was a member of the gun club, and he made the baseball team. Afterward he matriculated at Princeton and graduated with a degree in literature in 1910. From Princeton, he went on to Harvard Law School where he served on the editorial board of the *Harvard Law Review*. In fall 1913 he engaged in advanced research at the University of Heidelberg, and, after completing his studies abroad, he returned to Birmingham and established himself as a partner in the firm, Percy, Benners, and Burr.

Percy's mother, Mattie Sue, was from the prominent Spalding family of Athens, Georgia. Mattie Sue's father, Billups Spaulding, was a wealthy cotton broker who held various prestige positions in insurance and banking. Mattie Sue was herself a graduate of the Lucy Cobb Institute in Athens (then considered one of the nation's finest girls' schools) and the prestigious Miss Finch's School in New York.

The Percy family was well connected on a number of levels, not least significant of which was the family tie to the Percys of Greenville, Mississippi. Walker's great uncle (his paternal grandfather's brother) was U.S. Senator Leroy Percy. Senator Percy's son, William Alexander Percy, was the noted author of *Lanterns on the Levee*. Uncle Will would become a strong influence on Walker's literary development particularly after he became Walker's guardian during Walker's teen years.

Perhaps certain stereotypes are true. The Percys were, at least on the surface, typical examples of a period that saw the revival, even expansion of the Southern gentry, a class of men, in particular, who were given to such gentlemanly professional pursuits as law, brokering, medicine (increasingly), and (in increasingly fewer cases) planting. They cultivated ties with people and institutions of influence on the ivy stretch of the Eastern seaboard, particularly at Princeton and Harvard and in Europe, particularly in Germany and England. On general terms, they were ardently involved in politics, they promoted the arts, they appreciated literature, they liked golf and tennis, and they loved to hunt and drink.

Given our Arthurian theme and the ubiquitous presence of Southern cultural thought in Percy's fiction, this period of Southern history should be examined in relationship with medieval thought, particularly the brand of medieval thought, implied in Malory, in which there is a celebration of heroic and righteous ideals accompanied by an implicit understanding that these ideals have been or soon will be lost in the chaos of modern consumer culture. The period that circumscribed Percy's life, both the legacy inherited from his family and his own formative years were not marked by the simple progressivism that fueled much of America at this time. The cultural South of the Birmingham Percys was a privileged but remorseful space that felt an inert and ever-present pull of a lost past that some naively hoped to re-create but that the modern economy and increasingly enlightened standards for human rights would never support. Therefore, the future for the South on one level involved the hopeless effort to recover a past—a time gone by that existed more strongly in the imagination than perhaps it did in any real sense—that many of Percy's class understood could and should not be recovered.

This lament for a heroic, bygone era when all was, well, like Camelot, is a common sentiment produced generation to generation throughout time. Indeed, the theme of regret for a lost and more ideal past is central to Malory and to the French cycles from which he drew much of the Arthurian legend. However, in American history, this sentiment was and perhaps still is strong in the admittedly naive and uniquely romantic (and we should add well-to-do) white Southerner's view of the past. Perhaps the naive version of this ideal is best stated by Percy's Binx Bolling in *The Moviegoer*, when Binx comments on his uncle's zeal for Tulane football. When Uncle Jules describes a goal-line stand, "it is like King Arthur standing fast in the bloodred sunset against Sir Modred and the traitors" (30). One can well imagine Uncle Jules drawing the same parallel from Robert E. Lee's stand at Appomattox had this memory in his time not still been tainted by real despair.

Percy's father and grandfather were well-born and well-positioned professionally but they also were responsible men who were capable of taking full advantage of their birthrights. It is ironic that in this atmosphere of advantage and strong accomplishment, Walker's father and grandfather both suffered from severe bouts of depression. Whatever the personal sources for their malaise, it is difficult to separate their personal discomforts from their culture, a culture that produced and still produces shrill defiance among whites in certain quarters. Among thinkers, this culture bred and still breeds frustrated and often guilt ridden reflections on the unfortunate lost of extrinsically pure heroic ideals, often accompanied by the appropriate dismissal of an intrinsically flawed and unjust social system. The idea of the present and the future being inextricably entwined in a lost and botched past was strong in Percy's South, the idea is also a central theme in Medieval Christian thought, and the attendant frustration and guilt emitted from this idea had arguable purchase on personal emotions of a ruling class on the wane.

Whatever the possible personal or cultural causes of discontent, the early years of Walker's life were circumscribed by depression and suicide. In the year that Percy was born, his grandfather published an article in the *Birmingham Age-Herald* against the United States going to war in Europe. On February 8, 1917, after Woodrow Wilson publicly signaled American intention to side with the allies, Grandfather Walker, who had been undergoing treatment for depression in Baltimore, returned home before this treatment was complete. On February 8, he shot himself "accidentally" (according to the local paper), but many close to him suspected suicide or, given that he was an experienced hunter, purposeful negligence. Twelve years later, on July 9, 1929, while Walker and his brothers were off at camp, Walker's father went to the attic of their home, stripped to his underwear, and shot himself with a twenty-gauge shotgun. This time, there was no question about the intentions of the deceased.

Walker's infancy and childhood therefore were book ended by horrific, and, indeed, apocalyptic events. Otherwise, young Walker enjoyed a comfortable upbringing. At one point, his family moved from their home on Arlington Avenue to the local country club, where Walker's father (then president of the club) built a more modern style house "across the road from the sixth green and seventh tee" (Samway, 16). Young Walker and his brother eventually attended the superbly staffed Birmingham University School. The Percys were the type of family who "summered" and the boys would often enjoy portions of their breaks from school at the Greenville Percys' summer home in the mountains at Brinkwood, near Sewannee, Tennessee, or at various camps patronized by people of similar rank and background.

Shortly after LeRoy Percy's death, his widow moved with Walker and his brothers to her family home in Athens, Georgia, a much smaller university town that was quaint and comfortable. The Percys were warmly received by the maternal family and local friends and the transition, in spite of the bleak reasons for the move, seems to have been a positive experience for thirteen-year-old Walker and his brothers. Samway notes that their day-to-day life remained roughly the same and that "the surroundings certainly were different, but not the social customs" (29). Walker apparently made friends quickly in Athens and, during the next year, he attended Athens High School, and rooted for the local high school and college football teams.

During this period Senator Percy's wife (Uncle Will's mother), Camille, had been suffering from ill health. She died on October 7, 1929, and her husband became ill shortly thereafter and died before Christmas of the same year. Left in the family home in Greenville without his parents, Uncle Will invited Mattie Percy and the children to come live with him in Greenville. Percy later reflected that Uncle Will "was the fabled relative, the one you liked to speculate about. His father was a United States senator and he had been a decorated infantry officer in World War I. Besides that, he was a poet" (quoted in Samway, 34). Uncle Will was at that time an affable, forty-five-year-old bachelor and world traveler who no doubt made an enormous sacrifice by taking on the guardianship of the three children.

Mattie Sue and the children moved to Greenville, to the opulent "big house" of the Percy cousins, in summer 1930. Certainly Walker's mother had in mind putting the children in the secure hands of a beloved cousin, but later, a number of rumors circulated that Mattie Sue fell in love with Will, indeed that she had proposed marriage and that Will refused. This is speculation at best and perhaps more the outgrowth of local gossip than any real occurrence (Samway, 55).

At the heart of the Delta region, Greenville at that time was a town at once remote and yet charged with literary and cultural activity, much of it spawned and cultivated by Uncle Will. William Percy was a true Roosevelt Democrat who was not quiet about his distain for the mistreatment of African Americans in his community and who also forwarded open disdain for the "white trash" consciousness that called for morality while simultaneously promoting racism and unruly behavior. He was an ardent supporter of the arts and passed on his interests, both political and artistic, to his nephews.

During the early years of the Depression, Will Percy's house became a standard stop for those making a literary tour of the South, and there were visits from such imminent people as Carl Sandburg and William Faulkner. It was in Greenville that Percy first associated with the novelist-to-be, Charles Bell, and the now celebrated historian, Shelby Foote. Percy and Bell never became close and eventually had a breach over Bell's inclusion of the Percy family history in one of his novels.

Foote, however, though a year behind Percy in high school, became a lifelong intellectual soul mate and best friend. Percy and Foote both began writing at this period, an activity no doubt provoked by their concurrent philosophical interests and spurred forward by friendly competition.

Percy wrote poetry and articles for his Greenville High School student newspaper *The Pica* (according to Foote, who became the paper's editor, *The Pica* was voted the best high school newspaper in the United States around 1935). It is interesting to note that one Percy piece published in *The Pica*, entitled "The Passing of Arthur," shows an early interest in the Arthurian legend.

Just when it seemed that Percy had settled into a normal, albeit artistically charged life, an event that seems sublimely unjust brought yet another tragedy into young Walker's life. While driving with Walker's younger brother, Phin, Mattie Sue drove off a bridge into a nearby creek. Phin managed to escape from the car, but his mother drowned. No autopsy was performed, but, because Mattie Sue was in poor health, it is thought that the cause of the crash may have been a heart attack.

As Samway notes, Percy was inclined to view the death of his mother as yet another family suicide (56). The death, of course, left Percy and his brothers grief stricken. Uncle Will now had to take full charge of their parenting, a role that he accepted selflessly and with unending dedication. The summer after the Mattie Sue's death (and preceding Walker's senior year of high school), Will took the boys on an extended trip to the American West, and soon afterward legally adopted the boys and made them heirs to his estate.

After high school, Percy attended the University of North Carolina at Chapel Hill, where he enjoyed the normal campus life of well-appointed young men from his background. Percy apparently made friends easily and soon pledged the Sigma Alpha Epsilon fraternity. He performed well in school, and though he had his sights on medical school, he also expanded his humanistic learning. He wrote several articles for the local *Carolina Magazine*, traveled to Germany the summer after his freshman year, and studied the German language.

After graduating from North Carolina, Percy took up residence in New York, where he attended the Columbia College of Physicians and Surgeons in 1941. While at Columbia, he underwent psychotherapy for two years. Percy obviously had unresolved issues related to the deaths of his parents, but he also had an intellectual interest, particularly in Freud, that piqued his curiosity in the practice of psychotherapy itself. His treatment began under the auspices of the noted psychoanalyst, Harry Stack Sullivan, who at one point stayed at Will Percy's home for over a month to study race relations for the American Council on Education. When Sullivan left New York, he recommended Dr. Janet Rioch. Percy began seeing Rioch for treatment four to five days a week and continued for a period of two to three years (Samway, 104–5). At that time, Percy revered Freud and would later note that he "elevated" the philosopher "far beyond the point that even he [Freud] would place himself" (104). Percy himself admitted that the experience of psychoanalysis was positive but, on the whole, inconclusive.

Percy received his medical degree from Columbia in 1941. At this point, he returned to Greenville and, for a short period of time, practiced medicine. While assisting with blood counts and urinalyses at a local clinic he met Mary Bernice ("Bunt") Townsend, a medical technician, while she was taking his blood. The two soon began dating and eventually the courtship led to marriage.

Now a full-fledged medical doctor, Percy began his internship at Bellevue Hospital on the lower east side of New York in January 1942. The Bellevue internship was coveted by the finest young doctors because the largely immigrant clientele provided a range of illnesses for treatment and study. Because of the conditions in the surrounding area—the lack of hygiene and impoverished living conditions—tuberculosis was commonplace. At this time the treatment of this unnervingly infectious disease, which not long before had killed more people in America than any other illness, was undergoing innovation and the study of TB was of course a high priority in the nation's medical centers, particularly inner city centers like Bellevue. Percy worked long hours, often at the hospital's morgue, where he did autopsies on "floaters" or discovered corpses that had not been claimed after five days.

In the same month that Percy began his internship, Uncle Will, who had been ill for some time, died from cardiovascular disease at the age of fifty-six. Though this was not a sudden, tragic death such as he had experienced with his parents, it was nonetheless another great loss. Percy was now twenty-six and of course no stranger to human tragedy. However, since the age of fourteen, Will Percy had been Walker's second father, his beloved patron and kinsman. It should be noted, too, that the Japanese attack on Pearl Harbor had occurred less than two months prior to Will's death. While a biographer can often be overzealous in cross-referencing the impact of historic events with individual lives, it is certain that this was another difficult time for Percy.

In March, Percy was diagnosed (in fact he diagnosed himself) with tuberculosis. Percy himself felt that he contracted the disease while performing more than one hundred autopsies on Bellevue corpses; however, what was known about the spread of the disease, even at that time, suggests that this cause of infection was highly improbable. Indeed, given the many living TB patients in the hospital and the tenacity of the TB bacterium in airborne environments, it is probable that Percy caught the disease from a living patient. Samway points out also the scientific fact that TB can lie dormant throughout one's life (many of Percy's classmates at Chapel Hill tested positive for TB). Also, Percy's aunt died from TB, and he "had been in contact with her in his early teens" (122).

Regardless of how Percy caught the disease, it was certain that he needed to retreat to one of the many TB sanatoria that populated the country at this time. He spent roughly the next three years mostly in rural upstate New York at the Trudeau Sanatorium on picturesque Saranac Lake in the Adirondacks. During this extended period of recovery, Percy read philosophy, notably Kierkegaard, Camus, and Sartre. At one point he commented that "[T]hree years at Trudeau was like four years at Chapel Hill from the viewpoint of reading good books" (127). Percy did not have many visitors during this period, but Shelby Foote visited him and noted that, while Percy did not look well, he at least seemed content in his solitude. Much has been made of Percy's retreat from the world during his illness, but Samway points out that Trudeau was in fact a social place among patients well enough to socialize and that Percy enjoyed intellectual exchanges, as well as social contact with women who were referred to as "cousins." Percy later stated that having TB was "the best thing that ever happened" to him (136).

Still Percy was alone if not entirely lonely during the years of World War II. This period would play out in his fiction later when his main characters demonstrate in thought and action a sense of distance from their peers, and an outsider's perspective that is given to alienation and abstraction.

After being released from Trudeau with a satisfactory if not entirely clean bill of health, Percy began teaching pathology at Columbia. He soon had a relapse, and, in 1945, entered the Gaylord Farm sanatorium in Connecticut for roughly four to five months. In summer 1945, the war now over, Percy was discharged from Gaylord (184). The diagnosis and recovery period for Percy had lasted roughly the same period as World War II. Percy had spent perhaps the most calamitous period of the history of humankind in almost complete seclusion and retreat.

At this point he returned to Greenville and then on to Brinkwood (19). In summer 1946, Percy and Shelby Foote traveled west to New Mexico in search, among other things, of a healthy climate for Walker (he still had to remain constantly vigilant about his condition). They lodged for a period south of Santa Fe at Rancho La Merced (139). There, he corresponded with Bunt, who at that time was working in New Orleans. Soon afterward he flew to New Orleans from New Mexico and proposed to her. On November 6, they married in the First Baptist Church in New Orleans. Because of the recent death of Bunt's mother, it was a quick and small wedding attended only by a few close family and friends.

After the wedding the Percys settled in at Brinkwood. Though not a sanatorium, the mountainous environment was good for rest and relaxation. Though Percy at one point had considered returning to medical practice, his health was still not good. In August 1948, the Percys traveled to New Orleans for an extended visit and ended up moving into town for a period. They adopted a child and soon after moved with their new daughter, Mary Pratt, across Lake Pontchartrain to the quaint town of Covington. Several years later Bunt became pregnant and, in July 1954, Ann Boyd Percy was born. Soon afterward the Percys discovered that Ann was deaf and were relentless in making sure that she should be schooled at home rather than institutionalized. According to Samway, "they wanted the best care for her, even if it meant they had to dramatically change their lives" (177).

From 1947, as a newlywed, Percy began writing seriously, but with limited success. His first full-length book project, "The Charterhouse," reached 1,100 pages and was received as ponderous and not publishable. Similarly, he was unable to find a publisher for "The Gramercy Winner," his next book-length manuscript. These works coincided with other essays and reviews on philosophical topics that were well-received in intellectual journals.

While at Brinkwood and later in New Orleans, Percy and his wife began their thoughtful and deliberate conversion to Catholicism. Percy had been interested in religion for some time. His interest was spiritual, but heavily supplemented of course by a profound intellectual interest in philosophy. Percy's conversion to Catholicism was accompanied by a study in earnest, on the one hand, of the specific beliefs and practices of the church, and on the other of its philosophic foundation in the thoughts of the church fathers, particularly Augustine.

Poverty was certainly not among Percy's many misfortunes. It appears that he and his family were able to live comfortably on the income from the Percy estate and other sources, so there was time for Percy to cultivate his craft. And over time Percy succeeded finally in producing his first published novel, *The Moviegoer*, a breakthrough accomplishment that won the National Book Award in 1962. Now in his mid-forties, Percy had endured a very long struggle indeed for literary acceptance and success.

One can only speculate about how Percy's philosophical and religious thoughts developed during his childhood, his education, and his subsequent illness and initial disappointments as an author. It is tempting to draw parallels between his own troubled childhood and early adulthood and the tragic cultural and historic events that preceded and circumscribed his life and work. Such a connection is on the surface sophomoric, but it would help to illuminate the various cultural circuits that charged Percy's fiction and, in particular, the medieval and Arthurian elements that later ran through his work.

Certainly we see in Percy's life to this point a theme of calamity, disorder, and despair. On a personal level, Percy was driven to isolation, so, whatever sense of alienation he may have developed due to the tragic circumstances of his childhood, this sense of existing apart from the normal world was fortified in a very real way by an extended physical separation from friends, relatives, and career in his early adulthood. During this time he had to face death head on, but unlike the warriors of yore or the soldiers of his generation, he had to confront his mortality in quiet and extended contemplation.

It is no wonder that he was drawn to philosophy and, ultimately, the spiritual quest, specifically as it was forwarded in the Christian existentialist meditations of Soren Kierkegaard. Percy wanted a religious position that he eventually found through faith (and the Catholic Church), a position that at least allowed for some historically fixed and stabilized theological framework. If one were to try to describe the core of high medieval thought and culture, it would be that medievalism is precisely the same effort to order an otherwise chaotic world. This is evident in the distinct hierarchies of the medieval (or Catholic) church—in its administration and in its spiritual metaphysics (or cosmos)—and the parallel political hierarchies of medieval government. Both church and state valued loyalty, fealty, and humility as essential to the preservation of order.

Modern cultural critics are often quick to point out the differences between modern and medieval thought, between a world that was primitive albeit with a sense of order and heroism as compared to the modern world, in which we are more sophisticated but rudderless. But is frankly more accurate to admit their similarities. However ordered or heroic the medieval world may appear to the modern looking back, it is certain that the Arthurian legend, particularly as it is transposed and forwarded in Malory, is the outgrowth of the same feelings of lost values and chaos that has troubled moderns.

On one level, Percy's training in science, and the appearance of science in his writing, seem distinctly unmedieval in thematic character. On another level, though, particularly when his narrators attempt to order their worlds in terms of a personal spiritual search or quest, whether for faith or love, Percy's fiction is at times distinctly medieval in form and function. Will Barrett's contemplative character in *The Last Gentleman*, when offset by the unruly mercantilism of the Vaught family, may indeed illuminate a waning of gentlemanly or noble behavior in an absurd postmodern world. However, the questing knights of the Round Table, too, are the last knights in a kingdom soon to collapse under war, greed, brutality, and, eventually, chaos. "Love" may be "in the ruins" in Percy's futuristic third novel, but love is persistently ruinous in the medieval legends of courtly romance, particularly in the case of Lancelot and Guinevere.

With the exception of *Lancelot*, which contains direct allegorical allusion to the Arthurian legend, Percy's references to medieval lore in his other works are more oblique. Without exception, however, his narratives contain a spiritual search for meaning in life—spiritual meaning which also means the recovery of spiritual meaning—and this search or quest is distinctly Arthurian, the product of a heroic warrior culture trying to recover spiritual strength and communal order.

As a Southerner, this recovery was more than fictional for Percy. He became an ardent supporter of the desegregationist movement from the 1950s onward and based his support on the fundamental tenets of Christian faith. He was not a member of the naive class of Southerners who wanted to return to the autocratic and fictional antebellum periods of their imaginations, but one who felt strongly that an individual should seek a spiritual position and community with others through right action and good works, albeit in an absurd modern world in which meaning has gone topsy turvy.

To identify the Arthurian elements in Percy's fiction, one would have to take a modified view of particular elements of the Arthurian cycle as it is presented in Percy. Any attempt to draw direct allegorical parallels between the legend and Percy's plots will be thwarted by Percy's own view of absurdity in modern existence. The medieval version of the Arthurian narrative on the whole includes the rise of Arthur, the establishment of Camelot, the fallout after the exposure of Lancelot's love affair with Guinevere, the grail quest to restore an impotent king and kingdom, the revelation of the grail and then the final fall of Arthur to the army of his illegitimate son, Modred.

Percy's early narratives tend to begin after the main characters have already taken a fall perhaps brought on more by the scientific godlessness of the twentieth century than for specific personal reasons. In his first novel, *The Moviegoer* (1961), Percy introduces Binx Bolling, a young man who is a stockbroker in New Orleans looking forward to his thirtieth birthday and upcoming nuptials with Kate. Binx should be comfortable: he has what appears to be a good career, a promising life after marriage, and, as he points out, such creature comforts as "a first class television set, an all but silent air conditioner, and a very long lasting deodorant" (7). Yet he has fallen into the "everydayness" of life and realizes that the only way to avoid the despair or malaise of this banality is to search, to "be onto something" because "not to be onto something is to be in despair" (13).

This observation is vintage Kierkegaard and echoes the epigraph of the novel, that "the specific character of despair is precisely this: it is unaware of being despair." The key point here though is that the quest itself, not just the result of the quest, has intrinsic spiritual value. This point is as much the essence of Arthurian narratives during the Middle Ages as it is the outgrowth of modernist Christian existentialism. In *The Moviegoer*, Binx does begin his search, eventually wandering away, both physically and mentally, from the comfortable "desert" of his basement apartment on Elysian Fields Avenue and begins a transformation into meaningful existence through revelations afforded by the death of his religiously faithful half-brother, Lonnie, and his own acceptance of Kate's love. Of course obtaining the grail in Arthurian narrative is more about the inner character of the knight in pursuit. The pure knight of legend does not achieve the grail through his ability to gain insight or revelation as much as he manages to place himself in a position to be revealed unto. This spiritual positioning, one gained through the sheer willingness to search, is as much at the core of Percy's narrative as it is the old stories of the grail quest.

Similarly, the *The Last Gentleman* (1966), Percy's second novel, features a "lost" hero, whose life, like Percy's, is circumscribed by the indeterminable meaning of his father's suicide. In this story the main character, Will Barrett, takes a long and obvious pilgrimage to the real desert of New Mexico as part of his quest for a meaningful spiritual life. Like Binx, Will is another young man lost in everydayness but in New York instead of New Orleans. He is working as a "humidification engineer" at Macy's, and views himself as a scientific man who views the world as a scientist and often specifically from a safe distance through an actual telescope. Will has already learned to avoid the everydayness that plagued Binx at the beginning of *The Moviegoer*, and he has taken to "engineering" his life "according to the scientific principles and self-knowledge" he has gained from psychoanalysis (41). Though Will really thinks that he is "onto something" it is ironically and painfully clear that he has gotten off track. Will happens upon his quest after running into Kitty McVaught and getting caught up in the workings and personalities of the McVaught family, a curiously eccentric family from Alabama. Will travels to the South, then on to New Mexico, where terminally ill Jamie McVaught has a deathbed conversion. Bearing witness to Jamie's conversion, Will presumably works himself out of his own fugue state and returns to Alabama presumably to marry Kitty and to get on with his life. Again Percy winds his narrative around the search, but, unlike the symbolically concrete search for the grail in the legends of the holy knights, Percy gives his narrative a post-modern twist by leaving the reader wondering exactly what was revealed to gentlemanly Will in his modern spiritual desert.

By the mid sixties, Percy had settled into his life in Covington and in his first two novels seemed to be looking back to the perplexities of young adulthood, specifically the issues that he confronted during his own life and artistic development. The cultural sites for his fiction, ranging from New York, through the South to New Orleans and then West to New Mexico, are clearly reflective of his own travels. Indeed, Samway suggests that the ending of *The Last Gentleman* occurred to Percy when he stopped in Santa Fe when returning from a family trip to Jackson Hole, Wyoming (226). However, Percy was no stranger to the New Mexico desert as he had traveled there earlier for an extended stay during his own recovery period from TB. The everydayness from which Binx is escaping, the self-induced hypnotic spell that Will must break away from, the encounters with death and suicide experienced by both characters, are strongly reflected in Percy's own life and in the tragedies of his childhood, his extended psychoanalysis, and his enduring recovery periods in isolation. Indeed, Percy himself was a lost soul in search of spiritual meaning, and this search, however contorted through the lens of scientific modernity, is at the core the same struggle as that of the Arthurian knight through the wasteland. These themes would be visited again in *The Second Coming*, in which an older Will Barrett is still the mock heroic searcher wandering through an ironic and often comic modernist landscape that places a pristine golf course next to a vulgar spate of upstart religious denominations.

After the 1966 publication of *The Last Gentleman*, Percy had secured his place among the highly celebrated literary novelists of his generation. He was offered invitations to speak, teach, and participate in such prestigious roles as being a judge for the National Book Award. Percy was particular about when and where he made public appearances and as a result earned a reputation over the years as being a bit of a hermit. As Samway has clearly documented, this view is undeserved. Percy, though highly protective of his health and privacy—particularly in situations that required potentially harsh business negotiations or other heated discussions—traveled frequently and was very active in the literary and also the political world of his day (Samway, 266).

The novels that followed *The Last Gentleman*, particularly *Love in the Ruins* and *Lancelot*, led Percy's readers to wonder if he had lost a screw, given the graphic sex and violence and the ravings of the insane or nearly insane that appeared in these novels. It is certain that Percy became frustrated with the race issue and the inability of society to overcome this problem. He was actively involved in the Civil Rights movement to bring racial unity to the South and the nation as well. When he was confronted with the persistent resistances put up by the local school to desegregation and even threatened by the

Klan, he wrote that even in the village of Covington, he felt "more of an outsider" than ever (257). In this mood, it seems, he began to attack the enemy, so to speak, with the sometimes harsh ironic social critiques presented in his next novels.

In *Love in the Ruins* (1971) Percy, in medieval fashion, allegorizes a future postapocalyptic world, a utopia that seems on the surface to be as pristine as Camelot in the subdivision of Paradise Estates, where much of the novel is located. The main character, Tom More, has invented a scientific device, a lapsometer, which can trace the spiritual lapses of the brain and which, More believes, will cure the human race of its spiritual ills. However, the world of Paradise Estates is also fractured by racial divides and by upper-middle class social and, yes, sexual dysfunctions. The sense of the personal quest is present here, but this time only through thick layers of ironic and often hilarious social critique. Tom More is not the man for all seasons but a psychiatrist with his own psychiatric problems and a weakness for booze and women. The novel at one point turns into an action story as the hero (who has been tempted by a devil by the name of Art Immelmann) races against time to save both the suburbanites and the subalterns of the surrounding swamp. Tom More's utopia is quite different from that described by the earlier Thomas More, and the theme of the novel seems, as does the writing of Sir Thomas More, more postmedieval than medieval or Arthurian per se.

The same could be said of *Lancelot* (1977), Percy's fourth novel and another work that examines postapocalyptic life in reference to another postmedieval figure, Lancelot Andrews, the seventeenth-century divine so instrumental in the administration of the 1611 version of the King James Bible. Eventually the deranged narrator likens himself to the medieval knight of legend, however, and Percy also makes another namesake connection with the character Percival, who is Lancelot's confidant. Still, the heroic elements of the Arthurian legend are taken on at a sharp slant and in distinct contrast to the typical ideals of the genre as it has been carried forward from the medieval period. The heroic battles, the holy quests, the poetic diversions of idyllic love, are twisted and distorted in Percy's novel by a deranged hero into a story that puts a horrid spin on the classic legend.

Specifically, the Lancelot in Percy's work is a sometime lawyer living in his old family home of Belle Isle. Until he sees clues of his wife's, Margot's, infidelity, Lancelot has been basically sleepwalking through life. When several Hollywood types arrive to film a movie, the hero begins to sense the full extent of the sexual licentiousness that surrounds him, and in a semideranged state of rage and jealousy, he decides to go on a quest for evil and specifically to establish scientific proof of evil. Working with his brilliant and devoted assistant, he manages to capture on film the full exploits of his wife and daughter in their sexual engagements with the actors on site. He kills his wife's lover, Jacoby, with a knife (a type of scaled-down version of Excalibur), and sets fire to his house, thus killing Margot and two actors.

Lancelot therefore takes on the theme of adultery as central to the destruction of civilization. Infidelity on such a scale reflects the happenings in Camelot, with the major exception that in the legend it is Lancelot, himself, who commits adultery, whereas in Percy, Lancelot is the jilted one. Similarly, the quest for the grail in the legend is a holy quest, whereas in Percy it is a quest to find precisely the opposite. In terms of Percy's treatment of the old legend, one is left with the impression that the heroic and Christian elements of the old legend have been thwarted in the mind of a deranged and even criminal hero, however, a hero for whom the reader feels sympathy given the severity of the transgressions against him.

Percy's later work extends his earlier themes and also the lives of two earlier characters, Will Barrett and Tom More. In *The Second Coming* (1980), Will Barrett is a retired Wall

Street lawyer who, though rich and comfortable, suffers from melancholy and suicidal ideation. Barrett's father committed suicide, and Barrett himself contemplates the same, to the degree that he embarks on a mock serious spiritual quest into a mountain cave, in search of God but only to find that he has developed an excruciatingly painful toothache. Barrett runs across Allison Huger, an escaped mental patient who cares for him and helps him find his way from the laments of this profound case of male menopause. Again, we see the spiritual quest and again the tradition of the eventual sublime revelation is turned on its head through a narrative that, though serious enough, pokes some fun at modern existence and even at the main character.

Tom More emerges again in *The Thanatos Syndrome* (1987), literally from prison where, again, there is trouble in utopia, although not completely unwelcome trouble, as everyone seems content and sexually energized. With his cousin, Lucy Lipscomb, More discovers a government plot to anesthetize locals, robbing them of free will by spiking the area's drinking water with a special chemical. Percy uses this forum to satirize middle- and upper-middle-class America, and in doing so he provides a critique of the sixteenth-century utopia of Thomas More, which, one might argue, is carried forward from the Arthurian depiction of Camelot. It is only through this type of stretch that one finds Arthurian influence in either *Love in the Ruins* or *The Thanatos Syndrome*.

It should be mentioned in passing that Percy also wrote nonfiction and produced two works: *The Message in the Bottle* (1975), a series of essays, and *Lost in the Cosmos* (1983), a "self-help" book to examine the basic questions of existence. He also contributed essays to such publications as *Harpers*, the *Georgia Review*, and *Commonweal*. Percy's nonfiction is replete with sharp-witted critiques of the spiritual and intellectual vacuity of modern consumer culture and sloppy hypocrisies found in twentieth-century politics. He was specifically interested in the role of writers and thinkers who wish to promote meaning beyond the banalities of day-to-day, material life but was always the gentleman who knew how to soften the hard knocks with good humor and playfulness.

Percy's writing career spanned over four decades. Once settled in Covington, Percy maintained a strong commitment to family and community, local and national politics, and golf. He was a deeply committed father and grandfather, and also retained his faith. At one point he was appointed adviser to Pope John Paul II on American religious culture. He taught writing courses at Loyola University and at Louisiana State University and reviewed manuscripts for the National Endowment for the Arts and his own PEN-Faulkner committee. Percy continued to travel frequently throughout his career and personally provided insight and guidance to many of his contemporaries, both writers and intellectuals. On May 10, 1990, Walker Percy died from complications resulting from cancer.

One could argue that Percy's fiction and nonfiction generally extend the legacy of the Arthurian legend simply in its commitment to questing for higher ground in modern times. This quest, in both the medieval and modern world, takes place in a spiritual geography that is disorienting, and in a culture where honor and chivalry are depreciated. For Percy the spiritual grail, though elusive, was still the ubiquitous, once and future aim for a post-modern culture trapped in the confusion of day-to-day existence.

PRIMARY WORKS

The Moviegoer. New York: Knopf, 1961; London: Eyre & Spottiswoode, 1963; *The Last Gentleman.* New York: Farrar, Straus & Giroux, 1966; London: Eyre & Spottiswoode, 1967; *Love in the Ruins.* New York: Farrar, Straus & Giroux, 1971; London: Eyre & Spottiswoode, 1971; *The Message in the Bottle.* New York: Farrar, Straus & Giroux, 1975; *Lancelot.* New York: Farrar, Straus & Warburg, 1977; London Secker & Warburg, 1977; *The Second Coming.* New York: Farrar, Straus & Giroux, 1980; London Secker & Warburg, 1981; *Lost in the Cosmos.* New York: Farrar, Straus & Giroux, 1983; *The Thanatos Syndrome.* New York: Farrar, Straus & Giroux, 1987; London: Andre Deutsch, 1987.

Papers

Walker Percy's papers are held by the Southern Historical Collection of the Louis Round Wilson Library at the University of North Carolina, Chapel Hill.

SECONDARY SOURCES

Allen, William Rodney. *Walker Percy: A Southern Wayfarer.* Jackson: University Press of Mississippi, 1986; Bloom, Harold, ed. *Modern Critical Views: Walker Percy.* New York: Chelsea House, 1986; Brinkmeyer, Robert H. *Three Catholic Writers of the South.* Jackson: University Press of Mississippi, 1985; Bugge, John. "Arthurian Myth Devalued in Walker Percy's Lancelot." In *Lancelot and Guinevere: A Casebook,* ed. Lori J. Walters, 181–91. New York: Garland, 1996; ———. "Merlin and the Movies in Walker Percy's Lancelot." *Studies in Medievalism* (Fall 1983): 39–55; Coles, Robert. *Walker Percy: An American Search.* Boston: Little, Brown, 1978; Coulter, Lauren Sewell. "The Problem of Merlin's Pardon in Walker Percy's Lancelot." *Southern Literary Journal* 33 (2001): 99–107; Crowley, Donald J. "Walker Percy's Grail." In *The Grail: A Casebook,* ed. Dhira B. Mahoney, 525–43. New York: Garland, 2000; Crowley, Donald J., and Sue Mitchell Crowley, eds. *Walker Percy: Critical Essays.* Boston: G. K. Hall, 1989; Dale, Corinne. "Lancelot and the Medieval Quests of Sir Lancelot and Dante." *Southern Quarterly: A Journal of the Arts in the South* 18 (1980): 99–106; Desmond, John F. *Walker Percy's Search for Community.* Athens: University of Georgia Press, 2004; Hardy, John Edward. *The Fiction of Walker Percy.* Urbana: University of Illinois Press, 1987; Hobson, Linda Whitney. *Understanding Walker Percy.* Columbia: University of South Carolina Press, 1988; Lawson, Lewis A., ed. *Following Percy: Essays on Walker Percy's Work.* Troy, NY: Whitson, 1987; Lee, Jennifer. "The Sorceress and Her Inquisitor: Lancelot's Demonic Woman." *Southern Quarterly: A Journal of the Arts in the South* 37 (1999): 169–79; Lister, Paul A. "Sir Walker and Sir Lancelot." In *The Arthurian Myth of Quest and Magic: A Festschrift in Honor of Lavon B. Fulwiler,* ed. William E. Tanner, 77–89. Dallas: Caxton's Modern Arts Press, 1993; O'Gorman, Farrell. "Languages of Mystery: Walker Percy's Legacy in Contemporary Southern Fiction." *Southern Literary Journal* 34 (2002): 97–119; ———. "Walker Percy, the Catholic Church, and Southern Race Relations, c. 1947–1970." *Mississippi Quarterly: The Journal of Southern Cultures* 53 (1999–2000): 67–88; Poteat, Patricia Lewis. *Walker Percy and the Old Modern Age: Reflections on Language, Argument, and the Telling of Stories.* Baton Rouge: Louisiana State University Press, 1985; Smith, C. E. "The Unholy Grail in Walker Percy's Lancelot." *Religion and the Arts* (1999): 385–407; Taylor, L. Jerome. *In Search of Self: Life, Death, and Walker Percy.* Cambridge, MA: Cowley, 1986; Tharpe, Jac. *Walker Percy.* Boston: Twayne, 1983; ———, ed. *Walker Percy: Art and Ethics.* Jackson: University Press of Mississippi, 1980; Tolson, Jay. *Walker Percy: The Making of an American Moralist.* New York: Simon and Schuster, 1990; Wilhelm, Arthur W. "Moviemaking and the Mythological Framework of Walker Percy's Lancelot." *Southern Literary Journal* 27 (1995): 62–73.

THOMAS WINN DABBS

MARY STEWART

(September 17, 1916–)

What separates Stewart's Arthurian novels from contemporary works of the same genre is that she relates the Arthurian legend from the viewpoint of Merlin. He, not Arthur, is the protagonist in the first three books: *The Crystal Cave* (1970), *The Hollow Hills* (1973), and *The Last Enchantment* (1979). The focus shifts to Modred in *The Wicked Day* (1983). Not only does Stewart change prominent characters from the usual telling, she shifts the time as she places her tales in fifth-century Britain as opposed to the twelfth-century England Arthurian legend readers normally see. Even with the shift of seven centuries, Stewart maintains historical accuracy with the details of places, customs, religion, clothing, and life in general.

Lady Mary Florence Elinor Stewart was born September 17, 1916, in Sutherland, County Durham, England, to Frederick Albert and Mary Edith (née Matthews) Rainbow. Her father was a clergyman with the Church of England. At the age of five, her first published poem appeared in a local parish magazine. She attended Skellfield School before going on to the University of Durham where she received her bachelor of arts degree with first-class honors in 1938. In 1939 she was awarded a diploma in theory and practice of teaching. By 1941 she had been granted her master of arts degree. From 1940 to 1941, Stewart was head of English and classics at Abbey School, Malvern Wells, England. She returned to the University of Durham later in 1941 to assume a lecturer position and remained there until 1945, when she married Frederick Henry Stewart, a noted geologist. She continued as a part-time lecturer between 1948 and 1955.

The Stewarts moved to Edinburgh, Scotland, in 1956 when Sir Henry accepted a position at the University of Edinburgh. After the move, she decided to forgo teaching and concentrate on writing full time. The only time prior to 1955 that she did not teach was during World War II when she served in the Royal Observation Corps. The change to writing full time proved to be the right decision as her books have met with great success throughout her career. In 1960 she received the British Crime Writers' Association

Award for *My Brother Michael*. The Mystery Writers of America acknowledged her with their award in 1964 for *This Rough Magic*. By 1968 she was named a fellow at Newnham College, Cambridge. Her first book concerning the Arthurian legend, *The Crystal Cave*, garnered the 1971 Frederick Niven Award. In 1974 Stewart was awarded the Scottish Council Award for her children's book, *Ludo and the Star Horse*. Her husband was knighted the same year for his contributions to science.

In Stewart's early work she is a proponent of the suspenseful historical romance genre. Her gothic overtones have the protagonist, a charming young woman, caught in events outside her normal realm. The events are not only perilous but can also be life threatening. As with all romances, the hero and love interest of the unsuspecting heroine helps to solve the mystery, to survive the adventure, and to save the damsel from any duress. Her characters maintain a code of conduct not unlike the chivalric code of the Arthurian court where honorable behavior and a code of ethics are observed.

Her early novels have similar plots and the locals of each are in exotic, romantic, and foreign places, giving readers mini vacations from their day-to-day routines while offering the reassuring sameness that all will be well by the last page. Readers seem to embrace this sameness of work rather than becoming bored with it as evident by the majority of her titles atop the best-seller lists for numerous weeks.

New York Times reviewer Anthony Boucher, a Stewart fan from the beginning, maintained in his often-quoted review of her first novel, *Madam, Will You Talk?* (1955), "a backward glance will reveal so many whopping coincidences and inadequate or inconsistent motivations that you can't believe a word of it; but so unusually skillful is this young Englishwoman in her first novel that you really don't care. You've had too enjoyable a time" (March 18, 1956). He continued his praise with his assessment that her second novel, *Wildfire at Midnight* (1956), "is rich in uncertainty, excitement and sheer narrative flow" (September 9, 1956). Most critics responded with similar encouraging comments concerning Stewart's first works. She maintains she only wanted to be a good storyteller.

By the time *Thunder on the Right* was published in 1957, the critics continued with their generosity. Many cited her same formula of romance, setting, suspense, and adventure as reasons to engage in "good recreational reading" as the critic from *Booklist* advised on June 1, 1958, or the appreciation of her endings claimed another critic came about through her characters' convenient illnesses and personality shifts, which were not quite believable but nevertheless worked. Even Anthony Boucher thought Stewart's "credulity may be a bit stretched" in his *New York Times* (May 18, 1958) review. However, readers continued to buy Stewart's tried and true formula.

The critics' accolades returned with the publication of *Nine Coaches Waiting*, Stewart's 1959 novel. At 342 pages, this novel was her longest work to date. Not only was this tale the usual romantic story, her writing began to be compared to that of fellow suspense writer Daphne du Maurier's work *Rebecca* and Charlotte Brontë's *Jane Eyre*. It appeared Stewart had found her literary niche. She continued in the same romance suspense genre for another seven books, but with the publication of *My Brother Michael* in 1960, she began adding historical and classical references, along with offering more of her finely wrought details of country and people that endeared her readers. Anthony Boucher, still the fan, assures readers of the fact that although her previous books' "plots are . . . Eurydecian—they cannot stand a backward glance. But in *My Brother Michael* even this flaw vanishes" (*New York Times*, April 10, 1960).

With the comparison of Stewart to du Maurier and Brontë, Phoebe Adams of *Atlantic* contends she "would not count her as a threat to the laurels of Ngaio Marsh" (April 1962) after reading *The Ivy Tree* (1961). Other critics found the work containing typical Mary Stewart writing; her plot is intricate, the countryside detailed, and she continues "a sharp delineation of her stock characters" (*Library Journal*, December 15, 1961).

As the popularity of her books grew, a new market opened for an unusual audience. The Walt Disney Company decided to adapt her 1962 book, *The Moon-Spinners*, to the big screen. This proved to be an opportune marriage. Disney's child star, Hayley Mills, still under contract, had passed puberty. The role of Nicola Ferris, an English girl on vacation on the isle of Crete, who stumbles into the predictable Stewart mystery almost appears to have been written for Mills. She brings the character to life with the exuberance and naiveté Stewart places on her pages. The characters and situations of the novel meshed in a way not completely accomplished in her previous works, and in turn through the motion picture.

In her following novel, *This Rough Magic* (1964), Stewart keeps her Grecian locale, but moving from Crete to Corfu. Again, she turns a bit more toward the historical with both the title and the setting. The title comes from William Shakespeare's *The Tempest*, and Corfu may be the island where Prospero and Miranda escape. One reviewer for *Best Sellers* claims "no hesitancy in judging this polished and lively novel as highly recommended" (August 15, 1964).

The critics were less generous with *Airs Above Ground* (1964) and *The Gabriel Hounds* (1967). Some said she needed to slow down in her publishing output. Averaging one book a year, Stewart seemed to be losing her effectiveness of her descriptions, characters, and plot that kept her atop the best-seller lists for the last decade. Even those critics who had offered favorable reviews and overlooked the inconsequential flaws of her past works did not do so now. Longtime supporter Anthony Boucher of the *New York Times* contends *The Gabriel Hounds* to be "poverty-stricken in plot and character" (October 15, 1967), and Stewart herself may have felt the same.

For a while she wanted to change direction in her writing, but her publishers had tried to dissuade her. "The publishers didn't want me to write *The Crystal Cave* in the first place, because they were doing so well with the earlier books. Publishers never want you to change," she confesses in an interview with Raymond H. Thompson in April 1989. But it was her love of history and the classics that offered the change she seemed to need as she explains to *Contemporary Authors*:

> I always planned that some day I would write a historical novel, and I intended to use Roman Britain as the setting.... But then, quite by chance, I came across a passage in Geoffrey of Monmouth's *History of the Kings of England*, which described the first appearance of Merlin, the Arthurian "enchanter." Here was a new story, offering a new approach to a dark and difficult period, with nothing known about the "hero" except scraps of legend. The story would have to come purely from the imagination. (vol. 59)

From Stewart's imagination, she conjured up a history for the character of Merlin few had even thought to consider. No other authors concerned themselves with his heritage, his background, his relationship with King Arthur, or how he became the king's prophet. By supplying her readers with answers, her next novel proved to be neither plot poor nor character famished.

That Stewart falls into the popular culture category of writers cannot be denied; yet, her prose is not diminished by the fact. With the publication of the widely popular *The*

Crystal Cave in 1970, Stewart received the highest critical response of any of her novels to date along with an entirely new legion of readers. This novel became the first in what is to become known as the Merlin trilogy.

Called a "good rattling yarn" by a *Book and Bookman* critic (August 1970), Stewart starts at the end of Merlin's life to begin her novel. She contends she "originally had no intention of writing more than one novel" in an interview with *Contemporary Authors* (vol. 59). By the time readers arrive at the end of the book, they have no doubts of another one forthcoming. Stewart asserts in *Contemporary Authors, New Revision Series, Volume 1–4*, "the novelist has all the more responsibility laid on him to create a world where the individual is still seen to matter, and where right is still paramount." For the individual to matter and might be right (as T. H. White contends), and for Stewart's statement to remain viable, her believable portrayal of Merlin hinges on the fact she makes him human-flesh and blood, and as such, along with his "gift from the gods," he feels the same emotions that the rest of us do. Reminding readers of this fact makes her Merlin that much more identifiable to her audience: they feel the alienation he suffers in his grandfather's court; understand the love he has for his mentor, Galapas; share the bonds of friendship he has with Cerdick and Cadal; are relieved as Merlin once the identity of his father is known; and become as stoic as he is by some of the directions he must go to bid the gods' wishes. "The gods only go with you, Myrddin Emrys, if you put yourself in their paths," Galapas reminds him (61). Merlin's humanness becomes an icon for the trilogy and sets him apart from the awe-inspiring depictions of previous tales and from T. H. White's semi-Alzheimer character.

With each book of her Merlin trilogy, Stewart changes the iconography of the character to demonstrate the different facets of his life. In *The Crystal Cave* the icon comes from the title and aids readers' understanding of the character's statement "I'm just a man." However, Stewart changes the cave icon as Merlin grows and develops. The first appearance of the iconographic cave appears in the prologue to *The Crystal Cave*. Readers are privy to a private conversation between two people that neither reader nor participants understand the significance of until much later. The exchanges takes place just prior to Merlin's conception. He is conceived in the cave where he will experience a rebirth, and much later, his demise. The next cave readers find him in is the old disused Roman hypocaust, or hot water heating apparatus under the King of Wales's, his grandfather's, palace. In this underground area he overhears human conversations and becomes aware of the stars speaking. Through his eavesdropping, some, like his cousin Dinnas, begin to wonder at his powers. The first real indication Stewart offers readers of Merlin's soon-to-be famous sight occurs in his grandfather's private garden. His uncle, Prince Camlach, befriends and consoles him there after his mother, Lady Niniane, has refused King Gorlan's marriage proposal by offering the bastard Merlin an apricot. Merlin refuses, saying the apricot is "black inside" (33). Camlach, taken aback by the child's refusal, splatters the apricot against the castle wall. For a moment, Merlin has self-doubts of what he has seen: "I stood where I was, watching the juice of the apricot trickle down the wall. A wasp alighted on it, crawled stickily, then suddenly fell, buzzing on its back to the ground. Its body jack-knifed, the buzz rose to a whine as it struggled, then it lay still" (34). With Stewart's descriptive first-person prose, both readers and character alike have an epiphany: Merlin is awed by this newly discovered but still awkward power, and readers anticipate the unfolding of his history that leads him to become what legends are made of.

With the need to learn more about his power, sight, and ability, Merlin discovers Galapas, a hermit living in a cave not far from his grandfather's castle. Merlin begins his apprenticeship with the elder and in so doing, finds the second iconographic cave: the cave within the cave—the crystal cave. Within the walls of Galapas's home lies the unseen crystal cave. Here is where Merlin experiences his first true visions. Here is where he learns of the change in leadership occurring as he sits in the crystal cave, his impending death at his Uncle Camlach's hand, and the murder of Cedrick, his beloved servant and caretaker. Stewart creates a rebirth for Merlin as the guiding force in the fate of his beloved Brittany.

Galapas becomes the father figure Merlin lacks. With the hermit's guidance and sight, the child slowly matures. He learns flora and fauna; how to gather and distill herbs in potions; continues his harp lessons begun by Queen Olwen, his grandfather's second wife; listens to the gods speaking in the wind; and discovers he is "a whistle for that wind" (60). Not only does he increase his "magical" ability, he also learns the importance of relationships with other people no matter their standing in life. This mutual respect between royalty and commoner aids Merlin later in life when his gods are not always present to help.

Stewart's Merlin is so likeable because of his humanity; he has no pretentiousness about him, and he constantly reminds people that he is merely a man; even though, he soon discovers his father is Ambrosius, Duke of Brittany. Stewart explains to Thompson that in creating Merlin's past, why she made him the king's son: "I made him Ambrosius's son because he is referred to as Merlinus Ambrosius at some point. That gave me the connection." Stewart's connection enables her Merlin to hone his skills in languages, mathematics, engineering, medicine, mankind, and human natures. He learns from the master craftsmen of court and the blind singer equally.

Merlin comes completely of age in yet another cave—Vortigern's cave. Vortigern's cave is actually where Stewart's idea for *The Crystal Cave* began. She explains in the Thompson interview that while reading Geoffrey of Monmouth's *History of the Kings of Britain*: "I came to the part where the young Merlin, aged seventeen or so, is brought in front of Vortigern who intends to make a human sacrifice of him, and I thought that's my story." This particular cave proved the birthplace not only of Stewart's story, but also as the place Merlin comes of age and assumes his place in the world of the Arthurian legend. Vortigern wants to sacrifice Merlin because his wise men and magicians have told him to "seek out a lad who never had a father, and slake the foundations with his blood" (228), and he will have no further trouble with the construction of his castle walls. At this point in Stewart's story Merlin cannot reveal his parentage but considers "ironically enough, what they had got was no devil's child, nor even a boy who once had thought to have powers in his hands. All they had got was a human youth with no power beyond his human wits" (229). Merlin's life is spared, not because of any magic, but through the engineering knowledge he gained in his father's court. He does, however, with his sight see the downfall of Vortigern by his father, along with his mother's death. While trying to convince Ambrosius that he does not control this sight, he prophesizes death for his father and foresees Arthur. "And you shall live again in Britain, and for ever, for we shall make between us a king whose name will stand as long as the Dance stands, and who will be more than a symbol; he will be a shield and a living sword" (309).

Stewart deviates from Thomas Malory's story line in that she has Merlin transform Uther, his uncle in her story, into Gorlois, Duke of Cornwall, in order to bed Ygraine, his wife. Stewart's human Merlin accomplishes the transformation through clever make-up instead of magic. From this union Arthur is conceived, but as with the original tale, the night ends tragically. The Cornish king is killed in battle, and Merlin kills Brithael and loses Cadal, his faithful servant in the process of granting Uther's desires. Stewart concludes *The Crystal Cave* with the fiasco. Uther cannot see that his bastard will not be thought of as Gorlois and Ygraine's child no matter how hard Merlin tries to convince him. "I'll not acknowledge the bastard I begot tonight" as his only response (372). At the end of the book, readers find Merlin to be where he began—alone.

In *The Hollow Hills*, Stewart changes the iconography of Merlin to focus on the sword that brings Arthur to the throne as King of Britain and Uther's rightful heir. Since Merlin is the main focus of Stewart's work and not Arthur, she concentrates on her enchanter's life as he awaits the right time for Arthur's true identity to be revealed. "The main story in that book is the search for the sword. I'd been trying to bring in some of The Grail tradition, which of course has nothing to do with the real King Arthur. . . . everyone who is worth his salt has a Grail, and everybody's Grail is different. I thought, well, that sort of search is a good idea. In Merlin's case, of course, it was the search for the sword, and so that became the Grail," Stewart explains to Thompson. After safely delivering the baby Arthur to Moravik, Merlin's own childhood nurse, he sets off to visit some of the places he studied while growing up in Ambriosus's court. This action he maintains will keep the king's enemies from discovering the hiding place of Arthur.

His sight enables him to watch as the baby grows and is taken to live in Count Ector's court as ward. Ector's realm is where Emyrs, as Arthur is called, resides unknown to Uther's enemies and where he and Merlin will reunite. During Merlin's travels, the image of the sword he first saw while speaking with Ygraine appears in unusual places as though he is being drawn in its direction. Viewing a "silken tessarae" or tapestry in Ahdjan's home in Constantinopolis, Merlin learns Maximus's sword is somewhere in Britain, continuing the idea of the quest. Merlin returns to Britain as his sight tells him the time is nearing for Arthur's identity to become known. While making his way toward Ector, he discovers the sword's meaning through Stewart's unusual weaving of events. After mistakenly being captured by the Old Ones in what Stewart says is one of her favorite scenes in the book, Llyd of the hollow hills explains the legend of the sword: "The sword was laid down by a dead Emperor, and shall be lifted by a living one. It was brought home by water and by land, with blood and with fire, and by land and water shall it go home, and lie hidden in the floating stone until by fire it shall be raised again. It shall not be lifted except by a man likewise born of the seed of Britain" (240).

Merlin sets out to find the holy man who might provide more information, and through a series of coincidences, he comes to Macsen's Tower, a fort containing Maximus's home in the center. From this point, he sees the tower of his sword visions, a pagan temple for the god Mithras. As he surveys the derelict temple, he offers a prayer and is answered by a voice instructing him: "Throw down my altar. It is time to throw it down." (260). Awakening from the trance, Merlin finds the altar overturned and in its depths are Macsen's sword and a chalice. The sword he takes; the chalice he leaves, and the first part of the quest ends for Stewart's enchanter.

Stewart forges and connects links in her narrative like links of mail. She has Merlin continue on to the Chapel in the Green where he finds Prosper, the hermit, almost dead. Before the hermit's death, he explains that the chapel is also called the place of the sword and "the sword will come back to the shrine, to stand here for a cross" (270). Merlin assumes the hermit's place; takes care of the chapel; hides the sword on "the floating stone" in the depths of Caer Bannog, the island in the lake nearby; and watches "Emrys."

The first time the child enters the chapel he tries to lift a sculpted sword from the altar, saying, "That was the queerest thing. I thought it was real. I thought, 'There is the most beautiful sword in the world and it is for me.' And all the time it wasn't real" (292). Stewart provides her own interpretation of the sword in the stone when she has Emyrs bring Mascen Wledig's sword from its island hiding place, and to keep it for the rightful king, he watches as Merlin turns it into the stone sword of the altar.

Emyrs proves himself in battle, and before Uther dies he names Arthur as heir and the rightful king. King Lot demands more evidence, and like the other legends, Stewart has her child king pull the sword from the stone altar in a "white blaze of fire" that appears as Merlin's last act of enchantment as King Arthur is accepted as the "man likewise born of Britain."

What Ambrosius and Merlin envisioned for Britain has come true; the only thing Merlin's sight did not allow him to see, and thus to prevent, is the seduction of Arthur by his half-sister, Morgause. Merlin meets her briefly in *The Hollow Hills* when he comes to attend to Uther's battle wounds. Merlin defines her as Uther's bastard. As Gandar's assistant, she desires to meet Merlin to learn his magic. She does not comprehend when he explains the gift is not his to give. While the child is disappointed, she is not stopped in obtaining the alchemy education she desires. The next encounter readers have with Morgause occurs when Merlin brings Emyrs to court, and she seduces Arthur. Stewart stays with the legend in this aspect but with one notable difference—Morgause *knows* who Arthur is when the incestuous acts occurs. Where the Morgause character of Stewart's sources does conceive a child by her half-brother, she does so with some sort of innocence. Stewart offers no innocence to anything her Morgause does, only treachery. "I switched characters," Stewart tells Thompson when she speaks of Uther's daughters. In previous tales, Morgan le Fay is Arthur's half-sister of dubious claim. She is the high priestess of magic and Merlin's nemesis. Stewart's Morgan is the legitimate daughter of Uther and Ygraine, who, like her mother, will sacrifice herself for the good of the kingdom—at least on the surface.

As *The Last Enchantment* begins, Stewart extends Morgause's guile to ensnare King Lot from Morgan. By outwitting her sister, Stewart has her characters return in part to the familiar legend and provides the continuity for Modred.

"Merlin is dead." Stewart opens *The Wicked Day* (1983), her concluding novel in her Arthurian quartet. Modred lives; he, like the young Arthur, has been sent into safe hiding, and Stewart creates a new history for him not unlike the past she gave Merlin. Stewart explains in the author's note that readers know very little of Modred and no explanation of why he has the villainous role. She points to the fact that previous tales of Modred's treachery "are filled with absurdities," and given the opportunity, she would have liked "to have rewritten the story completely, and set Arthur, with Modred at his side against the Saxons." Any temptation she might have entertained she resisted due to her own writing. In her previous books she has Merlin prophesizing Arthur's destruction by Modred. She creates a Modred unlike previous portrayals: "I tried to iron out the absurdities of the old story, and add some saving greys to the portrait of a black villain" (367).

Stewart creates a Modred not unlike Arthur. Morgause fears Lot's retaliation and sends Modred away to be reared unaware of his parentage. When the young Medraunt, the fisher boy, comes to Arthur's court, his parentage is explained much the same way Arthur's was conferred to him. Morgause manages to retain some spell on all her sons, but once Modred realizes Gabran, Morgause's lover, killed his "parents," the bond between them weakens as the bond with Arthur grows. Stewart's reworking of the legend has Arthur and Modred on friendly terms. He is also Arthur's firstborn here, and thus heir to the throne. Stewart also differentiates this story from her previous three by narrating it in third person as opposed to the first person narrator she uses throughout Merlin's story.

Even without the focus on Merlin in this book, Stewart manages to have the enchanter's presence felt. From the opening sentence, the demise of the magician remains incomprehensible. And Stewart plays on both the readers' and characters' denial of loss with hints throughout as to the prophet's whereabouts. "'Merlin is still alive, after all,'" Cei tells the Orkney boys (130), and Merlin continues his counsel for a time. Then all learn: "Merlin was no longer with the court; since his last illness he had lived in seclusion, and when the king removed to Caerlon the old enchanter retired to his hilltop home in Wales, leaving Nimue to take his place as Arthur's advisor" (157). Stewart continues the duality of her enchanter as she has Nimue explain, "'I am Merlin'" (199, 201). The explanation Stewart has for this lies in the fact that she wrote each book as if it were her only or last book concerning the Arthurian legend, and she could not change anything from her previous works. "In *The Last Enchantment* Merlin says he never met or spoke to Modred," she tells Thompson. "Thus when I wrote *The Wicked Day*, I couldn't let Modred meet Merlin."

Instead Modred seeks Nimue to ascertain if there is anything he can do to undo Merlin's prophesy—including taking his own life. Stewart gives Modred a resolve of rightness previously unseen in his character. "'I owe him much and none of it evil'" portends of Stewart's "saving greys" in her characterization. When Nimue is unable to provide the answers he desires, Modred sets off on his own quest to find Merlin and the answer.

Once Modred reaches Bryn Myrddin, Merlin remains as enigmatic as before, but the sorcerer provides the answer to Modred's quandary:

> It was not even a curse. It was a fact, something due to happen in the future, that had been seen by an eye doomed to foresee, whatever the pain of seeing. It would come, yes, but only as, soon or late, all deaths came. He, Modred was not the instrument of a blind, brutal fate, but of whatever, whoever, made the pattern to which the world moved. *Live what life brings; die what death comes.* (235)

Stewart tries every way to change the legend. Modred saves Guinevere and tries to save the treaty between Arthur and the Saxons. Arthur has no desire to fight his son. It is this humanness of Stewart's characters that separates them from all other writers' conventions. She begins *The Crystal Cave* with Merlin's assertion of being only human and continues *The Wicked Day* with Nimue imploring Arthur not to "be blinded by prophecy . . . fate is made by men, not gods" (351). If the Nimue-Merlin can convince Arthur that as a man he actually holds power over the gods instead of the reverse, the destruction might end before it has begun. She reminds him "the time will come, is coming, has come, when you and your son may hold Britain safe between your clasped hands, like a jewel cradled in wool. But loose your clasp, and you drop her, to shatter, perhaps for ever" (351). Arthur realizes he, like everyone else in the world, controls his own destiny. Stewarts offers a lesson for all to heed.

Some times fall beyond human control. These deeds do not belong to the gods but to human frailty. One innocent act by a human creates havoc in a world seemingly meshed since time unremembered; it is the killing of an adder. "The straight speaking, the truths laid down during the talk by the truce table, the faith and the trust so nearly reaffirmed, all vanished" (356) as Stewart concludes her novel and interpretation of the legend.

In the epilogue, readers remain on the battlefield. "Arthur certainly isn't dead at the end of my book. I leave the resolution open, because he may well have been taken off in a coma, to be nursed or heaven knows what. Anyway, the legend leaves him alive. I didn't kill Merlin either," she reminds Thompson.

She left them both alive but writes no more of their tales. She continues with her suspense romance novels. In 1983, *Thornyhold* was published. She then changed directions in her writing career by releasing a book of poetry, *Frost on the Windows and Other Poems* in 1990. *The Stormy Petrel* was published in 1991 and was followed four years later by *The Prince and the Pilgrim* (1995) and *Rose Cottage* in 1997. Such is her unusual treatment of Merlin and his place in the Arthurian legend that her books remain highly popular and still in print. The books have also come required reading for high school literature classes and staples for the college Arthurian legend course.

Like each preceding writer Stewart embraces the Arthurian legend as her own. She retains the basic premises of the tales but continues adding new levels to the myths and legends few bothered to consider. Her interpretation of certain aspects of the characters adds a dimension not seen since T. H. White's retelling of the tale. Without fully relying on any one source she conjures up a world as real and as believable as any in the Arthurian world.

PRIMARY WORKS

Madam, Will You Talk? London: Hodder & Stoughton; New York: Morrow, 1955; *Wildfire at Midnight*. New York: Appleton, 1956; *Thunder on the Right*. London: Hodder & Stoughton; New York: Morrow, 1957; *Nine Coaches Waiting*. London: Hodder & Stoughton; New York: Morrow, 1958; *My Brother Michael*. London: Hodder & Stoughton; New York: Morrow, 1960; *The Ivy Tree*. London: Hodder & Stoughton, 1961; New York: Mill, 1962; *The Moon-Spinners*. London: Hodder & Stoughton; New York: Morrow, 1962; *This Rough Magic*. London: Hodder & Stoughton; New York: Mill, 1964; *Airs Above the Ground*. London: Hodder & Stoughton; New York: Mill, 1965; *The Gabriel Hounds*. London: Hodder & Stoughton; New York: Mill, 1965; *The Wind Off the Small Isles*. London: Hodder & Stoughton, 1968; *The Crystal Cave*. London: Hodder & Stoughton; New York: Morrow, 1970; *The Little Broomstick* (children's fiction). Leicester, UK: Brockhampton Press; New York: Morrow, 1971; *The Hollow Hills*. London: Hodder & Stoughton; New York: Morrow, 1973; *Ludo and the Star Horse* (children's fiction). Leicester, UK: Brockhampton Press; New York: Morrow, 1974; *Touch Not the Cat*. London: Hodder & Stoughton; New York: Morrow, 1976; *The Last Enchantment*. London: Hodder & Stoughton; New York: Morrow, 1979; *A Walk in Wolf Wood*. London: Hodder & Stoughton; New York: Morrow, 1980; *The Wicked Day*. London: Hodder & Stoughton; New York: Morrow, 1983; *Thornyhold*. New York: Morrow, 1988; *Frost on the Window and Other Poems*. New York: Morrow, 1990; *The Stormy Petrel*. London: Hodder & Stroughton; New York: Morrow 1991; *The Prince and the Pilgrim*. London: Hodder & Stoughton; New York: Morrow, 1995; *Rose Cottage*. London: Hodder & Stoughton; New York: Morrow, 1997.

Collections

Three Novels of Suspense. New York: Mill, 1963. Comprises *Madam, Will You Talk?, Nine Coaches Waiting*, and *My Brother Michael*; *The Spell of Mary Stewart*. New York: Doubleday, 1968. Comprises *This Rough Magic, The Ivy Tree*, and *Wildfire at Midnight*; *Triple Jeopardy*. London: Hodder & Stroughton, 1978. Comprises *My Brother Michael, The Moon-Spinners*, and *This Rough Magic*; *Selected Works*. London: Heinemann, 1978. Comprises *The Crystal Cave, Wildfire at Midnight*, and *Airs Above the Ground*; *Mary Stewart's Merlin Trilogy*. New York: Morrow,

1980. Comprises *The Crystal Cave, The Hollow Hills,* and *The Last Enchantment; Mary Stewart: Four Complete Novels.* New York: Avenel Books, 1983. Comprises *Touch Not the Cat, The Gabriel Hounds, This Rough Magic,* and *My Brother Michael.*

SECONDARY SOURCES

Dean, Christopher. "The Metamorphosis of Merlin: An Examination of the Protagonist of *The Crystal Cave* and *The Hollow Hills*." In *Comparative Studies of Merlin from the Vedas to C. G. Jung,* ed. James Gollnick, 63–75. Lewiston, NY: Mellen, 1992; Fries, Maureen. "The Rationalization of the Arthurian 'Matter' in T. H. White and Mary Stewart." *Philological Quarterly* 56 (1977): 258–65; ———. "Teaching White, Stewart, and Berger." In *Approaches to Teaching the Arthurian Tradition,* Approaches to Teaching World Literature, vol. 40, ed. Maureen Fries and Jeanie Watson, 113–17. New York: Modern Language Association of America, 1992; Hermans, Harold J. "The Women in Mary Stewart's Merlin Trilogy." *Interpretations: A Journal of Ideas, Analysis, and Criticism* 15, no. 2 (Spring 1984): 101–14; Hildebrand, Kristina. *The Female Reader at the Round Table: Religion and Women in Three Contemporary Arthurian Texts.* Uppsala, Sweden: Uppsala University Press, 2001; Jurich, Marilyn. "Mithraic Aspects of Merlin in Mary Stewart's *The Crystal Cave*." In *The Celebration of the Fantastic: Selected Papers from the Tenth Anniversary International Conference on the Fantastic in the Arts,* Contributions to the Study of Science Fiction and Fantasy. vol. 49, ed. Donald E. Morse, Marshall B. Tymn, and Csilla Bertha, 91–101. Westport, CT: Greenwood, 1992; Nelson, Marie. "King Arthur and the Massacre of the May Day Babies: A Story Told by Sir Thomas Malory, Later Retold by John Steinbeck, Mary Stewart, and T. H. White." *Journal of the Fantastic in the Arts* 43 (2000): 266–81; Watson, Jeanie. "Mary Stewart's Merlin: Word of Power." *Arthurian Interpretations* 1, no. 2 (Spring 1987): 70–83; Wiggins, Kayla McKinney. "'I'll Never Laugh at a Thriller Again': Fate, Faith, and Folklore in the Mystery Novels of Mary Stewart." *Clues: A Journal of Detection* 21, no. 1 (Spring/Summer 2000): 49–60.

M. TAYLOR EMERY

ROSEMARY SUTCLIFF
(December 14, 1920–July 22, 1992)

Rosemary Sutcliff is regarded as one of the twentieth century's most outstanding writers of belletristic children's literature. Acclaimed for her meticulous research and ability to bring historical periods to life through precise details and lifelike characters, she was awarded the British Library Association's Carnegie Medal, the Boston Globe-Horn Book Award, and the Phoenix Children's Book Award. In 1975 she was named a fellow of the Royal Society of Literature and an officer of the Order of the British Empire for her contributions to children's literature. In all, she wrote more than fifty books for children and adults, some of which were translated into fifteen languages. While best remembered for historical novels set in Roman Britain, her Arthurian trilogy, *The Sword and the Circle* (1981), *The Light beyond the Forest* (1979), and *The Road to Camlann* (1982), are considered the finest retellings of the original legend for youth. Moreover, her *Sword at Sunset* (1963), along with T. H. White's *Once and Future King*, is regarded as one of the two greatest Arthurian novels of the twentieth century. Reflecting on Sutcliff's craftsmanship and style, critic Robert Payne (*New York Times Book Review*, May 26, 1963) maintains, "Sutcliff is a spellbinder. While we read, we believe everything she says. She has hammered out a style that rises and falls like the waves of the sea."

The daughter of George Ernest Sutcliff, an officer in the Royal Navy, and Elizabeth Lawton Sutcliff, Rosemary Sutcliff was born in East Clanden, Surrey, on December 14, 1920. The small family spent the first ten years of her life following her father to various stations, from Malta, to Streatham (London), to Chatham Dockyard, to Sheerness Dockyard, finally settling in North Devon, where they remained until her mother died in the 1960s. In an interview with Justin Wintle and Emma Fisher, author Alan Garner comments that children's authors often have two things in common—they were deprived of the usual primary schooling and they were ill and left to their own company. Sutcliff's isolated childhood truly fits Garner's paradigm. In *Is Anyone There?* (1978) Sutcliff remarks, "I had a lonely childhood and growing-up time. My parents loved me and I loved them, but I could never talk to them about the problems and fears and aching hopes inside me that I had most need to talk about to someone. And there was no one else." At the age of two, she was afflicted with Still's disease, a kind of juvenile arthritis, which kept her in and out of hospitals for painful remedial operations and out of conventional schools until she was nine years of age. Her mother's obsessive personality also contributed to Sutcliff's isolation. During Sutcliff's illness, her mother became overly anxious, rejecting any outside help and demanding unconditional love and devotion in return; truly, she thought it unwise for her daughter to desire any companionship but hers. Hampered in her physical movement by the poly-arthritic disease, Sutcliff spent much of her time sitting still and observing. While the surrounding countryside might have been denied the young Sutcliff as a playground, the changing seasons of the North Devon landscape produced what Margaret Meek terms "a pitch of Keatsian sensibility" in Sutcliff's powers of observation, something that translated into "brilliantly etched details of hills, downs, coastline and villages" in her fiction for young adults.

Sutcliff was educated at home by her mother until the age of nine. In her memoir, *Remembered Hills* (1984), she describes a difficult relationship with her mother, but grants that "very few of the worthwhile things in this world are all that easy." Elizabeth disciplined her daughter harshly, but also read to her willingly, raising the young child on a diet of Beatrix Potter, A. A. Milne, Charles Dickens, Hans Christian Anderson, Whyte Melville, Kenneth Grahame, and Rudyard Kipling. Kipling's *Jungle Books*, *Just-So Stories*, and *Puck of Pook's Hill* were especially meaningful to the young Sutcliff. Indeed, she credits Kipling for awakening her passion for Roman Britain. Elizabeth never tired of reciting Norse, Celtic, and Saxon myths and legends to her impressionable, imaginative child and delighted in reading the historical novels she loved as well. Of these, King Arthur and Robin Hood attracted her "very strongly as a child," Sutcliff noted in an interview with Raymond H. Thompson. Interestingly, Sutcliff did not learn to read until she was nine years of age. At that time, she was enrolled in Miss Beck's Academy, a rather unorthodox school for children of service families. When the family returned to North Devon, she enrolled in St. George's School but left school—"mercifully early"—at fourteen. During this time, Sutcliff's illness required frequent absences from school for operations to repair the damages of her arthritic condition. In the hospital library, she found L. M. Montgomery's *Emily of New Moon*, a novel that recounts a young girl's adventures and her attempts to be a writer. For Sutcliff, it was a magical novel, but when she left the hospital, the book was left behind.

After ending her formal education at fourteen, Sutcliff trained as a painter at Bideford School of Art from 1935 to 1939. She passed the City and Guilds examination, became a member of the Royal Society of Miniature Painters, and was advised to make the painting of miniatures her profession. One of her miniatures, a depiction of a fifteenth-century knight in armor, was displayed at the Royal Academy and was quickly sold. World War II broke out when Sutcliff was eighteen. About this time, she visited a local book shop to read J. G. Frazer's *The Golden Bough*, a massive work that contained the concepts of sacred kingship and primitive religion that inform her historical novels in various ways. In an interview with Thompson, she states that the idea of a historical Arthur came from reading what she describes as "two intriguing books by some absolute crackpot called Dayrel Reid": *The Battle for Britain in the Fifth Century* and *The Rise of Wessex*. Sutcliff adds, "I was fascinated by this idea, and I set off looking for all the other clues that I could find. Then, little by little, other people, like Geoffrey Ashe, began to write about the historical Arthur, and I read their books as they came along . . . I was convinced that there was a real man in the middle."

Sutcliff was never fully committed to painting, and at the age of twenty-five, gave it up, declaring, according to Meek's monograph, that it "was becoming more of an exercise than an art. . . . Writing was more satisfactory." Not long after the end of the war, Sutcliff wrote her first book, *Wild Sunrise*, a romantic story of Cradoc, a young British chieftain, at the time of the Roman invasion. In her memoir, Sutcliff declares that she was happy that the narrative is now lost because "so much of me was in it, naked and defenceless." Shortly before the end of the World War II, she wrote another story, whose loss she did lament. The story centers on the relationship of a lonely young girl and an embittered young man, but in the end, Ait went wrong because, Sutcliff notes, she was too inexperienced to direct the plot to a convincing end. Some of its themes re-emerge in *The Eagle of the Ninth* (1954). Her first book, a retelling of Saxon and Celtic myths for children, was submitted to Oxford University Press by a friend. In their rejection letter, the editors suggested she write a version of the Robin Hood story for them, and Sutcliff produced *The Chronicles of Robin Hood* (1950), which was accepted. In the eighteen months it took to have the manuscript typed up and returned to her, Sutcliff wrote *The Queen Elizabeth Story*, published the same year.

Sutcliff's first four books are classified as books for younger children. In *The Chronicles of Robin Hood*, based upon the ballads, the emphasis is on the enchantment of the greenwood, the faithfulness of the sworn band of outlaws, and just retribution for the Sheriff of Nottingham, rich merchants, and barons who trample the weak. Robin's outlaws, however, are sworn to protect women, children, and honest poor men. Despite characters that are larger than life, Meek, in *Rosemary Sutcliff*, maintains that *The Chronicles of Robin Hood* shows that Sutcliff had the compelling narrative skill of the undoubted storyteller from the very beginning. *The Queen Elizabeth Story*, Sutcliff's first original children's story, provides insight into the author's isolated childhood. Perdita, the story's heroine, is a little girl who loves stories and is accustomed to playing alone. The book is for young girls who still believe that fairies can grant wishes on Midsummer's Eve. Meek finds Perdita "decorative, but puppet-like," her brother much too obliging, and her brother's friend much too attentive to a little girl. However, in Perdita's loyal friend, Adam Hilyarde, a lame orphan who aids her in achieving her wish to see the Queen before her next birthday, Meek finds seeds and strengths of books to come. "He is," she notes, "the first of a line of heroes whose inner life is as significant as their actions." A reviewer for *Junior Bookshelf* (July 3, 1950) notes, "The writing has considerable charm. It is simple and unaffected and displays an aptness in choice of epithet, a feeling for detail and a freshness appropriate to the scene. Only in Aunt Phoebe's story is there a somewhat false ring."

The feeling of sheltered seclusion found in *Robin Hood* and *The Queen Elizabeth Story* persists in both *The Armourer's House* (1951) and *Brother Dusty-Feet* (1952). In *The Armourer's House*, set in Henry VIII's London, the heroine, Tamsyn, has been taken to live with her armorer uncle, his wife and family. Her cousin Piers has dreams of voyages to the Indies, and together they act out their fantasies in the attic. Throughout the work, childhood is idealized; the aunt and uncle are sympathetic and scholarly, and the home is warm, secure, and comfortable. Irene Smith, in a review in the *New York Times Book Review* (October 26, 1952), finds "the richly detailed atmosphere of Henry VIII's London is the main attraction of the book. . . . The author's emphasis upon background deprived the story of full development; there are numerous events but no real plot." Sutcliff's fourth book, *Brother Dusty-Feet*, tells of the adventures of Hugh Copplestone and his dog Argus, who run away from wicked Aunt Alison to join a band of strolling players. As they trek across England together, the band provides a charmed circle for Hugh. In addition to Hugh's adventures with a palmer, a quack doctor, and a Tom o'Bedlam, Sutcliff includes retellings of the legends of St. George and St. Aldhelm that she enjoyed as a child.

As reported in *Townsend: A Sense of Story* (1971), Sutcliff notes that these "early works all seem to have been written so easily." Indeed, she goes on to explain, "They *were* written so easily, for in those early days I didn't know how hard it is to write books—at least books that satisfy the deep inner inquiring something in oneself." "Nobody," she goes on to say, "had told me about the strains and stresses of creating; I learned them for myself as time—and books—went by and I became more and more of a perfectionist." Townsend concurs with Sutcliff's own assessment of her early works, as he did not find much promise in them. Granting that the backgrounds are "solid," and the storytelling "effective," he declares the books' chapters are "strung like beads on a thread," and while the characters are nice little girls (Perdita and Tamsyn) and brave little boys (Hugh), "there is no real life in any of them." Moreover, he maintains, "the tone of voice is condescending, and simplicity can sink into naivety or be misleading."

In 1953 Sutcliff published *Simon*, her first critically recognized historical novel, one that marked an important transition in her career. A far more complex novel intended for an older age group than her first four books, *Simon* is set during the English Civil War and takes place over several years. Simon, a Roundhead, is forced to fight his childhood friend, Amias, a Cavalier. In moving away from historical legend to real history, Sutcliff depicts battles and setting with an imaginative power and scope scarcely hinted at in her first four books. Not all critics, however, share Meek's conclusion that Sutcliff has created a hero who "has depths of sense and sensibility unusual in adventure heroes"; Townsend maintains that "the conflict of loyalties in a friendship that cuts across the civil war lines is rather obvious, and the hero a dull fellow."

From 1954 to the end of the decade, Sutcliff produced an impressive and critically acclaimed series of historical novels. "With her first major novel, *The Eagle of the Ninth* (1954), Sutcliff brought a new dimension into historical fiction for children, indeed into children's literature,"claimed Sheila Egoff in *Thursday's Child*. *The Eagle of the Ninth*, *The Silver Branch* (1957), *The Lantern Bearers* (1959), and *Outcast* (1955) all take place in that period when the Romans were evacuating Britain. The first three titles, considered Sutcliff's "Roman British" trilogy are connected by protagonists who share a family line and a ring passed down through generations. *The Eagle of the Ninth* recounts the story of Marcus Flavius Aquila, a young Roman centurion who is wounded in his first battle in Britain. With his freed slave, Esca, he goes to find out what happened to his father's legion, the legendary Ninth, when it marched beyond the wall in 17 AD and mysteriously disappeared. "The detail of life in a Roman garrison and in the more primitive camps of the ancient Britons sound like eyewitness report," maintained Lavinia R. Davis in a *New York Times Book Review* (January 9, 1955). Moreover, she asserts that "their adventures, whether in battle, on the lonely hills, or in the forbidden temple where the Eagle was finally found, are invariably exciting and credible." The work was Sutcliff's favorite among her own books. As she explains in an interview in *British Children's Authors* (1976), "I'm so fond of it because when I wrote it I was going into the hospital to have an operation. . . . I was scared stiff and I wanted, really, someone to keep me company. I created Marcus and had him for a companion. I've always felt rather special towards him, as though he was a friend who's been with me in a tough corner."

The Silver Branch, the second book in the Roman British trilogy, takes place at a time when Saxon war bands are invading Britain. Its theme is an extension of the light and dark theme found first in *Simon*, "one that informs *The Eagle of the Ninth*, and *The Lantern Bearers* as well," asserts Meek. As she explains, "The light is what is valued, what is to be saved beyond one's lifetime. The dark is the threatening destruction that works against it." Egoff notes similarities in characters as well. The characters are all given "universal, human problems" yet remain "vital and recognizable in their own time," she claims. Moreover, because Sutcliff's perennial theme is that of "personal responsibility, particularly if the protagonist is in a position of leadership," she finds an epic quality permeating Sutcliff's major novels. *The Silver Branch* centers on Justin, a junior surgeon, and his centurion kinsman, Flavius Aquila (descendants of Marcus Flavius Aquila), during the reign of Carausius. After two years of exile, they lead a ragged band of the loyal underground against barbarians who threaten to destroy the hope of a civilized Britain. A reviewer writing for *New York Herald Tribune Book Review* (May 11, 1958), praised Sutcliff's integration of historical research and imagination, adding: "The plot is swift and compelling, rising to a free climax in the wild scene of battle and flame in the basilica of Calleva (Silchester), in which the 'lost' eagle again plays a part. The characters are interesting and varied, especially the daring heroes, the Emperor Carausius who hoped to steer clear of a knife in his back until Britain became strong enough to stand alone, perceptive and resourceful Aunt Honoria, and Cullen, the slave of the 'silver branch.'"

Sutcliff was awarded the 1959 Carnegie Medal from the British Library Association for *The Lantern Bearers*, the "most closely-woven novel of the trilogy," according to Meek. The novel focuses primarily on the conflict between Vortigern and Ambrosius and the decline of Roman Britain, presented through the eyes of Aquila, a Roman soldier who was "willfully missing" when the last of the Romans pull out so that he can defend Britain from its enemies. Townsend views Aquila's decision as evidence of a break between Sutcliff's strictly Roman British novels and the Arthurian ones that follow. *The Lantern Bearers* marks one of the first attempts at a historical setting for King Arthur and ends three days before the start of Sutcliff's adult novel *Sword at Sunset* (1963).

In an interview with Thompson, Sutcliff claims that both books are part of the same story, despite a shift in narrator from Aquila in *The Lantern Bearers and* Arthur himself in *Sword at Sunset*. Convinced that the legendary hero had a basis in a real person, Sutcliff turned to several sources in an attempt to reconstruct the man behind the legend, including these she revealed to Meek: R. G. Collingwood's *Roman Britain*; I. A. Richmond's *Pelican History of English*, Vol. I; Rollestan's *Myths and Legends of the Celtic Race*; P. Quenell's *Everyday Life in Roman Britain* and *Everyday Life in Saxon, Viking, and Norman Times*; Arthur Weigall's *Wanderings in Roman Britain, Wanderings in Anglo-Saxon Britain*; H. D. Trail's *Social England*, Vol. I; Sir Arthur Bryant's *The Makers of Realms*; and Reed's *Battle for Britain in the Fifth Century*.

Aquila, the narrator of *The Lantern Bearers*, is embittered and lonely, and according to Meek, "bears within himself the conflict of dark and light, the burden of his time and of himself." Aquila's world is shattered when Saxons enslave him and his sister, Flavia, kill their father, and destroy their farm. Aquila eventually escapes with the help of his sister, now married to a Saxon with a Saxon son. The remainder of the story centers on Aquila's redemption, aided by a kindly bee-keeping friar, Brother Ninnias, the Roman British leader, Ambrosius, whose friend he becomes, and Ness, his Celtic wife from a marriage arranged by Ambrosius. Aquila proves himself a valiant leader, and in the course of the struggle against the Saxons, he meets the nephew of Ambrosius and son of the late

Utha, Artorius, better known as Artos, the Bear. At the end of the novel, the future King Arthur, now twenty, has become a superb leader and rebel, gathering to him all the best and most gallant of the young warriors. The Saxons have been defeated, and Ambrosius Aurelianus has been crowned High King of Britain. Looking over the crowd of young warriors gathered for the coronation, Aquila ponders whether they will be remembered for their deeds. Eugenus, looking at Artos, replies, "You and I and all our kind they will forget utterly, though they live and die in our debt. Ambrosius they will remember a little, but he [Artos] is the kind that men make songs about to sing for a thousand years." "The characterizations are vivid, varied and convincing," maintained Margaret Sherwood Libby in the *New York Herald Tribune Book Review*. "The plot, both interesting and plausible, has its significance heightened by the recurring symbolism of light in dark days."

In between the books of the trilogy, Sutcliff published several other books, including *Outcast*, which recounts the story of a slave, Beric, who has no tribe and no identity and whose miseries as an outcast anticipate Aquila's torments in *The Lantern Bearers*. In addition, she published *The Shield Ring* (1956), the story of a young Viking boy who wishes to prove himself a worthy warrior during the time of the Norman invasion; *Lady in Waiting* (1956), aimed at adult readers; *Warrior Scarlet* (1958), the story of fifteen-year old Bronze Age boy, who earns the mantle of manhood despite a crippled right arm; and *The Bridge Builders* (1959), a short story of life on the Roman Wall, and *The Rider of the White Horse* (1959). In 1960, she published *Houses and History*, and *Rudyard Kipling*, a Walck Monograph. *Dawn Wind*, set at the end of the sixth century when the Britons fought their last battle against the Saxons and lost, was published in 1961 as was *Beowulf*, part of the Bodley Head library of historical retellings.

During the 1960s, Sutcliff's mother died, and she and her father moved to Sussex. Barbara Talcroft finds Sutcliff's kingship themes became most developed early in the decade, culminating in *Sword at Sunset* (1963) and *The Mark of the Horse Lord* (1965). Sutcliff has reported that Frazer's theories about primitive society, particularly his concepts of an eternal vegetation myth, had a major influence on her, and Talcroft analyses Sutcliff's use of the mythic themes of king and goddess, maimed ruler, and dying god in the historical novels. In *The Sword at Sunset*, Artos is the sacrificial king, dedicating himself to his people and land, and eventually dying for them. In *The Mark of the Horse Lord*, Phaedrus, a freed gladiator impersonates the lost prince of a Western Scottish tribe, inherits his highland kingdom, and voluntarily dies that the tribe may be saved.

The Sword at Sunset is the continuation of *The Lantern Bearers*. Sutcliff claims that one day she was "ready" to construct Arthur as a Dark Age leader, although she knew from a very young age that she would eventually find and reconstruct him. In her introduction to *The Sword and the Circle*, Sutcliff states, "Many people believe, as I do, that behind the legends of King Arthur as we know them today, there stands a real man. No king in shining armor, no Round Table, no fairy-tale palace at Camelot, but a Roman-British war leader, who when the dark tide of the barbarians came flooding in, did all that a great leader could do to hold them back and save something of civilisation."

While many people may believe in a historical Arthur, Sutcliff's viewpoint is an unusual one that has barely been explored in historical fiction. Always one to delve into historical backgrounds before beginning to write a novel, she devoted most of her research to the life and history of the Dark Ages and then worked Arthur into that setting. In her 1986 interview with Thompson, she claims never to have written a book in which she had been so deeply involved either before or since. Working from six o'clock one morning until two o'clock the next, Sutcliff took eighteen months to complete the novel. At times, she claims, it seemed as if the material was "being almost fed through me, rather than being the result of my own research." She had difficulty starting the novel, but after three false starts, realized the story had to be told in the first person, something with which she had no experience. She acknowledged that after completing the novel, getting back into a woman's skin was difficult, so absorbed had she become in living and thinking like a man.

In reviewing *Sword at Sunset* for *The New York Times Book Review*, Payne remarks, "the best historical novels, history goes out of the window and love remains." Furthermore, Payne argues that the novel is "only theoretically concerned with King Arthur, for it is 'unconvincing' as history and has almost nothing to do with the familiar Arthur of folklore." Sutcliff's retelling of the Arthurian legend "blends legend, historical scholarship and masterfully humane storytelling to illuminate the misty and romantic era that preceded the Dark Ages," remarked a reviewer for *Chicago Tribune Books* (March 8, 1987). Her Artos (Arthur) is neither the Arthur of history books nor the legendary Arthur of Tennyson or Malory; truly, he is only remotely associated with ancient England. True to Sutcliff's vision of a historical Arthur, there is no magical realm; indeed, there are no Merlin, no sword in the stone, no Camelot, no Round Table. Christopher Dean claims the novel is realistic fiction set in the distant past. Always, he claims, a rational rather than a supernatural explanation emerges for the story's events. For example, when Artos unwittingly commits incest with Ygerna, his half sister, he talks of "the magic mist" and the air filled with the "bloom of enchantment," and deems her "a witch," but the rational explanation is clear enough: Ygerna drugged his wine, and under its sway, Artos is seduced. In the same way, when the birth of Artos and Guenhumara's (Guinevere's) daughter comes on suddenly at the peak of a great storm, Artos, in desperation, finds her a place of safety in the village of Druim Dhu, the leader of the Dark People, despite Guenhumara's fears of these aboriginal inhabitants of England. When her baby dies, Guenhumara accuses the Dark People of having sucked the life out the infant to save a weak child of their own. But Artos does not accept a supernatural explanation for Guenhumara's fear, attributing it to nothing but an "ill dream."

The Sword at Sunset, like so many of Sutcliff's earlier works, depicts a Roman-British civilization desperately holding out against the dark forces of murderous Picts and Saxons, thirty years after the last of the Roman Legions left Britain. Arthur is presented as a British warlord, a supreme ruler, who, with his "Companions," is fighting to attain a few more years of civilization. Arthur is more man than myth, a man of culture to be sure, but one fighting very real battles and coping with the threat to a united Britain. While the novel is focused primarily on the battlefield, Sutcliff has not discarded all the traditional aspects of the Arthurian legend. Traditional companions Kay and Gwalchmai (here a healer) have parts; Arthur courts and marries Guinevere and discovers her in the arms of Bedwyr, a part later played by Lancelot; and she eventually goes into her nunnery. For Thompson, *Sword at Sunset* is deservedly one of the most admired historical novels about King Arthur. He notes, "*Sword at Sunset* brings Arthur down to earth without removing any of the glory or wonder." Townsend, however, finds the novel the least satisfactory of Sutcliff's Roman and post-Roman books, for "here the incorporation of legendary material into the historical framework has been achieved at the cost of nearly all its vitality. Arthur, or Artos, has become a standard Sutcliff warrior, and even then not convincing as a narrator; and Miss Sutcliff's Guenhumara is a feeble figure beside the Guinevere of legend."

Between the publication of *Sword at Sunset* and *The Mark of the Horse Lord* Sutcliff published *The Hound of Ulster* (1963), the story of Cuchulain, *A Saxon Settler* (1965), and *Heroes and History* (1965). She received the first Phoenix Award of the Children's Literature Association in 1985 for *The Mark of the Horse Lord*, considered by many her finest work. The award was established to honor a book published twenty years earlier, which did not receive a major award at the time of its publication, but which, from the perspective of time, is deemed worthy of special recognition for its high literary quality. The novel is set in Roman-occupied Britain in the second century and centers on the adventures of Phaedrus, a freed gladiator, who bears a remarkable resemblance to Midir, the lord of the Horse People (the Dalriada of Scottish history). He is pressed into impersonating the blinded king, whose throne has been usurped by the evil Liadhan, queen of the Picts. If Phaedrus fails to overthrow Liadhan, he, like so many kings of ancient myth, will be a temporary king, sacrificed at the end of a fixed term. Bit by bit, he comes to sense that he is the real chief, choosing death in the end to preserve the tribe.

Like Talcroft, Egoff maintains that the sense of sacrifice in the novel derives from ancient myths, although the incidents themselves are Sutcliff's own. Sutcliff's "mastery of the period enables her to choose the exact detail of dress, speech, customs, and the wild land itself to make the background vivid," asserted Elizabeth Hodges, in a review for *The New York Times Book Review* (November 7, 1965), and Egoff points out that the images of light and darkness that fill her work, the sounds of the battlefield, the horrors of the gladiator arena, are not unlike the images from the ancient myths from which they derive. Above all, claims Egoff, even when portraying the most horrible tragedies, Sutcliff insinuates that they are necessary steps a civilization must take on a long, arduous climb to real humanity.

Between the publication of Sutcliff's adult novel, *Sword at Sunset*, and her critically acclaimed trilogy of the Arthurian myth for children, she published more than a dozen works, including a widely praised retelling of the Irish legend *The High Deeds of Finn MacCool* (1967) and the tragic Celtic love story of *Tristan and Iseult* (1971), for which she won the Boston Globe-Horn Book Award.

Other works included *The Flowers of Adonis* (1969), the story a fifth-century BC Athenian general and statesman, *The Capricorn Bracelet* (1973), a collection of stories covering six generations of Aquila descendants fighting for Rome in the Scottish border country. *Blood Feud* (1977), a book for older children; *Sun Horse, Moon Horse* (1977), whose hero, Lubrin, like Phaedrus in *The Mark of the Horse Lord*, that his tribe may be saved; and *Song for a Dark Queen* (1978), which received the Children's Rights Workshop Award.

While Artos of *The Sword at Sunset* might be unrecognizable to readers of Thomas Malory, his retellings of the legends of King Arthur and the knights of the Round Table provide the material for Sutcliff's Arthurian trilogy for young readers, *The Light beyond the Forest; The Quest for the Holy Grail; The Sword and the Circle: King Arthur and the Knights of the Round Table*; and *The Road to Camlann: The Death of King Arthur*. In her preface to *The Sword and the Circle* (the first part of the trilogy, chronologically), Sutcliff claims that "we should have lost something beautiful and mysterious and magical out of our heritage" were the legends of King Arthur to be lost. In acknowledging the sources for the thirteen Arthurian stories in the work, she reports of following Malory in the main, if not "slavishly." Geoffrey of Monmouth's *British History* is the source of Vortigern and Merlin, Utha and Igraine and the dragon light in the sky; *Sir Gawain and the Green Knight* comes from a Middle English poem; Tristan and Iseult derive from

Godfrey of Strasburg's version and, in outline, from the Irish tragedies of *Deirdre and the Sons of Usna Diarmid and Grania. Geraint and Enid* is from an ancient Welsh book, *The Mabinogion*, and *Sir Gawain and the Loathely Lady* comes from a Middle English ballad. The sources of the early part of Sir Percival's adventures are an Early English poem and *Conte de Graal*, but the end is truly her own invention. *Beaumains, the Kitchen Knight* comes from Malory, although Sutcliff contends that this tale "seems to have come entirely out of Malory's own head."

In *The Sword and the Circle: King Arthur and the Knights of the Round Table*. Sutcliff adheres to the magical, chivalric, and medieval setting of the court of King Arthur of legend rather than the harsh, realistic setting in *Sword at Sunset*. She holds the thirteen familiar Arthurian tales together by interweaving references to the movements of such characters as Merlin, Sir Lancelot, Sir Gawain, and Morgan la Fay throughout the chapters. The book begins before the birth of Arthur and describes his education with Sir Ector and foster brother Kay, his pulling of the sword Excalibur from the stone, the magic of Morgan la Fey, his seduction by his half-sister Margawse, and the birth of their son, Mordred. In recounting Arthur's marriage to Guenever, the assembling of the knights of the Round Table, and the adventures of the homely Lancelot, the fiery Gawain, and his brother Garetha as Beaumains, Sutcliff "is constantly sensitive to the pageantry of color and rejoices in echoing the sounds and scents of nature," wrote a *Horn Book* (February 1982) reviewer. The book closes with "the Coming of Percival," and in its final pages, Arthur reveals to Lancelot what Merlin prophesied on the day Guenever brought the Round Table as her dowry: When Percival comes, the mystery of the Holy Grail would follow in less than a year. With it would come the final flowering of Britain, and nothing would ever be the same again.

A Light Beyond the Forest: The Quest for the Holy Grail, the first book of the Arthurian trilogy published, is the only full modern retelling of the grail story. With flawless prose and straightforward narrative, Sutcliff recounts the mystical search that Bors, Perceval, Galahad, and Lancelot embark upon in an effort to deliver the Waste Land from a religious curse. Despite Sutcliff's reliance on the traditional legends for setting and plot, Egoff contends that Sutcliff probes beyond the formalized Malory characterizations to a more psychological exploration of these four unique individuals. Lancelot is presented as a truly tragic figure, for his illicit love for Guenever shuts him out from God. His son Galahad is presented not as a simple symbol of purity, but as a man whose Christian virtue is difficult, compelling, and personal. While Donald K. Fry, in a review *School Library Journal* (August 1980), found Sutcliff's retelling to be "sentimental and overexplained," a contributor to *Horn Book* (August 1980) declared that "a few archaic words unobtrusively add color to a narrative note worthy for the grace and clarity of its prose."

The Road to Camlann: The Death of King Arthur, the final book in the trilogy, is focused on the destruction of the Round Table, the love between Lancelot and Guenever in their later years, the wars and the last battle, ending with Lancelot's death. Margery Fisher, in a review in *Growing Point* (March 1982), finds the work reminiscent of medieval poetry, perhaps accounting for "the delicate natural touches that refresh a tale of intrigue and cruelty." The final disbanding of Arthur's knights is brought about by the destructive element in the love between Guenever and Lancelot and the incestuous love between Arthur and his stepsister. It is this parentage that has caused Mordred's jealousy and spurred him on to subvert Arthur's authority and peace of mind. This, Fisher notes, is the felt contrast between their passion and the courtly restraints in which it has to be expressed. The destructive element in this love is recognized as one cause of the final dispersal of Arthur's knights. Furthermore with equal importance, the incestuous parentage of Mordred, an interpretation of historical chronicle and fifteenth-century narrative, is finely done in its grave pictorial. Paul Heins comments in *Horn Book* (February 1983) that Sutcliff has tightened and simplified the tragic end of the Round Table. Fry is some what disappointed with Sutcliff's final book in this review for *School Library Journal* (January 1983): "Her earlier volumes succeeded brilliantly in capturing the notion of an invisible transcendent world behind events, curiously missing in this conclusion." However, he adds, "her Mordred rises to new heights of evilness. Other than Malory, I can think of no better introduction to the whole sweep of Arthurian stories and values." In assessing the trilogy as a whole, Marcus Crouch *Junior Bookshelf* review (December 1981) asserts: "Sutcliff's trilogy stands as a valiant attempt to bring the often tragic, violent and sensual tales within the compass of children's understanding without cutting the heart from them."

After her father's death in the early 1980s, Sutcliff lived with a housekeeper and two small dogs in her home in Walberton, Sussex, not far from Arundel. Despite becoming more disabled with arthritis, she continued to write every day. In 1983 she published *Bonnie Dundee*, followed the next year by her memoir, *Blue Remembered Hills*, which told of her life from an infant until her first book was accepted at Oxford University Press. *The Roundabout Horse* and *Flame-Coloured Taffeta* were published in 1986, and *Blood and Sand A Little Dog Like You* published in 1987. *Little Hound Found* was published in 1989, followed by *The Shining Company*, in which Sutcliff returned to the post-Roman British setting of some of her earlier fiction.

Sutcliff was writing on the morning of her sudden death on July 22, 1992, in Chichester, Sussex. She had finished the second draft of a historical novel containing the saga of the Aquila family's descendents and their emerald ring. Tentatively called *The Saga of Bjarni Sigurdsun,* the story tells of a young Norseman, who is exiled from his settlement and returns with a British bride and an emerald ring, thus accounting for the reappearance of the ring among the Norse settlers in the Lake District in *The Shield Ring*. Some of her completed manuscripts, *Chess-Dream in a Garden* (1993), *The Minstrel and the Dragon Pup* (1993), *Black Ships Before Troy: The Story of the Iliad* (1993), and *The Wanderings of Odysseus: The Story of the Odyssey* (1996) were published after her death. Sutcliff is more likely to be remembered for historical fiction for young children more than for her works with Arthurian legend.

Newer theories of Arthur as mythical and historical figure have replaced those that informed Sutcliff's writings, and her method of storytelling, like Kipling's who inspired her, is somewhat out of fashion. Sutcliff's major historical works are, according to Egoff, "a virtually perfect mesh of history and fiction." In the writing of Rosemary Sutcliff. Talcroft asserts that "as we look back over the children's literature of the twentieth century, Rosemary Sutcliff will prove to be one of the outstanding writers of historical fiction for children and young adults, especially in her recreation of the earliest societies in Great Britain." She continues, "Thus what one perceives is that Sutcliff begins with a very well stored mind and an affinity for a given period in the distant past that she sets forth as if it were something she herself had once experienced, richly remembers, and recounts— much as some ordinary person talks about the memories of childhood or a trip." Similarly, Philip contended that "to call the books historical novels is to limit them disgracefully." "Sutcliff does not bring history to the reader," continued Philip, "but involves the reader in the past—not just for the duration of a book, but forever. She can animate the past, bring it to life inside the reader in a most personal and lasting way." Sutcliff immerses herself and the reader in the time period that she is relating, and "her method of settling on the felt details that remain in the mind, driven along the nerves of the hero, is even more convincing than the historian's account," upheld Meek. "Sutcliff's name," declared Evans, "will be remembered and revered long after others have been forgotten."

PRIMARY WORKS

The Chronicles of Robin Hood. London: Oxford University Press, 1950; New York: Walck, 1950; *The Queen Elizabeth Story.* London: Oxford University Press, 1950; New York: Walck, 1950; *The Armourer's House.* London: Oxford University Press, 1951; New York: Walck, 1951; *Brother Dusty-Feet.* London: Oxford University Press, 1952; New York: Walck, 1952; *Simon.* London: Oxford University Press, 1953; New York: Walck, 1953; *The Eagle of the Ninth.* London: Oxford University Press, 1954; New York: Walck, 1954; *Outcast.* London: Oxford University Press, 1955; New York: Walck, 1955; *Lady in Waiting.* London: Hodder & Stoughton, 1956; New York: Coward McCann, 1957; *The Shield Ring.* London: Oxford University Press, 1956; New York: Walck, 1956; *The Silver Branch.* London: Oxford University Press, 1957; New York: Walck, 1958; *Warrior Scarlet.* London: Oxford University Press, 1958; Walck, 1958; *The Lantern Bearers.* London: Oxford University Press, 1959; New York: Walck, 1959; *The Bridge Builders.* Oxford, England: Blackwell, 1959; *The Rider of the White Horse.* London: Hodder & Stoughton, 1959; New York: Coward McCann, 1959; republished as *Rider on a White Horse.* New York: Coward McCann, 1960; *Houses and History.* London: Batsford, 1960; *Knight's Fee.* London: Oxford University Press, 1960; New York: Walck, 1960; *Beowulf.* London: Bodley Head, 1961; New York: Dutton, 1962; republished as *Dragon Slayer.* London: Bodley Head, 1961; published as *Dragon Slayer: The Story of Beowulf.* New York: Macmillan, 1980; *Rudyard Kipling.* London: Bodley Head, 1960; New York: Walck, 1961; bound with *Arthur Ransome*, by Hugh Shelley, and *Walter de la Mare*, by Leonard Clark. London: Bodley Head, 1968; *Dawn Wind.* London: Oxford University Press, 1961; New York: Walck, 1962; *Sword at Sunset.* London: Hodder & Stoughton, 1963; New York: Coward McCann, 1963; *Hound of Ulster.* London: Bodley Head, 1963; New York: Dutton, 1963; *A Saxon Settler.* London: Oxford University Press, 1965; *Heroes and History.* London: Batsford, 1965; New York: Putnam, 1965; *The Mark of the Horse Lord.* London: Oxford University Press, 1965; New York: Walck, 1965; *The New Laird* (radio script). Stories from Scottish History, BBC Scotland, May 17, 1966; *The Chief's Daughter.* London: Hamish Hamilton, 1967; *The High Deeds of Finn MacCool.* London: Bodley Head, 1967; New York: Dutton, 1967; *A Circlet of Oak Leaves.* London: Hamish Hamilton, 1968; *The Flowers of Adonis.* London: Hodder & Stoughton, 1969; *The Witch's Brat.* London: Oxford University Press, 1970; New York: Walck, 1970; *The Truce of Games.* London: Hamish Hamilton, 1971; *Tristan and Iseult.* London: Bodley Head, 1971; New York: Dutton, 1971; *Heather, Oak, and Olive: Three Stories.* Contains *The Chief's Daughter*, *A Circlet of Oak Leaves*, and *A Crown of Wild Olive.* New York: Dutton, 1972; *The Capricorn Bracelet.* London: Oxford University Press, 1973; New York: Walck, 1973; "History Is People." In *Children's Literature: News and Reviews,* ed. V. Haviland, 305–13. New York: Scott Foresman, 1973; *The Changeling.* London: Hamish Hamilton, 1974; *We Lived in Drumfyvie,* Sutcliff and Margaret Lyford-Pike. London: Blackie, 1975; *British Children's Authors: Interviews at Home.* Chicago: American Library Association, 1976; *Blood Feud.* London: Oxford University Press, 1977; New York: Dutton, 1977; *Shifting Sands.* London: Hamish Hamilton, 1977; *Sun Horse, Moon Horse.* London: Bodley Head, 1977; New York: Dutton, 1978; *Is Anyone There?* ed. Sutcliff and Monica Dickens. New York: Penguin, 1978; *Song for a Dark Queen.* London: Pelham, 1978; *The Light Beyond the Forest: The Quest for the Holy Grail.* London: Bodley Head, 1979; *Three Legions: A Trilogy.* Contains *The Eagle of the Ninth*, *The Silver Branch*, and *The Lantern Bearers.* London: Oxford University Press, 1980; *Frontier Wolf.* London: Oxford, 1980;. London: Hamish Hamilton, 1981; *Eagle's Egg.* London: Hamish Hamilton, 1981; *The Sword and the Circle: King Arthur and the Knights of the Round Table.* London:

Bodley Head, 1981; New York: Dutton, 1981; *The Road to Camlann: The Death of King Arthur.* London: Bodley Head, 1981; *Bonnie Dundee.* London: Bodley Head, 1983; *Blue Remembered Hills.* London: Oxford University Press, 1984; *The Roundabout Horse.* London: Hamish Hamilton, 1986; *Coloured Taffeta.* London: Oxford University Press, 1986; published as *Flame-Colored Taffeta.* New York: Farrar, Straus, 1986; *Mary Bedell* (play). Produced in Chichester, UK, 1986; *The Best of Rosemary Sutcliff.* London: Chancellor, 1987; *Blood and Sand.* London: Hodder & Stoughton, 1987; *A Little Dog Like You.* London: Orchard, 1987; New York: Simon and Schuster, 1990; *Little Hound Found.* London: Hamish Hamilton, 1989; *The Shining Company.* London: Bodley Head, 1990; New York: Farrar, Straus, 1990; *Chess-Dream in a Garden.* London: Candlewick, 1993; *The Minstrel and the Dragon Pup.* Candlewick, 1993; *Black Ships before Troy: The Story of the Iliad.* New York: Delacorte, 1993; *The Wanderings of Odysseus: The Story of the Odyssey.* New York: Delacorte, 1996.

Papers

A collection of Sutcliff's manuscripts—including a manuscript and two typescripts for *The New Laird;* a small red composition book with notes for the books *The Red Dragon, The Lantern Bearer,* and *The Amber Dolphin;* and notes on several other topics—is housed at the Kerlan Collection, University of Minnesota.

SECONDARY SOURCES

Dean, Christopher. "The Metamorphosis of Merlin: An Examination of the Protagonist of *The Crystal Cave* and *The Hollow Hills.*" In *Comparative Studies of Merlin from the Vedas to C. G. Jung,* ed. James Gollnick, 63–75. Lewiston, NY: Mellen, 1992; Egoff, Sheila A. *Thursday's Child: Trends and Patterns in Contemporary Children's Literature.* Chicago: American Library Association, 1981; Meek, Margaret. *Rosemary Sutcliff.* New York: Walck, 1962; Montgomery, L. C. M. *Emily of New Moon.* New York: A. L. Bark, 1923; Reid, T. Dayrell. *The Battle for Britain in the Fifth Century: An Essay in Dark Age History.* London: Methuen, 1944; Talcroft, Barbara L. *Death of the Corn King: King and Goddess in Rosemary Sutcliff's Historical Fiction for Young Adults.* Metuchen, NJ: Scarecrow Press, 1995; Thompson, Raymond H. Interview with Rosemary Sutcliff. Walburton, UK, August 1996. Available at http://www.lib.rochester.edu/camelot/intrvws/sutcliff.htm; ———. *The Return from Avalon: A Study of the Arthurian Legend in Modern Fiction.* Westport, CT: Greenwood, 1985; Townsend, John Rowe. *A Sense of Story: Essays on Contemporary Writing for Children.* Philadelphia: Lippincott, 1971; Wintle, Justin, and Emma Fisher. *The Pied Pipers: Interviews with the Influential Creators of Children's Literature.* New York: Paddington Press, 1974.

MAUREEN MARMION HOURIGAN

THOMAS BERGER

(July 20, 1924–)

Thomas Berger was born in Cincinnati, Ohio, July 20, 1924, and grew up in nearby Lockland. He attended Miami University in Oxford, Ohio, in 1941, and transferred to the University of Cincinnati in 1942. He enlisted in the army in 1943, and was stationed in Berlin with the first American occupation forces. He graduated from the University of Cincinnati in 1948, accepted a position as a librarian with the Rand School of Social Science in New York, and married Jeanne Redpath on June 12, 1950. He continued his studies at Columbia University, where he began, but did not finish, a thesis on the fiction of George Orwell.

Berger's first novel, *Crazy in Berlin*, was published in 1958. Its central character, Carlo Reinhart, reappeared in *Reinhart in Love*, *Vital Parts*, and *Reinhart's Women*. Jack Crabb, the hero of *Little Big Man*, a story of the American West first published in 1964, also makes more than one appearance. Played by Dustin Hoffman, he appeared in a 1970 film directed by Arthur Penn, and returned in 1999 as the narrator of *The Return of Little Big Man*. Berger's novels also include *Who Is Teddy Villanova?* (a detective novel), *Killing Time* (an experiment with crime fiction), *Orrie's Story* (a retelling of the classic myth of Orestes), and *Robert Crews* (a transformation of Daniel Defoe's *Robinson Crusoe*). His *Arthur Rex: A Legendary Novel*, as its full title suggests, can, like the later published *Orrie's Story* and *Robert Crews*, be considered a work of fictional transformation.

Brooks Landon writes that "little, if anything, in [Berger's] writing could be termed autobiographical in any strict sense" (7), but *Crazy in Berlin*, published thirteen years after his service in a medical unit as a member of the first U.S. occupation forces in Berlin in summer 1945, clearly draws upon Berger's after-the-war experience. *Reinhart in Love*, published four years after *Crazy in Berlin*, shows Carlo Reinhart, home again, adjusting to work experience (he is apprenticed to a realtor), college classes (he reads whole texts instead of just the excerpts included in a comparative literature anthology), and marriage (which involves life in a Quonset hut in Vetsville and gallant service to a newly pregnant wife) may also be taken to reflect events of Berger's life (in a loose sense). Here Reinhart, who can perhaps be regarded as a comic transformation of Berger himself, having discovered that a high school friend has duped him into believing that he, the friend, possesses a great writing talent, finds that "the great thing about literature, as opposed to science, was that if asked about a book you could make up something quite as appropriate as—perhaps even better than—the particulars you had forgotten" (*Reinhart in Love,* 286).

This suggests a narrative strategy Berger may have used in several of his works. He purportedly bases the story of *Little Big Man,* a novel published two years after *Reinhart in Love,* on the records of one Jack Crabb, a white orphan raised by Cheyenne Indians who survives the battle known as Custer's Last Stand. Years later, the 111-year-old survivor returns, having merely faked his death to get out of a publishing contract, to continue his story in *The Return of Little Big Man* (1999). *Orrie's Story* (1990), which calls upon a story from classical tradition, provides a more direct example. Here the Greek chorus of Orestes becomes a group accustomed to assemble at the Idle Hour Bar & Grill, and Orestes becomes Orrie, a young college student who accidentally kills his mother as she attempts to defend her lover, the uncle who cuckolds Orrie's father—who plays the role of a returning war hero, who, incidentally, never went to war. The same narrative "strategy" serves Berger's purposes in *Robert Crews* (1994), as Bob Crews, a twentieth-century Crusoe who suffers from fear from flying, plunges to an island where he (his shipmates have perished in the crash) must fashion a shelter and find food for himself—and for a transformed Friday, a woman whose husband has cruelly mistreated and abandoned her. And it seems—and here Berger stays much closer to his sources—that he relied on a comparable transformation process when he wrote *Arthur Rex: A Legendary Novel.*

John Steinbeck prefaces his *Acts of King Arthur and His Noble Knights* with a personal story of the profound effect on his thinking of "a cut version of Caxton" an aunt gave him when he was a child. "I think," Steinbeck writes, "my sense of right and wrong, my feeling of noblesse oblige, and any thought I may have against the oppressor and for the oppressed, came from this secret book" (xii). Berger provides no personal preface for his retelling of the Arthurian legend. He simply begins his *Arthur Rex* at the beginning of his story, with a Book I that bears the title "Of Uther Pendragon and the fair Ygraine; and how Arthur was born."

Arthurian echoes that suggest a comparable early influence can be found, however, in Berger's earlier fiction. For example, in *Crazy in Berlin* he describes Carlo Reinhart as a "questing beast" whose needs, for the moment, are adequately satisfied (248), and invokes the concept of knighthood to explain the power of psychology, which confers "a permanent upper hand" upon its practitioner (422). In *Reinhart in Love,* his second novel, Berger's hero addresses Genevieve, the woman he will marry, as *Guinevere,* the explanation being that "whenever he tried to make himself understood, he thought irrelevantly of King Arthur" (183). Here too, as Reinhart "enters [Genevieve] fiercely," he thinks that "for the first time in his life he was doing what everybody everywhere approved." At this moment he acquires "the endurance of Galahad, who had the strength of ten because his heart was pure" (204). In the same novel Reinhart, collecting his childhood belongings for a move to Vetsville with his bride, finds "a dog-eared copy of King Arthur, with 'Carlo R., age 10' in a childish mess on the flyleaf" (207). And, to cite one example from Berger's later fiction, the hero of Berger's Orestes transformation finds "a letter opener, supposedly a replica of King Arthur's Excalibur, made in Japan, [that] he had purchased in a novelty store" among his belongings (*Orrie's Story,* 170). Finally, Berger does, Brooks Landon reports, "fondly mention 'his own boyhood King Arthur . . . the work of one Elizabeth Lodor Merchant, Head of the Department of English, William Penn High School, Philadelphia, Penna,' a gift from his father at Christmas 1931" (6–7).

Berger does not write of a wondrous childhood discovery of a fictional world. He does not exult, as Steinbeck did in a March 30, 1959, letter to his editor Elizabeth Otis, in words that came to him with "the strength and sureness of untroubled children or fulfilled old men" (*Steinbeck: A Life in Letters*, 622). But Steinbeck was engaged in a task of *translation* when he wrote *The Acts of King Arthur and His Noble Knights*. Berger was writing a *transformation*, a re-creation of inherited legend, when he wrote *Arthur Rex*.

This does not mean that reflections of Malory's syntax are not to be found in his headings for individual units of the Arthurian legend, but Berger turns that syntax to his own purposes. His use of Malory's "How _____" and "Of ____" headings are, with predictable frequency, followed by "Now ____" sequences.

The repeated "how . . . now" pattern Berger uses in his ninth novel oddly recalls a reprimand to which he gave attention in his second. Having asked why his father must start every sentence with the word "now," Splendor Mainwaring, Berger's young language critic, continues, " 'When do you think these remarks take place if not in the present, namely *now?*' " (*Reinhart in Love*, 54), and his question may indirectly suggest a reason for Berger's later repetition of "now" as a preparatory adverb. It is as if, even as he relies on Malory's syntax, Berger, with remarkable consistency, adds the repeated "now" to prepare the reader for the unfolding of a legendary story in his own re-created narrative present.

Other representations of Malory's characteristic usage also figure in the narrative style of Berger's *Arthur Rex*. Even minor characters like the dwarf who providentially appears with the cart Sir Launcelot needs to rescue Queen Guinevere (who, at this point, has been imprisoned by the evil Meliagrant) employ "like unto" connectives and a question syntax that, to readers of our time, seems to involve an inversion of a natural subject-verb order. The dwarf asks Launcelot, "What want you of me then?" (*Arthur Rex*, 168), when contemporary English would of course read "What do you want from me?"

Berger's characters, then, use earlier constructions that recall the language of Malory, but they do not use *just* the early forms of Middle English. Agravaine, attempting to inspire the envy of his older brother Gawaine, employs Middle English second person pronoun and verb forms to assert "Thou wert first knight . . . until he [Launcelot] came to Camelot" (195), but goes on to mention "our youngest sib, baby Mordred" (196). And thus Berger, even as he captures a sense of the past through his use of distinctive syntactic patterns and diction, injects a sense of the present, "the age of the cad," to use a descriptive phrase that Brooks Landon attributes to Berger himself.

Nevertheless, the first similarity to strike the eye of a reader determined to double-read *Arthur Rex* and the Everyman edition of *Le Morte d'Arthur* gives rise to a strong sense of uncrossed time boundaries. Malory's first five chapter headings read:

I: How Uther Pendragon Sent for the Duke of Cornwall, and Igraine His Wife, and of Their Departing Suddenly Again;
II. How Uther Pendragon Made War on the Duke of Cornwall, and How By the Means of Merlin He Lay by the Duchess and Gat Arthur;
III: Of the Birth of King Arthur and of His Nurture;
IV: Of the Death of King Uther Pendragon; and
V: How Arthur Was Chosen King, and of Wonders and Marvels of a Sword Taken Out of a Stone By the Said Arthur.

while Berger's first two titles read:

> I. Of Uther Pendragon and the Fair Ygraine;.How Arthur Was Born, and
> II: How Uther Pendragon Died; and How Arthur Took the Sword from the Stone;
> and of the Challenge to King Arthur by the Irish Ryons.

The "How . . ." and "Of . . ." constructions that served Malory's purposes clearly continues to serve Berger's structural intentions. But Berger draws with great consistency upon a second continuity marker. The first word of the first sentence of Berger's Book I is "Now," and the first sentence of his second chapter, which introduces the early years of Arthur's life, is "*Now* [italics mine] Merlin had no facilities for caring for a babe." Berger's "now" signal does not come until the second sentence of Chapter III (the early victories by which Arthur consolidated his power are given very brief attention in a single opening sentence), but this time marking "Now" introduces a key figure in the story of Arthur's life—the wife of King Lot, Margawse, Arthur's half sister. And this leads to a fully developed scene, not to be found in Malory, of a still-sleepy young man awakening to the recognition that he has just committed "the vile sin of incest unknowingly unlike the pagan kings and queens of Egypt with whom it was customary" (66), which, with its explanatory extension, can stand as an example of the Berger style as well. Much of the humor of Berger's apparently self-mocking narrative style can be seen to arise from knowledgeable, confidently expressed, judgmental sentence completions like this.

Berger's repeated "Now" gets the sequence of events moving and helps to establish a sense that events are unfolding before the eyes of the reader, and its repeated use, often in combination with expansions that refer to incest and sodomy, is linked to a second function. Berger's added commentaries help to establish a comic authorial presence. The manner with which his narrator communicates his judgment of incest will be called upon again and again as issues involving the topic of homosexuality, which seems to trigger a recurrent vocabulary relying on words like "sodomites" and "sods," arise. It even enters to strengthen approval of Gawaine's reformed behavior when this important Round Table figure is said no longer to be "the unrestrained lecher of old," but neither has he become "as enervate as a eunuch" (202).

The jocularly judgmental incest and sodomite-sod sequences Berger employs clearly have no a source in Malory. It is, however, immediately apparent that he draws the names of his characters directly from his sources, and equally evident that he takes pleasure in adding names as he introduces what could be a bewilderingly extended cast. Fortunately, Berger takes pains to fill in the genealogy of key characters (he, for example, does not allow us to forget that Gawaine has three younger brothers named Gaheris, Agravaine, and Gareth), and to distinguish between bearers of the same name. Elaine the daughter of King Pelles who gives birth to Galahad, for example, is not the same Elaine who dies for the love of Launcelot; and Isold, the wife of King Mark who loves and is loved by Tristram, is not Isold of the White Hands.

The Tristram-Tramtrist alternation Berger employs is present in Malory (Tristram goes by the name Tramtris in Ireland [*Morte* I, 249]), along with an explanation of its "born in sorrow" meaning, but Piss-tram is Berger's invention. King Pelles, the father of Elaine the mother of Galahad is a character straight from Malory, but the rhyming phrase with which Berger's Pelles identifies himself as "a king whom shame hath maimed" (*Arthur Rex,* 352) has no equivalent in his source. Sir Launcelot takes on a number of names in Malory's and other accounts of the deeds of the man who was the greatest knight of Arthur's time (until his son Galahad distinguishes himself in the search for the Holy Grail). He is the knight of the cart as he accepts a humiliation he feels he deserves (and here Malory himself gives credit as he does a number of times to "the French book"). He is also "Sans Loy," which Berger has him explain means "a knight without law" when he tells King Pelles of his love for Guinevere. But there is no counterpart in Malory for the sequence of names Arthur calls upon as he attempts to refer to Percival, King Pellinore's youngest son (Pellinore, Berger more than once reminds the reader, is the king who seeks the questing beast) as Pernival, as Percinell, and finally Purslaine— and they are intended, not really to disparage the deeds of Percival, but to show an effect of aging on the mental acuity of the king. But Arthur is always Arthur. Berger does not give his hero a child's name, as T. H. White does when he calls the young Arthur "Wart" in "The Sword in the Stone," the first book of his *Once and Future King* sequence.

This is not to say that even as Berger respects the legend he inherits he takes no liberties. He consistently tells the story of Arthur straight, just as he finds it, and then, just as consistently, takes the telling a step further. Consider, for example, Arthur's exchange with Merlin immediately after he draws the sword that entitles him to kingship.

Having just rebuked Merlin for his use of blasphemy, which may be forgiven the son of an imp, young Arthur says, with great solemnity,

> I shall be a Christian king because Christ was Our Saviour, and not because of expediency, political or spiritual. Loving and fearing God, I shall display no device but His Cross, and around me I shall gather, at a circular table at which no seat is more favored than the next, a body of knights as devout as they are brave. Our purpose shall be solely to serve the Right, by destroying the Wrong. There shall be no material magnificence, no personal aggrandizements, and no wars except in defense. (34)

The effect of this speech, in the "now" of Berger's narration, is that of an exaggerated, adolescent self-righteousness.

Berger does seem to take liberties with the character of Arthur's queen, who becomes, in her later years, capable of childish jealousy, but as early as Chapter I of Malory's Book Three, Merlin warned that "Guenever was not wholesome for him to take to wife, for . . . Launcelot should love her, and she him again" (*Morte* I, 71). The liberties Berger takes with the queen, then, are liberties of diction, not freedom with the facts.

The past language–present language with which guards stationed outside Guinevere's chamber, attributed as it is to less than worthy characters, nevertheless constitutes, with its use of double meanings, a certain defamation of character. This is the exchange, as Berger represents it:

> "And fucking well chamber'd he [Launcelot] is . . . For 'tis a rare queen these days
> can be told from a quean."
> "Dost believe he swyveth her?"
> "Else I never heard a groaning." (198)

and, even without consulting a Middle English dictionary for the "queen-quean" connection, the reader can readily see the point. And finally, at the conclusion of Guinevere's story, a certain diminution of dignity comes through in the name of the convent to which she retreats, the home of the Little Sisters of Poverty and Pain.

Guinevere was, until she married and was succeeded by Isold, the most beautiful maiden of Britain. This detracts in no way from her physical beauty, since she then becomes "the most beautiful queen." Launcelot, until he is succeeded by his son Galahad, who proves his surpassing virtue in the search for the Holy Grail, is the most noble knight of the Round Table. After his son's virtue is seen to exceed his own his position in the Berger hierarchy becomes that of "the most noble *sinful* knight." Launcelot remains, however, in both Malory and in Berger's transformation, despite his conflict of allegiance to his king and the woman he loves, despite his bouts of madness, a fully honorable and admirable man.

The presence of Sir Gawaine in the larger legend of King Arthur provides Berger with an opportunity to deal with the question Chaucer's Wife of Bath posed in her tale: what do women want most? In Berger's *Arthur Rex* this challenge presents itself with the appearance of a lady in distress. As the action begins, Arthur has just taken up a sword he supposes to be Excalibur (but it has been replaced by Morgan la Fey's dwarf with another, inferior sword), and Arthur and Gawaine set forth upon their chivalric mission. They meet Sir Gromer Somir Joure, now the possessor of Excalibur, who challenges the king to answer the question, "What do women most desire in the world?" (*Arthur Rex*, 243), his intention being to humiliate the king. Sir Gromer Somir Joure will return the sword if Arthur returns in one year with the correct answer, but the king will be at his mercy if he does *not* return with the correct answer.

Arthur tries to turn to the lady in distress for an answer, but she has disappeared. His strategy then becomes to get the answer from the first woman he puts it to, and, if this does not work, to ask Guinevere. Guinevere's answer, "My lord, what a woman desireth most is not the same from one time to another" (315), reinforces the king's belief that no woman knows her own mind. He turns to other women of the court and, getting answers he recognizes as efforts to please him, continues to fail to find a satisfactory answer. Nuns provide pious answers, which serve his purpose no better than the answers of strumpets from Ireland, Germany, and France. And the single answer provided by all the men he asks—"Women most desire to be desirable to men"—is no better.

Gawaine having returned by this time from a failed search for Launcelot (almost a year has passed), the two determine to return, answerless, to satisfy their obligation to Sir Gromer Somir Joure. They are met by an old hag, who has the answer, but wants something in exchange for it: Arthur must marry her. He cannot, of course, since he is already married to Guinevere, but Gawaine will save his king by offering himself in marriage to the old hag. The hag answers the question in response to Sir Gawaine's promise, but the reader is not yet told what it is. The answer is revealed when King Arthur tells Sir Gromer Somir Joure that "What women most desire in this world is ... *to rule over men*." King Arthur's life is saved, and Gawaine and Dame Ragnell (Berger now provides the old hag's name) are married.

Gawaine, kissing his bride, finds that she has been marvelously changed. But now he is presented with this choice: will he have Dame Ragnell fair by day or fair by night? Gawaine gallantly replies, "My dear sweet Ragnell, when thou art plain I shall not forget that thow wert beautiful not long before and that it will never be long before thou art beautiful once more" (*Arthur Rex*, 325). Gawaine now says that the choice must be Ragnell's alone, since she is obligated to answer only to God. And finally, with a detail to be found in John Gower's retelling of the story but not in Chaucer's "Wife of Bath's Tale," the reader learns that the old hag was bewitched, and, according to Berger, she was bewitched by Morgan la Fey.

This is not the first extended story in which Sir Gawaine plays a key role, nor will it be the last. Berger also includes the story of Sir Gawaine and the Green Knight in his reconstruction of Arthurian legend, and, in typical fashion, makes the basic elements to be found in the story told by a writer known only as "the Gawaine poet" or "the Pearl poet" fit his own style of narration. Berger's Green Giant enters the hall of King Arthur, demands that his challenge be accepted, then states what that challenge is: a knight bold enough to take the consequences must step forward and behead him. Gawain accepts the challenge and beheads the giant, and the giant's head rolls on the floor, unceremoniously kicked by other knights who function as members of the audience as it is in Berger's Middle English source. But in Berger's version the head rolls further. It is said to go "a-rolling the vast length of the hall of Camelot, [strike] the far wall, and [come] rolling back to the very feet of King Arthur," laughing all the way (153). The Green Giant then rises from the floor, places his head again on his shoulders, and issues his meet-me-again-in-a-year-and-a-day challenge.

Berger's Gawaine, seeking his opponent when the year-and-a-day has passed, meets with more challenges to his virtue than his predecessor ever faced. Those "temptations" not surprisingly include three golden-haired boys (who do not tempt Gawaine at all), his host's beautifully seductive wife (who is really the Lady of the Lake in disguise), and such delicacies as the "pickled testicles of tiger" (200–203). (Berger, characteristically, does not resist the temptation of sound play as he develops this sequence.) As this version of the story reaches its conclusion, Gawaine, though he does not prove himself to be without fault (he does not answer all questions with complete honesty), has sufficient courage to kneel before the Green Knight for the blow he must accept in return for the blow he dealt a year before in King Arthur's court. And he is spared. Gawaine is permitted to continue his loyal service to his king and to enjoy, at least until the time when war becomes inevitable, the peace of a prosperous middle age.

The last words of Thomas Berger's *Arthur Rex: A Legendary Novel* are "we must leave king Arthur, who was never historical, but everything he did was true" (499). Leaving *The Quest for Arthur's Britain* to Geoffrey Ashe and his fellow historians, it may nevertheless be possible in concluding to give brief attention to this question: how "true" to his source[s] *is* Berger's novel? Michael Malone reports that Berger "spoke *jokingly*" [italics mine] about a scriptwriter who had "apparently read 'none of Malory, Chretien de Troyes, Wolfram von Eschenbach, Alf Tennyson, Dick Wagner's Tristan and Parsifal,'" so this may seem to be a deliberately misguided effort. But Berger also refers, in the same letter from which Malone quotes, to "the many other forerunners whose works I ransacked" and expresses his negative judgment of the scriptwriter's work by saying, "This unbelievable trashy practitioner had *invented* his own Arthurian narrative!" (93), thus expressing a disapproval that suggests his own much stronger sense of obligation to his sources. But again, nothing in Berger's recorded communication presents itself for comparison with the sense of dedication Steinbeck's published letters express.

Two selections, drawn from a correspondence that began in 1963, may, however, provide a degree of insight into the personal context from which Berger's Arthuriad emerged. Zulfikar Ghose's "Observations from a Correspondence: From Thomas Berger's Letters," presents this December 7, 1969, quotation that does, at least, suggest the state of mind with which Berger began the work that would result, nine years later, in the publication of *Arthur Rex*:

I had an idea for a new novel on a contemporary theme, but realized after three days' work that I so loathed current reality that I could not write it. Therefore, I began my own version of the Arthurian tales, and this 6 July 1976 letter would seem to announce a second beginning:

I have begun my Arthurian narrative, somewhat shakily as always at the outset. In preparation I have read Geoffrey of Monmouth's *History of the Kings of Britain.* . . . *Arthur Rex* seems to have grown from Berger's need to go back to the past for a story worth the telling, and it also seems that he prepared for his task by embarking on the kind of study he attributed to Carlo Reinhart. He would not be satisfied until he had read, and tried to understand, the whole text. But it also needs to be said that part of what makes his retelling pleasurable for readers who already have a general knowledge of the story comes from Berger's employment of his individual transformation strategies. Berger diligently probes his sources, then does not stop when he has simply retold the story he finds there.

To cite one example, this is his account of King Pellinore's defeat of a knight as large as a tree and as black as night who had abducted a woman:

Then the knight raised his great sword in two hands high over his head, but before he could bring it down Pellinore smote him across the waist, cutting him through the belly, and next he gave him such a stroke upon the helmet that it parted down to the nasal, as did the head within it, the which was sliced as if it were a melon, and when King Pellinore took his blade away, the knight's brains did spew out of both parts of his cleft skull. (103)

Nor does he hesitate to exaggerate the male appetite for female flesh, as in his reference to the knight who cannot be satisfied unless he is provided with *two* virgins to satisfy his lust, or the female pleasure in asserting her right to control, as in the disdain of the damsel Percival rescues which continues to show itself all the way to Camelot (380–88).

Berger does not restrain his own use of pejorative adjectives, as when he tells "how the vile Mordred made common cause with his wicked aunt Morgan la Fey." Indeed, perhaps to present a more fully rounded characterization, he permits the child Mordred to tell how Margawse and his supposed father King Lot (Arthur, of course, is his real father) expose Mordred in a wasteland. Berger's Mordred introduces himself to his aunt Morgan le Fey with these words:

Lady . . . I am Mordred, and I am ten years old. Having lately been exposed by my parents, I owe no fealty to anyone. If this evil which you serve will give me an home, I shall be its willing vassal. (219)

and to express this judgement of Margawse and Lot:

If they were malefactors of true mettle, they would have murdered me outright and not submitted me to an ordeal which might well go awry and fail in its purpose— as indeed it hath. (220)

Nor does Mordred hesitate to utter these words of wisdom on the subject of father-son relationship:

A child "loves" his father because he is afraid of him, and this fear is the other face of hatred. Whereas a father "loves" a son while the boy is small, because he as yet has no fear of him, and this so-called love is therefore disguised contempt. Then the boy grows up, and he and his father arrive at a kind of equilibrium of power, and this truce is again called "love." Finally the elder becomes a dotard, which is to say through age he has become as weak as a child, and in power (which is the only quality worth considering on earth or in Heaven) the father that become a son, and he fears his new parent and is in turn despised by him. And once again this is called filial-paternal love. (222–23)

Berger's Mordred's speech may have the sound of twentieth-century psychological jargon, and his own narrative style may abound with references to "sods" and "sodomites" and "eunuchs." His Sir Gareth may at one point be addressed as "an insolent impostor" and his Lynnette may be an "impudent bitch," but his King Arthur still seems, even as his ability to name all his knights begins to fail, the king that Malory honored in *Le Morte d'Arthur,* Berger carries his respect for Arthur through to the end of his story.

When young Arthur pulls the sword from the stone and becomes king he is not the king his father was. Uther Pendragon's claim to be the greatest king of his time rested upon the facts that "he killed many men and took many maidenheads wherever he went" (21). Arthur may not remain as naively committed to idealism as he was in the early chapter in which when he reprimands Merlin for blasphemy, but he nevertheless remains a modest king who dedicates himself to the cause of peace.

Berger gives short shrift to the early wars in which Arthur defeated the eleven kings and the Emperor Lucius, but when King Leodegrance praises his courage in war his Arthur responds with commendable modesty. Since Excalibur makes him invincible, his success is not the result of his own action. This Arthur says, "I go to war only to defend Britain or such an ally as yourself. It is necessary to subdue enemies, but I get no satisfaction from the fighting itself, as I am told did Uther Pendragon. Indeed, war to me seemeth but a brutish enterprise" (70).

Berger's Arthur may briefly wish for the inspiration to unselfish behavior that war can provide (300), but his desire for peace is strong enough to enable him to rise above the taunts of Mordred as the story nears its climax. Even at this point he would, if he could, take the steps necessary to establish a situation in which peace could be maintained.

Arthur is not possessed by the single-minded love that ennobles Launcelot, for whom Malory's Sir Ector, Arthur's foster father, delivers this eulogy:

"Ah, Launcelot ... thou were head of all Christian knights, and now I dare say ... thou Sir Launcelot, there thou liest that thou were never matched of earthly knight's hand. And thou were the courteoust knight that ever bare shield. And thou were the truest friend to thy lover that ever bestrad horse. And thou were the truest lover of a sinful man that ever loved woman. And thou were the kindest man that ever struck with sword. And thou were the goodliest person that ever came among press of knights. And thou was the meekest man and the gentlest that ever ate in hall among ladies. And thou were the sternest knight to thy mortal foe that ever put spear in the rest." (*Morte* II, 400)

In contrast to the love and dedication of Launcelot, both as he is portrayed in Malory's *Morte d'Arthur* and Berger's *Arthur Rex*, King Arthur—and Berger's King Arthur particularly—seems downright ungallant. In fact, when Leodegrance proposes that Arthur accept his daughter Guinevere, along with his Round Table, that great cart wheel he acquired from a giant, he seems more pleased to have acquired the Round Table than he is to have gained a wife. And when the war that results from the escalation of hostilities between the followers of Gawaine and those of Launcelot has brought Berger's version of the story of Arthur to a climax from which there is no turning back, Arthur regrets the loss of the Round Table more than the loss of his queen, for, as he says, he could have ladies enough, but there was, and could be, only one Round Table of noble knights.

King Arthur, to the end, whether his story concludes, as in Malory, with the misinterpretation of a sword raised to strike an adder, or with Berger's transformation of the adder to the "serpent's tongue" with which Mordred brings his pagan followers "to a murderous frenzy in which they would have smote their own brothers" (476), remains an ideal king who wants peace for his people.

These are the details of the catastrophic conclusion as Berger presents them. Arthur, hoping for a peaceful settlement as he approaches Mordred, displays a banner bearing a picture of the Mother of God. Mordred responds with taunts about "the cuckold St. Joseph" and refers to Launcelot, who has "crowned [the king] with antlers" (*Arthur Rex*, 479). Arthur, more concerned with preserving the peace than with defending himself against personal insult, responds by acknowledging Mordred as his son, expressing his willingness to abdicate, and laying Excalibur on the ground as Mordred requests. Mordred lays his own sword down in return but, instead of instructing his followers to hold their peace, he commands them to attack. Mordred then seizes Excalibur, Arthur's magic sword, and plunges it deep into his father's bosom. Mordred does not fall on the field of battle as he does in Malory's account. Arthur is, however, carried off, having received a mortal wound, as he was in *Le Morte d'Arthur*.

As Berger manipulates the time sequence, Arthur is visited by Gawaine after, not before, the forces meet, but Gawaine's message remains the same: the king must kill his son Mordred. Arthur now draws the sword from his own body (and Berger connects this act with the act of drawing the sword from the stone that first established his right to rule) and goes forth to kill Mordred, a mission he successfully accomplishes.

The familiar story of Arthur's twice-repeated dying wish that Bedivere return Excalibur to the Lady of the Lake follows, the three ladies appear to carry him to his unknown destination, and the legend of the death of King Arthur is quickly told and in a manner that remains true to the story as Berger found it. The story Berger retells, with all its play of language, remains a legend of a *dux bellorum*, a leader dedicated to the cause of peace. Once his early wars were over Berger's Arthur takes no revenge against the hosts he had defeated (*Arthur Rex,* 36). He goes as far as he can, and further than Malory's Arthur went, to establish an honorable compromise with his rebel son. And he is honored in his passing from this world.

PRIMARY WORKS

Crazy in Berlin. New York: Charles Scribner's Sons, 1958; *Reinhart in Love*. New York: Charles Scribner's Sons, 1962; *Little Big Man*. New York: Dial Press, 1964; *Killing Time.* New York: Dial Press, 1967; *Vital Parts*. New York: Richard W. Baron, 1970; *Other People* (play). Produced in Stockbridge, MA, July 1–11, 1970; *Regiment of Women*. New York: Simon and Schuster, 1973; *Sneaky People*. New York: Simon and Schuster, 1975; *Who Is Teddy Villanova?*. New York: Delacorte Press/Seymour Lawrence, 1977; *Arthur Rex: A Legendary Novel*. New York: Delacorte Press/Seymour Lawrence, 1978; *Neighbors*. New York: Delacorte Press/Seymour Lawrence,1980; *Reinhart's Women*. New York: Delacorte Press/Seymour Lawrence, 1981; *The Feud*. New York: Delacorte Press/Seymour Lawrence, 1983; *Nowhere*. New York: Dial Books for

Young Readers, 1985; *Being Invisible*. Boston: Little, Brown, 1987; *The Houseguest*. Boston: Little, Brown, 1988; *Changing the Past*. Boston: Little, Brown, 1989; *Orrie's Story*. Boston: Little, Brown, 1990; *Meeting Evil*. Boston: Little, Brown, 1992; *Robert Crews*. New York: William Morrow, 1994; *Suspects*. New York: William Morrow, 1996; *The Return of Little Big Man*. Boston: Little, Brown, 1999.

SECONDARY SOURCES

Ashe, Geoffrey. *The Quest for Arthur's Britain*. Chicago: Academy Chicago Publishers, 1987; Benson, Larry D., ed. *The Riverside Chaucer*, 3rd ed. Boston: Houghton Mifflin, 1987; Ghose, Zulfikar. "Observations from a Correspondence: From Thomas Berger's Letters." Available at http://www.compedit.com/bergerobserv.htm; Gollancz, Israel, ed. *Sir Gawain and the Green Knight*. London: Oxford University Press, 1940; Landon, Brooks. *Thomas Berger*. Boston: Twayne, 1989; Madden, David W. "An Interview with Thomas Berger." In *Critical Essays on Thomas Berger*, ed. David W. Madden. 151–72. New York: G. K. Hall, 1995; Malone, Michael. "Berger, Burlesque, and the Yearning for Comedy." In *Critical Essays on Thomas Berger*, ed. David W. Madden. 89–99. New York: G. K. Hall, 1995; Malory, Sir Thomas. *Le Morte D'Arthur*, 2 vols. London: J. M. Dent, 1953; Steinbeck, Elaine, and Robert Wallsten, eds. *Steinbeck: A Life in Letters*. New York: Viking Press, 1975; Steinbeck, John. *The Acts of King Arthur and His Noble Knights*, ed. Chase Horton. New York: Farrar, Straus and Giroux, 1976; Taylor, Beverly, and Elisabeth Brewer. *The Return of King Arthur*. Cambridge: D. S. Brewer, 1983; Wells, John Edwin, ed. *A Manual of the Writings in Middle English, 1050–1400*. 1916. Reprint, New Haven, CT: Yale University Press, 1937; Wheeler, Bonnie. "The Masculinity of King Arthur: From Gildas to the Nuclear Age." *Quondam et Futurus: A Journal of Arthurian Interpretations* 2, no. 4 (Winter 1992): 1–26.

MARIE NELSON

MARION ZIMMER BRADLEY

(June 3, 1930–September 25, 1999)

Marion Zimmer Bradley is idolized by science fiction and fantasy fans for her critically acclaimed *Darkover* novels, which, broadly, explore the conflict between the communal and technologically advanced Terrans and the individualistic and antitechnological Darkovans. She is best known to the general reading public, however, for her best-selling, female-centered retelling of Arthurian legends, *The Mists of Avalon*, and its less successful prequels *The Forest House* and *Lady of Avalon*. A fourth novel set in early Britain, *Priestess of Avalon*, co-authored and finished by Diana L. Paxson, was published posthumously. A prolific writer with more than one hundred works spanning nearly half a century and the genres of pulp romance, confessions, daily horoscopes, detective fiction, gothic, fantasy, and science fiction, as well as literary criticism and essays, she has been recognized by male and female fans alike as a groundbreaker for women in genres dominated by male writers. While Bradley declined to identify herself as a feminist, she nevertheless served as a role model to young feminists both in her professional life and through her fiction, which depicts strong female protagonists and posits utopian societies where men and women share an egalitarian existence.

Bradley was born on a dairy farm on June 3, 1930, in East Greenbush near Albany, New York, and, according to her friend Ann Sharp who delivered a eulogy at her funeral, was descended from poet Anne Bradstreet. Growing up during the Great Depression and World War II, Bradley escaped the poverty and abuse of her childhood by burying herself in books and music. In her acknowledgements in *The Mists of Avalon*, she cited her grandfather, John Roscoe Conklin, for whetting her interest in Arthurian romance and legend and said that she had "virtually memorized" Sidney Lanier's *The Tales of King Arthur* by the time she was fifteen. The *Prince Valiant* comic strip was another important early influence, as were Malory's Arthurian works. Her love of "medieval" romance led in turn to an interest in mysticism and by extension the "occult," which she pursued through a careful reading, at age fourteen, of Frazer's multivolume *Golden Bough*, an influential work on comparative religion, and other works on religion, archaeology, folklore, and musicology.

Despite this early love of literature, writing was in fact her second career choice. The radio nurtured her love of both fiction and music and she hoped to use her writing to support musical training with the eventual goal of becoming a professional opera singer. She claimed that she had written as long as she could remember and even dictated to her mother who recorded her stories before she learned to write. Bradley became a science fiction and fantasy fan in her teens, began writing for student publications and fanzines, and anticipated her later work as editor for *Marion Zimmer Bradley's Fantasy Magazine* and *Swords and Sorcerers* when, as a high school student, she published an amateur magazine for science fiction fans. She sold her first work in 1949 in an amateur fiction contest for *Fantastic/Amazing Stories.* That same year she married her first husband, Robert Alden Bradley, a railroad stationmaster she met through a science-fiction letter column and with whom she had one son, David Bradley. Her first professional publication appeared in a 1952 issue of *Vortex Science Fiction.* Although she began publishing her work fairly regularly, financial instability from being the family's sole support coupled with poor health prevented her from pursuing a musical career. Instead, she became a professional writer and a lifelong music lover and amateur singer, describing herself in the original volume of *Contemporary Authors* as "basically a musician." After high school graduation, Bradley attended New York State College for Teachers in Albany from 1946 to 1948. She later returned to college at Hardin Simmons University in Abilene, Texas, where she received her bachelor's degree in psychology in 1964. Following a divorce that year from Robert Bradley, she married fellow writer Walter Breen, father of her daughter Moira Breen Stern and son Patrick Breen. She pursued graduate work at the University of California, Berkeley, from 1965 to 1967.

A look at a bibliography of her works reveals the breadth of topics Bradley covered in her early years. She described this time of transition from fan and amateur who "published in the letter columns of the old pulp magazines [and] fanzines published by other young science fiction or fantasy fiction enthusiasts" to professional writer in her essay "Fandom: Its Value to the Professional." Following such short stories as "Centurion Changeling," "The Climbing Wave," "The Stars Are Waiting," and "The Wind People," which appeared throughout the 1950s, Bradley emerged as a full-fledged professional with the publication in 1961 of her first novel *The Door Through Space*, an expanded version of a 1957 magazine story. As the decade progressed, Bradley had a lively career as a writer of lesbian pulp fiction, part of what she later termed "the pulps and the sleazo paperbacks that put [her] through college," with such titles as *My Sister, My Love,* in 1963 under the pseudonym Miriam Gardner, and *No Adam for Eve,* in 1966 as John Dexter. At the time, Bradley was supporting a sick husband and two small children, reportedly rising early in the morning to write so she could tend to her family during the day. These pseudonymous works do not appear in the official bibliography maintained by her estate, because Bradley claimed that she would have used her name if she had wanted people to know she had written them. They were considered pornographic material at the time, and, additionally, she felt that the editor had altered at least one book so much that the work's character was destroyed. Although she later declined to claim works published under pseudonyms, such romance fiction—coupled with her work in 1960 on *Checklist: A Complete, Cumulative Checklist of Lesbian, Variant, and Homosexual Fiction in English*—may have laid the groundwork for her later mature work, which explored psychosexual development and frequently featured gay, lesbian, or sexually ambivalent characters.

Although times were difficult financially and personally, Bradley developed a large network of friends and colleagues. In 1966, drawing on her love of the European Middle Ages, Bradley and her brother and sister-in-law, along with a group of science fiction and fantasy fans, held a large medieval-themed party taking care that the food, costumes, speech, and entertainment—which included music, dancing and jousting—were as authentic as possible. After the party, several participants met to discuss forming a medieval re-enactment organization, which developed into the Society for Creative Anachronism, an international organization with thousands of members who attempt to re-create life in the Middle Ages.

It was also during this time that she published the first of what became an extremely popular series with cult status among science fiction and fantasy enthusiasts and what the editors of the *Encyclopedia of Science Fiction* called "perhaps the most significant planetary romance sequence in modern science fiction." Bradley always insisted that the nearly thirty Darkover novels were not a series: they were cobbled together out of various bits of her early writing and each book was meant to stand on its own. Fans and subsequent printings, however, have established a loose chronology for the created universe and many of the characters develop and achieve self-realization across several of the works. Fans, sometimes in collaboration with the author, added to the Darkovan world in novels and short stories and through a thriving Internet culture that continued even after Bradley's death. As a group, the collection recounts the history of, according to critic Lester del Rey in a March 3, 1977, review in *Analog Science Fiction/Science Fact,* "one of the most fully realized of the worlds of science fiction." All Darkovans are descendants of explorers from Earth (Terrans) who colonize the Planet Darkover, develop as an isolated and unique culture, and are eventually rediscovered by the Terran Empire. *The Sword of Aldones* and *The Planet Savers,* both appearing in 1962, are the first of the Darkover novels. Bradley was nominated for the Hugo Award in 1963 and the Nebula Award in 1964 for the former, which tells the story of Lew Alton, son of a Darkovan father and a Terran mother, who experiences isolation and conflicts due to his "mixed" heritage. In the second novel, the themes of isolation and conflict occur within the single character Jason Allison, who suffers from a dissociative personality disorder. While *The Sword of Aldones* ends without reconciliation, *The Planet Savers* sets the tone of successful union found in the subsequent novels as Jason's dominant personality, cold and impersonal, successfully integrates with the secondary personality Jay, who is outgoing and friendly. The third Darkover novel, *Star of Danger,* appeared in 1965, and Bradley continued writing them until her death in 1999, when she was at work on the *Clingfire Trilogy.* Bradley said many times that as an author she was unconcerned with consistency, and she freely altered elements of the universe to suit the narratives' present needs. In other cases, she rewrote or expanded earlier novels, particularly her early works, which she considered somewhat juvenile. For example, *The Sword of Aldones* was revised into the psychologically complex *Sharra's Exile* (1981); *The Bloody Sun* (1967), which she called her first mature work, was extensively revised and reissued in 1979. Despite her feelings about that work, in the late 1960s she resolved never to write another Darkover novel. She credited Anne McCaffrey and her recommendation to read Ursula LeGuin's *Left Hand of Darkness* with her revitalized interest in the series. She explained years later, "I was tired of writing the same novel over and over again. I was tired of reading the same novel over and over again." After encountering LeGuin's work, however, she wrote, "Maybe there was still some good science fiction after all!"

She re-entered the Darkover world in 1971 with *The World Wreckers*, and began what most critics consider Bradley's mature Darkover period with the *Heritage of Hastur* (1975). In it Bradley combines an adventure story with the profound exploration of spiritual, sexual, social, and psychological themes that mark both her Darkover and non-Darkover work. Lew Alton reappears in this story, whose events predate those in *The Sword of Aldones*, along with fellow protagonist Regis Hastur. Following form, the characters experience isolation and conflict: Alton, because of his parentage as in the first novel, and Hastur, because he lacks telepathic powers and feels unprepared for a leadership position. Reconciliation occurs for Hastur as he discovers his telepathic powers and accepts the role of Regent-heir to the aristocratic Comyn Council, while Alton bitterly vows to leave Darkover. One of the best received novels during this time period is *The Forbidden Tower* (1977), for which Bradley received the Invisible Little Man Award in 1977 and the Leigh Brackett Memorial Sense of Wonder Award in 1978. The plot centers on four challengers to the laws and sacred traditions of Darkover. Bradley uses the device of telepathy to explore the emotionally and physically intense relationship of the twin sisters Ellemir and Callista and their lovers Damon and Andrew, occasionally linking the four into one entity through a psychic connection. The novel contains the familiar conflict between Terrans and Darkovans, and as the four rebel against society, they are faced with a kind of cultural relativism as they break down prejudices and preconceived notions about other cultures even as opposition grows against the Forbidden Tower that they have erected. Critic Paul McGuire III, in *Science Fiction Review* (1978), noting the undercurrent of isolation and personal and cultural conflict that runs throughout her works, called this "the most confined of Ms. Bradley's novels, the isolation ultimately is that of a person within himself, separate in mind and body from others."

Three of the Darkover novels have been of particular interest to feminist readers. *The Shattered Chain* (1976), *Thendara House* (1983), and *City of Sorcery* (1983) concern the Renunciates, a Darkovan sisterhood that resists the patriarchy of Comyn society by forming an alternative family group. In this traditional social hierarchy, women are regarded as a group in need of protection by male "protectors" who control them or marry them off to preserve the genes and telepathic ("psi") powers of the aristocracy. Two orders of women set themselves apart from this rigid order, which can also include explicit emotional and physical abuse and rape in addition to implicit abuse of the social system. The Priestesses of Avarra and the warriors of the Sisterhood of the Sword join forces to become the Order of Renunciates, also known as the Free Amazons, and all must take an oath to renounce the protections of and responsibilities toward to men. Having eschewed the "protection" of the patriarchy, the Renunciates are required to take responsibility for themselves and make their own decisions, and such problems as explored in both these novels illustrate the difficulties inherent in making choices. According to Susan Shwartz in "Marion Zimmer Bradley's Ethic of Freedom" (1982), the choices made by Bradley's female characters are "pain-filled" and constrained by their position in society. In the first of this trilogy, *The Shattered Chain*, "[the] Amazons . . . became a metaphor for female and human conditions on Darkover and elsewhere of being bound by old choices, refusing to remain so, and—through enduring the pain of choice—arriving at new solutions and restored integrity." Rohana disguises herself as a Free Amazon to rescue her relative Melora and Melora's daughter Jaelle from a despot who kidnapped the older woman and kept her chained up with other women in Dry Town, where she was forced to be his concubine. Following their rescue, Melora dies giving birth to a son, and Jaelle joins the sisterhood. The shattered chains of the title are the literal chains that bind the women of

Dry Town and the metaphorical chains of the restraining attitudes of the men and women. For Schwartz, the most important metaphorical shattering, of "intellectual and spiritual chains," occurs in the character of Rohana, who realizes that her prejudicial beliefs about the Amazons—that, for instance, they seduce young girls and neuter women—are unfounded. Liberated from these ideas, Rohana is likewise freed to pursue intellectual independence.

Thendara House contains a similar premise. Magdalen Lorne, a Terran raised on Darkover, disguises herself as a Free Amazon and tries to rescue her ex-husband from bandits. Jaelle, from the previous novel, and a group of real Renunciates find out her true identity and force her to take their oath. Despite the circumstances, Magdalen honors the oath and joins the group. The theme of sexual exploration occurs here when conflicts arise between Jaelle's love for Peter Haldane and her feelings for Magdalen. She marries Peter but eventually returns to the sisterhood where she and Magdalene become lovers and "freemates," in a relationship similar to marriage. In the final novel of the trilogy, *City of Sorcery*, Jaelle and Magdalen have become full members of the rebellious Forbidden Tower and embark on a search for the mythic city of sorcery. In their quest, they encounter physical hardship as they cross perilous mountain peaks, are threatened by "natural and supernatural dangers," and eventually must battle the evil sorcery of the Dark Sisterhood.

Although her fictive events and female characters—going all the way back to Cassiana in the 1954 "Centaurus Changeling"—have been held up as models of utopianism and feminism, Bradley claimed that she was not a feminist. According to her friend Ann Sharp, she defined feminism as political activism, and declined even to identify herself publicly within the political spectrum. Part of her reluctance to place a label on herself, however, might have been simply a matter of semantics, given that Bradley herself was a woman unbound by traditional mores and the restrictions placed upon women in her youth. In a 1975 letter printed in the *Witch and the Chameleon,* Bradley explained that she had grown up on a farm and always perceived women as men's equals and that she had never experienced sexism within the science fiction culture. Her experience with feminism was as an extremist and separatist movement, and the perceived focus on housework struck her as strange: for her, "mucking out the barn" was far more difficult than cleaning house. Yet for all that, a decade and a half later in the introduction to *Jamie, and Other Stories* (1992), Bradley cited the women's movement, rather than space exploration, as the most important twentieth-century occurrence.

Furthermore, Bradley insisted emphatically that literature is not political or propagandist: "Any attempt to put politics into fiction should be treated with the utmost contempt—not to mention the editor's ultimate weapon, the rejection slip!" Readers, however, might quibble with her on this point when they encounter her literary championing of other socially progressive ideas during the middle years of her career. Despite her harsh words above, she conceded that "[on] the other hand, if you write with conviction and honesty, your views will be clear enough." Although the feminist movement had support from many quarters during the 1970s, the movement for gay rights did not enjoy the same level of debate. In *The Heritage of Hastur,* the young Lord Regis Hastur awakens both his psychic abilities and his homosexual identity and claims control of his life through his love for his friend Danilo Syrtis and as heir to the Comyn telepathic dynasty. A non-Darkover novel, the mainstream *The Catch Trap* (1979), tells the story of two gay circus performers in the 1940s. Reportedly the novel that Bradley's family considered her best, it also became her first best seller. Trapeze artist Tommy Zane, experiencing the same sort of personal and cultural conflict present in the Darkover novels, struggles to fit into the Flying Santellis family and their life in a traveling circus while coming to terms with his sexuality. In the end, Zane willingly sacrifices his flying career to become a catcher for his lover, Mario Santelli. Just as her strong female characters may have mirrored Bradley's experience as an independent woman, her depictions of gay characters may have been influenced by her personal experience. Her second husband was gay, and for many years she worked as a pastoral counselor at the Gay Pacific Center.

The Catch Trap was not her only non-Darkovan work from this era. In 1978, she wrote *The Ruins of Isis*, about Cendri Owain who discovers, and is shocked by, a matriarchal society on the planet Isis where men are subjugated. Reconciliation for the protagonist comes she joins with her husband in a loving, egalitarian relationship and the two work for legal, social, and educational equality for the men and women of Isis. *The Endless Universe* (1979)—an expanded version of her 1975 *The Endless Voyage*—addresses the social construction of gender, race, and racism in a tale about androgynous space travelers who have lost all skin color and reproductive abilities because of exposure to radiation. The Explorers, as they are called, live in a discrimination-free environment on their ship, perhaps as a result of their physical characteristics, although the novel leaves this point open to debate.

In 1982 Bradley produced the work that led to her greatest fame and mainstream recognition, making the *New York Times Bestseller List* for four consecutive months on its release and earning her the 1984 Locus Award for best fantasy novel. *The Mists of Avalon* recounts the legends of King Arthur from the viewpoint of the female characters and is considered by many Arthurian scholars an important addition to the chronicles. The novel is told from the viewpoint of three women, Igraine, Viviane, and Morgaine. Although Morgause does not act as narrator, she is central to the plot. She, Igraine, and Viviane are sisters, daughters of the former priestess of Avalon and different fathers. Together, the four women represent the archetypal faces of the goddess, whom they worship. Bradley's goddess, which she claimed she drew from modern Wicca and Druid revivalists, is reflected in Jung's breakdown of the female psyche, which comprises the polar opposites maiden/mother and wise woman/warrior. Igraine is the mother figure, the Magna Mater. Viviane, as the oldest daughter, has inherited the mantle of the priestess and is called the Lady of the Lake; she notes the resemblance of the four to the goddess and primarily represents the wise woman. Morgaine begins as the maiden and moves through the other aspects; and Morgause, whom we learn about through the voices of the others, represents the dark face of the goddess, the Devouring Mother who stands in contrast to the nurturing Great Mother. In the midst of and in contrast to the Pagan goddess-figures stands Gwynhyfar, described by Spivack as "[almost] an iconographical image," and "a lost innocent, pure and lovely, totally helpless."

Unlike many other modern retellings of the medieval Arthurian legends, Bradley's version includes all the major episodes, drawing mostly from Malory's fifteenth-century collection, an important influence on and long-time favorite of the author. Although she makes minor alterations in the plot and characters, de-emphasizing, for example, the identification of Arthur through the sword in the stone and mentioning but not elaborating on the Round Table, Bradley covers the entire life of Arthur. The most dramatic change, however, according to Spivack, is in the meaning: the women's perceptions "create a moving, vivid account of the Arthurian legend with its spiritual meaning deeply rooted in the religious struggle between matriarchal worship of the goddess and the patriarchal institution of Christianity," a conflict between what Bradley terms "the cauldron and the cross."

Igraine, who begins the narrative, has been raised a Druid on the holy Isle of Avalon and possesses sorcery skills and the Sight. When she is fifteen, she marries the Romanized Christian leader Gorlois and then gives birth at age sixteen to Morgaine. Despite losing touch with her mystical heritage, Igraine is informed by Viviane that she is fated to give birth to a Great King who will unify all of Britain. Still a young bride, Igraine accompanies Gorlois to London for the king-making council who must decide upon a successor to the dying High King Ambrosius. There, she meets Uther Pendragon, leader of the Britons, and at first sees him only as the clumsy, rude, and womanizing man that he appears to be on the surface. Nevertheless, she enjoys talking with him, which leads to Gorlois's jealousy when he finds them deep in a religious discussion. In addition, and central to Viviane's plan that the blood line of Avalon be joined with the native British, Igraine dreams that she encounters Uther in a previous life, a dream in keeping with the belief among goddess worshipers in reincarnation. Unbeknownst to Igraine, Uther shares the same dream-vision, in which they learn that they were as closely united as two sides of the same soul at a time when Uther was a priest of Atlantis. In the shadow of Stonehenge, the two bind themselves to each other and to Britain. After the dream, Igraine discovers that Gorlois has planned treachery toward Uther. In an episode that circumvents the implied rape of the traditional versions, with her long-buried sorcery skills she sends her spirit to warn him. Uther avoids the treachery and appears disguised as Gorlois, recognized only by Igraine, on a night in midwinter, an auspicious time to conceive the future High King. They learn shortly after that Uther has died in battle, and the two marry, at first seeming to fulfill Viviane's plan. The marriage is a happy one, but their love for each other leads to the neglect of Morgaine and their son Arthur. Morgaine cares for Arthur until are they old enough to be sent away—she to the Isle of Avalon for priestly training and he to Sir Ectorious for fostering. Meanwhile, Igraine wears the moonstone pendant that symbolizes her faith in the goddess, yet reluctantly begins to observe Christian tradition for political purposes while at Tintagel and later at Camelot. Following Uther's death, she retires to a convent, but dies renouncing Christianity and regretting that Morgaine, who has the sight and thus should know of her impending death, has not come to visit her. Although Igraine symbolizes the maternal aspect of the goddess, she has been a less than ideal mother to her two children.

On the other hand, Viviane, who has acted as a kind of mentor to Igraine, takes her parental responsibilities more seriously even as she, as priestess of Avalon, represents the wise woman and the ancient secrets of the goddess. As a young woman, she gives birth to Balan after a ritual mating with the Horned One during Beltane. In this ceremony, a Virgin Huntress mates with the young man who hunts down the King Stag. Viviane's friend Priscilla gives birth around the same time to Balin, and then raises the two boys. After many years, at age thirty-nine, Viviane has another son called Galahad, who later takes the name Lancelot and is raised at King Arthur's court, a slight variation on the traditional versions that conflates two grail knights of disparate legends. Despite her motherhood, Viviane's main purpose lies in her sacred duties—which over her lifetime manifest in the goddess aspect of warrior and, as part of the wise woman, old crone. Like Igraine, she has the gift of sight, with the ability to see both the near and distant future, as well as the capability of performing sacred magic and interpreting for others the will of the goddess. Intimately involved with birth and death, Viviane eases Priscilla's suffering at the time of her death, which will prove to be her downfall. Her actions arouse the vengeance of Balin who suspects her of causing his mother's death.

Many times we find her "manipulating" the fates of the other characters to achieve her primary goal, the unification of Britain. For example, she arranges for the conception of Gwydion, later known as Mordred, by Arthur and Morgaine to further the bloodline. When Arthur ascends the throne of High King, as Lady of the Lake she presents him with not only Excalibur but with the Sacred Regalia of the Druids, a spear, cup, and platter, upon which Arthur swears to follow the sacred magic of those who crowned him king and to "deal fairly with both Druids and Christians." Viviane senses that her grand plan is failing, however, when Arthur, under the influence of the Christian Gwenhwyfar, begins to favor Christianity. He carries the banner of the Virgin Mary at the battle of Mt. Badon instead of the dragon banner, allows the Christian priests to outlaw Beltane rites and profane the sacred Druid groves, and institutes the Order of Knighthood as a sacrament. Viviane dies trying to rectify Arthur's treachery. She travels to the court on the day of the king's Pentecostal feast, when the king hears petitions from his subjects, in of hopes of convincing him to reaffirm his oath to the goddess. As she begins her plea, the crowd is at first stunned by her imperious beauty and then shocked as the vengeful Balin rushes forward and splits her head with an axe.

The third narrative voice is that of Morgaine, who first appears as a child, caring for little Arthur but resenting their mother Igraine for her neglect. She receives religious training on the Isle of Avalon and is initially shocked to discover that she will participate in the ritual mating with her brother, whom she has not seen in seven years and who does not recognize her. Christianity condemns the act as incest, and Arthur is overcome by guilt when he discovers her identity the next morning, but in the fertility-centered goddess worship sex is always an affirming and empowering act. She conceives Gwydion and leaves Avalon to give birth in Orkney at the home of Morgause and Lot. Following the secret birth, Morgaine leaves the baby to be reared by the couple and returns to Arthur's court. Once there, she enters into a painful relationship with Lancelot. She loves him, but knows that he is in love with Gwenhwyfar, and, even more problematically, with Arthur.

The apparent homosexual relationship between Lancelot and Arthur has been the subject of some scholarly discussion. As noted earlier in this essay, Bradley was recognized as sympathetic to issues affecting homosexuals, both fictitious and real. Yet James Noble, in "Feminism, Homosexuality, and Homophobia in *The Mists of Avalon*" (1994), argues that despite her attempts to demythologize Lancelot's sexuality and, presumably, challenge the masculinist assumptions of the traditionally patriarchal Arthurian world—and thus of our own society—in the end she ultimately subverts and denies his sexuality. He notes that at first glance, Lancelot's characterization contrasts with the stereotypical "limp-wristed, effeminate male whose interests and ideologies set him apart from the stereotypical heterosexual male." Morgaine, who introduces Lancelot, thinks that "she has never seen so masculine a creature before." Masculinity in this case reflects that standard of men as active and independent. When Viviane wants Lancelot to stay in Avalon for seven years, he refuses saying he wants to be in Britain fighting the Saxons "where the real struggles of life are taking place" and haughtily states that he has lived and will continue to live in a world where men do not ask for permission from women. Sexually, Lancelot appears to like women. He is physically attracted to Morgaine the first time he sees her as a child, and the apparently sexually precocious girl notes that he looks at her with the same love and desire, "almost worship," that he earlier focused on Gwenhwyfar. The two spend an afternoon together at the Ring of Stones, and Lancelot is disappointed that Morgaine will be unable to have sexual relations with him since she is promised to the goddess.

What Noble terms a "reverential response" to women later reappears when Lancelot looks at Gwenhwyfar "as if she were the statue of the Virgin on the altar at the church" and again when Lancelot tells Morgaine he cannot sleep with her because such a relationship would risk causing her "hurt and dishonor." Such seems to be the case throughout Lancelot's sexual history, as readers learn toward the end of the novel that the affair with Gwenhwyfar included little actual intercourse. In fact, intercourse occurred only in the early years, at Arthur's request. Fearing that he is the cause of Gwenhwyfar's infertility, the king suggests that Lancelot should try to impregnate her. The result is a *ménage à trois* of Arthur, Lancelot, and Gwenhwyfar, during which, Lancelot confesses to Morgaine, he experienced something he had never felt before as he made love to Arthur—in what terms remains ambiguous—and also makes clear that his love for Gwenhwyfar is inextricably tied to his love for Arthur: "I—I touched Arthur—I touched him. I love her, oh, God I love her, mistake me not, but had she not been Arthur's wife, had it not been for—I doubt even *she*—." Prior to this admission, Lancelot has told Morgaine that he has always been sexually attracted to men, but had experimented with many women, always unsatisfactorily.

Morgaine identifies his "problem" during their own sexual encounter, when she feels that their relations are unnatural and blasphemous in that he profanes the goddess by refusing to give himself over to her will. Instead, his lovemaking, while "careful, sensuous, [and] deliberate," is as reverent as his general attitude toward women and thus denies her complete sexual abandon and fulfillment. As Karin Fuog pointed out in "Imprisoned in the Phallic Oak: Marion Zimmer Bradley and Merlin's Seductress" (1991), *The Mists of Avalon* demythologizes women's sexuality and turns it into a source of empowerment and pride. She points to Nimue's post-coital feeling of triumph— following a coupling with Kevin, the grotesquely misshapen spiritual heir to Merlin— which leads in turn to her self-actualization. Igraine's decision to pursue Uther sexually leads her to the same feeling of independence and self-determination. Morgaine, sexually oppressed by Lancelot, finds such positive benefits with other men: with Kevin she is "healed," and with Accolan, the young son of King Uriens of North Wales, she reawakens her lost sexual identity and falls in love for a second time.

Lancelot, however, is denied such empowerment and affirmation in his own sex life. Noble finds that Bradley's treatment of Lancelot subsequent to his revelation to Morgaine mirrors Morgaine's reaction to the news: "Morgaine put out her hand to stop him. There were things she could not bear to know." Likewise, the novel offers no resolution to Lancelot, as if Bradley herself does not know what to do with the situation. Instead, Noble argues, Bradley symbolically punishes him by building a rift between him and Arthur following their sexual encounter. Gwenhwyfar accuses Arthur of touching Lancelot with more love than he has ever shown her, and Arthur reacts with rage toward his wife and a cooling attitude toward his best friend. Along with losing this close friendship, Lancelot must endure an unhappy marriage to Elaine, whom he marries out of a sense of duty and honor. Finally, Lancelot enters the priesthood. Many readers view this episode as a moment of closure signifying that he has at last made peace with his life; in contrast, Noble infers that he has been cast out of the traditional societal order because there is no place for a homosexual within the patriarchy.

However unsatisfying Lancelot's end may be to readers, it is perhaps less bitter than that of the other characters. Although Morgaine achieves fulfillment through her relationship with Accolon, a much younger man, she is disappointed to learn that Arthur desires to marry her off to the old king instead. Having left her role as maiden of the goddess behind, she adapts to her role as mother, acting the good Christian wife and queen, as she ministers to her aging and ailing husband and nurtures his young son Uwaine. At the same time, she continues to represent the wise woman. She is one of the few well-educated women at the Christian court, possessing knowledge of Latin, Greek, and clerical skills. Despite her outward show of Christian worship, she worries about Arthur's failure to keep his oath to the Druids and plots to destroy Camelot, thereby saving Avalon. She attempts to retrieve the Sacred Regalia from Arthur and convinces her lover Accolon, father of her unborn child, to challenge Arthur to a duel. Accolon is killed, and Morgaine miscarries the baby. Despite the tragic outcomes of her machinations, Morgaine is not the villainous trickster or shape-shifting loathly lady of the old Arthurian legends. Although she resolves to bring down Arthur for his betrayal of Avalon, her actions result from religious convictions and she remains a sympathetic character. It seems, however, that her good intentions lead to evil outcomes; her realization of this irony leads her to question the Sight and the will of the goddess. Despite her doubts, she regains the Holy Regalia, and at the end of the novel reaffirms the cycle of life instituted by the goddess as she accompanies the mortally wounded Arthur to the Isle of Avalon.

Although we do not hear their stories in their own voices, two other women, Morgause and Gwenhwyfar, play central roles in the epic. Morgause, the least developed of the main female characters, represents the destructive force of the goddess, the Devouring Mother, primarily through her dominating sexuality and excessive ambition. She and Lot have what might be termed an open marriage, and even after her son Gareth dies she sleeps with the man who has been charged with staying with her during her grief. Power-hungry, she acts as a political advisor to her husband, and advises Gwydion—who accidentally kills Ninian, a young priestess of Avalon whom he loves, in anger—to mask the death as accidental by throwing the body from a cliff. Gwenhwyfar is a devout Christian and provides a stark contrast to the Celtic Pagan women. She first encounters the older side of Britain when she is a child living in a convent near Avalon. One day while wandering in the forest, she gets lost in the mist, and Morgaine finds her and takes her back. In the patriarchal Christian world, she grows up dependent on men for direction and protection, and when her father organizes a marriage with Arthur, she agrees unquestioningly. In spite of her intentions to be a good wife, she meets and falls in love with Lancelot on the way to Camelot. Determined to honor her marriage vows, she sets about being a good wife to Arthur, a good queen to her subjects, and, most importantly, a good Christian intent on bringing her religion to the kingdom by enforcing strict adherence to Christian worship and moral standards. In contrast to the joyful sexuality of the matriarchal world of Avalon, Gwenhwyfar's sexuality is constrained by her faith, and when Arthur suggests that she commit adultery with Lancelot, she is horrified. Nevertheless, to please her husband, she acquiesces. Despite her subjection to men, she does stand firm in her devotion to Christianity, and it is her insistence that Arthur reject the practice of the Druids in favor of her God that contributes to the fall of Camelot, rather than her adultery as it is in most versions of the story.

This conflict between Druidism and Christianity—Bradley's cauldron and cross—is reflected by several contrasts in the book: the old ways of the Celts versus the new ways of the romanized Britons; the female empowerment of the goddess religious set against the oppression of women by the Christian patriarchy; and the desire for the spiritual resolution advanced by the mystical Avalon as opposed to the total rejection of religious faith in favor of human power. Arthur's failure to protect Druidism leads to Morgaine's determination to destroy him, via the character of Gwydion, in adulthood known as Mordred and who, according to Charlotte Spivack in her 1992 essay, "Morgan Le Fay: Goddess or Witch?," personifies all the elements of the conflict. Following Morgaine's retrieval of the Sacred Regalia, the cup of which Arthur's court has mistaken for the Holy Grail, the knights of the Round Table embark upon a quest for the lost object. Mordred alone stays behind, rejecting the god of his father and the goddess of his mother and choosing instead to follow the path of earthly glory. In the end, Mordred and Arthur reject both religions as they fight to the death.

Because of the vivid depiction of Druidism in *The Mists of Avalon,* Bradley herself was considered a high priestess of neo-paganism by many of her fans, some of whom, for example, flocked to hear her speak at the Heartland Pagan Festival in the early 1990s. In an interview with Carrol Fry, excerpted in Fry's 1993 essay, "The Goddess Ascending: Feminist Neo-Pagan Witchcraft in Marion Zimmer Bradley's Novels," she recounted that since the publication of the novel many readers "treated [her] as the great mother of the New Age." One of them even wrote a letter saying they had met on the astral plane. She responded with humor in a note from her secretary reading, "Mrs. Bradley does not meet anyone on the astral plane except by prior arrangement. Her husband wouldn't like it."

Although the official web page maintained by the Marion Zimmer Bradley Literary Works Trust states that she did not participate in goddess worship or witchcraft, she had a lifelong interest in the occult and told Nancy Faber in the May 16, 1983, issue of *People* magazine that she was a believer in neo-paganism, which rejected "the Christian belief in man's dominion over the earth." In her 1986 essay, "Thoughts on Avalon," Bradley wrote that she feared that *The Mists of Avalon* might be perceived by some Christians as an attack on their religion rather than on "the enormous bigotry and anti-feminism that have become grafted on to Christianity." For her, these elements had no connection with Christianity or Christ's teachings. Her own spiritual quest during these years involved seeking, in her words, "the female aspect of Divinity itself" and believing that the goddess was an extra dimension of God rather than a replacement. In 1980, she and her husband Breen were ordained as priests in a gnostic Catholic church. She believed during these years in clairvoyance, extrasensory perception, and reincarnation and co-founded the Centre for Nontraditional Religion in the carriage house on her property, where groups such as Wiccans held meetings. In later years Bradley turned to mainstream Christianity and was a regular communicant in the Episcopal Church at the time of her death.

In the same year that *The Mists of Avalon* appeared, Bradley continued the Darkover series with *Hawkmistress!* and then in the following years the Renunciate books *Thendara House* (1983) and *The City of Sorcery* (1984), and, in 1989, *Heirs of Hammerfell.* The bulk of her work during the 1980s involved non-Darkover writing, such as the science fiction *Warrior Woman* (1985), continuing the theme of strong women, and the fantasy novels *House Between the Worlds* (1981), a Science Fiction Book Club Selection, *The Inheritor* (1985), *Night's Daughter* (1985), *Fall of Atlantis* (1987), and *Dark Satanic* (1988). In 1987 she used the female-centered formula of *The Mists of Avalon* in *The Fireband,* a novel focusing on the women of the Trojan War. She began editing an anthology series for DAW Books, *Sword and Sorceress,* which followed Bradley's pattern in her own work by publishing stories with strong heroines, in 1984. In 1988, she used part of the profits from *Mists* to start *Marion Zimmer Bradley's Fantasy Magazine,* and, as editor, began in earnest to help young writers begin their own careers by providing both a venue for aspiring writers and advice on the profession. In a 1997 interview she said, "I've always felt that it's sort of a requirement that you teach everybody else what you know yourself."

Bradley enthusiastically embraced this philosophy. In the essay, "Advice to New Writers" (1980), she explained her no nonsense approach to writing: "The main way to get started as a writer is to write: apply the seat of the pants firmly to the seat of the chair and just get down to it. Having a thousand 'good ideas' in your head is no good; you have to get them on paper. Just sit down and do it." She recommended avoiding college creative writing classes, correspondence courses, and amateur writing workshops, where, she felt, "amateurs sit around and read their failures to each other." On the other hand, she believed that an extension course in fiction writing, books such as Dean Koontz's *Writing Popular Fiction* and Dick Perry's *One Way to Write Your Novel*, and regular reading of the magazine *Writer's Digest* were useful methods of studying the craft. Throughout the years, she was instrumental in the careers of several science fiction and fantasy authors. Mercedes Lackey, author of over forty novels and co-author with Bradley of *Rediscovery* (1994) and, with Elisabeth Waters and Andre Norton, *Tiger Burning Bright* (1995), was one of those who benefited from Bradley's professional generosity. "One way or another she really encouraged my career," she said. "Between providing a lot of positive feedback and a steady market for my stories [and] convincing her agent to take me. . . . I think she's in no small part responsible for where I am today. She's shoved a lot of us into professional careers." Another writer, Lawrence Schimel, recalled her professional generosity in an essay in *Lambda Book Report* (December 1999) published after Bradley's death. Not only did *Sword and Sorceress* publish his first short story, but its editor offered the young writer a job at her magazine. During the 1980s and 1990s, she belonged to a community of science fiction and fantasy writers called Greyhaven and continued to work one on one with writers as well as to conduct seminars and writing workshops (despite her earlier warnings about such things) and frequently spoke with English classes and judged writing competitions. She also offered the Darkover universe to other writers and proposed Darkover anthologies to DAW. Eventually, twelve such anthologies were published, including *The Keeper's Price and Other Stories* (1980), *Free Amazons of Darkover* (1985), and what was the final collection at the time of her death, *Snows of Darkover* (1994).

Bradley's first published collaborations, with her brother Paul Edwin Zimmer, were the science fiction *Hunters of the Red Moon* in 1973 and *The Survivors* in 1979. During the 1990s, however, she began collaborating more frequently. *Dark Trillium* (1990), with Norton and Julian May, is divided into three parts and tells the story of an evil sorcerer who conquers the kingdom of Ruwenda, kills the king and queen, and forces their three daughters into exile. The co-authors each write a part describing a princess's attempt to defeat the sorcerer. Its sequel, *Lady of the Trillium* (1995), written with Elisabeth Waters, takes place in the same setting, with the elderly Princess Haramis, protector and Archmage of Ruwenda, designating the reluctant young Princess Mikayla as her successor. Bradley collaborated in two other series during the last decade of her life. *Glenraven* (1996) and *Glenraven 2: In the Rift* (1998), both written with Holly Lisle are set in the country of Glenraven, the "last gate into Europe's mystical forgotten past," which falls between France and Italy. *Ghostlight* (1995), *Witchlight* (1996), *Gravelight* (1997), and *Heartlight* (1998), with Rosemary Edghill, are contemporary fantasy novels involving the sleuth Truth Jourdemayne and her investigations of paranormal and mystical events.

Also in the 1990s, Bradley returned to the world of Avalon with the prequels *The Forest House* (1994) and *The Lady of Avalon* (1997). At the time of her death, she was collaborating with Diana L. Paxson on a fourth novel of the series, *Priestess of Avalon*, which was finished by Paxson and published in 2001. *The Forest House* is set five hundred years before the Arthurian saga when the Romans have invaded and occupied Britannia and are moving ever closer to the Druidic society of the Forest House in a remote part of Britain. The narrative sets up the conflict between the old and the new, the Druids and the Christians, that reaches a climax in *The Mists of Avalon*. The novel opens with an accidental encounter between the Druid Eilan, a young woman called to the goddess, and Gaius Marcellus, a young Roman officer familiar with the language and customs of the native Britons through his mother, who had married his Roman father in hopes of forging an alliance in the early days of the occupation. Gaius falls into a bear pit and is rescued and nursed back to health by Eilan. He has sworn allegiance to the Roman leaders, and for a time keeps his identity a secret, using his British name Gawen. The two quickly fall in love, but Gaius's father Macellius, Prefect of the Camp of the Second Adiutrix Legion, and Eilan's father Bendeigid, son of the Arch-Druid Ardanos, deny them permission to marry. The two become lovers, however, during Samaine rites. Pregnant, Eilan is taken to the Forest House, where the last remaining Druid priestesses practice the ancient traditions of their religion and try to make peace between their people and the occupiers. Eilan secretly gives birth to a son, Gawen, and is chosen to succeed Lhiannon, the Priestess of the Oracle, as the new High Priestess.

In the meantime, Gaius returns to Rome to observe the Senate, fights against the Germans on the Continent, and then is unhappily married off to Julia, daughter of the Procurator of Britannia in Londinium, in a politically motivated match. Although she initially worships the gods of the Romans, Julia is drawn to the new Christian religion and its belief in resurrection after their daughter Secunda drowns and she delivers a stillborn son. Patricia Monaghan (1994) suggested that Bradley introduced "too many subsidiary characters for the reader's comfort" in the second half of the book. For example, the rebellion against the Romans led by Boadiccea (here called Boudica or Brigitta) has a small presence when she is captured as a hostage and brought to Gaius. Meanwhile, her children have been sent to the Forest House and Eilan for protection, even though the priestess believes that they should stay away from political entanglements. Yet political instability in Rome leads to civil unrest in Britain: Caillean, a senior priestess and Eilan's mentor, is attacked on the highway and badly wounded; drunken Roman Legions run rampant and threaten the maidens of the Forest House; and some of the Druids plan an uprising against their conquerors. In the final scene of the book, Gaius is captured by the Druids even as he is attempting to ward off a battle between them and the Romans and is sacrificed during the Samaine rites. The Druids learn that Gawen is Eilan's son, and she too is killed for her perceived treason. Caillean's voice ends the book, relating that Gawen has been taken away to a mist-obscured vale called Afallon.

Lady of Avalon links the events between *The Forest House* and *The Mists of Avalon*. Although technically still not Arthurian in scope, characters important to the events of the latter book, such as Merlin, Viviane, Igraine, Morgause, and Uther, appear. The book is tripartite in structure, covering three separate threats to Avalon, occurring in episodes set at the end of the first century, the third century, and the middle of the fifth century. Picking up where the last work left off, Gawen is being raised in Avalon by Caillean, who magically separates Avalon from the outside world and establishes a sisterhood of the goddess there. Gawen is acknowledged as the Pendragon and true Son of a Hundred Kings and given a magic sword. He is slated to be the Sacred King who will rule and save Britannia. He marries his true love Sianna at the Great Rites of Beltane and the two begin to rule as king and queen. He is soon killed by the Romans, but Sianna gives birth to his child and their descendants continue to influence Britannia. Gawen is reincarnated as Carausius, the future Emperor of Brittania. The High Priestess Dierna discovers him and mistakenly arranges a marriage that leads to his defeat. Vortimer, son of the High King, is the third to attempt to save the old ways. He unites with Viviane, the future High Priestess of Avalon, but Viviane will become the famed Lady of the Lake and guardian of the Grail. Her sister Igraine, whom she raises, is the one destined to be joined to Britannia's future leader. The third section introduces characters that appear in *The Mists of Avalon*. At the end of the book, the Faerie Queen speaks, musing on the swift passage of time and revealing that a "new age is coming, when Avalon shall seem . . . distant." She prophesies that future rulers will try to change that destiny but will inevitably fail.

Reaction to the two prequels was mixed. Many fans were disappointed by their lack of character depth, particularly when compared with *The Mists of Avalon*, but the two sold modestly well. A review in *Kirkus* (1994) described Bradley's writing in *The Forest House* as evidence of "one at ease in sketching out mystic travels" with an "unhurried pace and uncluttered staging," and Daneet Steffens, writing in *Entertainment Weekly* (May 20, 1994), called it "[meticulously] researched" and noted its "dark edge." Reviewing *Lady of Avalon*, Monaghan (1997) wrote that Bradley's female characters were "as usual, strong and vibrant" and gave attention to her heroic male characters as being particularly effective.

Although Bradley continued to be a prolific writer during the last decade of her life, she suffered from heart disease and, following a series of strokes, her public life appeared to slow down. She divorced her second husband in 1990. Her intellectual life, however, continued unabated. Following her death, friends recalled her continued love of reading and her habit of walking several blocks with a cane to her favorite bookstore in Berkeley. Her brother, Paul Edwin Zimmer, died from a heart attack on October 7, 1997, at the age of fifty-four, and Bradley herself suffered a massive heart attack on Tuesday, September 21, 1999. She died the following Saturday, September 25. The memorial service was held at St. Mark's Episcopal Church in Berkeley, where she had been a member for several years. The service followed the *Book of Common Prayer,* but Bradley placed her mark on the service by choosing the music, mostly Brahms, and the readings.

Following her death, several of Bradley's works in progress were finished by collaborators. Co-author Deborah J. Ross finished *The Fall of Neskaya* (2001), the first of the Darkover *Clingfire Trilogy,* which the two sketched out together before Bradley's death. Paxson—crediting Bradley for the story idea and outline—wrote *Priestess of Avalon,* another *Mists* prequel. Set in the late third and early fourth centuries, the novel tells the story of Eilan, later called Helena, who plans to spend her life as a priestess on Avalon. Instead, as the consort of Constantius, a Roman general, she gives birth to Constantine, the future emperor of Rome. Katy Miller, reviewing *for The Orlando Sentinel* (May 2, 2001), considered the book well written but criticized its unnecessarily heavy link to the other Avalon books and called it lacking the "magical touch" of Bradley. The book, however, and the others in the Avalon series received a boost from the TNT television mini-series *The Mists of Avalon,* which aired in July 2001. *Marion Zimmer Bradley's Fantasy Magazine* continued to publish works by new authors in the years following her death, and fans continued to flock to Darkover conventions and Avalon gatherings, attesting to Bradley's enduring impact on the science fiction and fantasy world.

PRIMARY WORKS

The Door Through Space. New York: Ace, 1961; *I Am a Lesbian* (as Lee Chapman). Derby: Monarch, 1962; *The Intruder and Other Stories.* New York: Ace, 1962; *The Planet Savers.* New York: Ace, 1962; *Seven from the Stars.* New York: Ace, 1962; *The Strange Women* (as Miriam Gardner). Derby: Monarch, 1962; *The Sword of Aldones.* New York: Ace, 1962; *The Planet Savers/The Sword of Aldones,* 1980. Revised and expanded as *Sharra's Exile.* New York: Ace, 1981; London: Arrow, 1983; *My Sister, My Love* (as Miriam Gardner). Derby: Monarch, 1963; *Spare Her Heaven* (as Morgan Ives). Derby: Monarch, 1963; *The Bloody Sun.* New York: Ace, 1964; London: Arrow, 1978. Rev. ed., New York: Ace, 1979; Boston: Gregg Press, 1979; *Falcons of Narabledla, The Dark Intruder, and Other Stories.* New York: Ace, 1964; *Twilight Lovers* (as Miriam Gardner). Derby: Monarch, 1964; *Castle Terror.* New York: Lancer, 1965; *Star of Danger.* New York: Ace, 1965; London: Arrow, 1978; Boston: Gregg Press, 1979; *Knives of Desire* (as Morgan Ives). San Diego: Corinth, 1966; *No Adam for Eve* (as John Dexter). San Diego: Corinth, 1966; *Souvenir of Monique.* New York: Ace, 1967; *Bluebeard's Daughter.* New York: Lancer, 1968; *The Brass Dragon.* New York: Ace, 1970; *Winds of Darkover.* New York: Ace, 1970; London: Arrow, 1978; Boston: Gregg Press, 1979; *World Wreckers.* New York: Ace, 1971; London: Arrow, 1978; Boston: Gregg Press, 1979; *Darkover Landfall.* New York: DAW, 1972; London: Arrow, 1976; Boston: Gregg Press, 1979; *Dark Satanic.* New York: Berkeley, 1972; New York: Tor, 1988; *In the Steps of the Master* (teleplay novelization). New York: Tempo Books, 1973; *Men, Halflings, and Hero-Worship.* Baltimore: T-K Graphics, 1973; *Hunters of the Red Moon,* by Bradley and Paul Edwin Zimmer. New York: DAW, 1973; *The Jewel of Arwen.* Baltimore: T-K Graphics, 1974; *The Necessity for Beauty: Robert W. Chambers and the Romantic Tradition.* Baltimore: T-K Graphics, 1974; *The Parting of Arwen* (as Elfrida Rivers). Baltimore: T-K Graphics, 1974; *The Spell Sword.* New York: DAW, 1974; London: Arrow, 1978; Boston: Gregg Press, 1979; *Can Ellen Be Saved?* (teleplay novelization). New York: Tempo, 1975; *The Endless Voyage.* New York: Ace, 1975; *Heritage of Hastur.* New York: DAW, 1975; Boston: Gregg Press, 1977; London: Arrow, 1979; *Drums of Darkness: An Astrological Gothic Novel.* New York: Ballantine, 1976; *The Shattered Chain.* New York: DAW, 1976; London: Arrow, 1978; Boston: Gregg Press, 1979; *The Forbidden Tower.* New York: DAW, 1977; London: Arrow, 1979; Boston: Gregg Press, 1980; *The Ballad of Hastur and Cassilda.* Berkeley, CA: Thendara House, 1978; *Storm Queen!* New York: DAW, 1978; Boston: Gregg Press, 1979; London: Arrow, 1980; *The Ruins of Isis.* Virginia Beach, VA: Donning, 1978; New York: Pocket, 1980; London: Arrow, 1979; *Bloody Sun/To Keep the Oath.* Boston: Gregg Press, 1979; *The Catchtrap.* New York: Ballantine, 1979; *The Endless Universe,* expanded version of *The Endless Voyage.* New York: Ace, 1979; *The Survivors,* with Paul Edwin Zimmer. New York: DAW, 1979; *The House Between the Worlds.* New York: Doubleday, 1980; *Two to Conquer.* New York: DAW, 1980; London: Arrow, 1982; *Survey Ship.* New York: Ace, 1980; *Children of Hastur.* Garden City, NY: Doubleday, 1981; London: Arrow, 1983; *House Between the Worlds.* New York: Del Rey, 1981; *Hawkmistress!* New York: DAW, 1982; London: Arrow, 1985; *The Mists of Avalon.* New York: Knopf, 1982; London: Joseph, 1983; *City of Sorcery.* New York: DAW, 1983; London: Arrow, 1986; *Oath of the Renunciates.* Garden City, NY: Doubleday, 1983; *Colors of Space.* New York: Monarch, 1983. Rev. ed., Norfolk, VA, 1983; *Thendara House.* New York: DAW, 1983; London: Arrow, 1985; *The Inheritor.* New York: Tor, 1984; *Free Amazons of Darkover,* by Bradley and the Friends of Darkover. New York: DAW, 1985; *Night's Daughter.* New York: Ballantine, 1985; London: Sphere, 1985; *Warrior Women.* New York: DAW, 1985; *Web of Darkness,* ed. Hank Stine. Virginia Beach, VA: Donning, 1983; Sevenoaks, UK: New English Library, 1985; *Web of Light,* ed. Hank Stine. Virginia Beach, VA: Donning, 1983; *Lythande.* New York: DAW, 1986; *Fall of Atlantis.* Riverdale, NY: Baen Books, 1987; *The Other Side of the Mirror and Other Darkover Stories,* by Bradley and the Friends of Darkover. New York: DAW, 1987; *Red Sun of Darkover,* by Bradley and the Friends of Darkover. New York: DAW, 1987; *The Best of Marion Zimmer Bradley.* New York: DAW, 1988; *The Firebrand.* New York: Simon and Schuster, 1987; London: M. Joseph, 1988; *Four Moons of Darkover,* by Bradley and the Friends of Darkover.

New York: DAW, 1988; *Heirs of Hammerfell.* New York: DAW, 1989; *Dark Trillium,* by Bradley, Andre Norton, and Julian May. Garden City, NY: Doubleday, 1990; *Domains of Darkover,* by Bradley and the Friends of Darkover. New York: DAW, 1990; *Witch Hill.* New York: Tor, 1990; *Leroni of Darkover,* by Bradley and the Friends of Darkover. New York: DAW, 1991; *Renunciates of Darkover,* by Bradley and the Friends of Darkover. New York: DAW, 1991; *Jamie, and Other Stories: The Best of Marion Zimmer Bradley.* Chicago: Academy Chicago Publishers, 1992; *Rediscovery: A Novel of Darkover,* by Bradley and Mercedes Lackey. New York: DAW, 1993; *The Forest House.* New York: Penguin, 1994; *Ghostlight,* by Bradley and Rosemary Edghill. New York: Tor, 1995; *Lady of the Trillium,* by Bradley and Elisabeth Waters. Bantam, 1995; *Tiger Burning Bright,* by Bradley, Andre Norton, Mercedes Lackey, and Elisabeth Waters. 1995; *Exile's Song,* by Bradley and Adrienne Martine-Barnes. 1996; *Glenraven,* by Bradley and Holly Lisle. Riverdale, NY: Baen Books, 1996; *Witchlight,* by Bradley and Edghill. New York: Tor, 1996; *Gratitude of Kings.* New York: Roc, 1997; *Gravelight,* by Bradley and Rosemary Edghill. New York: Tor, 1997; *Lady of Avalon.* New York: Penguin, 1997; *Glenraven 2: In the Rift.* Riverdale, NY: Baen Books, 1998; *Heartlight,* by Bradley and Rosemary Edghill. New York: Tor, 1998; *Traitor's Sun,* by Bradley and Adrienne Martine-Barnes. New York: DAW, 1999; *The Fall of Neskaya,* by Bradley and Deborah J. Ross. New York: DAW, 2001; *Priestess of Avalon,* by Bradley and Diana L. Paxson. London: HarperCollins, 2000; New York: Viking, 2001.

Other Works

"The Climbing Wave." In *Fantasy and Science Fiction,* February 1955. Reprinted in *If This Goes On,* ed. Charles Nuetzel. N.p.: BCA, 1965; "The Stars Are Waiting." In *Saturn,* March 1958. Reprinted in *The Dark Intruder and Other Stories.* New York: Ace, 1964; *Songs from Rivendell.* Privately printed, 1959; "The Wind People." In *If,* February 1959. Reprinted in *A Century of Science Fiction,* ed. Damon Knight. New York: Simon and Schuster, 1962. Also reprinted in *Women of Wonder,* ed. Pamela Sargent. New York: Vintage, 1975; *Checklist: A Complete, Cumulative Checklist of Lesbian, Variant, and Homosexual Fiction in English,* compiled by Bradley and Barbara Grier (as Gene Damon). Rochester, TX: privately printed, 1960; "Measureless to Man." In *Amazing,* December 1962. Reprinted as "The Dark Intruder" in *The Dark Intruder and Other Stories.* New York: Ace, 1964; "Phoenix," by Bradley and Ted White. In *Amazing,* February 1963. Reprinted in *The Best from Amazing,* ed. Ted White. New York: Manor, 1973; *El Villano en su Rincon,* by Lope de Vega, trans. Bradley. Privately printed, 1971; "The Jewel of Arwen." Baltimore: TK Graphics, 1973. Reprinted in *The Year's Best Fantasy Stories,* ed. Lin Carter. New York: DAW, 1975; *A Gay Bibliography.* New York: Arno Press, 1975; Letter in response to Vonda MacIntyre's review of *Darkover Landfall. Witch and the Chameleon* 3 (1975): 28–30; Letter in response to Vonda MacIntyre's review of *Darkover Landfall. Witch and the Chameleon* 4 (1975): 19–25; "The Day of the Butterfly." In *The DAW Science Fiction Reader,* ed. Donald A. Wollheim. New York: DAW, 1976; "Experiment Perilous: The Art and Science of Anguish in Science Fiction," by Bradley, Norman Spinrad, and Alfred Bester. In *Experiment Perilous,* ed. Andrew Porter. New York: Algol Press, 1976; "The Waterfall." In *The Planet Savers.* New York: Ace, 1976. Reprinted in *The Planet Savers/The Sword of Aldones.* New York: Ace, 1980; "The Keeper's Price," by Bradley and Elisabeth Waters. In *Starstone,* January 1978. Reprinted in *The Keeper's Price,* ed. Bradley. New York: DAW, 1982; "The Secret of the Blue Star." In *Thieves' World,* ed. Robert Lynn Asprin. New York: Ace, 1979. Reprinted in *Sanctuary,* ed. Robert Lynn Asprin. SFBC, 1982; "The Lesson at the Inn." In *Starstone,* June 1978. Reprinted in *The Keeper's Price,* ed. Bradley. New York: DAW, 1982; "Elbow Room." In *Stellar,* no. 5, ed. Judy-Lynn del Rey. New York: Ballantine, 1980. Reprinted in *The 1981 Annual World's Best Science Fiction,* ed. Donald A. Wollheim and Arthur W. Saha. New York: DAW, 1981; "The Hawkmaster's Son." In *The Keeper's Price,* ed. Bradley. New York: DAW, 1980; *Sword of Chaos,* ed. Bradley. New York: DAW, 1982; "Greyhaven: Writers at Work." In *Greyhaven,* ed. Bradley. New York: DAW, 1983; "The Incompetent Magicion." In *Greyhaven,* ed. Bradley. New York:

DAW, 1983; *Sword and Sorceress,* 18 vols., ed. Bradley. New York: DAW, 1984–2001; "Fandom: Its Value to the Professional." In *Inside Outer Space: Science Fiction Professionals Look at Their Craft,* ed. Sharon Jarvis. New York: Ungar, 1985; "Responsibilities and Temptations of Women Science Fiction Writers." In *Women Worldwalkers: New Dimensions of Science Fiction and Fantasy,* ed. Jane B. Weedman. Lubbock: Texas Tech Press, 1985; *Marion Zimmer Bradley's Fantasy Magazine,* ed. Bradley. 1988–2000; "The Devil Made Me Do It: Why Characters Act as They Do." *The Writer* 101 (1988): 16–17; "One Woman's Experience in Science Fiction." In *Women of Vision: Essays by Women Writing Science Fiction,* ed. Denise Du Pont. New York: St. Martin's Press, 1988; *Spells of Wonder.* Vol. 5.5 of *Sword and Sorceress,* ed. Bradley. New York: DAW, 1989; *Best of Marion Zimmer Bradley's Fantasy Magazine,* 2 vols. N.p.: Warner, 1994, 1995.

SECONDARY SOURCES

Arbur, Rosemarie. *Marion Zimmer Bradley.* Mercer Island, WA: Starmont, 1985; Benko, Debra A. "Morgan le Fay and King Arthur in Malory's *Works* and Marion Zimmer Bradley's *The Mists of Avalon*: Sibling Discord and the Fall of the Round Table." In *The Significance of Sibling Relationships in Literature,* ed. Jo Anna S. Mink and Janet D. Ward. Bowling Green, OH: Popular Press, 1992; Brackett, Leigh. *Marion Zimmer Bradley, Anne McCaffrey: A Primary and Secondary Bibliography.* Boston: G. K. Hall, 1982; Farwell, Marilyn R. "Heterosexual Plots and Lesbian Subtexts: Towards a Theory of Lesbian Narrative Space." In *Lesbian Texts and Contexts: Radical Revisions,* ed. Karly Jay, Joanne Glasgow, and Catherine Stimpson, 81–103. New York: New York University Press, 1990; Fry, Carrol L. "The Goddess Ascending: Feminist Neo-Pagan Witchcraft in Marion Zimmer Bradley's Novels." *Journal of Popular Culture* 27 (1993): 67–80; Hornum, Barbara. "Wife/Mother, Sorceress/Keeper, Amazon/Renunciate: Status Ambivalence and Conflicting Roles on the Planet Darkover." In *Women Worldwalkers: New Dimensions of Science Fiction and Fantasy,* ed. Jane B. Weedman, 153–64. Lubbock: Texas Tech Press, 1985; Hughes, Linda K. "The Pleasure Lies in Power: The Status of the Lie in Malory and Bradley." In *The Arthurian Yearbook II,* ed. Keith Busby, 99–112. New York: Garland, 1992; Hughes, Melinda. "Dark Sisters and Light Sisters: Sister Doubling and the Search for Sisterhood in *The Mists of Avalon* and *The White Raven.*" *Mythlore* 19 (1993): 24–28; Jones, Libby Falk. "Gilman, Bradley, Piercy, and the Evolving Rhetoric of Feminist Utopias." In *Feminism, Utopia, and Narrative,* ed. Libby Falk Jones and Sarah Webster Godwin, 116–28. Knoxville: University of Tennessee Press, 1990; Kaler, Anne K. "Bradley and the Beguines: Marion Zimmer Bradley's Debt to the Beguinal Societies in Her Use of Sisterhood in her Darkover Novels." In *Heroines of Popular Culture,* ed. Pat Browne, 70–90. Bowling Green, OH: Popular Press, 1987; Leith, Linda. "Marion Zimmer Bradley and Darkover." *Science Fiction Studies* (1980): 28–35; Noble, James. "Feminism, Homosexuality, and Homophobia in *The Mists of Avalon.*" In *Culture and the King: The Social Implication of the Arthurian Legend,* ed. Martin B. Shichtman and James P. Carley, 288–96. Albany, NY: SUNY Press, 1994; Russ, Joanna. "Recent Feminist Utopias" In *Future Females: A Critical Anthology,* ed. Marleen S. Barr, 71–75. Bowling Green, OH: Popular Press, 1981; Sheppeard, Sallye J. "Arthur and the Goddess: Cultural Crisis in *The Mists of Avalon.*" In *The Arthurian Myth of Quest and Magic: A Festschrift in Honor of Lavon B. Fulwiler,* ed. William E. Tanner, 91–104. Dallas: Caxton's Modern Arts Press, 1993; Shwartz, Susan. "Marion Zimmer Bradley's Ethic of Freedom." In *The Feminine Eye: Science Fiction and the Women Who Write It,* ed. Tom Staicar, 73–88. New York: Ungar, 1982; Spivack, Charlotte. *Merlin's Daughters: Contemporary Women Writers of Fantasy.* Westport, CT: Greenwood, 1987; Tobin, Lee Ann. "Why Change the Arthur Story? Marion Zimmer Bradley's *The Mists of Avalon.*" *Extrapolation* 34 (1993): 147–57; Volk, Sabine Birke. "The Cyclical Way of the Priestess: On the Significance of Narrative Structures in Marion Zimmer Bradley's *The Mists of Avalon.*" *Anglia* 100 (1990): 400–428.

ALISON GULLEY

PERSIA WOOLLEY
(November 8, 1935–)

Persia Woolley is one of the few authors dealing with the Matter of Britain to focus on developing the character of Guinevere beyond the two-dimensional character usually presented in earlier versions of the story. According to her note to the first volume of the series, *Child of the Northern Spring*, for writers who follow the Victorian view of the characters, Guinevere is "either the shadow substance of a king's ill-made choice or the willful and spoiled beauty who ruins the kingdom without compunction" (7). Woolley turns the character into the more historically accurate view of a Celtic queen as partner and co-ruler, portraying her first as a bright, inquisitive child in the kingdom of Rheged who grows into a woman who captivates all who come in contact with her, and who relies on the responsibilities of a proper Celtic queen to govern the major decisions she encounters during her life.

Woolley was born November 8, 1935, the only child of Lois and William Higman. She grew up in Auburn, California, a small gold rush town east of Sacramento, where her father was the principal of Placer High School and her mother was the city librarian. According to a February 4, 2003, e-mail interview with her, the Matter of Britain was not a particular interest to her as a child, although her mother did give her a Howard Pyle volume that was being culled from the shelves. She revealed in a July 22, 1990, interview with Alix Madrigal of the *San Francisco Chronicle* that she spent most of her childhood in a world of her own imagination, fed by her love of storytellling. In 1953 she graduated from high school on Wednesday, packed on Thursday and left town on Friday for the Berkeley campus of the University of California, where she studied architecture. Her education was interrupted in 1956, when she married James P. Woolley, an engineer. Together they had two children, Natasha and Christopher, before divorcing in 1958. The experience of being a single mother led Woolley to pen her first two books: *Creative Survival for Single Mothers* (1974) and *The Custody Handbook* (1979). The former was one of the first books written about the challenges of being a divorced mother, while the latter analyzed different ways to share the children following the divorce. Following the publication of these books, she was the keynote speaker at the National Conciliation Court conference in 1978, and spoke at many conferences on the subject of child custody, including American Bar Association meetings and family mediator conventions.

On December 3, 1960, the Majestic Theater in New York City premiered *Camelot*, Alan Jay Lerner and Frederick Loewe's musical adaptation of T. H. White's novel *The Once and Future King*. Woolley read the novel in 1961, and the possibilities of the story became clear to her, though she would do nothing with the idea for about twenty years. In 1963, blending her education with practicality, Woolley found work running an architect's office. She shifted her sights in 1967 when she went to work for the *Harper's Bazaar* magazine, running their Los Angeles office. In 1969 she went to work for *Entertainment World* magazine, where she was in charge of distribution and promotion. By 1970 she had moved to San Francisco, becoming a contributing editor for *Entertainment World*, *Show Magazine*, and *After Dark* magazine while doing freelance interviews for the *San Francisco Chronicle*. After spending 1971 working in public relations in San Francisco, she began a one-year stint as the writer, producer, and host of "The Paisley Teahouse," a live television program in San Francisco, which provided her the opportunity to interview various artists and musicians.

In 1978 she married Dr. Edward Garwin, a physicist at Stanford University with several children, giving her the experience of being a stepmother. According to a February 4, 2003, e-mail interview with her, even though she happened to travel with her husband to a number of Arthurian places in Britain in 1978, the notion of doing a novel on the subject did not surface until fall 1980, when the idea of telling the tales as experienced by Gwen in real time with real people struck her. She began her considerable research with the numerous Arthurian works of Geoffrey Ashe (who soon became a friend) and John Morris's *The Age of Arthur*. She eventually started writing her historically accurate novels in 1981, signing a contract with Poseidon Press/Pocket Books four years later for the first volume, *Child of the Northern Spring*, which finally appeared in 1987.

The story begins with sixteen-year-old Guinevere's reluctant departure from Rheged to become Arthur's queen. During the ride south, under the aegis of Merlin and Bedivere, various experiences of the journey cause her to remember back to different episodes from her childhood. The first memory takes her back to when she was nine: although she almost had an opportunity to study at the sanctuary with Vivien, the Lady of the Lake, she did begin her studies with a Druid priest; then after a very hard winter that brought much famine to her country, she lost her mother and little brother. Another memory recalls the circumstances behind the arrival of the dark-haired Kevin, her first love, and his cousin Brigit, an Irish lass and a Christian, who becomes Guinevere's companion, eventually accompanying her to Arthur's court. To pass the time on the journey, Bedivere tells the story of how Arthur became High King, participating with Uther in his final battle against the Saxons, and she learns that Merlin was Uther's nephew (son of brother Ambrosius Aurelius—defeater of Vortigern). When they finally meet, her future husband and his command of the people's respect intrigue Guinevere; conversely, her ability to size people up and make others comfortable in her presence intrigues Arthur. They finally marry in a rushed ceremony because the kingdom is being attacked from the west while all of the leaders have gathered for the wedding. Arthur rushes off to fight off the invaders in a battle in which he is injured. After he heals, all the knights gather once again at Caerleon for a wedding feast, where, per Guinevere's suggestion, the tables are arranged in a circle so there is no head or foot.

Child of the Northern Spring was followed in 1990 by *Queen of the Summer Stars.* The story continues, addressing the events of the next eight years of Arthur and Guinevere's marriage, including her struggles to become pregnant and to create the romantic kind of relationship with Arthur that her parents had. The story ends with revelation of Arthur's illicit, though unwitting, relationship with his sister Morgause, culminating in the child Modred's arrival at court to become a page on his eleventh birthday. After Morgause is slain by her son Agravain for bedding the son of the man who had killed her husband, Guinevere's accepts Modred as the child she could never have. In between, Guinevere is captured and raped by her cousin Maelgwn, the king of Gwynedd; when Lancelot comes to her rescue, she falls in love with the dark haired knight who reminds her of her first love Kevin. The Irish princess Isolde marries King Mark of Cornwall, but she loves Tristan, Mark's nephew; they eventually run away together, seeking sanctuary at Arthur's court. Arthur sends them under the auspices of Guinevere on to Lancelot's estate Joyous Gard located in Northumbria on the North Sea, just north of Hadrian's Wall. Here they spend three idyllic months before Isolde decides to return to Mark to keep him from attacking Arthur's kingdom. Ettard and Pelleas become engaged, but they break up when Gawain beds Ettard. She slinks back to a home she inherited from Queen Igraine, while Pelleas winds up finally settling down after falling in love with Nimue, who has replaced Merlin at court. Kevin returns briefly to the story as a priest, bringing much comfort to the many members of the court who seek his council. The book ends as Camelot is built at Cadbury.

The third volume of the series, *Guinevere: The Legend in Autumn,* appeared a year later. By the time the third volume was completed and published in autumn 1991, Woolley had been to Britain on four research trips, staying in hostels, and hiking over Roman ruins and Celtic hill-forts. Thoroughly absorbed by her topic, she became a scholar of Dark Age Britain, studying the religions (Celtic pagan, Celtic Christian, and Roman Christian), economics and taxation, military strategies, social anthropology (particularly in the comparison of Anglo Saxon, northern Briton, and Romano Briton), the architecture of all three cultures, and technology, as well as the sources and significances of the Arthurian legend, collecting a library of almost three thousand books, pamphlets, maps and such for the project in her quest to render Guinevere's story as accurately as possible.

The third book in the trilogy begins as Guinevere is imprisoned, awaiting her fate: to be burned at the stake for treason. Gareth and Enid keep her company as she reviews her life since Camelot was built when she was twenty-six. During this period Guinevere and Modred develop a healthy, productive stepmother/stepchild relationship even though Arthur refuses to admit Modred is his son. Eventually, Arthur gives Modred a position of responsibility as envoy to the Federates, the loyal Saxon settlers, though he rejects most of Modred's suggestions regarding the handling of these immigrants. Life is so calm that the companions decide to create a purpose for themselves, going on quests for the grail, which has a special meaning for all of the religions represented at court. Galahad eventually succeeds, returning the cup to cure King Pellam of Carbonek, who has been dying for many years, which has turned his kingdom into a Waste Land; the cup cures Pellam, who promptly dies making Galahad ruler until he too dies in sacrifice to the land. After being challenged, Gawain confronts the Green Man at the Perilous Chapel and lives to tell of his adventure. Meanwhile, Lancelot's distress over the death of his son Galahad leads him to Guinevere for solace, which is interrupted when Agravain and his followers break in, charging them with treason against the king. When Lancelot escapes, Guinevere faces the charges alone in Arthur's experimental court of peers, who judge her guilty. Arthur's distress at the decision causes him to arrange for Lancelot to rescue her, though

Gareth is accidentally killed in the process. Guinevere and Lancelot spend a year at Joyous Gard before instigators provoke Arthur into threatening a war if she does not return. To maintain peace, she returns to Arthur while Lancelot accepts exile in Brittany. The Saxons led by Modred rise up against Arthur, who, after being severely wounded, is taken away by Morgan, who had agreed to take care of Arthur if Guinevere would give up her position as high queen and retire to a nunnery.

All three volumes of the trilogy were "Book of the Month Club" alternates, and to date the trilogy has been published in Dutch, Portuguese, Italian, and Russian; at the present time, the trilogy is being extensively marketed in German. In 1994 the trilogy was made into a television movie for Lifetime TV, produced by Hearst Entertainment. Although her trilogy has been out of print here for a while, Woolley still receives e-mails from fans who have just discovered the series or her personal Web site.

With the completion of the series, life moved on for Woolley. In 1987 she had moved back to her hometown of Auburn, becoming the first director of the town's Arts Council. Since 1992 she has spent time working on a very large Michneresque historical novel set on the western slope of the Sierra Nevada mountains, peopled with Old California Mexican settlers, the pioneers, gold-rush miners, empire builders, and first generation of California-born Yankees. Because publishers are not currently interested in publishing this type of novel, the manuscript remains only half completed. Instead, in the past four years she has turned her attention to the Trojan War, seeking to humanize the archetypal characters of that legend much as she humanized those of Camelot. In addition, Writer's Digest Books asked her to draw on her writing experience to develop the volume *How to Write and Sell Historical Fiction* in 1997. In 1998 she began writing regularly for the *Auburn Sentinel*, a weekly, locally owned and focused newspaper, writing news stories and personal profiles, reporting on arts and culture, with the occasional philosophical column thrown in. She has written interviews on people such as Leonard Nimoy, Dalton Trumbo, Dale Brown, Norman Mailer, Sir Richard Attenborough, Geoffrey Ashe, and Robert Duval. She frequently does day-long workshops on the art of writing at conferences, plus lectures and speaking engagements for public and private groups such as Sacramento Reads, as well as schools such as the University of Minnesota at Duluth, the University of Nevada at Reno, and Evergreen College in San Jose.

Very little has been written critically specifically about Woolley's Arthurian trilogy beyond an entry in *The New Arthurian Encyclopedia* and book reviews in diverse places like the *Library Journal, Publishers Weekly,* the *New York Times Book Review, The Washington Post,* and the *San Francisco Chronicle.* In her note to the first volume of the series, she herself presented as her goal in writing this trilogy to look behind the myths long associated with the Matter of Britain and retell the stories "in terms of human, rather than legendary, perspectives" (7), focusing on the psychological motivation of the characters, an idea which has not been seriously addressed by the critics.

In her 1991 book *The Reclamation of a Queen,* Barbara Gordon-Wise acknowledges that Woolley's novels "have few if any magical elements" (7). However, returning the focus to the traditional view of Arthurian material, Gordon-Wise goes on to observe that "the Arthurian material itself is primarily mythical and mystical, thus qualifying these novels as fantasy" (7). Gordon-Wise does place Woolley's Guinevere without a doubt among the "Revisionist Guineveres" found in the books authored by Parke Godwin (*Beloved Exile,* 1984), Sharan Newman (the trilogy *Guinevere* [1981], *Chessboard Queen* [1983], and *Guinevere Evermore* [1985]), and Gillian Bradshaw (*In Winter's Shadow,* 1982) (117). She finds that, in marked contrast with previous portrayals of the queen, in these works, the "Revisionist" Guinevere is clearly portrayed as a Celtic queen, imbued with all of the qualities attributed to a Celtic goddess: "fertility, sovereignty, courage, autonomy and initiative" (117).

The only major study of any of Woolley's trilogy is Oliver Andresen and Glenn Marin's 1992 "Analysis of *Queen of the Summer Stars* by use of the Literary Profundity Scale" for the spring issue of *Quondam et Futurus: A Journal of Arthurian Interpretations*. This article first describes the Literary Profundity Scale, which consists of approaching a work of literature from five different directions, or planes, to assist the reader in interpreting the author's theme. By considering various episodes of the second book from the physical, mental, moral, psychological and philosophical planes, Andresen and Marin determine "the compelling narrative is Guinevere's relationship with Sir Lancelot" (83), which, for them, makes the novel useful as a teaching tool.

The only other study of Woolley's trilogy is an online article addressing "Balin and Balan," which is part of the Camelot Project at the University of Rochester. This uncredited article observes that, in the *Child of the Northern Spring*, Woolley presents the two characters as "two sides of the same personality," clearly noting a psychological approach to their story at least, thereby starting to fulfill Woolley's stated goal.

Even though her works are recent enough to have not yet made their way into the mainstream of literary criticism, Woolley is significant for the thoroughness of her portrayal of her major characters and her attention to rounding out most of the minor characters. Readers find few miscellaneous knights, pages, or servants, for example, who are not given some kind of a background to place them fully within the context of the story. This attention to detail along with what Lee Tobin McLain identified in his 1997 article titled "Gender anxiety in Arthurian romance" for *Extrapolation* as an "attempt to work out changes in gender expectations via the Arthurian legend" makes Woolley's trilogy a leader in the modern interpretation of the Matter of Britain, providing contrast with Marion Zimmer Bradley's manifesto of modern society's denunciation of religious interference in politics while also addressing this issue in Woolley's unique way.

PRIMARY WORKS

Creative Survival for Single Mothers. Berkeley, CA: Celestial Arts, 1974; *The Custody Handbook*. New York: Simon and Schuster, 1979; *Child of the Northern Spring*. New York: Poseidon Press, 1987; *Queen of the Summer Stars*. New York: Poseidon Press, 1990. Reprinted as *Guinevere: Queen of the Summer Stars*. London: Grafton, 1991; *Guinevere: The Legend in Autumn*. New York: Poseidon Press, 1991; *The Portable Writers Conference*. Sanger, CA: Quill Driver Books, 1997; *How to Write and Sell Historical Fiction*. Cincinnati, OH: Writer's Digest Books, 1997; "Pastel Artist Reif Erickson: Following Your Bliss." *Perspectives*, March/April 2000, 12–13; "Capturing a Glimpse of the Profound: Watercolorist Michael Anello." *Perspectives*, May/June 2000, 13–16; "A Gaze from the Depths of a Dream: A Portrait of J. Randall Smith." *Perspectives*, July/August 2000, 8–11; "The Shape of Worship: From a Formal Christian Church to a Native American Roundhouse, the Architecture of Where We Worship Runs the Gamut." *Perspectives*, November/December 2000, 4–5; "End Paper: Singing the World into Creation." *Perspectives*, November/December 2000, 18.

SECONDARY SOURCES

Andresen, Oliver, and Glenn Marin. "An Analysis of *Queen of the Summer Stars* by Use of the Literary Profundity Scale." *Quondam et Futurus: A Journal of Arthurian Interpretations* 2, no. 1

(1992): 82–97; "Balin and Balan." The Camelot Project at the University of Rochester: Arthurian Texts, Images, Bibliographies, and Basic Information, ed. Alan Lupack and Barbara Tepa Lupack; available at http://www.lib.rochester.edu/camelot/balmenu.htm; Gordon-Wise, Barbara Ann. *The Reclamation of a Queen: Guinevere in Modern Fantasy*. Westport, CT: Greenwood, 1991; Madrigal, Alix. "The Arthurian World According to Woolley." *San Francisco Chronicle*, July 22, 1990, 3; McClain, Lee Tobin. "Gender Anxiety in Arthurian Romance." *Extrapolation* 38, no. 3 (1997): 193–99; Richards, Stanley, ed. *Great Musicals of the American Theatre*, vol. 2. Radnor, PA: Chilton, 1976.

PEGGY J. HUEY

MARGARET ELEANOR ATWOOD
(November 18, 1939–)

Born in Ottawa, Ontario, Canada, on November 18, 1939, Margaret Atwood spent childhood summers reading Grimms' fairy tales in wilderness settings, where her father, Carl Atwood, pursued research in forest entomology. In her 1999 Empson Lectures at the University of Toronto, she recalls the reading and storytelling traditions that shaped her early years and the intense moment in 1956 when a poem formed itself in her mind as she walked home from school: "My transition from not being a writer to being one was instantaneous, like the change from docile bank clerk to fanged monster in 'B' movies" (*Negotiating*, 14). A prolific output of poetry, fiction, and literary criticism over four decades confirms the writer's identity that Atwood felt at that moment.

Atwood's parents, Carl Edmund Atwood and Margaret Dorothy Killam, first took their daughter to the field when she was six months old. Her brother, Harold Leslie, two years older, became a close companion. Because the family accompanied Carl to the field for several months a year, Atwood attended school only irregularly until the eighth grade. She received an early education from her mother, who had worked as a dietician and nutritionist. Her reading materials included what someone thought to pack, but she also recalls a thriving interest in comic books. Although Atwood was somewhat frail and regularly in need of extra rest, she was expected to help with quotidian life in the forest.

Looking back at possible cultural influences, Atwood recalls the general focus on and adaptation to World War II, which had begun the year of her birth. The early experience she shares with other writers is that of "books and solitude" (*Negotiating*, 7). The transition to urban life in a post-war split-level house thrust her unexpectedly into the manipulations of pre-adolescent girls and a general discomfort over the atomic bomb and McCarthyism. More pleasant inspirations include the music of Patti Page, radio soap operas such as *The Green Hornet* and *Inner Sanctum,* and, a few years later, Elvis Presley.

Whether recounted formally by degree and institution or shared as confession by Atwood herself, Atwood's education comprehended the canonized literary traditions, as well as emerging trends discussed in defiant whispers by the counterculture in their black turtle-necks and dancers' tights during the days of the Beat generation. She studied writing at Victoria College, University of Toronto, graduating in 1961. Northrop Frye is often cited as a literary influence; his *Anatomy of Criticism* first appeared in 1957. In 1962 she received a master's degree in English from Radcliffe College, and she pursued doctoral level studies at Harvard, researching "The English Metaphysical Romance" (Stein, xviii).

Atwood first engaged with Medieval literature as an honors undergraduate at the University of Toronto, reading *Sir Gawain and the Green Knight* and Tennyson's *Idylls of the King*. Graduate study in Victorian literature returned her attention to Tennyson, and she supplemented this reading with "works on the history and archaeological research of the Arthurian period" (Thompson). Among her first publications is a sequence of poems entitled "Avalon Revisited," which appeared in the Canadian journal *Fiddlehead* in 1963. She published under the initials "M. E. Atwood," and later observed that she did so because she "did not want anyone important to know [she] was a girl" (*Negotiating*, 14).

Asked to discuss the poems in a 1991 interview, Atwood noted that she remembered few details about the creative process that produced them. She spoke of Arthurian legend as one of many "myths and traditions" that helped her shape a poetic voice in the early 1960s. She observed that she experimented with the sequence as a mean of incorporating narrative into lyric form, as Tennyson had done in *Idylls*. Among the characters of Arthurian legend, she emphasized the women, noting that Vivien was "most important" to her. More generally, Arthurian legend was a tradition that she "felt free . . . to adapt to [her] own purposes . . . just as others had done" (Thompson).

Those readers who feel free to interpret "Avalon Revisited" may do so in the context of Arthurian legend or for their contribution to the Atwood oeuvre. The Arthurian dimension of the sequence lies more with Tennyson than with Geoffrey of Monmouth, particularly in its development of Guenevere and its striking yet less-than-idyllic imagery: "The incautious couple by the trees / Trip on the skull, and part / As apples pale in the descending sun" ("Elaine in Arcadia," *Fiddlehead*, 11).

If Tennyson's Avalon serves as a metaphor for Victorian England, Atwood's milieu resounds with echoes of mid-twentieth century modernism. Returning to "the ultimate Avalon," Arthur "is not there. No hero / Paces the blighted grounds" ("The King," *Fiddlehead*, 13). Reflecting the passing of high modernism into a media-inspired world where all stories have already been told, the sequence narrates few details of Arthurian legend, but rather asks the reader to step in for a close-up of the ruins. Vivien's mirror, for instance, "Lies shattered into slivers of the dead / Eyes that watched the intricate castles / Crumble when he bent his head" ("Recollections of Vivien," *Fiddlehead*, 10). Such a stance toward narrative and storytelling may have emerged from an awareness of Marshall MacLuhan's presence "just down the road at an adjacent college" (*Negotiating*, 23), one voice in the debate she has called the "yelling over myth and media and literature" (*Negotiating*, 23).

Those familiar with Atwood's later poetry will recognize an intense, almost violent feminine impulse in the sequence as well. Both Vivien and Elaine, in their respective poems, figure in the doom that pervades. The jealous Elaine is "inverted in the water," locked in the sinful embrace of Lancelot and Guinevere, and forced to "sing the song their bodies made / Changed to a mawkish wail. . . ." Likewise, Vivien's "cold inverte-brate arms" haunt and trap the inhabitants of Broceliande, "breeding the overthrow of holy spires." In the widely anthologized later poems "This Is a Photograph," "You Fit into Me," and "Siren Song," Atwood continues to draw images of power, pain, and inti-macy in romantic relationships.

The Avalon poems, as the author herself has observed, appropriate myth for her own artistic purposes. Writing on the more widely read and studied early poetry, including *Double Persephone* (1961), *The Circle Game* (1966), and *The Animals in That Country* (1968), Karen F. Stein observes that both locale and character serve as mythic forces rather than specific places or individuals. The Avalon poems have yet to make that detachment. Vivien, Guenevere, and Elaine appear in sharp psychic outline, casting their influence and becoming physically trapped—in a tapestry, as a water reflection—in a state of punishment or regret. They do, however, show an early tendency of the poet to shift among mythic images. Guinevere, in "The Betrayal of Arthur," takes on the role of Eve in the Garden of Eden: "She was the garden, she became the tree / that lured his will within the reach of choice" (*Fiddlehead*, 11). In "The Apotheosis of Guinevere," the queen becomes bound in her "flat tapestries," recalling multiple mythological and fairy tale figures. Yet, with Eve escaping individuality and becoming tree or garden, and with Guinevere trapped in the tapestry like a figure on Keats' Grecian urn, the movement toward Stein's notion of mythic forces has clearly begun.

Having won the E. J. Pratt award for *Double Persephone* in 1961, Atwood gained further prominence in 1966, when *The Circle Game* brought her the Governor General's Award, a prestigious national honor. With the publication of the novel *The Edible Woman* in 1969, Atwood's reputation further expanded, as both popular and scholarly audiences responded with interest and acclaim. Since that time, Atwood has not only maintained a prolific output of fiction, poetry, and other writings, she has helped to shape a Canadian nationalist literature and built a complex profile as a popular writer and feminist academic. She has served as writer-in-residence at York University; University of Toronto; University of Alabama; Trinity University, San Antonio, Texas; and she has held the Berg Chair in English at New York University. Among those institutions granting her honorary degrees are Concordia University, Queen's College, University of Guelph, Mount Holyoke College, University of Waterloo, Oxford University, University of Toronto, and Trent University.

Atwood is currently lecturer of English at the University of British Columbia, Vancouver. Among her many literary awards are the Molson Award, a Guggenheim Fellowship, Toronto Arts Award, Governor General's Award, *Los Angeles Times* Fiction Award, and Trillium Award. The French and Canadian governments have honored her writing career with numerous recognitions.

Atwood supported a deeply personal and exhaustive biography published by Natalie Cooke in 1998. In this book, *Margaret Atwood: A Biography,* together with *Negotiating with the Dead*, a thematic self-portrait of Atwood's identity as a writer, readers and scholars glimpse a quick-witted thinker and disciplined writer. Both books address the intersection of Atwood's career and the public discourse on gender issues. Similarly, scholarly readings of her fictionalized quests for female identity and gender-based power struggles make a substantial contribution to feminist literary studies. While pursuing commercial exposure of her fiction and poetry, Atwood has fended off narrow biographical readings and sought a more subtle public discussion of feminist issues than the popular media is prepared to pursue. Today literary scholars further these aims through participation in the Margaret Atwood Society, which sponsors online discussions and sessions at the Modern Language Association Conventions.

Recurrent among Atwood's accomplishments and reflections is her role in establishing a Canadian nationalist literature. Atwood taught a course in Canadian women writers at York University in 1971. In 1972 she published *Survival: A Thematic Guide to Canadian*

Literature and set off on a tour of the country to discuss this work and a nationalist literature. The guide, which was greeted with strong reactions both positive and negative, presented a Canadian literary renaissance, particularly its poetry, as an "explosion" (quoted
in Cooke, 198) and sparked a vigorous debate that continues today. In the early 1980s
she edited volumes of Canadian verse and short fiction written in English. Seeking inter-
ludes from public exposure, Atwood has from time to time returned to the Canadian wilderness. These retreats have intensified the author's connection with her rural roots and
heightened her commitment to environmental concerns. Lecturing at Oxford University
in 1991, Atwood charmed an unexpectedly large British audience in a series of four lectures that Clarendon Press published in 1995 under the title *Strange Things: The Malevolent North in Canadian Literature.*

The novel *Surfacing,* also published in 1972, is widely read as an individual quest for
gender and national identity in Canadian settings, past and present, rural and urban. The
short story collection *Wilderness Tips* (1991) challenges an innocent and overly simplistic
myth of the wilderness. Although Atwood does not seem to object to the status accorded
her as a major world woman writer, she has also devoted considerable energy to envision-
ing a Canadian literary tradition that she and her compatriots consider representative of
their art and accurate in terms of history and culture.

Atwood concludes the 1991 interview with a firm assertion that she has no plans to
write additional Arthurian poems. Certainly her writings reflect an intellectual grazing
across historical, mythic and generic boundaries. A pervading irony and a postmodern
impulse toward pastiche discourage any single paradigm by which to interpret her characters, settings, and conflicts.

A systematic look at Atwood criticism, however, reveals one further connection with
the medieval world in the form of gothic sensibility. Hardly a single novel or poetry collection has been free of such an association. Writing about *Lady Oracle* and *The Robber
Bride,* for instance, Hilde Staels observes, "At the core of the Gothic sensibility is fear—
fear of ghosts, women's fear of men, fear of the dark, fear of what is hidden but might
leap out unexpectedly, fear of something floating around loose which lurks behind the
everyday" (153). Establishing such conventions and readerly expectations, and noting
that "Gothic narrative suggests the co-existence of the everyday alongside a shadowy
nightmarish world" (153), Staels places Atwood squarely in the tradition of female writers
who have favored the genre: Ann Radcliffe, Mary Shelley, the Brontës, Daphne DuMau-
rier, and Jean Rhys. Atwood herself has related *Lady Oracle* to Jane Austen's *Northanger
Abbey.* The concern over twentieth-century women's struggle for identity that pervades
Atwood's fiction and verse finds a natural venue in a genre that reminds even today's
woman—fictional and real—of the "menace and mystery" that bring doubt to all efforts
at self discovery, independence, and voice.

Interlocking frames of fiction and pseudo-autobiography allow *Lady Oracle* to indulge
in and simultaneously comment upon the gothic. The protagonist, Joan Crawford Foster, writes costume gothic romances under the nom de plume Louisa K. Delacourt. Foster hides this work from Arthur, her political activist husband, out of a fear that he will
lose his respect for her. Ironically, income from these writings supports the couple while
he pursues a graduate degree. While Arthur claims that his politics defends working
women, Foster justifies her escapist fiction as the true salvation of those trapped in what
Arthur calls "meaningful work": "Why refuse them their castles, their persecutors and
their princes, and come to think of it, who the hell is Arthur to talk about social relevance? . . . The truth was that I dealt in hope, I offered a vision of a better world,

however preposterous" (35). The narrative of Delacourt's gothic romance *Stalked by Love* is woven among autobiographical segments recalling an obese childhood and Foster's staged suicide and escape to Italy. Joining these narrative threads is the voice of a third persona, the commercially acclaimed author of a poem of literary merit, named Lady Oracle by the poem's promoters. The poem, as the narrator observes, is a gothic bodice-ripper gone awry. With two-thirds of her identity always in fear of discovery, the remaining third risks an attempt at self-expression and a sense of accomplishment. In many ways, and especially as the narrative threads become entangled, the protagonist becomes the villain she most fears. Inside the narrative of *Stalked by Love,* the generically conventional maze draws in its victim, just as Joan is positioning herself to confront the villain from whom there is no escape.

Ann McMillan reads *Lady Oracle* as a blend of two strains of gothic romance: gothic fantasy and gothic naturalism. In the former, the heroine helps to transform her rescuer into a hero through a change in her own perceptions, particularly her admission of love for him. In the latter, "the heroine is acted upon by external societal forces she can neither understand not control" (48). Typically, this heroine ends in death or madness. McMillan suggests that Atwood mixes these gothic traditions to produce a heroine whose transformation brings maturity and insight. Under this paradigm, Joan enters a figurative maze in search of men capable of nurturing or threatening her. Through identification with the heroines she has created in gothic romances, Joan eventually sees the moral folly of the deceptions she has used to escape and ultimately trap herself.

Susan Rosowski observes in *Lady Oracle* a similar process of self discovery through immersion in gothic fantasy. In her reading of the novel, Joan comes to question "the Gothic dimensions that exist *within* our social mythology" (197). Joan's acknowledgement that she has never participated honestly in a human relationship unravels her psychological dependence upon others and upon the fantasy itself. For Rosowski, this self discovery would lead naturally to the creation of a personal mythology to replace a social mythology flawed by gothic fear and horror. She notes that Joan fails to reach this stage of awareness or development.

While gothic paradigms lend insight into the novel, none ventures a comment upon the final actions and thoughts of the heroine. In fact, the climactic action and comic resolution of the novel remain bathed in an irony that runs along the historical/generic spectrum of the gothic romance towards modernist absurdity and paralysis. The reference to a Disney movie as metaphor is among numerous allusions that splinter a focused reading and remind us of the novel's contemporary context.

The poems of *Circle Game* and *Power Politics* evoke contemporary images to suggest the presence of gothic horror in everyday life. Judith McCombs finds in these volumes repeated evocations of the female hero-victim "tempted by male Others whose power animates and captivates, whose guises enthrall, whose love spells death" (5). *Power Politics* illustrates the heroine's collusion with this dangerous hero, albeit in catastrophic terms. Indeed, the heroine is inevitably crushed by the hero and, at his insistence, "lie[s] mutilated beside" him. This verse concludes with the questions "How can I stop you" and "Why did I create you," confirming the heroine's willing victimhood. Further, in this poetry and in *The Journals of Susanna Moody,* nature, specifically the dark, chaotic, wilderness, encloses the struggle spatially and increases its intensity.

Gothic elements in *The Robber Bride* are even more fragmented and blended with contemporary life than those in *Lady Oracle* and the poetry. In a feminine inversion of the fairy tale *The Robber Bridegroom*, the absent Xenia is constructed through the narratives of three women whom she victimized during her lifetime. The additional gothic element employed in this novel is the "demonic woman" rendered from beyond the grave. The three narrators ground an ongoing relationship upon their tales of this transgressive figure and thus assure the continued presence of the danger she represents. In the mind of the narrator Tony, a military historian, Xenia evokes the memory of Dame Giraude, a thirteenth-century female warrior who engaged in a successful battle against the Catholic forces of Simon de Montfort (Staels, 167). Another of the narrators, Charis, links Xenia to the biblical Jezebel. These associations, together with the narrators' urge to keep this other woman story alive, once again presses gothic fear and mystery up against contemporary life and notions of female identity.

PRIMARY WORKS

Double Persephone. Toronto: Hawkshead Press, 1961; "Avalon Revisited." *Fiddlehead* 55 (1963): 10–13; *The Circle Game*. Toronto: Contact Press, 1966; *The Animals in That Country*. Toronto: Oxford University Press, 1968; *The Edible Woman*. Toronto: McClelland and Stewart, 1969; *The Journals of Susanna Moodie*. Toronto: Oxford University Press, 1970; *Procedures for Underground*. Toronto: Oxford University Press, 1970; *Power Politics*. Toronto: House of Anansi Press, 1971; *Surfacing*. Toronto: McClelland and Stewart, 1972; *Survival: A Thematic Guide to Canadian Literature*. Toronto: House of Anansi Press, 1972; *You Are Happy*. Toronto: Oxford University Press, 1974; *Lady Oracle*. Toronto: McClelland and Stewart, 1976; *Selected Poems I, 1965–1975*. Toronto: Oxford University Press, 1976; *Dancing Girls and Other Stories*. Toronto: McClelland and Stewart, 1977; *Days of the Rebels, 1815–1840*. Canada's Illustrated Heritage. Toronto: Natural Science of Canada, 1977; *Up in the Tree*. Toronto: McClelland and Stewart, 1978; *Life Before Man*. Toronto: McClelland and Stewart, 1979; *Two-Headed Poems*. Toronto: Oxford University Press, 1980; *Bodily Harm*. Toronto: McClelland and Stewart, 1981; *True Stories*. Toronto: Oxford University Press, 1981; *Second Words: Selected Critical Prose*. Toronto: House of Anansi Press, 1982; *Bluebeard's Egg*. Toronto: McClelland and Stewart, 1983; *Murder in the Dark: Short Fiction and Prose Poems*. Toronto: Coach House Press, 1983; *Interlunar*. Toronto: Oxford University Press, 1984; *The Handmaid's Tale*. Toronto: McClelland and Stewart, 1985; *Selected Poems II: Poems Selected and New, 1976–1986*. Toronto: Oxford University Press, 1986; *The CanList Foodbook: Pen to Palate—a Collection of Tasty Literary Fare*. Toronto: Totem Books, 1987; *Cat's Eye*. Toronto: McClelland and Stewart, 1988; *Barbed Lyres: Canadian Venomous Verse*. Toronto: Key Porter Books, 1990; *For the Birds* (children's fiction). 1990; *Selected Poems, 1966–1984*. Toronto: Oxford University Press, 1990; *Wilderness Tips*. Toronto: McClelland and Stewart, 1991; *Good Bones*. Toronto: Coach House Press, 1992; *The Robber Bride*. Toronto: McClelland and Stewart, 1993; *Morning in the Burned House*. Toronto: McClelland and Stewart, 1995; *Princess Prunella and the Purple Peanut* (children's fiction). 1995; *Strange Things: The Malevolent North in Canadian Literature*. Oxford: Clarendon Press, 1995; *Alias Grace*. Toronto: McClelland and Stewart, 1996; *The Labrador Fiasco*. London: Bloomsbury, 1996; *Eating Fire: Selected Poetry, 1965–1995*. London: Virago, 1998; *Two Solicitudes: Conversations*. With Victor-Levy Beaulieu. Toronto: McClelland and Stewart, 1998; *The Blind Assassin*. Toronto: McClelland and Stewart, 2000; *Negotiating with the Dead: A Writer on Writing*. Cambridge: Cambridge University Press, 2002.

SECONDARY SOURCES

Cooke, Natalie. *Margaret Atwood: A Biography*. Toronto: ECW Press, 2000; McCombs, Judith. "Atwood's Haunted Sequences: *The Circle Game, The Journals of Susanna Moodie*, and *Power Politics*." In *Margaret Atwood*, ed. Harold Bloom. Philadelphia: Chelsea House, 2000; McMillan, Ann. "The Transforming Eye: *Lady Oracle* and Gothic Tradition." In *Margaret Atwood:*

Vision and Forms, ed. Kathryn Van Spanckeren and Jan Garden Castro. Carbondale: Southern Illinois University Press, 1988; Rosowski, Susan J. "Margaret Atwood's *Lady Oracle*: Fantasy and the Modern Gothic Novel." In *Critical Essays on Margaret Atwood,* ed. Judith Combs. Boston: G. K. Hall, 1988; Staels, Hilde. "Atwoodian Gothic: From *Lady Oracle* to *The Robber Bride.*" in *Margaret Atwood,* ed. Harold Bloom. Philadelphia: Chelsea House, 2000; Thompson, Raymond H. Interview with Margaret Atwood. Toronto, March 25, 1991. Available at http://www.lib.rochester.edu/camelot/intrvws/atwood.htm.

REBECCA DUNCAN

ARTHURIAN ART

Arthurian art, like Arthurian literature, was primarily created during three distinct periods; the more raw and robust medieval works were stepping stones for the elegance and morality of the Victorian era which was immediately followed by the linear and abstract qualities of the Edwardian period. After the medieval period during which Arthurian art was created all over Europe, King Arthur, as a quasi-historical king of the Britons primarily inspired English artists; however, some modern American examples of Arthurian art merit mention as well. While this section will examine each of these times chronologically, it seems valuable to first note the qualities that typify Arthurian art.

While there is some questioning and subversion in all periods except the earliest medieval times—for example, a funny King Arthur with a crafty fox face—the Gothic style has remained remarkably consistent for eight centuries. Castle exteriors with turrets and drawbridges as well as castle interiors with ornately canopied beds, chamber walls with elaborate wall hangings, and giant tables in enormous mead halls all vary little with time. The stock characters and motifs are mostly of the nobility: kings, queens, lords, ladies, and knights are all primarily identified by fancy garments—with crowns and ermine edged robes designating royalty. Peasants are also clearly delineated by aprons and sturdy, less ornate clothing.

Scenes are usually one of four sorts: courtly life in a castle, religious celebrations inside a church, marvelous visions or lonely moments on a forest quest, or jousting at tournaments. Castles' interior scenes stress the material opulence of furniture, clothing, and jewels. Tournament and battle scenes often reflect details of armor, weaponry, and horses. It is the paintings of questing knights, usually in pairs or alone, that show scenes of wondrous visions often including the grail chalice, giants, dwarfs, angels, unicorns, white stags, lions, or dragons. Apparently, it is tired and lonely men to whom such apparitions appear as they are never part of the scenes of everyday feudal life. Normal folks may have been convinced of the existence of dragons and unicorns, but only questing knights or damsels in distress are captured in art alongside such creatures.

Motivation for questing, leaving the safety and society of family and friends, varied: a political desire to conquer new territories, a feudal obligation to serve an overlord and protect his vassals from potential danger abroad, or an amorous desire to win and justify a lady's favor. Usually shown riding alone, the questers are all relying upon personal ethics rather than the social conventions of castle life or the Christian virtues of Catholic believers. A knight is tested in all manner of ways, and perhaps the most interesting Arthurian art reflects a lone knight's psychological state of inner turmoil as he does not find that which he seeks or conversely finds himself ill equipped spiritually or emotionally for the challenges he faces. The grail quest adventures were breeding grounds for such frustrations because while all the knights of Camelot journeyed out in search of the grail, only the spiritually purest one, Galahad, could discover the chalice, while the other men were doomed to failure. Much Arthurian art reflects various aspects of the grail quest and knights enduring various tests or challenges.

Fitting because Arthur was considered in his semihistorical context to be the first Christian king of a united Catholic Britain and because his knights were on a quest for a Christian vessel, Arthurian art originates—in terms of the earliest extant piece chronologically—with church decorations, predominantly sculptures. Of course, such art is still intact because the church had the means both to create and to protect valuables. It is not until later in the medieval period that representations of Arthurian characters abound in illuminated manuscripts, tapestries, paintings, and other secular decorations found in private homes. Speculation naturally runs rampant because scholars have so little materials that remain intact from the early medieval period, while they have a wealth of inventories of private homes that list pieces of art specifically or potentially decorated by Arthurian characters.

An Arthurian artist usually depicts a famous moment frozen from the tales and helps the viewer identify the subject by various timeless symbols and signs, like Arthur's heraldic sign of three gold crowns on a red or blue background (symbolizing his dominion over England, Brittany, and Scotland), Galahad with a red cross on a white background, or Tristram with a harp, hawk, or chessboard. Sometimes, as did the Victorian William Morris and his company under the stained glass panes at Harden Grange, artists added very helpful narrative summaries at the bottom of a scene that tell the viewer exactly what is being depicted.

Much like the Bible, the Matter of Britain—because its origins are primarily the most ancient of Welsh, Celtic, and Germanic fertility myths—has multileveled metaphysical meaning; these tales are as old as human time and filled with archetypal characters to whom have been added many layers of attributes over the years. After employing the stock medieval costumes, the Arthurian artist must focus on allegorical symbols and setting to place the viewer into the narrative. Further, colors are also important indicators of personality traits, especially in the clothing, with generally the following typically medieval meanings—even when used in later periods: Blue=fidelity, Gold=divinity, White=purity, Black=vile, Green=amour, Grey=sadness, and Yellow=hostility.

Even in the Arthurian legends of literature, identification of characters and setting relies upon visual signs, so discussing the meaning of a picture using the same conventional system of symbols is not too difficult. Plus, the art is generated by the literature rather than vice versa. For example, in artwork, Lancelot is a knight riding on a cart or balancing on a sword bridge above waters or riding past a lady in a tower because he did these things first in a story. Merlin is a bearded old man in a long, dark gown sometimes wearing a tall, pointed hat in pictures because the artist had been given this description in words. Such patterns impose order and actuate memory through symbols, making the viewer recall the entire story while seeing only a few well-placed devices.

Just as Arthurian literature takes a wide variety of forms, such as chronicle, romance, epic and mock-heroic, so, too, Arthurian art can be found in sculpture, stained glass, decorative boxes, metalwork, tiles, wall hangings, illuminated manuscripts, lithographs, and paintings. It is believed that the oldest surviving example of Arthurian art is a sculpture carved between 1120 and 1130. It is in the Modena Cathedral in Northern Italy; conveniently, there is a band above the sculpture with a list of names of the characters, including "Artus de Britannia." The relief depicts a castle where Mardoc holds Winlogee (Guinevere) prisoner. This Winlogee is derived from an early version of a Welsh folktale, wherein her character is a powerful fee and a Persephone figure who is queen of both the underworld and of vegetation. Gawain and Arthur attempt to rescue Winlogee, but in literature it is Lancelot who is ultimately her rescuer. The men's conical helmets with attached nose pieces and long, pointed shields are useful for dating the subject of the piece to an early period. The Lancelot, Guinevere, and Arthur triangle is among the more common subjects of Arthurian art, perhaps because it has all of the most dramatic, passionate elements entwined within it.

The next oldest extant piece of Arthurian art is the mosaic tile floor of a cathedral in Otranto. This beautiful and intricate flooring was created around 1165. One of the scenes is entitled "Rex Arturis" and shows a crowned man carrying a club and riding a goat. This rather odd and comical figure may be of particular significance in terms of the Welsh story of Arthur's combat with the giant cat of Lausanne, as a cat attacking a man appears in the same scene. Still the goat remains a puzzling addition to the legends, and may, perhaps, reflect a tale now lost. It could also be a subversion, one artist showing humor, or sharing distain for this king by relegating him to riding such an ungallant animal, but it probably is not because it is an early cathedral work.

The oldest intact Arthurian mural has been dated around 1200. It is called "Iwein at the Magical Fountain" and again characters are identified by labels using the Latin forms of their names. In eleven scenes Iwein rides into a forest, fights a giant, and several other knights. The hero's sword, sheath, and horse are hit as the castle gate closes on them. Iwein is helped by a lady and marries her rich sister. This Arthurian plot is apparently taken from Hartmann von Aue's "Iwein" (finished sometime before 1200), which contains the episode of the castle gate closing on Iwein's horse—incorporating several scenes stemming from ancient mythology, wherein the entrance to the underworld has a gate that cuts off limbs.

The oldest extant illustrated manuscript dates from just a bit later. It is a prose *Lancelot* that was probably decorated in Paris around 1220. It contains fifty-seven illustrations within very large initials, forty-four of which are the letter "O" so that the roundel is the common shape of the art. Included within one of the "O's" is Arthur beheading a giant. The twelfth and thirteenth centuries gave rise to vernacular literature and literacy; illustrated manuscripts often involved such secular subjects because monks no longer controlled this type of art. Books were illustrated by various artists, ink makers, and book binders who did not necessarily have particularly strong religious ties. During this time the five most popular nonreligious subjects of illustrated books were the Fall of Troy, Chanson de Roland, King Alexander, the Roman de la Rose, and the many branches of Arthurian legend.

While there are other extant murals and tapestries, the next significant piece is the giant Winchester Round Table probably produced around 1250. It is eighteen feet in diameter and hangs over the dais in Winchester Castle's hall. It is included as evidence of an actual historical Arthur by William Caxton in his preface to Sir Thomas Malory's *Morte d'Arthur* (1485). Although it was used by several English kings, most notably Henry VII and later Henry VIII who displayed it to the Emperor Charles V, as proof of lineage, or as evidence of their ancient line of kings, the table certainly is not the one used by the real King Arthur—if he even actually existed—because of its comparatively late date. The table was probably designed for a Tudor king who wanted some visualization of his potential dynastic ties to show visiting rulers from notably older lineages.

On the Winchester Round Table, Arthur holding a sword is the only figure but spokes with the names of twenty-four knights radiating out of the circle are also present. These knights are all the ones noted by Malory as sitting at the table with Arthur and departing on the grail quest. The alternating spokes are the Tudor colors of green and white, and the documented examinations of the table by various visiting political leaders reminds us that the Arthurian legends themselves were repeatedly reinvented as a veneer for sociopolitical gain through many centuries. The table was obviously built for manipulative purposes just after 1250 to emulate Arthur's table as mentioned by early Arthurian writers. A round table is first mentioned as a part of King Arthur's castle by Wace in *Roman de Brut* (1154) as a means of avoiding potential protocol problems in seating the knights at meals and meetings.

While continental European countries were primarily interested in artistically decorating romances, the illustrated manuscripts crafted in England are more commonly of historical or quasi-historical chronicles showing Arthur's lineage through other English kings. The British people were always acutely aware of their country's position among some other European civilizations as a relative newcomer in terms of having one king of a unified country. While they could not produce a ruler of Charlemagne's stature, they could encourage belief in the great warlord king, Arthur. Arthurian legends made the monarchy appear to begin around 450 AD with King Arthur unifying the nation, rather than as was recorded with Egbert, King of Wessex, becoming king of all England in 827.

Tracing ancestry back to the ancient Picts through Drustan of Talorc, it must now be mentioned that the largest portion of intact Arthurian art is connected with the Tristram branch of the legends. The triangle of uncle, uncle's wife, and hero was of early Irish origin, but became localized in the Arthurian legends in Tintagel Castle, high on rock cliffs overlooking the sea in Brittany. Tintagel Castle is also where Uther Pendragon, with Merlin's assistance, had relations with Igraine, wife of Gorlois, Duke of Cornwall, to produce the infant Arthur. The addition to the Tristram tale of the two Iseults and the story of the black-and-white sails also show ancient Arabic and Greek influences, so the Tristram legends may have both the oldest and the farthest-reaching branches within the Matter of Britain. The tale lent itself easily to French conceptions of courtly love with many pictures of the lovers sharing wine, playing chess, or sitting under a tree, and, since so many secular manuscripts were illustrated in Paris, there are numerous extant copies of books with many pictures concerning the Tristram and Iseult tragedy.

The oldest visualization of the Tristram story is on an ivory box, probably intended as a lady's jewel case, dated around 1200 from Cologne. It is engraved with pictures telling the entire Tristram tale. Other boxes and tiles, dated from about the same time, also display scenes from the Tristram cycle, reflecting the great popularity of the tale. The most common scene portrayed is the "Tryst beneath a Tree" wherein King Mark spies on the lovers from behind branches. It is clear that artists hated Mark and rooted for Tristram and Iseult's love to prevail because the king is always shown stalking the lovers as he lurks in the bushes with an evil expression on his unattractive face. Mark is also frequently shown in profile, which is artistic shorthand for a character who has malice on his mind. The entire tale is condensed in and therefore recalled by this one evocative scene.

While medieval inventories list enormous numbers of decorative items made of metals, most were destroyed by their owners when taken to a goldsmith for refurbishing into a more contemporary design. Pillaging in war was certainly problematic in the secular world, but usually large cathedrals had sealed vaults to protect valuables through the centuries. Further, in smaller churches where the crosses or candlesticks at least remained intact, intricate patterns do not reflect Arthurian subjects, probably because of some of the immoral characters. One metal piece in the Victoria and Albert Museum is a salt cellar from 1482 made in the shape of a ship model that shows Tristran and Isode on board the ship stopping a chess game to gaze lovingly at each other as they hold hands across the board.

More inclusive of Tristram's adventures as a knight—rather than his prowess in amour—is a tile pavement in an abbey near Windsor. The tiles, which display thirty-five scenes of the hero's life, was apparently funded by Henry III in 1270. As one would expect of a religious retreat, only three tiles deal with the lovers while the rest are action scenes. The area is called the "King's Walk," apparently because Henry visited and not to reflect upon Tristram who was not a king, but a lusty warrior knight.

There are six German medieval embroidery pieces representing the Tristram story. The finest were created by nuns in the Cistercian Convent of Wienhauser in Hanover in the fourteenth century. The earliest of these Cistercian pieces is dated around 1310. Several quilts made by Sicilian needle workers as wedding gifts around 1395 depict the Tristram adventures. Also, Tristram and Lancelot are among six heroes posed around Venus on a tray of the popular type called *desco da parto* that is now in the Louvre. These trays were gifts given to a mother on the birth of her child, and this particular tray has been dated at around 1400 because of the heroes' clothing. Rays of light emanating from between Venus's legs mark the tray with a frank sensuality, perhaps concentrating upon the power and the value of the source of life to cheer a new mother.

A castle called Schloss Ronkelsten on the outskirts of Bolzano, Italy, has extensive murals in several rooms intended to display the owners' refinement and elegance via his knowledge of chivalric literature. Triumvirates abound so we find Arthur, Charlemagne, and Godfry of Bologne as the three greatest Christian heroes; Perceval, Gawain, and Iwain are noted as the three best knights. The three sets of best lovers includes Tristran and Isolde. King Arthur frequently appears in depictions of the nine worthies along with Hector, Alexander, Julius Caesar, Joshua, David, Judas Maccabeus, Charlemagne, and Godfrey. Fifteen scenes from Gottfried von Strassburg's *Tristan* adorn the castle's ladies' chamber, and seem excessively bloody for a room meant for relaxation. There is, however, a scene of Tristram naked in the bath that would surely titillate the ladies.

The castle's new owner as of 1388 probably commissioned the murals sometime soon after rights to the building were acquired. It should be noted that there are several dwarves in these Arthurian murals and in many other such medieval works, especially from Italy. Dwarves abound as symbols of gentilesse or they are just included for good luck. Often a dwarf wears the same armor or ornately embellished gown as his or her patron when they are both painted together. It was rare for members of the nobility to be without their dwarves, and so they are often included in artwork. This adoration of the childlike adult can be seen in the tale of Percival who knows nothing of the world.

The Perceval story was very popular in the medieval period and many examples of visual depictions from that cycle survive. There are seven known illustrated manuscripts of the Perceval tale, perhaps because the many Christian elements relevant to this knight's story made religious copyists and artists more willing to spend the time on it; naturally, they were more likely to undertake pictorial representations that involved some portion of Jesus's life, such as the Holy Grail, and then to protect such an effort. Beyond its Christian elements, the grail legend is ultimately linked to the most ancient fertility myths wherein the land is only as healthy as its leader; the productivity of the people, of the land, and of the Fisher King were viewed as one. When the king, like Arthur, does not reproduce or leave an heir, the women and livestock are barren, and the land produces only ash. Famine is caused by the cursed leader and can only be lifted through him.

In the grail legend, the king has a wound in his thigh that can only be healed by someone who asks the correct question and thus fixes his "broken sword" and restores health to the wasteland, the women, and the ruler. The king has a chalice that feeds him or an older king a mythical substance that keeps him alive; the cauldron of plenty is found, in ancient mythology, as a magical substance that maintains life in a time of peril. This chalice, or the Holy Grail, in the Fisher King's castle, is traditionally believed to be the vessel used by Jesus to serve wine at the Last Supper and also used to collect Jesus's blood as He hung on the cross. Drinking from the cauldron of plenty or the grail chalice often changes the character's sphere of reality, for example, making a hero remain in fairy land forever or taking a person to heaven.

Legend has it that this chalice was brought to England by Joseph of Arimithea and then lost. The knights of Camelot ride out on a quest to find the missing Holy Grail; most do not return from the hunt alive. On his quest, Percival finds the grail castle and the Fisher King, but does not ask the necessary question. Ultimately, Galahad the Pure finds the Holy Grail and is then taken up to Heaven along with it. During the thirteenth and fourteenth centuries, the *Queste del Saint Grail* was one of the most frequently illustrated manuscripts. As one would imagine, this portion of the Arthurian legends was especially popular also during the highly moral Victorian era when Galahad was held up as an example of perfect manhood.

The grail picture most often reinvented by artists is the chalice processional through a castle before the wandering eyes of feasters. Usually a beautiful, young girl ends the processional holding the jewel encrusted, golden grail. The girl is frequently identified as the "grail maiden," or Elaine, who, along with Lancelot, the best secular knight, produced Galahad, the pure Christ figure able to attain the vessel on a quest because it is God's will. The grail is placed on a table by the maiden, reflecting both the Last Supper and the significance of Arthur's Round Table and its brotherly love. Indeed, all of the symbolism involved in grail literature and art is multileveled, reflecting biblical exegesis, Arthurian legend, and often ancient fertility myths of Welsh and Celtic origin. Church beliefs and church illustrators had large influence on *L'Estorie del Seint Graal* as seen in the nearly perfect correspondence of Christian symbolism with Arthurian legends.

Often illustrated was *Perceval* or *Le Conte du Graal* (c. 1191) by Chrétien de Troyes in which Percival is shown as a *dümmlingkind*, a naive boy raised in the wilderness. The manuscript of *Parzival* in the Bavarian State Library in Munich (that was probably published in Strasburg between 1228 and 1236) has Parzival nearly committing fratricide and seeing a champagne like grail cup. A later manuscript from the same shop and probably created by the same scribe shows women with long, crimped hair and wimple head coverings typical of the time. The dragon in the manuscript resembles a Disney character with its long ears and blue legs. These miniatures are very neat and detailed, unlike the sloppy work done later.

The boy Percival's chivalric education contains many atypical spiritual elements leading to the hero finding but not attaining the grail, called a dish in Chrétien's work that apparently serves communion wafers and foreshadows Galahad's vision at Sarras that implies the Ascension. In Arthurian typology, Galahad symbolizes Jesus, while Percival is fallen man with the potential for redemption. It is Galahad who heals the maimed Fisher King and restores the wasteland to a fertile abundance, but the tongue-tied Percival did find the Fisher King first; his mistake was in not asking the correct question because he had been told that knights do not speak excessively.

Medieval illustrators of *Percival, L'Estoire,* and *Le Queste* used pictorial representations to make Christian significance clearer while still emphasizing critical Matter of Britain moments; for example, Galahad drawing a sword from a stone just as Arthur did to become king, or transubstantiation shown by a cross inside the grail. While such visualizations are different, they are helpful and a departure from the many battle illustrations necessary because of Arthurian plots that are moved along by fighting and generally end in some sort of bloodbath; they are forerunners to Shakespeare's tragedies that also denouement with nearly everybody being killed. Arthur's story ends in a giant battle scene where all the knights kill each other, as do Mordred and Arthur, leaving only Bedivere alive to return the sword Excalibur to the Lady of the Lake. Such Arthurian stories as *Mort Artu* depend upon scenes of mortal combat as do most French volumes before the mid-1300s. Such illustrations highlight various weapons like swords, shields, and spears. To show serious slaughter, we see heaping piles of bodies after a battle or boats full of infants that the king has ordered to be drowned. The intent is gory and clear despite problems with perspective, proportion, and angularity.

The Black Death and the Hundred Years' War did nothing good for the art and literature of France and England. Little artwork exists in England from 1330—80. By the end of the fourteenth century, illustrated manuscripts were a luxury commissioned by individual patrons. To ensure their own immortality, patrons and their families are used in the pictures to depict famous characters. Powerful Italian families long ago entranced with Arthurian legends heard from Norman knights and Breton minstrels were often wealthy enough to employ their own scribes and illustrators within their own castle walls who incorporated their family coats of arms into pictures. Medieval Italians seemed especially interested in Arthur of Britain, and there was now a new artistic style to suit the connoisseurship of artistic patrons. The Byzantine conventions—wherein there was no concern for proportion and horses were larger than trees or people were bigger than castles—gave way to the new Giottesque style; suddenly figures have normal size and volume and everything seems more three dimensional.

Tapestries, bed curtains, and bench coverings in medieval castles apparently had lots of Arthurian images woven into them, but material decorations of the sort used frequently in domestic life tended to disintegrate fairly rapidly from use and cleaning. As with the metalwork, various medieval home inventories note such fabrics as having Arthurian characters, often with a patron's face for one of the heroes, but they have been lost. Lots of castles had great halls adorned with knights jousting in tournaments. Depictions of medieval women are few, perhaps because of their limited role in society. Generally, ladies are bored looking, tournament spectators. The more robust male roles are obviously more interesting to paint, particularly knights in armor on horseback going into battle, into a jousting contest, or on a quest. By the end of the fifteenth century, knighthood had ended and so did the popularity of Arthurian legend in literature and art.

Malory, with his *Morte D'Arthur,* was already looking longingly back at a lost time of the brotherhood of loyal feudal knights. When William Caxton reissued the text in 1498, it was illustrated with twenty-one woodcuts of a clumsy, stiff nature. The illustrator was apparently familiar with the text, so the drawings are fully accurate, except for a few notable differences, like the dragon who has transmuted into a monster with three human heads. The next bit of Arthurian literature is Edmund Spenser's *Faerie Queen* (1590) that mentions Arthur and creates a childhood for him previously never touched upon in literature. Prince Arthur meets many challenges and dreams of the Fairy Queen, who is ultimately the future Elizabeth Tudor, the Virgin Queen, for whom Spenser wrote the work. It has only one woodcut of the Red Cross Knight killing a tiny dragon, depicted as much smaller than the text would indicate.

Around the mid-1500s, the historicity of King Arthur began to be seriously doubted by all real scholars, so John Milton's *History of Britain* (1655) notes that Arthur's reign seems unlikely; rather than write about Arthurian legends as he had planned, Milton instead penned *Paradise Lost*. Whether or not King Arthur ever actually existed is still in question today with strong cases being argued for either side. The material also became unpopular because of its many Catholic associations that Protestants disagreed with, and because of its strong association with the Stuarts, particularly through James who was considered by many of his subjects not just Arthur's successor but to *be* an actual reincarnated Arthur. The Hanover's dynasty traced its roots to Germanic Saxons and so a mythic king of the Celtic ancient Britons became undesirable politically.

Enlightenment values of rationalization and classicism made works about the great king, surrounded by fees and other mythological creatures, seem like a crude mockery of reasonable literature. There was also the problem of Arthur being given the sword that made him invincible by the Lady of the Lake, a witch who lived underwater. By the late eighteenth century, an academic interest in history, medieval literature, and romance renewed attention, but Arthur as a subject in a painting did not grace the walls of the Royal Academy again until 1826. That work is *Henry II's Discovery of the Relics of King Arthur in Glastonbury Abbey* by George Cattermole. Here Arthur has not been shipped off to Avalon by three mourning queens and will not be returning when his people most need him—but has died and is buried at Glastonbury.

In 1817 Robert Southey reprinted the 1634 *Le Morte D'Arthur*. This text provided the impetus for the Pre-Raphaelite Brotherhood, whose members—chiefly William Morris, Edward Burne-Jones, and Dante Gabriel Rossetti—greatly admired all things medieval by the 1850s. The Pre-Raphaelites's attention to details of the medieval period had little to do with the sudden public interest in the great King Arthur and the knights of the Round Table in Camelot. In 1847 an oil painting called *King Arthur Carried to the Land of Enchantment* by William Bell Scott was exhibited by the Royal Academy. This quote from *Le Morte* Book XXI, Chapter vii, was attached to the title in the catalog:

> Some men say in many parts of England, that Arthur is not dead; but by the will of our Lord Jesu, carried into the place that he will come again and win the Holy Cross. And men say that it is written on the tomb, "Arthurus, rex quondam, Rex futurus."

This messianic idea of a once and future Christian king was often repeated during the very moralistic Victorian period. The people needed Arthur to return in a sanitized form to encourage their national identity.

Alfred, Lord Tennyson's *Idylls of the King* (1859) cleaned up Malory and added plenty of didacticism to make the story more attractive still to Victorian audiences. The entire failure of Camelot is here blamed upon Guinevere's ongoing lust for Lancelot, and Arthur's incestuous tryst that produced Modred the patricide is omitted, as is Arthur's biblical echo wherein he slays all of the male babies born during a certain period to prevent his son/nephew from growing up. Arthur, of course, is as unsuccessful as Herod was. At this time in England, women were considered angels of the house, and Tennyson made Enid, the "Patient Griselda" figure of lore, into the perfect wife. Enid and the grail damsel were painted for ladies to emulate, while young men were given pictures of Galahad.

In 1847 William Dyce was commissioned to decorate the Queen's Robing Room with scenes from the *Le Morte*, proving that Arthur had found his place as part of the national mythology. The frescoes were treated as personifications of virtuous qualities: "Religion," depicting the vision of Sir Galahad and his company; "Courtesy" showing Tristram harping to a modest and sweet Isolde; "Generosity" reminding the viewer that Lancelot spared Arthur's life at Joyous Garde. "Mercy" showing Sir Gawain swearing to be merciful and "never be against ladies" after he accidentally kills the wife of a knight who had come between them in a fight. The last fresco was left unfinished at Dyce's death in 1861. It was completed later by C. W. Cope, another Westminster painter and called "Hospitality" and showing the admission of Sir Tristram to the fellowship of the Round Table. This painting was the only one in which Prince Albert wanted Arthur included. The legendary king is here at his round table with knights in armor all around him, as well as lovely ladies, minstrel singers, and a white horse galloping into a mead hall. The Queen's Robing Room is successful as a group Gothic revival works stressing neo-Platonic idealism, Aristotelian materiality, allegory, symbolism, and Christian didacticism. The artists of Westminster complained Prince Albert was too involved and constantly checking their work. While these new palace paintings were unseen by the general public, the people were aware of them and more interested than ever in elegant, moral Arthurian characters.

In 1851, perhaps taking its cue from the Queen's Robing Room frescoes, the fledgling Pre-Raphaelite Brotherhood undertook decorating the walls of the Oxford Union Hall, a debate area, library, and reading room, of the great university. The unfinished works have a quality of luminosity attained by applying pure color over white backgrounds. They are also outstanding for their deviation in subject from Christian views to sexual entanglements. Rossetti, Morris, Arthur Hughes, and Val Prinsep are the artists. Rossetti's mural was *Sir Launcelot's Vision of the Sanc Grail*, focusing on the sexual guilt that prevents Launcelot, the bravest of all the knights, from seeing the grail; his vision instead is of Guinevere, and she stands in an apple tree, an obvious allusion to Eve, with her arms outstretched in the branches. Launcelot's lust for the queen costs him the quest and eventually his position as Arthur's right hand and best friend. Rossetti said that he intended to paint a second mural of Launcelot's pure of heart son, Galahad, attaining the grail, but he never did accomplish it.

In 1857 Rossetti painted a small watercolor, *The Damsel of the Sanct Grael*, showing a single, beautiful, full length, golden-haired young woman carrying a cup full of blood and a basket of bread. The grail is again Rossetti's subject in 1864 in a painting called *Sir Galahad, Sir Bors, and Sir Percival Receiving the Sanc Grail*; the crowded picture also includes the damsel of the grail, a dove, Percival's dead sister, and a host of angels. As an artist, Rossetti never left an area empty if he could possibly squeeze in some sort of symbolism.

Morris's Oxford Union mural was called *How Sir Palomydes Loved la Belle Iseult with Exceeding Great Love Out of Measure, and How She Loved Him Not Again but Rather Sir Tristram*. Burne-Jones painted *The Beguiling of Merlin*. All chose Arthurian material about the power of beautiful women to seduce men. This was, of course, completely the opposite direction from Dyce's murals in the Queen's Robing Room, and it was intentional. When these young men—and others who were equally interested in the more robust, raw, and sexual aspects of medievalism, particularly Arthurian legend—formed the Pre-Raphaelite Brotherhood, it is no wonder that their artwork focused on eroticism. The Pre-Raphaelite Brotherhood, by the time of Rossetti, Waterhouse, Burne-Jones, and later Frederich Sandys and Aubrey Beardsley used beautiful women to represent all the beauty in the universe, as well as eternal truth and goodness. Whereas the romantics were always worried about the vice of a femme fatale, the Pre-Raphaelite Brotherhood glorified the seductive powers of lovely women they called "stunners."

The exalting of the sexual aspects of the Arthurian legend by the Pre-Raphaelites was probably a reaction to Alfred Tennyson's "The Lady of Shalott" first published in 1832 and then again in his *Idylls of the King*. The Pre-Raphaelite Brotherhood took their material from Malory but admitted to reading aloud from Tennyson's more sanitized versions at their meetings. The first to paint an Arthurian work after the brotherhood formed was F. G. Stephens with his *Mort D'Arthur* (1849). The unfinished somber work shows the loyal knight Bedivere lifting King Arthur's body away from the desolate landscape. The group continued to develop communal beliefs about the legends that led to a cross fertilization of poems and paintings. One such correspondence is Morris's poem "The Defense of Guinevere" (1858) and Rossetti's pen and ink drawing of *Sir Lancelot in the Queen's Chamber* (1857), which were both composed at about the same time and focus upon sexual intrigue and infidelity. In Rossetti's drawing, Lancelot looks out the window with fear and guilt and holds his sword. Guinevere stands with her hand to her head, about to faint, as her attendants reflect the horror of what is about to happen.

The great knight Lancelot's infidelity had effects of another sort and caused a flurry of nineteen paintings of the Lady of Shalott to be exhibited at the Royal Academy between 1861 and 1913. She is a young girl whose love for Lancelot was never acknowledged by him. Following even a quick perusal of these representations, one is startled by the great variety; the paintings are amazingly dissimilar, and the lady's hair and clothing are many different hues. The character's popularity must be attributed to Tennyson's renditions of her, first in "The Lady of Shalott" (1832) and next in the seventh idyll of *Idylls of the King*. It has been noted that the abundance of symbolic detail in Tennyson's second poem about the Lady was caused by his complex reactions to Pre-Raphaelite art.

Elaine, the lily maid of Astolat, was developed from Malory's character. She lives in purposeful naiveté in a tower where her life is devoted first to art and then to Lancelot, whose worship of the queen destroys any possibility that Elaine's love will be returned. The rejection causes the lady to desire death as the only way she can fashion herself into the queen's competitor. Hence, her elaborate death scene—lying in a boat, clutching a letter to Lancelot in her cold hands, when she is rowed up the River Thames to Camelot by her old, mute male servant—inspired an amazing number of paintings.

Sometimes the lady is shown weaving a tapestry in her high tower, and sometimes she is dying or already dead, but generally she is a still, static character. However, there is one notable exception in the work of William Holman Hunt who designed the illustration of the lady for a reprint of Tennyson's *Idylls*. His first drawing of her in 1850 in pen and chalk foreshadows the wildness of his 1857 version. The scene captures the moment in Tennyson's first "Lady" poem where the weaver looks from her mirror that reflects the world she captures in art, to an actual window in hopes of seeing Lancelot more clearly. The mirror cracks, and the woman is then cursed in the poem, so Hunt shows the thread all wild about her. In Hunt's later version, the lady is actually imprisoned by the loosened threads of her weaving and her long hair stands electrified all about her head as she strains to see Lancelot ride away.

Elizabeth Siddel, associated also with the Pre-Raphaelites, created a similar scene in 1853. The lady looks beyond the crucifix in her window, the symbol of salvation, out to Lancelot, who is her damnation. We see the cracked mirror and the unwoven loom. Rossetti's drawing of 1857 concentrates upon Lancelot gazing upon the lady as she lies dead in her boat reflecting the poem lines where Lancelot says "She has a lovely face; God in his mercy grant her grace, The Lady of Shalott." (169–71). Ultimately, the most famous of the lady paintings is one by John William Waterhouse, *The Lady of Shalott* (1888), where she is between the two worlds of life and death. The curse has come upon her, so she sits in a boat, about to push off toward Camelot. Her weavings drag in the water as they hang from the boat. Her three candles have gone out just as her life is about to be extinguished. Her exquisite beauty and palpable anguish are intense.

Tennyson also inspired artwork reflecting men who are doomed by love. In 1857 he released the idyll that included the story of Nimüe, the seductive Lady of the Lake who beguiles Merlin, overpowers him with magic, and leaves him in a trance of longing for her forever. Burne-Jones had earlier painted the Oxford Union hall mural of this story and returned to the subject when Tennyson's poem came out. Burne-Jones shows the large, powerful figure of Nimüe looking back at Merlin as she is leaving him stranded in a constant, trancelike state of desire. Nimüe here is a scary witch with a Medusa-style head covering, but she is still attractive as is Vivien in Frederick Sandys's 1863 painting of her. Vivien, her beautiful face surrounded by peacock eyes, holds the poison hemlock.

The greatest Arthurian femme fatale, who according to Tennyson caused the deaths of all of Arthur's knights, was painted as a languid, tired lovely woman by Morris in 1858. His oil painting of Guinevere has at times also been identified as Iseult, as both women occupied the artist/poet's thoughts. A woman in medieval costume has just risen from a rumpled bed and is clasping her belt around her waist as she dresses. Her little dog is curled up in the still-warm bed. She is solitary and deep in sorrowful contemplation. Her cramped quarters suggest this is the point in the saga when Mordred has Guinevere locked in a tower as he attempts to steal the king's position.

Also evoking high pathos are the many renditions of Arthur's death. Four were painted in a very short time span: Arthur Hughes's *The Knight of the Sun* (1860); James Archer's *La Mort d'Arthur* (1861); John Mullaster Carrick's *Mort d'Arthur* (1862); and Joseph Noël Paton's *The Death Barge of Arthur* (1862). Archer's painting is probably the best and the most famous. It shows four sad women and Arthur lying with his head in the lap of one. The king is staring and nearly dead. The barge waiting to take them to Avalon, land of the blessed dead, is in the water in the background, and Merlin and Nimüe talk on the beach. An angel with the grail chalice hovers by a tree. Between the painting of these four works, Albert, Victoria's beloved Prince Consort died in 1861. Albert was only forty-two and very popular. His death eventually brought about a decline in the popularity of the monarchy in England, particularly because Victoria was criticized for her prolonged bereavement that lasted forty years until her death.

The Arthurian revival began waning with Albert's death and when Edward VII was crowned in 1901, that time of idealization of monarchy and chivalry was long past. The new king was a corpulent fifty-nine-year-old of dubious moral character who did not inspire interest in British nobility. There was a shift away from painting men of action toward portraying still female forms, such as a repentant Guinevere, a patient Enid, and of course more of the dying Lady of Shalott between 1890 and 1914. The Celtic revival of the 1890s influenced a resurgence of interest in Arthurian legend as it is rooted in Celtic folklore, but the English still preferred all Saxon elements generally, and considered the Anglo-Saxon race the great conquerors of the world. Thus, in effect, admiring chivalry gave way to applauding the brutality required of attack.

The cheery, virtuous side of the legends was, however, kept alive by illustrations for juvenile books, particularly those decorated by Walter Crane, Arthur Rackham, and Aubrey Beardsley. Books teaching decorum and exemplary behavior to boys of necessity expunged parts of the legends and any offensive characters. Walter Crane's watercolors and drawings in Henry Gilbert's *King Arthur's Knights: The Tales Re-Told for Boys and Girls* (1911) were colorful and imaginative. Arthur taking the sword from the stone or presiding at the Round Table are the sorts of scenes inspiring to children. With Crane's picture "Sir Galahad Is Brought Back to the Court of King Arthur," viewers are enthralled by the handsome youth's beautiful blond hair and aquiline nose of the Anglo-Saxon type so admired by the English who believed in the supremacy of classic features.

The most influential pictures of these children's books were Rackham's eighty-seven illustrations for Alfred W. Pollard's abridgement of Malory, *The Romance of King Arthur and His Knights of the Round Table* (1917). Costumes, architecture, and landscape are realistically portrayed. The various monsters are somehow convincingly included in typically medieval scenes. The constant juxtaposition of beauty and evil lends the art its freshness. There may be a monster hiding around any corner and very nearly blending into the realistic countryside.

Beardsley's illustrations for the new J. M. Dent *Morte d'Arthur* brought to a close the Celtic revival's penchant for allegory and moral iconography. As a nineteen-year-old boy, Beardsley rocked the art world with his linear, black and white decorative pages for the new *Morte*. Bare, asymmetrical, and filled with characters who look a bit mad, the Beardsley style was a perfect reflection of modern British sensibilities. He produced 585 chapter headings, borders, and initials, and full and double page illustrations for the text. This new version was widely acclaimed except by William Morris, who threatened Beardsley with a lawsuit.

Many of Beardsley's decorative, energetic lines and abstract flowers are of the art noveau type. The knights are not the war heroes of old, but lie around passively, contemplating the world around them, even smelling the flowers. Britons were shocked by Beardsley's hermaphroditic knights who looked like skinny females, as well as his masculine looking women. The Victorian dichotomy of women as Angel of the House or Demonic Femme Fatale is here subverted in women who are strong and enervating. This shift led to works like Andre Derain's woodcut illustrations for *L'enchanteur pourrisant* (Paris, 1909); one particularly troubling picture is "Vivien Dances on Merlin's Tomb," an all black-and-white picture of a naked woman dancing on a buried skeleton.

Towards the end of his life, William Morris turned his attention to illuminated manuscripts and founded Kelmscott Press to emulate in modern books the beauty of thirteenth and fourteenth century French manuscripts. Morris's energy had been engaged in creating stained glass for various buildings as well as with encouraging medieval looks for household furniture, wall papers, sculptures, and other decorative arts for the home that continue to be popular today. For his books, Morris insisted that the quality of paper, ink, and drawings be the best. Kelmscott Press's most famous work is a beautiful *Chaucer* (1896) because Burne-Jones, Morris's chief illustrator, died before a planned production of a Malory text had begun.

Morris's Malory would most likely have been the best; however, since it was not even undertaken the greatest illustrated work is probably the deluxe, three-volume edition of

Malory that was illustrated by Robert Gibbings in 1936. Gibbings owned the press, The Golden Cockerel, and did all of the printing and decoration of this extraordinary text. Gibbings's knights have a zestful activeness suggesting the chivalric action so popular almost a century earlier. The woodcuts' elongated forms and decorative designs are all of a simple and elegantly abstract quality. "The Last Battle," Gibbings's wood engraving of the *Morte*'s scene of Mordred killing his father, Arthur, is moving and tense with rounded plants and curved human shapes highlighting the straight edges of the lance and sword.

While previously in America the British penchant for bringing back their medieval period had seemed absurd and affected, there developed a great feeling of nostalgia by the early 1900s. A country in its infancy, struggling with the effects of industrialization and immigration, suddenly chose to embrace the national myths of England as its own sometime after the publication of Mark Twain's *A Connecticut Yankee in King Arthur's Court* (1889). The cowboy of the Wild West became a knight chivalrously performing heroic deeds. American art and art movements were imitative and there was no adoption of the native American form, so for the arts and crafts movements here, Morris's decorative arts were copied almost exactly. Handicrafts included furniture, wood figures, rugs, and pottery all covered in artwork originating in England or found in English narratives.

The Boston Public Library is a good example of the Gothic Revival reflected in America. Edwin Austin Abbey was asked in 1890 to paint a frieze 180 feet by 8 feet in the library's delivery room. Abbey chose to reflect the Holy Grail legends in fifteen scenes, moving from Galahad's infancy to his vision of the unveiled chalice. The Holy Grail was also featured in Princeton University's dining hall as a stained glass bay window designed by Charles Connick. For Princeton University Chapel's stained glass windows (1931), Connick also used a few scenes from Malory's *Morte*—along with Dante's *Divine Comedy*, Milton's *Paradise Lost*, and Bunyan's *Pilgrim's Progress* to signify man's search for God.

The habit of critiquing historical, political, social, and cultural events or people through Arthuriana entered popular culture, especially before World War II. For example, in Hal Foster's *Prince Valiant* comic strip, medieval knights battled Nazis disguised as Huns. Camelot endured in America as a prototype of leadership both monumentally effective and ultimately ineffective, a kind of government intended to be pure and stable, but destroyed in the end. From his Celtic background, military achievements, regal persona, and administration style to his brutal death, Camelot was the perfect symbol of John F. Kennedy and his presidency.

Drawings of Kennedy as Arthur both serious and comedic abound, and can be seen as the root of contemporary use of Arthuriana. The modern American outpouring of thousands of Arthurian novels, television programs, movies, drawings, scholarly and popular articles proves that the habit of recreating the Camelot narrative to discuss social problems cannot be kicked. That this phenomenon has occurred primarily in America is odd, but much like the early English kings who built and displayed a fake Round Table in order to look more rooted, perhaps Americans cling to Arthur as a means of feeling more substantial. In response to the many late twentieth century antifeministic terms used to describe Arthur's court, there are now many retellings and art works with a feminist slant: women-oriented spiritualism, goddess worship, wicca groups, matriarchal communities led by three queens and examples of powerful, dominant women as medieval warriors.

While Americans admire the moral qualities implied by some aspects of the legends, they tend to use more Arthurian names and pictures as hooks for advertising than any other purpose. They also use them more than any other nationality, perhaps lamenting a lack of their own royalty. Despite the fact that there are more Americans of Germanic ethnic descent than any other, they are still greatly attached to England's national mythology and want to live in the Camelot Trailer Park or have dinner at the Excalibur Restaurant. Americans have ignored the mythology of our indigenous peoples and did little to promote stories like Johnny Appleseed and Paul Bunyan.

Arthurian comic books, graphic novels, board games, and computer games all appeal largely to an audience of adolescent males which reminds one of the Victorian youth in England who read illustrated Arthurian juvenile manuscripts. However, one wonders about the necessity of hook names with X-rated comics like *Arthur Sex* and *Camelot Uncensored* or the online Excalibur porn site. Realizing that historical literature need not be mimetic, not an imitation of events in the world, but narrative designed as discourse about the world removes questions of King Arthur's actual existence as a man and allows us to focus upon his life as a symbol. Apparently even the modern commercial employment of King Arthur as product endorser has been unable to render him an empty signifier; the once and future king continues to reign.

Arthurian legends are a complex reworking of previously existing narratives and ideologies that are ever both anachronistic and contemporary. Following suit, the art always stems from the stories. The costumes, characters, and settings generally are intended to reflect the early medieval period, but the themes of fate, guilty passion, and loyalty are universal, not in the sense of timeless meaning, but because new writers and artists in each period care enough to mutate or reinvent the lesson to be gleaned about Camelot's tragedy; thus aesthetic judgments about the point of Arthuriana change based upon the historical present. Arthurian themes have ever lent themselves well as a veneer for social criticism; each new interpretation pleads and persuades, making a particular point by shifting the focus to change the significance. Whether Arthur existed as a real human being or not is insignificant inasmuch as his primary job is to provide, as a huge mythological figure, a unifying form for an enormous variety of art and literature about the early medieval period. The historicity, even if it does not accurately reflect historical reality, is one particularly fascinating aspect of Arthurian legends.

SELECTED SOURCES

Alexander, J. J. G. *Italian Renaissance Illumination*. New York: G. Braziller, 1978; Altick, Richard D. *Paintings from Books: Art and Literature in Britain, 1760–1900*. Columbus: Ohio State University Press, 1985; Bentley, D. M. R. "The Pre-Raphaelites and the Oxford Movement." *Dalhousie Review* 57 (1977): 523–37; Brinkley, Roberta F. *Arthurian Legend in the Seventeenth Century*. 1932. Reprint, New York: Octagon, 1967; Casteras, Susan P. *Images of Victorian Womanhood in English Art*. London: Associated University Presses, 1987; Denomy, Alexander J. "Courtly Love and Courtliness." *Speculum* 27 (1953): 44–63; Ditmas, E. M. R. "The Cult of Arthurian Relics." *Folklore* 85, no. 2 (1966): 91–104; Evans, Joan. *Art in Medieval France, 987–1498*. Oxford: Oxford University Press, 1948; Faber, Geoffrey. *Oxford Apostles: A Character Study of the Oxford Movement*. London: Faber and Faber, 1974; Fitzgerald, Penelope. *Edward Burne-Jones: A Biography*. London: Hamish Hamilton, 1975; Gay, Daly. *Pre-Raphaelitism in Love*. London: Fontana, 1990; Gerould, G. H. "Arthurian Romance and the Date of the relief at Modena." *Speculum* 10 (1935): 355–76; Göller, Karl Heinz. "Arthur: Saint and Sinner." *Avalon to Camelot* 2, no. 1 (1986): 11–12; Goodman, E. L. "The Prose Tristan and the Pisanello Murals." *Tristania* 3, no. 2 (1978): 23–25; Gribble, Jennifer. *The Lady of Shalott in the Victorian Novel*. London: Macmillan, 1983; Houghton, Walter E. *The Victorian Frame of*

Mind, 1830–1870. New Haven, CT: Yale University Press, 1957; Jenkins, Elizabeth. *The Mystery of King Arthur*. London: Michael Joseph, 1975; Lee, J. A. "The Illuminating Critic: The Illustration of the Cotton Nero AX." *Studies in Iconography* 3 (1977): 17–46; Loomis, Roger Sherman, ed. *Arthurian Legend in Medieval Art*. London: Oxford University Press, 1938; Loomis, Roger Sherman. "The Legend of Arthur's Survival." In *Arthurian Literature in the Middle Ages: A Collaborative History*, 2nd ed., ed. Roger Sherman Loomis, 64–71. London: Clarendon Press, 1979; Mancoff, Debra N. "'An Ancient Idea of Chivalric Greatness': The Arthurian Revival and Victorian History Painting." In *The Arthurian Tradition: Essays in Convergence*, ed. Mary Flowers Braswell and John Bugge, 127–43. Tuscaloosa: University of Alabama Press, 1988; ———. *The Arthurian Revival in Victorian Art*. New York: Garland, 1990; ———. *The Return of King Arthur: The Legend Through Victorian Eyes*. New York: Harry N. Abrams, 1995; Nevison, John L. "A Show of the Nine Worthies." *Shakespeare Quarterly* 14 (1963): 103–7; Nutt, Alfred. *Studies on the Legend of the Holy Grail with Especial Reference to the Hypothesis of Its Celtic Origin*. London: David Nutt, 1888; Pearsall, Derek, ed. *Manuscripts and Readers in Fifteenth-Century England: The Literary Implications of Manuscript Study*. Totowa, NJ: D. S. Brewer, 1983; Pointon, Marcia. *William Dyce, 1806–1864*. Oxford: Oxford University Press, 1979; Poulson, Christine. "Arthurian Legend in Fine and Applied Art of the Nineteenth and Early Twentieth Centuries: A Catalogue of Artists." *Arthurian Literature* 9 (1989): 81–142; Rorimer, J. J., and M. B. Freeman. "The Nine Heroes Tapestries at the Cloisters." *Metropolitan Museum of Art Bulletin*, new ser., 7 (May 1949): 243–60; Scherer, Margaret. *King Arthur in Art and Literature*. 1945. Reprint, New York: Metropolitan Museum of Art, 1974; Sewter, A. C. *The Stained Glass of William Morris and His Circle*. 2 vols. New Haven, CT: Yale University Press, 1974–1975; Simpson, Roger. *Camelot Regained: The Arthurian Revival and Tennyson, 1800–1849*. Cambridge: D. S. Brewer, 1990; ———. "Update II: Arthurian Legend in Fine and Applied Art of the Nineteenth and Early Twentieth Centuries." *Arthurian Literature* 11 (1992): 81–96; Stein, Richard L. "The Pre-Raphaelite Tennyson." *Victorian Studies* 24 (1981): 279–301; Taylor, Beverly, and Elizabeth Brewer. *The Return of King Arthur: British and American Literature since 1900*. Cambridge: D. S. Brewer, 1983; Watkinson, Ray. *William Morris as Designer*. 1979. Reprint, London: Studio Vista, 1990; Whitaker, Muriel. "The Arthurian Art of David Jones." *Arthuriana* 7, no. 3 (Fall 1997): 137–56; ———. *The Legends of King Arthur in Art*. Cambridge: D. S. Brewer, 1990; Wroot, H. E. "Pre-Raphaelite Windows at Bradford." *Studio* 72 (November 1917): 69–73.

LAURA COONER LAMBDIN AND ROBERT THOMAS LAMBDIN

SELECTED READINGS

Alama, Pauline J. "A Woman in King Arthur's Court: Wendy Mnookin's *Guenever Speaks*." *Quondam et Futurus* 2.2 (Summer 1992): 81–88.

Alcock, Leslie. *Arthur's Britain: History and Archaeology, AD 367–634*. London: Allen Lane/Penguin, 1971.

Allen, Judson Boyce. "The Medieval Unity of Malory's *Morte Darthur*." *Mediaevalia* 6 (1980): 279–309.

Allen, Mark. "The Image of Arthur and the Idea of King." *Arthurian Interpretations* 2.2 (Spring 1988): 1–16.

Allen, Rosamund. "Eorles and Beornes: Contextualizing Lawman's *Brut*." *Arthuriana* 8.3 (Fall 1998): 4–22.

Archibald, Elizabeth, and A. S. G. Edwards, eds. *A Companion to Malory*. Cambridge: D. S. Brewer, 1996.

Ashe, Geoffrey. "A Certain Very Ancient Book." *Speculum* 56 (1981): 301–23.

———. *The Discovery of King Arthur*. New York: Anchor/Doubleday, 1985.

———. "The Origins of the Arthurian Legend." *Arthuriana* 5.3 (Autumn 1995): 1–24.

———, ed. *The Quest for Arthur's Britain*. New York: Praeger, 1968.

Atkinson, Stephen C. B. "'Now I Se and Undirstonde': The Grail Quest and the Education of Malory's Reader." In *The Arthurian Tradition: Essays in Convergence*, ed. Mary F. Braswell and John Bugge. Tuscaloosa: University of Alabama Press, 1988, 90–108.

Baetzhold, Howard G. "The Course of Composition of *A Connecticut Yankee*: A Reinterpretation." *American Literature* 33.2 (May 1961): 195–214.

———. "'The Autobiography of Sir Robert Smith of Camelot': Mark Twain's Original Plan for *A Connecticut Yankee*." *American Literature* 32.4 (January 1961): 456–61.

Bartlett, Anne C. "Cracking the Penile Code: Reading Gender and Conquest in the *Alliterative Morte Arthure*." *Arthuriana* 8.2 (Summer 1998): 56–76.

Batt, Catherine. "Malory and Rape." *Arthuriana* 7.3 (Fall 1997): 78–99.

Batts, Michael. *Gottfried von Strassburg*. New York: Twayne, 1971.

Beal, Rebecca S. "Arthur as the Bearer of Civilization: *The Alliterative Morte Arthure*, ll. 901–19." *Arthuriana* 5.4 (Winter 1995): 33–44.

Beatie, Bruce A. "Arthurian Films and Arthurian Texts: Problems of Reception and Comprehension." *Arthurian Interpretations* 2.2 (Spring 1988): 65–78.

Benson, Larry. *Art and Tradition in Sir Gawain and the Green Knight*. New Brunswick, NJ: Rutgers University Press, 1965.

———. *Malory's Morte Darthur*. Cambridge, MA: Harvard University Press, 1976.

———, ed. *King Arthur's Death: The Middle English Stanzaic Morte Arthur and the Alliterative Morte Arthure*. Revised by Edward E. Foster. Kalamazoo, MI: TEAMS (The Consortium for the Teaching of the Middle Ages) in association with the University of Rochester by Medieval Institute Publications, 1994.

Berkove, Lawrence. "*A Connecticut Yankee*: A Serious Hoax." *Essays in Arts and Sciences* 19 (1990): 28–44.

Blacker, Jean. "Where Wace Feared to Tread: Latin Commentaries on Merlin's Prophecies in the Reign of Henry II." *Arthuriana* 6.1 (Spring 1996): 36–52.

Blanch, Robert J. "George Romero's Knightriders: A Contemporary Arthurian Romance." *Quondam et Futurus* 1.4 (Winter 1991): 61–69.

Blumreich, Kathleen M. "Lesbian Desire in the Old French *Roman de Silence*." *Arthuriana* 7.2 (Summer 1997): 47–62.

Bogdanow, Fanni. "A Little Known Codex, Bancroft ms. 73, and Its Place in the Manuscript Tradition of the Vulgate Queste del SArthurian Interpretations Graal." *Arthuriana* 6.1 (Spring 1996): 1–21.

Boos, Florence. "William Morris, Robert Bulwer–Lytton, and the Arthurian Poetry of the 1850s." *Arthuriana* 6.3 (Fall 1996): 31–53.

Boyd, David L. "Sodomy, Misogyny, and Displacement: Occluding Queer Desire in *Sir Gawain and the Green Knight*." *Arthuriana* 8.2 (Summer 1998): 77–114.

———. "Tennyson's Camelot Revisited: An Augustinian Approach to the *Idylls*." In *The Arthurian Tradition: Essays in Convergence*, ed. Mary F. Braswell and John Bugge. Tuscaloosa: University of Alabama Press, 1988, 163–74.

Brewer, Elisabeth. *Sir Gawain and the Green Knight: Sources and Analogues*. 2nd ed. Woodbridge, UK: D. S. Brewer, 1992.

———. *T. H. White's The Once and Future King*. Cambridge: D. S. Brewer, 1993.

Brodman, Marian Masiuk. "Terra Mater–Luxuria Iconography and the Caradoc Serpent Episode." *Quondam et Futurus* 2.3 (Fall 1992): 38–45.

Bromwich, Rachel, ed. and trans. *Trioedd Ynys Prydein: The Welsh Triads*. 2nd ed. Cardiff: University of Wales Press, 1978.

Bromwich, Rachel, A. O. H. Jarman, and Brynley F. Roberts, eds. *The Arthur of the Welsh: The Arthurian Legend in Medieval Welsh Literature*. Cardiff: University of Wales Press, 1991.

Brown, Emerson, Jr. "Review of *Approaches to Teaching the Arthurian Tradition*." *Arthuriana* 4.1 (Spring 1994): 84–87.

Bruce, Christopher W. *The Arthurian Name Dictionary*. New York: Garland, 1998.

Bruce, James Douglas. *The Evolution of Arthurian Romance from the Beginnings Down to the Year 1300*. 2 vols. 2nd ed. Baltimore: Johns Hopkins University Press, 1928.

Brumlik, Joan. "The Knight, the Lady, and the Dwarf in Chrétien's *Erec*." *Quondam et Futurus* 2.2 (Summer 1992): 54–72.

Bryan, Elizabeth J. "Truth and the Round Table in Lawman's *Brut*." *Quondam et Futurus* 2.4 (Winter 1992): 27–35.

Bulger, Thomas. "Mark Twain's Ambivalent Utopianism." *Studies in American Fiction* 17 (1989): 235–42.

Bullough, Vern L. "Medieval Concepts of Adultery." *Arthuriana* 7.4 (Winter 1997): 5–15.

Bumke, Joachim. *Courtly Culture: Literature and Society in the High Middle Ages*, trans. Thomas Dunlap. Berkeley: University of California Press, 1991.

Busby, Keith. *Gauvain in Old French Literature*. Amsterdam: Rodopi, 1980.

Buschinger, Danielle. "Les Problèmes de la Traduction des Textes Médiévaus Allemands dans les Langues Modernes." *Arthuriana* 4.3 (Fall 1994): 224–32.

Carley, James P. "Polydore Vergil and John Leland on King Arthur: The Battle of the Books." *Arthurian Interpretations* 15.2 (Spring 1984): 86–100.

Carpenter, Christine. *The Wars of the Roses: Politics and the Constitution in England, c. 1437–1509.* Cambridge: Cambridge University Press, 1997.

Chrétien de Troyes. *Lancelot, or the Knight of the Cart,* trans. Ruth Harwood Cline. Athens: University of Georgia Press, 1990.

———. *Perceval, or the Story of the Grail,* trans. Ruth Harwood Cline. Athens: University of Georgia Press, 1983.

———. *Romans Arthuriens,* ed. Michel Zink. Paris: Livre de Poche, 1994.

———. *Yvain, or the Knight with the Lion,* trans. Ruth Harwood Cline. Athens: University of Georgia Press, 1975.

Cochran, Rebecca. "Swinburne's Concept of the Hero in The Tale of Balen." *Arthurian Interpretations* 1.1 (Fall 1986): 47–53.

———. "Edwin Arlington Robinson's Arthurian Poems: Studies in Medievalisms?" *Arthurian Interpretations* 3.1 (Fall 1988): 49–60.

Cohen, Jeffrey Jerome, and the Members of Interscripta. "The Armour of an Alienating Identity." *Arthuriana* 6.4 (Winter 1996): 1–24.

Collins, Frank. "A Semiotic Approach to Chrétien de Troyes's *Erec et Enide.*" *Arthurian Interpretations* 15.2 (Spring 1984): 25–31.

Curley, Michael J. "Arthurian Literature of the Middle Ages: A National Endowment for the Humanities Summer Seminar for Secondary School Teachers." *Arthuriana* 4.4 (Winter 1994): 392–401.

Curtis, Jan. "Byzantium and the Matter of Britain: The Narrative Framework of Charles Williams's Later Arthurian Poems." *Quondam et Futurus* 2.1 (Spring 1992): 28–54.

———. "Charles Williams's 'The Sister of Percivale': Towards a Theology of Theotokos." *Quondam et Futurus* 2.4 (Winter 1992): 56–72.

———. "A Confluence of Pagan-Celtic and Christian Traditions in Charles Williams's 'Bors to Elayne: The Fish of Broceliande.'" *Arthuriana* 6.1 (Spring 1996): 96–111.

Curtis, Renée L. "The Perception of the Chivalric Ideal in Chrétien de Troyes's *Yvain.*" *Arthurian Interpretations* 3.2 (Spring 1989): 1–22.

Dalrymple, Scott. "Just War, Pure and Simple: *A Connecticut Yankee in King Arthur's Court* and the American Civil War." *American Literary Realism* 29 (Fall 1996): 1–11.

Day, Mildred Leake. "Scarlet Surcoat and Gilded Armor: The Literary Tradition of Gawain's Costume in *Sir Gawain and the Green Knight* and *De ortu Waluuanii.*" *Arthurian Interpretations* 15.2 (Spring 1984): 53–58.

Dean, Christopher. *Arthur of England: English Attitudes to King Arthur and the Knights of the Round Table in the Middle Ages and the Renaissance.* Toronto: University of Toronto Press, 1987.

———. "The Many Faces of Merlin in Modern Fiction." *Arthurian Interpretations* 3.1 (Fall 1988): 61–78.

Dick, Ernst S. "The German Gawein: *Diu Crône* and *Wigalois.*" *Arthurian Interpretations* 15.2 (Spring 1984): 11–17.

Dillon, Bert. *A Malory Handbook.* Boston: G. K. Hall, 1978.

Dittmar, Mary Lynne. "A Psychologist Responds to 'A Little Acknowledged Theme.'" *Quondam et Futurus* 1.4 (Winter 1991): 36–38.

Doherty, John J. "'A land shining with goodness': Magic and Religion in Stephen R. Lawhead's Taliesin, Merlin, and Arthur." *Arthuriana* 9.1 (Spring 1999): 57–66.

Donahue, Dennis P. "The Darkly Chronicled King: An Interpretation of the Negative Side of Arthur in Lawman's *Brut* and Geoffrey's *Historia.*" *Arthuriana* 8.4 (Winter 1998): 135–47.

Douglass, Rebecca M. "Missed Masses: Absence and the Function of the Liturgical Year in *Sir Gawain and the Green Knight.*" *Quondam et Futurus* 2.2 (Summer 1992): 20–27.

Dumville, David. "Sub-Roman Britain: History and Legend." *History* 62 (1977): 173–91.

Eckhardt, Caroline D. "Prophecy and Nostalgia: Arthurian Symbolism at the Close of the English Middle Ages." In *The Arthurian Tradition: Essays in Convergence,* ed. Mary F. Braswell and John Bugge. Tuscaloosa: University of Alabama Press, 1988, 109–26.

Edwards, Elizabeth. *The Genesis of Narrative in Malory's Morte Darthur.* Cambridge: D. S. Brewer, 2001.

Entwhistle, W. J. *Arthurian Legend in the Literatures of the Spanish Peninsula.* London: Dent, 1925.

Everett, Dorothy. "Layamon and the Earliest Middle English Alliterative Verse." In *Essays on Middle English Literature*, ed. Patricia Kean. Oxford: Clarendon Press, 1955, 23–45.

Falsani, Teresa Boyle. "Parke Godwin's Guenevere: An Archetypal Transformation." *Quondam et Futurus* 3.3 (Fall 1993): 55–65.

Farrell, Thomas J. "Life and Art, Chivalry and Geometry in Sir Gawain and the Green Knight." *Arthurian Interpretations* 2.2 (Spring 1988): 17–33.

Farrier, Susan E. "Erex saga and the Reshaping of Chrétien's *Erec et Enide*." *Arthurian Interpretations* 4.2 (Spring 1990): 1–11.

Fehrenbacher, Richard. "The Domestication of Merlin in Malory's *Morte Darthur*." *Quondam et Futurus* 3.4 (Winter 1993): 1–16.

Ferrante, Joan M. *The Conflict of Love and Honor: The Medieval Tristan Legend in France, Germany, and Italy.* The Hague: Mouton, 1973.

Field, Peter J. C. "Caxton's Roman War." *Arthuriana* 5.2 (Summer 1995): 31–73.

———. *The Life and Times of Sir Thomas Malory.* Arthurian Studies, no. 29. Cambridge: D. S. Brewer, 1993.

———. "Malory and the French Prose *Lancelot*." *Bulletin of the John Rylands University Library of Manchester* 75.1 (Spring 1993): 79–102.

———. *Malory: Texts and Sources.* Cambridge: D. S. Brewer, 1998.

———. "Malory and *The Wedding of Sir Gawain* and *Dame Ragnell*." *Archiv fur das studium der neuren sprachen und literaturen* 219 (1982): 374–81.

———. *Romance and Chronicle: A Study of Malory's Prose Style.* Bloomington: University of Indiana Press, 1971.

Finke, Laurie A., and Martin B. Shichtman. "No Pain, No Gain: Violence as Symbolic Capital in Malory's *Morte d'Arthur*." *Arthuriana* 8.2 (Summer 1998): 115–33.

Fleissner, Robert F. "Sir John Falstaff Atilt with Sir Gawayne: A Mock-Arthurian Reversal." *Arthurian Interpretations* 1.1 (Fall 1986): 35–38.

Flood, John L. "Arthurian Romance and German Heroic Poetry." In *The Arthur of the Germans: The Arthurian Legend in Medieval German and Dutch Literature*, ed. W. H. Jackson and S. A. Ranawake. Cardiff: University of Wales Press, 2000, 231–41.

Fowler, David C. "The Quest of Balin and the Mark of Cain." *Arthurian Interpretations* 15.2 (Spring 1984): 70–74.

Fox-Friedman, Jeanne. "Howard Pyle and the Chivalric Order in America: King Arthur for Children." *Arthuriana* 6.1 (Spring 1996): 77–95.

Frappier, Jean. *Chrétien de Troyes: The Man and His Work*, trans. Raymond J. Cormier. Athens: Ohio University Press, 1982.

Fries, Maureen. "The Arthurian Moment: History and Geoffrey's *Historia regum Britanniae*." *Arthuriana* 8.4 (Winter 1998): 88–99.

———. "Boethian Themes and Tragic Structure in Geoffrey of Monmouth's *Historia Regum Britanniae*." In *The Arthurian Tradition: Essays in Convergence*, ed. Mary F. Braswell and John Bugge. Tuscaloosa: University of Alabama Press, 1988, 29–42.

———. "From the Lady to the Tramp: The Decline of Morgan le Fay in Medieval Romance." *Arthuriana* 4.1 (Spring 1994): 1–18.

Fulton, Helen. "A Woman's Place: Guinevere in the Welsh and French Romances." *Quondam et Futurus* 3.2 (Summer 1993): 1–25.

Fuog, Karin E. C. "Imprisoned in the Phallic Oak: Marion Zimmer Bradley and Merlin's Seductress." *Quondam et Futurus* 1.1 (Spring 1991): 73–88.

Furtado, Antonio. *The History of the Kings of Britain*, trans. Lewis Thorpe. Harmondsworth, UK: Penguin, 1966.

———. "From Alexander of Macedonia to Arthur of Britain." *Arthuriana* 5.3 (Autumn 1995): 70–86.

————. "Geoffrey of Monmouth: A Source of the Grail Stories." *Quondam et Futurus* 1.1 (Spring 1991): 1–14.

————. "The Arabian Nights: Yet Another Source of the Grail Stories?" *Quondam et Futurus* 1.3 (Fall 1991): 25–40.

————. "'Arthur Had an Affair with an Amazon'—Says Senator Carucius." *Quondam et Futurus* 2.3 (Fall 1992): 31–36.

————. "A Source in Babylon." *Quondam et Futurus* 3.1 (Spring 1993): 38–59.

————. "From Alexander of Macedonia to Arthur of Britain." *Arthuriana* 5.3 (Autumn 1995): 70–86.

Furtado, Antonio, and Paulo A. S. Veloso. "Folklore and Myth in *The Knight of the Cart*." *Arthuriana* 6.2 (Summer 1996): 28 43.

Gamble, Giles Y. "Power Play: Elizabeth I and The Misfortunes of Arthur." *Quondam et Futurus* 1.2 (Summer 1991): 59–69.

Gardner, Edmund G. *Arthurian Legend in Italian Literature*. London: Dent, 1930.

Gates, Robert, ed. *The Awntyrs off Arthure at the Terne Wathelyn: A Critical Edition*. Philadelphia: University of Pennsylvania Press, 1969.

Geoffrey of Monmouth. *Historia Regum Britanniae*, ed. Neil Wright. Cambridge: D. S. Brewer, 1985.

Gilmore, Gloria Thomas. "Le Roman de Silence: Allegory in Ruin or Womb of Irony?" *Arthuriana* 7.2 (Summer 1997): 111–23.

Girouard, Mark. *Return to Camelot: Chivalry and the English Gentleman*. New Haven, CT: Yale University Press, 1981.

Glowka, Arthur Wayne. "Malory's Sense of Humor." *Arthurian Interpretations* 1.1 (Fall 1986): 39–46.

Goodman, Jennifer R. *Malory and Caxton's Prose Romances of 1485*. New York: Garland, 1987.

Goodrich, Peter, ed. *The Romance of Merlin*. New York: Garland, 1990.

Gottfried von Strassburg. *Tristan, with the Surviving Fragment of the Tristan of Thomas*, trans. A. T. Hatto. Harmondsworth, UK: Penguin, 1960.

Goyne, Jo. "Parataxis and Causality in the Tale of Sir Launcelot du Lake." *Quondam et Futurus* 2.4 (Winter 1992): 36–48.

————. "Arthurian Wonder Women: The Tred of Olwen." *Arthuriana* 9.2 (Summer 1999): 5 10.

Gray, James Martin. *Thro' the Vision of the Night: A Study of Source, Evolution and Structure in Tennyson's Idylls of the King*. Edinburgh: Edinburgh University Press, 1980.

Greene, Wendy Tibbets. "Malory's Merlin: An Ambiguous Magician?" *Arthurian Interpretations* 1.2 (Spring 1987): 56–63.

Griffith, Richard R. "The Political Bias of Malory's *Morte Darthur*." *Viator* 5 (1974): 365–86.

Grimm, Kevin. "Editing Malory: What's at (the) Stake?" *Arthuriana* 5.2 (Summer 1995): 5–14.

————. "Knightly Love and the Narrative Structure of Malory's Tale Seven." *Arthurian Interpretations* 3.2 (Spring 1989): 76–95.

————. "The Reception of Malory's *Morte Darthur* Medieval and Modern." *Quondam et Futurus* 2.3 (Fall 1992): 1–14.

Gross, Gregory W. "Secret Rules: Sex, Confession, and Truth in *Sir Gawain and the Green Knight*." *Arthuriana* 4.2 (Summer 1994): 146–74.

Haghofer, Natascha U. *The Fall of Arthur's Kingdom: A Study of Tennyson's The Holy Grail*. Salzburg: University of Salzburg Press, 1997.

Hahn, Stacey L. "The Motif of the Errant Knight and the Royal Maiden in the Prose *Lancelot*." *Arthurian Interpretations* 3.1 (Fall 1988): 1–15.

Hall, Louis B., ed. *The Knightly Tales of Gawain*. Chicago: Nelson-Hall, 1976.

Hamel, Mary. "Adventure as Structure in the *Alliterative Morte Arthure*." *Arthurian Interpretations* 3.1 (Fall 1988): 37–48.

Hanks, D. Thomas. "Malory, Dialogue, and Style." *Quondam et Futurus* 3.3 (Fall 1993): 24–34.

———. "Malory's Book of Sir Tristram: Focusing *Le Morte Darthur*." *Quondam et Futurus* 3.1 (Spring 1993): 14–31.

———, ed. *The Social and Literary Contexts of Malory's Morte Darthur*. Cambridge: D. S. Brewer, 2000.

Harrington, David V. "The Conflicting Passions of Malory's Sir Gawain and Sir Lancelot." *Arthurian Interpretations* 1.2 (Spring 1987): 64–69.

Hartmann von Aue. *Erec*, trans. J. W. Thomas. Lincoln: University of Nebraska Press, 1982.

———. *Iwein*, ed. and trans. Patrick M. McConeghy. New York: Garland, 1984.

Harty, Kevin. "Cinema Arthuriana: Translations of the Arthurian Legend to the Screen." *Arthurian Interpretations* 2.1 (Fall 1987): 95–113.

———. *Cinema Arthuriana: Essays on Arthurian Film*. New York: Garland, 1991.

———. "Looking for Arthur in All the Wrong Places: A Note on M. Night Shyamalan's *The Sixth Sense*." *Arthuriana*. 10 (4) Winter 2000: 57–62.

———. "Cinema Arthuriana: A Bibliography of Selected Secondary Material." *Arthurian Interpretations* 3.2 (Spring 1989): 119–37.

———. "Television's *The Adventures of Sir Lancelot*." *Quondam et Futurus* 1.4 (Winter 1991): 71–79.

———. "The Knights of the Square Table: The Boy Scouts and Thomas Edison Make an Arthurian Film." *Arthuriana* 4.4 (Winter 1994): 313–23.

Haug, Walter. "Reinterpreting the Tristan Romances of Thomas and Gotfrid: Implications of a Recent Discovery." *Arthuriana* 7.3 (Fall 1997): 45–59.

Helm, Joan. "The Celestial Circle: Fées, Philosophy, and Numerical Circularity in Medieval Arthurian Romances." *Arthurian Interpretations* 3.1 (Fall 1988): 25–36.

———. "Nature's Marvel: Enide as Earth Measure in an Early Arthurian Manuscript." *Quondam et Futurus* 1.3 (Fall 1991): 1–24.

———. "Erec, the Hebrew Heritage: Urban Tigner Holmes Vindicated." *Quondam et Futurus* 2.1 (Spring 1992): 1–15.

Herman, Harold J. "The Women in Mary Stewart's Merlin Trilogy." *Arthurian Interpretations* 15.2 (Spring 1984): 101–14.

———. "Sharan Newman's Guinevere Trilogy." *Arthurian Interpretations* 1.2 (Spring 1987): 39–55.

———. "Sir Kay, Seneschal of King Arthur's Court." *Arthurian Interpretations* 4.1 (Fall 1989): 1–31.

Hess, Scott. "Jousting in the Classroom: Teaching the Arthurian Legend." The Round Table: Teaching King Arthur at Harvard. *Arthuriana* 9.1 (Spring 1999): 133–38.

Hinton, Norman D. "The Language of the Gawain-Poems." *Arthurian Interpretations* 2.1 (Fall 1987): 83–94.

Hodges, Laura F. "Steinbeck's Dream Sequence in *The Acts of King Arthur and His Noble Knights*." *Arthurian Interpretations* 4.2 (Spring 1982): 35–49.

———. "Steinbeck's Adaptation of Malory's Launcelot: A Triumph of Realism over Supernaturalism." *Quondam et Futurus* 2.1 (Spring 1992): 69–81.

———. "'Syngne,' 'Conysaunce,' 'Deuys': Three Pentangles in *Sir Gawain and the Green Knight*." *Arthuriana* 5.4 (Winter 1995): 22–31.

Hoffman, Donald L. "The Third British Emperor." *Arthurian Interpretations* 15.2 (Spring 1984): 1–10.

———. "The Ogre and the Virgin: Varieties of Sexual Experience in Malory's *Morte Darthur*." *Arthurian Interpretations* 1.1 (Fall 1986): 19–25.

———. "Malory's Tragic Merlin." *Quondam et Futurus* 1.2 (Summer 1991): 15–31.

———. "Isotta Da Rimini: Gabriele D'Annunzio's Use of the Tristan Legend in His *Francesca da Rimini*." *Quondam et Futurus* 2.3 (Fall 1992): 46–54.

———. "Pomorex: Arthurian Tradition in Barthelme's *The King*, Acker's *Don Quixote*, and Reed's *Flight to Canada*." *Arthuriana* 4.4 (Winter 1994): 376–86.

————. "Perceval's Sister: Malory's Rejected Masculinities." *Arthuriana* 6.4 (Winter 1996): 72–83.

————. "Guenevere the Enchantress." *Arthuriana* 9.2 (Summer 1999): 30–36.

Hoffman, Donald L., and Maureen Fries. "In Memoriam Jeanne T. Mathewson." *Quondam et Futurus* 1.4 (Winter 1991): 106–8.

Hopkirk, Susan. "The Return of the King: Arthur in Canada." In *Pioneering North America: Mediators of European Culture and Literature*, ed. Klaus Martens and Andreas Hau. Wurzburg, Germany: Konigshausen & Neumann, 2000, 184–92.

Howard, Donald, and C. K. Zacher, eds. *Critical Studies of Sir Gawain and the Green Knight*. Notre Dame, IN: University of Notre Dame Press, 1968.

Howey, Ann F. "Queens, Ladies, and Arthurian Interpretations: Arthurian Women in Contemporary Short Fiction." *Arthuriana* 9.1 (Spring 1999): 23–38.

Howlett, D. R. "The Literary Context of Geoffrey of Monmouth: An Essay on the Fabrication of Sources." *Arthuriana* 5.3 (Autumn 1995): 25–69.

Hughes, Linda K. "'All That Makes a Man': Tennyson's *Idylls of the King* as a Primer for Modern Gentlemen." *Arthurian Interpretations* 1.1 (Fall 1986): 54–63.

Hyatte, Reginald. "Tristran's Monologues as a Narrative Model in Thomas's *Roman de Tristan*." *Arthurian Interpretations* 15.2 (Spring 1984): 32–41.

Ihle, Sandra N. "The Art of Adaptation in Malory's Books Seven and Eight." *Arthurian Interpretations* 15.2 (Spring 1984): 75–85.

Ingham, Patricia Clare. "Masculine Military Unions: Brotherhood and Rivalry in *The Avowing of King Arthur*." *Arthuriana* 6.4 (Winter 1996): 25–44.

Jackson, W. H. "The Arthurian Material and German Society in the Middle Ages." In *The Arthur of the Germans: The Arthurian Legend in Medieval German and Dutch Literature*, ed. W. H. Jackson and S. A. Ranawake. Cardiff: University of Wales Press, 2000, 280–92.

Jackson, W. T. H. *The Anatomy of Love: The Tristan of Gottfried von Strassburg*. New York: Columbia University Press, 1971.

Jaech, Sharon L. Jansen. "The Parting of Lancelot and Gaynor: The Effect of Repetition in the *Stanzaic Morte Arthur*." *Arthurian Interpretations* 15.2 (Spring 1984): 59–69.

Jamison, Carol Parrish. "A Description of the Medieval Romance Based upon *King Horn*." *Quondam et Futurus* 1.2 (Summer 1991): 44–58.

Jankofsky, Klaus P. "'America' in Parke Godwin's Arthurian Novels." *Arthurian Interpretations* 4.2 (Spring 1990): 65–80.

Jeffrey, David Lyle, ed. *A Dictionary of Biblical Tradition in English Literature*. Grand Rapids: Eerdmans, 1992.

Jung, E., and M-L Von Franz. *The Grail Legend*. Boston: Sigo, 1986.

Kaylor, Noel Harold, Jr. "Teaching Diversity of Medieval Thought in Undergraduate Courses." *Arthurian Interpretations* 4.1 (Fall 1989): 32–42.

Keen, Maurice. *Chivalry*. New Haven, CT: Yale University Press, 1984.

Keller, Joseph. "The Ambiguity of Prowess: Knights, Sorceresses, and Enchanted Places—Chiefly in Malory." *Arthurian Interpretations* 1.1 (Fall 1986): 1–11.

————. "Paradigm Shifts in the Grail Scholarship of Jessie Weston and R. S. Loomis: A View from Linguistics." *Arthurian Interpretations* 1.2 (Spring 1987): 10–22.

Kellogg, Judith L. "Economic and Social Tensions Reflected in the Romances of Chrétien de Troyes." *Romance Philology* 39 (August 1985): 1–21.

Kelly, Douglas. *The Romances of Chrétien de Troyes: A Symposium*. Lexington, KY: French Forum, 1985.

Kelly, Kathleen Coyne. "Malory's Body Chivalric." *Arthuriana* 6.4 (Winter 1996): 52–71.

————. "Malory's Multiple Virgins." *Arthuriana* 9.2 (Summer 1999): 21–29.

Kennedy, Beverly. "Notions of Adventure in Malory's *Morte Darthur*." *Arthurian Interpretations* 3.2 (Spring 1989): 38–59.

————. "Adultery in Malory's *Le Morte d'Arthur*." *Arthuriana* 7.4 (Winter 1997): 63–91.

————. *Knighthood in the Morte d'Arthur*. Cambridge: D. S. Brewer, 1992.

Kennedy, Edward Donald. "Malory's Guenevere: 'A Woman Who Had Grown a Soul.'" *Arthuriana* 9.2 (Summer 1999): 37–45.

Kennedy, Elspeth. *Lancelot and the Grail: A Study of the Prose Lancelot*. Oxford: Clarendon Press, 1986.

Kenney, Alice P. "Yankees in Camelot: The Democratization of Chivalry in James Russell Lowell, Mark Twain, and Edwin Arlington Robinson." *Studies in Medievalism* 1.2 (Spring 1982): 73–78.

Kibler, William W., ed. *The Lancelot-Grail Cycle: Text and Transformations*. Austin: University of Texas Press, 1994.

Kim, Jongsoon. "Mark Twain's Ambivalence Toward Progress: A Study of *Connecticut Yankee in King Arthur's Court*." *Journal of English and Literature* 36.4 (1990): 643–57.

Kindrick, Robert L. "The Administration of Justice in Malory's Works." *Arthurian Interpretations* 2.1 (Fall 1987): 63–81.

Kindrick, Robert L., ed., with the assistance of Michele R. Crepeau. "William Matthews on Caxton and Malory." *Arthuriana* 7.1 (Spring 1997): 3–133.

Kinoshita, Sharon. "Two for the Price of One: Courtly Love and Serial Polygamy in the Lais of Marie de France." *Arthuriana* 8.2 (Summer 1998): 33–55.

Kirchhoff, Frederick. "'The Glory and Freshness of a Dream': Arthurian Romance as Reconstructed Childhood." *Arthuriana* 6.3 (Fall 1996): 3–13.

Kirk, Elizabeth D. "'Wel Bycommes Such Craft Upon Cristmasse': The Festive and the Hermeneutic in *Sir Gawain and the Green Knight*." *Arthuriana* 4.2 (Summer 1994): 93–137.

Knepper, Wendy. "Theme and Thesis in *Le Chevalier de la Charrete*." *Arthuriana* 6.2 (Summer 1996): 54–68.

Knight, Stephen. *Arthurian Literature and Society*. New York: St. Martin's Press, 1983.

Kordecki, Lesley C. "Twain's Critique of Malory's Romance: *Forma tractandi* and *A Connecticut Yankee*." *Nineteenth-Century Literature* 41.3 (December 1986): 329–48.

Krishna, Valerie, trans. *Five Middle English Arthurian Romances*. New York: Garland, 1990.

Labbie, Erin F. "The Specular Image of the Gender-Neutral Name: Naming Silence in Le Roman de Silence." *Arthuriana* 7.2 (Summer 1997): 63–77.

Lacy, Norris J. "Arthurian Film and the Tyranny of Tradition." *Arthurian Interpretations* 4.1 (Fall 1989): 75–85.

————. "The Arthurian Ideal in Pierre Sala's *Tristan*." *Arthurian Interpretations* 1.2 (Spring 1987): 1–9.

————. *The Craft of Chrétien de Troyes: An Essay on Narrative Art*. Leiden: Brill, 1980.

————. "Medieval French Arthurian Literature in English." *Quondam et Futurus* 1.3 (Fall 1991): 55–74.

————. "Emergent Direct Discourse in the Vulgate Cycle." *Arthuriana* 4.1 (Spring 1994): 19–29.

————. "From Medieval to Post-Modern: The Arthurian Quest in France." *South Atlantic Review*. 65 (2) Spring 2000: 114–33.

————, ed. *Medieval Arthurian Literature: A Guide to Recent Research*. New York: Garland, 1996.

Lacy, Norris J., ed. and trans. *Béroul. Romance of Tristan*. New York: Garland, 1989.

Lacy, Norris J., Geoffrey Ashe et al., eds. *The Arthurian Handbook*. 2nd ed. New York: Garland, 1997.

————. *The New Arthurian Encyclopedia*. Updated paperback ed. New York: Garland, 1996.

Lacy, Norris J., Douglas Kelly, and Keith Busby, eds. *The Legacy of Chrétien de Troyes*. 2 vols. Amsterdam: Rodopi, 1987–1988.

Lagorio, Valerie M. "Foreword." *Interpretations A Journal of Idea, Analysis, and Criticism: Arthurian Interpretations* 15.2 (Spring 1984): v.

Lagorio, Valerie M., and Mildred Leake Day, eds. *King Arthur Through the Ages*. 2 vols. New York: Garland, 1990.

Lambdin, Laura. "Swinburne's Early Arthurian Poems: Shadows of His Mature Vision." *Quondam et Futurus* 3.4 (Winter 1993): 63–76.

Lambert, Mark. *Malory: Style and Vision in Le Morte Darthur.* New Haven, CT: Yale University Press, 1975.

Lancelot-Grail: The Old French Arthurian Vulgate and Post-Vulgate in Translation, ed. Norris J. Lacy. 5 vols. New York: Garland, 1993–1996.

Last, Rex, ed. *The Arthurian Bibliography.* 3 vols. Cambridge: D. S. Brewer, 1985. Supplement 1979–1983. Cambridge: D. S. Brewer, 1987.

Layamon. *Brut*, ed. G. L. Brook and R. F. Leslie. Published for the Early English Text Society. London: Oxford University Press, 1963.

Leckie, R. William, Jr. "Mutable Substance: The Diamond Helmet and the Death of Gahmuret in Wolfram's *Parzival.*" *Arthurian Interpretations* 3.2 (Spring 1989): 23–37.

Life, Page West. *Sir Thomas Malory and the Morte Darthur: A Survey of Scholarship and Annotated Bibliography.* Charlottesville: Bibliographical Society of the University of Virginia, 1980.

Littleton, Scott, and Linda Malcor. *From Scythia to Camelot: A Radical Reassessment of the Legends of King Arthur, the Knights of the Round Table, and the Holy Grail.* New York: Garland, 1994.

———. "Some Notes on Merlin." *Arthuriana* 5.3 (Autumn 1995): 87–95.

Loomis, Roger Sherman, ed. *Arthurian Literature in the Middle Ages: A Collaborative History.* Oxford: Clarendon Press, 1959. 2nd ed., Oxford: Clarendon Press, 1961.

———. *The Development of Arthurian Romance.* New York: Harper and Row, 1963.

Loomis, Roger Sherman, and Laura Hibbard Loomis. *Arthurian Legends in Medieval Art.* London: Oxford University Press, 1938.

Lumiansky, R. M. *Malory's Originality.* Baltimore: Johns Hopkins University Press, 1963.

Lumpkin, Bernard. "The Once and Future Course: Teaching the Arthurian Legend." The Round Table: Teaching King Arthur at Harvard. *Arthuriana* 9.1 (Spring 1999): 130–33.

Lupack, Alan. "A Bibliography of Critical Studies of Mark Twain's *A Connecticut Yankee in King Arthur's Court.*" *An Arthuriana/Camelot Project Bibliography.* Available online at http://www.lib.rochester.edu/camelot/acpbibs/twainbib.htm.

———. "The Arthurian Legend in America: A Moderated Discussion on 'Arthurnet.'" *Arthuriana* 4.4 (Winter 1994): 291–97.

———. "Merlin in America." *Arthurian Interpretations* 1.1 (Fall 1986): 64–74.

Lupack, Alan, and Barbara Tepa Lupack. "F. Scott Fitzgerald's 'Following of a Grail.'" *Arthuriana* 4.4 (Winter 1994): 324–47.

MacBain, Danielle Morgan. "Love Versus Politics: Competing Paradigms of Chivalry in Malory's *Morte Darthur.*" *Quondam et Futurus* 2.3 (Fall 1992): 22–30.

MacDonald, Aileen A. *The Figure of Merlin in the Thirteenth Century French Romance.* New York: Edwin Mellen Press, 1990.

Machann, Clinton. "Tennyson's King Arthur and the Violence of Manliness." *Victorian Poetry* 38 (2) Summer 2000: 199–226.

Maddox, Donald. *The Arthurian Romances of Chrétien de Troyes: Once and Future Fictions.* Cambridge: Cambridge University Press, 1991.

Mahoney, Dhira B. "Hermits in Malory's *Morte Darthur*: The Fiction and the Reality." *Arthurian Interpretations* 2.1 (Fall 1987): 1–26.

Malory, Sir Thomas. *Caxton's Malory*, ed. James W. Spisak. 2 vols. Berkeley: University of California Press, 1983.

———. *Works*, 3 vols., 3rd ed., ed. Eugene Vinaver, rev. P. J. C. Field. Oxford: Clarendon Press, 1990.

Mancoff, Debra N. *The Arthurian Revival in Victorian Art.* New York: Garland, 1990.

———. "Introduction: William Morris and King Arthur." *Arthuriana* 6.3 (Fall 1996): 1–2.

———. "Problems with the Pattern: William Morris's Arthurian Imagery." *Arthuriana* 6.3 (Fall 1996): 55–68.

———. "*Rex Quondam Rexque Ens.*" *Quondam et Futurus* 2.3 (Fall 1992): 55–68.

Mandel, Jerome. "Elements in the Charrette World: The Father-Son Relationship." *Modern Philology* 62 (1964): 97–104.

————. "Proper Behavior in Chretien's *Charrette*: The Host-Guest Relationship." *The French Review* 48 (1975): 683–89.

Marie de France. *The Lais of Marie de France*, trans. Glyn S. Burgess and Keith Busby. Harmondsworth, UK: Penguin, 1986.

Mathewson, Jeanne T. "Sir Gawain and the Medieval School of Comedy." *Arthurian Interpretations* 15.2 (Spring 1984): 42–52.

McCarthy, Terence. *An Introduction to Malory*. Cambridge: D. S. Brewer, 1991.

McDonald, William C. "Wolfram's Grail." *Arthuriana* 8.1 (Spring 1998): 22–34.

McFarland, Timothy. "The Emergence of the German Grail Romance: Wolfram von Eschenbach, *Parzival*." In *The Arthur of the Germans: The Arthurian Legend in Medieval German and Dutch Literature*, ed. W. H. Jackson and S. A. Ranawake. Cardiff: University of Wales Press, 2000, 54–68.

Meister, Peter. "Arthurian Literature as a Distorted Model of Christianity." *Quondam et Futurus* 1.2 (Summer 1991): 32–43.

Mickel, Emanuel J., Jr. *Marie de France*. New York: Twayne, 1974.

Moorman, Charles. "'Yet Some Men Say ... that Kynge Arthure Ys Nat Ded.'" In *The Arthurian Tradition: Essays in Convergence*, ed. Mary F. Braswell and John Bugge. Tuscaloosa: University of Alabama Press, 1988, 188–99.

Moorman, Charles, and Ruth Minary. *An Arthurian Dictionary*. Chicago: Academy Chicago, 1990.

Morris, Rosemary. *The Character of King Arthur in Medieval Literature*. Cambridge: D. S. Brewer, 1982.

Muller, Ulrich, and Werner Wunderlich. "The Modern Reception of the Arthurian Legend." In *The Arthur of the Germans: The Arthurian Legend in Medieval German and Dutch Literature*, ed. W. H. Jackson and S. A. Ranawake. Cardiff: University of Wales Press, 2000, 303–23.

Nennius. *Nennius: British History and the Welsh Annals*, ed. and trans. John Morris. Chichester, UK: Phillimore, 1980.

Nickel, Helmut. "Why Was the Green Knight Green?" *Arthurian Interpretations* 2.2 (Spring 1988): 58–64.

Nitze, W. A. *Arthurian Romance and Modern Poetry and Music*. Chicago: University of Chicago Press, 1940.

Owen, D. D. R., ed. *Arthurian Romance: Seven Essays*. New York: Barnes and Noble, 1971.

Parins, Marylyn Jackson. "Malory's Expurgators." In *The Arthurian Tradition: Essays in Convergence*, ed. Mary F. Braswell and John Bugge. Tuscaloosa: University of Alabama Press, 1988, 144–62.

————. *Sir Thomas Malory, the Critical Heritage*. London; New York: Routledge, 1995.

————. "Two Early 'Expurgations' of *Morte Darthur*." *Arthuriana* 7.3 (Fall 1997): 60–77.

Parry, Joseph D. "Narrators, Messengers, and Lawman's *Brut*." *Arthuriana* 8.3 (Fall 1998): 46–61.

Paxon, Diana L. "Marion Zimmer Bradley and *The Mists of Avalon*." *Arthuriana* 9.1 (Spring 1999): 110–26.

Pearsall, Derek. "Teaching 'The Story of Arthur.'" The Round Table: Teaching King Arthur at Harvard. *Arthuriana* 9.1 (Spring 1999): 127–30.

Peyton, Henry Hall, III. "Wagner and the Arthurian Legend." *Arthuriana* 11 (1) Spring 2001: 93–107.

Phillips, Graham, and Martin Keatman. *King Arthur: The True Story*. London: Century Random House, 1992.

Pickens, Rupert T. "Arthur's Channel Crossing: Courtesy and the Demonic in Geoffrey of Monmouth and Wace's *Brut*." *Arthuriana* 7.3 (Fall 1997): 3–19.

————, ed. *The Sower and His Seed: Essays on Chrétien de Troyes*. Lexington, KY: French Forum, 1983.

Pickford, Cedric E., and Rex Last, eds. *The Arthurian Bibliography, I: Author Listing*. Cambridge: D. S. Brewer, 1981; and *II: Subject Index*. Cambridge: D. S. Brewer, 1983.

Pigg, Daniel F. "Language as Weapon: The Poetics of Plot in Malory's 'Tale of Sir Gareth.'" *Quondam et Futurus* 2.1 (Spring 1992):16–27.

Pigott, Stuart. "The Sources of Geoffrey of Monmouth." *Antiquity* 15 (1941).

Plummer, John F. "Frenzy and Females: Subject Formation in Opposition to The Other in the *Prose Lancelot*." *Arthuriana* 6.4 (Winter 1996): 45–51.

Poag, James F. *Wolfram von Eschenbach*. New York: Twayne, 1972.

Pochoda, Elizabeth. *Arthurian Propaganda: Le Morte Darthur as an Historical Ideal of Life*. Chapel Hill: University of North Carolina Press, 1971

Psaki, Regina F. "The Modern Editor and Medieval 'Misogyny': Text Editing and *Le Roman de Silence*." Arthuriana 7.2 (Summer 1997): 78–86.

Ragland, Ellie. "Psychoanalysis and Courtly Love." *Arthuriana* 5.1 (Spring 1995): 1–20.

Ranawake, Silvia. "The Emergence of German Arthurian Romance: Hartmann von Aue and Ulrich von Zatzikhoven." In *The Arthur of the Germans: The Arthurian Legend in Medieval German and Dutch Literature*, ed. W. H. Jackson and S. A. Ranawake. Cardiff: University of Wales Press, 2000, 38–53.

Reiss, Edmund, Louise Horner Reiss, and Beverly Taylor. *Arthurian Legend and Literature: An Annotated Bibliography, I: The Middle Ages*. New York: Garland, 1984.

Ricciardi, Marc. "'Se What I Shall Do as for My Trew Parte': Fellowship and Fortitude in Malory's 'Noble Tale of King Arthur and the Emperor Lucius.'" *Arthuriana* 11 (2) Summer 2001: 20–31.

Riddy, Felicity. *Sir Thomas Malory*. Leiden and New York: Brill, 1987.

Rider, Jeff. "The Perpetual Enigma of Chrétien's Grail Episode." *Arthuriana* 8.1 (Spring 1998): 6–21.

Ringel, Faye J. "Pluto's Kitchen: The Initiation of Sir Gareth." *Arthurian Interpretations* 1.2 (Spring 1987): 29–38.

Robertson, D. W., Jr. "The Concept of Courtly Love as an Impediment to the Understanding of Medieval Texts." In *The Meaning of Courtly Love*, ed. F. X. Newman. Albany, NY: SUNY Press, 1968, 1–18.

———. "Some Medieval Terminology with Special Reference to Chrétien de Troyes." *Studies in Philology* 48 (1951): 669–92.

Robertson, Kellie. "Geoffrey of Monmouth and the Translation of Insular Historiography." *Arthuriana* 8.4 (Winter 1998): 42–57.

Rockwell, Paul. "Remembering Troie: the Implication of Ymages in the *Roman de Troie* and the *Prose Lancelot*." *Arthuriana* 7.3 (Fall 1997): 20–35.

Rollo, David. "Three Mediators and Three Venerable Books: Geoffrey of Monmouth, Mohammed, Chrétien de Troyes." *Arthuriana* 8.4 (Winter 1998): 100–114.

Romance of Tristan, trans. Renée L. Curtis. Oxford: Oxford University Press, 1994.

Rosenberg, Samuel N. "Merlin in Medieval French Lyric Poetry." *Quondam et Futurus* 1.4 (Winter 1991): 1–18.

Rossignol, Rosalyn. "The Holiest Vessel: Maternal Aspects of the Grail." *Arthuriana* 5.1 (Spring 1995): 52–61.

Rowe, John Carlos. "How the Boss Played the Game: Twain's Critique of Imperialism in *A Connecticut Yankee in King Arthur's Court*." In *The Cambridge Companion to Mark Twain*, ed. Forrest Robinson. Cambridge: Cambridge University Press, 1995, 175–92.

Sacker, Hugh D. *An Introduction to Wolfram's Parzival*. Cambridge: Cambridge University Press, 1963.

Salda, Michael N. "William Faulkner's Arthurian Tale: Mayday." *Arthuriana* 4.4 (Winter 1994): 348–75.

Samples, Susann. "Guinevere: A Re-Appraisal." *Arthurian Interpretations* 3.2 (Spring 1989): 106–18.

———. "Guinevere: A Germanic Heroine." *Quondam et Futurus* 1.4 (Winter 1991): 9–22.

Sanders, Arnold A. "Malory's Transition Formulae: Fate, Volition, and Narrative Structure." *Arthurian Interpretations* 2.1 (Fall 1987): 27–46.

Sandler, Florence Field. "Family Romance in *The Once and Future King*." *Quondam et Futurus* 2.2 (Summer 1992): 73–80.

Saunders, Corinne J. *The Forest of Medieval Romance: Avernus, Broceliande, Arden*. Cambridge: D. S. Brewer, 1993.

Scherer, Margaret. *King Arthur in Art and Literature*. New York: Metropolitan Museum of Art, 1945.

Schwartz, Debora B. "The Horseman Before the Cart: *Le Chevalier de la Charrete* and Intertextual Theory." *Arthuriana* 6.2 (Summer 1996): 11–27.

Sears, Theresa Ann. "'And Fall Down at His Feet': Signifying Guinevere in Chrétien's *Chevalier de la Charrete*." *Arthuriana* 6.2 (Summer 1996): 44–53.

Shichtman, Martin B. "Percival's Sister: Genealogy, Virginity, and Blood." *Arthuriana* 9.2 (Summer 1999): 11–20.

Shichtman, Martin B., and James Carley, eds. *Culture and the King: the Social Implications of the Arthurian Legend*. Albany, NY: SUNY Press, 1994.

Simpson, Roger. "William Fulford: An Arthurian Reclaimed." *Quondam et Futurus* 1.1 (Spring 1991): 56–72.

———. "Merlin and Hull: A Seventeenth–Century Prophecy." *Quondam et Futurus* 3.1 (Spring 1993): 60–65.

———. "A Minor Road to Camelot: Once a Week, 1859–1867." *Arthuriana* 4.1 (Spring 1994): 46–69.

———. "The Nannu Oak: Bulwer Lytton and his Midsummer Knight at the Westminster Round Table." *Arthuriana* 7.3 (Fall 1997): 124–36.

———. *Camelot Regained: The Arthurian Revival and Tennyson, 1800–1849*. Cambridge: D. S. Brewer, 1990.

Sir Gawain and the Green Knight, ed. and trans. William Vantuono. New York: Garland, 1991.

Sklar, Elizabeth S. "Adventure and the Spiritual Semantics of Malory's *Tale of the Sankgreal*." *Arthurian Interpretations* 2.2 (Spring 1988): 34–46.

Sleeth, Charles R. "Gawain's Judgment Day." *Arthuriana* 4.2 (Summer 1994): 175–83.

Sloane, Patricia. "Richard Wagner's Arthurian Sources, Jessie L. Weston, and T. S. Eliot's *The Waste Land*." *Arthuriana* 11 (1) Spring 2001: 30–53.

Smith, Evans Lansing. "The Arthurian Underworld of Modernism: Thomas Mann, Thomas Pynchon, Robertson Davies." *Arthurian Interpretations* 4.2 (Spring 1990): 50–64.

———. "The Narrative Structure of T. H. White's *The Once and Future King*." *Quondam et Futurus* 1.4 (Winter 1991): 39–52.

Spearing, Anthony C. *The Gawain-Poet*. Cambridge: Cambridge University Press, 1970.

———. "Public and Private Spaces in *Sir Gawain and the Green Knight*." *Arthuriana* 4.2 (Summer 1994): 138–45.

Staines, David. *Tennyson's Camelot: The Idylls of the King and Its Medieval Sources*. Waterloo, Canada: Wilfrid Laurier University Press, 1982.

Stanley, E. G. "Layamon's Antiquarian Sentiments." *Medium Ævum* 38 (1969): 23–37.

Stephenson, Will, and Mimosa Stephenson. "Proto-Modernism in Tennyson's 'The Holy Grail.'" *Quondam et Futurus* 2.4 (Winter 1992): 49–55.

Sterling-Hellenbrand, Alexandra. "Women on the Edge in *Parzival*: A Study of the 'Grail Women.'" *Quondam et Futurus* 3.2 (Summer 1993): 56–68.

Stock, Lorraine Kochanske. "Arms and the (Wo)man in Medieval Romance: The Gendered Arming of Female Warriors in the *Roman d'Eneas* and Heldris's *Roman de Silence*." *Arthuriana* 5.4 (Winter 1995): 56–83.

———. "The Importance of Being Gender 'Stable': Masculinity and Feminine Empowerment in *Le Roman de Silence*." *Arthuriana* 7.2 (Summer 1997): 7–34.

Stone, Gregory L. "Chrétien de Troyes and Cultural Materialism." *Arthuriana* 6.2 (Summer 1996): 69–87.

Struve, Laura. "The Public Life and Private Desires of Women in William Morris's 'Defence of Guenevere.'" *Arthuriana* 6.3 (Fall 1996): 15–28.

Sturges, Robert S. "Chrétien de Troyes in English Translation: A Guide to the Issues." *Arthuriana* 4.3 (Fall 1994): 205–23.

———. "Chrétien's *Knight of the Cart* and Critical Theory." *Arthuriana* 6.2 (Summer 1996): 1–10.

———. "Epistemology of the Bedchamber: Textuality, Knowledge, and the Representation of Adultery in Malory and the *Prose Lancelot*." *Arthuriana* 7.4 (Winter 1997): 47–62.

———. "La(ca)ncelot." *Arthurian Interpretations* 4.2 (Spring 1990): 12–23.

Surles, Robert L. "Mark of Cornwall: Noble, Ignoble, Ignored." *Arthurian Interpretations* 3.2 (Spring 1989): 60–75.

Sutton, Anne F., and Livia Visser-Fuchs. "The Dark Dragon of the Normans: A Creation of Geoffrey of Monmouth, Stephen of Rouen, and Merlin Silvester." *Quondam et Futurus* 2.2 (Summer 1992): 1–19.

Swinburne, Algernon. "Under the Microscope." In *Swinburne Replies: Notes on Poems and Reviews*. Syracuse, NY: Syracuse University Press, 1966.

Takamiva, Toshiyuki, and Derek Brewer, eds. *Aspects of Malory*. Cambridge: D. S. Brewer, 1981.

Taylor, Beverly, and Elisabeth Brewer. *The Return of King Arthur: British and American Arthurian Literature since 1900*. Cambridge: D. S. Brewer, 1983.

Thomas, Alfred. "King Arthur and His Round Table in the Culture of Medieval Bohemia and in Medieval Czech Literature." In *The Arthur of the Germans: The Arthurian Legend in Medieval German and Dutch Literature*, ed. W. H. Jackson and S. A. Ranawake. Cardiff: University of Wales Press, 2000, 249–56.

Thomas, Patrick Michael. "Circle as Structure: The Tristan of Thomas." *Quondam et Futurus* 1.3 (Fall 1991): 41–54.

———. "Tristan and the Avatars of the Lunar Goddess." *Quondam et Futurus* 2.3 (Fall 1992): 15–21.

Thomas of Britain. *Tristan*, ed. and trans. Stewart Gregory. New York: Garland, 1991.

Thompson, Ayanna. "'It lives dispersedly in many hands, And every minstrel sings it differently': Tennyson and the Comparative Approach to 'The Story of Arthur.'" The Round Table: Teaching King Arthur at Harvard. *Arthuriana* 9.1 (Spring 1999): 138–41.

Thompson, Raymond H. "Morgause of Orkney, Queen of Air and Darkness." *Quondam et Futurus* 3.1 (Spring 1993): 1–13.

———. *The Return from Avalon: A Study of the Arthurian Legend in Modern Fiction*. Westport, CT: Greenwood Press, 1985.

Tichelaar, Tyler R. "Creating King Arthur's Children: A Trend in Modern Fiction." *Arthuriana* 9.1 (Spring 1999): 39–56.

Toledo Neto, Silvio de Almeida. "Liuro de Josep Abaramatia and the Works of Robert de Boron." *Quondam et Futurus* 3.3 (Fall 1993): 36–45.

Tolhurst, Fiona. "The Britons as Hebrews, Romans, and Normans: Geoffrey of Monmouth's British Epic and Reflections of Empress Matilda." *Arthuriana* 8.4 (Winter 1998): 69–87.

Tolmie, Jane. "Can We Talk about 'Multiple Versions of the Same Thing' in a Meaningful Way?" The Round Table: Teaching King Arthur at Harvard. *Arthuriana* 9.1 (Spring 1999): 141–43.

Torregrossa, Michael. "Camelot 3000 and Beyond: An Annotated Listing of Arthurian Comic Books Published in the United States, c. 1980–1998." *Arthuriana* 9.1 (Spring 1999): 67–109.

Ulrich von Zatzikoven. *Lanzelet*, trans. Kenneth G. T. Webster. New York: Columbia University Press, 1951.

Van Der Schaff, Baukje Finet. "*The Lai de Tyolet* and *Lancelot and the Whitefooted Stag*: Two Romances Based on a Folktale Motif." *Arthuriana* 4.3 (Fall 1994): 233–49.

Van Domelen, John E. "'Take Down, Callipe, Your Trumpet': A Poet of the Third Dark Age Celebrates a Hero of the Second." *Arthurian Interpretations* 4.1 (Fall 1989): 55–74.

Vinaver, Eugene. *Form and Meaning in Medieval Romance*. Leeds, UK: Maney, 1966.

———. *Malory*. Oxford: Clarendon Press, 1929.

———. *The Rise of Romance*. Oxford: Clarendon Press, 1971.

Wace. *Le Roman de Brut*, 2 vols., ed. I. Arnold. Paris: Champion, 1938–1940.

Wambach, Annemarie. "Strickers Daniel von dem blühenden Tal Ein 'klassischer' Artusroman?" *Arthuriana* 6.1 (Spring 1996): 53–76.

Warren, Michelle R. "Making Contact: Postcolonial Perspectives through Geoffrey of Monmouth's *Historia regum Britannie*." *Arthuriana* 8.4 (Winter 1998): 115–34.

Waters, Elizabeth A. "The Third Path: Alternative Sex, Alternative Gender in *Le Roman de Silence*. *Arthuriana* 7.2 (Summer 1997): 35–46.

Watson, Jeanie. "Mary Stewart's Merlin: Word of Power." *Arthurian Interpretations* 1.2 (Spring 1987): 70–83.

Watson, Jonathan. "Affective Poetics and Scribal Reperformance in Lawman's *Brut*: A Comparison of the Caligula and Otho Versions." *Arthuriana* 8.3 (Fall 1998): 62–75.

Weinberg, Carole. "Þ at kinewurde bed [a bed fit for a king]: Thematic Wordplay in Lawman's *Brut*." *Arthuriana* 8.3 (Fall 1998): 33–45.

Wheeler, Bonnie, et al., eds. *The Malory Debate: Essays on the Texts of Le Morte Darthur*. Cambridge: D. S. Brewer, 2000.

Whitaker, Muriel. "The Arthurian Art of David Jones." *Arthuriana* 7.3 (Fall 1997): 137–56.

———. *Legends of King Arthur in Art*. Cambridge: D. S. Brewer, 1990.

Wilson, Robert H. "Malory in the *Connecticut Yankee*." *University of Texas Studies in English* 27 (1948): 185–205.

Withrington, John. "'He Telleth The Number of the Stars; He Calleth Them All by Their Names' The Lesser Knights of Sir Thomas Malory's *Morte D'Arthur*." *Quondam et Futurus* 3.4 (Winter 1993): 17–27.

Wolfram von Eschenbach. *Parzival*, trans. A. T. Hatto. Harmondsworth, UK: Penguin, 1980.

Zimmer, H. *The King and the Corpse*. Princeton, NJ: Bollingen, 1956.

INDEX

Boldface page numbers indicate main entries.

Acts of King Arthur and His Noble Knights, 128, 269–71, 324

Aelfric, 49–50

Aeneas, 50

Agravaine, 232, 279, 325, 326

Albion and Albanius, 157

Alliterative verse, 93

Ambraser Heldenbuch, 60

Ambrosius Aurelianus, 4, 20, 32, 312, 315, 316

Andreas Capellanus, 106

Anglo-Saxons, 8, 9, 20, 45, 47, 48, 49, 53, 93, 104, 375

Annales Cambriae, 1, 31

Annals of Tigernach, 1

Arnold, Matthew, xviii, 135, **165–74**, 187, 195, 220

Arofel, 75

Art, Arthurian, **364–78**

Arthur Rex (Berger), 323, 324, 328–31

Art of Courtly Love, 105

Atwood, Margaret Eleanor, **357–63**

Aurelius, 51, 52

Avalon, xx, 33, 56, 117, 269, 320, 343, 346, 358, 359, 374

Baden, 3, 9, 20, 21, 341

Balan, 269

Balen, 196, 197, 269

Balin. *See* Balen

"Balin and Balan," 196, 207, 214, 355

Ban, 188, 189

Bassas, 19

Beard, Daniel Carter, 224–25, 226

Beauchamp, Richard, 129

Bede, 2, **7–15**, 47, 158

Bedivere, 26, 232

Beowulf, 49

Berger, Thomas, **323–33**

Bertilak, 97, 98, 99, 101, 102, 106

Blauncheflour, 188

"Bob and Wheel," 105

Boccaccio, Giovanni, 70, **110–19**, 120, 121, 154

Book of Merlyn, The, 279, 284

Bors, 233, 253

Bradley, Marion Zimmer, **334–50**

"Breton Hope," 27

Britons, 17, 18, 20, 21, 26, 30, 32, 45, 51, 52, 340

Brut (*Hystoria Brutonum*), 45, 48–50, 56, 253

Brutus, Brute, 30, 31, 50, 147, 158

Büchlein, Das (The Little Book), 60

Burne-Jones, Edward, 176, 186

Cabal, 21

Caccia di Diana, La, 111

Cadwallader, 30, 33, 56

Caen, 23, 24

Cair Guorthegrin, 21

Calilburnus, 33

Camelot, ix, xx, 87, 97, 98, 126, 134, 135, 138, 187, 189, 194, 196, 200, 209, 219, 232, 233, 238, 268, 282, 296, 298, 317, 325, 329, 343, 353, 369, 374, 377

Candle in the Wind, The, 276, 283

Caradoc of Llancarfan, 1, 2, 5

Carlyle, Thomas, 222

Caxton, William, 128, 132, 370

Celts, x, 18, 25, 31, 50, 251, 252, 312, 355, 375

Ceowulf, 8

"Chapel at Lyoness, The," 179

Chaucer, Geoffrey, xiii, 56, 70, 83, 103, 110, **120–27**, 128, 133, 138, 141, 143, 154, 160, 328

Chevalier au lion, Le, 60

Child of the Northern Spring, The, 352

Chivalry, 38, 81, 83, 86, 88

Chrétien de Troyes, xii, xiii, xiv, xvii, 8, 26, 27, **37–44**, 58, 60, 71, 72, 100, 102, 103, 104, 113, 133, 166, 244, 253, 329, 369–70

Chronicles (Froissart), 81, 82, 83, 84, 85

Cleanness, 91, 92, 93, 94–96, 105

Clemens, Samuel Langhorne. *See* Twain, Mark

Cligés, 37, 39, 41

Coleridge, Samuel Taylor, 202

"Coming of Arthur, The," 211

Conception Nostre Dame, La, 24

Connecticut Yankee in King Arthur's Court, 218–26, 250, 280, 376

Corbaccio, 110, 115–16

Crystal Cave, The, 301, 303–6

Culhwch and Olwen, 101

Dame Ragnell, 328

"Day before the Trial, The," 187, 189–90

"Death of Merlin, The," 270

Decameron, 110, 113–14

De casibus virorum illustratum, 110, 116–17

De Excidio et Conquestu Brittania, 2, 3, 4, 20

"Defence of Guenevere, The," 178, 189

Defence of Guenevere and Other Poems, The, 178, 187

Der arme Heinrich (Lord Henry), 65–66

Diu Klage (The Lament), 60

Dryden, John, **154–64**

Dubglas, 18

Ecclesiastical History, 8, 158

Edward III, 82, 105, 120

Elaine, 209, 210, 283, 326, 342, 358, 359, 369

Eleanor of Acquitaine, 27, 37, 48

Elegia di Madonna Fiammetta, 110, 113

Eliot, T. S., 128, 218, 230, **241–48**, 253

Emerson, Ralph Waldo, 219, 230

Empedocles on Etna, and Other Poems, 165, 166

Enid, 38–39, 61, 62–63, 353

"Enid" (Tennyson), 209

Enite. *See* Enid

Erec, 37, 38–39, 61

Erec (Hartmann), 59, 60

Erec et Enide, 37, 38–39, 40, 41, 59

Escaldos, 40

Excalibur, xx, 26, 28, 33, 134, 269, 270, 319, 324, 328, 332, 370

Faerie Queen, The, xviii, 110, 138, 139–40, 141–43, 371

Feirefiz, 73, 74

Filocolo (Labor of Love), 111

Filostrato, 111

Fisher King, xiv–xv, 42, 123, 241, 244, 245, 246, 247, 253, 256, 369

Forest Home, The, 334

Fortuna, 107

Fragmente, 3

Frazer, Sir James George, 253, 312, 334

Froissart, Jehan, **81–89**, 178

Gahmuret, 73, 74

Galahad, 112, 134, 136, 232, 235, 253, 256, 283, 319, 324, 327, 328, 340, 353, 369, 370, 376

"Galfridus Arthuris," 31

Ganhumara. *See* Guinevere

Gardeviaz, 77

Gareth, 213, 279, 326, 353

Gareth and Lynette, 214

Gauvain. *See* Gawain

Gawain, 37, 41, 61, 63, 64, 74, 79, 98–100, 122, 125, 232, 233, 234, 279, 283, 319, 325, 326, 328, 329, 332, 353, 366

"Gawain, Ewain, and Marhalt," 270

Gawain-Poet, The, **90–109**

Geoffrey of Monmouth, xi, xviii, 8, 16, 21, 24, 25, 26, 27, **30–36**, 45, 47, 50, 52, 53, 54, 56, 102, 133, 158, 211, 253, 305, 318, 330

"Geraint and Enid," 209

Gildas, **1–6**, 20, 33

Glein, 18

Godefroy de Leigny, 41

Golden Bough, The, 253, 312, 334

Gorlois, 27, 32, 52, 305, 340

Grail, ix, 41, 42, 134, 190, 238, 241, 244, 288, 327, 347, 368, 372, 376

Gral, 77, 78

Green Chapel, 97, 99

Green Knight. *See* Bertilak

Gregorius, 64–65

Gregory the Great, 2

Große Heidelberger Liederhandschrift, 71

Guendoloena, 34

Guenhumara. *See* Guinevere

Guinevere, xii, xv, 32, 39, 41, 55, 62, 106, 107, 112, 113, 116, 134, 136, 178, 189, 190, 209, 212, 232, 233, 238, 253, 269, 270, 282, 283, 295, 296, 317, 324, 325, 327, 328, 331, 341, 342, 343, 351, 352, 353, 354, 358, 359, 365, 371, 372

Guinevere (Woolley), 353

Gwenhwyfar. *See* Guinevere

Hallam, Arthur, 201, 206

Hartmann von Aue, **58–69**, 70

Henry II, 24, 27, 28, 48, 368

Henry III, 48

Henry V, 129

Henry VI, 59

Herseloyde, 73

Heywood, Thomas, **146–53**

Historia Brittonum, xi, 16, 17, 18, 19, 20

Historia Regum Britanniae (History of the Kings of Britain), xi, 16, 21, 24, 25, 27, 30, 31, 33, 34, 45, 47, 50, 133, 149, 158, 211, 253, 305, 318, 330

History of the English Church and People, A, 8, 9, 10

Hollow Hills, The, 301, 306–7

"Holy Grail, The" (Tennyson), 211, 213, 215

Holy Grail and Other Poems, The, 212

Howells, William Dean, 224, 225

Hundred Years' War, 81, 83, 86, 88, 92, 129

Idylls of the King, 128, 138, 167, 196, 204, 206, 208–15, 219, 236, 253, 258, 358

Igraine. *See* Ygraine

Ill-Made Knight, The, 276, 279, 282–83, 371

Iseult, 39, 112, 135, 166, 188–89, 191, 234, 237, 238, 367–68, 372

Isolde. *See* Iseult

Iwein, 59, 60, 61–62, 63–64

James I, 157

Jersey, 23

Jesus Christ, x, xiii, 19, 26, 42, 189, 244, 252, 370

Joseph of Arimethea, 42, 197, 244, 369

"Joyeuse Garde," 187, 191, 195

Joyous Gard, 232, 233, 234, 353, 354, 372

Jutes, 9

Kalogrenant, 63

Kay, 40, 102, 317

Keii, 63

King Arthur, or The British Worthy, 158

"King Arthur's Tomb," 178–79, 190

"King Ban," 187

Knight of the Cart, The, 26, 37, 40–41, 100, 104

"Knight with the Two Swords, The," 269

Lady of Avalon, 334

Lady of Shalott, 205, 210, 373

"Lady of Shalott, The" (Tennyson), 176, 202, 203, 204, 209, 373

Lady of the Lake, x, 26, 347, 370

L'amorosa visione, 110, 112

Lancelot, 37, 41, 103, 113, 114, 116, 134, 136, 187, 190, 232, 233, 253, 254, 271, 272, 277, 279, 282, 283, 295, 298, 319, 325, 326, 328, 331, 332, 341, 353, 354, 358, 365, 366, 368, 371, 372, 373

Lancelot (Percy), 288, 295, 298

Lancelot (Robinson), 230, 233, 236, 238

"Lancelot" (Swinburne), 187, 190–91

Lancelot (*The Knight of the Cart*), 26, 37, 40–41, 100, 104

"Lancelot and Elaine," 210

"Lancelot's Quest of the Grail," 207

Lantern Bearers, The, 315–16

Last Enchantment, The, 301

Last Gentleman, The, 297, 298

"Last Pilgrimage, The," 195

"Last Tournament, The," 167, 213

Laudine, 40

"Launcelot" (Lewis), 253

Lawman. *See* Layamon

Layamon, xiv, 25, **45–57**, 253

Le Bel, Jean, 84

Leodogran, 212
Lewis, C. S., 175, **249–64**
Life of Merlin, 147–48, 149
Life of St. Illtud, 2
Light beyond the Forest, 311, 319
Livre de faits d'Arrthur, 33
Locrin, 27
Lord Henry, 59
Love in the Ruins, 298
Love Song of J. Alfred Prufrock, The, 241–42
Lucan, 232
Lunite, 40

Mabinogion, 209
Malory, Sir Thomas, xv, xvii, 26, 28, 34, 56,
      103, **128–37**, 166, 171, 177, 178, 179,
      187, 189, 190, 196, 208, 218, 219, 235,
      253, 254, 256, 261, 267, 268, 271, 278,
      284, 289, 290, 305, 317, 318, 320, 325,
      326, 327, 331, 332, 334, 367, 370, 373
Marc, Mark, 169, 170, 188–89, 191, 194,
      195, 234, 353, 367
Marie de France, 27, 37, 114, 166
Mary, 19, 38
"Matter of Britain, The," 33, 110, 112, 113,
      114, 138, 278, 351
Maud, 207, 209, 210
"Maying of Guenevere, The," 179
Meleagant, 40–41
Meliador, 81, 83–84, 85–88
Merlin, ix, xx, 20, 21, 30, 32, 33, 34, 43, 45,
      50, 52, 56, 133–34, 136, 103, 147, 158,
      171, 202, 208, 215, 231, 232, 235, 236,
      238, 252, 256, 269, 270, 280, 301, 303,
      304, 305, 306–7, 308, 309, 319, 327, 346,
      352, 353, 365–66, 374
Merlin (Robinson), 230, 231–33, 235,
      236, 238
"Merlin and the Gleam," 215
"Merlin and Vivien," 207, 214, 215
Metamorphoses, 42
Mirabilia (Marvels), 17, 21
Mists of Avalon, The, 285, 334, 339,
      344, 346
Modred, ix, xi, 27, 32–33, 55, 102, 112, 117,
      134, 202, 232, 233, 280, 283, 290, 296,
      307, 308, 319–20, 325, 330, 331, 332,
      341, 344, 353, 370
Mordred. *See* Modred
Morgaine. *See* Morgan le Fay
Morgan le Fay, x, 34, 106, 223, 234, 253,
      270, 271, 319, 328, 330, 340, 341, 342

Morgause, 194, 280, 281, 285, 307, 319,
      326, 330, 339, 343, 353
Morris, William, xviii–xix, 34, 165, **175–84**,
      185, 187, 188, 189, 190, 375–76
Morte d'Arthur (Malory), xvii–xviii, 56,
      128, 130, 131, 132–37, 166, 177, 189,
      190–91, 196, 221, 257, 261, 268, 278,
      282, 325, 331, 332, 367, 370, 373
"Morte d'Arthur" (Tennyson), 206–7, 210,
      212, 215, 253
Myrddin. *See* Merlin

Nennius, xi, **16–22**, 33
Nimüe, 207, 208, 252, 253, 308, 353, 374
"Noble Tale of Sir Lancelot of the Lake,
      The," 270–71
Norman Conquest, 24, 28
Normandy, 24
Normans, 27, 49
Northumbria, 7, 8, 10
"Nun's Priest's Tale, The," 120, 123–24

Once and Future King, The, 128, 153,
      276, 277, 281–82, 283, 284, 285,
      311, 327, 352
"Orkneys, The," 279–80, 283
Osmond, 158
Ovid, 42

Parzival, 70, 71, 72–74, 77, 78, 79
"Passing of Arthur," 212, 214
Patience, 91, 92, 93, 94, 99
Pearl, 91, 92, 96–97, 99, 105
"Pelleas and Atarre," 213
Perceval, 37, 41–42, 72, 112, 244, 253, 368
Perceval (*The Story of the Grail*), 26, 41–42,
      71, 98, 102, 103, 104, 244, 253
Percy, Walker, **288–300**
Petrarch, 83, 120
Philippa of Hainault, 83, 84
Poenitentiae, 3
Pope, Alexander, 3
Pound, Ezra, 241, 243
Pre-Raphaelites, 242, 371, 372
"Pridwin," 33
Prince and the Pauper, The, 224
Prophetiae Merlini, 30

Queen of Air and Darkness, The, 276
Queen of the Summer Stars, 353
"Queen's Pelasance, The," 194
"Queen Yseult," 187, 188–89

Quest for the Holy Grail, The (Sutcliff), 318
Quest of Bleheris, The, 252, 261
Quest of the Holy Grail, 254

Red Cross Knight, 141
Remedia Amoris, 42
Road to Camlann, 311, 319–20
Robert de Chesney, 31, 33
Robert I, 23
Robinson, Edwin Arlington, **230–40**
Rollo, 27
Roman de Brut, xiii, 23, 25, 27, 28, 47,
    253, 367
Roman de Rou, 23, 27, 28
Romans, xi, 2, 3, 9, 19, 20, 51, 54, 64, 102,
    169, 315
Romeo and Juliet, 39
"Ron," 33
Rondel, 87
Round Table, ix, xiii, xx, 25, 26, 28, 38, 45,
    54, 63, 87, 88, 106, 112, 117, 122, 134,
    232, 317, 319, 326, 331, 339, 367, 369

"Sailing of the Swallow, The," 194
St. Finian, 2
St. Peter at Wermouth, 7
Saxons, 4, 9, 17, 18, 20, 32, 148, 157, 158,
    312, 316, 352
Schionatulander, 77
Scott, Sir Walter, 219
Second Coming, The, 297, 298–99
Shepheardes Calender, 139
Sigune, 77
"Sir Galahad: A Christmas Mystery," 179
"Sir Gareth," 213
Sir Gawain and the Green Knight, xvii, 90, 91,
    92, 93, 96, 97–107, 253, 318, 358
"Sir Lancelot and Queen Guinevere:
    A Fragment," 202, 203–4
"Sir Pelleas," 212
"Sir Thopas," 120, 123, 143
Spenser, Edmund, xviii, **138–45**, 371
"Squire's Tale, The," 120, 122, 123
Steinbeck, John, 128, **265–75**, 324, 325, 329
Stewart, Mary, **301–10**
The Story of the Grail, 26, 41–42, 71, 98, 102,
    103, 104, 244, 253
Sutcliff, Rosemary, **311–22**
Swift, Jonathan, 3
Swinburne, Algernon Charles, xviii, 128, 136,
    165, 167, **185–99**
Sword and the Circle, 311, 318

Sword at Sunset, 311, 316–17, 318
Sword in the Stone, The, 276, 278–79, 280,
    284–85

Tale of Balen, The, 186, 189, 195–96, 198
Taliesin, 18, 34, 51
Tennyson, Alfred, Lord, xviii, 34, 56, 128,
    138, 165, 167, 171, 176, 193, 196,
    200–217, 219, 235, 253, 258, 289,
    317, 329, 358, 371, 373, 374
Teseida, 112
Tintagel, 32, 234, 340
Titurel, 76–78
Tolkien, J. R. R., 252
Tristan, 39, 42, 112, 113, 114, 135, 166,
    167, 186, 188, 234, 237, 318, 326,
    367–68, 372
Tristan (Hartmann), 59–60
"Tristan and Iseult" (Arnold), 165,
    168–71, 187
Tristram. *See* Tristan
Tristram (Robinson), 230, 235, 237, 238
Tristram of Lyonesse, 167, 186, 189, 192–95
Troilus and Criseida, 111
Twain, Mark, 128, **218–29**, 250, 280, 376

Uther Pendragon, ix, 27, 32, 50, 52, 63,
    78, 148, 280, 305, 318, 324, 331, 340,
    346, 352

Victoria, 221, 224, 226
Vie de St. Marguerite, La, 24
Vie de St. Nicholas, La, 24
Vita Gildae auctore monacho Ruiensi, 1
Vita Goeznouei, 33
Viti Merlini, 30, 50
Vivien, 171, 208, 209, 232, 236, 339, 340,
    341, 346, 359
Vortigern, 4, 9, 20, 21, 32, 52, 148, 305,
    312, 352

Wace, xiii, **23–29**, 34, 45, 47, 49, 50, 52, 53,
    54, 56, 253, 367
Walter of Oxford, 25, 33
War of the Roses, 129, 131
Waste Land, The, 241–46, 253
"Wedding of King Arthur, The," 269–70
Wenceslaus of Bohemia, 83, 86, 87
White, T. H., 128, 253, **276–87**, 304,
    327, 352
Wicked Day, The, 307–8
"Wife of Bath's Tale, The," 120, 124–25, 328

Willehalm, 70–71, 74–76, 78
William of Malmesbury, 8, 31, 102
"Williams and the Arthuriad," 258
Wolfram von Eschenbach, **70–80**, 329
Woolley, Persia, **351–56**
World War I, 236, 241, 291

World War II, 242, 245, 283, 284, 294, 357, 376

Ygraine, ix, 27, 32, 280, 305, 339–40, 346, 353
Yseult. *See* Iseult
Yvain, 37, 39–40, 59, 103

About the Editors and Contributors

LAURA COONER LAMBDIN is a lecturer in management at the University of South Carolina's Moore School of Business. She has written or edited six books and had many articles published in scholarly journals.

ROBERT THOMAS LAMBDIN teaches in the management department at the University of South Carolina's Moore School of Business. He has published many articles and books on pedagogy, Old and Middle English literature, and Jane Austen.

ALBRECHT CLASSEN is University Distinguished Professor of German Studies at the University of Arizona. He has published more than forty monographs, editions, anthologies, translations, and textbooks, and close to four hundred scholarly articles. He has received numerous teaching awards, and in 2006 he received the AATG Outstanding German Educator Award and the Checkpoint Charlie Foundation Scholarship for outstanding achievement in furthering the teaching of German in schools of the United States. He is editor of *Tristania* and co-editor of *Mediaevistik*.

THOMAS WINN DABBS is a professor of English literature at Aoyama Gakuin University in Tokyo. He is the author of *Reforming Marlowe* and is currently completing a book on teaching the Bible in Japan.

MICHAEL JAMES DENNISON teaches English at the American University of Beirut in Lebanon. He is a poet, playwright, scholar of comparative literature, and author of *Vampirism: Literary Tropes of Decadence and Entropy*.

REBECCA DUNCAN is an associate professor and director of undergraduate research at Meredith College in Raleigh, North Carolina. She has published essays on Virginia Woolf, Jane Austen, and Yann Martel, as well as digital media on information literacy.

M. TAYLOR EMERY is an instructor of English at Austin Peay State University. Professor Emery teaches composition and world literature.

PRISCILLA GLANVILLE teaches literature and composition for the College of Lifelong Learning, Portsmouth. Her publishing areas are widespread, but Dr. Glanville has a passion for nineteenth-century British literature.

CANDACE GREGORY-ABBOTT holds a doctorate in medieval studies from Yale University and is an assistant professor in the history department of California State University–Sacramento. Her dissertation was on the diocese of York, England, the Lollard heresy, and church reform. She has presented many conference papers and published articles on women in the late Middle Ages, medieval heresy, class identity in fifteenth-century England, and the Middle Ages in film. She teaches a variety of medieval courses.

JOHN DENNIS GROSSKOPF is dean of teaching and learning at North Florida Community College, where he teaches a variety of composition and literature courses, including "King Arthur and His Stories." Professor Grosskopf has published articles on medievalism and has presented many conference papers about Old and Middle English literature.

ALISON GULLEY is an associate professor of English and coordinator of the literature program at Lees-McRae College in Banner Elk, North Carolina, where she teaches medieval and Renaissance literature as well as "Women and Literature." She has published several articles on women's spirituality in the Anglo-Saxon era.

MAUREEN MARMION HOURIGAN is an associate professor at Kent State University–Trumbull. Dr. Hourigan teaches composition, women's literature, and Great Books. Her scholarly interests include the influences of gender, class, and culture on students' writing abilities.

PEGGY J. HUEY is an assistant professor at the University of Tampa. A person of wide-ranging interests, she previously published articles on various examples of "Breton Lais" in Greenwood Press's *Encyclopedia of Medieval Literature*, and has entries on various short stories in the forthcoming *Facts on File Companion to the American Short Story*. In addition, she has in print a chapter about the squire (and his tale) in *Chaucer's Pilgrims: An Historical Guide to the Pilgrims in The Canterbury Tales*; a discussion of "Sanditon" in *A Companion to Jane Austen Studies*; and articles exploring the Magrath sisters in *Crimes of the Heart*, John Hersey's *A Bell for Adano*, and the mythology of the *Harry Potter* series.

JAMES KELLER is professor of early modern literature and chair of English and theatre at Eastern Kentucky University. He is the author of four monographs: *Princes, Soldiers, and Rogues: The Politic Malcontent of Renaissance Drama*; *Anne Rice and Sexual Politics*; *Queer (Un)Friendly Film and Television;* and *Food Film, and Culture*. He has also published three edited collections with Dr. Leslie Stratyner: *Almost Shakespeare*, *The New Queer Aesthetic on Television*, and *Fantasy Fiction into Film*. Dr. Keller's current projects include a monograph tentatively titled *V for Vendetta: Shadow Text and Intertext*, and a fourth edited collection, *South Park and Cultural Criticism*. He is also the author of more than forty articles and chapters on a variety of subjects, including early modern literature, film, gender studies, and cultural studies.

EDWARD DONALD KENNEDY is a professor of English and comparative literature at the University of North Carolina–Chapel Hill. He has written *Chronicles and Other Historical Writing* (vol. 8 of *A Manual of the Writings in Middle English*, ed. A. E. Hartung), has edited *King Arthur: A Casebook*, and has published numerous articles on

French and English medieval Arthurian romance and medieval chronicles. He is the editor of *Studies in Philology*.

SIGRID KING teaches English at Carlow University in Pittsburgh. She is a scholar of early modern literature, Shakespeare, and seventeenth-century women playwrights. She is the editor of *Pilgrimage for Love: Essays in Early Modern Literature*.

KEVIN MARTI is an associate professor of English at the University of New Orleans. His publications have focused on the Gawain Poet, Dante, and Chaucer.

RICHARD B. MCDONALD is an associate professor of medieval literature at Utah Valley University. He specializes in language theory as it relates to medieval mystics and teaches a wide variety of traditional medieval courses for undergraduates. Dr. McDonald is also the associate director of the center for the study of ethics.

MARIE NELSON has taught Old English, history of the English language, "Chaucer and Chaucer's Women," and "Heroes in Transformation," along with introductory linguistics and writing courses at the University of Florida. She has published essays in *Speculum, Neophilologus, Oral Tradition*, and other journals. Now a professor emerita, she continues to teach "Writing about Language" for the University of Florida's Honors Program.

CAROL L. ROBINSON teaches at Kent State University–Trumbull. Her current interests include Pier Paolo Pasolini's cinematic interpretation of Geoffrey Chaucer's Wife of Bath, adaptations of medieval Arthurian women of power into film, and gender identity in medievalist film and video games. Currently, Dr. Robinson is co-editing a book on neomedievalism in film, television, and video games titled *The Medieval in Motion* and working on an analysis of hypertext, Sir Gawain and the Green Knight, and an American Sign Language neomedieval adaptation of "The Wedding of Sir Gawain and Dame Ragnel."

MARCUS A. J. SMITH is associate professor of English at Loyola University in New Orleans. He is also a practicing attorney.

FIONA TOLHURST earned her Ph.D. from Princeton University and is an associate professor of English at Alfred University. Among the classes Dr. Tolhurst teaches are "Tales of King Arthur," "Arthurian Literature," "Chaucer," and "The Middle Ages in Literature and Film." She has published widely, primarily about women in medieval literature.

JENA TRAMMELL is an associate professor of literature at Anderson College. She has written extensively and presented often at conferences concerning John Dryden.

RAYMOND M. VINCE was a visiting instructor in English at the University of South Florida, teaching American literature, modern literature, and "The Bible as Literature." Other interests include Hemingway, Fitzgerald, Norman Mailer, medieval literature, heroism in war, and the spy novel. His article on "Alienation" appeared in *The New Dictionary of Theology* (1988), and he has a forthcoming article on *The Great Gatsby*, Einstein, and the transformations of space-time in *The F. Scott Fitzgerald Review*. He is assistant editor of the *Mailer Review*. With previous careers as a scientist and a priest, he holds a Ph.D. in English from the University of South Florida and four degrees in theology, English, logic, and the scientific method from the Universities of London and Bristol in England.

JULIAN N. WASSERMAN was a professor of English at Loyola University New Orleans and a widely published medieval scholar. He died in 2003.